The Corporation, Law, and Capitalism

Historical Materialism Book Series

The Historical Materialism Book Series is a major publishing initiative of the radical left. The capitalist crisis of the twenty-first century has been met by a resurgence of interest in critical Marxist theory. At the same time, the publishing institutions committed to Marxism have contracted markedly since the high point of the 1970s. The Historical Materialism Book Series is dedicated to addressing this situation by making available important works of Marxist theory. The aim of the series is to publish important theoretical contributions as the basis for vigorous intellectual debate and exchange on the left.

The peer-reviewed series publishes original monographs, translated texts, and reprints of classics across the bounds of academic disciplinary agendas and across the divisions of the left. The series is particularly concerned to encourage the internationalization of Marxist debate and aims to translate significant studies from beyond the English-speaking world.

For a full list of titles in the Historical Materialism Book Series available in paperback from Haymarket Books, visit:
https://www.haymarketbooks.org/series_collections/1-historical-materialism

The Corporation, Law, and Capitalism

A Radical Perspective on the Role of Law in the Global Political Economy

Grietje Baars

Haymarket Books
Chicago, IL

First published in 2018 by Brill Academic Publishers, The Netherlands

Published in paperback in 2020 by
Haymarket Books
P.O. Box 180165
Chicago, IL 60618
773-583-7884
www.haymarketbooks.org

ISBN: 978-1-64259-187-3

Distributed to the trade in the US through Consortium Book Sales and Distribution (www.cbsd.com) and internationally through Ingram Publisher Services International (www.ingramcontent.com).

This book was published with the generous support of Lannan Foundation and Wallace Action Fund.

Cover design by Jamie Kerry and Ragina Johnson.

Printed in the United States.

10 9 8 7 6 5 4 3 2 1

Library of Congress Cataloging-in-Publication data is available.

For my parents

The law locks up the man or woman
Who steals a goose from off the common,
But leaves the greater villain loose
Who steals the common from under the goose.
The law demands that we atone
When we take things we do not own
But leaves the lords and ladies fine
Who takes things that are yours and mine.
The poor and wretched don't escape
If they conspire the law to break;
This must be so but they endure
Those who conspire to make the law.
The law locks up the man or woman
Who steals the goose from off the common
And geese will still a common lack
Till they go and steal it back.

– Fifteenth-century English rhyme

∴

Contents

Preface

Famously, Marx said, in the *11th Thesis on Feuerbach*: 'Philosophers have interpreted the world in various ways, but the point is to change it'.[1] Aside from the academic purpose of the work, with this book, I have one specific practical aim.

In this book I examine both legal scholarship and legal practice. The examination of practice is inspired by the work of practising lawyers I have met over the years and also by my own time in practice. Michael Sfard, one of the best-known anti-occupation lawyers working in the Israeli court system, has expressed the need for academic reflection on cause lawyering practice, and, in particular, to analyse how such practice may constitute the lifeblood of the system of oppression it is seeking to overturn. He observes that practising lawyers' ethics prevent them from turning away individual clients whose lives might be marginally improved through litigation, in favour of the 'collective struggle' (which may be helped by, say, boycotting the courts).[2] The onus of finding the way through this dilemma, he argues, is on legal academics. Legal academics in his view have the obligation to rise above the perspective of individual cases and provide practitioners with a better understanding of how human rights litigation in mass abuse cases works to sustain the system.

> By uncovering the truth about the limited success of human rights victims in a given legal system, and by pointing to the processes that transform these limited successes into regime-empowering tools, academic debate is likely to weaken these tools. Since at least some of the perils listed [in Sfard's article] are vested in the image-creating force which ... opposition grants the regime, revealing them may diffuse their sting. This can only be done by academics. And they have failed to do so for all too long.[3]

Sfard and practitioners like him are not helped by the fact that almost all of academia, especially in the human rights field (and in the 'business and human rights' field), is unwaveringly 'pro-human rights', and without Sfard's sobering (demystifying) practice experience, adhere to the romantic notion of human

1 Marx 2000f, p. 173. The central hall of the Humboldt University in Berlin (Marx's alma mater) at Unter den Linden 6 still prominently displays this statement, apparently much to the chagrin of the current board of the university, who cannot take it down as the hall in its entirety was declared a 'listed building' before the end of the GDR. This, interestingly because of law, they cannot change.

2 Sfard 2009, p. 49.

3 Ibid.

d international criminal law as the liberal saviour, and more broadly, eing generally, or at least in principle, a good thing.[4] Engels exhorts us e off our law-glasses', to set aside our *juristische Weltanschauung*,[5] and to cease seeking solutions to world problems in law, against our better knowledge. Kropotkin provocatively scorned, 'Instead of themselves altering what is bad, people begin by demanding a law to alter it'.[6] It is my aim to show how a historical-materialist approach to business and human rights, and to 'corporate acountability', can offer a critical, analytical, 'real world' perspective, which I hope responds in some small way to Sfard's critique.[7] Moreover, I hope that it will give impetus and affirmation to those seeking to change the world beyond law, in spite of law, and, ultimately, against law.

---

4 Fox 1993.

5 Lit. 'juridical worldview', Beirne 1977, p. 199.

6 Kropotkin 1886, p. 1.

7 Ollman 2003, p. 20.

Acknowledgements

On the long journey with this book I have sought out and encountered many fascinating, inspiring and stimulating people from all walks of life: academics of every type including lawyers, anthropologists, sociologists and historians, judges, prosecutors and defenders, trade union activists, diplomats and parliamentarians of all colours and nationalities, squatters and anarchists, ex-detainees and prisoners of war, generals and footsoldiers, refuseniks and resistance fighters, company directors and private military contractors, middle management and civil service bureaucrats, cause lawyers and City types (and those that are both). I am grateful to all of them. Especially, in order of appearance:

This book started with Joel Bakan's *The Corporation* (the film and the book), which echoed many of the experiences of the relationship between capital and law I had had as a commercial solicitor at Bird & Bird in the City of London and which led to my return to academia. I am grateful to my Ph.D. supervisor Catherine Redgwell at UCL for giving me the space and freedom to explore an untrodden path and for her faith in my ability to do so sensibly, and to Riz Mokal for his friendship during these years. My early work has benefitted enormously from discussions with Jason Beckett, Akbar Rasulov and Jörg Kammerhoffer. My time as an in-house solicitor at Habitat enabled me to understand the real-life effects of the intricacies of global corporate group structures as well as the relationship between human rights, contract law and international production chains. I am grateful for Andrea Shemberg's invitation to be part of the Expert Panel for the International Commission of Jurists' first Business and Human Rights Report (*Corporate Complicity and Legal Accountability: The Report of the ICJ's Expert Legal Panel on Corporate Complicity in International Crimes*), and the opportunity to volunteer with the Business Leaders Initiative on Human Rights – both when the CSR debate was only just morphing into the BHR debate. Life and my view of (international law) took a different turn, however, when faced with a different reality in Palestine. I am grateful to Azem Bishara for providing the impetus for this life-changing decision, Aeyal Gross, Arthur Neslen and Rachel Shabi for the soft landing, and especially Anne Paq (who I'm grateful to count as one of my closest people, wherever she is in the world), Lymor Goldstein and Nadav Frankovitch for deeply inspiring friendships. My gracious institutional hosts in Palestine included Mudar Qassis at the Institute of Law (with whom I first visited Gaza), Birzeit University, Muhammed Shelaldeh at the Palestinian School of Law, Al-Quds University, Assaf Likhovski at the CEGLA Center, and Ronen Shamir (who has become an important intellectual ally) also at Tel Aviv University.

Most importantly in this period, Munir Nusseibeh and Radi Darwish, with whom I created the Al-Quds Human Rights and International Humanitarian Law Clinic. I treasure this opportunity to work with many gifted students, passionate, driven and tenacious human rights professionals, especially those who became close friends: Mahmoud Abu Rahma of Al-Mezan, Smadar Ben Natan, and Miri Weingarten of PHR-I, as well as Sahar Frances of Addameer and Sha'wan Jabarin at Al-Haq prominently amongst many others. At Diakonia I am grateful for the sustaining political solidarity with Wa'el Abu-Nemeh especially, for the chance to investigate and report on corporate human rights and IHL violations in the West Bank and Gaza with Joakim Wohlfeil and for the opportunity to organise the 'Enforcing IHL' conference with many international human rights litigators in Brussels. Important friends at this time, and still today, Simon Boas, Vivian Korsten, Anne de Jong, Amber Houssian, Suzanne Goedeken and Liza Franke – as well as many others. The late Samer 'Asli' (Rest in Peace and Power), Mohammed Jaradat, Fady Swaitti and Ibrahim Burnat were solid companions. I owe deep thanks to Yehuda Shaul, Dalit Baum, Shir Hever and Jonathan Pollak who showed me how to carve a politically meaningful path in a politically messy world.

While in Palestine my mind was blown when reading China Miéville's 'Between Equal Rights: A Marxist Theory of International Law', and my understanding was challenged, deepened and shaped through the many discussions with China, Robert Knox, Paavo Kotiaho, Irina Ceric and Alessandra Asteriti, as well as, and most enjoyably over large jigsaw puzzles, Hannah Franzki.

Moving to Berlin I found a stimulating temporary home (thanks to Tsafrir Cohen) at the European Centre for Constitutional and Human Rights – thank you especially to comrade Kamil Majchrzak – and the late Michael Ratner – as well as an intellectual community with Florian Jeßberger and Jochen Bung at Das Franz-von-Liszt-Institut for International Criminal Law, Humboldt University, Berlin. Benedikt Naarman and Reut Paz were great study buddies while Antonia, Sarah K, Anna, Üner and their crew sustained me socially. The Universal Jurisdiction and strategic litigation squad included legal warriors Ward Ferdinandusse, Liesbeth Zegveld, Maria LaHood and Daniel Machover most importantly, as well as true comrade Ben Hayes.

I am grateful to Francesca Marotta for allowing me to experience the UN Human Rights system from the inside as one of the lawyers on Justice Richard Goldstone's Fact Finding Mission on the 2008–09 'Operation Cast Lead' Israeli assault on Gaza, and working me harder than anyone ever has before or since.

I thank my thorough and stimulating Ph.D. examiners Susan Marks and Douglas Guilfoyle, and my colleagues at City, University of London, especially my dear friend and office mate, may he rest in peace as well as power, Riccardo Montana, and my comrades Ioannis Kalpouzos, Marios Costa and Mazen Masri.

My fascination with the corporation has led me to set up the Critical Corporation Project together with André Spicer, David Whyte, Paddy Ireland, Tom Hadden, Peter Fleming, Martin Parker, David Quentin, David Hansen-Miller, Liam Campling, Andrew Sanchez and a host of others, in a 3-year ESRC-funded seminar series and edited collection: *The Corporation: A Critical, Multidisciplinary Handbook*, and an exciting series of activist workshops with the Radical Housing Network, Concrete Action, Corporate Watch and a launch event with my book's inspiration, Joel Bakan.

This also led to the opportunity to teach 'The Corporation in Global Society' at David Kennedy's Harvard IGLP Workshops in Doha, Bogota and Bangkok together with my more senior, always brilliant, and slightly less Marxist intellectual twin Dan Danielsen, to organising two joint conferences on Corporate Power and Resistance with the Corporation in Global Society Research Group at Harvard's Institute of Global Law and Policy in June 2014. Moreover, it led to many of our 'Critical Corporation' crew joining Dan Danielsen and Jennifer Bair in the Law and the Global Value Chain Research Group. I owe a lot to the IGLP gatherings, not least the encounters and discussions with Alejandra Azuero, Swethaa Ballakrishnan, Genevieve Painter, Honor Brabazon, Christopher Gevers and many others.

I have presented the research in this book at numerous fora including the Melbourne 'Hidden Histories of War Crimes Trials' event, and am grateful to UCL, IGLP and City for generous funding. I am especially grateful to Glenn Morgan and Bobby Bannerjee for the opportunity to present my research at LAEMOS in Havana, Cuba, in March 2013 and Susanne Soederberg and Laureen Snider for including us in the 'Critical Perspectives on Corporate Power' CRN at the Law and Society Association Annual Meeting in Boston in 2013, Seattle in 2015 (kayaktivism!) and Mexico City in 2017. My next project 'Queering Corporate Power' has been inspired by many of you.

At Brill/Historical Materialism and TAT Zetwerk, Danny Hayward, Jennifer Obdam and Cas Van den Hof and colleagues have been supportive, encouraging and patient. Jay Boggis and Zee Ahmed provided eagle-eyed editing under high pressure with humour and grace. Deep thanks go to the anonymous reviewer.

Finally, and above all, to my queer family Cloe, Sib, Lamble, Usch, Goz, Leila, Rosa, Saio, Çeylan, Jo and the kickabout crew, my brothers from another mother David, Vanja and comrade Tomaso, oldest friend in London Holly, even older friend Tessa in Den Haag and my home family: Jasmijn, Marijn, Eva, Milou, Kees and Annet.

∵

Some of the chapters have appeared in previous form:

A shorter version of Chapter 2B was published as Baars 2015.
An earlier version of Chapter 3A was published as Baars 2013.
An earlier version of Chapter 4A was published as Baars 2014a.
Earlier versions of Chapter 6 were published as Baars 2016 and Baars 2017.

Abbreviations

AFPS	Association France Palestine Solidarité
AIA	Association Internationale Africaine
ATCA	Alien Tort Claims Act
ATS	Alien Tort Statute
BACAR	Banque Continentale Africaine au Rwanda
BASF	Badische Anilin- und Soda-Fabrik
BIT	Bilateral investment treaty
CAT	Convention Against Torture
CCL	Control Council Law
CCR	Centre for Constitutional Rights
CEO	Chief Executive Officer
CERD	Charter of Economic Rights and Duties of States
CETA	Comprehensive Economic and Trade Agreement
CIA	Central Intelligence Agency
CICL	Corporate International Criminal Law
CIL	Customary International Law
CL	Criminal law
CLS	Critical Legal Studies
CNN	Central News Network
Co	Company
Corp	Corporation
DEICo	Dutch East India Company
DEST	Deutsche Erd- und Steinwerke
DLH	Dalhoff, Larsen and Horneman
DRC	Democratic Republic of Congo
ECCHR	European Center for Constitutional and Human Rights
EDO	Earl Dodge Osborn
EU	European Union
FBI	Federal Bureau of Investigation
FDI	Foreign direct investment
FDN	Fond Defense National
FEC	Far Eastern Commission
FRG	Federal Republic of Germany
FRUS	Foreign Relations of the United States
FYR	Former Yugoslav Republic
GATT	General Agreement on Tariffs and Trade
GCC	Global Capitalist Class

GDR	German Democratic Republic
GWC	Global Working Class
HGW	Hermann-Göring-Werks
HRW	Human Rights Watch
ICC	International Criminal Court
ICJ	International Court of Justice
ICL	International criminal law
ICSID	International Center for the Settlement of Investment Disputes
ICESCR	International Convention of Economic, Social and Cultural Rights
ICTR	International Criminal Tribunal for Rwanda
ICTY	International Criminal Tribunal for the Former Yugoslavia
IG	Industriegesellschaft
IHL	International humanitarian law
IHRL	International human rights law
IL	International law
ILC	International Law Commission
ILIP	International law of investment protection
ILP	International legal personality
IMF	International Monetary Fund
IMT	International Military Tribunal
IMTFE	International Military Tribunal for the Far East
JAG	Judge Advocate General
JCE	Joint Criminal Enterprise
JCS	Joint Chiefs of Staff
JSC	Joint Stock Corporation
LoC	Library of Congress
Ltd	Limited
MaNGO	Market-oriented non-governmental organisation
MNC	Multi-national corporation
MP	Member of Parliament
MPEPIL	Max Planck Encyclopedia of Public International Law
MRND	National Republican Movement for Democracy and Development (French: Mouvement républicain national pour la démocratie et le développement)
NAFTA	North American Free Trade Agreement
NATO	North-Atlantic Treaty Organisation
NGO	Non-governmental organisation
NIEO	New International Economic Order
NMT	Nuremberg Military Tribunal
OECD	Organisation for Economic Cooperation and Development

OMGUS	Office of the Military Government of the United States
OSI	Open Society Institute
OTC	Oriental Timber Company
PCA	Permanent Court of Arbitration
PCIJ	Permanent Court of International Justice
PoW	Prisoner of War
RAID	Rights and Accountability in Development
Res	Resolution
RTLM	Radio Télévision Libre Mille Collins
RUF	Revolutionary United Front
SCAP	Supreme Commander of the Armed Forces
SCSL	Special Court for Sierra Leone
SD	Sicherheitsdienst
SMT	Soviet Military Tribunals
SS	Schutzstaffel
STL	Special Tribunal for Lebanon
SWNCC	State War Navy Coordinating Committee
TNC	Transnational corporation
TPP	Trans-Pacific Partnership
TRC	Truth and Reconciliation Commission
TTIP	Transatlantic Trade and Investment Partnership
TVPA	Torture Victims Protection Act
TWAIL	Third World Approaches to International Law
UK	United Kingdom
UN	United Nations
UNCITRAL	United Nations Commission on International Trade Law
UNCLOS	United National Convention on the Law of the Sea
UNGA	United Nations General Assembly
UNSC	United Nations Security Council
US	United States
USD	United States Dollar
USSR	Union of Socialist Soviet Republics
VOC	Verenigde Oostindische Compagnie (Dutch East India Company)
WB	World Bank (International Bank for Reconstruction and Development)
WCCLR	United Nations War Crimes Commission
WTO	World Trade Organisation
WVHA	Wirtschaft und Verwaltungshauptamt
WWI	First World War
WWII	Second World War

CHAPTER 1

Introduction: 'Das Kapital, das immer dahinter steckt'[1]

1 Introduction

Much has changed in the world since this book was first conceived over ten years ago. We currently have a corporate CEO in the White House. In his presidential election campaign, Donald Trump spoke about ISIS ('Islamic State' militants):

> We're going to bomb the shit out of 'em, … ISIS is making a tremendous amount of money because they have certain oil camps, certain areas of oil that they took away. They have some in Syria, some in Iraq. I would bomb the shit out of 'em. I would just bomb those suckers. That's right. I'd blow up the pipes … I'd blow up every single inch. There would be nothing left. And you know what, you'll get Exxon to come in there and in two months, you ever see these guys, how good they are, the great oil companies? They'll rebuild that sucker, brand new – it'll be beautiful. And I'd rig it, and I'll take the oil. And I said it, I'll take the oil.[2]

In May 2017, after Trump had gained the presidency, his 'go-to guy' Erik Prince, founder of Blackwater (now called Academi), the company that profited greatly from the part-privatisation of the second US-led war in Iraq, spoke on Fox News. Prince proposed that Trump should deploy an 'American South Asia Company' to manage the occupation of Afghanistan, doing away with expensive US soldiers, and returning from a '1st Infantry Division model' back to an 'East India Company model'.[3] According to Jeremy Scahill, Intercept journalist and author of a book on Blackwater,[4] Prince was clearly touting for business

1 Literally, 'the capital that always lurks behind it'. I owe this phrase to Fabian Schellhaas, who used it in his presentation in March 2010 at Prof. Werle's Doktorandenseminar at the Humboldt University of Berlin.

2 Campaign speech, *Donald Trump*, 16 November 2015.

3 Tucker Carlson Tonight, *Fox News*, 17 May 2017 (*Erik Prince on Tucker Carlson*).

4 Scahill 2007.

through the public medium of Fox News, the one news source he knew Trump would watch.[5] Prince would provide something Trump might just love: an occupation for profit, not for security, expressly and openly.[6] Back in 2003 Tony Blair needed to emphatically deny the suggestion that the second Iraq war was a war for oil, insisting it was humanitarian, and above all legal. In 2017, however, the 'war on terror' rhetoric has been so successful, the climate of fear created and the hunger for punishment (of a 'terrorist state' like Afghanistan) so profound and widespread, that Trump would likely be supported by a significant sector of the US public if he 'bombed the shit out of ISIS' and brought home the Iraqi oil with the help of Exxon. The US President would likely be cheered on by many for paying Prince and his private army to go into Afghanistan to exploit the 'trillion dollars' worth of minerals, and another trillion dollars' worth of oil and gas'[7] – rather than be called a war criminal by a million people in his capital,[8] as happened to Tony Blair. Anno 2017, corporations are the natural and accepted partners in such global 'adventures', just as they were in the time of the British East India Company. The 'war crimes law' that was invoked by people across the world to condemn leaders like Tony Blair and G.W. Bush has also given rise to a discourse of 'corporate accountability', which includes the idea that businesses should be held to account criminally for complicity in human rights and other abuses.

My key argument in this book is that rather than thinking of corporate accountability as capable of restraining corporate value extracting activity, we should think of it as *facilitating* corporate profit making and corporate capitalism as a whole. I will show how, counterintuitively, international criminal law has helped, and continues to help, corporations gain and maintain a legitimate role in the management of global affairs.

This is a book about the relationship between law and capital, or, put differently, about the role of law in capitalism. It is a Marxist legal scholar's task to take the role of law in facilitating, structuring, 'congealing' global capitalism seriously. I deliberately use the word 'congealing' 'incorrectly' so as to call attention to the presence of agency where we normally do not perceive it. Law, as made by lawmakers/lawyers, and *law users* in varying degrees, directs and shapes and sets future outcomes according to, ultimately, the logic of capit-

5 'There's something about Jared', *Intercepted Podcast*, 31 May 2017.
6 'Erik Prince's dark plan for Afghanistan: Military occupation for profit, not security', *Salon*, 3 June 2017.
7 *Erik Prince on Tucker Carlson*.
8 'Why was the biggest protest in World history ignored?', *Time*, 15 February 2013.

alism. It is an appeal to understand the nature of the corporation, that ubiquitous 'phenomenon' (owned and run by people) that touches every area of our lives, and that forms global capitalism's main engine, as a masterpiece of legal technology. I write in conversation with the authors, scholars and activists, who are committed to addressing the fact that the corporation has the power to do unprecedented harm within our societies and environments, urging us to deepen our critical stance. It is above all a book that shows that precisely *because of law's relationship to capital,* law cannot, categorically, be successfully employed to prevent or remedy the many negative effects produced around the world by corporate capitalism. Public interest litigation can sometimes provide temporary relief, a legal rule can curb some corporate behaviour some of the time, treaty or contract negotiation involving corporations can be key in people's everyday life or death struggles, but it can never bring about the structural change that is needed to *overcome* global corporate capitalism's devastating realities. This is because law and capital, besides producing that local, specific, temporary relief, also *produce* global corporate capitalism's devastating realities. In the past ten years, lawyers' and academics' concern about the devastating realities around us has led to, amongst other things, a call for corporations to be held to account for 'corporate complicity' in human rights violations through international criminal law prosecution. I illustrate the relationship between law and capital by means of a counter-narrative to this call. I describe the historical conditions and processes that produced this call, why it is popular, why it has not yielded the desired results, and why it is not only doomed to fail in the long run, but also ultimately counter-emancipatory. Letting go of the 'corporate accountability' fantasy will generate the space we need to formulate a different answer to 'the question of the corporation', and different answers to global corporate capitalism more broadly, beyond the law. The first step to producing these answers is the recognition of the intimate, symbiotic relationship between law and capital and the nature of the corporation.

1.1 *'Global Corporate Rule is Here' and the Liberal Approach*

The theme of 'business and human rights' appears as an obvious choice for a case study on the relationship between law and capital. This theme has become a hot topic in the news and the subject of many legal studies but also other academic, civil society and policy publications in the past ten to fifteen years. While ongoing war, especially in the Middle East, global financial crises, global inequality and climate change may be listed as the world's top problems, the role of corporations in these problems is receiving increasing attention.

'Business and human rights', 'corporate complicity' in states' human rights abuses, the need for 'corporate accountability', closing the 'accountability gap' and combatting 'corporate impunity' are popular new slogans.[9] The voluminous literature in this field tells a common and seemingly straightforward story, which I briefly sketch here.[10]

Many authors on this topic start from the finding that 'global corporate rule is here'. Bakan, a legal scholar and author of the groundbreaking general audience book (and documentary movie) *The Corporation: The Pathological Pursuit of Profit and Power*, opens as follows:

> Today, corporations govern our lives. They determine what we eat, what we watch, what we wear, where we work, and what we do. We are inescapably surrounded by their culture, iconography, and ideology. And, like the church and the monarch in other times, they posture as infallible and omnipotent, glorifying themselves in imposing buildings and elaborate displays. Increasingly, corporations dictate the decisions of their supposed overseers in government and control domains of society once firmly embedded in the public sphere. The corporation's rise to dominance is one of the remarkable events of modern history.[11]

The legal sociologist Ronen Shamir starts one of his many interventions on the global, or multinational corporation thus:

> Multinational corporations (MNCs) dominate the global economy, accounting for two-thirds of global trade in goods and services. Of the one hundred largest world economies, fifty-one are corporations. The top two hundred corporations generate 27.5 percent of the world gross domestic

9 This literature normally takes a broad view of 'human rights' and often also includes discussion of what lawyers would designate 'international humanitarian law' and 'international criminal law', especially in the discussion of corporate complicity and corporate accountability, e.g., Bernaz 2016.

10 The 'devastating realities' mentioned here, and their relationship to corporations, have been approached in various other ways beside the one I focus on here. Obvious examples include Corporate Social Responsibility (which I discuss in Chapter 6), the tightening of corporate governance rules, the discussions around the 'purpose of the corporation' (see Chapter 2A) and, in the UK new Section 172 of the Companies Act 2006, which stipulates that the corporate directors must consider the interests of 'stakeholders' in their decision-making (see further Chapter 2A). For an overview of the distinctions and overlaps between the CSR and BHR debates, and the variety of actors and legal and 'voluntary' regimes potentially engaged, see Bernaz 2016.

11 Bakan 2005, p. 5. Muchlinski starts his monograph with the following observations: 'Mul-

> product and their combined annual revenues are greater than those of the 182 states that contain 80 percent of the world population. The combined sales of four of the largest corporations in the world exceed the gross domestic product of Africa.[12]

Similarly, the Transnational Institute, headed by Susan George and 'a lead facilitator in the global political movement to end corporate impunity', publishes infographs in its series of 'Corporate Power' Reports bearing out similar facts.[13]

These authors point out that corporate power (of course, we mean here predominantly, but not only, the power of the large multinationals) includes the power to do much harm, and their writings are replete with examples of business implications in situations of war, civil conflict, labour exploitation, land grab, other human rights abuse and serious environmental harm. Commonly cited examples include the fact that 141 corporations were implicated in the Congolese genocide[14] or that Shell was behind the killing of Ogoni Valley human rights activist Ken Saro Wiwa,[15] that Western clothing retailers' price-squeeze indirectly led to the deaths of over a thousand Bangladeshi workers in the Rana Plaza factory collapse,[16] or more broadly that (Western) multinationals (a result of 'recent globalization') are causing, financing, or more generally directly or indirectly profiting from the human rights violations and international crimes that are occurring around the world (although mostly in the Global South) on a daily basis.[17] Then, it is argued, the inability (or unwillingness) of (often 'weak') host states to act so as to safeguard the human rights of

---

tinational enterprises (MNEs) are perhaps the most talked about forms of business association in the contemporary "globalizing" world and economy. It is often said that the major MNEs have a turnover larger than many nation states, that they are powerful enough to set their own rules and to sidestep national regulation. They appear to be a power unto themselves'. Muchlinski 2007a, p. 3. For another version of this introduction, see Zerk 2006, pp. 7–14; Sornarajah 2010, p. 23; McLean 2004, p. 363; Hertz 2001, pp. 8–9; for book-length contemplations of the issue, see Vernon 1971; Korten 2001; Klein 2001; Barnet and Muller 1974. 'Global corporate rule' is a phenomenon asserted and analysed across disciplines; see, e.g., Crouch 2011; for a useful overview from a political science perspective, see Fuchs 2013, p. 77; see also Hertz 2001, pp. 8–9, as well as, generally, Vernon 1971, Korten 2001.

12 Shamir 2005, p. 92.

13 *Transnational Institute*, The State of Power, 2016: Democracy, Sovereignty and Resistance.

14 Stewart 2010.

15 E.g., Zerk 2006, p. 23.

16 E.g., *The Telegraph*, 29 April 2013.

17 E.g., Stephens 2005.

those people at risk due to (mainly) Western MNC behaviour leads to 'corporate impunity' – which needs to be addressed at the international level.[18]

Legal, NGO and activist publications in this genre typically hold that the various 'soft law' (non-binding) corporate social responsibility (CSR) mechanisms that have been created over the past 30 years by the United Nations, the OECD, industry bodies and corporations individually, fail to constrain corporations because of their lack of enforceability, which leaves an 'accountability gap'.[19] Simultaneously, the past 20 years have seen the exponential growth of international criminal law ('ICL') – the regime and institutions of international law that provide a venue for the prosecution of (certain) international human rights and humanitarian law violations. This moves the authors to present an analysis of the question whether corporations, these newly important global actors, in fact have binding legal obligations in existing international human rights law (sometimes international humanitarian law is also included), and whether they can thus potentially commit an international law crime through (grave) violation of such obligations.

Based on how they answer that question, these authors proceed in one of a number of directions.

If it is found that, yes, corporations have binding obligations under international law,[20] one comes up against the obstacle that currently none of the international courts or tribunals have explicit jurisdiction to try corporations (as legal persons) for violations of these obligations.[21] The next logical, and practical move is then normally to propose that corporations accused of violating their obligations, be brought before the courts in their home states. This could be where international criminal law is part of, or has been incorporated into, domestic law, or where civil actions are permitted on the basis of violations of international law 'extraterritorially' (home liability for acts committed outside the home jurisdiction, i.e. usually in the Global South).[22] If the finding is that ICL does not (yet) recognise corporate liability, the call is normally that such norms ought to be created.[23] In response to the growing debate, in 2005 Kofi Annan, who was then UN Secretary General, appointed John Ruggie (a well-known international relations scholar) as his Special Representative on Business and Human Rights to 'identify and clarify standards of corpor-

18 Kinley and Augenstein 2013, p. 271.
19 For an overview, see Bernaz 2016.
20 E.g., Clapham 2006; Deva and Bilchitz 2013; Černič and Van Ho 2015; Bernaz 2016.
21 In Chapter 4 I discuss the recent trial of corporations at the Special Tribunal for Lebanon (which is an international criminal tribunal), in the 'Contempt Cases'.
22 E.g., the well-known Alien Tort Statute cases in the US – see Chapters 4 and 5.
23 E.g. Zerk 2006, p. 299.

ate responsibility and accountability regarding human rights'.[24] His conclusion was that there is 'an emerging norm of corporate responsibility for international crimes'.[25]

The preferred *long-term* option of 'business and human rights' scholars and practitioners is for a new treaty, creating or setting out the binding obligations in international human rights law of corporations. These obligations should be matched by criminal liability, and either the International Criminal Court (ICC) statute should be amended in order for the Court to be able to prosecute corporations for international crimes, or a special tribunal for business must be established.[26] The UN Human Rights Council in 2014 adopted a resolution sponsored by Ecuador and South Africa, deciding to establish the 'Open Ended International Working Group for a binding treaty on business and human rights' (OEIWG) to work out the details of precisely such an arrangement and produce a draft treaty for governments to consider.[27] The idea of corporate liability in international criminal law has, in other words, gained traction in the scholarly and professional communities. Almost invariably both academic and

---

24 Introduction by the Special Representative to his work: 'In July 2005, UN Secretary-General Kofi Annan appointed me as his Special Representative (SRSG) on Business and Human Rights. The new administration of Ban Ki-moon extended the assignment. My mandate was created in response to division regarding the draft Norms on Business and Human Rights which were put to the UN Commission on Human Rights in 2004 but failed to gather intergovernmental support. Instead, the Commission recommended that the Secretary-General appoint a Special Representative to advance the debate on business and human rights. Commission Resolution 2005/69 requested the new SRSG to identify and clarify standards of corporate responsibility and accountability regarding human rights; elaborate on state roles in regulating and adjudicating corporate activities; clarify concepts such as "complicity" and "sphere of influence"; develop methodologies for human rights impact assessments and consider state and corporate best practices'. Available at: http://www.reports-and-materials.org/Ruggie-introduction-to-portal-Jul-2009.doc.

25 *Ruggie* (2007) *Mapping Report*, para 33.

26 Stoitchkova 2010; Stewart 2012; Van den Herik 2010, p. 350; Ezeudu 2011, p. 11; Voiculescu 2007, p. 399; Kyriakakis 2017a, pp. 221–40; Kinley et al., in McBarnet et al (eds) 2007; Burchard 2010b, p. 919; Clapham 2008, p. 899; 'business and human rights' specifically has also become a theme outside of law, for instance, in international relations, e.g., Mwangi, Rieth and Schmitz 2013; Deitelhoff and Wolf 2013; Deva and Bilchitz 2013 and 2017; *Stop Corporate Impunity* 2014, 'The International Peoples Treaty on the Control of Transnational Corporations' (n.d.).

27 The first two sessions of the OEIGWG were 'dedicated to conducting constructive deliberations on the content, scope, nature and form of the future international instrument'. Building on the first session held in July 2015, the second session in October 2016 continued the discussion so as to enable the OEIGWG Chairperson-Rapporteur to 'prepare elements for the draft legally binding instrument for substantive negotiations at the commencement of the third session' (see: https://www.ohchr.org/en/hrbodies/hrc/wgtranscorp/pages/igwgontnc.aspx).

policy-oriented texts in this genre do not refer to individual liability of the directors, managers or others inside the corporation, but only to the corporate entity itself. The conclusion is always this: 'Corporations must be held accountable!'[28]

At first glance this narrative sounds eminently reasonable. If we think about it, and beyond the examples in this body of literature, corporations are indeed deeply involved in all the world's main problems today, ranging from war (arms and private military companies and those benefiting from access to oil, or rebuilding contracts), poverty (companies implicated in creating food deserts in the Global North, and controlling access to essential medicines, seeds and land in the South), a polluted environment (the energy consumed by massive servers containing our search engine and social media data), and gendered, racialized violence in the North (private prisons, the involvement of private companies in refugee detention, healthcare, benefits assessments and transport).[29]

The solution sounds plausible until one stops to consider the deadlock that appears – mainly below the surface, but which is sometimes verbalised – in some of this literature: the reason there are corporate 'crimes' and there is corporate impunity is *because* corporations rule.

The foreign investment law scholar Muthucumaraswamy Sornarajah succinctly sums up the problem: 'The need for regulation of this private power through the instrumentality of international law is a necessary fact which has not been adequately addressed, largely because the existence of such power itself ensures that no control is brought about'.[30] The legal scholar Dan Danielsen has pointed out that while much of the literature on corporate regulation and accountability starts with the unstated – and counterfactual – assumption that states can (that is, have the power to), and will (can be moved to), 'govern' the corporation, the reality is much more complex.[31] He explains that large states and corporations co-produce sets of rules, regulations and policies that represent a certain (constantly renegotiated) balance between the powers, capabilities and interests of each. When corporations rule, the balance inevitably tips in their favour. As will become clear in the course of this book, it is not simply this correction to the counterfactual but mainstream assumption about states' ability and desire to restrain corporate power that is needed. Also

28 E.g., Zerk 2006; Černič 2010; Bernaz 2016; and Baars 2007.

29 In the UK such corporate activities are monitored, for example, by CorporateWatch: https://corporatewatch.org/. Of course, there are other solid reasons why one might not prefer the carceral solution – for an abolitionist perspective, see Davis 2003.

30 Sornarajah 2010, p. 240.

31 Danielsen 2015. For more on this, see further below.

the very fact that such a counterfactual belief could be so widely held is significant, and warrants our analysis, in itself. In this book, I therefore also explain how this assumption, and subsequently this deadlock, came into being, what the power of this piece of legal ideology is, and how we can subvert it so as to create space to imagine a different response to global corporate capitalism. As such I provide a counter-narrative to the popular mainstream literature on the call for the use of international criminal law to restrain business in conflict, in order to make a much broader argument about the 'actual' relationship between law and capital, and what we could call its 'progeny', the corporation. What this leads to is a realisation that working out alternative social and economic models ought to be our main focus.

1.2 *This Book: a Counter-narrative*

In this book I use a Marxist theoretical framework and method. Marxist theory has garnered renewed interest in the past decade, perhaps for obvious reasons. Marxist legal theory has likewise experienced a revival and vigorous redevelopment, for example in the writings of China Miéville, Robert Knox and Ntina Tzouvala, whose work emphasises the co-constitutive nature of capitalism and law.[32]

Hugh Collins, the acrid but astute critic, explains Marxist approaches to law:

> The typical legal theory dispensed in law schools presents descriptions of law, analysis of legal concepts, and inquires into the demands of justice, based upon assumptions about the legitimate authority of the power which is exercised through the institutions of a modern legal system … [whereas] Marxism is bent upon the overthrow of the existing apparatus of domination, [and thus] its objectives in the study of law differ markedly … The principal aim of Marxist jurisprudence is to criticise the centrepiece of liberal political philosophy, the ideal called the Rule of Law … By exposing the structures of domination and subverting the beliefs and values which sustain them, Marxists seek to pave the way towards a revolutionary social transformation.[33]

'Exposing the structures of domination and subverting the beliefs and values which sustain them' accurately describes the main aim of this book. More specifically, I seek to achieve this task as outlined by Chris Arthur: 'The task … is

32 Miéville 2006, 2008, 2009; Knox 2009, 2010, 2012, 2016a, 2016b; Tzouvala 2016.

33 Collins 1982, p. 1. I have reversed the order of Collins's sentences here; he starts his text with 'The principal aim …'.

tracing ... both the relationships that are expressed in the legal superstructure and those that it ideologically spirits away'.[34]

The claim that adequate regulation of corporations does not exist, because corporate power prevents it, points us to the 'structures of domination' mentioned by Collins above. Sornarajah's demand for legal controls are caused by, and part of, 'the beliefs and values which sustain them' mentioned in the same quote. Marxist theory elucidates who is dominating, through what structures, and what the role of those structures is in the domination. Specifically, in this book I look at the role of law in expressing, affecting, abstracting, shifting and spiriting away the relationship between those who in criminal law terminology would be known as the 'perpetrator' and the 'victim'. Through law, this relationship becomes one between legal persons, and one of the focal points of this book is what happens to the human relationship when it is 'legalised', especially when the legal person is a reified *corporate* person. Although the 'business and human rights' debate (and practice) is broader than this, I specifically focus on the International Criminal Law aspect of it. In Sections 2–4 below I set out the specifics of the Marxist theory of law that I employ to do so.

1.3 *The Structure of the Book*

I have divided some of the chapters into A and B Sections (or at one point A, B, and C), which each contain one side of a story, in order to show and emphasise the dialectical interrelation between (and interpenetration of) the two sides.

Proposing a radical new approach requires going to the root of the problem. The first point for discussion in this book, then, is the nature of capitalist law, which I examine in the second half of this chapter. Few mainstream *or* critical legal texts (or indeed texts in other areas) question the notion that law is inevitable, and mostly a good thing,[35] nor do they deal with the question of where the *form* of law came from (as opposed to where law's *content* – particular legal norms, or all legal norms – came from), how and why it was created or why *law* specifically was selected as opposed to other forms of social organisation.[36] The *commodity form theory of law*, the Marxist legal theory as put forward by Evgeny Pashukanis in 1924 and elaborated in particular in the area of international law by China Miéville in 2004, provides a clear and persuasive explanation of *where law comes from* and *why it (was) developed*.[37]

34 Arthur, Editor's Introduction, in Pashukanis 1978, p. 31.

35 On this, see the anarchist psychologist Fox 1993.

36 E.g., Miéville 2006, pp. 59–60.

37 Miéville 2004.

The second task of this counter-narrative is to construct an alternative account of the corporation. Mainstream legal scholarship also treats the corporation ahistorically and as unquestionably 'natural' and 'good' – at least good most of the time. Company law textbooks generally contain a page or less on the history of the corporation, and several display an unquestioningly explicit pro-corporate stance. The specific field of economic history describes particular companies' development mainly teleologically. There is little to no critical scholarship on the corporation in law or in other disciplines.[38] In this book I provide a comprehensive, interdisciplinary account of 'the corporation in international law', engaging literature and insights from history, sociology, criminology and other disciplines.

Employing the commodity form theory of law, I show that the corporation came from somewhere. I establish that what has come to be capitalism's main motor, the corporation, was developed as a legal concept to 'congeal' relations of production (where 'calculable law' enabled literal 'accountability' of risk in legal relations) and minimise capitalists' risk-exposure while maximising surplus value extraction. In other words, the corporation was constructed as a 'structure of irresponsibility'[39] – precisely to ensure 'corporate impunity' (and the impunity of the individuals behind the corporation). The corporation became 'capital personified', an amoral calculator, driven by the profit imperative, or the imperialism at the heart of the corporation. Moreover, I show what 'global corporate power' consists of and where it came from – how, from the sixteenth century onwards, the corporation served as an instrument of imperialism, causing the global spread of capitalism and the global adoption (imposition) of capitalist law – law's 'capitalising mission' – for example through the colonial Dutch and British East India Companies as well as the dozens of other companies involved in corporate imperialism and the corporate scramble for Africa. In order to protect corporate power/corporate capitalism, an epistemological divide between the 'private' (where corporations have legal personality) and 'public' (where they do not) international law spheres was created in the late nineteenth to early twentieth century. This divide functions to shield 'the economic' and its corporate agents from political and humanitarian concerns and responsibilities, including responsibility for harm resulting from involvement in conflict. Investment law is one example of an area where the vast power this accords corporations vis-à-vis states has recently come to the fore. The 'law on the protection of foreign direct investment', as it is known in full,

38 But see Baars and Spicer (eds) 2017, and further below.
39 This term is used by Glasbeek 2010.

is created and serves to protect the property and profits of precisely those multinationals accused of wrongdoing in the Global South. In Chapter 2, I *reconnect* the ideas and concepts from increasingly separate areas of law such as company law and criminal law, international criminal law, international economic law and public international law, at the same time also reconnecting domestic and international law, exposing overlaps as well as significant deliberate, planned gaps, erasures and blind spots. I further highlight the real-world effects of such conceptual separations within the 'international law enterprise'.

Having examined the roots of law and the corporation, in Chapter 3 I move on to examine exactly how the relationship between law and capitalism plays out when the question of the responsibility of business actors (companies as well as individuals) arises in international law. Here I narrow my focus to examine international criminal law (ICL).

After World War Two, ICL was developed ostensibly as an accountability mechanism – performing an important ideological function as the completion piece (based on the idea that law only makes sense when it can be enforced and violators can be punished) of the international law enterprise. Rather than providing genuine accountability, however, I show that ICL functioned in the Nuremberg trials of the industrialists implicated in World War Two, and the sparse trials of businessmen on the Eastern (Japanese) front, to *conceal* rather than address the economic causes and imperialist nature of the war – and, effectively, through this, exclude economic actors from the scope of ICL. Moreover, the trials after World War Two served, despite the progressive efforts of individual lawyers (eventually turning into a theatre of the absurd) to legitimise through 'capitalism's victors' justice' the global economic hegemon's position, and enabled capital's further expansion through colonisation.

ICL lay dormant (at least in terms of application on the supranational level) during the Cold War but after 1989 it was rediscovered and to some extent *reimagined* and rewritten. In Chapter 4A I describe and evaluate the conscious creation (mostly by academic lawyers) of the tool of international criminal law post-Cold War, liberal and legalist ICL discourses which figure the new ICL as the completion of the international law enterprise, and a liberal saviour. ICL's foundational narratives each build up their 'pre-fab', constructive critique, while foreclosing radical interrogation of the existence and purpose of ICL itself. I contrast this with Pashukanis's comments on the commodified, visceral element of criminal law and introduce the notion of ICL's 'canned morality'. Then in Chapter 4B I examine lawyers' work in abstracting relationships of responsibility in the development of ICL's 'modes of participation' and 'degrees of liability' – which – I argue – make ICL in fact eminently applicable to business scenarios. Yet, ICL is actually (and deliberately) a very field which excludes through 'planned impunity' most 'crimes', and se serve predominantly as a ruse where 'expert' doctrinal debate obscure tifies) lack of application. In Chapter 4C I investigate ICL's internal contradictions on the interplay of individuality and collectivity, and the putative liability of the corporation as a 'legal person' – which contrasts with the 'individualisierung' of ICL elsewhere – proposed by academic lawyers and others.

The almost complete non-application of ICL to business in conflict (even in situations where businesspersons/companies were clearly implicated) betrays the 'capitalist logic' of IL, I argue in Chapter 5, where we see that, as in Nuremberg and Tokyo, ICL is used to create narratives that exclude the economic causes of conflict, to shield particular actors, and to form a 'distraction' for the implementation of far-reaching economic (liberalising, capitalising) reforms.

ICL's strong emotive appeal (I show in Chapters 4 and 6 how this forms an element of law's ideology) has led both legal scholars and 'cause lawyers' (mostly members of the white Western professional classes) to continue to advocate and seek 'corporate accountability' in ICL. In response to the perceived 'corporate impunity', however (Chapter 6), 'cause lawyers' and human rights activists have tried to hold businesses to account through strategic litigation, and have failed. In the final part of the book, I argue that, counterintuitively, *through this practice*, and combined with (legalised, weaponised) 'corporate social responsibility', 'corporate accountability' becomes part of corporate ideology, an instrument of legitimisation for the liberal capitalist enterprise. Especially, by performing the 'concession' of including it as a subject of ICL capitalist elites would complete the corporation's reification and ideological identity as a political citizen exercising legitimate authority within 'global governance'. The relationship between law and capitalism therefore constructs corporate impunity, while at the same time keeping this fact largely hidden from us through its promise of accountability, forever deferred.

In conclusion, I argue that while emancipation from corporate power *cannot* be achieved through law, its promise lies in the alternatives (such as countersystemic activism, building alternative modes of production, abolitionist and transformative justice work) and, with that, human emancipation.[40]

40 'What is to be done?' is the classic phrase attributed to V.I. Lenin, which emphasises the need to turn theory into *praxis* in Marxist thought. I pose the question here but offer only limited examples of what others are attempting *to do* in relation to the issue in Chapter 6.

1.4 *Debates Intervened in, Limitations, Future Research*

This book builds directly on a number of key texts by Miéville,[41] Marks,[42] Knox[43] (theory of IL), Glasbeek[44] (company law), Shamir[45] (sociology of CSR), Pearce and Tombs,[46] and Tombs and Whyte[47] (corporate criminology). I critically examine, integrate, apply and elaborate on these texts. My text is written mostly from within legal scholarship but is supplemented with history, economics, business, etc. so as to combine legal theory, black letter doctrine and legal practice to come to a holistic understanding of the operation of law in society. While my desire has been to break (even sub-)disciplinary silos and illuminate blind spots, inevitably this wide range carries the risk in reality of omission, reduction and limited depth. Much more can and must be said on many of the topics in this book in future works.

Scholars in history,[48] sociology[49] and management studies[50] have also critically examined the corporation in the context of global capitalism. This book incorporates the findings of some of these studies into its discussion on law, integrating them and building on them to a point beyond individual disciplinary boundaries.

The book produces a narrative of IL that takes into account the nature and significance of the corporate form – while despite 'global corporate rule' often being proclaimed, the corporation has been notably absent from accounts of IL. For the first time, the topic of business and human rights is discussed using the dialectical method – taking into account the context, materialist history and structure. The benefit is that this allows us to break the deadlock in current thinking on the issue and to stop seeing the status quo as inevitable or unchangeable but instead as one stage in a process. Also, for the first time the commodity form theory of law has been applied in a sustained way to a specific societal problem. A secondary benefit of this is that the application of the commodity form theory to a real-world problem shows that the commodity form theory 'works' and gives us specific answers to and insights into

41 Especially Miéville 2006.
42 Especially Marks 2003; Marks 2001, p. 109; Marks 2009, p. 1; Marks 2011, p. 57.
43 Knox 2009, p. 413; Knox 2012, p. 21; Knox 2016, p. 81.
44 Especially, Glasbeek 2002.
45 Especially, Shamir 2010, p. 531.
46 Especially, Pearce and Tombs 1990.
47 Especially, Tombs and Whyte 2003, p. 217.
48 See, e.g., Harris 2000; McQueen 2009; Taylor 2006; Yamamoto 2011, pp. 806–34; Stern 2011.
49 E.g., Whyte 2008; Tombs and Whyte 2003, p. 217.
50 Jones and Spicer 2009; Fleming and Spicer 2007; Fleming and Jones 2013.

specific problems. This makes this book one of the very few[51] critical analyses of company law and the phenomenon of the corporation in the global political economy – from a legal-historical perspective. Because of the often-made claim that 'corporate rule is here' it would appear obvious and urgent that such an examination be made. Nevertheless, this book is still one of the few[52] critical analyses of both the nature and practice of international criminal law. Considering that ICL is now 'in fashion' – the 'accountability tool of choice' – it is timely to critically engage with it. This book offers a response to current, highly topical real-world questions, not only those faced by, for example, the US Supreme Court,[53] but also by the victims of corporate abuses. It provides fresh research on the impact of international criminal law on domestic justice systems and includes discussion of past and recent cases that have not been analysed in the literature before and builds on the author's experience in practice. Through uncovering archival materials not previously discussed in the literature, and through unearthing long-forgotten court decisions, the book subverts commonly held beliefs regarding the Nuremburg and Tokyo processes. Finally, it tests, for the first time, the widespread expectation of corporate accountability through the mechanism of international criminal law.

The context of this set of questions is a time when, despite indications that we should have learnt our lesson from recent financial crises, 'Reports of the death of the Washington Consensus have been greatly exaggerated'.[54] It is also a time of renewed popular anti-capitalist resistance, most visibly in the global 'Occupy' movement, but also the significant rise in mutual aid activism, alternative media and growth in the food sovereignty movement.[55] As such, it would seem an auspicious moment to investigate the issue of corporate 'excess', the fallacy of the legal accountability fantasy, and to propose a radically different perspective on corporate capitalism.

51 Ireland, Grigg-Spall, and Kelly 1987; Ireland 1999, p. 32; Ireland 2002, p. 120; Ireland 2009, p. 837.

52 But see the works of Tallgren and Megret: Tallgren 2002a, p. 561; Tallgren 2002b, p. 297; Mégret n.d.; Mégret 2008; Mégret 2002, p. 1261; Schwöbel (ed.) 2014.

53 *Kiobel v. Royal Dutch Petroleum* Co., 621 F.3d 111, 123–24 (2d Cir. 2010).

54 E.g., Rasulov 2010; and Sornarajah 2010, p. 77, who speaks of a 'retreat of liberalism'.

55 See, e.g., http://www.occupytogether.org/, Mutual Aid Disaster Relief, see: https://mutualaiddisasterrelief.org/, It's Going Down Podcast, see: https://itsgoingdown.org/category/podcast/ and Global Justice, 'What is Food Sovereignty?', see: https://www.globaljustice.org.uk/what-food-sovereignty.

retical Framework

Commodity Form Theory of Law – a Brief Outline

larxism: A General Theory,[56] Evgeny Pashukanis outlines the commodity form theory of law, which holds that law (the legal system) came about as a result of the class struggle between the feudal lords and their subjects, and was fundamental in the transition from feudalism to capitalism, from privilege to law, and, as Maine had said it prior to Marx, from status to contract.[57] The emergence of law as we know it today is explained by the emergence of capitalism in medieval Europe, and *vice versa*. This is the point of departure of the commodity form theory of law. Pashukanis's key puzzle is why law specifically – as law – emerged as the means to regulate human relationships and what the 'lawness' of legal rules and a legal system consists of.

Pashukanis explains that the juridical element in the regulation of human conduct enters where the isolation and opposition of interests begins. This is 'tie[d] closely to the emergence of the commodity form in mediating material exchanges'[58] as described by Marx in *Capital I*.[59] At this point man comes to be seen as a legal subject, having legal personality, the bearer of rights as opposed to customary privileges and duties. Man (white *bourgeois* man) as a commodity-owner is a legal owner. Thus, the logic of the commodity form is the logic of the legal form.[60]

In *Between Equal Rights*, Miéville elaborates that, while in commodity exchange, each commodity must be the private property of its owner, freely given in return for the other at a rate determined by their exchange value, each agent in the exchange must be, first, a property owner and, second, formally equal to the other agent(s).[61] Whereas previously, the formally unequal individuals implied by the hierarchical command relations of feudalism (and other prior forms of social organisation) engaged in unfree transactions, in the transition (from feudalism) to capitalism another specific form of social regulation became necessary, to formalise the method of settlement without

56 Pashukanis 1978.

57 Maine 1861, Chapter V. Maine of course had a different normative appreciation for this transition; for instance, 'old law fixed a man's social position irreversibly at his birth, modern law allows him to create it for himself by convention', Chapter IX; Miéville 2006, p. 285.

58 Arthur 1978, p. 13.

59 Marx 1976, pp. 163 ff.

60 Arthur 1978, p. 13.

61 Miéville 2006, p. 78. Miéville has applied his theoretical approach in Miéville 2008 and 2009.

affecting either party's formally equal status. '*That form is law*'.[62] This form was also simpler than the complicated and specific rights and obligations of actors in feudal transactions and therefore significantly more efficient, making it possible to vastly increase economic interactions between commodity owners.[63]

The change occurs gradually, imperceptibly at the time of the growth of the urban middle class, of land enclosures, of technological development enabling the production of a surplus to be taken to market. In Pashukanis's words, 'only the development of the market creates the possibility of – and the necessity for – transforming the person appropriating things by his labour (or by robbery) into a legal owner. There is no clearly defined borderline between these two phases. The "natural" changes into the juridical imperceptibly, just as armed robbery blends quite directly with trade'.[64] Eventually, and '[o]nly when bourgeois relations are fully developed does law become abstract in character. Every person becomes man in the abstract, all labour becomes socially useful labour in the abstract, every subject becomes an abstract legal subject. At the same time, the norm takes on the logically perfected form of abstract universal law'.[65] Accompanying the development of the economy based on the commodity and on money, human relations become legal relations, all property is transformed into moveable property, including labour power.[66] The *cash nexus* is introduced into all relationships,[67] including – for our purposes significantly – relationships of responsibility.

While legal forms regulate relationships between autonomous legal subjects, the subject is the 'cell form' of the legal system, a basic element of which is contestation (struggle over property). In Chapter 2A I describe the becoming of legal subjects of collectivities (polities, corporations, etc.), and later, (increasing categories of) individuals, in the atomisation process of modernity.

62 Miéville 2006, p. 79 (emphasis in original). 'The owners of commodities were of course proprietors even before they acknowledged one another as such, but in a different, organic, non-legal sense'; Pashukanis 1978, p. 121. See also Cohen 2000, pp. 217 ff., who explains the relationship prior to law as one of power.

63 I am grateful to Jay Boggis for this insight.

64 Pashukanis 1978, p. 124.

65 Pashukanis 1978, p. 120. Of course legal personhood was then, and still is to some extent, dependent on class, race, status as a slave, prisoner or 'free person', gender expression, ability, migration status and many other factors.

66 Pashukanis 1978, p. 40; Marx 1976, pp. 125 ff.

67 Pashukanis 1978, p. 40. On the concept of cash nexus, see Caudwell 1905, p. 69: '[the] cash nexus ... replaces all other social ties, so that society seems held together, not by mutual love or tenderness or obligation, but simply by profit'.

.ly, for law, the fundamental question arises, why the machinery of state .on is created in the form of an impersonal apparatus of public power, .rate from society.[68] Pashukanis argues that, although the emergence of the state was enabled by law, it was not *necessary*.[69] It was not necessary because of the coercion inherent in the form of law itself (see below). Miéville attaches great significance to this point for the 'lawness' of international law, which exists without an overarching authority.[70] On the usefulness of the state for law, nonetheless,

> coercion cannot appear [in a society based on commodity production] in undisguised form as a simple act of expediency. It has to appear rather as coercion emanating from an abstract collective person, exercised not in the interest of the individual from whom it emanates – for every person in commodity-producing society is egoistic – but in the interest of all parties to legal transactions. The power of one person over another is brought to bear in reality as the force of law, that is to say as the force of an objective, impartial norm.[71]

This is the power, the violence, and the *legitimacy* of law.

2.2 *The Form and Violence of Law: Property (and Sovereignty) as 'Mine-Not-Yours'*

A crucial point in this brief exposition of the commodity form theory of law is that of the fundamental nature of property ownership as a legal right. In *Between Equal Rights*, Miéville explains:

> For the commodity form itself, dispute, coercion and violence are inherently implied. The notion of 'mine' necessary to ownership and commodity exchange is only meaningful inasmuch as it is 'mine-*not-yours*'. The fact that something is 'mine' necessarily defines it in opposition to a counterclaim, whether or not that counterclaim is in fact made. Disputation, and hence the legal form itself, lurks at the heart of the most peaceful private property relation.[72]

---

68 Pashukanis 1978, p. 139.

69 Ibid: 'The state authority introduces clarity and stability into the structure of law, but does not create the premises for it, which are rooted in the material relations of production'.

70 Miéville 2006, pp. 124–31.

71 Pashukanis 1978, pp. 143–4.

72 At fn. 99 on pp. 95, 96–7 (emphasis in the original).

Miéville argues, 'Superordinate and abstract coercion is contingent to the legal form itself'.[73]

The contestation over property ownership which gave rise to 'law as we know it' also positions property ownership as the *Grundnorm*[74] of all legal systems, the norm at the basis of other norms[75] of law as a system of rules, institutions, processes and practices. This fact means that legal systems' rules and processes are oriented towards, and find their *raison d'être* in, upholding, protecting and enforcing the norm of property ownership, and that legal systems operate according to the logic of capitalism. This aspect is key in this book.

3 'Developing the Form on the Basis of the Fundamental Form'

Without departing from the main tenets of the commodity form theory of law, I adjust a number of Miéville's parameters to better fit some aspects of Marxist theory *and* the questions I seek to answer. These relate to my use of a notion of 'law' rather than his differentiation between national/international law (3.1); the concept of global classes in preference over Miéville's emphasis on the international state-system (3.2); and my foregrounding of imperialist economic violence (3.3) perpetrated and participated in by the various types of members of the global capitalist class rather than inter-state war per se. In Sections 3.4 and 3.5 I sketch the application of the commodity form theory to my two focal points: ICL and the corporation.

3.1 *Law: Inter-polity Law and Proto-law*

According to Pashukanis, the 'development of international law as a system was evoked not by the requirements of the state, but by the necessary conditions for commercial relations between those tribes which were not under a single sphere of authority'.[76] In other words, '(proto-) international law predates domestic law'.[77] Miéville picks up this point and adds that this 'has nothing to do with any putative ontological primacy of the international sphere: it is, rather, because law is thrown up by and necessary to a systematic com-

73 Miéville 2006, p. 288.

74 This is a somewhat bastardised use of Kelsen's concept (Kelsen 2008).

75 Cf. Hohfeld 1913–14, pp. 21–3.

76 Pashukanis 1978, p. 89. As Weber puts it, 'the oldest commerce is an exchange relation between alien tribes'. Weber 1982, pp. 195–8.

77 Miéville 2004, p. 289.

change relationship, and it was between organised but disparate hout such overarching authorities rather than between individu- such relationships sprang'.[78] Of course this means such law would be more accurately described as 'inter-polity law'. Miéville omits one further thing, namely that it is also inaccurate to speak of *domestic* law at this point, or of a concept of the domestic beyond the tribal community.[79] While my adjustment does not fundamentally alter Miéville's point about the lack of overarching authority at law's origin, an additional point can be made about the common root of international and domestic law: one did not predate the other, in fact, both share the same root, as 'law' undifferentiated, predating the state system.[80] At this point law/the legal form was not universalised: 'The law only held where and when commodity exchange was likely to occur'.[81] In this book I emphasise the common root and form of domestic and international law. A second point for the purposes of this book can also be made – namely that in the transitional period law's first persons, the formally equal legal persons between whom the transaction enabled by law took place, being polities, were collectivities. As will become clear below, this point is obvious when seen in its historical context, if not through today's liberal individualist spectacles. In Chapter 2A, I discuss the transition from tribal and familial collectivities governed by moral and kinship ties to individual and 'artificial' separate legal persons for corporations governed by legal rules, focusing specifically on the reasons for this development.

3.2 *Global Classes*

My main departure from Miéville (closely connected to the above) is my emphasis on the global nature of the class system at the helm of which we find mainly (but not exclusively) white male members of the Western elites – active both in business and governance, who have at their disposal law, be it international or domestic, or the currently popular notion 'global governance'.[82] Pashukanis writes on international law: 'Bourgeois see international law as a function of some ideal cultural community which mutually connects indi-

78 Miéville 2004, p. 289.

79 In international law scholarship it is customary to speak of 'domestic law' – meaning national law, in opposition to international law. As states with centralised authority in the modern sense did not emerge until at least 1648, one cannot speak before this point about separate realms of 'national' (or domestic) and 'international' law in any meaningful way. Cf. Teschke 2009.

80 Cf. Neff 2010, pp. 6–7.

81 Miéville 2006, pp. 128 ff.

82 Baars 2011, p. 429. The notion of global class is the subject of debate, see, e.g., Anievas 2008.

vidual states. But they do not see that this community reflects (conditionally and relatively, of course) the common interest of the commanding and ruling classes of different states which have identical class structures'.[83] Contra Pashukanis's hint at global class society at the basis of IL, Miéville takes a (liberal) statist perspective on IL, viewing states as the 'atom', the 'fundamental contending agents' of IL.[84] My view is that we are not only dealing with similar class structures in different states, but that those classes (or rather, members of the same class) are also connected globally, by virtue of mutual/identical interests globally and often also actually as members of global business communities and other class networks.[85]

If we accept with Pashukanis that the State was a 'convenient' but not a necessary result of capitalist law,[86] then we can begin to envisage a 'pluralist' Marxist perspective where states are not the atom of IL, but instead where individuals and corporations and states and other 'legal persons' compete in complex ways on a predominantly transnational (global) plane.[87] Miéville (following Pashukanis) argues that the overarching and abstract coercion that the state represents on the domestic plane takes the form of interdependence under the conditions of balance of power[88] – which is a somewhat outdated, realist international relations perspective.[89] Instead, a pluralist perspective better fits with Miéville's assessment of the origin of law: 'The development of law as a system came about as a result of the commercial requirements of disparate groups (tribes, polities) that existed before the state system and thus before any overarching enforcing authority existed. *Ius gentium* (the law of nations) was the prototype of the legal superstructure in its pure form'.[90] I elaborate on this development, and global class, in Chapter 2.

3.3 *Conflict, Violence, Imperialism, Structural Violence and Oppression*

Miéville argues that violence and coercion are inherent in the commodity relationship itself (as in the 'mine-not-yours' illustration above): in international law, 'self-help – the coercive violence of the legal subjects [states] themselves –

83 Pashukanis 2006, p. 324.
84 Miéville 2006, p. 173.
85 Global business communities: Moses 2008, p. 7; governance elites: Shamir 2010; Krisch 2009. On the notion of global class, see also Chimni 2011; Rasulov 2008; Sklair 1997.
86 Miéville 2006, p. 124.
87 For a similar critique of Miéville's emphasis on states as the main actors in IL, see Knox 2009, esp. pp. 418–23.
88 Miéville 2006, p. 129.
89 E.g., Krasner 1999, pp. 43ff.
90 Miéville 2006, p. 130.

.he legal relation'.[91] Yet Miéville himself makes the classic liberal mis- acing *war* at the centre of IL, which (as explained above) he conceives ıst system. In line with my view of a 'pluralist' global class society I inclu… the myriad other forms of coercion found in today's global capitalism, and broaden the focus from military violence (war) to include the everyday violence of capitalism where the capitalists own the means of production and therefore the ability (power) to exploit all others.[92] This violence is the opposite of *human emancipation*.[93] It is *exploitation* in Marx's sense of the extraction of surplus value from a workforce with no choice but to subject itself to the wage labour system, the unfreedom inherent in the structural determination, the oppression inherent in a society structured along hierarchies of race, class, gender, ability, etc. It *does* at times take the form of war/physical violence, but much more commonly, it is the everyday exploitation, encroachment and unfreedom the global racialised and gendered proletariat, the wretched of the earth,[94] endure, by virtue of the inequality inherent in the capitalist mode of production.

Relatedly, Miéville agrees with Pashukanis that 'the better part of international law's norms refer to warfare'.[95] This may have been the case in Pashukanis's time, but it is no longer the case today. Much is 'international economic law', including also examples of internationalised law in the form of agreements between the various global ('multinational') enterprises and between international organisations and 'developing' states, such as loan agreements.[96] Even if we do agree with Pashukanis that the real historical content of international law is the struggle between capitalist states, and with Miéville that that content is 'an ongoing and remorseless struggle for control over the resources of capitalism, that will often *as part of that capitalist ("economic") competitive process* spill into political violence', we must take that 'remorseless struggle' (cause) and its inherent structural violence as a starting point rather than the often-occurring military/political violence (means, or effect).[97]

91 Miéville 2006, p. 133.
92 For a similar perspective, see Knox 2009, pp. 423–5.
93 Marx 2000c, p. 54.
94 Pottier, E. (n.d. 1890–1900); Fanon 1963.
95 Miéville 2006, p. 136 (citing Pashukanis 2006, p. 322).
96 See, e.g., Qureshi 2011.
97 Miéville 2006, p. 139 (emphasis in the original).

3.4 *The Commodity Form Theory and Corporations*

The commodity form theory of law allows us to explain and understand the process of development (the *abstraction*) of the legal concept of the corporation out of earlier forms of social organisation, as well as the way in which relationships of responsibility are expressed, abstracted, and shifted by means of what we now call 'company law'. I argue in this book that such relations of responsibility (in the non-legal sense) are profoundly affected by the creation of the corporation as a separate person in law, in more than one way, which I explain in Chapter 2 and illustrate in Chapters 3 and 4. I also comment on the role of the corporation in the global political economy more broadly, and the ideological moves law provides for corporate capitalism's legitimation.

3.5 *The Commodity Form Theory and (International) Criminal Law*

When all relationships become legal relationships and members of society become atomised individuals in competition with one another (a process which has reached its climax in today's neoliberalism), the violation of certain norms constitutes a crime. Criminal law transforms an issue of society at large (certain effects of the prevailing mode of production) to an issue (deviancy) of an individual, for which the individual may expect to 'pay' in time or money.[98] The introduction of the corporate legal person into criminal law further changes the relationship between the wrongdoer and the person(s) affected by the 'crime' – I elaborate on this in Chapters 4 and 6. I focus on ICL because it has become the 'accountability tool of choice' for matters of international concern.[99] Criminal law has a special ideological 'weight', and, according to Pashukanis, '[c]riminal law is the sphere in which legal relations attain their maximum intensity and, as such, [it] was the dominant bourgeois form of regulation'. In particular ICL has been invested with the expectation of it 'becom[ing] the central pillar in the world community for upholding fundamental dictates of humanity'.[100] Criminal law, more than any other area of law, functions as society's 'moral guide' and is thus a powerful ideological tool that can be deployed at opportune political moments in the service of capitalism, as 'canned morality'. When there is a public call for 'something' to be done, criminal prosecution of one or two individuals can serve as a powerful ideological, pacificatory device, which of course has a direct material impact when resistance is subdued and 'business as usual' can continue for everyone

98 Pashukanis 1978, p. 177.
99 E.g., Drumbl 2011, p. 23.
100 Cassese 2003, p. 18.

aside from those prosecuted.[101] Criminal law can have this function also when it is not (intended to be) enforced, or enforced only on certain persons and not on others. In Chapters 3, 5, and 6, I discuss these questions. In Chapter 4, I also discuss the making and demarcating of international criminal law – the meta-debates on what is, or even should be considered, an international crime and who can be 'an international criminal' (an ICL subject) in the movement towards including the corporate legal person which is tied up with the impunity/punity dialectic.

4 Beyond 'Nebulous Left Functionalism': Further Considerations on Marxism and Law

Some further attention must be paid to key concepts in Marxist theory and how these affect an analysis of the book's topic. Marx and Engels themselves never made law a direct object of their inquiry, although they treat it with varying degrees of depth in their works.[102] The *Communist Manifesto* is a natural starting point on certain key ideas that inform this book, in particular class struggle. Further, in *Capital* Volume I (Part VIII) Marx elaborates on the primitive accumulation and the repressive use of law in the transition to capitalism. Other texts by Marx of relevance to this book are *On the Jewish Question* (for the concept of 'human emancipation' which is contrasted with 'legal emancipation', below Chapter 6, Section 5) and *Critique of the Gotha Programme* (on the notion of compromise and 'tinkering on the surface').[103] Finally, the *German Ideology* offers an impetus toward the critique of the ideological function of law.[104] Below, I add considerations of determination and totality (4.1), the structure *vs.* agency question (4.2), and law's emancipatory potential (4.3).

4.1 *Law 'Congealing Capitalism': Determination, Overdetermination and Totality*

Akbar Rasulov explains that

> the development of a consistently Marxist approach to international legal studies must begin … with the production of a general systematic account

101 And, of course, those affected by the 'crimes', but these disappear from view when 'justice' has been administered.

102 Cain 1979, p. 62.

103 Marx 2000c, pp. 46–64, Marx 2000a 610–16.

104 Marx 2000e, pp. 175–206.

> explaining the basic interrelationship between the historical patterns structuring the global division of labour (and the corresponding extraction of surplus value) and the corresponding institutional forms of the international legal order – in particular, with a view to establishing the latter's causative contribution to the burgeoning contradiction between the immanent logic of the global productive forces and the corresponding system of the global relations of production.[105]

Some legal scholars, such as Susan Marks, consider that economic factors, *among a range of other factors*, set limits on the ways in which law may develop.[106] Others, including Rasulov, consider this determination strictly: 'the terms on which other social factors [such as race, gender etc.] *overdetermine* the effects of class struggle are themselves determined, *in the last instance*, by the logic of class struggle'.[107] In other words, *everything* (all social phenomena) can ultimately be explained in economic terms. As I will show below (Chapter 2), Pashukanis's General Theory conforms to this latter point of view, and I also employ this here. The form and content of law are determined by the mode of production. Law '*congeals capitalism*'. Whatever material relations exist, we design law, or law functions, so as to confirm, support, congeal or concretise them.[108]

If 'everything' is determined by the economic base of society, then it follows that everything is interrelated. Global capitalism has 'create[d] a world in its image'.[109] According to Bertell Ollman: 'Capitalism ... stands out from earlier class societies in the degree to which it has integrated all major (and, increasingly, most minor) life functions in a single organic system dominated by the law of value and the accompanying power of money but also in the degree to which it hides and seeks to deny this singular achievement'.[110] In Marxism the concept of totality 'refer[s] to the actuality that phenomena in the world are interrelated, and hence can only be properly understood when viewed as elements within larger social systems, including the system of global capitalism'.[111] For an example of a very specific interpretation of the concept

105 Rasulov 2010, p. 257.
106 Marks 2008, p. 3.
107 Rasulov 2010, p. 261, emphasis added.
108 But see the works of authors such as Angela Davis, Selma James, Angela Harris, Kimberlé Crenshaw, etc. My next project involves developing a more complex account of the role of the corporation in the gendered, racialised, embodied, etc. global political economy.
109 Marx and Engels 1969, *Communist Manifesto*, p. 47.
110 Ollman 2003, p. 3.
111 Marks 2007, p. 15.

ity, in Chapter 2B, I cite the work of the legal scholar and historian Eric , who uses Immanuel Wallerstein's Marxist-inspired 'world systems theory'.

I am interested in this dialectical (or, perhaps, *panlectical* to reflect the sense that all factors interact with each other) relationship between the material world in which certain intellectual concepts arise – in this case in the sphere of law and business in conflict – how these ideas are translated into legal academic discourse and abstract legal concepts, and then sets of processes, rules, and institutions, that in turn affect material reality. One step in that process is the abstraction performed by lawyers and the fitting of the abstract concepts into a set of ideas which come to have some internal coherence, a legal system with a (measure of) internal logic *of itself*[113] – visible at least to lawyers – and *outwardly* creating the illusion of objectivity, *autonomy*.[114] As I try to show, scholars describing, representing, interpreting and *abstracting* the world tend to seek (or give) internal coherence in (to) a narrative, which in itself reflects the 'totality' of material reality more or less accurately, at any given point in time, and which affects material reality when such narratives influence, or are transformed into, legal decisions/rules. This is the dialectical process of *law(yers) congealing capitalism*.[115]

4.2 *Lawyers Congealing Capitalism: Who Constructs the Structure?*

Marx's methodology of historical materialism takes the 'base' of the material reality of economic relations to determine the ideological 'superstructure', which includes the political and legal superstructure.[116] The content of ideas such as law, religion, and culture are determined by (or representations of) economic reality (the base), which is determined by the ownership of the means of production, and evolves as a result of a dialectical relationship between the two opposites: 'all history is the history of class struggle'.[117] Putting it schematically, while according to Pashukanis/Miéville the legal *form* itself belongs to the base,[118] the *content* of norms is supplied by the superstructure, and the evolutionary dialectic between base and superstructure (between material reality

112 Wilson 2008, pp. xi–xiv.
113 Generally, Kennedy 1987.
114 Pashukanis 1978, p. 93.
115 For a detailed exposition of this process in the 'making of ICL', see Chapter 4.
116 Marx 2000d, p. 425; see, generally, Cohen 2000; Rasulov 2010, p. 261, Marks 2008, pp. 2–3, Ireland 2002, p. 126.
117 Marx and Engels 1969, p. 40.
118 Miéville 2006, pp. 88, 96; Pashukanis 1978, p. 93.

and ideas) is what causes change (progress) in society.[119] Where, then, is the individual in this? What is 'our' agency?[120] Engels said, 'Men make their histories themselves, only in given surroundings which condition it and on the basis of actual relations already existing, among which the economic relations, however much they may be influenced by the other political and ideological ones, are still ultimately the decisive ones, forming the red thread which runs through them and alone leads to understanding'.[121] Man can move only within the parameters of existing economic structures. The temptation then is to see or treat those structures as 'given', inevitable or even natural. Omitting structure from the discussion then has the effect of 'spiriting it away' and rendering what remains meaningful in its own right, containing its own origin and solution. Those who benefit from the current economic system would benefit from this ideological move, while it blinds those who are oppressed by it to possible emancipatory interventions. Marks warns critical legal scholars, who, perhaps contrary to mainstream lawyers, generally are 'attentive to the "false necessity" that treats social reality as naturally arising, rather than historically constructed',[122] not to fall into the trap of '"false contingency" ... according to which injustices appear random, accidental and arbitrary'.[123] Bringing structure back into the picture, she speaks of 'planned misery'[124] (the structural oppression experienced in particular by the 'bottom billion' in global society) in the way that I will discuss 'planned impunity' (of business actors involved in the specific acts that make up that oppression) in Marxist terms. The key question, then, appears to be: 'Who constructs the structure?'

Marx emphasised that current class structure of society, and indeed the economic structure of feudal society, was not simply a result of the 'luck of the draw' as to who was born a prince and who a pauper, nor was it because some worked hard and others were lazy. In the chapters in *Capital* on primitive accumulation, Marx describes the active, deliberate construction of class society,[125] which was also harrowingly described by E.P. Thompson in *The Making of the English Working Class*.[126] Since in the commodity form theory of law, law is an integral part (a *sine qua non*) of the economic structure of capitalist soci-

119 In *Preface to A Critique of Political Economy* Marx outlines the base-superstructure metaphor: Marx 2000d, pp. 425–6.
120 Generally, Callinicos 2004; specifically, Thompson 1963.
121 Engels 1894, para. 2(a).
122 Marks 2008, p. 15.
123 Ibid.
124 Marks 2011, pp. 57–78.
125 Marx 1976, pp. 871 ff.
126 Thompson 1963.

ety, the 'constructors' of law must be part of my inquiry. There is no structure without agency.[127] The dialectic between the individual agency of the jurist, academic author, lawmaker (lawyers, broadly understood) and the structure of law and economic relations is where capitalism is constituted. As noted above, lawyers, through law, *congeal* capitalism. I deliberately use the verb *to congeal* incorrectly here, to emphasise the hidden agency behind a process that seems 'natural'.[128]

While Miéville quotes Ralph Miliband's argument that judges make law that accommodates the interests of the class to which they themselves generally belong, he continues to argue that on the international level this is not the case.[129] My argument throughout this book is that this *is* the case, that international law is made by the pluralist conglomerate of global administrators (bureaucrats, oligarchs, global Hofmafia (Philip Allott),[130] the global judicial cocktail party (Anne-Marie Slaughter),[131] global handmaidens (Philip Alston),[132] global invisible college (Oscar Schachter),[133] global experts (David Kennedy))[134] *as members of a particular class*, the global capitalist class. In my upcoming chapters I pay particular attention to the personalities behind the content (and ideology) of law, in order precisely to elucidate the dialectic between their agency and the structure (including their class membership) within which they exist, and which they simultaneously construct, consciously or otherwise.

As Ollman has pointed out, those few who benefit from capitalism use a 'mixture of force and guile to order the lives and thinking of the great majority who would benefit most from radical change'.[135] Susan Marks has described and analysed the various different interpretations of the concept of ideology.[136] The interpretation she encourages critical international lawyers to use is 'the role of ideas and rhetorical processes in the legitimation of ruling power'.[137] I

---

127 On the structure versus agency debate generally, see Callinicos 2004.

128 Likewise, there is agency behind a jelly pudding congealing: someone made or acquired, selected, and mixed the ingredients, someone poured the mixture into a bowl, placed it in the fridge, where the jelly set. Through the actions of the maker, the pudding *was* congealed.

129 Miéville 2006, p. 121, quoting Miliband 1969, pp. 124–6.

130 Allott 2002, pp. 380–98.

131 Slaughter 2005, p. 96.

132 Alston 1997, p. 453.

133 Schachter 1977, p. 217.

134 Kennedy 2016.

135 Ollman 2003, p. 11.

136 Marks 2000, pp. 8–10; see also pp. 18–25.

137 Marks 2008, p. 7.

will focus in particular on the ideological function of law both in supporting and legitimating structures in society. One fundamental ideological function of law is that it presents itself as the explicit man-made mechanism for regulation and normative ordering of society, and thus the go-to place for solutions to society's problems. Because of the particular range of solutions law offers, it even limits what we might meaningfully (productively) consider as problems. Integral to law's ideology, finally, is law's ability to present *itself* as a solution rather than as 'part of the problem', or part of what creates problems in the world. Law's ideology therefore underlies advocates' choice for a *legal* solution even 'against better knowledge'.[138]

4.3 *Law's Emancipatory Potential Queried*

Two final points on law and Marxist theory of relevance to this book warrant elaboration in this section. They are the question of law's emancipatory potential[139] and the prospect for law in post-capitalist society. As Marx famously held, 'all history is the history of class struggle' – progress in society is the result of the struggle between classes over their opposing interests. Of what utility is law in the struggle of the working class (including, specifically, those affected by the involvement of business in conflict) against the powerful corporations, and/or the individual businesspersons at their core? Miéville states, 'Given the widespread though mistaken belief that law is counterposed to power and war, the desire for a rule of law is not surprising. Its extension is held to be an emancipatory project, internationally and domestically'.[140] Yet, since law, in the commodity form theory of law, is an inherently capitalist instrument (*qua* form, regardless even of content) based and built on the *Grundnorm*[141] of private property ownership and inhering between formally equal legal subjects, it cannot but serve the interests of capital and reflect the underlying economic relations. As Marx said, 'Right cannot be higher than the economic structure of society'.[142] Legal struggle can at times yield progressive results (Chapters 3A, 5 and 6), but, on law's emancipatory potential, we can generalise Arthur's statement:

> No amount of reformist factory legislation can overcome the basic presupposition of the law: that a property freely alienated belongs to the pur-

138 Phrase quoted by Susan Marks in Marks 2009 and used by Sloterdijk 1987, a direct translation of the Dutch idiom 'tegen beter weten in'.

139 See further Baars 2011.

140 Miéville 2006, p. 315.

141 This is a concept used by Hans Kelsen in his *Pure Theory of Law* to denote the basic norm that underlies a legal system, Kelsen 2008.

142 Marx 2000a, p. 615.

> chaser, and hence that the living labour of the worker becomes, through exchange, available for exploitation by capital.[143]

As a corollary to this, it can be said that law's form is not an empty vessel into which we can pour any content.[144] Because of law's *form*, there is no possibility of communist (or indeed any kind of post-revolutionary) law.[145]

5 Conclusion

It could be said that by adopting the commodity form theory of law, the narrower of the two main questions of this book would be answered very quickly. If law is a tool to perpetuate class rule, then of course the application of ICL will not counter business involvement in imperialist wars and other situations of exploitation and abuse, if such is economically rational. However, the story does not end here. As inspiration and guidance for the dialectical method in this book, I use Bertell Ollman's *Dance of the Dialectic*.[146] Ollman describes Marxist dialectics as 'a way of thinking that brings into focus the full range of changes and interactions that occur in the world'.[147] Replacing common notions of 'thing' with notions of 'process' and 'relation' allows us to understand how processes have developed up to the 'now' point, and how they may continue to develop into the future, as well as how they relate to other processes. As such, it takes us away from considering that things just 'are' (this perception is an effect of ideology)[148] and points us towards processes of continual change. Moreover, it allows us to discern our role in shaping the past, as well as realise our power to affect the development into the future.[149] The 'seed of the new' is present in the contradictions in the current situation. In particular, understanding how the very work of 'corporate accountability' does not tame, but rather *legitimates* capitalism, points us in a new direction. Examining exactly the 'whys' and 'hows' of the relationship between law, capital, and the corporation should allow us to identify and realise the ways in which we can shape a different future.

---

143 Arthur 1978, p. 31.
144 Arthur 1978, p. 29.
145 Cf., e.g., Stuchka 1988, p. 180.
146 Ollman 2003.
147 Ollman 2003, p. 12.
148 Ollman 2003, p. 14.
149 Ollman 2003, p. 20.

CHAPTER 2

The Roots, Development, and Context of the Le Concept of the Corporation: the Making of a Structure of Irresponsibility and a Tool of Imperialism

1 Introduction to Chapter 2

The previous chapter argued that one of the key obstacles to resolving 'the question of the corporation' (and ultimately the question of corporate capitalism itself) is the gap in our understanding of the relationship between law, capital and the corporation. Our failure to see law as the 'congealing' of property relations and the company as a legal superstructure arising from the relations of production leads us to treat corporations ahistorically and as natural, and neutral or indeed beneficial phenomena. Corporate form 'naturalisation' conceals the distributive effects and relations of exploitation that lie at its base and thus affects our ability to confront the material effects of corporate power. This chapter therefore seeks to fill that gap and dispel that silent assumption, through describing and analysing the roots and the development of the concept of the corporation in what came to be 'domestic' law, on the one hand (Part A), and the place of the company in what became 'international' law, on the other (Part B). This historical-materialist analysis will show, firstly, how the formal legal concept of the company was developed through organisational forms such as boroughs and guilds during the transition to capitalism – around the same time as the modern state form – to replace relations of kinship and trust with ones of contract, partly to ensure the acquisition, and then stability of ownership, of the means of production and to enable the extraction of surplus value. As a corollary to this, through what Weber calls 'calculable law', responsibility becomes a commodified concept capable of being expressed in terms of value (and therefore of being exchanged). Secondly, I will show how the formal legal concept of the corporation with separate legal personality was reified in law (and in the public imagination as the personification of capital: Monsieur Le Capital),[1] in order to externalise as much as possible

1 Neocleous 2003, p. 147, citing Marx 1981, Vol. 3, Ch. 48.

the individual as a legally relevant agent in a specific context, to extinguish individual responsibility for 'corporate' actions by hiving off risk and displacing potential liability, and to render 'accountable' and exchangeable that which is not externalised. This construction makes the corporation capitalism's main motor.[2] Public 'buy-in' through cheap share offerings (and much later, institutional investment) ensures that a significant section of the population has a stake in capitalism's success. The corporate form enables, and even (through its profit mandate) demands, 'irresponsible' behaviour wherever it leads to the maximisation of shareholder return, which is the 'imperialism *at the heart of* the corporate form' – the corporation's inherent, imperialist character.[3] The specific characteristics of the corporation were each developed, in a dialectical conversation, as a result of specific historical circumstances and in order to facilitate the advent of bourgeois capitalism. The historical examples in this chapter also show that in instances where the corporate form does not (perfectly) achieve the displacement of risk, political leaderships and the judiciary, as members of the same class, generally assist in the protection of capital. Moreover, the current explicitly pro-capital body of scholarly and instructive work in company law (important elements of 'corporate ideology')[4] aids the legitimisation and consolidation of the *status quo* and stifles the question of 'why' the corporation.

Also in international law the corporation is not generally part of the story. Yet, a historical-materialist re-telling of the story of the corporation in international law (Part B) shows that the corporation was a main vehicle for spreading capitalism and capitalist law around the world, as a vehicle of the commodification of racialised others in the slave trade and later colonisation, and later as a vehicle of concealed 'neo-colonialism' (or, more accurately, continued colonialism). These are *manifestations* of the 'imperialism *of* the corporate form' or the corporation's imperialist 'behaviour'. The development of what became international law consistently follows the logic of capitalism, and through it, corporate interests are protected, at times through obscuring corporations' violent past (and present), through instigating a public/private divide in international law, and thus walling off the corporate domain from public international law regulation, and through creating *sui generis* regimes such as 'interna-

2 Glasbeek 2010, p. 249.

3 I use the term *imperialism* more broadly here than the commonly used Marxist understanding of imperialism as a specific phase of capitalism, but, with Miéville, as one of the 'defining structural elements of actually-existing capitalism', which is manifested in myriad ways and forms (2006, p. 273).

4 Baars 2016.

tional law of investment protection' and mechanisms such as investment arbitration which is privatised pro-capital dispute resolution between states and corporations. International law and the (multinational) corporation are thus co-constitutive, and, as I will show, international law developed such regimes as were needed, including human rights and humanitarian law (and eventually ICL), to protect and further corporate capitalism – and ultimately also to carve out a legitimate role for corporate governing power.

2A The 'Back Story' of the Legal Concept of the Business Company

1 Introduction to 2A

It is said that the corporation, in its various, comparable legal forms, has become the predominant medium for 'doing business' – or, in Marxist terms – surplus value extraction, worldwide. According to Farrar:

> The company, incorporated under the successive Companies Acts, is a dominant institution in our society, all the more so with the retreat in recent decades of the government-owned or public sector of the economy from a number of areas in which it previously had been a monopoly or near-monopoly provider of services or, less often, of goods.[5]

The company has become the most popular *legal* vehicle for business, in comparison with various forms of partnership (the more recent introduction into English law is the Limited Liability Partnership which approximates the corporate form).[6] This is the case in the UK, but also in the rest of the world, where the Anglo-Saxon model has been adopted or imposed. The multinational or transnational enterprise, or global corporate group, is 'perhaps the most talked about form of business association in the contemporary "globalising" world and economy'.[7] This is the form that is able to amass the power discussed in

5 Davies 2003, p. 1 (first sentence of the book).

6 *Limited Liability Partnerships Act, 2000*. Before 1789, partnerships were the main form of business association in England as elsewhere (e.g., Getzler 2006, p. 16).

7 Muchlinski 2007a, p. 3. A multinational corporation in the legal sense is a group of corporations linked to each other through shareholding and (usually) service contract – usually in the form of one or more parent (or holding) companies presiding over a network of wholly or partly owned subsidiaries and joint ventures.

Chapter 1. And yet, its origins are rarely discussed. This chapter examines where the *corporate form* came from and how each of its key elements was developed in its specific historical context.

A milestone in the development of the concept of the corporation is the acceptance of the notion that the corporation has a separate legal personality from its members, the persons who created it and those who own it. As the early twentieth-century legal scholar John Dewey noted in relation to this particular aspect of the corporate form, controversies surrounding corporate legal personality

> and [its] introduction into legal theory and actual legal relations, express struggles and movements of immense social import, economic and political ... To answer this question [of how legal doctrine and external factors relate] is to engage in a survey of the conflict of church and empire in the middle ages; the conflict of rising national states with the medieval Roman empire; the struggle between dynastic and popular representative forms of government; the conflict between feudal institutions, ecclesiastic and agrarian, and the economic needs produced by the industrial revolution and the development of national territorial states; the conflict of the 'proletariat' with the employing and capitalist class; the struggle between nationalism and internationalism, or trans-national relations, to mention only a few outstanding movements.[8]

As will become clear in this chapter, the same can be said of the other aspects of the corporate legal form. Thus, this chapter uncovers which particular struggles took place resulting in the aspects of the concept of the corporation as we know it today, focusing in particular on what happens to the question of responsibility in the incremental development of the corporation. As will become clear, the history of the corporation is part of the Western/European history of social organisation, and the development of modern capitalism more generally. I will show how the idea of corporate personality, for example, came about partly as a papal 'mystification' of power and partly as a result of the organisation of the nascent urban middle classes into guilds and boroughs, which still shared reward and responsibility and which were able to leverage their collective weight against feudal lords and kings. I discuss how these commercial organisations then gave rise to partnerships (such as the early trading companies), which served as a precursor to the abdication of personal/collective respons-

8 Dewey 1926, p. 664 (footnote omitted).

ibility to the company per se, and the protection of the company's own capital through entity shielding. In the transition to capitalism then the capitalists-to-be appropriated the means of production and simultaneously created the now landless poor as the workforce for its factories. Development of the corporate form in the Industrial Revolution reflects the dynamic of synergy and competition between state and capital until the corporation reaches its modern form in *Salomon* and the contemporary multinational corporate group – the form that allows the accumulation of capital (power) spoken of in Chapter 1.

As Section 3 below shows, neither mainstream legal scholarship nor, surprisingly, critical legal scholarship has so far put '[c]apital's *seemingly natural and eternal forms*' into question.[9] I have already suggested that this silence affects our ability to understand the relationship between law, capital, and the corporation and, as a consequence, our ability to respond in a meaningful way to questions of responsibility in general and the question of liability and business involvement in conflict in particular, alongside the broader question of corporate capitalism. In order to see how this ideological silence came about and is sustained on the back of various economic struggles, I start with a discussion of the epistemology of the corporation in law.

2 Epistemology of the Corporate Legal Form

2.1 *Writing the History out of the Corporation through Legal Textbooks*

UK (technically, English and Welsh) company law textbooks, which are also used for teaching law undergraduates in former British colonies and mandates,[10] expend diminishingly little time on the history of the concept of the corporation.[11] Gower and Davies' sixth edition (1997) contained two chapters on the history of company law in the introductory section to the volume, because, as Davies stated:

> this book is concerned with modern company law, but there are some branches of modern English Law which cannot be properly understood without reference to their historical background, and company law is one

9 Ireland 1987, p. 163. I will discuss some exceptions below.

10 For example, outside the UK they are used in Israel.

11 Boyle and Birds 2014 (six pages of history: pp. 1–6), Davies, Lowry, and Reisberg 2009 (one page, at pp. 8–9); Pennington 2001, Girvin, Frisby, and Hudson 2010, Dignam and Lowry 2009, Davies 2012, Hannigan 2016, Mayson, French and Ryan 2015–16, Davies and Worthington 2016 (no history); Morse 2005 (two and a half pages on the development of company law on pp. 4–6).

> of them; indeed, of all branches of law it is perhaps the one least readily understood except in relation to its historical development, a somewhat extended account of which is therefore essential.[12]

Nevertheless, the seventh edition from 2003 omits the two historical chapters in favour of a 'more functional introduction',[13] congruent with most of the English, but also continental European[14] and North American[15] textbooks on company law. Societal context is also not a favourite topic of scholars writing on company law – company law is generally taught from the 'inside' – from the point of view of the corporation, its structure, mechanics, directors, and shareholders.[16] Company regulation is usually discussed in terms of expediency from the point of view of the business enterprise, and, more generally, the market. Kraakman et al. (who exceptionally have written significantly on the history of company law)[17] describe the majority view: 'the appropriate role of corporate law is simply to assure that the corporation serves the best interests of its shareholders or, more specifically, to maximise financial returns to shareholders or, more specifically still, to maximise the current market price of corporate shares'.[18] This is because

> the maximization of shareholder returns is, in general, the best means by which corporate law can serve the broader goal of advancing overall

12 Davies 1997, p. 18 (footnote omitted).

13 Davies 2003, p. vi.

14 Meier-Hayoz and Forstmoser 2007, Böckli 2004, Kalls and Nowotny et al. 2008 (very brief description of history), Wilhelm 2009 (seven pages on 'Die Zeit bis zum AktG von 1965' commencing on p. 21, 'Die AG ist die Rechtsform der Industrialisierung'), Raiser and Veil 2006 (two pages on eighteenth and nineteenth century), Di Sabato 1995, Cozian, Viandier, and Deboissy 2005 (p. 2 debates the nature of the company of the past: 'Les temps ont changé et les querelles académiques ne sont plus de mise. La mode est aujourd'hui au libéralisme et au recul d'État. L'ère des nationalisations est révolue, celle des privatisations est envoie d'achèvement. Le nouveau droit des sociétés, qui est encore à construire, ce signalera par la confiance restituée aux associés, et la réhabilatation de la liberté contractuelle. C'est l'ère de la deregulation'.), van Schilfgaarde 2017 (two pages of history).

15 Henn and Alexander 1983 (eight pages of history).

16 For example, Davies's 2003 chapter 'Advantages and Disadvantages of Incorporation' discusses these issues from the point of view of 'the company' (including, to some extent, investors) and not of, say, workers, society large, consumers, etc. Davies holds that, as incorporation has generally worked to the advantage of companies, 'The main policy issue, therefore, has been how small firms should have easy access to the corporate form' (Davies 2003, pp. 27–44).

17 E.g., Hansmann, Kraakman, and Squire 2006.

18 Kraakman et al. (eds) 2009, p. 28.

> social welfare. In general, creditors, workers, and customers will consent to deal with a corporation only if they expect themselves to be better off as a result.[19]

This view is the modern incarnation of Adam Smith's famous aphorism: 'It is not from the benevolence of the butcher, the brewer, or the baker, that we expect our dinner, but from their regard to their own self-interest. We address ourselves, not to their humanity but to their self-love, and never talk to them of our own necessities but of their advantages'.[20] The role of company law in capitalism is expressed in the opening line of *Pettet's*: 'At the heart of the UK capitalist system, the free market economy, lies company law'.[21] This attitude is reflected in most company law books and forecloses critique of the corporation that does not see the corporation as inevitable, or in principle a good thing. It posits an enabling relationship between law and capitalism, or at least that relationship in the area of 'corporate law'.[22] It is my argument in this book, and in the commodity form theory of law, that the 'maximisation of shareholder returns', once called the 'end of history of corporate law', not only constitutes the purpose of corporate law, but, in fact, that the accumulation of capital and the extraction of surplus value drives *all* law.

2.2 *Legal Theory and the 'Big Idea' of Company Law*

Legal education in company law avoids historicisation, contextualisation, and critique, conforming to critical legal scholar Duncan Kennedy's argument that legal education seeks to reproduce society's (capitalism's) structural hierarchies.[23] Outside of the textbooks, one place where one might expect some ana-

19 Ibid.

20 Smith 1994 [1776] I.2.2.

21 Lowry 2012, p. 3.

22 Hansmann and Kraakmann 2001. Much has been written on the 'shareholder value' model and its impending replacement with a more 'socially efficient' model (e.g., Hansmann 2006; Talbot 2010; Keay 2008 and 2010; Stout 2012; on the 'Enlightened Shareholder Model' as adopted in the UK through the 2006 Company Act – in particular, s. 172, see the Company Law Review Steering Group's report 'Modern Company Law for a Competitive Economy: Developing the Framework' (URN 00/656) London: DTI, 2000; Haldane, Andrew (Chief Economist, Bank of England) 'Who owns a company?' – speech given at the University of Edinburgh Corporate Finance Conference on Friday 22 May 2015). However, once corporate social responsibility, or board representation of workers and consumers, for example, 'make business sense' they follow the logic of capitalism, the logic of shareholder value, even if by a different name.

23 Kennedy 1983.

lysis of corporate power is in jurisprudence (legal theory). However, there is only a limited body of legal *theoretical* scholarship on the corporation.[24]

The modest body of company law theory is predominantly aimed at 'problem solving' and can be divided into a number of quite distinct schools of thought. The first, 'hegemonic', school, is that of 'contractarians' – law and economics scholars who are closely allied to economic theorists of the firm and concerned with reducing the transaction cost of law while optimising such economic benefits as it may deliver.[25] A second body of theory is concerned with improving the firm in terms of organisational efficiency,[26] and mainly focuses on corporate governance.[27] A minority of theorists, sociologists, and socio-legal scholars is concerned with the company's organisational nature and dynamics including gender and other diversity on corporate boards,[28] and includes studies of 'corporate crime' (e.g., Wells)[29] (below and Chapter 4). Finally, there is the company 'stakeholder' debate, which allows consideration of factors and constituencies outside the corporation *per se*[30] (and was in the UK adopted in s. 172 of the 2006 Companies Act[31] – see Chapter 6).

What connects these diverse groups of scholars is that they all accept the inevitable existence of the corporation in its current legal form.[32] This includes what is called the 'big idea of company law': the company's separate legal

---

24 For an overview, see French 2009, pp. 158–9; Stokes 1986. Mainstream jurisprudence has a sizeable literature on legal personality generally (e.g., Kelsen 2008, p. 66), but very few scholars of legal theory engage with corporate law, and thus scholarship on legal personality does not cover or explain corporate legal personality. An exception is Hart, who nevertheless concludes we must put aside the question of 'what is a corporation' in favour of 'under what types of conditions does the law ascribe liabilities to corporations'? (Hart 1983, p. 43). For critical perspectives within law on corporate purpose and corporate governance, however, see Talbot 2013, 2014, and 2015.

25 Talbot 2015, p. 1.

26 E.g., Farrar 2008.

27 Talbot 2015, p. 1.

28 E.g., Wheeler 2016; O'Kelly and Wheeler 2012; Rosenblum 2014; Williams 2002.

29 E.g., Wells 2001.

30 Overview: French 2009, p. 32; Keay 2008 and 2010.

31 Which requires *consideration* only of stakeholders' interests: s. 172 Companies Act 2006.

32 It is not always possible to distinguish between the various strands: for example, there are the 'law and economics' approaches of Roscoe Pound and others, the socio-legal approaches of Wheeler et al., and then there is the 'law and socioeconomics' of scholars such as Dallas (Dallas 1988). Some scholars, especially in the 'stakeholder' debate, advocate legislative change forcing the adoption of 'board representation' of stakeholders including employees (or indeed workers' councils as per the German model corporation), e.g., Keay 2008 and 2010.

personality[33] – or capital personified. It is this separate legal pers
law and existing only by virtue of law, that is made capable of own
being a party to contracts, and being a claimant or defendant in
lack of explanation of the phenomenon of corporate legal perso
authors such as Lowry to suggest that, in relation to the corporat main characteristic, 'a certain flexibility of mind [is] needed to deal with the legal creation of corporate personality'.[35] While remaining unexplained, the corporate legal person, and the corporation more generally, has now become a natural accepted part of our existing system, even though '[t]here are few topics which seem more thoroughly theoretical ... [and which have been] declared by the courts to be the basis of their decisions and upon which rights in valuable property have been determined and enormous sums of money distributed'.[36]

The exact nature in law of the corporate legal person once did 'arouse ... the excited attention of all who have discussed legal theories and of not a few who have professed a profound disinclination to such discussion',[37] but is no longer the subject of theoretical debate. Nevertheless, and although few contemporary authors make this explicit, different understandings of the nature of corporate personality do affect black-letter accounts of company law.[38]

For example, French et al. adopt an 'artificial entity' theory of corporate personality, which holds that incorporation creates an artificial separate person, produced by human artifice but treated in law as real.[39] This perspective is related to the individualist approach to business involvement in crime, which I discuss in Chapter 4. The 'real entity' theorists, on the other hand (associated with Von Gierke and presently, for example, with Teubner),[40] consider the corporation as an entity that amounts to *something qualitatively different* from an aggregation of individuals. This perspective underlies 'system criminality' arguments like those made by Nollkaemper (Chapter 4). Finally, the pragmatic 'concession theorists' regard as entities those who have been accorded separate personality by statute, or registration – where the exact content of

33 French 2009, p. 3.
34 Ibid.
35 Dignam 2009, p. v.
36 Radin 1932, p. 643.
37 See, e.g.: Machen 1911; Geldart 1911; Hohfeld 1923; Radin 1932; Maitland 1936; DuBois 1938, Nekam 1938; Cooke 1950. For later treatments, see, e.g., Hurst 1970. For a non-Anglo-Saxon view, see Bastid 1960.
38 French 2009, p. 159.
39 French 2009, p. 153, see also Schilfgaarde 2006, p. 1; Radin 1932.
40 Von Gierke 1958; Teubner 1988.

that personality depends on policy considerations.[41] This category corresponds to pragmatic approaches to legal person liability (e.g., Van den Herik, below Chapter 4). Contractarians (by far the largest group) regard the firm as a 'nexus of contracts', emphasise freedom of contract (here, the freedom to carry on business activities without state interference) and deny the existence of, or ignore, separate personality.[42] This, the dominant theory, seems least amenable to the idea of corporate crime, and comes closest to the idea that relations of responsibility are subsumed by 'risk transactions' – which I return to below and in Chapters 4 and 6. A final way of thinking of (corporate) legal entities is as 'pools of assets' as per leading US corporate lawyers Hansmann and Kraakman: 'Individuals (or rather, their personal estates) and corporations are thus both examples of *legal entities*, a term we use to refer to legally distinct pools of assets that provide security to a fluctuating group of creditors and thus can be used to bond an individual's or business firm's contracts'.[43] Indeed this perspective is an accurate and usefully 'demystified' description of the nature of corporate personality in capitalist law – that in fact aligns with the Marxist description of the corporation as 'capital personified'. It is the *legal ideology* (why this entity is allowed to exist and function in this way) that needs further analysis.

Critical Legal Studies (CLS) and other critical and Marxist scholars,[44] however, are generally silent on company law.[45] Notable exceptions include the Marxist scholars Neocleous and Ireland, whom I cite here. Ireland, querying why such scholars leave unanswered the 'perplexing questions' raised by company law, considers this particularly surprising considering that the corporation is a major site of relations of domination and subordination.[46] The 1980s US CLS scholar Stanley has suggested:

41 E.g., Stone 1972.

42 Contractarian theory of the corporation '[c]onceptualises the relationship between management and shareholders in a public company as one of contract – a "corporate contract" – in which joint wealth would be maximised as a result of atomistic market-mediated actions' (Easterbrook and Fischel 1991; cf. Clark 1986).

43 Hansmann et al. 2006, p. 1337.

44 Critical Legal Studies emerged in the US in the 1970s as a left-progressive movement employing insights from Marxism and the Frankfurt School to understand the role of law in society's structures of oppression and to instrumentalise law for emancipatory goals. See Unger 2015, Ch. 1, pp. 3–41.

45 But see, e.g., Ireland 2008, Hadden 1977, Stanley 1988, De Vroey 1975, Neocleous 2003. Thus far feminist legal critique of corporate law has been inchoate – the (as yet unchallenged) conclusion of Lahey 1985. Hadden, Stanley, De Vroey and Neocleous have long since moved on from writing about company law. While some authors explicitly label their work as 'critical' or 'marxist', they tend to lack a *theory of law*.

46 Ireland 1987, p. 149.

> This may be because as a subject traditionally firmly entrenched within the orthodoxy of exposition and the black letter/textbook heritage it has no appeal for the radical lawyer, not giving itself easily to either critical or contextual analysis. Alternatively, and I hope this is the case, company law may be of such importance within the C.L.S. agenda of critique that no scholar has yet dared to venture into the mire which constitutes the legitimation system of the capitalist mode of production, the underpinning mechanism for the reproduction of capitalist society.[47]

After Stanley wrote this decades ago, the critical silence remains just as perplexing, and illustrates the hold corporate ideology has – at least on legal scholars.[48]

2.3 *Writing the History Back into the Corporation*

The lack of inquiry into the origins and nature of company law has served to 'normalise' (and legitimise or at least neutralise) this area of law,[49] and (viz. Gower's omission of historical chapters, *supra*) can be connected to the claim of capitalism's, and indeed the corporation's, end of history.[50] Apart from the historical-materialist methodological requirement to return to history to discover how we got here, the undoing of the ideological move of normalisation should provide an impetus for Marxist and other critical scholars to take a 'turn to history' – comparable to that currently underway in international law (see Chapter 2B, Section 1.1).[51] So here I start, as an 'explorer ... into a region where sign-posts are too few',[52] in reconstructing the story of the corporation from the Western canon.[53] I concentrate on UK company law (it is predictably accepted

---

47 Stanley 1988, p. 97.

48 There is, however, a relatively lively critical-theoretical literature, mostly in criminology, on corporate crime/crimes of the powerful, e.g., Whyte 2008, Tombs and Whyte 2003, Snider 1993, 2000, Tombs and Snider 1995, Bittle 2015, Bittle and Snider 2015 (see further Ch. 4).

49 On 'normalisation' as an ideological strategy, see Marks 2000, p. 19.

50 Fukuyama 1992, Marks 2000, pp. 33–5; on the corporation's end of history, see Hansmann and Kraakman 2001, Hansmann 2006.

51 Ireland 2008, Hadden 1977, Stanley 1988 and De Vroey 1975 all delve into company law history. Such a turn to history is also notable in current policy statements such as that of the Chief Economist of the Bank of England (Haldane 2015).

52 Maitland 1900, p. vii.

53 Outside of the metropole, e.g., Islamic jurists 'to meet a need of their arena' (at 202) developed the doctrine of '*dhimma*', which is 'generally defined as a presumed or imaginary repository that contains all the rights and obligations associated with a person' (at 203). Traditional scholars agree that bodies such as the *waqf*, Islamic Public Treasury, schools, orphanages, hospitals, mosques and other charities can have '*dhimma*' separate

in the Western canon) because 'corporate law evolved from centuries of English law and was incorporated wholesale into US law' and thus 'prevails today'.[54] I supplement the summary accounts found in Davies,[55] Farrar,[56] with specialist works (Dubois[57] and Hunt),[58] and works of general legal history from the early twentieth century (Pollock and Maitland).[59] After Holdsworth's 16-volume *History of English Laws* published between 1903 and 1966,[60] the standard text on English legal history (*Oxford History of the Laws of England*) only in 2010 added a (positivist)[61] section on the history of company law starting at 1820 (Cornish et al.).[62] The main continental authors I rely on are Von Savigny[63] and Von Gierke,[64] whose ideas are said to have influenced Anglo-Saxon legal development significantly,[65] while the work of Harris,[66] who – besides Ireland[67] – is the only contemporary specialist in company law history, provides an instructive comparative perspective. Legal scholars Neocleous (mentioned above), Deakin, Getzler, Hansmann, Kraakman and Squire, Grear and McLean have also made useful contributions.[68] Beyond this, (economic) history[69] and Weber's sociological works including, especially, *General Economic History*[70] are informative.[71]

from its employees and administrators, while 'modern Islamic law scholars' also extend the concept to commercial companies (Zahraa 1995, p. 204).

54 Blumberg 1993; Kraakman 2009, which is a comparative study of corporate law across jurisdictions. On the absence of the corporate form in Islamic law, see Kuran 2005.

55 Davies 1997.

56 Farrar 1998.

57 DuBois 1938.

58 Hunt 1936.

59 Pollock and Maitland 1911, Maitland 1898.

60 Holdsworth 1926.

61 See McLean 2013 who criticises the Oxford handbooks for providing histories of law 'from within' and being devoid of socio-economic context.

62 Cornish et al. 2010.

63 Von Savigny 1840.

64 Gierke 1903.

65 Harris 2006.

66 Harris 2000; Harris 1994, Harris 1997, Harris 2005; Harris 2006.

67 Ireland 1987; Ireland 2002; Ireland 2009; Ireland 2016.

68 E.g., Neocleous 2003; Deakin 2017; Getzler 2006; Hansmann, Kraakman and Squire; Armour, Hansmann and Kraakman 2009; Grear 2007; McLean 2004.

69 See, e.g., Braudel 1982; Blackford 2008; Stern 2013; Brandon 2015; Yamamoto 2016.

70 Weber 1982, esp. 202–35; see also Roth and Wittich 1978, esp. 705–31.

71 There are significant discrepancies between, e.g., Dubois, Holdsworth and Maitland. For example, Maitland dates the Bubble Act *after* the crash of the South Sea Company's shares, likely due to inaccurate conversion of historical English calendars. Other differences are more complex, e.g., the disagreement on when corporations were first endowed with separate legal personality. Seeking the *correct* answer to these questions is not the

While uncovering the history of company law it also becomes evident that the legitimacy of the corporate form *has* at various times in history been questioned, even by the 'father of the free market', Adam Smith himself (see below at Section 4.1). 'Backlashes' against the corporation spurring debate on the desirability of the corporate form have occurred at very specific points in history, namely the middle to the end of the nineteenth century,[72] the 1920/30s,[73] the 1970s,[74] and in recent years.[75] These were periods of profound economic change (crisis) – I discuss this further below and in Chapter 6.

In the course of this chapter it will become clear that the history of the company is also closely linked with what we now (in legal scholarship) look at mainly through the lens of international law: the history of colonialism, and also of the slave trade, and of course with the advent of global imperialist capitalism generally, and in particular the coincidence and potential relations between war, capitalism and corporations – in other words: the *political economy of international law*. I develop the international law angle more fully in Part B of this chapter.

3 The Creation of Market Society: Legal Relations and Legal Entities

As noted in Chapter 1, law universalised in the period of transition from feudalism to capitalism.[76] Instances of capitalism had existed in some shape or form in many eras, but in this period it came to penetrate the provision of everyday wants, and labour power was commodified – for example, when serfs became day labourers. Law enabled these processes. The universalisation of law was thus not an isolated movement, but one that came as an integral part of greater societal changes in the transition to capitalism. Capitalism did not just mean the introduction of the market in the economic sphere; it meant the creation of the *market society*.[77] This is a society organised according to the rules of the

---

purpose of this book. Harris provides a thorough comparative analysis based on primary sources, and I rely mainly on his findings in these instances.

72 E.g., Cook: 'Plutocracy has appeared in a new guise, a new coat of mail – the corporation. The struggle of democracy against plutocracy – a struggle that is coming to the American people – will be between democracy and the corporation' (1891, p. 249).

73 E.g., Wormser 1931.

74 E.g., Hurst 1970, esp. pp. 30–44.

75 E.g., Broad 2002; Baars 2016.

76 See generally, Wood 2002; Pashukanis 1978, p. 44.

77 Woods 2002, pp. 23–4 and, generally, Thompson 1963. In his introduction to the second Russian edition of *General Theory of Law and Marxism*, Pashukanis responds to criticism

market imperative.[78] It also means the replacement of human relationships with legal relationships, the transformation of human individuals and (some) groups into legal subjects, and ultimately the creation of legal entities devoid of humans. The transition to capitalism came about as a result of a combination of specific historical circumstances, a change in the present factors. These were technology, mental conceptions, relation to nature, the nature and manner of production, social relations (including division of labour, gender relations), how daily life was led (reproduction), institutional arrangements including law and the state. Key to the transition is the development out of earlier forms of communal organisation of the corporate legal form with its specific functions (Sections 4.1.1–2). It is this corporation which comes to form the 'motor' of capitalism partly because of the way that the legal form 'distributes' risk, gain and responsibility. I discuss this here, together with an example of how this works out in the famous *Case of Sutton's Hospital* (4.1.3), the creation of the working class and the process of 'primitive accumulation' (4.2), and finally, the key concept of 'accountability' in law (4.3).

3.1 *The Legal Personality of Commercial Polities: from Collective Burden Sharing to Societas Delinquere non Potest*

Although the transition to capitalism only took hold in Northern Europe from the eighteenth century and into the nineteenth, in pockets of history economies have existed that have looked quite similar to capitalist market economies. In those, commercially successful and what one could call 'proto-capitalist' forms of manufacturing and trading enterprise existed as the main vehicles, or proto-legal technologies through which these economies operated. In the Roman Empire, for example, the slave-managed *peculium* resembled a (contractual) partnership – as did the thirteenth–fourteenth-century Italian *com-*

---

he received over his argument that law is essentially a capitalist 'invention': 'I have indeed maintained, and still do maintain, that the relations between commodity producers generate the most highly developed, most universal, and most consummate legal mediation, and hence that every general theory of law, and every "pure jurisprudence" is a one-sided description, abstracted from all other conditions, of the relations between people who appear in the market as commodity owners. But a developed and consummate form does not of course exclude undeveloped and rudimentary forms, rather to the contrary, it presupposes them' (Pashukanis 1978, p. 44). Engels suggests Roman law lies at the basis of current bourgeois law: 'Roman law, the first world law of a commodity-producing society, with its unsurpassably fine elaboration of all the essential legal relations of simple commodity owners (of buyers and sellers, debtors and creditors, contracts, obligations, etc.)' (Engels 1950 [1886]).

78 Woods 2002, p. 36.

pagnia partnerships such as the famous Medici Bank which had branches in various European cities including London.[79] Neither of these forms involved the creation of a legal entity as such, both relying on familial or master-servant relations formalised where needed into contract for their 'unity' and coherence. While no doubt influenced by, and similar to, these arrangements, the roots of the modern corporation as it emerged in English law lies in the polities (Chapter 1.3.1) into which English communal life in the second half of the Middle Ages was organised. These included, amongst others, 'townships and manors, hundreds and counties, franchises of various kinds and boroughs, and all over is the community of the whole realm'.[80] Law was created to structure these, but only in a 'peculiarly untheoretical and practical manner',[81] while these communities were seen as 'part of the natural order of things' in a society organised around the needs of communal agriculture and other feudal forms of cooperation, without a strong overarching central (national) authority.[82] Holdsworth describes how 'their doings, like the doings of individuals, were ordered as seemed to the judges and statesmen of this period reasonable and efficient'.[83] The thirteenth century then forms a midway point in England between 'the undiluted communalism of the earliest period [early Middle Ages] and the bureaucratic ideas of the [twentieth century]'.[84] What we can see in examining these polities' self-organising more closely is how they became increasingly conscious of the wider utility of their collective strength and the possibility to leverage this nascent collective 'personhood', including as against the nascent state. The borough and the guild were the two main forms of economic organisation that can be seen as the direct forebears of the modern corporation.

As noted in the introduction, the development of the notion of corporate legal personality was partly organic and partly mystical/ideological. In other words, the legal concept came about as a result of the dialectic between existing and emergent material relations, and superstructural 'abstracted' (proto-)legal ideas. In corporate ideology, the material comes to be explained, and ulti-

79 Generally, Hansmann, Kraakman and Squire 2006. For a discussion of partnership forms in early Islam, see Udovitch 1970.

80 Holdsworth 1925, Vol. II, p. 401.

81 Holdsworth 1925, Vol. II, p. 402.

82 Pollock 1911, Vol. I, pp. xiii–xv. Pollock enumerates the 'Sorts and Conditions of Men' in the law of the early Middle Ages as 'Earls and Barons, Knights, the Unfree, the Religious, the Clergy, Aliens, the Jews, Outlaws and convicted Felons, Excommunicates, Lepers, Lunatics and Idiots, Women, Corporations and Churches, and finally, the King and the Crown'.

83 Holdsworth 1925, Vol. II, p. 402.

84 Holdsworth 1925, Vol. II, p. 404.

mately justified and reproduced, by the metaphysical. John Dewey, writing in 1926, locates the roots of the idea of corporate legal personhood in the twelfth and thirteenth centuries – long before it was used by business enterprises. In Dewey's account, Pope Innocent IV promoted what later became known as the 'fiction' or artificial entity theory of corporate personality with an indefinite lifespan in order to preserve the great political power the papal empire was enjoying at that time.[85] According to the pope, because of their fictional personality, ecclesiastical chapters *as corporate bodies* could not be excommunicated, or be guilty of a delict – both useful attributes when the objective is to maintain power.[86] This notion then travelled to England where it came to be applied to business corporations and it became common knowledge of 'all English lawyers'[87] that the corporation has 'no body to kick and no soul to damn'.[88] Pollock agrees that 'the idea of the Church as the mystical body of Christ has had an important influence on the growth of the law of corporations; it did much towards fashioning for us the anthropomorphic picture of the many members in one body'.[89] At the same time, this linkage transplanted a key idea onto the business corporation – namely that *societas delinquere non potest* – a society cannot commit a crime – an idea that would persist until the twentieth century (see Chapter 4). Thus, in its earliest 'mystical' (in the sense of originating in religious ideas) conception, we see the employment of the legal 'corporation', on the one hand, for the personification of (a certain type of) power, and, on the other, for the *organisation* of responsibility and liability, two fundamentals the business enterprise would come to use to its benefit.

The common types of corporation in the twelfth to fourteenth centuries included 'counties, boroughs, hundreds, townships, manors, merchant gilds, trading gilds, chantries, deans and chapters, monasteries of various kinds, the universities, and the societies of lawyers which were developed into the Inns of Court'.[90] This section looks at boroughs and guilds, which became the organisational units playing a key role in the rise of the capitalist class – at least partly because of their ability to 'act as one person' wielding their collective capital.

85 Dewey 1926, p. 663. See also Maitland 1898 pp. xiv, 18, and Pollock 1911, p. 494.

86 Dewey 1926, p. 663.

87 Pollock 1911, p. 494.

88 Quote attributed to Lord Thurlow (1730–1806) by Coffee 1980–81.

89 Pollock 1911, p. 495.

90 According to Pollock 1911, Vol. I, p. 494, the Oxford and Cambridge universities claim to be the first British Corporations.

3.1.1 The Borough

Once the papally promoted idea of the *persona ficta* had become accepted in canon law and 'travelled' to England, it started to be used for common law bodies such as the boroughs and guilds.[91] Out of these, the borough stood out with greater distinctness from its individual members.[92] A second theory, the concession theory of personality, which emerges out of the competitive power struggle between polities and the emerging centralised state, also gained currency.[93]

The way the emerging state sought to assert its hegemony was to treat all collectivities as 'conspiracies' unless they were expressly granted a charter ('concession') by the crown. Some thirteenth-century boroughs were self-proclaimed, and some were indeed granted by royal charter.[94] The qualification 'borough' was a source of privilege, such as that of being free from the control of a sheriff. 'The external test in the past has been the separate appearance of the borough community before the justices ... in the future it will be its separate representation in Parliament'.[95] The borough's trading privileges, such as the freedom of toll throughout England – toll being the main source of income for a borough,[96] made the position of 'burgess' (or a borough elder) a valuable one. Risk in the borough was compensated by opportunity: while the burgesses of a borough could be liable in the court of a foreign borough for the debt of their fellow burgesses, conversely, many boroughs gave the burgess the right to share in bargains made by fellow burgesses.[97] Here we see the start of a form of organised sharing of commercial risk and gain. Internal decision-making in the borough was organised to enable the most efficient use of the borough's privilege, and a seal was used to express communal consent. The borough was quickly 'coming to be a more active, more self-conscious unit than the ordinary community ... not yet regarded as a corporate body – as an artificial person, separate from its members; but ... on the high road to the attainment of that status'.[98] The burghers were becoming aware of the potential benefit that a(n evolved) corporate form might bring them, the economic power they could

91 Holdsworth 1925, Vol. VIII, p. 474.
92 Holdsworth 1925, Vol. VIII, p. 475.
93 Dewey 1926, p. 666.
94 Holdsworth 1925, Vol. II, p. 385.
95 Holdsworth 1925, Vol. II p. 386 – perhaps foreshadowing *Citizens United v. Federal Election Commission*, Supreme Court No. 08-205, 21 January 2010.
96 Pollock 1911, p. 664.
97 Holdsworth 1925, Vol. II, p. 394.
98 Ibid. See further Holdsworth 1925, Vol. III, pp. 469–75.

wield, and were on their way to evolving into the 'bourgeoisie'.[99] It was precisely this that was to worry Hobbes when he spoke of corporations as 'worms in the entrails of natural man' (see below Section 4.1.4).

3.1.2 Guilds

Guilds sprung up within the heterogeneous borough as forms of group organisation around a specific economic activity.[100] Guilds could be roughly divided into merchant guilds and trade (or craft) guilds.[101] Some of these were run by foreign traders with a permanent post in a city, for example the German 'Hansards' in London.[102] The purpose of the trade guild was to restrict the practice of a particular skilled trade or the sale of a particular product (line) to a group with strict membership criteria.[103] Merchant guilds (which were listed in the Selden Society's *Select Charters of Trading Companies*, e.g., English Merchants in Prussia, Haevre Merchants, etc.)[104] exploited the royal grant of a trading monopoly in a particular commodity or the exploration (seeking commercial opportunity) in a particular area, or later, along a specific trade route. Once these merchant guilds took on a more permanent form, e.g., as *commenda* and later 'regulated companies' (below Section 5), with permanent accounting rather than accounting on the basis of single journeys/traders (developments in accounting were aided by the fourteenth-century switch from Roman to Hindu-Arabic numerals, and the availability of paper),[105] these also came to be perceived as 'legal persons' with a unique existence despite an ever-changing set of members. According to Cooke, the guilds were a necessary precursor to a capitalist economy, as

> the effect of this [institution of the 'Guild'] was necessarily to increase the wealth and power of the most efficient members. Through the craft guild and the trading company, associations of merchants were able to throw off local public control. The result of this was eventually to make the whole country one economic unit and to lead to national economic policies.[106]

---

99 Later chartered cities continued to operate much like businesses, with citizens becoming shareholders through paying shares in taxation (Weber 1982, p. 281).

100 Pollock 1911, p. 639.

101 See further, Pollock 1911, pp. 664–7.

102 Weber 1982, p. 281.

103 Cooke 1950, p. 22.

104 Holdsworth 1925, Vol. III, p. 199.

105 Hansmann, Kraakman and Squire 2006, p. 1367.

106 Cooke 1950, p. 34.

At the same time the guilds had an interest in state regulation th cial recognition by means of a 'concession' because this prevented n organisations – i.e., organisations without an express grant from th from rivalling their power.[107] At the base of the 'concession' lies the idea that the group that was granted the privilege of incorporation served a public purpose. This requirement, however, declined, according to Farrar, 'due to a number of factors – ... the increase of trade and manufacture and the growth of overseas trade, originally as privateering expeditions. This is the beginning of the rise of capitalistic enterprise'[108] – a publicly chartered body with a *private* purpose.

Pollock observes that at times guilds of knights or merchants aspired (and presumably occasionally succeeded) to 'boss' the town.[109] While the borough was an institution weighed down with various civic and administrative obligations, the new guild's almost purely economic objective gave the merchant and trading classes a more agile construct through which to translate their economic power into political power. The borough had to serve the interests of many, while the guild served a specific narrow class in the first instance. Here we see how increasingly purely economic enterprises compete effectively with more burdensome public bodies for power and influence.

3.1.3 Illustration on the Corporation and Responsibility

According to Baker, the mid-fifteenth century 'was the period in which the distinctions between bodies politic and natural persons, and between corporations and their individual heads and members, began to receive full examination by the courts'.[110] Even so, the courts in this period did not come to any firm conclusions, perhaps because 'it would have been such a large task to define the qualities of a corporation that it would have taken an entire vacation'.[111] This left space for imaginative use of the corporate concept.

All the same, Edward Coke, J. could describe the corporation in the *Case of Sutton's Hospital* (1612):

> And it is great reason that an Hospital in expectancy or intendment, or nomination, shall be sufficient to support the name of an Incorporation, when the Corporation itself is onely in abstracto, and resteth onely in intendment and consideration of the Law; for a Corporation aggregate

107 Later, in Chapter 6 we will see companies demanding regulation for the same purpose.
108 Farrar 1998, p. 16.
109 Pollock 1911, p. 639.
110 Baker 2003, p. 623.
111 Baker 2003, p. 623, citing Spelman's reading (Gray's Inn, 1519) 113 Selden Soc. 154.

> of many is invisible, immortal, & resteth only in intendment and consideration of the Law; and therefore … They may not commit treason, nor be outlawed, nor excommunicate, for they have no souls, neither can they appear in person … A Corporation aggregate of many cannot do fealty, for an invisible body cannot be in person, nor can swear, … it is not subject to imbecilities, or death of the natural, body, and divers other cases.[112]

This quote has come to be cited in the textbooks as 'the cornerstone of company law'.[113] Textbooks generally do not mention the facts of the case. Sutton, a businessman and money-lender and reportedly at the time of his death 'the richest commoner of England',[114] had intended to establish a hospital and school (on the grounds of the defunct London Charterhouse). Would-be heirs of Sutton (Sutton Jr. and Law) challenged his legacy on the basis that although Sutton had had a licence from the King to establish a hospital and a school for the poor, he had not yet actually built either.

What Sutton *had done*, however, was to create the Hospital *as a charity*, and to *sell* the school grounds and the *future* hospital to the charity's Board of Governors. Coke J. lists the governors established in the charter of the charity, who include not only *Coke himself* but most of the members of the King's Bench.[115] Sutton Jr. argued that, since the *actual* hospital did not exist, the charity had not been properly incorporated and was merely 'utopical and mathematical'. As such, it was argued, the charity did not have legal personality and hence no capacity to own property and the transaction was void.[116]

The transaction was, however, considered valid by the bench, which decided that in accepting the transfer they and the remainder of the Board had not acted in their 'political', but in their private capacity.[117] Moreover, it was held that a corporation *could be* something that existed *only in law*, and not in material reality.[118] What we see here, then, is an early example of the attempt at *defining* and then *using* the incorporate person as a pure abstraction for speculative gain and the evasion of 'liability' (here: the 'liability' or relationship of indebtedness towards natural heirs) – with the explicit and almost farcical cooperation of the court and many other leading figures in the ruling class.

---

112 *Case of Sutton's Hospital* [1612] 77 Eng Rep 960, 973 (citations excluded).
113 E.g., Dignam 2009, p. 313.
114 Description by London Metropolitan Archives, ACC/1876.
115 *Case of Sutton's Hospital* 140–1.
116 *Case of Sutton's Hospital* 8–9.
117 *Case of Sutton's Hospital* 137.
118 *Case of Sutton's Hospital* 104.

Moreover, this case shows an early example of what Hansmann, Kraak Squire have termed 'entity shielding': the protection of the firm's ass the creditors of its owners/shareholders.[119] What we also see, on another level and in another time, is the concealing/ideological function of ahistorical 'positivist' teaching *today* as the case is routinely taught without its little-known facts.[120]

3.1.4 Conclusions on the Incorporate Person

Despite the clumsy description given by the court in the *Case of Sutton's Hospital*, it was immediately clear to the legal and business audience that certain powers, capacities and liabilities affecting natural persons 'obviously' did not apply to corporate persons, while others, such as a power to own property, to contract, to sue and be sued, liability on contract, for wrongs done as the owner of property, were 'obviously' included.[121] There seemed to be an idea (ideology) of what the corporation was and what its proper role and treatment ought to be. More concretely, there was already a sense of the corporation becoming a creature with its own will, not subject to public control. In Pollock's words, '[t]he corporation vanishes as we pursue it'.[122]

The *Case of Sutton's Hospital* illustrates that law was going to be developed not on the basis of higher principles or policies, but on the basis of commercial expediency on a case-by-case basis. As the potential of the corporation 'as we know it' was realised, merchant classes were quick to take up the construct and use it to their advantage, and the courts had to deal with the difficult questions on an *ad hoc*, reactive basis. The most difficult questions, those relating to liabilities, were not answered in a clear and systematic manner in advance of the problems of liability arising. Indeed, 'the broad way in which the law was laid down indicate[d] a line of thought which will long tend to restrict the delictual capacity of corporations' and 'it is clear that the law on this subject was being constructed rather by considerations of expedience, than by any attempt to work out logically deductions drawn from the nature of corporate personality'.[123] The expedience in question was the expedience of business, of capitalism.

---

119 Hansmann, Kraakman, and Squire 2006.

120 The Charterhouse School was eventually built and has become one of England's top private schools, counting many lawyers and judges among its alumni.

121 Holdsworth 1925, Vol. VIII, p. 488.

122 Pollock 1911, Vol. I, p. 490.

123 Holdsworth 1925, Vol. VIII, p. 488. This is later mirrored by the legal personalities of international organisations in the ICJ's '*Certain Expenses Case*', see below Chapter 2B.

This flexible arrangement suited the bourgeoisie, who were becoming increasingly proactive in employing the economic power encapsulated in the legal construct of the corporation in their personal and class interest. This is precisely what worried the theorist of royal absolutism Thomas Hobbes. According to Webb, '[b]etween the Reformation and the French revolution in Western Europe corporate bodies connoted privilege and political inequality, and Hobbes spoke for his age when he compared them to "worms in the entrails of natural man"'.[124] Hobbes was a critic of the concept of the corporation, insofar as it challenged the power or authority of the absolute ruler of the Commonwealth – which he seemed to consider inevitable based on the nature of the corporation – its presence intrinsically does not serve the 'common good'. The corporation, he feared, would ultimately compete for power with the Crown, eating away at its rule.

3.2 *Primitive Accumulation and the Creation of the Working Class*

In addition to creating the legal constructs through which to organise and optimise one's business affairs, a key stage for the development of market society was, on the one hand, the appropriation of the means of production by one part of society and the simultaneous creation of the working class on the other. The former occurred according to what Marx in *Capital I* calls 'primitive accumulation' which reflects the idea that the difference in wealth in today's society (as in Marx's society of the nineteenth century) did not come about, simply put, because one part of the population was diligent and frugal, and the other 'lazy rascals', but, rather, as a result of 'conquest, enslavement, robbery, murder, in short, force'.[125] The future 'owners of the means of production' managed to acquire their wealth by physically divorcing the producer from the means of production,[126] while the working class was created as a result of this process. Starting in the late fifteenth century a 'massive land grab' occurred (caused mainly by the rise in wool prices and the gentry's desire to turn arable land into sheep walks)[127] in which the feudal lords managed to appropriate vast tracts of common land (and, with the Reformation, Church land), thereby turning themselves into 'landed gentry', while razing cottages and sometimes whole

124 Webb 1958, p. v., and see Hobbes 1651, Pt. II, Ch. 27.

125 Marx 1976, p. 874: The process 'operates two transformations, whereby the social means of production are turned into capital, and the immediate producers are turned into wage-labourers'.

126 Marx 1976, p. 475. Marx contrasts his 'primitive accumulation' with Adam Smith's concept of 'previous accumulation', which is the 'idyllic' version laying the origin of inequality in human nature rather than forcible expropriation (Marx 1976, p. 874).

127 Marx 1976, pp. 878–9.

villages.[128] First this occurred 'without the slightest regard to legal etiquette', but after the 'Glorious Revolution' of 1688[129] the landed gentry gained control of parliament, and 'legalised' the process through the Enclosure Acts.[130] '[T]he advance made by the eighteenth century shows itself in this, that the law itself now becomes the instrument by which the people's land is stolen'.[131] At other times still the appropriation of the means of production, in the form of land in this instance, was accompanied by heavy use of physical violence, for example during the 'Highland Clearances' in Scotland.[132] Such manorial farmers as remained created agricultural enterprises and sold their surplus produce at market.[133] 'The same people who had rebelled against [the concept of private] property had no choice but to approve it the next day as they met in the market as independent producers'.[134] Simultaneously the urbanisation of the dispossessed, now landless classes fed into the creation of a newly wealthy urban middle class (the burgesses, becoming the bourgeoisie) who were able to exploit their labour in industrial and craft production by creating factories.[135] While landed wealth controlled parliament, in the transitional period it began to invest in colonial ventures and later also industry when it became clear that the commercial class had started to gain position.[136] Industry gained its workforce partly through the forcible 'recruitment' of the poor from cottages and workhouses – including children particularly in the cloth industry in the North of England.[137] The poor were forced into the factories by means of repressive law, e.g., by criminalising vagrancy but also by laws prohibiting proletarians from rearing cattle or providing for their own subsistence in some other way.[138] Capitalism depends on 'free' labour: 'persons must be present who are

128 Generally, Marx 1976, pp. 877–95.

129 The so-called 'Glorious Revolution' 'brought into power, along with William of Orange, the landed and capitalist profit-grubbers' (Marx 1976, p. 844).

130 Marx 1976, p. 884.

131 Marx 1976, p. 885.

132 Marx describes this process in some detail, Marx 1976, pp. 890–3.

133 Weber argues: 'In England, the mere fact of the development of a market, as such and alone, destroyed the manorial system from within'. Weber 1982, p. 98. See also Merriman 2010, esp. Ch. 10.

134 Weber 1982, p. 124.

135 Blackford 2008, p. 12.

136 Intermarriage with the industrial middle class or nouveau riche 'saved' the British aristocracy from extinction – *Explainer* Museum of London Docklands, 21 September 2010. See also generally, Wood 2002 and Merriman 2010, pp. 350, 378–9.

137 Marx 1976, pp. 922–3.

138 Merriman 2010, pp. 382–5; Marx 1976, p. 877ff., generally, Thompson 1973; Baars 2011, pp. 417–18.

legally in the position, but are also economically compelled, to sell ɔor'.[139] The development of the institutions of capitalism, law, the state a… e *business enterprise*, formed an essential ingredient in the transition, alongside technological change and the cultural and ideological aspects of capitalism; together they created 'market society' and 'corporate ideology'.[140]

3.3 *Calculable Law, Risk Accounting and 'Accountability'*

Finally, to Marx's account of the transition to capitalism, Weber adds:

> In the last resort the factor which produced capitalism is the rational permanent enterprise, rational accounting, rational technology and rational law, but again, not these alone. Necessary complementary factors were the rational spirit, the rationalization of the conduct of life in general, and a rationalistic economic ethic.[141]

Weber's writing is a rich source on the role of law in society, compared to Marx's.[142] This is not to say that Marx considered law unimportant, but that he did not elaborate on this a great deal, which meant it was left to others, such as Pashukanis and indeed Weber, to fill the gaps.[143]

Weber's concept of rational accounting enables us to understand the relation between law, business and responsibility. 'Rational accounting, "the most general presupposition for the existence of this present day capitalism" as the norm for industrial enterprises, involves the appropriation of all physical means of production – land, apparatus, machinery, tools, etc. as disposable property of autonomous private industrial enterprises. It also involves freedom of the market, without irrational limitations, and technology rationalised to the highest degree'.[144] For capitalism to function, *accountability* was needed, meaning that an entrepreneur had to be able to predict and calculate every element of his business, including opportunity and risk, and including the cost of averting such risk. Double-entry bookkeeping enabled accountability, and the ability to see (and influence or manage) which profits or losses could be ascribed to whom. Weber explains how rational commerce (i.e., capitalist exchange) was the field where 'quantitative reckoning' first appeared. While

139 Weber 1982, p. 177.
140 See also Wood 2002, p. 15; Weber 1982, p. 343.
141 Weber 1982, p. 354.
142 Ibid. See also Weber 1978, esp. Vol. I, p. lxix; Vol. II, pp. 641–808; Wood 2002, p. 17.
143 Generally, Cain 1979; Weber 1982, pp. 275–7.
144 Weber 1982, pp. 276–7.

business was carried out by family firms, as a 'closed family affair', 'accountability was … unnecessary'[145] – it depended on the equitable assumption of risk, the equal exposure committed to by both parties was seen as a mark of integrity. In the transition to capitalism accountability became essential. Family, community and eventually also individual property became separated from the property of the business.

Capitalism also required law to be 'accountable' – the *development* of what Weber calls 'calculable law': 'The capitalistic form of industrial organization, if it is to operate rationally, must be able to depend on calculable adjudication and administration'.[146] As time progressed business became less and less dependent or based on familial/social relations and when capitalism matured the legal, *commodified* relationship took its place, in particular, or more prominently so, in business. It is only then that we can meaningfully speak of formal *legal* relations.[147] From an arrangement based on blood and trust, we gradually move to a formal *legal* relationship called a 'Trust' (or indeed a Partnership or Corporation). The corporation becomes an 'amoral calculator'[148] and the corporate construct allows, indeed forces, its human operators to be the same. This is the specific instance of the broader notion of the introduction of the *cash nexus* into all human relationships.[149] The genealogy of the notion of accountability (in the sense used by the 'business in conflict' authors discussed in Chapter 1) in this *accountability in a literal sense* lies at the heart of the 'commodified responsibility' conclusion I draw in Chapter 6.

3.4 *The Legal Forms, Limited Liability and 'Entity Shielding'*

Finally then a note on the specific legal forms that were created in the process of the transition to capitalism and from which the corporation derives. The Italian partnership forms used at the time when rational accounting was introduced, the *compagnia*, the *commenda* and the *societas*, spread through Europe – from the Italian city-states, up to Antwerp and then London – as part of the generally accepted 'law merchant'.[150] These are mentioned in the literature as the forerunners of the company as we now know it. The *compagnia*, family-based

145 Weber 1982, p. 225.

146 Weber 1982, p. 277.

147 As we shall see below, however, family relations and name still remain significant until after World War Two in some cases (e.g., *Krupp*, Ch. 3, § 5.2) and also today 'goodwill' can be a business's biggest asset.

148 Sutherland 1983, p. 236.

149 Pashukanis 1978, p. 40; Caudwell 1905, p. 69.

150 Generally, Weber 2003 [1889]. See also Harris 2000, p. 20; Farrar 1998, p. 16; Davies 1997, p. 19. For Grotius's interpretation of the *societas*, see below and van Ittersum 2006.

partnerships (mostly productive and service-based rather than trading), were set up to separate the members' assets from the business assets (thus introducing a form of limited liability). More important than the limited exposure and liability of the company's owners, however, became 'entity shielding' – an early example of which we saw in *The Case of Sutton's Hospital* above – the protection of the corporation from the owners' creditors.[151] The larger partnerships such as the Medici Bank mentioned earlier operated a form of entity shielding between different branches of the firm.[152] This meant that were a branch to fail, the others, or the Medici family fortune, would not be affected also. The latter construct we now commonly find in any larger firms and especially multinational enterprises. Although the 'entity shielding' effect of legal personality had also been achieved to various degrees prior to the availability of corporate personhood (through contract), separate legal personality, separating the company's property from its members'/owners' property, became the main technique to achieve this.

The *societas* was a more permanent form of partnership adopted amongst others by guilds, 'each partner being an agent of the others and liable to the full extent of his private fortune for partnership debts'. Partners invested capital and labour based on ability and shared profits based on needs and custom.[153] The private, unlimited liability was considered important in sectors where individual status and reputation were a major factor for trading partners and investors. Trading as collectivities, the members bore risk jointly – Weber calls this an 'organized community of risk'.[154] Examples go as far back as the *'lex Rhodia de iactu'* where in shipping expeditions, if at times of distress goods had to be thrown overboard, loss was borne equally.[155] Business was a personal affair, with business organisation mainly consisting of partnerships, and where the profitability of an enterprise depended on trust in a 'reputable merchant'. Partnerships were regulated internally to insure the relationship (and minimise the risk) between partners through contracts and informal bonds of reputation and kinship, and between partners and employees by extensive 'house rules'.[156]

151 Hansmann, Kraakman, and Squire 2006.

152 Weber 2003 [1889]; Hansmann, Kraakman, and Squire 2006, pp. 1364ff.

153 Holdsworth 1925, Vol. III, p. 198. The *commenda* in a similar form still exists in continental Europe, e.g., as the Société en Commandité in France and the Commanditaire Vennootschap in The Netherlands.

154 Weber 1982, p. 205.

155 Weber 1982, p. 204. Another example was the 'Sea loan' – because of the extraordinarily high risk of sea ventures, an interest rate of up to 30 percent was paid to lenders, while in case of the loss of the ship, the lender would not receive repayment.

156 Blackford 2008, p. 1, describing how employees of the leading business Herries & Com-

There was no conceptual or practical separation between 'business' and 'personal' in general.[157] Similarly, the family household accounts and thus wealth was not separated from the commercial accounts of members of the family.[158]

Although the *commenda* left no direct descendent in England, the influence of this idea indirectly affected the form of the commercial enterprises which in England and elsewhere emerged in the seventeenth century. The *commenda* was used for trading partnerships (first around the Mediterranean and up and down the European rivers, later beyond), generally a cross between a partnership and a loan and involved one person (the commendator) advancing money to a trader on the basis that he would receive a return which varied with the profits – originally for one specific transaction such as a particular shipping voyage.[159] The lender shared in the profit but was liable only to the extent of their share paid into the partnership (i.e., if a loss was suffered this did not lead to the lender having to pay out over and above losing the investment) – as an early finance capitalist. It was on this type of arrangement that the later merchant adventurers (such as the Company of Royal Adventurers Trading to Africa – later known as the Royal African Company – which was England's foremost slave trading company)[160] and colonial enterprises would initially be based. In sum, it was with this idea of risk-free (but potentially profitable) investment combined with the creation of a separate corporate form that the modern corporation was created.[161]

According to Holdsworth, 'it was through the *commenda* that the idea of a society in which the capitalist could invest and limit his liability came into the commercial law of Europe'.[162] During the transition from feudalism to capitalism, this form enabled wealthy landowners to invest in a manufacturing or trading venture while not being involved in the day-to-day running of it. It formed an important way for European aristocracy to safeguard its economic position by channelling its capital into commerce and industry.[163] Partners could be anonymous 'sleeping partners' who were spared the indignity of being seen to engage in business, especially so when such business failed. Moreover,

pany required employees to keep the business fully informed of where they lived and ate.

157 For example, for protection of group wealth and joint liability, members of the Hanseatic League were not allowed to marry outside the group.

158 Weber 1982, pp. 225–6.

159 The *commenda*, see Davies 1997, p. 20; Harris 2000, p. 20; Farrar 1998, p. 16.

160 Williams 1966 [1944], p. 30.

161 Harris 2000, p. 16.

162 Holdsworth 1925, Vol. III, p. 197.

163 Harris 2000, p. 30.

once the burgesses realised the power of the city *versus* the state, and once guilds were able to 'boss' the town, and when the protection of *corporate* assets separate from personal/familial assets became a possibility and even a *priority*, the foundations of *corporate power* were laid.

The transition to capitalism took place in a period of intensely violent conflict.[164] The synergy between business and conflict stimulated both. This includes the *legal* development of the corporation. Weber notes, because of the risk of pirate attacks, single ships (each organised as a single venture in accounting terms) normally joined together into a 'caravan' and were either armed themselves or joined by an armed convoy.[165] This then 'by commercial necessity' led to the formation of public companies with a more *permanent* form, joint accounting structure and protection of the company's assets in case of a member's insolvency: the joint stock corporation – the forerunner of today's multinational corporation.[166] This *commenda* form was first used for the Dutch and British East India Companies, and once England became the commercial hegemon in the world, this form was developed there and adopted widely.[167]

4 From the Joint Stock Corporation to the MNC

4.1 *Merchant Adventurers, Slave-Traders and Colonisers Inc.*

In the second half of the sixteenth century and following, once the basic building blocks were present, the corporate form was developed in practice and through the cases on partnership liabilities being decided in the Chancery courts, which interpreted the rules on debt priority so as to give business the effects of separate personality, asset partitioning (or entity shielding) and limited liability.[168] The 'joint stock corporation' ('JSC') was based on financial elements of the guild combined with the corporate form,[169] a 'concrete, profit-oriented form',[170] that grew out of the sixteenth-century trading enterprises used by merchant adventurers. Their proliferation as part of the colonial enterprise (more about this in Chapter 2B) resulted in the formation of 'regulated

164 Brandon 2010.
165 Weber 1982, p. 208.
166 Harris 2000, p. 39.
167 Hansmann, Kraakman, and Squire 2006, pp. 1377–8.
168 Generally, Getzler 2006.
169 Getzler 2006.
170 Harris 2000, p. 39.

companies', effectively extending the guild system into overseas trade.[171] These companies were awarded Royal Charters providing for incorporation and the grant of a trading privilege, often a trading monopoly, such as the trade in a certain commodity and/or on a certain trade route or from a certain colony. As one of the earliest examples, in 1555 the Merchants Adventurers of England for the Discovery of Lands Unknown, also known as the Muscovy or Russia Company, were incorporated to exploit the sole right to travel to Russia or further north.[172] The concept of 'joint stock' appeared in the mid-sixteenth century.[173] Davies tracks the rapid development: from 1614 there was joint stock to which members could subscribe varying amounts for a period of years. In 1653 a permanent joint stock was introduced, and in 1692 individual trading on private accounts was forbidden to members.[174] Members shared profits and losses of all business activities of the corporation, as well as all overheads.[175] From this point, the company traded as a single entity.[176] Notably, the JSC's shares were fully tradeable (the Amsterdam Stock Exchange – founded in 1602 by the Dutch East India Company – being the first public market for shares[177] and shares changing hands 'vigorously' since the 1690s),[178] and the courts allowed the protection of the firm itself from the personal debts of the shareholders giving the firm strong asset shielding, which made the JSC form very popular and successful.[179]

The legal development of the joint stock corporation took place within the specific context of a small number of merchant enterprises, in a specific time. '[F]rom the mid-sixteenth to the mid-seventeenth century, a mechanism was developed for raising money in return for shares, for dividing profits among shareholders, for transferring shares among members and to outsiders, and for keeping accounts of joint stock concerns for long durations'.[180] For the Crown, granting monopolies was a convenient way to raise increasing military expenditure while avoiding the parliamentary supervision attached to other forms of revenue such as taxation.[181] In effect, the 'conduct of war by the state

171 Farrar 1998, p. 17.
172 Baker 2003, p. 623.
173 Harris 2000, p. 24.
174 Davies 1997, p. 20.
175 Harris 2000, p. 33.
176 Morse 2005, p. 5.
177 Braudel 1983, pp. 433 ff.
178 Hansmann, Kraakman, and Squire 2006, p. 1385.
179 Hansmann, Kraakman, and Squire 2006, pp. 1378–9.
180 Harris 2000, p. 25.
181 Harris 2000, p. 41.

a business operation of the possessing classes'.[182] Here we see the ...l for synergy between state and corporation (a 'military-mercantilist ...ex'), rather than the competition above. War loans could potentially be ve... lucrative if the war was won, with its spoils, which were shared out among investors as 'profits'. Other benefits for the Crown included using the corporations as an indirect means of foreign policy through warfare or colonisation[183] (see below under Part B, Section 2), and – in the case of the triangular slave trade – as the main source of capital which funded the industrial revolution.

4.1.1 Jobbers and Bubbles at the Birth of the Modern Corporation

Opening up the share market to the public caused a momentous phase in the development of company law. In 1600 the British East India Company was granted a monopoly of the trade with the Indies by Royal Charter.[184] It was the first to combine incorporation, overseas trade and joint stock raised from the general public.[185] Moreover, after the 'bourgeois revolution' of the English Civil War (1642–51) and the 'Glorious Revolution' of 1688–89[186] the business climate changed, monopoly ownership was no longer as important and in particular, the British East India Company, the Bank of England and the South Sea Company (known as 'moneyed companies') re-emerged as leaders in public finance and gained political importance.[187] In the English revolution, a massive social and economic upheaval, the forces of parliament and the City of London, representing the British capitalist class, mobilised popular forces to end remnants of feudal monarchical absolutism. Substantial sales of land led to loss of Crown income, while the corporations had access to vast public pools of money through the stock market. As the Crown came to depend on these companies for loans, their power grew. By 1714, 39 percent of the public debt was owed to the three 'moneyed companies'.[188]

Harris emphasises that the institution of the business corporation is not a product of industrialisation, but of the earlier mercantilist era. This origin is the cause of the corporation's specific features of stock structure, monopol-

182 Weber 1982, p. 280.

183 Weber 1982, p. 282, fn. 2.

184 Harris 2000, p. 24.

185 Farrar 1998, p. 17. Similarly, in the Netherlands, the Dutch Vereenigde Oostindische Compagnie (Dutch East India Company) was established in 1602 by Charter explicitly granting shareholders limited liability, and issued its holders with paper certificates that could be traded on the Amsterdam Stock Exchange (ibid).

186 Merriman 2010, pp. 226–31.

187 Harris 2000, p. 53.

188 Head 2008, p. 3.

istic rights, financial linkage to the crown and public law r the environment changed, the legal form proceeded on 'an path'. According to Harris then, in the period of industrialisa according to its own logic rather than being determine 'needs' of the time.[190] Ireland considers that the underlying ining logic is that of capitalism, which emerges in the While the 'industrial revolution' did not initially consist in a sudden and dramatic technological change, it did cause major changes in the social organisation of production. The development of law did follow the logic of capitalism as did the change in social organisation, which was to a large extent enabled by law.[191]

Consolidating these views leads to the view that the corporation is a product of capitalist logic already present in the mercantilist era, and that it adopts its identifying (and still current) characteristics during the time of changing social organisation of labour in industrialisation. One major factor here is the reification of the company share as property rights enabling the 'pure finance capitalists' to invest without any involvement in, or risk from, the activities of the corporation and while being able to freely exchange these shares at will. We can observe here the results of the dialectic between form and content. Mercantilism required maximum flexibility and minimum exposure, which we still have now, and which suits capitalism.

Only with Enlightenment individuality – and the commodification of risk/-calculability that the legalisation of human relations entailed – did the idea of collective liability lose traction and was the corporation created as a separate legal person as opposed to it remaining an aggregate of persons. This, with 'limited liability', allowed the externalisation of risk to the outside world. Savigny's fiction theory (the corporation is a legal fiction) lost favour to Gierke's real theory (the corporation is a real entity created by law). At the same time, and as described by Ireland, in English law the separation of the legal entity from its (constituent) members occurs. Risk was thereafter not socialised among the members but among society at large – and the natural environment.

The key point here is that raising money from the general public also shifted (or devolved) the majority of the risk to it; that is, the risk was 'socialised'. Despite the obvious bubble-bursting repercussions the general public was and stayed somehow willing to take on this risk. This is perhaps a result of the capitalist culture that started to emerge.

---

189 Harris 2000, p. 56.

190 Harris 2000, p. 58.

191 Ireland 2002, p. 134.

.2 The Big Bang of Modern Company Law: When the Bubble Burst

The story of the South Sea Company illustrates the changing dynamic between the state and corporation. The British South Sea Company, a joint stock company, was founded in 1710 with the dual objectives of the exploitation of a monopoly of all trade to the Spanish colonies in South America and to take on the government's burden of national debt accrued as a result of the War of the Spanish Succession (1701–14).[192] The company took a gamble on both the outcome and cost of the war. In exchange the company was rewarded with solid government support for the business. The Bank of England, which had been founded in return for money lent to the government by a group of individuals, was outbid by the South Sea Company, which had bribed government members.[193] When rumours started circulating that the country might go bankrupt because of the size of the debt, the Company persuaded the government to convert the debt to shares in the company which were offered to the open market.[194] This move allowed for a dramatic expansion of the national debt.[195] The converted bonds were sold riding the wave of the popularity of the share trade. There was what we would now call 'consumer confidence' in the years following the war which ended with the Treaty of Utrecht in 1713. There was increased wealth, no longer confined to the upper classes, and an excitement about the luxury goods that could be acquired from foreign lands. Stocks were busily traded by stockjobbers working from the coffee houses on and around Exchange Alley in the City of London.[196] The hype surrounding the South Sea shares fuelled share prices generally and led to numerous genuine and less genuine companies being set up. Stockjobbers set up stalls on the street, selling shares in companies 'for importing jackasses from Spain', 'securing perpetual motion', 'an undertaking which would in due time be revealed'.[197] With penny shares everyone (of the petty bourgeois or middle class) could and *did* invest. This in turn reflects a popular acceptance of (a literal 'buy-in' to) the ideology of capitalism.

The South Sea shares were valued at around 100 pounds each in January 1720, and over 1,000 pounds in December of the same year. The company apparently bribed ministers and persuaded the government to pass the so-called

192 Davies 1997, p. 24.

193 Holdsworth 1925, Vol. III, p. 213.

194 Farrar 1998, p. 17.

195 Harris 2000, p. 62.

196 After a fire destroyed many coffee houses in 1748, a group of jobbers set up a club and built a new coffee house called New Jonathan's. It was later renamed the Stock Exchange, see the London Stock Exchange, Our History (n.d.).

197 Wormser 1931, p. 21.

'Bubble Act',[198] which required all companies to have charters, and declared all undertakings 'tending to the common Grievance, Prejudice and Inconvenience of His Majesty's Subjects' illegal and void.[199] The Act exempted the South Sea Company (and the East India Company) from all its substantive restrictive provisions,[200] and it ex post facto legalised certain departures from the debt conversion scheme made by the Company, which 'demonstrated the company's ability to manipulate Parliament at will'.[201]

The Act did nothing to stem the popularity of South Sea shares. Eventually the burst of the bubble came – possibly as a result of proceedings against rival companies (Farrar suggests these may have been instigated by South Sea).[202] The shares were back down to around 100 pounds each within days and many lost their fortunes. 'Everyone – merchants, professors, doctors, clergymen – even the Canton of Berne [had] invested in the company'.[203] An enquiry took place and exposed a 'web of deceit, bribery and corruption',[204] which involved members of the Royal Household and Government.[205] The overwhelming public sentiment was one of a vacuum of accountability following the crash.[206] However, instead of punishment, the South Sea directors received the King's gratitude for their friendship in dealing with the government debt, and King George made baronets of John Blunt and William Chapman.[207]

There were calls for the company directors to face a 'Roman style execution', but instead a sum of two million pounds was made available for compensation.[208] Some MPs were expelled from parliament and MP and South Sea Director Aislabie was tried and found guilty of 'most notorious, dangerous and infamous corruption that he had encouraged and promoted the dangerous and destructive execution of the South Sea scheme'.[209] Rather than facing jail time,

198 Ibid.
199 Bubble Act s.18.
200 Bubble Act s.23, 24, 26–29 – these also protected two newly established insurance companies.
201 Harris 2000, p. 68.
202 Farrar 1998, p. 18, and Gower 1952.
203 Farrar 1998, p. 18.
204 South Sea Company Harvard Business School Project: http://www.library.hbs.edu/hc/ssb/index.html.
205 Davies 2003, p. 26.
206 South Sea Company Harvard Business School Project.
207 Harris 2000, pp. 72–3.
208 Farrar 1998, p. 18.
209 *Case of Aislabie* (1721) and see Novak 2003, p. 574.

however, Aislabie was able to return to his stately home in Yorkshire and dedicate the remainder of his life to redesigning the estate's parkland.[210]

4.2 *Bubble Aftermath: Effects on Company Law Development*

Many commentators describe the Bubble Act as reactionary and prohibitive legislation aimed at impeding the rise of the joint stock company as a form of business organisation.[211] Harris, on the other hand, argues that the South Sea Company, which organised the national debt conversion scheme, also instigated the Bubble Act, 'because small bubble companies had become an annoying factor in the stock market of 1720'.[212] Indeed, the South Sea Company and a number of others were explicitly exempted, and the South Sea Company continued to exist for over another century.

The Bubble share-craze, by advancing the links between the various financial markets in Western Europe, 'facilitated, for the first time, the emergence of an integrated and efficient international financial market'.[213] While the bubble had been a disaster for the thousands who lost their money in this first time mass-socialisation of risk, and despite an outcry over the lack of accountability, the public continued to assume corporate risk in the years and indeed centuries to follow, which is testament to the strength of corporate capitalist ideology. One explanation for this is the individualising tendency of capital: 'Of course, not all of the people subscribing to the schemes believed they had any true merit. All they wanted to do was get in early and sell at a higher price to a bigger fool ... Every fool aspired to be a knave'.[214]

The Bubble Act did not impede economic development, nor did it hinder the development of company law.[215] After the Bubble 'PR fiasco' the state created some distance between itself and business, making it difficult to obtain a Charter or Statute. The effect was that lawyers began to create the same effect as 'joint stock' incorporation by means of ingenious drafting, using amongst others the 'deed of settlement' construct – a cross between a trust and an association, and effectively granting limited liability.[216] Property would be vested in a board of trustees, management would be delegated to a board of directors, although whether they could be sued remained unclear – and 'obscurity on

210 Woodland Trust, Aislabie walk leaflet.

211 Harris 2000, p. 60; Maitland 1936, p. 208; Holdsworth 1925, Vol. VIII, p. 221.

212 Harris 2000, p. 61.

213 Harris 2000, p. 80.

214 MacKay 2001 [1841].

215 Blackford 2008, p. 39.

216 Farrar 1998, p. 19.

this point was by no means a disadvantage from the point of view of th pany'[217] – and even 'strangely enough [use of this type of companies] seems to have been encouraged rather than frowned upon by the Government'.[218] The agents of change in the period following the Bubble Act were businessmen and lawyers. The latter, trained on the job (often in business),[219] developed law in a more pragmatic 'managerialist' direction compared to other countries. Such legal scholars as there were at Oxford and Cambridge Universities exclusively read Roman and Canon law and did not concern themselves with everyday business. Law was further developed by 'overworked common-law judges and Lord Chancellors [whose] agenda was shaped by the disputes that reached their halls'.[220] Some legal texts were also written by retired judges and 'barristers on the margins of their profession, who aimed at supplementing their legal fees'.[221] There was no space for theoretical discussions on, for example, the nature of legal personality in the writings of those authors, who mainly focused on the 'how' of company law. Then as now, company law was directed by the practical concerns of entrepreneurs and their attorneys, and lawyers, judges, and businessmen all needed legal rules that could be easily and predictably applied.[222] An alternative explanation may be that then (as indeed now) a separation between high public life and the world of business suited the ruling elite, and enabled it to create an ideological separation/distance between themselves and the exploitative goings-on that supplied their income. Company law in this period was made privately, for private purposes.

4.3 *1844: The First Modern Companies Act*

The expansion of the railways finally brought a push for company law reform. Railway companies needed to raise large amounts of capital from the public.[223] The Bubble Act was eventually repealed in 1825,[224] and the first 'modern companies act', The Joint Stock Companies Act 1844,[225] was enacted – properly adopting the deed of settlements company and endowing it with the 'qualities and incidents' of corporations, except limited liability.[226] Significantly, the

217 Davies 2003, p. 29.
218 Dubois 1938, p. 216.
219 Weber 1978, pp. 785–8.
220 Harris 2000, p. 111.
221 DuBois 1938, pp. 83–4; for an earlier example of such text, see, e.g., Kyd 1795.
222 Harris 2000, p. 112.
223 Davies 2003, p. 31.
224 Farrar 1998, p. 19.
225 7 & 8 Vict, cx.
226 Farrar 1998, p. 19.

company's profit mandate was included in the statutory definition of the company.[227] According to Farrar, 'The effect of this legislation was to shift from the *privilege* of incorporation by Royal or Statutory grant to *the right of incorporation* provided the statutory conditions were fulfilled'.[228] Incorporation could then be achieved upon registration with the newly established Registrar of Companies. This shift was indicative of a shift in the balance of power in society from crown to the bourgeoisie-dominated parliament, and thus their private economic interests. The public/private conceptual divide stems from this period and when for the first time corporations could be formed without any explicit state interference, a private sphere was created into which corporations shifted.[229] This 'conceptual innovation … lay at the core of the longer term revolution'.[230]

Contracting for limited liability became 'cumbrous and expensive' with such large corporations.[231] Despite the difficulties inherent in attempting to sue a fluctuating body of members and the even greater difficulties of levying execution – which made the personal liability of the members largely illusory,[232] the fact that a debt of £10 could land one in debtors' prison was a strong incentive to try to limit (shift) one's exposure.[233] Any lingering insecurity over whether contractual limited liability would stand up in court was taken away in 1852 in *Hallett v. Dowdall*.[234] Subsequently it was provided for in the 1855 Limited Liability Act,[235] which, according to Gower, was passed with 'almost indecent haste'.[236] As limited liability had already been introduced by statute in the US and France, the Board of Trade promoted the measure to 'help vitalise British business' and stop 'British' companies from incorporating abroad.[237]

227 S. II 7 & 8 Vict, CX.
228 Farrar 1998, p. 19, emphasis added.
229 Harris 2000, p. 284.
230 Ibid.
231 Farrar 1998, p. 19.
232 Davies 2003, p. 32.
233 Harris 2000, p. 131. Related to this, in the nineteenth century bankruptcy became a privilege rather than a punishment (Harris 2000, p. 132). One of the criticisms of limited liability was that it takes away the right of the creditor. However, creditors would often also themselves be able to benefit from limited liability, and in 1856 creditors' remedies were improved through the system of winding up, which achieved its current form in 1929 (Farrar 1998, p. 22).
234 *Hallett v. Dowdall* (1825) 21 LJQB 98.
235 Limited Liability Act 1855 (18 & 19 Vict. c.47).
236 Farrar 1998, p. 21.
237 Farrar 1998, p. 20.

The 1855 Act contained safeguards, such as the requirement that a company must have at least 25 members and a minimum subscribed capital, which were 'brushed aside in the name of laissez-faire'[238] in the 1856 Joint Stock Companies Act[239] and shortly thereafter the Companies Act of 1862,[240] which was dubbed the 'Magna Carta of cooperative enterprise'.[241] Many industrial enterprises took the opportunity to incorporate under this act.[242] The modern corporation had been born.

From Wilhelm we learn that in France and Germany the run-up to the 'modern corporation' had been similar to the developments in the UK, even down to the popular demand for share ownership in the first half of the 1800s, leading to the establishment of bogus companies – in France, for example, there was a joint stock company 'pour le marriage de l'Amérique et de l'Afrique'.[243] In France the main companies legislation was introduced in 1856, and the General Assembly of the German Confederation in 1868 adopted the *Allgemeines Deutsches Handelsgesetzbuch* (drafted with the participation of many merchants) regulated joint stock companies and the 'Kommanditgesellschaft auf Aktien'.[244] As such, the legal developments in these countries mirrored those in the UK, while the development of capitalism had followed broadly similar paths there, too.[245]

The corporation, as it came to exist in law in the mid-nineteenth century, has not changed fundamentally since. All the key characteristics were in place.

4.4 *Another Look at Separate Personality*

Of the key company characteristics that 'solidified' at this time it is necessary to pause once again at the concept of legal personality. When, with the joint stock company and later the modern corporation, share ownership is deliberately spread out over the general public, the risk of the economic activity of the corporation is externalised, and it becomes in 'everyone's' interest that the company do well, and that, for instance, economic policies adopted by the government favour business. According to Marx:

---

238 Farrar 1998, pp. 20–1.
239 Joint Stock Companies Act 1856 19 & 20 Vict. c.47.
240 Companies Act 1862 25 & 26 Vict. c.89.
241 Farrar 1998, pp. 20–1; see also Hadden 1977, p. 22.
242 Farrar 1998, p. 21.
243 Wilhelm 2009, p. 22.
244 Wilhelm 2009, pp. 22–6.
245 Generally, Weber 1982.

> Capital, which is inherently based on a social mode of production and presupposes a social concentration of means of production and labour-power, now receives the form of social capital (capital of directly associated individuals) in contrast to private capital, and its enterprises appear as social enterprises as opposed to private ones. This is the abolition of capital as private property within the confines of the capitalist mode of production itself.[246]

Taking this understanding it is possible to *vindicate* Pashukanis:

> It is now the capitalist *project* which must use wage-labour to accumulate, as opposed to the individual capitalist. A necessary corollary of this was the development of the juridical form to allow for a corporate body to be the owner of a commodity and therefore retain legal personality. This was not a 'new' legal form but a development of the legal form Pashukanis outlines *on the basis of that form itself*.[247]

This move is enabled by the development of the corporate ideology.

Ireland et al. argue, 'it is the emergence of the joint stock company share as a new form of fictitious capital that underlies the doctrine of separate personality and, therefore, the basic conceptual structure of contemporary company law'.[248] This change is reflected in the definition of the company which moved from 'persons form[ing] themselves into an incorporated company' in 1856, to 'persons form[ing] an incorporated company' in 1862.[249] The company had then become, and has remained since, something 'external' to its members, a *separate* legal person.[250] What caused the momentous change in the 1850s–60s, according to Ireland et al., was 'the changing economic and legal nature of the *joint stock company share*. The share became property, "realty" in its own right, as opposed to a mere claim based on a contractual relationship'.[251]

Explaining the change in Marxist terms, it is pointed out that 'such transformations can only take place under certain historical conditions – conditions in which labour power has become a commodity'. Ireland et al. use the Marxist distinction between money capitalists (who invest) and industrial capitalists

246 Marx 1981, p. 567.
247 Miéville 2005, p. 108 (emphasis in the original).
248 Ireland 1987, p. 149.
249 Companies Act 1856 s. 3, Companies Act 1862, s. 6.
250 Ireland 1987, p. 149.
251 Ireland 1987, p. 153, emphasis added.

(who utilise the funds). 'Interest represents a relationship between the two capitalists and, as such, necessarily entails antagonism between them as they contest the division of surplus value'.[252] Yet, the common drive to maximise surplus value extraction is stronger than (and intensified by) this competition. For instance, the pressure to maintain or raise stock prices may force industrial capitalists to take measures they might otherwise not have considered.

Marx describes the process of reification of money capital as, '[the thing] which embodies ... the social relationship ... acquire[s] a fictitious life and independent existence'.[253] Thus, 'the conception of capital as a self-reproducing and self-expanding value, lasting and growing eternally by virtue of its innate properties, is thereby established'.[254]

What enabled this development to occur was the development of a secondary market for these company shares. According to Ireland, the UK railway system's development in the early nineteenth century led to the popularisation and proliferation of shares available and readily traded.[255] With this 'a gulf emerged between companies and their shareholders and between shareholders and their shares'.[256] Companies owned the industrial capital and shareholders the 'fictitious' share capital which they could sell at will without affecting the size of the industrial capital. Ireland states that, at this point, the company became a singular entity, separate from shareholders, 'emptied of people'.[257] 'Both the company and the share had been reified'.[258] What the description of this process of course highlights is the centrality of law as 'one of the primary social practices through which actual relationships embodying class power [are] created and articulated'.[259] Through law, '[c]apitalist social relations come to be reified and depersonalised; that is, that class relations under developed capitalism cease to be personal but come, to a significant extent, to be embodied in things, some of which – like the joint stock company share – are constituted *in law* as autonomous forms of property'.[260] This is the process that Marx calls 'commodity fetishism'.[261] Linked to this is the congealing of the corporate purpose of profit extraction in the 1844 Act: the legitimation of the narrow

252 Ireland 1987, p. 155.
253 Marx 1972, p. 483.
254 Marx 1972, p. 394.
255 Ireland 1987, p. 159.
256 Ibid.
257 Ibid.
258 Ibid.
259 Ireland 1987, p. 161, quoting Klare 1979.
260 Ireland 1987, pp. 161–2.
261 Marx 1976, pp. 163–77.

profit mandate, economic-rational decision-making to the exclusion of moral considerations. In the words of Stanley:

> Capitalist societal relations are expressed in the reflection of the alienated individual to the mode of production. Thus the legitimisation of the mode of production through regulation of the corporate form bears witness to the legality of the process of alienation. Law is both constituted by capitalist social relations and constitutive of them. Central to this process of creation, articulation and reproduction of class relationships is the idea of alienation which is clearly seen in law through the process of the legitimisation of both the corporate entity and the relationship of the individual to that entity through the mode of production.[262]

The relationship of the individual worker, the person affected by the activities of the corporation, the 'victim' becomes a relationship with *the corporation*, no longer with the individuals inside it, the corporation has been lifted up above them, or, emptied of them. The corporation becomes 'capital personified',[263] or *Monsieur Le Capital*.[264] The relationship between 'outsider' and the corporation becomes one of exchange, as formal legal equals. Chapter 6 examines how this affects the relationship of responsibility between the corporation and those affected by its operations.

4.4.1 The Finishing Touch: Salomon

The 1897 case of *Salomon v. A. Salomon & Co. Ltd*.[265] put the new company law to the test. Salomon had been a successful leather merchant for many years. In 1892, he decided to create a limited company, Salomon & Co Ltd, with himself, his wife and five of his children as shareholders. He then purchased the business (acting as its managing director) *from himself* for £39,000 – a sum rather larger than a reasonable estimate of its value.[266] Within a year the company went into liquidation and the company assets were not sufficient to pay the unsecured creditors.

The question facing the House of Lords and the lower courts before them was whether to 'interpret the law literally or whether to consider more its pre-

262 Stanley 1988, p. 97.
263 Neocleous 2003, p. 158.
264 Marx 1981 p. 969.
265 *Salomon v. A. Salomon and Co. Ltd* [1897] AC 22.
266 Lord Mcnaghten in *Salomon* at 49.

sumed spirit and intention'.[267] The court came down firmly on the s former, allowing an abstraction from material reality not seen since tl *Sutton's Hospital*.

While limited liability had ostensibly been created in order to stimulate arms-length investment in business ventures where investors had little oversight or input, *Salomon* showed how it could be used to the investor's advantage in the opposite situation: the main person active in the company was able to 'incorporate' and thus limit his *own* liability for the consequences of his own decisions and actions. At the time of *Salomon* incorporation required seven shareholders, and the decision confirmed that this could be one active, controlling shareholder and six nominal participants.[268] The House of Lords understood that in the case of *Salomon*, the six other shareholders besides Mr. Salomon were mere 'dummies', '[b]ut when once it is conceded that they were individual members of the company distinct from Salomon, and sufficiently so to bring into existence in conjunction with him a validly constituted corporation, I am unable to see how the facts to which I have just referred can affect the legal position of the company, or give it rights against its members which it would not otherwise possess'.[269]

Lord Halsbury in the same case comments:

> [I]t seems to me impossible to dispute that once the company is legally incorporated it must be treated like any other independent person with its rights and liabilities appropriate to itself, and that the motives of those who took part in the promotion of the company are absolutely irrelevant in discussing what those rights and liabilities are ... I can only find the true intent and meaning of the Act from the Act itself; and the Act appears to me to give a company a legal existence with, as I have said, rights and liabilities of its own, whatever may have been the ideas or schemes of those who brought it into existence.[270]

At this point then company law receives its current form. Protection and furthering of business interest is not a right, but a normalised entitlement: 'Persons are entitled to incorporate companies for the purpose of separating their business affairs from their personal affairs'.[271] The following chapters will also

267 Hicks 2008, p. 96.
268 Under the UK Companies Act 2006, one person can incorporate alone: Art. 7.
269 Lord Herschell in *Salomon*, 43. See further in Harris 2000, pp. 40–1; Davies 2016, pp. 29–32.
270 Lord Halsbury in *Salomon*, 30–1, emphasis added.
271 French 2009, p. 146.

touch on the effect of compartmentalising 'business' from 'personal' in the psychological, or *mens rea* sense: corporate anomie.[272] The corporation 'absorbs' any bad faith (or worse) on behalf of the individual: as per Lord Halsbury in Salomon: 'the motives of those who took part in the promotion of the company are absolutely irrelevant in discussing what those rights and liabilities are'.[273]

In 1891 Cook wrote:

> Fifty years ago wealthy men were identified with their investments, Today, with a few exceptions, the great enterprises are not connected in the public mind with individual names … If corrupt and unscrupulous, the odium and disgrace rests upon the corporation and not upon the individual. Take it all in all, the corporation is as perfect and heartless a money-making machine as the wit of man has ever devised.[274]

The reified corporation was complete.

4.5 *The Modern Leviathan: The Multinational Corporate Group*

From the *Salomon* decision evolved the corporate group consisting of subsidiary companies owned by parent companies based and operating in one or more jurisdiction, each having separate legal personality. Enterprises are vertically integrated and constituted as multinational corporate groups containing sometimes hundreds of discreet corporations domiciled in a variety of jurisdictions but forming a single economic unit and responding to a common management strategy.[275] The structure of multinational corporate groups is generally 'optimised' so as to afford maximum protection of corporate interests through locating assets and interests in specific ('friendly' or 'conducive') jurisdictions, for example, intellectual property in The Netherlands, capital in the Bahamas, and so on, and through creating relationships (contractual and ownership) between different parts of the corporate groups to efficiently distribute and protect revenue streams.[276] Production has mostly moved to the Global South, while capital (and thus power and direction) has stayed in the North/West. It is mostly these 'companies' (more accurately, groups of companies) that are

272 Passas 2009, p. 153.
273 Lord Halsbury in *Salomon*, 30.
274 Cook 1891, pp. 250–1.
275 Vagts 1970, p. 740; generally, Muchlinski 2010.
276 Muchlinski 2007, pp. 203 ff.

accused of the human rights and other violations discussed in Chapter 1, and that indeed control much of the economy.[277]

The case of *Adams v. Cape* illustrates how the corporate group structure serves the interests of capital in a multinational enterprise. Cape Industries is a UK parent company whose subsidiaries mined asbestos in South Africa, which was then shipped to a Texas subsidiary. Workers in Texas became sick with asbestosis and sued the parent company in a US court, and subsequently attempted to enforce the judgment in their favour through the UK Court of Appeal. The court stated that although the corporate group had apparently been constructed deliberately so as to immunise the parent company from the claims that its board members *already expected* to arise out of its trade in asbestos, it held that 'the court is not free to disregard the principle of *Salomon v. Salomon & Co Ltd* merely because it considers that justice so requires'.[278] Thus we see how the individual 'moral' actors disappear behind the corporate construct, and the group structure is used to insulate not only the individuals but other companies in the group from (financial) risk through the particular group's legal structure, which is optimised (amongst others) through the use of a technique known among corporate lawyers as 'defensive asset partitioning'.[279] In the twentieth and twenty-first centuries, we have seen corporate groups form ever more sophisticated structures that can isolate and shift value, risk, and responsibility on the global level while continuing global accumulation of wealth and the exploitation of Third World labour much like its joint stock forebear.[280] The following chapters focus mainly on these transnational businesses, complex legal structures based on the single company operated by individuals.[281]

277 Vitali 2011.

278 *Adams v. Cape Industries plc* [1990] BCLC 479 520.

279 On this notion, see generally, Kraakman 2009, pp. 135–6. There have been exceptional cases where such structures have failed and the 'corporate veil' has been lifted, including in another case against Cape, brought by Lubbe and around 3,000 others (including children) who contracted asbestosis as a result of working at Cape's South African subsidiary: *Lubbe et al. v. Cape* [2000] UKHL 41.

280 For a commentary, see Mwaura 2012.

281 While there has been some movement driven by activists and campaigners towards increasing transparency and with that, responsibility, within the 'global value chain' through transparency and vigilance-type laws such as the Californian 'Transparency in Supply Chains Act' (S.B. 657, 2010) and the French 'duty of vigilance' law adopted by the National Assembly in February 2017, in reality these are very difficult to police and enforce.

5 Conclusion to 2A

This chapter has highlighted the development from joint shouldering of risk and reward by familial and other groups bound by relationships of trust pre-capitalism, to the creation of market society and the introduction of 'calculable law' and the staged development of the modern corporation. Calculable law allows the business unit to base its decisions not on normative considerations, but on economic rationality. Responsibility becomes *accountability*. The creation of separate legal personality follows this logic: 'The most rational actualization of the idea of the legal personality of organizations consists in the complete separation of the legal spheres of the members from the separately constituted legal sphere of the organization'.[282] Aside from the *formal* legal aspects, the ideological aspects of reification/anthropomorphisation, the socialisation of shareholding as a factor in the legitimisation of the narrow profit mandate ('shareholder primacy'), serves to render the corporation a 'structure of irresponsibility',[283] which is 'capitalism congealed' and which serves to conceal (and enrich) the individual businessperson. Corporate groups form ever more sophisticated structures that can isolate and shift value, risk, and responsibility on the global level. I also showed that this situation is normalised, rendered neutral, by means of court decisions, through the business-led development of law which stayed largely isolated from philosophical/ethical enquiry, and by means of current 'positivist' teaching of, and scholarship on, company law. For example, a key element of 'corporate ideology', 'limited liability', which is actually liability *socialised* over broader society and the natural environment, combined with profit for a limited group, is not generally seen as a controversial or unnatural concept. This corporate ideology serves to produce knowledge, policy, and legal decisions and instruments that perpetuate capitalism and reproduce current socio-economic hierarchies.

Moreover, as Berle and Means wrote in their 1930s classic *The Modern Corporation and Private Property*: 'The corporate system has done more than evolve a norm by which business is carried on. Within it exists a centripetal attraction which draws wealth together into aggregations of constantly increasing size, at the same time throwing control into the hands of fewer and fewer men'.[284] The corporate form, the company as an 'amoral calculator',[285] induces its indi-

282 Weber 1978, p. 707.

283 Whyte 2008, p. 104.

284 Berle 1991, p. 18.

285 Sutherland 1983, pp. 236–8, who argues the corporation comes closer to 'economic man' than any person or organisation.

vidual operatives to make 'economically rational' amoral decisions – a form of capitalist *anomie*.[286] This anomie is expressed well by Steinbeck in *Grapes of Wrath*, when he describes one of the many farmland repossessions during the Depression in the United States:

> *We're sorry. It's not us. It's the monster. The bank isn't like a man.*
> *Yes, but the bank is only made of men.*
> *No, you're wrong there – quite wrong there. The bank is something else than men. It happens that every man in a bank hates what the bank does, and yet the bank does it. The bank is something more than men, I tell you. It's the monster. Men made it, but they can't control it.*

Market society then is one with the corporation, capital personified, Monsieur Le Capital driving the corporation as the engine of capitalism, accumulating power without responsibility – by means of the imperialism at the heart of the corporate form – the elephant in the room that is allowed to stay concealed through the workings of corporate ideology. Moreover, while the structure of capitalism produces this process, the individual human beings behind or within the corporation (as in Steinbeck's novel) come to feel shielded or powerless and thus without responsibility as to the devastating outcomes of corporate capitalism.

In Part B, using the examples of slave labour and pillage ('accumulation by dispossession')[287] in three different periods in history, I will show the effects of the imperialism *at the heart of* the corporate legal form. In 1848, Marx and Engels wrote in the *Communist Manifesto*: 'The need of a constantly expanding market for its products chases the bourgeoisie over the entire surface of the globe. It must nestle everywhere, settle everywhere, establish connections everywhere'.[288] It is to this corporate behaviour – the imperialism *of* the corporate form – on the global level, and in international law, that I turn next.

286 Passas 2009, p. 155; Bakan calls the corporation 'psychopath' (Bakan 2005, p. 134).

287 Below, Ch. 2B.

288 Marx and Engels 1969, p. 46; Veitch 2007, p. 44.

2B The Corporation and the Political Economy of International Law[289]

1 Introduction: the Corporation and Capitalism in International Law

In this section I elaborate on the argument made in Chapter 1 (s.3) that international law also finds its roots in the transition to capitalism, is an essential part of it (indeed, a *sine qua non*), and developed according to the logic of what Kingsbury has called 'commercial sociability', or the logic of capitalism[290] in order to create a global market society.

I start with a short overview of the epistemology and sources on this topic (s.1.1). In Sections 1.2–1.3 I discuss the origins and development of IL using again the commodity form theory of law – based on Pashukanis's *Essay on International Law*[291] and Miéville's monograph, which I further modify here. In Section 2, paying particular attention to the role (agency) of individual lawyers such as Grotius, I discuss the major significance of the corporation in the early development of IL. Elites (the global capitalist class) have used the legal technology of the corporation to channel their activities, amongst others, in overseas trade especially the triangular (slave) trade, fighting trade wars and, importantly, as a colonising entity (a tool for colonisation) in various specific ways which I illustrate here. Moreover, the corporate form created a template for the creation of the state form – which is shown by way of the Congo Corporation example – and the phenomenon of 'corporate sovereignty'. I include colonisation (and imperialism more broadly) as a form of conflict and discuss the *corporate* scramble for Africa in this light.

In Section 3 on corporations in the twentieth century, I comment on the significance of the historical development of the idea of (international) legal personality of both state and corporation in this story. I focus specifically on nationalisation/expropriation cases, as these are most relevant to the 'business and human rights' theme. Likewise 'decolonisation' is a site for conflict, in particular over the metropolitan states' (elites') continued access to Third World natural resources, labour and markets more broadly. To deal with these, new rules and regimes of IL are shaped through a collaboration of state and cap-

289 A shorter version of Chapter 2B has been published as 'From the Dutch East India Company to the Corporate Bill of Rights: Corporations and International Law', in *Political Economy and Law: A Handbook of Contemporary Practice, Research and Theory*, edited by U. Mattei and J. Haskell, Cheltenham: Edward Elgar 2015.

290 Kingsbury 2010, p. 33.

291 Pashukanis 2006, p. 321.

ital, giving credence to the claim of a 'global capitalist class'. This sometimes occurs visibly, for example through states' espousal of corporate claims in international fora such as the ICJ (s.3.4). A new field of IL has developed to manage conflict between capital and (mainly) Third World states and publics in favour of capital: the international law of investment protection (ILIP). The law in this field allows (among other things) corporations as parties to concession agreements and under Bilateral Investment Treaties (BITs) and more recently also North-North multilateral trade agreements to 'litigate' against states on the international level in arbitration including through the International Centre for the Settlement of Investment Disputes (ICSID).[292] In doing this, capitalists managed to lift their interests out of host state domestic jurisdiction and into international law, and then to separate off certain questions of international law to the realm of 'private international law', thereby excluding or concealing 'public' and 'domestic' interests, and in particular of course corporations' / capitalist elites' role in continued imperialist violence (both physical and economic) through the exploitation of labour and what David Harvey has called 'accumulation by dispossession'.

Legal scholarship and practice have aided capital through the creation of epistemological separations (shielding) of certain issue-areas of law from others, through 'fragmentation', and the creation of a public international law (PIL) and a private international law realm in IL. The public realm has come to be governed by the logic of peace, and the private by the logic of the market, a situation that has come to appear self-evident and unproblematic.

In a final section I discuss how, even though contemporary international law on the one hand includes the reified corporation as a 'participant' in areas of 'private' international law (such as in the law on 'investment protection'), in 'public' international law it remains largely invisible.[293]

1.1 *Epistemology: Sources in International Law/History of International Law*

In order to locate the corporation in the history of international law, and in international legal practice, some creativity is required. The history of interna-

292 The Centre 'provides facilities for conciliation and arbitration of investment disputes between Contracting States and nationals of other Contracting States', and was established by means of the 1965 Washington Convention on the Settlement of Investment Disputes between States and Nationals of Other States, 575 UNTS 532 (*1965 ICSID Convention*).

293 I use 'Private IL' to mean the IL that regulates aspects of the 'private sphere', and not in the technical sense of 'conflict of laws'.

tional law, like the history of company law, has been a neglected area.[294] The past 20 years, however, have seen something of a 'turn to history' in both mainstream and critical international legal scholarship.[295]

Earlier works of authors in the recent surge in history of IL work tended to focus on the writings of legal philosophers, the history of ideas or of a 'sensibility' of IL and less so the historical-material context in which those jurists operated.[296] An exception was Grewe, whose monumental *Epochen der Völkerrechtgeschichte* was translated into English by Michael Byers and published in 2000[297] but considered a 'problematic, even disturbing book' by Koskenniemi for its silences on Nazi era atrocities, failure to mention the holocaust, and revisionism in relation to the Versailles Treaty.[298] Considering the dearth in history of IL work, I do use Grewe's earlier chapters, which despite showing 'Nietzschian admiration of the realist perspective',[299] yields useful non-doctrinal material. In contemporary IL few authors discuss the 'why' of the emergence of law/international law – the development of law is often represented as a 'self-unfolding of ideas' or even through a 'teleology of freedom'.[300] Often too law and legal concepts appear (e.g., in judicial decisions or in the literature) seemingly as if out of nowhere, yet are presented as 'elementary' and obvious. Thus fundamental (foundational) contradictions are obscured: for example, the idea of statehood being both antecedent to and a product of IL.[301] Critical IL scholars such as Koskenniemi, Kennedy, Craven and Skouteris, as well as postcolonial IL scholars such as Anghie, provide useful correctives to the teleological readings.[302] Yet, as I argue below, in 'public' or general international law and history of international law scholarship, the political economy of international law remains largely concealed even in critical, and indeed even in *Marxist*, IL scholarship.[303]

294 Miéville 2006, p. 153; but see Nussbaum 1954; Verzijl 1968; Grewe 1984.

295 E.g., the 1999 founding of the *Journal of the History of International law/Revue de l'histoire de droit international* and the writings of Kennedy 1997; Berman 1998–99; Lesaffer 2002; Koskenniemi 2002; Koskenniemi 2004; Simpson 2004; Neff 2006; Kennedy 2012. See also Craven 2016.

296 Koskenniemi 2002, p. 2.

297 Grewe 1984; 2000.

298 Koskenniemi 2002.

299 Koskenniemi 2002, p. 747.

300 Miéville 2006, p. 155.

301 Craven 2010, p. 203.

302 Primarily, Kennedy 1983; Koskenniemi 1989; Craven 2007; Skouteris 2009; Anghie 2007.

303 But see the work of critical scholars Orford 2001; Alston 1997; Kennedy 2013; and Marxist scholars Rasulov 2008; Rasulov 2010; Carty 2008; Cutler 2003; Cutler 2008. See also Koskenniemi 2016a.

International legal scholarship, moreover, has had a blind spot when it comes to the notion of the corporation and the multinational enterprise[304] – which should seem surprising considering the latter's obvious significance in the global political economy and our daily lives. Current IL scholarship – which is divided into relatively discrete fields such as 'Public International Law' (PIL), 'Private International Law' and branches of these, including under PIL, 'International Economic Law', 'International Human Rights Law', 'International Environmental Law', etc. – appears to view the corporation either as external and/or irrelevant to its field of study, or (in 'international economic law' or more specifically, e.g., 'international law of investment protection' [ILIP])[305] to treat corporations (including multinationals) as self-evident, 'natural', and, most important, inevitable facts of life.[306] A notable example in the latter category is Peter Muchlinski's monograph *Multinational Enterprises and the Law*, first published in 1995.[307] The division of IL into various autonomous and highly technical and specialised subfields – the 'fragmentation of IL' – has been discussed in the International Law Commission as a cause for concern.[308] 'Constitutionalisation' of the international (or rather, global) legal field – where 'global governance'[309] happens – has been proposed as a corrective, and I will come back to this in Chapter 6.[310]

In Chapter 1, I discussed in some detail the emergence of a field of 'business and human rights'. This field forms part of a broader human rights mainstreaming or 'Human Rights and ...' effort in mainstream and critical scholarship[311] (which includes 'business and human rights', 'trade and human rights', 'development and human rights') spurred by the multidimensional global economic, environmental, and social problems of the past years, and developing on the back of a trend of 'humanisation' in IL that is in the mainstream literature often

304 Johns 1995, p. 19. But see Somers 2001; Nussbaum 1954, pp. 27–35, 203–7; Grewe 2000, pp. 345–57, 546–52; Verzijl 1968 – section on nationalisation and the private/public IL; generally Neff 1990; Miéville 2006, pp. 107–8; Wilson 2008, pp. 189–260, 400–15; Gathii 2010 esp. Chs. 5, 6, 7.

305 Strictly speaking, an amalgamation of public, private, and domestic law as well as soft law and business custom.

306 Allott is an exception: Allott 2002, 8.65. Key works of IL theory and history do not mention the corporation, for example, Koskenniemi 2002, but see the publication of Johns 2016.

307 Muchlinski 2007.

308 Report of the study group on the fragmentation of international law, finalised by Martti Koskenniemi, UN Doc. A/CN.4/L.682 13 April 2006 (*ILC Fragmentation Report* (2006)). See also Koskenniemi 2007; Benvenisti 2007; and Peters 2016.

309 See, e.g., Mieville 2005, p. 304 ff.

310 Peters 2016; and Kennedy 2006–07.

311 See Frankenberg 2010 for an encyclopaedia entry on critical theory in IL scholarship.

said to have started with the abolition of slavery in IL,[312] and the start of legalised 'humanitarian' limits on warfare[313] (the latter, interestingly, instigated by imperial businessman Henry Dunant).[314] The trend in critical international legal scholarship follows, and to some extent critically mirrors, the mainstream scholarship discussed in Chapter 1. At first glance this development appears to correct for IL's fragmentation, and to make visible the real-world relationships between various problems IL is called on to address. However, without a historical-materialist understanding of where today's problems come from (and the role of law in their creation), and without a theory of the relationship between the corporation, law and capitalism, such writing remains incomplete at best.

The turn to history and to economy has left significant gaps – for example, the section in the 2012 *Oxford Handbook on the History of International Law* entitled 'Actors' has chapters on Peoples and Nations; States; Peace Treaties (!); Minorities and Majorities; *Hostes humani generis*: Pirates, Slavers and other Criminals; International Arbitration and Courts; International Organisations and Peace Movements – but not corporations – although they are included under 'Themes'.[315] This creates the impression that rather than being a persona co-creating international law, and one to which IL applies, the corporation is merely a passive/natural phenomenon of relevance to IL – like Territory, Religion, War and Peace and The Sea. On the other hand, 'Theorising the Corporation in International Law' was included in the recent *Oxford Handbook on the Theory of International Law*.[316] It has also given rise to some writing about the corporation in the context of the history of early colonialism.[317] These scholars are able to make use of a small surge of publications by historians on the colonial corporation.[318] The main debates in current historical scholarship on the corporation occur around the question of the nature of the corporation as political, economic or hybrid. As such, and as pointed out by Marxist historian Pepijn Brandon, these authors presuppose the possibility of separation between 'politics' and 'economics'. Brandon shows that it is in fact this ideological (illusion of) separation that has historically allowed space for corporate power to grow unchallenged.[319] It is also this same ideological move that con-

312 E.g., Bernaz 2016, especially Ch. 2.
313 E.g., Rodley 2014, p. 785.
314 Moorehead 1999.
315 Fassbender and Peters 2012.
316 Johns 2016.
317 Miéville 2006, pp. 107–8; Stephen 1999; Gathii 2010.
318 Stapelbroek 2012, p. 15; Stern 2011; Taylor 2006.
319 Brandon 2017.

tinues to cause a blind spot for many of today's historians, legal and other scholars when it comes to the corporation.

The final set of writings or rather set of unique pieces are those that do discuss the corporation in IL, in particular, in the context of global governance and global legal pluralism.[320] I will come back to these in the final section of this chapter and in Chapters 4 and 6.

The historical-materialist retelling of the story of the origins of international law, and its relationship to the corporation, centres these blind spots and takes cognisance of the socio-economic conditions in which they arose. Marx said that 'capital comes dripping from head to toe, from every pore, with blood and dirt'.[321] However, while it is clear that the transition to capitalism and capitalism itself was and is a 'bloody business', most historical and especially legal literature has been cleansed of any evidence of this. This is, of course, not necessarily an innocent move. As Miéville has written, 'Law disguises its own brutal core'.[322] As I try to show in this book as a whole, there are many indications of continuity between primitive accumulation in Europe (e.g., Britain's clearances, see Chapter 2A), colonial practices (this chapter), corporate involvement in World War Two (Chapters 3A and 3B) and *current* multinationals' practices in the Third World mentioned throughout this book – and not just in 'bloody' violence but also in economic, structural violence.[323]

Miéville observes that 'it is only through examining the changing nature of exchange and market relations across communities and eventually nation-states that the changing nature of international law can be made sense of'.[324] The (proto-)state was first conceptualised as a unit of economic activity.[325] Moreover, I argue, it is also only through examining the changing nature of market relations and the concomitant development of international law that we can really understand the creation and role of the corporation in the political economy of international law. The first, striking discovery one makes when attempting to describe the origins of capitalism, law/international law, and the corporation is that their emergence occurs (gradually) in the same period, and is closely interlinked. The creation of trading corporations was profoundly implicated in the spread/export (and eventual *universalisation*) of capitalism, the state form, and the content and institutions of international law. The key

320 Danielsen 2006; 2016.

321 Marx 1976, p. 926.

322 Miéville 2006, p. 194. Victims' accounts have rarely been recorded: Renton 2006, pp. 34–6.

323 Harvey proposes the term 'accumulation by dispossession' to emphasise the continuity between 'primitive' accumulation and current practices: Harvey 2003, p. 145.

324 Miéville 2006, p. 156.

325 Craven 2010.

point here about the corporation is that it exists and operates over an extended period of time and needs laws and arrangements that will allow it to make long-term plans and to enforce contracts that were made long ago and sometimes in distant places. In this way, IL becomes a function of the corporation's size and duration. I start by examining the corporate roots of IL and the early development of law around corporate activity in trade wars.

1.2 *Towards International Law*

Neff stresses the fact that natural law writers in the pre-modern age considered the whole of human (and often also non-human) society 'to form a single moral and ethical community', and that 'no body of law existed that was applicable *uniquely* to international relations as such'.[326] Such universalist natural 'law', however, would more appropriately be called philosophical theory, where it existed only inside the heads and treatises of the scholars of the time (i.e., in the realm of ideas) without reflecting actually existing material reality of human relations, or indeed having much impact on them.[327] Seen through the prism of the commodity form theory of law, such law as actually existed is pre- or proto-law at most, except insofar as it inhered between trading polities. It is from the pluralist everyday practice of city-states and other types of polities trading as economic units (e.g., boroughs and guilds: Chapter 2A) that a '*ius inter gentes*'[328] is eventually developed, although generally inhering only for the duration of specific exchanges without becoming systematised (or universalised).[329] Early examples of law developing around inter-polity trade were the bilateral agreements for the protection of merchants, both on land and sea, the latter receiving the benefit of rules such as those in the '*Consolato del Mare*' which sought to govern amongst others the right of neutral traders in wartime.[330]

Such 'law merchant' operated on a pragmatic basis, mostly between European traders and to a more limited extent their Asian and African counterparts, until the 'discovery' of America by Columbus profoundly changed the socio-political space. Faced with a 'new world', the Portuguese and Spanish superpowers of the time divided the known world between them in the Treaty of

326 Neff 2010, pp. 6–7.

327 Although natural lawyers of the time might have argued that the laws were to be discovered in nature or 'reason' – Grotius himself.

328 Grewe 1984, pp. 163 ff.

329 Miéville contradicts himself at p. 167 when he states, 'The simple fact of relations between polities is not enough even to claim the legal form'.

330 Neff 2010, p. 8.

Tordesillas of 1494.[331] In the treaty a line (*raya*) was drawn across the world between Spanish and Portuguese spheres of hegemony. This was not the first such line, but it was the first *global* line. It was essentially 'a feudal line between two princes'[332] in a rapidly altering world. A 'premodern line of division was drawn onto a newly (post-feudal) scientific conception of the world, for the purposes of the exploitative distribution of a global order between two burgeoning mercantilist states'.[333] The question arose (perhaps mainly in the minds of scholars) how to view the new world, which was not part of the *res publica Christiana* but also not classed as 'enemy'. Once the Spanish learnt about the Aztec gold, this question became all the more salient. The Spanish theologian and jurist Francisco de Vitoria answered it by denying the 'Indians' sovereignty (as this right was reserved for Christians), but by 'granting' them 'dominion' over their territory, a *reciprocal* right of ownership.[334] '[T]he mere "discovery" of the Americas does not give the Spanish ownership "any more than if it had been they who had discovered us"'[335] – which was clearly a rhetorical possibility only. Of course having ownership meant having the hypothetical capacity to trade (in this case, specifically, to sell). In *De Indis Noviter Inventis*, de Vitoria concluded that the Spanish conquest of the native kingdoms in the New World had been 'legal' as the 'Indians' had 'unlawfully' attempted to exclude Spanish traders (effectively preventing them from 'buying' Aztec treasures). This is an early example of legal doctrine being developed – through the ideological claim that the principle of free trade was at the time in the *res publica Christiana* considered a natural law as well as a religious right[336] – to serve the commercial desire to acquire the Aztec gold. Moreover, while the Aztecs' 'right of free trade' was emphasised, celebrated and exploited, any other 'rights' the Aztecs may have claimed were conveniently ignored.

Moreover, in addition to gold and other treasures, the main 'commodity' the European explorers accumulated from the 'newly discovered' places were slaves. The Portuguese justified the capture of African slaves on the basis of

331 Miéville 2006, p. 171.

332 Ibid.

333 Miéville 2006, p. 175.

334 De Victoria 1964 no pagination: Summary of Third Section. See, generally, Anghie 2007, pp. 1–31.

335 Miéville 2006, p. 177, quoting De Victoria 1964 no pagination: Third Section.

336 Neff 1990: 'Free trade is the international law of God' (p. 38); see also pp. 15–17. The 'Indians', through the right of dominion, also had to be posited as having some measure of legal personality.

conversion to Christianity, while to the Dutch the trade in slaves was permitted when they were acquired as part of the 'spoils of war' – a concept that came to be very broadly understood.[337]

At this point the *res publica Christiana* was crumbling and the 'Spanish Age' of 1492–1648 was also the period of transition to capitalism. The *raya* was soon replaced by 'lines of amity' which were agreed between the now up and coming French, Dutch and English economic powers.[338] Rather than dividing the world between them, these were lines that demarcated a European sphere (where international law ruled), and a space beyond. Beyond the lines of amity, the European powers considered the world – including its inhabitants – as being up for grabs and, through and with their trading companies, they competed with each other to colonise the remaining world and enslave its people.[339] This is when the previously 'universal' law becomes a *European* international law – with 'no law beyond the line'.[340]

Eventually in 1648, Spain – in the Peace of Münster, which ended the Thirty Years War – recognised the United Netherlands as another economic power and simultaneously recognised Dutch colonial possessions.[341] The lines of amity became irrelevant as European powers came to recognise each other's 'title' to the various parts of the rest of the world, and 'European international law' became universal once again.[342]

1.3 *The Commodity Form Theory in International Law*

As discussed above (Chapter 2A, Section 4), in Europe around 1648, strong, centralised governments began to get the upper hand over the diffuse feudal power structures.[343] Provinces and city states joined, or merged into, 'national' unions. As Miéville has written:

> The legal form – the form whereby the bearers of abstract rights and commodities confront each [*sic*] – has existed in various historical conjunctures, but it was only with the rise of sovereign states that international law can be considered to have been born, and it is with the triumph of

337 Drescher and Finkelman 2012, p. 896.
338 Grewe 1984, p. 184.
339 Miéville 2006, p. 182; Grewe 1984, pp. 181 ff.
340 Miéville 2006, p. 184; Grewe 1984, p. 192. See also, generally, Anghie 2007, Ch. 2.
341 *1648 Peace of Münster* forming part of the series of treaties signed in May and October 1648 together making up the Peace of Westphalia.
342 Grewe 1984, p. 270; Miéville 2006, p. 183.
343 But see Teschke 2009; cf. Neff 2010, p. 11; also Brandon 2011.

> capitalism and its commodification of all social relations that the legal form universalised and became modern international law.[344]

Thus when the bourgeoisie came to dominate the proletariat in the West and 'organised itself into separate state-political trusts' we can properly speak of international law.[345] When the bourgeoisie completed the process of separation of state from private rule, the state gained subjectivity in international law,[346] or 'international legal personality' ('ILP'). That the new international law was something qualitatively different from feudal law is exemplified by the fact that states denied the binding nature of pre-existing dynastic treaties (including the fact that the lines of amity had been feudal agreements between princes).[347] As indicated above, bourgeois international law operates on two levels. On the one hand, where (mainly) European nations compete over, and divide amongst themselves, the rest of the world, the previously intra-class international law (Vitoria) replaced feudal struggles and 'primitive accumulation' with inter-class diplomatic, contractual exchange[348] (post-1648 international law). In sum, inter*national* law comes about when polities converge into (or are submerged in) states, and states obtain legal personality by virtue of relating to each other as formally equal legal persons. 'It is during this period that the categories concomitant to that trade – the legal forms – begin to universalise ... As trade became global, and definitional to sovereign states, the international order could not but become an international *legal* order'.[349]

Both movements were mutually reinforcing:

> There can be no doubt ... that the great revolutions that took place in trade in the sixteenth and seventeenth centuries, along with the geographical discoveries of that epoch, and which rapidly advanced the development of commercial capital, were a major moment in promoting the transition from the feudal to the capitalist mode of production. The sudden expansion of the world market, the multiplication of commodities in circulation, the competition among European nations for the seizure of

344 Miéville 2006, p. 161 (emphasis in original).
345 Pashukanis 2006, pp. 322–5.
346 Pashukanis 2006, p. 327.
347 Ibid.
348 Pashukanis 2006, p. 325.
349 Miéville 2006, p. 200.

> Asiatic products and American treasures, the colonial system all made a fundamental contribution towards shattering the feudal barriers to production.[350]

Pashukanis posits that '[t]he real historical content of international law is the struggles between polities/states for resources'.[351] Miéville emphasises how it is the formal legal equality masking the material inequality between the Europeans and the non-Europeans that 'gave [law] in service to the strong – the coloniser'.[352]

Miéville locates colonialism in the *content* and also in the *form* of international law:

> The colonial encounter is central to the development of international law. But this centrality is not reducible to the colonialism of content, the fact that certain legal categories were invested with Western bias, though the fleshing out of such historical specificities is important. Colonialism is in the very form, the structure of international law itself, predicated on global trade between inherently unequal polities, with unequal coercive violence implied in the very commodity form. This unequal coercion is what forces particular content into the legal form.[353]

Law disguises this as noted above: 'law disguises its own brutal core'.[354] Succinctly put, 'international law *is* colonialism'.[355] In this book, I argue that as well as the historically specific 'colonialism', exploitation, domination and imperialism are the very form, the very structure, of international and indeed *all* law.

As signalled above (Chapter 1, Section 3.2), I consider that Miéville could (or perhaps *should*) have taken his Marxist theory one step further (away from liberalism). Where Pashukanis remarks that 'international law owes its existence to the fact that the bourgeoisie exercises its domination over the proletariat and over the colonial countries',[356] one can read into this a perception of a global class structure. This, of course, follows with Marxist theory's (or communism's) inherently internationalist (or, properly, *global*) outlook. States, like

350 Marx 1981, p. 447, cited by Miéville 2006, p. 199.
351 Pashukanis 2006; Miéville 2006, pp. 325ff.; and Miéville 2004, p. 292.
352 Miéville 2006, p. 177.
353 Miéville 2006, p. 178 (emphasis in original).
354 Miéville 2006, p. 194.
355 Miéville 2006, p. 169.
356 Pashukanis 2006, p. 325.

corporations, as I showed in Chapter 2A, are fetishised (or reified) legal abstractions created for particular purposes and which nonetheless (and maybe partly consequently) come to have some 'real-world' actuality. They are in their own peculiar way part of the 'material base'. Miéville's statist framing of IL, however, is a lapse into liberalism. For the purposes of a Marxist theoretical critique we need to both understand the workings and effect of the reification of the state and the fragmentation and bracketing of IL as a seemingly separate field of law, and simultaneously demystify the state, IL, and the corporation.

Miéville continues his explication of the commodity form theory of international law by describing how the guarantee as between formally 'equal states' in the absence of a superior authority rests in the balance of forces.[357] 'The historically progressive generalisation of "equal rights" is the generalisation of the abstract legal subject'.[358] Eventually, as Miéville surmises by quoting Marx, 'between equal rights, force decides'.[359] In his discussion on the essence of class struggle, which is to be found in the struggle over the working day, Marx continues after this short phrase: 'Hence is it that in the history of capitalist production, the determination of what is a working-day, presents itself as the result of a struggle, a struggle between collective capital, i.e., the class of capitalists, and collective labour, i.e., the working-class'.[360] From this fragment we can deduce that the 'force' Marx means is not necessarily physical violence (war), as Miéville seems to say, but rather the 'force' of domination and exploitation through ownership of the means of production, the ultimate *unfreedom* of labour. The capitalist class still has at its disposal the feudal 'power' to coerce, but it is the achievement of capitalism that this is no longer (or rarely) necessary. The capitalist class coerces by virtue of its ownership of the means of production, while the modern capitalist *Rechtsstaat* coerces *through law* backed up by the legitimate threat, or use, of physical and economic force.

Ultimately, therefore, the real regulating factor in the world is the *economic imperialism* of the global capitalist class, first and foremost.[361] Law, law's institutions and law's bureaucracy have, to some extent, been developed (mostly by lawyers) to have their own internal logic (coherence, rhetoric),[362] but this logic follows the logic of economic imperialism and is based on the *commodity form*. As I argue below, modern-day economic imperialism (as illustrated in

357 Pashukanis 2006, p. 331.
358 Miéville 2006, p. 88.
359 Miéville 2006, p. 292.
360 Marx 1976, *Capital*, Vol. 1, Ch. 10.
361 But see Marks 2007, esp. p. 211.
362 See, generally, Kennedy 1987.

Chapter 1 and discussed further in Chapter 6) is administered first and foremost through the construct of the corporation or corporate participation in global governance, through its international 'management committees', the Bretton Woods institutions, arbitral tribunals, and legal tools such as bilateral investment treaties, conditional loan agreement, etc., by (or at the behest of) the capital-owning classes.[363]

2 Corporations, Law and Capitalism

Having set out the historical-doctrinal development of international law above, I argue that the creation of trading corporations is profoundly implicated in the spread/export (and eventual *universalisation*) of capitalism, the state form and the content and institutions of international law. A number of situations, events and phenomena show the effects of this continuing development. These can roughly be divided into three closely interlinked categories: (1) the origin of the concept of international law, states and corporations around the same time (2.1); (2) the close relationship between state and corporation exemplified in their concurrent development in history (2.2 and 2.3); and (3) the use of corporations in the slave trade, colonisation, accumulation and the spread of capitalism exemplified in the corporate scramble for Africa (2.4–6). First, I examine the corporate roots of IL and the early development of law around corporate activity including in trade wars.

2.1 *Grotius: 'Father of International Law' and Corporate Counsel to the Dutch East India Company*

Hugo de Groot (Grotius), who was later named the 'father of international law', in his younger years made his mark as the legal advisor to the Dutch East India Company (Vereenigde Oostindische Compagnie or 'VOC' in Dutch)[364] – the Dutch predecessor and equivalent of the British East India Company in all essential aspects. Through a historically contextualised analysis of Grotius's work, we can gain some insight into the role of corporations and trade wars in the early development of international law during the period of mercantilism.

In 1603, one of the VOC's captains, Jan van Heemskerk, had captured a loaded Portuguese merchant ship, the *Santa Catarina*. Some of the VOC's shareholders objected to the capture on religious/moral grounds. Grotius was commissioned

363 On this, see also, e.g., Rasulov 2008; Rasulov 2010.

364 Corporate counsel in the sense that he was employed to write a legal brief, not 'in permanent employ': Wilson 2008, p. 7. See further Stapelbroek 2012; Van Ittersum 2006.

to write a defence of the seizure, which he did in *De Iure Praedae* (On the law of prize). In Grotius's professional view, the capture was justified on the basis of law, honour and expedience.[365]

De Iure Praedae also contained *Mare Liberum* – which introduced the idea that the seas are 'global commons', free for all states to navigate with a view to exploration and plying trade.[366] The text provided a justification for breaking up various (foreign) trade monopolies, motivated by the fact that Grotius viewed the facilitation of global free trade to be the overarching purpose of IL. Rules had to be made and agreed upon, however, between the major seafaring nations about how to tackle piracy (which was a major obstacle to free trade), who was allowed to pass through and travel where, etc., and, of course, what the repercussions were for non-compliance with these rules. Indeed, the first Dutch-Anglo war was fought over the disagreement between Grotius's idea of *Mare Liberum* versus the English idea of closed seas as described by Selden in *Mare Clausum*. This idea was implemented through the English Navigation Acts, a series of laws aimed at protecting English trading monopolies through stipulations that goods could only enter English harbours on board English ships.[367] The fear among the British elite was that *Mare Liberum* would lead to Dutch control of the open seas, and that closing markets or erecting significant barriers would protect the British economy. In the words of Walter Raleigh, 'Whoever rules the waves rules commerce; whoever rules commerce rules the wealth of the world, and consequently the world itself'.[368] Eventually, a compromise was agreed, and a three-mile zone (the reach of protection by cannon fire, important for local security, but also for coastal fishing)[369] was to be considered 'territorial waters' with the remainder open seas free for trade. The British and Dutch merchants themselves were naturally not particularly interested in the big 'philosophical' questions of *mare liberum* or *mare clausum* per se, but rather in how these ideas could be operationalised to ensure the effective policing of their commercial interests on the high seas.[370]

---

365 Wilson 2008, p. 7. To satisfy any possible type of doubt entertained by his countrymen, Grotius treated the question from the point of view of whether the capture was legally justified (Chs. II–XIII), honourable (Ch. XIV) and expedient (Ch. XV). The publication of Grotius's text was apparently pre-empted by a Dutch court order in favour of retaining the prize (Fruin 1925, p. 26); Grotius 2005. *De Iure Praedae* contained an early version of Grotius's influential work *De Iure Bellis ac Paci*.

366 Grotius 2004, Ch. 8 (not paginated).

367 Grewe 1984, p. 318; Mieville 2005, pp. 204–6.

368 Ferro 1997, p. 47.

369 Craven 2012, p. 862.

370 Grewe 1984, p. 345.

Grotius considers states, as well as other 'human associations' such as the Dutch East India Company, to have rights and obligations comparable to private individuals.[371] Grotius's conception of the legal realm therefore seems to be one without divisions between the domestic and the 'international', but rather one in which one legal space is organised according to the logic of commerce. The contemporary theorist Benedict Kingsbury shows an awareness of this: 'Grotius had developed his doctrine of the state of nature and the natural right to punish against the backdrop of the need to show that the Dutch East India Company, even if acting on its own behalf as a private actor, had the right to wage war against the Portuguese fleet in Southeast Asia'.[372] But Kingsbury fails to add that Grotius created his broader jurisprudential theory on the basis of (t)his particular class's commercial interest.

Grotius's theory gained broad acceptance among legal scholars over the years, detached from its context, to become a standalone legal-philosophical representation.[373] This theory, and Grotius's larger role as the 'father of IL', is *now* primarily seen as 'about war and peace', which obscures the commercial imperative behind his work.[374] Perhaps this should be regarded as a teleological reading of history, viewed from the current perspective, or fitting in the current dominant discourse where international law is 'about' and 'for' peace, common values of justice, human rights etc. (cosmopolitanism, constitutionalism; see below, Section 5).[375] Yet when retelling the story in this way, we can see how international law was significantly shaped to suit the interest of one particularly important corporation, the VOC, in relation to the idea of a just war and free trade, and that the international rules still in existence today regarding territorial waters originated as a compromise reached on the basis of the respective economic power of British and Dutch trading empires.

Indeed, according to Wilson, '[t]he defence of the VOC came to serve as a template for a wider re-conceptualisation of the trans-national space within which the Company operated'.[376] Further, in 1601 Grotius was appointed the 'national Historiographer of Holland', which meant both that he was a 'self-conscious producer of republican and patriotic texts' and that he worked in

---

371 Grotius 1925, p. 105.

372 Kingsbury and Straumann 2010, p. 41.

373 Wilson 2009, pp. 51, 128.

374 The commercial logic of international law is also evident in Pufendorf, who described how *cultura*, the state of life produced by human industry, and commerce, which emerge to overcome humans' natural state of *imbecilitas* and *indigentia*, correspond with the formation and flourishing of society; cf. Kingsbury and Straumann 2010, p. 33.

375 Also Koskenniemi 2010.

376 Wilson 2008, p. xii.

close proximity to ('in the immediate political orbit of') tl general' (landsadvocaat) Johan van Oldebarnevelt.[377] As suc to exercise great influence not only on the development of but also on what became domestic law: 'the Text [*sic*] "trar tional requirements of the World-Economy into the terms oi prudence'.[378] Thus we see how one individual, representativ particular company's interest, came to leave a particular mark on current international and domestic law.

With the perspective Grotius's story brings to mind, it is possible to re-cast our understanding of the state and corporate form. Miéville argues that for law to 'work' and a legal system to come into existence (and for capitalism to mature), the creation of a state is not necessary. The same can be said of the corporation. However, as shown in 2A, both are conducive to capitalism and both operate along its logic. As I discussed in Chapter 2A, as the explorers wanted to undertake more ambitious expeditions, they sought to raise finance among a wider group of persons. It made sense to do so in a wider, but more or less homogenous and increasingly centrally regulated market/locality, where the traders could also find customers for the goods, and where they would be willing to risk large sums of money. As many directors of the trading companies were also active in the local and provincial administration (e.g., in the Dutch Republic),[379] the centralisation of administration and regulation came about as a matter of rationality. Perhaps then it is possible to draw a parallel here with the European (proto-)state form and the large trading companies on the domestic level from the point of view of the elites, who developed both the state and corporate form as conducive to the development and spread of capitalism.[380] While the physical shape of modern European states is a remnant of feudalism / pre-capitalist absolutism[381] (in the sense that the national boundaries were drawn around the feudal estates of lords and larger provinces of lords sworn to the same king), conversely the eventual *form* of the state is a construct of capitalism / the capitalist class. In the domestic and in the global sphere, there seems to be in the first instance great convergence between (proto-)state and corporate interests with corporations forming an extension of such states, rather than (proto-)states forming a 'bureaucracy' for the facilitation of the eco-

377 Wilson 2008, p. 14.
378 Ibid.
379 Brandon 2011, p. 127.
380 Miéville 2006, p. 201; Marx 1981, p. 451.
381 England and The Dutch Republic were anomalies in Europe and had representative governments; see, e.g., Merriman 2010, p. 208.

omy.[382] In due course (as the ideological forms 'congeal'), the state and the corporation each gain their sphere of activity and authority (private/public) internally and on the global level.[383] In Chapter 6, I discuss the current status of these, now once again converging, spheres.

2.2 *Concurrent Development: Corporations, States and Colonialism*

In this section I take a closer look at the interrelation between (proto-)states and corporations as putative 'subjects' of the new field of international law, and the role of particular legal concepts such as sovereignty in the practice of colonialism by the elites heading such polities, (proto-)states and corporations. Miéville posits, 'Sovereignty is the legitimising principle by which that subject in modern international law – the state – faces others'[384] – and indeed faces others as sovereign, *legal* equals. However, during the period of exploration and later colonisation, it was not 'states facing each other as sovereigns' in the space 'beyond the line', it was the captains and merchants of trading corporations that both interacted with each other and with non-European polities. This meant that European elites, making up the pre-modern states, were able to deal indirectly with the non-European polities without being forced to recognise them as states. Grewe suggests that corporations were used in the colonisation process to prevent the nascent state form from spreading beyond Europe:

> The most important [effect on the development of international law] was the dual position taken by the trading companies: semi-public, semi-private, which enabled the avoidance of a complete transfer of the European state-form, with its extensive legal consequences and its characteristics of sovereignty – nation, territory, borders – to the overseas colonial space.[385]

He continues, 'It was through the fact that it was the corporations and not the states themselves, that encountered each other, and that were considered (or at least held out to be) more or less independent, that a *particularly elastic system of colonial international law* was constructed'.[386] Apparently, '[p]oliticians were

---

382 Weber 1982, p. 338 ff.

383 Craven 2010, p. 211, describes the consequences of the personification of the state and the concomitant (ideological) separation between the internal sphere and the external relations.

384 Miéville 2006, p. 184.

385 Grewe 1984, p. 346.

386 Grewe 1984, p. 346, emphasis added.

well aware that the legal status of their colonial possessions was problemat The East India Companies were the perfect agents to police this "transitional colonialism, because of their indistinct legal status'.[387] The East India companies could do things that if done by the 'politicians' would be considered acts of war. This use of the corporation required the corporation to be viewed as something quite distinct from the pre-modern state, yet equally formed as an extension or instrument of this body. In this way, the large trading corporations were the main tools in the colonisation process (not least for England and the Netherlands), and they represented the legal and organisational form through which the colonial powers annexed their conquered territories to the motherland. Likewise, the settlement of North America took place through the use of chartered companies. Settlement companies such as the Virginia Company – whose aim it was, through private individual appropriation and settlement of land and (commonly) the cultivation of coffee, tea, sugar and tobacco plantations (utilising slave labour), to increase states' productive land – would assert the sovereignty needed to grant land rights to settlers even before such authority over the territory could be said to have arisen. This curious inversion[388] is another example of law's pragmatic 'invention' in the service of capitalism. The legal-economic form of the corporation allowed the assertion of political power, not simply vice versa. As a very 'direct' example of this, through the Plymouth Company, the Puritans of the *Mayflower* hoped to gain the political freedom and independence in New England that they had been denied in Europe.[389]

In certain situations, corporations thus mirrored or wore the mask of (an as yet not clearly defined or circumscribed) 'state sovereignty', which sometimes extended well beyond the power to grant land rights. Wilson uses the term 'Corporate Sovereignty' to describe the nature of the VOC's operations in the seventeenth century.[390] The main French, English and Dutch colonial companies were endowed with delegated sovereign rights by way of their charters. Among these was, for example, the grant by Charles II to the British East India Company in 1661 with the express right to send war ships, personnel, and armoury for the defence of the Company's factories and trading posts and to decide over war and peace with all non-Christian peoples. In 1677 the right to coinage was added. Dutch and French companies similarly delegated sovereign powers, such as the right to wage wars of trade and territory with other European entit-

387 Miéville 2006, p. 184.
388 Craven 2012, pp. 77–8.
389 Grewe 1984, pp. 348–9.
390 Wilson 2008 (Wilson's capitals).

ies. At the same time, ideological separateness allowed such wars to take place 'beyond the line' and thus not to affect the internal European peace.[391] The second Anglo-Dutch war mentioned above had started in 1664 with attacks by the Royal African Company on the Dutch trading posts in Guinea but did not become a 'European' war until the following year.[392] Conversely, when European powers were engaged in war 'at home', this did not necessarily affect their trading relationships overseas, nor did it mean their posts and territory outside Europe would be attacked.[393]

There are direct parallels to be drawn here between other, contemporary instances of protection of trade in times of conflict (about which more below, Chapter 5).[394] 'Business' and 'politics' are each assigned a separate conceptual realm despite their obvious entanglement.

> The close relation between a state-authorised monopoly and the state itself … meant that the boundaries between the company and the state were permeable, and the monopoly trade could be used to underpin political (state) control. *The monopoly nature of these companies was the means by which their parent state retained control over its colonial possessions in an era of increasingly bounded sovereignty.*[395]

The strength of the nascent capitalist 'military-industrial complex' lies in the capitalist class's ability to split and reunite at will, its interests appearing sometimes political (or public) and at other times commercial (or private). It is *law* that enables this conjecture.[396] Whether acting as 'corporation' or 'state' (I use these terms loosely here), the logic of capital was paramount, which was also clear when the British East India Company reduced its workforce to slave-like conditions such that when the Great Bengal Famine arrived in 1769, over half of the 30 million strong population died.[397]

The interests of the European traders, settlers and investors (which included, of course, European statesmen) were protected further by the way they man-

391 Grewe 1984, p. 352.

392 Grewe 1984, p. 318.

393 Grewe 1984, p. 353.

394 'The victory of the bourgeoisie, in all the European countries, had to lead to the establishment of new rules and new institutions of international law which protected the general and basic interests of the bourgeoisie, i.e., bourgeois property. Here is the key to the modern law of war' (Pashukanis 2006, p. 325).

395 Miéville 2006, p. 207 (emphasis in original).

396 See also Pashukanis 2006, p. 327.

397 Robin 2012.

aged to uphold the idea that their national laws travelled with them wherever they went overseas. They managed generally to enforce the application of 'imperial law' in the colonies and extraterritorial application of imperial law in the trading enclaves (e.g., in China, Japan), with disputes being referred to the imperial courts.[398] The implication of this was that local rulers could not expropriate traders' property or pass laws that negatively affected the foreign merchants' operations.[399] As I will show below (s.3) this state of affairs is in some ways effectively still current.

While power was the final arbiter in disputes between the European traders and their counterparts and 'gunboat diplomacy' was still the method of choice to enforce compliance,[400] it was felt towards the end of the nineteenth century that legal doctrine needed to be constructed to justify the use of force.[401] This signals the growing 'maturity' of the 'international rule of law' and of global capitalism, where coercion predominantly occurs through means other than *direct* use of physical violence: means including law.

2.3 *The Nineteenth-Century Trading Corporations Preparing the Ground for States in the Western Image*

While the company and crown/state interests had coincided effectively as class interest in the mercantilist period, the increasing ideological public/private and political/economic division also brought about real competition between merchants and statesmen. The old colonial companies' monopolies were slowly reconciled to the idea of free trade. The old trading companies of the first colonisation period (sixteenth–eighteenth centuries) continued to exist into the nineteenth century but their independence, power and significance had long dissipated. The British Crown, for instance, took over direct control of India from the British East India Co. by means of the 1773 Regulating Act.[402] Anghie surmises, 'The direct involvement of European states in the whole process of governing resulted in a shift from the vulgar language of profit to that of order, proper governance and humanitarianism'.[403] The language of profit is shifted over to 'private' IL while 'public' IL becomes the human face of capitalist IL. Koskenniemi describes the transfer of control over India differently and argues it occurred in order to lessen the burden on the taxpayer. For the British,

398 Sornarajah 2010, pp. 19–20, fn. 56. See also Koskenniemi 2016.
399 Subedi 2008, p. 7.
400 Hopkins 1980, p. 779, for an example in the context of Britain's annexation of Lagos.
401 Sornarajah 2010, p. 20.
402 *The Regulating Act for India 1773*, 13 Geo. 3 c. 63 (*Regulating Act*).
403 Anghie 2007, p. 69.

'[d]uring 1815–1870 the slogan "trade, not rule" formed the core of British overseas policy'.[404] '[M]onopoly companies had outlived their usefulness as agents of colonialism', explains Miéville. 'India was simply too profitable to be left in the control of a company which was structured to treat it as a treasure-chest. By taking it over *politically* the British state helped institutionalise the separation of politics and economics associated with mature capitalism'.[405] The outcome, however, was that though '[o]stensibly aimed at checking the oppression of the Company's rule the real effect of the Act was to systematise the exploitation of India'.[406]

When European states in the nineteenth century *did* want to create new (although dependent) states to govern the colonised areas or settle new ones, they used a mostly *new* set of corporations to ensure those states took exactly the shape that they wanted (and presumably had exactly the leaders they wanted).[407] According to Koskenniemi: '[t]he end of informal empire meant that European public institutions – in particular, European sovereignty – needed to be projected into colonial territory'.[408] Britain intensified what Koskenniemi calls 'informal' influence through the proliferation of a new type of chartered company: 'By the time the scramble [for Africa] was over, more than 75 percent of British acquisitions south of the Sahara were acquired by chartered companies'.[409] Many of these companies sought alliances with local leaders, but often proved to be ineffective at administering territory. When these territories needed to be recognised as sovereign in their own right, however, the form (including institutional form and law) and content of that sovereignty had already been constructed.

404 Koskenniemi 2001, p. 112.

405 Miéville 2006, p. 234.

406 Ibid. Another effect of the *Regulating Act* – which exempted the financially ailing East India Company's tea from import duties – was rather momentous too. When this favourable treatment was discovered by rival American traders, Company tea was thrown into the Boston Harbour. The 'Boston Tea Party' became one of the major acts of revolt leading to the American Revolution.

407 Grewe 1984, p. 546; Anghie 2007, pp. 77–8. In South America, rather than corporations, the political act of recognition was employed. At the same time as Latin American colonies were gaining independence from Spain, the US issued the Monroe Doctrine, which stated its proprietary claim on Latin American countries while *at the same time* recognising them as sovereign states: Miéville 2005.

408 Koskenniemi 2001, p. 121.

409 Koskenniemi 2001, p. 117.

2.4 *The Corporate Scramble for Africa*

The corporate scramble for Africa had as its main aim the creation of markets, and the establishment of those institutional conditions necessary for these markets to function and be integrated into global capitalism. This logic included a reinterpretation of slavery to not only function as the precursor to the creation of 'free' labour but also to constitute a generative condition for the market economy.[410] Slaves were eventually to morph into workers and consumers. The scramble marked the start of a new phase of instrumentalisation of the corporate form in colonialism – the third category of mutual implication of international law, global capitalism and the corporation identified above. This instrumentalisation occurred behind an *outwardly* clearer separation (and 'deniability') between the state sphere and a vast network of private companies given wide rein to run the colonies. For example, in 1881 the British North Borneo Company was founded, in 1886 the Royal Niger Company, in 1888 the Imperial British East Africa Company, and in 1889 the British South Africa Company.[411] The latter was run by Cecil Rhodes, under a charter giving him practically a free hand to administer the area (his 'irresponsible policy' is said to have 'almost inevitably' led to the Boer War).[412]

Similarly, what was to become German South West Africa was acquired in 1882 by a tobacco merchant from Bremen, with the Zanzibar region being administered by the German East Africa Company and the Imperial British East Africa Company.[413] Vast tracts of land were granted by the German government to the Deutsche Kolonialgesellschaft, which proceeded with a policy of settler colonialism, granting many German farmers and entrepreneurs generous concessions.[414] German companies active on the ground included a railway company, the company running the ports, Deutsche Bank and various mining companies. New German settlers began to question whether the colony might not be better off without the 'black problem', or, the presence of an indigenous people, the Herero. One colonial leader is quoted as saying,

> I do not concur with those … who want to see the Herero destroyed altogether. Apart from the fact that a people of 60,000 or 70,000 is not so easy

410 Craven 2012 p. 884.

411 Grewe 1984, p. 548.

412 Grewe 1984, p. 120.

413 Grewe 1984, pp. 118–20.

414 *Hereros v. Deutsche Afrika-Linien Gmblt & Co*, 6 F3d 1684 (3rd Cir. 2001) (*2001 Hereros Complaint*). The Herero genocide became the subject of (unsuccessful) compensation litigation in the US in 2001.

> to annihilate, I would consider such a move a grave mistake from an economic point of view. We need the Herero as cattle breeders … and especially as labourers. It will be quite sufficient if they are politically dead.[415]

This plea was apparently rejected by the companies and Imperial Germany,[416] which sent in General von Trotha, who had just suppressed the Arab rebellion in German East Africa, and who responded, 'I shall annihilate the African tribes with streams of blood and streams of gold'.[417] After the brutal crushing of the Herero uprising by the German army, German military rule returned. The around 15,000 surviving Herero were placed in concentration camps maintained by (amongst others) the Woermann shipping company, where they were subjected to slave labour, rape and medical experimentation.[418] Almost half those put to work building railways died. This example highlights the 'deniability' factor of arms-length outsourcing of the colonial enterprise.[419]

In 1881 Portugal founded the Mozambique Company. In 1900, French Equatorial Africa was divided up between 40 French concession companies.[420] These new companies were a 'different beast' altogether from the old trading companies, as they did not have the right to wage war, nor a trading monopoly, and were placed under strict state control.[421] Ahead of the Berlin Conference in 1884, German Chancellor Bismarck (who had inaugurated Germany's colonial policy, actively promoting German colonial enterprise so as to find new markets for developing German industry[422]) expressed the demarcations of this manner of 'corporate sovereignty' as follows:

---

415 2001 *Hereros Complaint* para. 92.

416 The Hereros Complaint denotes the Deutsche Bank, the Terex Corporation then Orenstein-Koppel, which built railways and ran mines, and the Woermann Line shipping and ports company together as the 'German Colonial Enterprise'.

417 2001 *Hereros Complaint* para. 95.

418 2001 *Hereros Complaint* 114–24. The German geneticist Eugen Fischer experimented on 'mulatto' offspring of German settler men and Herero women to explore his ideas about 'racial hygiene', which he was later to teach, as Chancellor of the University of Berlin, to Josef Mengele.

419 In fact, German responsibility for the Herero Genocide was acknowledged only in 2004. Cf. Speech by Federal Minister Heidemarie Wieczorek-Zeul, 'The suppression of the Herero uprising' speech at the commemorations of the 100th anniversary of the suppression of the Herero uprising, embassy of the Federal Republic of Germany Windhoek website, 14 August 2004; see also Norimitsu Onishi, 'Germany Grapples with Its African Genocide', *New York Times*, 29 December 2016.

420 Renton 2006, p. 29. This area corresponds with what is today Chad, Gabon, Central African Republic and the Republic of the Congo.

421 Grewe 1984, p. 548.

422 Dawson 1973, pp. 146–7.

> My intention, as approved by the Emperor, is to leave the responsibility for the material development of a colony as well as its inauguration to the action and enterprise of our seafaring and trading citizens, and to proceed less on the system of annexing the transoceanic provinces to the German Empire than that of granting charters, after the form of the English Royal Charters, encouraged by the glorious career which the English merchants experienced in the foundation of the East India Company; also to leave to the persons interested in the colony the government of the same, only granting them European jurisdiction for Europeans and so much protection as we may be able to afford without maintaining garrisons. I think, too, that a colony of this kind should possess a representative of the Imperial Authority with the title of Consul or Resident, whose duty it would be to receive complaints, while the disputes which might arise out of these commercial enterprises would be decided by one of our Maritime or Mercantile Courts at Bremen, Hamburg, or somewhere else. It is not our intention to found provinces but commercial undertakings.[423]

Another reason to use companies in the colonial process is that when an undertaking proves to be unprofitable, it can simply be dissolved or sold at a loss. If a territory becomes a province, the state has to support it, to some extent, even during unprofitable times. Bismarck in the quote above describes a manner of 'outsourcing' *avant la lettre* of the colonial enterprise. The new arrangement seemed designed to reap all possible benefits, while any commercial risk the company took remained with the company.[424] This flexible approach allowed the state to use the company when it suited state interests, and to distance itself when it did not. The late-nineteenth-century trading company concept influenced European and colonial forms of governance and was in turn influenced by non-private dynamics. '[T]he colonial territory was now fundamentally divided up, organised and governed according to the principles and concepts of the inter-state law that was developed in Europe'.[425] At the same time, one of the main means of spreading capitalism and creating states in the image of the modern European state was the replacement of local laws with the laws and legal concepts of the colonial state and institutions under the tutelage of the imperial institutions. For example, Hopkins describes how notions of *collective* ownership of property prevalent in the colonies were replaced by European notions of private property, because 'to establish a virtuous circle of develop-

423 Dawson 1973, pp. 150–1.
424 Grewe 1984, p. 550.
425 Grewe 1984, p. 552.

ment it was necessary to export commercial institutions and approved property rights'.[426] Conversely, Craven describes the 1918 decision of the Privy Council, *In re Southern Rhodesia*, where it was held that the British South Africa Company had the right to alienate certain land in Southern Rhodesia – the 'absence of indigenous knowledge of the institution of private property ... effectively allowed the extinguishment of all native title through the fact of settlement'.[427]

Another way for a company to gain entry to a 'colony' was to buy up or refinance a government's sovereign debt. This is how the Firestone company gained a 99-year lease over one million acres of Liberian land, which it transformed into a rubber plantation, removing villagers from their land and recruiting them as workers at gunpoint.[428] By 1929, some 350,000 Liberians were reportedly forced into employment by Firestone in circumstances comparable to those in Leopold's Congo. Liberia was not a colony in the technical sense, but since its founding by the American Colonization Society in 1847, it was indebted to the company as its sole creditor.[429] This could be presented as a good thing: the former Liberian president noting that since Firestone had taken control of Liberia, border disputes promptly ceased.[430] Colonial-styled corporations were not simply expressions of foreign imposition; their formats allowed them to be instrumentalised by *host* state elites under the rationalities of order and self-determination.

2.5 *The Congo Corporation and the State Form*

The story of the Congo shows in one example how companies became vehicles for the transfer of the European state form. In 1876 the *Association Internationale Africaine* (AIA) was founded at the behest of the Belgian King Leopold II, apparently motivated for the sake of private gain and political intrigue.[431] In 1878 the International Congo Society was founded (also chaired by King Leopold), which formed the profit-seeking front for the more 'philanthropic' AIA. The 1884 Berlin West Africa Conference recognised the society as sovereign over what became known as the Congo Free State and as a member of the international community by the major powers present at Berlin.[432] Renton, Seddon and Zeilig describe the rule of Leopold in The Congo within the broader

426 Hopkins 1980, pp. 777–98.

427 Cf. Craven 2010, p. 50; *In re Southern Rhodesia* [1919] A.C. 211.

428 *John Roe I et al. v. Bridgestone Corporation et al.* (*2005 Firestone Complaint*) 7 November 2005.

429 Ibid, p. 38.

430 Ibid.

431 Grewe 1984, p. 551.

432 Renton, Seddon and Zeilig 2006, p. 24.

context of turn-of-the-nineteenth-century colonial Africa. King Leopold's company took control of the rubber and ivory trades, while giving much of the land of the Congo to concessionary businesses that would build infrastructure and control the territory. These companies were granted the right to levy taxes, which meant the previously self-sufficient non-monetary economy had to develop to produce surplus and the population had to offer itself up as wage labour. New companies were also founded to exploit the mineral wealth, the Union Minière du Haut Katanga (1905) amongst many others, mostly owned directly or indirectly by King Leopold. A large bureaucracy was set up and run by around 1,500 European civil servants. One of the Congo's richest resources proved to be rubber, called 'red rubber' after the brutal regime in which it was harvested. King Leopold's corporate rule created a 'slave society', and more generally, '[u]nder direct European or American rule, forced labour became widespread throughout the continent, and an "economy of pillage" became the norm'.[433] In Marx's words, capitalism came 'dripping with blood' as the creation through subjugation of a rapidly increasing workforce was symbolically 'accounted for' by its members, when the imperial soldiers (and village elders) had to evidence with body parts that a shortfall in the (unrealistic) rubber collection target was punished by death:

> The baskets of severed hands, set down at the feet of the European post commanders, became the symbol of the Congo Free State … The collection of hands became an end in itself. *Force Publique* soldiers brought them to the stations in place of rubber; they even went out to harvest them instead of rubber … They became a sort of currency. They came to be used to make up for shortfalls in rubber quotas, to replace … the people who were demanded for the forced labour gangs; and the *Force Publique* soldiers were paid their bonuses on the basis of how many hands they collected.[434]

Dismissing the idea that Leopold's rule was a return to feudalism, arguing that the process was more complex than Lenin's analysis that colonialism is simply another expression, in a grander form, of the general tendency between businesses that was typical of the capitalist systems, Renton and colleagues consider that 'the most striking feature of Leopold's rule was its similarity to an older form of accumulation, simple theft'.[435] We can see here the direct cor-

433 Renton, Seddon and Zeilig 2006, p. 29.
434 Forbath, p. 1977, p. 374, quoted in Renton at al. 2006, p. 32.
435 Renton, Seddon and Zeilig 2006, p. 29.

respondence between the process of the forcible creation of a wage-labour force and the expropriation of land (and other natural resources) in the Congo (and indeed the rest of the African continent) and 'primitive accumulation' in Britain (see Chapter 2A above). Moreover, direct correspondence can be seen between the Congolese (and Rhodesian and Liberian) examples and the corporate imperialism of the twentieth century – what David Harvey describes as 'accumulation by dispossession'. Renton and Zeilig point out that the Congolese population declined sharply (from around 20 million in 1891 to 8.5 million in 1911) as a result of disease, massacre and forced labour. The main 'winners', as they see it, were King Leopold, the shareholders of his companies, and the various banks involved in financing the enterprise.[436]

King Leopold was able to successfully hold on to his possession partly because he 'presented himself as the inheritor of the liberal ideal'. However, '[b]eneath the high-flowing rhetoric, financial calculations were evidently being made'.[437] The end of the corporate Congo was brought about by three factors: first, resistance and rebellions in the Congo itself;[438] second, a reform movement in Europe and the US; and third, commercial interests by rivals – all in addition to the classic European rivalries with the ultimately unsuccessful British government effort to end Leopold's regime on the basis that the Congo was a 'British discovery'.[439] In contrast, the reform effort proved a more effective check on Leopold. Missionary reports of the extraordinary cruelty of Leopold's regime helped spark a popular campaign to urge Belgium to take the Congo into government control or to allow it to be independent (or even to transfer it to British rule). The campaign included Booker T. Washington, Mark Twain, Arthur Conan Doyle and Joseph Conrad as well as others. In addition, world powers began to realise the significant mineral wealth in the Congo. This included the US, which would later use Congolese uranium to bomb Hiroshima and Nagasaki.[440] In 1908 Belgium 'nationalised' the King's private corporate empire, and in 1913 opened it up to 'free trade'. The British-Belgian company Union Minière stayed, recruiting (often at gunpoint) workers for its copper mines from the whole surrounding region (what is now Rwanda, Zambia, and Uganda).[441] The Congo example shows deniability of the state-corporate link –

436 Many foreign mining companies, including the US companies Ryan and Guggenheim, bought concessions. The biggest company, *Union Minière du Haut-Katanga*, was part-financed by Midlands, Barings and Rothschilds. Renton, Seddon and Zeilig 2006, p. 29.

437 Renton, Seddon and Zeilig 2006, pp. 32, 33.

438 Renton, Seddon and Zeilig 2006, pp. 30–7.

439 Anghie 2007, p. 92.

440 Anghie 2007, p. 3.

441 Anghie 2007, p. 52.

the Congo company state was portrayed as King Leopold's private adventure or folly. At the same time, it (and the corporate scramble for Africa more generally) did create the conditions for and realisation of capitalism in areas previously relatively untouched by Europe's 'capitalising mission'.

2.6 *The Berlin Conference: Legalising Corporate Imperialism*

The Berlin West African Conference has broader significance than simply in relation to the Congo. In their rivalries, European states began to fear for the validity of their agreements with non-European powers, since the titles to their territories were concluded with colonised people otherwise considered 'uncivilised' and without legal agency. The Europeans managed to safeguard their interests and make these 'unequal treaties' part of general IL by giving them a literal, positivist reading and endorsing them as valid (ignoring whether they had been made under duress or deceit).[442] Anghie notes the fact that most colonial territories were acquired by force combined by formal 'legal' acts of local chiefs signing over 'all our country ... all sovereign rights ... and all and every other claim absolutely, and without any reservation, to Her Most Gracious Majesty ... and heirs and successors, for all time coming'.[443] What is witnessed here is the concrete example of how primitive accumulation may be legalised and how an 'agreement' forming feudal proto-law is turned into what we now consider 'law'. The particular challenge in the context of the Berlin Conference (where 'humanitarianism and profit-seeking were presented in proper and judicious balance')[444] was that the interests at hand had to locate the non-European world in the international law framework somehow. To do so, the conference participants passed the *Berlin Act* which regulated freedom of navigation and trade, as well as the rules on the acquisition of new territory.[445] Its most infamous provision, Article 35, obliged parties to establish authority in the African territories 'insofar as necessary to ensure free trade'.[446] At the same time, protectorates were excluded from this obligation, which 'allowed the British, for instance, to uphold their unlimited commercial empire while at the same time avoiding the financial and administrative burdens ... [of] formal occupation'.[447] Thus, the *Berlin Act* systematised and *legalised* the scramble for Africa, and at the same time *extended* the rhetoric of the civilising mission to

442 Hopkins 1980, pp. 71–3.
443 Hopkins 1980, p. 92.
444 Hopkins 1980, p. 69.
445 Koskenniemi 2001, p. 123.
446 *1885 Berlin General Act* Art. 35.
447 Koskenniemi 2001, p. 124.

cover (up) the economic motivations of colonisation: '[n]ow, because trade was the mechanism for advancement and progress, it was essential that trade be extended as far as possible into the interior of all these societies'.[448] The 'capitalising mission' was thus re-branded as the 'civilising mission'. (In the upcoming chapters I show that it becomes rebranded as a 'development mission' and an 'ICL/transitional justice mission' – while forever remaining truly a 'capitalising mission'.) The motivations underlying colonialism have been described as purely 'political', 'economic' or even religious, but 'civilisation' in the nineteenth century came to be understood as including the *values* (aims) of capitalism,[449] paving the way for further corporate exploitation in the twentieth and twenty-first centuries. I will come back to this in the following chapters.[450]

3 Corporations in IL in the Twentieth Century

Into the twentieth century, corporations continued to be involved in imperialist endeavour (e.g., the 'banana wars' in Central and South America),[451] and state-governing elites continued to act as private property owners[452] within institutional configurations that were at once formally equal and materially unequal. For example, Captain Smedley Butler described the military 'racketeering' of US foreign policy on his 1930s lecture tour around the United States:

> I spent 33 years and 4 months in active service as a member of our country's most agile military force – the Marine Corps ... And during that period I spent most of my time being a high-class muscle man for Big Business, for Wall Street and for the bankers. In short, I was a racketeer for capitalism ... Thus I helped make Mexico and especially Tampico safe for American oil interests in 1914. I helped make Haiti and Cuba a decent

448 Koskenniemi 2001, p. 97. In the *1885 Berlin General Act* Preamble: 'WISHING, in a spirit of good and mutual accord, to regulate the conditions most favourable to the development of trade and civilization in certain regions of Africa, and to assure to all nations the advantages of free navigation on the two chief rivers of Africa flowing into the Atlantic Ocean'. Echoes of this clause can later be found in Articles 74 and 76 of the *United Nations Charter*.

449 Hopkins 1980, p. 778.

450 For example, British Prime Minister Palmerston, who 'shared ... the notion of a civilizing mission ... believed that the standard of morals was linked to the standard of living, and that both would be raised by the growth of world trade' (Hopkins 1980, p. 778).

451 Litvin 2004, p. 113ff.

452 Merriman asserts that rivalry over colonial possessions caused World War One. Merriman 2009, p. 859.

> place for the National City Bank boys to collect revenues in. I helped in the raping of half a dozen Central American republics for the benefit of Wall Street. The record of racketeering is long. I helped purify Nicaragua for the international banking house of Brown Brothers in 1909–12. I brought light to the Dominican Republic for American sugar interests in 1916. I helped make Honduras 'right' for American fruit companies in 1903. In China in 1927 I helped see to it that Standard Oil went its way unmolested.[453]

The sense that what Captain Butler was describing was somehow shocking or at least an uncomfortable stretching of the doctrine of diplomatic protection (the state's obligation to protect the rights and interests of its citizens abroad) signalled the urgency to construct some semblance of separation between the economic and political realms in IL. In the early twentieth century, on the back of the abolition of the slave trade (according to many an economically motivated move both through the creation of a free labour force and enhancing the image of previously slave trading companies),[454] and early examples of what we now call international humanitarian law, IL started to gain specifically liberal humanitarian content – with the seed of an ICL (Chapter 4A).[455] By creating an ideological divide separating 'clearly' economic activities by private actors from political/public/state activities, it became acceptable to shield the former from 'interference' by the latter, or, in other words, to let the former be ruled by the market in private international law, and the latter (ostensibly) by liberal humanitarian concerns in public international law.[456] The conceptualisation of free trade as a value in itself – a remnant from the Grotian era – renders this separation legitimate.

---

453 Butler 2003; Smedley Butler was later asked by a number of leading businessmen to form a militia and conduct a coup against Franklin D. Roosevelt, which he refused to do; see Special Committee on Un-American Activities, Investigation of Nazi Propaganda Activities and Investigation of Certain Other Propaganda Activities, 73rd Congress, 1934.

454 Generally, Ashworth 1987; Williams 1966; Rodley 2014.

455 E.g., the *1907 Hague Regulations*.

456 Cutler 2001, p. 261. Cutler argues that 'the [public/private] distinction [in international law] is not reflective of an organic, natural or inevitable separation, but is an analytical construct that evolved with the emergence of the bourgeois state'. Cutler lays the origin of this divide earlier than I would in IL. In my view, the real public/private divide in IL came about only between say 1880 and 1910 with the 'completion', the regularisation of the basic framework of the global IL system FORM which was to continue with the League of Nations, the Hague/Geneva conventions, Nuremberg, the UN charter and finally the Bill of Rights CONTENT. This divide also encapsulated the divide in law, the formal if not the real divide between states and corporations on the international plane (viz. Bismarck's words above).

The international protection of capital through law rather than military force also signals the impending completion of the IL project. In what has been described as one of the last instances of 'gunboat diplomacy', in 1902 the British and German navies bombarded Caracas and blockaded the Venezuelan coast to force Venezuela to repay British and other bondholders.[457] This was an instance of use of state force for the interest of 'private' members of the capitalist class. The Venezuelan foreign minister Luis María Drago complained about the blockade in a letter, stating that 'the public debt cannot occasion armed intervention nor even the actual occupation of the territory of American nations by a European power'. A version of this 'Drago doctrine' was eventually adopted in the 'Drago-Porter Convention' of 1907[458] – and is closely related to the (now obsolete) doctrine of state immunity for commercial acts.[459] Henceforth states could be subjected to arbitration on state debts, yet an opening was left for the use of force if a debtor state refused an offer of arbitration, prevented the reaching of a compromise or failed to submit to the award.[460] Legal, economic coercion thus became war by other means.[461] As Gathii puts it, 'the move toward arbitration and away from the use of force to enforce contract debts shifted the concerns of weak, mostly non-Western countries from the fear of forcible interventions to the bias against them in the rules, processes and outcomes of arbitral forums'.[462] Gathii argues that although Drago was influenced by classical doctrines of international law, he was misguided to think that the rules and institutions of international law were neutral and apolitical alternatives to the use of force.[463] Drago's was thus an act of anti-imperialist resistance that failed by virtue of the *systemic* constraint of IL due to the *form* of IL. Moreover, the use of *legitimate* physical force to preserve commercial interests also continues.[464]

457 Drago and Nettles 1928, p. 204; Gathii 2010, p. 147, Miles 2013, p. 68. For the much earlier but similar story of *the United States and Paraguay Navigation Company Claim*, see Miles 2013, pp. 56–9.

458 The Convention Respecting the Limitation of the Employment of Force for the Recovery of Contract Debts, October 18 1907, 36 Stat. 2241, T.S. 537 (also called '*1907 Hague Convention on Debt Recovery*').

459 Gathii 2010, p. 148.

460 *1907 Hague Convention on Debt Recovery*.

461 The origins of modern arbitration are said to lie in the Treaty of Amity, Commerce and Navigation of 1794 (also known as the 'Jay Treaty'), which set up mixed arbitral commissions for the resolution of disputes between citizens of the US and Great Britain (Collier and Lowe 1999, p. 32).

462 Gathii 2010, p. 151.

463 Gathii 2010, p. 153.

464 Miles 2013, p. 69.

Thirdly, 'extraterritorial' capital investment protection grew, from its roots in the case-by-case diplomatic protection of aliens and their property into a separate substantive regime (international law of investment protection or ILIP) that sits or at least has its centre of gravity on the private side of IL. How this emerged can be illustrated through the story of what became known as the 'Calvo Doctrine'. Inspired by the writings of the Argentinean foreign minister and jurist Carlos Calvo, the Latin American politicians insisted that equal treatment of (the plentiful and mostly US) foreign investors to domestic actors satisfied the requirements of international law.[465] Clearly, it was not enough merely to assert such equal (or indeed unequal) treatment satisfied *domestic* law in the state where foreign parties held investments.[466] Moreover, Western investors argued that there was in fact an 'international minimum standard'[467] of treatment that had to be satisfied and was part of the 'general principles of law recognised by civilisation'.[468] Any standard of protection falling below this bar (or indeed any state proposing such a standard) could be considered 'uncivilised' and ignored. What that standard *was*, however, remained open to interpretation.[469] Normally it would be the standard of the investor's country,[470] thus replicating the foreign merchants' (and through it the GCC's) position outlined above.

The discourse of 'positivism' that had become dominant by the early twentieth century with its notion of international law as a system of rules between consenting states also served to conceal the role of class and the corporation in international law.[471] First and foremost, the development of ILIP per se distracts from the question of the merits of the protection of capital vis-à-vis, say, the protection of local community or the environment. Second, it conceals the role of the corporation in the global political economy, which, as we now know, is more powerful than that of most states. Despite earlier notions of 'corporate sovereignty' and effective corporate legal personality in IL, the twentieth-century notion of corporate personality became circumscribed and contested. As corporations are non-subjects, business people are able to wield the col-

465 Gathii 2010, p. 21.

466 Nationalisation of foreign corporate investment also took place after the Russian Revolution and the spread of Communism in Europe; however, generally lump sum payments were made in settlement (Gathii 2010, p. 21).

467 Root 1910.

468 Schwarzenberger 1955, using the phrase found in *ICJ Statute* Art. 38.

469 Key arguments concern whether the standard includes norms of international human rights and environmental law: Subedi 2008, p. 11.

470 Subedi 2010, p. 10.

471 Koskenniemi, 2007; Anghie 2007, Chapter 2.

lective power of the corporation *and* construct normative regimes 'below the radar' of public IL. One particularly 'lucrative' area in this sense, the regime of investment protection, is entirely aimed at serving their specific interest while not *formally* affecting 'public' law notions of statehood and sovereignty.[472] The effect of positivism and the public/private divide is that it constructs a sphere of liberty where the global capitalist class can pursue (overseas) economic interests with little oversight. The discourse of 'responsibility' is situated in the 'constitutional'/'political' part of international law and 'corporate activity' enclosed in the 'private' domain of international law[473] resulting in a significant ideological hurdle that must be overcome before one might be associated with the other.

In this section I illustrate how the various rhetorical processes (the public/private divide, the definition of key concepts in IL such as sovereignty and personality) are employed to support, strengthen and 'spirit away' (Chapter 1, Section 2) global class relationships. The 'international law of investment protection' is a key site for the analysis of international class law in the twentieth century.[474] Technically (doctrinally), ILIP is a misnomer because a majority of the rules of ILIP are generated by businesspersons (and their lawyers and arbitrators), as members of the global capitalist class through their contractual relations and private and hybrid arbitration, and are thus to the positivist lawyer not 'law' as such.[475] However, through the prism of the commodity form theory of law we can see it as having the same structure and following the same logic. The ILIP regime was developed to safeguard corporate interests in the decolonisation process and during/after moments of political change and conflict in

472 Cf. Pellet 2010, p. 6.

473 Pellet 2010, p. 3. Pellet cites P. Reuter, 'Trois observations sur la codification de la responsabilité internationale des États pour fait illicite', in *Le droit international au service de la paix, de la justice et du développement – Mélanges Michel Virally*, Paris: Perdone, 1991, p. 390. Note that the notion of the international responsibility of corporations receives no further attention in Crawford, Pellet and Olleson's otherwise seemingly exhaustive volume, whereas there *is* a chapter on 'Injuries to Corporations' (see Lowe 2010, p. 1005).

474 See, e.g., Pellet 2010, p. 6. For one particularly 'schizophrenic' assessment of the separation: 'FDI is a politically sensitive issue as the taking of control is sometimes perceived as an attempt to weaken national sovereignty and national interest. In our view, well-designed regulations should help overcome this possible perverse effect of FDI and reassure those countries that have such fears. Therefore, we advocate the gradual elimination of the political side of FDIs as it only brings uncertainty and maintains unfounded fears, even if we are aware of how difficult a task this is because FDI has political implications'. Lael-Arcas 2010, p. 178.

475 Sornarajah 2010, p. 79; Moses 2008, pp. 7–8.

the Third World outside of the decolonisation process – and entrenches corporate interests in IL (the imperialism of the corporate form) into the present.[476] One way such interests were, and are, safeguarded was through adjusting the *content* of the principle of sovereignty (s.3.1). One effect of investment protection through one of its key tools – investment arbitration (s.3.2) – has been that *corporate* international legal personality is actualised and difficult to deny even by positivists. One way around this conundrum has been to bracket the content (or incidence) of corporate legal personality in IL to *exclude* responsibility (s.3.3). In Chapters 4 and 6, I will show that this bracketing becomes untenable and is dismantled in a (counterintuitive) way by, and *favourable* to, the GCC. The growing acceptance of the notion of pluralist global governance in IL requires, presupposes and produces it (Chapter 6).

3.1 *Concession Agreements and Unequal Sovereigns*

Before the corporate colonialism of the nineteenth century could move to global liberal capitalist statehood of the twentieth century, the ground for 'self-determination' and 'decolonisation' had to be prepared so as not to affect Western corporate interests in the Third World. The European capitalist class had to publicly divest itself of political responsibility for the periphery while retaining its private material hold. The technique, following the late nineteenth-century informal empire companies, was the granting of concession agreements with wide powers and long terms – some being concluded in the context of mandates and trusteeships, others directly. Moreover, the *physical* shape of future states was made subject to these interests. For example, 'France and Great Britain were intent on gaining control over the oil resources in their Middle Eastern mandates and they went so far as to redraw the boundaries of the mandate territories of Palestine, Mesopotamia and Syria in order to enable a more efficient exploitation of their oil reserves'.[477] This is a striking example of the form of law affecting material reality – all around the shape of corporate activity.

While decolonisation is often presented as allowing 'peoples' to exercise their right to self-determination, Craven has suggested that it may be more accurate to describe decolonisation as a process of *determination*, where Third World populations (not necessarily divided along the lines of 'peoples' or nations) are shoe-horned into a particular conception of liberal capitalist statehood shaped and 'made available' to them by the global capitalist class.[478] The

476 See generally, Miles 2013.

477 Anghie 2007, p. 144; cf. Higgins 1999.

478 Craven 2007, p. 260; cf. Simpson 2004.

newly decolonised states are 'unequal sovereigns' in the sense that their sovereignty is recognised by the metropole/global capitalist class conditional upon (amongst others) continued free access to markets and natural resources. As such, the opportunity to gain statehood presents the 'equal opportunity to be unequal'.

States and corporations from the metropole (or rather, the GCC through them) gained long-term control over prized natural resources in particular, by entering into concession agreements with the governors of colonised (or mandated, etc.) territories (often nationals of the colonial state or local elites in a position of loyalty to the colonial state).[479] Through these agreements, rulers would cede sovereign rights over vast areas of territory and/or rights over the exploitation of oil and mining products to foreign corporations for long periods of time.[480] For example, the Aminol concession was granted by the sheikh of Kuwait (then a British protectorate) in 1948 – with a royalty of two shillings and sixpence per barrel – for 60 years.[481] Similarly, the Ashanti goldfields concession in Ghana was to last for 100 years.[482] Many of these types of arrangements were made by Western companies throughout the Third World.[483] Their length and disadvantageous terms often led to disputes, especially when the new states' leaderships changed.[484] Such disputes rarely led to the metropolitan corporation losing its foothold, such that the imperial holds established in the late Middle Ages continue to be reproduced in the present. Moreover, it is some of these companies in particular that are now the subject of complaints in terms of human rights abuses and violations of the laws of war (see Chapter 5 below). The natural resource sector is one particular area where we can speak of the continuing practice of 'primitive accumulation' or 'accumulation by dispossession'.[485]

---

479 See generally, e.g., Cattan 1967; Cameron 2011; Higgins 1999.

480 Generally, Sornarajah 2010, pp. 38–41; Konoplyanik 2004, pp. 67–70.

481 *Aminol Award.*

482 Sornarajah 2010, p. 39.

483 E.g., in the plantation sector with companies such as Twinings and Lipton, see Sornarajah 2010, p. 41.

484 Anghie 2007, p. 224; and see also Nussbaum 1954, p. 125. Some of these agreements have been cancelled, while others have been turned into 'participatory agreements', partly through the changing power-balance in the oil sector and the support for the 'doctrine of permanent sovereignty over natural resources' contained in General Assembly Resolution 1803 (XVII) Permanent Sovereignty over Natural Resources, 14 December 1962, UN Doc. A/RES/1803 (*UN General Assembly PSNR Resolution*); Sornarajah 2010, p. 40.

485 Harvey 2003, pp. 137 ff.

3.2 *ILIP and Internationalisation*

To deal with these disputes – starting with concession agreement disputes – governing and business elites (the GCC) developed ILIP.[486] The key to ILIP is investor-state dispute resolution (ISDS), normally through arbitration, which allows the internationalisation of investment agreements, or 'lifting' them out of host state jurisdiction and into (private) IL. Many of these early ILIP arbitrations relate to newly independent governments wishing to change the concession terms with still-present metropolitan multinationals – often to raise the royalties on resource extraction or to nationalise such resources and their extraction infrastructure altogether. Early cases involve Mexico, Panama, and other Latin American countries, and were decided long before the so-called 'Hull formula' – articulated by US diplomat Cordell Hull and elevated into international law, sidelining the Calvo doctrine favoured in the Third World.[487] Some of the new leaders of former British and other mandates challenged the oil and gas deals made with metropolitan corporations in the period preceding their independence.[488] A series of arbitrations arose after a change in leadership in some countries where it was alleged the old regime had accepted bribes in return for the concession, e.g., in Indonesia after the fall of Suharto, after the departure of Marcos from the Philippines, Abacha in Nigeria and the fall of Bhutto in Pakistan.[489] Finally in the Middle East, Egypt's nationalisation of the Suez Canal Co. led to arbitration, while other Arab states in the early 1970s nationalised or abrogated concessions of major Western oil companies.[490] ILIP arbitration increases the material inequality of the new 'unequal sovereigns'.

The story of the *Abu Dhabi Award* is a good example.[491] This is the first, landmark decision where the arbitrator considered the contract between the sheikh and the company to be an 'internationalised contract'.[492] As such it was to be governed not by Abu Dhabi law (which in any case the arbitrator Lord Asquith

486 Sornarajah 2010, p. 20; Subedi 2008, p. 8.

487 Subedi 2008, pp. 16–18.

488 The tribunal in the *ARAMCO Award* found petroleum concessions to be governed by international law *ARAMCO Award* 156–68.

489 Sornarajah 2010, p. 75 (fn. 148). Sornarajah argues that a putative emerging norm of democratic governance ought to have consequences for investment agreements concluded with unrepresentative governments. Arguing that this is not currently the case, he concludes: 'Those who favour the existence of such a rule do not address the situation of foreign investment contracts made with totalitarian governments, which may indicate that the norm proposed is not to be uniformly applied but is a covert basis for undermining governments that states do not approve of' (2010, p. 76, fn. 151).

490 *LIAMCO Award, Texaco Award* etc.; Sornarajah 2010, p. 74.

491 *Abu Dhabi Award.*

492 *Abu Dhabi Award.*

considered did not exist: 'it would be fanciful to suggest that in this very primitive region there is any settled body of legal principles applicable to the construction of modern commercial contracts')[493] but by international principles of law. This new law of 'investment protection' bore an uncanny resemblance to English law: per Lord Asquith: 'albeit English municipal law is inapplicable as such, some of its rules are in my view so firmly grounded in reason, as to form part of this broad jurisprudence – this "modern law of nature"'.[494] Anghie comments that hereby the law of the Third World state is in effect *selectively* replaced by the law of England.[495] This is effectively so, while principles of English law are adopted into ILIP, which obviates the Third World state's jurisdiction. 'Elevating' these concession agreements into international law also meant that 'by entering into such contracts, Third World states, *in effect, were investing foreign corporations with international personality*'.[496] The state lost its ability to interfere with the activities of private parties for the benefit of its people as the principle of *pacta sunt servanda* (agreements must be honoured) now severely limited the ability of the state to change the terms of the international agreement, and in sum, the state and the corporation were positioned as 'formal legal equals' despite material difference both in bargaining power and in purpose.[497]

3.3 *Investment Arbitration: the Silent Revolution?*

The internationalisation of concession agreements is carried forward in contemporary foreign direct investment practice. Investors' (including shareholders') rights are now generally explicitly protected under the terms of Bilateral Investment Treaties ('BITs') and multilateral trade and investment agreements such as NAFTA, TPP and CETA, which are the hardened vehicles (protective constructs) provided by the home state accompanying most private foreign direct investment.[498] While the number of BITs in existence between states has skyrocketed to 2,321 in force in 2016,[499] multilateral agreements with investor protection have also started to proliferate in the past five years especially, with TTIP still under negotiation as at July 2017.[500] As with their earlier version, the

493 *Abu Dhabi Award*, para. 241.

494 Quoted in Anghie 2007, p. 229; *Abu Dhabi Award*, para. 242.

495 Anghie 2007, p. 229.

496 Anghie 2007, p. 232, emphasis added.

497 On the 'equal treatment', see Shalakany 2000, p. 419. On difference and coincidence of purpose, see Renton et al., who describe kickbacks etc. to local elites/leaders of the decolonised state: Renton et al. 2007, pp. 204–6.

498 See, generally, Jannaca-Small 2010.

499 Source: UNCTAD http://investmentpolicyhub.unctad.org/IIA.

500 There have been attempts at the creation of multilateral investment treaties: e.g., the

concession agreement, a key feature of most BITs and multilateral agreements is the arbitration clause, by which the two states agree that any disputes are to be resolved through arbitration. This typically *includes* those disputes between an investor and the host state (investor-state dispute settlement/ISDS). In other words, BITs enable the investor to ride on the back of the bilateral agreement, and *to stay out of the host state's court*.[501] Rather than seeking adjudication in courts of law, disputes arising from BITs are generally resolved through arbitration, either through ICSID, or through an arbitrator appointed under the UNCITRAL Arbitration rules or similar arrangement.[502] While BITs and other trade and investment deals that include ISDS are nominally reciprocal, in practice arbitration is almost exclusively initiated by a metropolitan corporate investor against a Third World state. Moreover, the arbitrators are private individuals, normally members of the metropolitan elite, who are class-bound to find in favour of capital.[503]

Originally many of the disputes arbitrated under such agreements related to the disputes over nationalisation of investors' assets where an incoming government sought to reverse the concession arrangements that saw all natural resources being exported out of a country for very little return,[504] but more recently disputes have arisen over more complex 'loss in value' on the part of investors. This includes loss which is termed 'regulatory takings', for example where a state's labour, environmental or consumer regulation causes an investor to have to spend money on adjustments for compliance. 'Stabilisation clauses' in most BITs require the host state to compensate any loss (usually

Abs-Shawcross Convention backed by the International Chamber of Commerce (a private institution), and the Multilateral Agreement on Investment (MAI), which both failed to gain sufficient support. Calls for the World Trade Organisation to draft such an instrument have, according to Sornarajah, 'served only to indicate the nature of the dissension among states as to what the rules on foreign investment at the global level are' (Sornarajah 2010, p. 80). Regional provisions on foreign investment include Chapter 11 of NAFTA and the ASEAN Comprehensive Treaty on Investments.

501 Moses considers this the main point of arbitration: Moses 2012, p. 1. In Chapter 5, I will show that corporate liability in international criminal law and CSR have the same objectives and effects.

502 Subedi 2008, p. 32.

503 Generally, Dezalay and Garth 1996; also, generally, Subedi 2008; Miles 2013.

504 Lowenfeld, pp. 585–6. The common principles of BITs are 'the understanding that international law is applicable to the relation between host states and foreign investors, that expropriation must be for a public purpose and must be accompanied by just compensation, and that disputes between foreign investors and host states should be subjected to impartial adjudication or arbitration' (p. 586).

including loss of future profits) caused by a change in host state law.[505] This has a limiting ('chilling') effect on the host state's ability to pass laws and take policy decisions it considers beneficial to its citizens or the natural environment,[506] or indeed to prosecute corporations once human rights law or environmental law violations have occurred, and injury has been suffered.[507] With the IMF and World Bank's drives towards the privatisation of, e.g., public services in Third World countries, the presence and effect of foreign corporations has only increased. Third World countries are forced to offer conditions attractive to Western multinational investors, which may well include a willingness to ignore 'irresponsible corporate practices'.[508] Through BIT arbitration, ILIP allows corporations to significantly affect the ability of Third World states/communities to manage distribution of resources, to maintain public health, and to manage the effects of exploitation and deprivation.[509] Multilateral arrangements such as NAFTA and a possible future TTIP could replicate this effect as between Western states, where corporations in the jurisdiction with the lowest regulatory barrier (e.g., the US on environment, food safety, health, and EU countries on banking regulation) can force down high regulatory barriers in other states.[510]

Subedi calls the idea of allowing private corporations direct access to international law mechanisms to resolve disputes with states a 'silent revolution':[511] as unequal sovereigns, Third World states engage with metropolitan states in BITs as formal legal equals and moreover with powerful multinational corporations as equals in arbitration. It is 'silent' because this state of affairs occurs (and is drawn into) the 'private side' of IL. Also, the corporation as an actor (with ILP) remains hidden in this private side of IL. Quite literally, moreover, most arbitrations happen behind closed doors in cosmopolitan hotels and are never reported. Alvarez has called BITs 'Bills of Rights for Foreign Investors'.[512] Although BITs carry reciprocal rights and obligations, due to the unidirec-

505 *Aminol Case*, Fitzmaurice Separate Opinion fn. 7; Cameron 2010, p. 104.

506 E.g., *Santa Elena v. Costa Rica Award*, *Metalclad Award*; cf. *Methanex Award*; Anghie 2007, p. 234. See also Sornarajah 2010, pp. 282–3.

507 See for example the *Chevron v Ecuador* arbitration, triggered by an Ecuadorian court judgement against Chevron for alleged environmental damage.

508 Human Rights Watch, Corporations and Human Rights, at https://www.hrw.org/legacy/about/initiatives/corp.html.

509 CEPAL FDI Arbitration and Water Report, p. 19.

510 See, e.g., War on Want, 'What is TTIP?', n.d.

511 Subedi 2008, p. 32.

512 Alvarez also calls *NAFTA* a 'Bilateral Investment Treaty on Steroids': Alvarez 1996–97, p. 304.

tional investment patterns, and through ILIP's basic techniques they significantly benefit the metropolitan shareholder of the Western-headquartered multinational corporation, and thus create an 'equal opportunity to inequality'.

3.4 *Corporations in the PCIJ and ICJ*

Although most of ILIP falls on the private side of IL, some of the basic principles of ILIP were developed in the public court system.[513] The Permanent Court of International Justice (PCIJ) and the International Court of Justice (ICJ)[514] in several cases have dealt with corporate interests represented by states, usually on the basis of aliens' right to diplomatic protection.[515] Some of these were related to concessions (*Mavrommatis* and *Anglo-Iranian*) and others to foreign investment in another sense. States could, and did, 'espouse' corporate interests in these fora, in particular in the area of ILIP. Aside from the need for home state espousal of a corporate interest, the court route was less popular mainly because the PCIJ and the ICJ's jurisdiction in disputes requires *host state* (adverse party) consent.[516] In many cases, also, there was reluctance on the part of home states to take questions on foreign investment to the ('public') international fora for fear of exposing the uncertainty in the law and losing the flexibility afforded by arbitration once norms were 'set' by court.[517] Moreover, it appears the ICJ itself preferred to defer jurisdiction *and* findings on IL to arbitration.[518]

Nevertheless, states have at times espoused the commercial interests of their private citizens, including corporations, at the PICJ and later the ICJ, and the courts have set some of the key principles of ILIP. From the point of view of epistemology it is also interesting to see how most of these cases (like the *Case of Sutton's Hospital* in Chapter 2A) are cited in current textbooks without their backstory, in particular as many of these cases deal with issues of 'business in

513 See, generally, Lael-Arcas 2010, Sornarajah 2010, pp. 79–87.

514 Which are housed in a building paid for and owned by the foundation of Scottish industrialist and philanthropist Andrew Carnegie alongside the Permanent Court of Arbitration and the Iran–United States Claims Tribunal, see http://www.icj-cij.org/information/index.php?p1=7 The Iran–US Claims Tribunal moved to its own premises in The Hague in 1982.

515 The constituent instrument also limits jurisdiction to disputes between states: *PCIJ Statute* Art. 34(1).

516 PCIJ Statute: Art. 34(1).

517 Sornarajah 2010, p. 37.

518 *Anglo-Iranian Case* 10; Sornarajah 2010, pp. 106–7; Higgins 1999, p. 87.

conflict'.[519] The back stories reveal class interest in these cases and the significance of law in corporate-state (GCC) imperialism.

In the *Mavrommatis Palestine Concessions* case[520] and the related case *Mavrommatis Jerusalem Concessions*[521] – the cases that set the precedent for state espousal of business interests – Greece attempted to protect the interests of a Greek[522] businessman by means of diplomatic protection. The espousal argument is based on a collectivist state view: 'a presumption that nationals are indispensable elements of a State's territorial attributes and a wrong done to the national invariably affects the right of the State'.[523] The case concerned a concession granted to Mavrommatis in 1914 by the Ottoman rulers of Palestine, which was arguably violated by the British when they took on the Palestine Mandate in 1920 and granted a partially conflicting concession to another company through the Zionist Organisation.[524] The conflicting part of the concessions included the construction of tramways in Jerusalem. The PICJ held the claim to be inadmissible with regard to the Jaffa concession but admissible with regard to the Jerusalem concession, on which it held that Mavrommatis was wrongly denied his concession and had to be compensated.[525] The main legal question on jurisdiction was answered thus: 'It is an elementary principle of international law that a State is entitled to protect its subjects, when injured by acts contrary to international law ... By taking up the case of one of its subjects and by resorting to diplomatic action or international judicial proceedings on his behalf, a State is in reality asserting its own rights'.[526] The case is now known as authority for what constitutes an international dispute.[527] With the

---

519 Higgins 1999. See, e.g., Lowenfeld 2008. Harris quotes only three paragraphs from the decision on jurisdiction in the *Mavrommatis Palestine* case: Harris 2004, p. 565.

520 Mavrommatis Palestine 1924.

521 Mavrommatis Jerusalem 1925.

522 An interesting point was that Mavrommatis in the concession document was described as a *Turkish* citizen. The Court did not let this stand in the way of Greece claiming diplomatic protection on his behalf.

523 Okowa 2010, p. 477.

524 See also Borchard 1925, who comments: 'One gets the impression on reading the correspondence, that Mavrommatis had lost his ability or willingness to go on with the concessions and desired to bring about their expropriation against indemnity; that the Rutenberg company and the Palestine Administration, sensing this, preferred not to exercise their power of expropriation, but invited Mavrommatis to go on with his concessions, in the belief that he would not avail himself of the privilege' (pp. 736–7). See also Bishop 2005, pp. 444 ff.

525 The difference lay in the timing of the concession vs. the terms of the Mandate and the fact that the Jerusalem concession had begun to be executed.

526 *Mavrommatis Palestine* 1924, p. 12.

527 Higgins 1999, p. 88.

backstory in mind, we can see this case as an example of competition between different capitalists' interests, while we can also observe joint interest between the espousing state and the industrialist.

The *Factory at Chorzów case*[528] concerned factories in (mineral-rich) Upper Silesia – formerly German territory part of which became Polish after the Silesian Uprisings of 1919 and 1921 – uprisings of a Polish-speaking working-class majority against a German-speaking elite who owned the mines and factories – many of whom moved to Germany 'proper' once part of Silesia became Polish. One of the questions before the Court was whether the property (land, moveable property and patents) belonged to Germany or to the German companies (Oberschlesische Stickstoffwerke A.G. and the Bayerische Stickstoffwerke A.G.).[529] The PICJ ordered restitution: full compensation to be paid to the companies (not to Germany). This case set the precedent for compensation in international law generally,[530] but its backstory is one of a decision on state borders in an effort to quell class conflict arising from accumulation by dispossession.[531]

The *Anglo-Iranian Oil Co. Case* of 1952 related to the property of a British company (later know as BP), which was subject to a nationalisation attempt by the Iranian government led by Prime Minister Mossadegh, who had been democratically elected. The property had been conveyed to the company in a concession granted by the shah of Iran in 1933. The ICJ concluded it did not have jurisdiction because the concession was a contract between the shah and the company, and not an international agreement to which the UK was a party.[532] Thus the 'public' ICJ decided to leave the matter to private resolution, perversely by *denying* internationality in this case whereas earlier arbitral awards had found such agreements to be 'internationalised' precisely in order to attract jurisdiction. The following year the government in Iran was overthrown *covertly* by the CIA in Operation Ajax, and a new shah was installed.[533] Shah Reza

528 At p. 453: 'reparation must, as far as possible, wipe out all the consequences of the illegal act and re-establish the situation which would, in all probability, have existed if that act had not been committed'. *Factory at Chorzów*.

529 These became part of the IG Farben cartel, see Ch. 3A below.

530 *Anglo-Iranian Oil Case*.

531 Author's correspondence with Kamil Majchrzak, 3 March 2011.

532 *Anglo-Iranian Oil Case*.

533 The events escalated into something of a trade war, with the Anglo-Iranian Oil Co. and other major international oil companies denying the new National Iranian Oil Co. access to markets in Europe or North America, filing suits to 'repossess' shipments of oil from Iran, and, allegedly, the British Royal Air Force threatening to bomb Iranian vessels (Lowenfeld 2008, p. 519); see also Sornarajah 2010, p. 20, who calls the overthrowing of the

Pahlavi commenced 'a massive programme of industrialization and modernization, principally through soliciting private investment and long-term contracts from firms in the United States'.[534] After the 1979 Islamic Revolution the Ayatollah Khomeini reversed many of the shah's policies, suspending contracts and expropriating property. After 'Iranian students' occupied the US Embassy in Tehran, the US froze Iranian bank accounts in the US. One of the results of the negotiation was the establishment of the Iran–United States Claims Tribunal, at which to date thousands of US companies and individuals have filed claims against Iran.[535] As many arbitrations relating to concessions and BITs between the metropole and the periphery followed the disposal of the original contracting (often unrepresentative) regimes, one can imagine, as in the case of regulatory takings, that such cases have a chilling effect on political change. Moreover, the Anglo-Iranian arbitration illustrates the combined use by the GCC of law and physical force in conflict.

One *unsuccessful* company case was *Interhandel*, where the claim was for the release (by the US) of funds belonging to a company that had (it was argued, by the US) formed part of the IG Farben cartel (see Chapter 4 below).[536] This case is generally cited for its findings on jurisdiction: The US had sought to exclude from the ICJ's jurisdiction disputes arising before 1946 – the year of the US's acceptance of ICJ jurisdiction.[537] The ICJ, however, declared the application inadmissable on the basis that local remedies had not been exhausted, as a domestic case was still pending.[538] Simmonds calls the decision 'illogical' and a missed opportunity for the ICJ to assert its jurisdiction.[539] At the same

---

Mossadegh, together with the Allende Government in Chile, the 'more obvious instances in recent history of forcible, though covert, interventions to assist foreign investment' (fn. 62). See also The White House, Office of the Press Secretary, The President's Remarks in a Speech at Cairo University, 4 June 2009.

534 Lowenfeld 2008, p. 542.

535 See the tribunal's website, at http://www.iusct.org/english/.

536 *Interhandel* paras. 26–30. *Interhandel* concerned to the General Aniline and Film Co. (GAF), the largest supplier of photographic materials in the US and producing products essential for the US arms industry during World War Two. It was argued that GAF was controlled by the German company IG Farben through a Swiss company called IG Chemie Companie. This company changed its name to Interhandel in 1940, at which point, the Swiss Government argues, the relationship with IG Farben ended. For further discussion of the context and the diplomatic negotiations and the domestic litigation leading up to this case, see Simmonds 1961.

537 Harris 2004, pp. 1047–8; Evans 2003, p. 494.

538 *Interhandel*, para. 27.

539 Simmonds 1961, p. 547.

time, perhaps the case shows the limits of the ICJ's power to enter into politically highly sensitive territory – where a decision on the merits would have had to examine US–German military/commercial ties before and partially during World War Two – which I will come back to in the next chapter.

At particular times, then, we can see the GCC's resort to public institutions such as the ICJ to set formal legal principles in situations where private arbitration proved inadequate or inappropriate. Such resort to public institutions appears to be prevalent with a 'less unequal' adversary, and in a 'more public' context such as a war/conflict. The effect of such public state espousal of corporate interests is a measure of naturalisation of the corporation in IL, while conversely publicly 'hiding' it behind the state it needs to represent it. In the next section I revisit the issue of corporate personality in IL. The other significant point to highlight, especially since it is not normally made in the mainstream literature, is that the cases brought by states always concern corporate *interests*, corporate *rights*, but never corporate *obligations* or *responsibility*.

3.5 *Island of Palmas Arbitration vs. Reparations for Injuries: International Legal Personality Revisited*

Wilson argues that Grotius's *De Indis / De Iure Praedae* 'operate[d] to legitimate international personality and authority of the VOC, a "pre-modern institutional form"'[540] – and that a clear relationship exists with the current debate on international legal personality of multinational/transnational corporations as well as the emergence of a 'neo-medieval' world order, for which '[m]ost important is the investiture of private non-state actors with Original Personality, particularly the TNC'.[541] Currently, the nature and content of corporate ILP are in contention.

Although the trading corporations had acted like 'corporate sovereigns' and as subjects of international law by entering into treaties as among the first of IL's persons, with the advent of positivism the corporation as ILP went away. Nevertheless, inevitably the question whether other bodies besides states could have 'international legal personality' came up formally, in the ICJ *Reparations for Injuries* Advisory Opinion of 1949. The case concerned the question of the capacity of the UN to claim reparation from the responsible state for the death of a person acting in the UN's official capacity (*in casu* Count Folke Bernadotte, who had been assassinated by the Stern Gang while on an official mission as the UN Peace Negotiator in Palestine) on behalf of the United Nations itself and

540 Wilson 2008, p. 128.
541 Wilson 2008, p. 127.

on behalf of the deceased.[542] The Court adopted a circular reasoning, holding that, where international organisations, in order to carry out the mandate given by states in their constitutive documents, needed to have the capabilities that come with international legal personality (such as *in casu* the capacity to bring an international claim), they should be considered to have personality.[543] International legal personality was quite simply 'indispensable' for the UN to be able to function.[544] The idea of the UN as a body in law separate from its members is clearly comparable to the corporation's separate legal personality in domestic law (Chapter 2A). Here too the 'fetishisation' occurred in a context of responsibility; this time it was the absorption by the separate legal personality of the loss borne by an individual or his family or his community – and the right to claim compensation on their behalf.

Some 20 years earlier, in the *Island of Palmas Case* at the Permanent Court of Arbitration (which was a territorial dispute over the island Palmas/Miangas between the US and The Netherlands), sole arbitrator Max Huber commented on the nature of the acts of the Dutch East India Company in 'acquiring' the island:

> [They] must in international law, be entirely assimilated to acts of the Netherlands State itself. From the end of the sixteenth until the nineteenth century, companies formed by individuals and engaged in economic pursuits (Chartered Companies), were invested by the state to whom they were subject with public powers for the acquisition and administration of colonies.[545]

Since 1677 the 'native' states had been 'connected with' the Dutch East India Company, 'which conferred upon the suzerain such powers as would justify his considering the vassal state as part of his territory'.[546] So, on the one hand, the Court accepted the Company's treaty with the 'natives' for the transfer of the Island of Palmas as valid, but on the other, it would not recognise the company's (or indeed the natives') international legal personality.

---

542 *Reparations for Injuries*, para. 174.

543 *Reparations for Injuries*, para. 178.

544 *Reparations for Injuries*, para. 178. In *Certain Expenses*, in an *obiter*, or perhaps even inadvertent sentence para. 168: 'Both national and international law contemplate cases in which the body corporate or politic may be bound, as to third parties, by an *ultra vires* act of an agent'. The Court seems here to show it is well aware of the international legal activities and status of bodies other than states.

545 *Island of Palmas Case*, para. 858.

546 *Island of Palmas Case*, para. 867.

Rather, I would suggest, the *Palmas* decision presents a pragmatic choice based on class interests, which reflects a desire to 'legalise' past corporate colonialism without bringing the corporation into 'public international law' as a responsibility-bearing entity, on the one hand, while *Reparations* represents a desire to create an additional (potential risk-absorbing) entity besides states, on the other.

Although in international law doctrine 'international legal personality' means 'being a subject of international law', this in itself is not necessarily always taken to mean 'subject of *all* international law'. Many legal norms are considered in the canon to address only a specific type or subset of 'legal subjects'.[547] In other words, although the *form* of subjectivity is the same, the content may be interpreted quite differently depending on whether the subject is a state, international organisation, corporation or indeed an individual.[548] In Chapter 4 I analyse the debate around the question whether the content of corporate international legal personality includes the possibility of liability for international crimes.

The *Barcelona Traction* case (*Belgium v. Spain*) of 1970[549] concerned the claims of Belgian shareholders who had lost money during the Spanish Civil War when the Franco government had placed restrictions on doing business in Spain. Barcelona Traction Light & Power Company Ltd (which ran the tramways in Barcelona) was registered in Canada. Belgium asserted the right to exercise diplomatic protection on behalf of shareholders, for the 'creeping expropriation' of their property.[550] The court held that shareholders have no rights independent from the company and only the home state of the company (Canada – which had chosen not to) could claim diplomatic protection against Spain.[551] This would indicate the reification of the corporation in international law similarly to domestic law – but thus far only in the economic sphere. The ICJ states, in para 38:

547 See generally, Schermers 2003, p. 992; and Klabbers 2003, p. 43.

548 *ILC Responsibility of IOs.*

549 *Barcelona Traction.*

550 *Barcelona Traction*, paras. 33–35.

551 *Barcelona Traction*, paras. 39, 88. The ICJ decided the *Barcelona Traction* case on the basis of the assumption that IL in this respect referred to the rules generally accepted by municipal legal systems in these matters. But concepts of corporate veil and the centralisation of all rights and duties in a single place may conflict with other existing rules of IL (at para. 5). IL allows piercing of the veil following from the principle of justice that requires reference to the substance and not merely to the legal form – citing *Cayuga Indians* 1926. However, practice does not follow any uniform pattern, the rules vary according to the person behind the veil.

> All it means is that international law has had to recognize the corporate entity as an institution created by States in a domain essentially within their domestic jurisdiction. This in turn requires that, whenever legal issues arise concerning the rights of States with regard to the treatment of companies and shareholders, as to which rights international law has not established its own rules, it has to refer to the relevant rules of municipal law.[552]

This paragraph lends itself to the interpretation that the corporation must be recognised as a matter of fact, not as a matter of international law. Strikingly, the ICJ mentions *rights* here specifically. The ICJ developed this point in the *Case of Ahmadou Diallo (Republic of Guinea v. Democratic Republic of the Congo)*. This case concerned the arrest, detention and compulsion of Diallo, a Guinean businessman, by the DRC:

> What matters, from the point of view of international law, is to determine whether or not these [companies] have a legal personality independent of their members. Conferring independent corporate personality on a company implies granting it rights over its own property, rights which it alone is capable of protecting. As a result, only the State of nationality may exercise diplomatic protection on behalf of the company when its rights are injured by a wrongful act of another State. In determining whether a company possesses independent and distinct legal personality, international law looks to the rules of the relevant domestic law.[553]

Again, the focus here is on rights, not ILP in general or (especially) responsibility. Crawford (UN Special Rapporteur responsible for the International Law Commission's Articles on State Responsibility for Wrongful Acts[554]) describes legal personality as 'the paradigm of responsibility in international law'.[555] Recognising that, as per the *Reparations for Injuries* Advisory Opinion there are other legal persons besides states, 'it would seem unproblematic to substitute the words "international organization" or "international legal person"

552 *Barcelona Traction Case*, para. 38.

553 *Ahmadou Diallo Case*, para. 61.

554 See the *ILC State Responsibility Articles*: esp. Article 33(2): [the content of a state's responsibility is] 'without prejudice to any right, arising from the international responsibility of a State, which may accrue directly to any person or entity other than a State'.

555 Crawford 2010, p. 17.

for "State" in Article 1 of the ILC Articles'.[556] Yet, 'it is doubtful whether [corporations] are in any meaningful sense "subjects" of international law'[557] and 'it is also very doubtful whether "multinational corporations" are subjects of international law for the purpose of responsibility ... From a legal point of view, the so-called multinational corporation is better regarded as a group of corporations, each created under and amenable to its own national law as well as to any other national legal system within which it operates'.[558] Pellet (in the same volume) suggests that corporations have both 'active' and 'passive' personality, meaning they may invoke the responsibility of other subjects of international law on the international plane in specific circumstances (essentially in the realms of investment), and on the other, be held accountable for their own internationally wrongful acts.[559] What we see here is that this area is in flux/contention. I argue in Chapter 6 that, following Wilson's suggestion, corporate ILP is now being 'pursued' by the GCC – even in the 'humanitarian' sphere, as part of a gradual move to the acceptance of a notion of pluralist global governance.[560]

More immediately telling than the deliberations around ILP in the various decisions is the fact that an individual businessman like Diallo was able to mobilise the ICJ for what were essentially his rights as an international businessman – in a similar manner as Mavrommatis had done several decades earlier. Rather than the USD 11 million compensation Diallo had claimed, the USD 95,000 the ICJ considered appropriate, caused dissenting judges Al-Khasawneh and Yusuf, invoking Frantz Fanon, or indeed *The International*, to note: '[T]he low standard of protection of shareholders under customary law is now confined to the wretched of the earth like Mr. Diallo ... we believe that this case sets a dangerous precedent for foreign investors unprotected by bilateral investment treaties'.[561]

556 Ibid.

557 Crawford 2010, p. 18.

558 Ibid.

559 Pellet 2010, pp. 7–8. Authors such as Brown Weiss have argued that non-state actors should be given the right to invoke state responsibility, which effectively corporations *already have*, in investment arbitration: Brown Weiss 2002, p. 816. See also Parfitt 2016.

560 Further, Baars 2011.

561 ICJ Diallo dissenting judgment of Al-Khasawneh and Yusuf. If there had been a BIT Mr Diallo would have had to make a claim as an individual shareholder/investor (because the companies were DRC-registered), which is not common in investment arbitration, but see the (now settled) Italian bondholders' 'class action' arbitration against Argentina (which is similar to the *Barcelona Traction* case – individual share/bondholders claiming) for loss that occurred as a result of Argentinian dictatorship abuses. Reuters, 4 February 2016 'World Bank arbitration on hold after Argentina debt deal with Italian creditors'. Another example of individuals claiming are the Zimbabwe white farmer cases resulting

In other words, facilitated by unequal treaties (BITs), concluded in the name of states, businesspersons, using particular (ideological, technical/legal, also epistemological) techniques including remaining outside the purview of public international law, by exercising personality only in private international law, asserting a *sui generis* position requiring its own set of rules, positing formal equality, etc. largely managed to escape the requirements of formal lawmaking and adjudication, the 'constitutional' elements of *public* international law. Likewise these arrangements remained outside of the 'liberal humanitarian impulse' and within the capitalist free market mandate, and outside of the IL *responsibility* domain. Yet, at the same time, we see the corporation making *some* headway as an ILP on the global level. In the following chapters we will see where this leads.

4 Class Law and Class Struggle in IL

International law, especially in the past 60 years and thus broadly in line with the general tendency of neoliberalism, has been said to be moving towards individualisation, both in the fields of rights and responsibilities, in particular in the creation of international human rights and humanitarian law, and its corollary international criminal law.[562] The explicit logic of capitalism, and the material effects it has produced, has created room for, and, I will argue, the need for, an outspoken discourse of 'humanitarianism'.[563] This needs to be seen in a context of an accompanying scholarly trend in which a plurality of actors is said to engage in global governance where both intergovernmental organisation, state and (only occasionally also) corporation function as normative agents.[564]

Above I have spoken mostly of events on the 'private' side of IL. On the 'public' side during the course of the twentieth century the discourse of law has gradually turned towards constitutionalisation, using the cosmopolitanism liberal humanitarian discourse. IL came to be seen as about, and for, peace and human rights.[565] 'Pluralist global governance', moreover, was supposed to

from Mugabe's expropriations of land from farmers who still had Swiss or German citizenship, allowing them to claim under, e.g., the Switzerland-Zimbabwe BIT. See, e.g., *Bernhard von Pezold and others v. Zimbabwe, ICSID Case No. ARB/10/15.*

562 E.g., McCorquodale 2010 p. 284.

563 E.g., Ashworth 1983; Meron 2006.

564 E.g., Sklair 1997; Kennedy 2006–07; Krisch 2010; also: Danielsen 2016; Kennedy 2016.

565 Generally, Meron 2006.

ensure close collaboration between states, the new supranational institutions, and, eventually, global corporations.[566]

This was of limited use in global class struggle. Apart from the earlier nationalising efforts by newly elected social democrat Third World leaders (e.g., Mossadegh), elements of such class struggle could be seen in the increasing assertiveness of newly decolonised Third World States and their allies in the 1960s and 1970s, expressed in a number of United Nations General Assembly Resolutions and Declarations including on Permanent Sovereignty over Natural Resources[567] and later the attempt to establish a New International Economic Order[568] and the Charter of Economic Rights and Duties of States.[569] While 120 of 138 General Assembly members supported the resolution, nearly all 'capital exporting states' voted against the Charter, abstained or did not vote.[570] The Third World states' assertion of ownership was the assertion of a

566 E.g., Mieville 2006, pp. 304ff.

567 The first such Resolution (*UN General Assembly PSNR Resolution*) is an ambiguous document, from which 'different interests could cite different provisions for their own purposes': Lowenfeld 2008, p. 489. The later two resolutions (GA Res 2158 (1966) and GA Res 3171 (1973)) are more favourable to host state rights, with the latter affirming 'that the application of the principle of nationalization carried out by States, as an expression of their sovereignty in order to safeguard their natural resources, implies that each State is entitled to determine the amount of possible compensation and the mode of payment, and that any disputes which might arise should be settled in accordance with the national legislation of each State carrying out such measures'.

568 General Assembly Resolution 3201 (S-VI). Declaration on the Establishment of a New International Economic Order, UN Doc. A/RES/S-6/3201, 1 May 1974 (*UN General Assembly New International Economic Order Resolution*).

569 The Charter includes, e.g.:
2. Each State has the right:
(*a*) *To regulate and exercise authority over foreign investment within its national jurisdiction in accordance with its laws and regulations and in conformity with its national objectives and priorities ...;*
(*b*) *To regulate and supervise the activities of transnational corporations within its national jurisdiction and take measures to ensure that such activities comply with its laws, rules and regulations and conform with its economic and social policies. Transnational corporations shall not intervene in the internal affairs of a host State ...;*
(*c*) *To nationalize, expropriate or transfer ownership of foreign property, in which case appropriate compensation should be paid by the State adopting such measures, taking into account its relevant laws and regulations and all circumstances that the State considers pertinent. In any case where the question of compensation gives rise to a controversy, it shall be settled under the domestic law of the nationalizing State ...*
Charter of Economic Rights and Duties of States, GA Res 3281 (1974) UN Doc A/RES/29/3281 (*UN General Assembly CERD*).

570 *UNGA CERD voting record.*

'mine not yours' nature. More precisely, however, it could also be seen as an assertion of *the right to dispose of oneself*.[571]

The class interest expressed in the New International Economic Order movement (which had sought to dismantle the master's house using the master's tools, international law) was absorbed into the international development agenda, which can be seen as having become a cloak for foreign direct investment (FDI) and a way of achieving competition among Third World countries for (public and private) 'development' loans. The term 'development' can be viewed as a euphemism for foreign direct investment, or, the global spread of capitalism and the corporate imperialist scramble for Third World resources, land and labour.[572]

Gathii argues that, through ILIP, the 'rules of international law have hollowed out the sovereignty of capital-importing States when they engage in transnational commercial activity'.[573] At the same time, Third World leaderships realise that 'foreign direct investment will not travel south without an arbitration clause in its luggage'.[574] Western MNC bargaining power as against the Third World state is congealed in this arbitration clause.[575] World Bank/IMF privatisation requirements leave Third World public services in (Western) private hands, while host state and private policing protects FDI property and personnel against host state citizens. As a result, many Third World states are no longer able to carry out important aspects of the 'public' function of the state internally – but are penetrated by the capitalising mission *through law*.[576]

When we connect the superstructural ideological developments discussed here to their material origins and effects, we are faced with an inherent tension between the trend to individualisation in IL and the corporation as putative subject of IL, as well as a contradiction between the position of the corporation as a subject of IL in some areas but not in others, the corporation's ability to *do* in IL, but not to be *done to*, in IL. The 'business and human rights' literature discussed in Chapter 1 appears to try to correct this, yet as always the story is more complex than this. If a lack of human rights is the problem, a solution can be proposed that does not disrupt the structures and basic premises of capitalism. The underlying question – and one of the 'red threads' through

571 Craven 2007, p. 259 ff.
572 Oxfam Land Grab Report.
573 Gathii 2010, p. 187.
574 Shalakany 2000, p. 422.
575 Viz., e.g., the statistic of Usman 2011, p. 294.
576 Subedi 2008, p. 2.

this book – is whether the law is capable of adopting a 'humanitarian' or perhaps anti-capitalist logic (the question of 'law's emancipatory potential') – and if not, what are we to make of the, apparently, humanitarian content of some IL, and moreover, how are we to achieve the stated aims of this humanitarian content, if not through law?

On the global level, institution building replicates the creation of states in the transition to capitalism (Chapter 2A, Section 4). As private rule-making, private provision of 'public' services, even private policing and private military become normalised and are considered legitimate (further discussed in Chapter 6), states lose much of their utility. 'Global governance' lifts many issues previously within the domestic jurisdiction of states to the international level of decision-making and coordination. Authority for this international regime is provided by the 'political' bodies and rule-sets, including the UN peace, human rights and development sectors, and in particular also the international formal legal infrastructure of the ICJ, and now also international criminal law and the ICC.

Yet, the liberal impulse expressed in 'humanitarian' rules, concepts, and institutions is not benign or innocent: 'The language of human rights is essential to the oversimplification of the roots of disorder in international society at present'.[577] At the same time, individuals are forced to become 'rights-entrepreneurs': in the same way that economic success is an individual's own responsibility, achieving one's 'human rights' becomes a matter of individual success or failure to negotiate in the state and supranational rights marketplace (see further Chapter 6). Moreover, as Pashukanis expressed it, 'law creates right by creating crime',[578] and rights violation can become used as a pretext for imperial intervention, as well as criminalisation of individuals, together 'legitimising' the party (or parties) acting as 'global policemen'.

5 Conclusion to 2B

Having looked at the specific ways in which law is employed by global classes – in ways that may affect responsibility for harm caused through their involvement in conflict – it seems possible to discern a number of structural trends. First, the deployment of the ideological devices of fragmentation and the public/private divide.

577 Carty 2007, p. 194.
578 Pashukanis 1978, p. 167.

Wilson surmises, 'the discursive separation of the private from the public as an autonomous legal realm effectively renders World Economy both a-political and extra-judicial, superseding the direct regulatory and legislative capacities of the "public", or "political", "Nation-State"'.[579] Similarly Anghie, 'one of the major responses of the West to the challenge of the Third World was to entrench neo-imperial economic relations in the private sphere'.[580] Also, 'public international law ... was ... used to further solidify the private realm and to enhance the immunity of private actors'.[581] This occurred through the espousal by states of corporate interests in courts, and through BITS. Positivism 'sealed' the artificial and deliberate split between a public and a private international law. Craven has shown that the public/private divide has particular consequences in the context of succession, which may also be seen as emblematic of IL in general. An 'implication of [the] separation between the public and private dimensions of succession ... is that the central function of the doctrine seemed to be to secure the primacy of capitalist relations of production – in which the relationship between the West and the periphery could be understood, above all else, in terms of the inclusion or exclusion of those societies that had not yet established the conditions for capitalism'.[582] Yet, securing the presence of Western corporations and creating (unequal, yet formally equal) states in the periphery in the Western image remedied this situation.

Sornarajah notes that 'the role of [powerful corporate] actors in the international legal system is seldom studied due to the dominance in the field of positivist views which stress that states are the only relevant actors in international relations. They provide a convenient cloak for hiding the absence of corporate liability'.[583] Once discovered by scholars in the business and human rights field, however, the logical sequence becomes the proposal of 'corporate liability' as the appropriate corrective to this situation. In the following chapters I show why it is not, or at least not from an emancipatory perspective. Additionally, scholars seem to prefer ignoring lawmaking by arbitrators and 'most highly qualified publicists' 'lest it shakes [*sic*] the hoary foundations on which their discipline is built'.[584] However, it would seem likely that those scholars, arbitrators and the 'most highly qualified publicists' (whose writings

579 Wilson 2008, p. 213; see also generally, Shalakany 2003.
580 Anghie 2007, p. 239.
581 Ibid.
582 Craven 2007, p. 45.
583 Sornarajah 2010, p. 6.
584 Sornarajah 2010, p. 5.

are named as a source of IL in Art. 38 of the Vienna Convention on the Law of Treaties)[585] are the very same.[586] Muthucumaraswamy Sornarajah comments:

> through the employment of private techniques of dispute resolution, they are able to create principles of law that are generally favourable to them. That they can bring about such outcomes through pressure on their states is obvious ... By employing low-order sources of international law such as decisions of arbitrators and the writings of 'highly qualified publicists', it is possible to employ vast private resources to ensure that a body of law favourable to multinational corporations is created.[587]

There is an element of competition/conflict of interest between *practising* lawyers, and (other) businesspersons, but ultimately the dynamic is that of class.

At the same time, business people are also effective users of IL – even if they are at times 'disowned' by politicians. They manage to find their way into the state-only institutions such as the PCIJ/ICJ, to have the basic parameters of law set (and in one case even 'through a curious combination of circumstances'[588] a specific tribunal to deal with (mainly) commercial interests – the Iran–United States Claim Tribunal). At the same time they manage to shape their rules elsewhere in more flexible environments – in arbitrations but also more generally through 'business as usual', namely repeat practice of major corporations, trendsetting in the field. With the participation of business elites in rule-creation the situation has changed little from that of the 1920s when, according to Pashukanis, international law was constructed around the common interest of the ruling classes of different capitalist states: 'international law owes its existence to the fact that the bourgeoisie exercises its domination over the proletariat and over colonial countries'.[589]

Fragmentation is one of the particular techniques (ideological moves) employed for this purpose, division between civilised and uncivilised, domestic and international, public and private, between old and new legal rules, and between 'functionally separate' regimes of law.[590] Benvenisti posits:

---

585 *1969 Vienna Convention on the Law of Treaties.*

586 E.g., the ICSID list of concluded cases as at 1 November 2016 lists, among others, Vaughan Lowe, P.M. Dupuy, Andreas Lowenfeld, Christian Tomuschat, Brigitte Stern, Philippe Sands, James Crawford, Laurence Boisson de Chazournes and Georges Abi-Saab as arbitrators.

587 Sornarajah 2010, p. 5.

588 See Lowenfeld 2008, p. 541ff.

589 Pashukanis 2006, p. 325.

590 The word *fragmentation* suggests the breaking up of a whole, while I argue here that the

> Powerful states labor to maintain and even actively promote fragmentation because it enables them to preserve their dominance in an era in which hierarchy is increasingly viewed as illegitimate, and to opportunistically break the rules without seriously jeopardizing the system they have created. Fragmentation accomplishes this ... by creating institutions along narrow, functionalist lines and restricting the scope of multilateral agreements ... [and] by suggesting the absence of design and obscuring the role of intentionality, fragmentation frees powerful states from having to assume responsibility for the shortcomings of a global legal system that they themselves have played the major role in creating. The result is a regulatory order that reflects the interests of the powerful that they alone can alter.[591]

Instead of 'powerful states', I have argued here, the GCC, members of governing and business elites, are the relevant actors, employing law, on a (racialised, gendered) capitalising mission, to create the global market society.

Anghie has described how 'international law [has] ... legitimized colonial exploitation'[592] – which, as I have argued, was an important phase in the transition to the global market society. Anghie focuses on the 'civilising mission' as the racist animator of colonialism. In my view, the 'civilising mission' functions mostly as a (*post hoc*[593]) ideological cloak for economically rational behaviour and is not an actual motivation in itself. This cloak continues to cover the 'failure to decolonise' or, rather, the continuing presence of racialised corporate imperialism *through* international law. In Miéville's words, 'International law is a constituent part of the dynamic of modernity'.[594]

This was explicit up to the end of the nineteenth century, but globalising IL required a 'humanitarian' makeover. In Craven's words: 'Decolonization was a moment of disciplinary anxiety and introspection; a moment at which the emancipation of the colonized world had to be accompanied by the simultaneous emancipation of the idea of international law'.[595] The ideological move of the 'decolonisation of international law' was intended to wash the blood of past

---

effort is to keep separate those 'fragments' that may never have been part of a whole. The motivations and effects described by authors cited here still apply, however.

591 Benvenisti 2007, p. 595.

592 Anghie 2007, p. 2.

593 It tends to be the lawyers, philosophers, and theologians who seek to provide legitimisation in retrospect.

594 Miéville 2006, p. 226.

595 Craven 2007, p. 6.

colonialism off the hands of law. *Contra* Craven, I argue that this process commenced much earlier, with liberal impulses finding their way into international law with the advancement of so-called humanitarian areas of law including the prohibition on slave trade and those on the means and methods of warfare in the late nineteenth century, with the increased visibility of the individual in IL, both of which rapidly progressed with the Nuremberg and Tokyo trials after World War Two.

In these, we partially see the 'public' and 'private' collide, the discourse of liberalism and the logic of capitalism speak against one another, the individual businesspersons practice 'corporate imperialism' but reappear out of the corporate structure, and the ideological play of humanitarian law turn absurd.

6 Afterword to 2A and 2B: the Modern Corporation and Criminal Law

The development of domestic law on 'corporate crime' in the UK (and the US) perfectly mirrors the process of reification, and eventually, anthropomorphisation, of the corporation. In the late nineteenth century, Judge Thurlow famously asked, 'Did you ever expect a corporation to have a conscience, when it has no soul to be damned, and no body to be kicked?'[596] When norms of crime and punishment were abstracted from religious, emotional sentiment and became 'accountable', attitudes towards corporate criminal liability began to change, most likely first for practical reasons, however, rather than as a result of academic theorising.[597] In the UK, from as early as 1842, a 'corporation aggregate' could be held criminally liable for failing to fulfil a statutory duty.[598] This follows the joint liability of earlier forms of organisation as discussed in Section 4.1 above, and the logic that it made sense to seek financial recompense from large (here, railway) companies rather than indict individual employees for 'minor' offenses. In 1917 vicarious liability of a corporation (as *legal person*) for the acts of its employees and agents became a possibility in another rail-

596 Quoted in Coffee 1980–81, p. 386.

597 Bush 2009, p. 1052; Canfield 1914; Edgerton 1927. No 'anthropomorphising' of the corporation, nor notions of '*corporate* corporate crime' (see Ch. 4 below) existed at this point: in *Edwards v. Midland Railway*, Justice Fry had held that 'it is equally absurd to suppose that a body corporate can do a thing willfully, which implies will; intentionally, which implies intent; maliciously, which implies malice'. *Edwards v. Midland Railway* (1880).

598 'A corporation aggregate may be indicted by their corporate name for disobedience to an order of justices requiring such corporation to execute works pursuant to a statute'. *Birmingham and Gloucester Rly* [1842]; Ormerod 2008, p. 247.

ase.[599] In the mid-1940s the UK courts[600] accepted corporate criminal ıty for crimes requiring a 'guilty mind' on the basis of the guilty mind of a ıtrolling officer',[601] in a construction that was a decade later to be described in memorable terms by Lord Denning:

> A company may in many ways be likened to a human body. It has a brain and nerve centre which controls what it does. It also has hands which hold the tools and act in accordance with directions from the centre. Some of the people in the company are mere servants and agents who are nothing more than hands to do the work and cannot be said to represent the mind or will. Others are directors and managers who represent the directing mind and will of the company, and control what it does. The state of mind of these managers is the state of mind of the company and is treated by the law as such.[602]

In Chapter 3 I uncover to what extent this reification 'holds' in the face of accusations of serious 'international' crimes. From this notion, eventually the current, fully anthropomorphised 'corporate *corporate* crime' discussed in Chapter 6 would evolve.[603] In Chapter 6, I also come back to the moralisation of the 'good' company through corporate social responsibility, and comment on the legitimising roles of CSR and corporate crime for corporate power.

---

599 *Mousell Bros v. London and North-Western Railway Co.* [1917] (employees of a company evading toll).

600 In the US a similar development took place, some years before the UK, on breach of statutory duty (1834) vicarious liability (1852), moving to attributing mens rea of an officer to the company in 1909: *People v. Corporation of Albany* (1834) (non-feasance); *State v. Morris* Essex (1852) (misfeasance); *New York Central & Hudson River Railroad Company v. US* (1909); Stessens 1994, pp. 496–7.

601 *DPP v. Kent and Sussex Contractors* [1944], approved in *Rex v. ICR Haulage* [1944]; Ormerod 2008, p. 248.

602 *HL Bolton (Engineering) Co. Ltd. v. T.J. Graham & Sons Ltd.* [1957], 172.

603 See also, e.g., Simester 2010, pp. 272 ff.; French and Ryan 2009, pp. 629 ff.

CHAPTER 3

Capitalism's Victors' Justice? The Economics of World War Two, the Allies' Trials of the German Industrialists and Their Treatment of the Japanese *zaibatsu*

1 Introduction to 3A and 3B

Telford Taylor, who was the Chief Prosecutor for the subsequent trials at Nuremberg, wrote in his memoirs:

> The root circumstances which gave rise to the laws of war as we know them today are part of the great waves of change that swept Western civilization in the eighteenth and nineteenth centuries ... humanitarianism played a part in the development of these laws, but the prime motivations were commercial and military. They were, in fact, very largely the product of what Dwight Eisenhower, when retiring from the presidency, called the 'military-industrial complex'.[1]

In the previous chapter I have shown how both what we now call 'domestic' and 'international' law were developed to further the interests of capital. I also showed how in domestic (company) law the notion of 'responsibility' became commodified and available for exchange, while in international law the company managed to stay out of the purview of responsibility by appearing as a legal person in some instances but not in others. I also commented on the relationship between capitalism and racialised imperialism, and on the notion of a global capitalist class, where the identity of military, state and commercial agents partly overlaps, and where their interests largely converge despite short-term clashes or competition between them. In this chapter, I note how the Nuremberg trials (the main trial but especially the trials of the industrialists) were the first instance of the processes of law that today's 'business and human rights' lawyers advocate being actualised. Here we saw for the first time corporate involvement in racialised imperialist war, genocide, slave labour on an

1 Taylor 1992, p. 5.

industrial scale, and other gross violations addressed in a court of law, indeed of international criminal law. However, rather than a momentous corporate accountability achievement, I show in this chapter that the international criminal law developed by the Nuremberg and Tokyo tribunals was in fact a *product* of the military-industrial complex in Japan and Germany, on the one hand, and the military-industrial and legal-political complex in the United States, on the other. Rather than restraining business involvement in conflict, the criminal trials following World War Two, in what I will call a display of 'canned morality', *served* the prevailing mode of production, by allowing 'liberal lawyers' to express their individual humanitarianism and through this to construct the ideological 'play' of the trials, while simultaneously creating a 'diversion' for far-reaching economic intervention.

In the immediate aftermath of the war, the Allies expressed their consensus (e.g., through the measures announced in the Potsdam Agreement)[2] that World War Two on both the Western and Eastern fronts had been a war for markets and resources carried out by a combination of the political and military might of the state of both Japan and Germany, and the resources, productive capacity and finance of the industrial giants. The means were matched by the motivation: the imperialist drive to expansion at the core of the capitalist state and corporation. In this chapter, I first discuss how and why the decision to hold criminal trials for the prosecution of the authors of the war was taken – and how this was explained to relevant publics. I also discuss the US post-war economic policies – and investigate the relation between the trials and the economic reforms implemented by the US in Japan and Germany/Europe. With the start of the Cold War 18 months after the end of World War Two, US foreign and economic policy changed dramatically. I show here that this change is reflected in the conduct, discourse and outcome of the trials, in particular in the US 'subsequent trials'. I argue that the change in US attitude towards the vanquished powers, from one of punishment to one of rehabilitation, turned the trials from morality plays into theatre of the absurd, with the trial judges going to great lengths to exculpate the defendants, often not without a sense of irony. Most important, with the commencement of the Cold War, the role of economic actors in instigating World War Two, which had once been a point of agreement among the Allies, became a point of sharp ideological divide. Henceforth the 'economic case', as it had been called in the main international trial at Nuremberg, has been ignored in the Western literature and remained visible only in GDR/Soviet discourse. Likewise, the omission of *zaibatsu* lead-

2 *1945 Potsdam Agreement* – excerpt in Appendix B.

ers from the Tokyo International Tribunal hid the Allies' expressed conviction that the war on the Eastern front had also been one of racialised economic imperialism.

Contrary to what we might have expected following the development of the corporate form as discussed in Chapter 2A, the construct of the corporation as a mechanism to minimise individual exposure failed to protect the directors and other high officials of some of the main German companies after the war. The 'progressive' liberal move to individual responsibility for what were previously considered 'state crimes' prevented the acceptance of corporate, rather than individual, liability for the businesses involved (although the possibility was debated and would find its echo decades later: Section 6.1.2; Chapter 4). The *anomie* – or imperialism at the core of the corporation (Chapter 2A) – is reflected in the way defendants describe their own roles and their own views on their (lack of) culpability (Sections 6 and 7). Moreover, the nature of imperialist corporate abuse (imperialism of the corporation) during World War Two, in both the East and West, shows great similarities with the accumulation by dispossession, as well as the physical violence, of the colonial period, as illustrated in Chapter 2B.

Part A of this chapter deals with the Allied responses to the economic aspects of World War Two in Germany, and Part B with Allied policy in the aftermath of World War Two in regard to Japan. In a joint conclusion to Parts A and B I compare the German and Japanese trajectories and draw broader conclusions about the relation between the particular material context existing at the time and the decision to employ international criminal law and ask what inferences can be drawn from the post-World War Two experience for the future application of ICL to corporate actors, leading to the questions I will seek to answer in the following chapters.

3A Germany: The Nuremberg International Military Tribunal, or, the Theatre of Law[3]

1 Introduction to 3A

Any discussion of Nuremberg and the subsequent trials is inevitably coloured by the availability of material. To explain the particular effect of a very partial availability of materials on the post-World War Two trials, I start this chapter with a brief discussion of the sources employed. This is followed by a dis-

3 An earlier version of Chapter 3A has been published as Baars 2013b.

cussion of the process that led to the decision to hold international criminal trials after World War Two and an exploration of the underlying motivations. In Section 4, I describe the lead-up to the main international trial at Nuremberg, with a particular focus on the treatment of the 'economic case', and the debates around the inclusion/exclusion of the industrialists – in order to highlight what has been forgotten in contemporary accounts of World War Two.[4]

Then in Section 6 I examine the Americans' decision to hold 'subsequent trials' at Nuremberg, partly motivated by the *lawyers'* expressed wish to try industrialists. As during the course of these trials US policy towards Germany/Europe changed dramatically (Section 5), I show how this change reflects in the trials – concretely, in material differences between the decisions in the subsequent trials compared with the International Military Tribunal ('IMT') judgment, in similar facts being judged differently, and legal concepts being explained and applied differently. More generally, I comment on the changed discourse in the subsequent proceedings, and pay attention to the representations made by the defendants and the judges on the role of business in conflict. Finally, I examine the aftermath of the trials, commenting on the post-trial treatment of the lawyers, and the further course of the industrialists. In Section 7 I comment on the other Allies' trials in their respective zones of occupation, including the prosecution of Röchling and colleagues by the French Occupation authorities, Tesch and Wittig by the British, and Topf by the Soviets. Each of these reveals the respective Ally's own political objectives.

1.1 *Sources*

The fact that 'Nuremberg'[5] and the subsequent proceedings were largely a US-dominated event is reinforced for today's researchers as most of the available materials are US-produced and published. Although I carried out this research in Germany, by far the most plentiful and detailed resources were the online US government archives, detailing the deliberations and discussions leading up to, and surrounding, the various US decisions, and trials. Some measure of similar material is available in the UK National Archives, in largely unorganised hard copy files. No documentation is available online for the UK military cases. Summaries of some cases are included in the 15-volume 'Law Reports of Trials of War Criminals' published by the United Nations War Crimes

4 E.g., Merriman 2009, Ch. 26.

5 I follow many commentators in using the term 'Nuremberg' as a shorthand to denote the post-World War Two Allied trials in Germany as a phenomenon.

Commission ('WCCLR')[6] – the remainder of the material is stored in paper form in the National Archives, while full texts for the French Röchling case are stored in archives in Germany and France.[7] Because of linguistic limitations I was unable to research Soviet cases except by means of one translated bundle.[8] In contrast, the US authorities have published a full record of the London Agreement negotiations, with minutes of private meetings, several drafts of the agreement, and reports by government officials.[9] Further records offering an insight into the decision-making around Nuremberg are available from the US Senate, e.g., Senator Kilgore's sub-committee investigating German industry.[10] In addition, many US intelligence documents were declassified in 2000, and were described and commented on in a 2007 working group report.[11]

The official record of the Nuremberg IMT trial is published in 'The Blue Series', a 42-volume series of books containing the official record of the proceedings. This is supplemented by 'The Red Series' or 'Nazi Conspiracy and Aggression', an 8-volume, 12-book series, with the subtitle 'Collection of Documentary Evidence and Guide Materials Prepared by the American and British Prosecuting Staffs for Presentation before the International Military Tribunal at Nurnberg, Germany'.[12] This series includes scanned original documents used in evidence, transcripts of pre-trial interrogations and summaries of investigations carried out by the US and British prosecution teams. The subsequent proceedings are published by the US government in a 15-volume set, the 'Trials of War Criminals Before the Nuremberg Military Tribunals Under Control Council Law No. 10' or the 'Green Series'.[13] All of these US resources are publicly available through the Library of Congress ('LoC') online collection.

---

6 *WCCLR*.

7 I am grateful to Fabian Schellhaas (Ph.D. Candidate at the Humboldt University of Berlin) for a copy of the *Röchling Case* decision from the German National Archive at Koblenz.

8 *Prozeßmaterialien*.

9 E.g., Report to the President by Mr Justice Jackson, United States Representative to the International Conference on Military Trials, June 6, 1945, published as Section VIII (p. 42) of the record of negotiations at the London Conference of June 26 to August 8, 1945, in Department of State Publication 3080, International Organization and Conference Series II, U.S. Government Printing Office, Released February 1949 (*Jackson Negotiations Report*), Report to the President by Mr Justice Jackson, October 7, 1946, published as document LXIII of *Jackson Negotiations Report* (*Jackson Final Report*).

10 *Kilgore Report*.

11 Nazi War Crimes and Japanese Imperial Government Records Interagency Working Group, Final Report to the United States Congress, Published April 2007 (*2007 IWG Report*).

12 *Blue Series*; *Red Series*.

13 *Green Series*.

The private archives of some of the key US personalities at the time yielded much material: the 'Morgenthau Diaries';[14] the Robert H. Jackson Center Research Archive;[15] the Telford Taylor Papers at Columbia Law School;[16] and the Hebert Nuremberg Files collection at Louisiana University Library, which includes scans of handwritten notes the judge took during the IG Farben trial as well as a draft dissenting judgment that was never submitted.[17] The Harold S. Truman Library and Museum holds interviews with many individuals involved in the trials in its oral history collection.[18] Finally, many of the US and other Allied lawyers involved in the trials have published personal memoirs and perspectives on the trials, including Ferencz,[19] Jackson,[20] Taylor,[21] Calvocoressi,[22] and Vishinsky.[23] British army investigator Airey Neave, who served the indictments on the Nuremberg defendants, published his memoirs.[24] One of the German defence lawyers at Nuremberg, Kranzbühler, has published his commentary[25] while a great number of the defendants have written autobiographies, including Schacht and Von Knieriem, the board member and corporate counsel of IG Farben.[26]

I have used the UK National Archives at Kew for the Tesch, Wittig and Mitsugu trials. Excerpts of the German post-World War Two trials are published online by the University of Amsterdam.[27]

Most scholarly writing on the issue also again comes from the US. Few British, or other European, legal scholars have reflected on Nuremberg, though some focus on specific legal questions.[28] In particular a number of German aca-

14 Parts of which are published in German: Schild 1970, p. 64 ff.; and in English in Blum 1959–67 (three volumes).
15 *Jackson Archive*.
16 *Taylor Archive*.
17 *Hebert Archive*.
18 *Truman Library*.
19 E.g., Ferencz 1999; *Ferencz Library*.
20 See also the bibliography in Taylor 1992, p. 680.
21 Taylor 1992.
22 Calvocoressi 1947.
23 A bibliography containing sources in various languages can be found in Frei 2006, pp. 603–46.
24 Neave 1982.
25 Kranzbühler 2008, pp. 433–44.
26 E.g., Schacht 1956; Von Knieriem 1953.
27 *Nazi Crimes on Trial* http://www.junsv.nl/.
28 E.g., Kelsen 1947, p. 165.

demic lawyers have provided descriptive accounts.[29] Unfortunately, Polish and Soviet primary sources and secondary literature are inaccessible to me insofar as it has not been translated – and little of it has been, although historians have published on them in English.[30] The zonal trials held by the Allies have received very little treatment in the academic literature.[31] A notable exception is the historian Norbert Frei's edited collection 'Transnationale Vergangenheitspolitik', which also includes chapters (and an extensive bibliography) on the treatment of World War Two war crimes suspects in Germany and many other European countries and the Soviet Union.[32] Frei and Schanetzky have also published a collection specifically on firms in the Third Reich.[33] Besides the case reports and associated documentation, the memoirs of prosecution lawyers Dubois[34] and Sasuly[35] provide the main insight into the background to these trials. There has been a recent surge in interest in the trials of the industrialists – unsurprisingly coinciding with the current interest in ICL in general and 'corporate responsibility' in particular, with new publications being published and prepared.[36]

Aside from the materials related to the trials specifically, the papers related to the US administration of Germany and Japan, the US Library of Congress has also published the declassified 'Enactments and approved papers of the Control Council, Coordinating Committee and Allied Control Authority for Germany'.[37] Alongside and long after the zonal trials had ended, many domestic

29 Noteworthy is the absence of 'Nuremberg' (and World War Two more generally) in Grewe 1984. For recent examples, see e.g., Burchard 2006, p. 800.

30 E.g., Hirsch 2008; Prusin 2003 and 2010. Prusin describes the seven cases of the Polish Supreme National Tribunal (Najwyższy Trybunał Narodowy – NTN): 'Established specifically for the purpose of prosecuting major Nazi perpetrators and collaborators, the NTN adjudicated seven high-profile cases between 1946 and 1948. During the course of these trials, 49 defendants were charged with war crimes and crimes against humanity. In fact, among the former Soviet satellites, Poland was the most consistent in investigating and prosecuting war crimes: between 1944 and 1985, Polish courts tried more than 20,000 defendants, including 5,450 German nationals'. None of the seven NTN trials involved business leaders, but one would think that several will have been among the latter cases.

31 But see, e.g., Ueberschär 1999, Bush 2009, Heller 2011.

32 Frei 2006.

33 Frei and Schanetzky 2010.

34 Dubois 1952.

35 Sasuly 1952; Sasuly 1947. The role of IG Farben in World War Two and the *IG Farben Case* has attracted by far the most commentary of all 'subsequent trials'; see, e.g., Borkin 1978; Ferencz 2002; Neumann 1963; Hayes 2000.

36 See Chapter 5 below; and see, e.g., Bush 2009; Jeßberger 2010; Frei 2010; Heller 2011; Van Baar and Huisman 2012; Karstedt 2015.

37 Library of Congress online collection: http://www.loc.gov/rr/frd/Military_Law/enactments-home.html.

courts in Europe and elsewhere continued to hear cases related to World War Two, although in Germany, 'Hitler's Elites', the doctors, businessmen, lawyers, journalists, and officers were able to continue or return to their posts without much upheaval.[38]

2 From War to Trials: Why 'Nuremberg'?

It is striking that the main ICL texts invariably describe *that*, and also *how*, in the practical sense, the Allies came to try the Nazi leaders at Nuremberg, but not *why* they did so.[39] It is as if criminal trials, and the development of an ICL, were simply the next logical step in the progression of the IL enterprise. In the context of this book, the *why* question is important, not least, as Falk puts it, because '[i]n a fundamental sense, as with human rights, it is difficult to comprehend why sovereign states should ever have been willing to validate such a subversive idea as that of the international criminal accountability of leaders for war crimes. It goes directly against the spirit and ideology of sovereignty'.[40] Answering this question allows us to reveal '*the relationships that are expressed in the legal superstructure and those that it ideologically spirits away*'.[41] In this section I examine how 'Nuremberg' and 'Tokyo' were explained publicly, while I also consider what may have been alternative underlying objectives and structural causes.

As early as 1942, in the Joint Declaraton for the Punishment of War Criminals, commonly referred to as the *St. James Declaration*, the Allies had vowed to 'place among their principal war aims the punishment, through the channel of organised justice, of those guilty of or responsible for [acts of violence against civilians contrary to international law, and in particular the 1907 Hague Conventions], whether they have ordered them, perpetrated them, or participated in them'.[42] The meaning of 'organised' was more straightforward than that of 'justice', which took longer to decide than contemporary accounts might suggest. The 16-member United Nations War Crimes Commission,[43] which

38 Frei 2003.

39 Cryer 2009; Werle 2009, p. 7; but see, generally, Simpson 2007, esp. Chs. 4 and 5.

40 Falk 1998–99, p. 710.

41 Arthur 1978, p. 31.

42 *1942 St James Declaration.*

43 The commission derives its name from the conference, where the participants called themselves 'the united nations' (Werle 2009, p. 8); on the establishment of the United Nations, the Commission became the UN's War Crimes Commission. For a short history of the Commission, see Current Notes, AJIL 39(3) 1945 pp. 565–79.

first met on 20 October 1943, immediately commenced collecting evidence of the commission of war crimes through its London office and national sub-commissions in the Nazi-occupied countries and in the Far East. Ten days later, on 30 October, in Moscow, Churchill, Stalin and Roosevelt issued the Moscow Declarations, and largely echoing the 1942 Declaration, added a 'Declaration on Atrocities' announcing 'German criminals … will be punished by joint decision of the government of the Allies'.[44]

While these declarations were mere statements of intent, perhaps mostly made to function as deterrents to the Nazis, they did put the question of trials on the agenda. The Declaration on Atrocities, largely drafted by Winston Churchill, was, according to Taylor, his attempt to bring the other allies round to a punishment of 'German criminals' without trial.[45] Churchill favoured summary execution.[46] The Soviets saw the Nazis' crimes as already clearly proven, and favoured holding short hearings just to determine punishment. In the US, Roosevelt's sudden death on 12 April brought to the fore President Truman, who was persuaded of the desirability of trials by Stimson, the lawyer at the head of the War Department. Eventually, when Hitler and Goebbels committed suicide on 30 April and 1 May 1945, Churchill also gave in to the idea of trials.[47] One way of viewing this moment is as the *triumph of liberalism* (*liberal legalism*) over the barbarism of the war (cf. the 'civilising mission' discourse above, Chapter 2B), and also over prior ways of dealing with the vanquished in the aftermath of war. While European leaders had failed to prosecute the German Kaiser after World War One,[48] now their United States counterparts would take the lead to 'stay the hand of vengeance'.[49]

This was the nascent hegemon's moment to shape the IL system of the future: 'Any legal position asserted on behalf of the United States w[ould] have considerable significance in the future evolution of International Law'.[50] According to Taylor, the idea of war crimes trials originated in US War Department and was 'pretty fully developed' there.[51] While negotiations were still ongoing, Stimson and his colleagues had already made significant progress in outlining the 'Nuremberg ideas', which included the conspiracy charge and the aggressive war charge. Stimson's personal conviction driving this effort was that

44 *1943 Declaration on Atrocities.*
45 Taylor 1992, pp. 28–31. What follows draws on Taylor 1992, pp. 1–40, unless otherwise stated.
46 Taylor 1992, p. 30.
47 Taylor 1992, pp. 32–3.
48 Werle 2009, pp. 4–6.
49 *Jackson IMT Opening Address.*
50 Taylor 1992, p. 73.
51 Taylor 1992, p. 4.

international law would be complete only if its violation would lead to *individual* criminal responsibility.[52] As a corollary to the outlawing of aggressive war in *Versailles*, IL needed individual criminal responsibility for initiating and waging such a war.[53]

On 2 May 1945, Truman appointed Robert Jackson, then Associate Justice of the Supreme Court, as Representative of the United States and Chief of Counsel.[54] On 3 May 1945 the Allied foreign ministers – who were in San Francisco for the United Nations' foundational conference – riding on the 'mood of liberal internationalism'[55] discussed and agreed upon Stimson's plan for war crimes trials. Subsequently, Jackson's negotiations report was presented as the official US position statement and placed before all delegations to the London Conference in August. Jackson, according to his own account, enjoyed an unusually wide margin of authority to negotiate an agreement in London, while 'the Foreign Ministers became engaged in other things'.[56] The contents of Jackson's report were adopted in the London Agreement of 8 August 1945.[57] All allies had sent legally trained negotiators.[58] Vishinsky, the Soviet representative, remarked, 'The reason we were able to get an agreement was that it was left to the lawyers instead of diplomats'.[59] Many of the London Agreement's negotiators later appeared as prosecutors or judges at the IMT.[60] Justice Jackson became the Nuremberg Tribunal's chief prosecutor, and with that one of the best-known names attached to the Nuremberg trials.

Taylor surmises that although the initial pressure for post-war trials came from the peoples of the German-occupied nations,[61] in a real sense the trial was conceptualised and pushed by a handful of elite US lawyers 'with a strong sense of noblesse oblige'.[62] The Allied Declarations, then, could be regarded as the public result of private efforts by (mainly US) government lawyers, who as part of their class and profession had a keen sense of the ideological and

52 Taylor 1992, p. 37.

53 See the discussion at *Jackson Negotiations Report*, pp. 65–7, 295, 327, 335.

54 Quoted in Taylor 1992, p. 39.

55 *Luban Lecture* 2007.

56 Jackson 1946, p. 4.

57 Final Report to the Secretary of the Army on the Nuernberg War Crimes Trials under Control Council Law No. 10, Telford Taylor, et al., (1949) (*Taylor Final Report*) with Appendix B: Nuremberg Trials: War Crimes and International Law 27 International Conciliation 1 April 1949, No. 450 (*Taylor IC*) at 247 [I follow the IC page numbering here, running 243–371].

58 Jackson 1949, p. 816.

59 Ibid.

60 E.g., the Soviet lawyer Nikitchenko.

61 And the American Jewish Conference and the War Refugee Board (Taylor 1992, p. 35).

62 Taylor 1992, pp. 4, 42.

material role and purpose of law. What is harder to grasp is the motivations of the US president in approving the idea: Did the president bend to the wishes of the lawyers or were there other reasons behind the decision? A hint of two further aims is given by Taylor: 'To give meaning to the war against Germany. To validate the casualties we have suffered and the destruction and casualties we have caused' and secondly, 'to establish and maintain harmonious relations with the other United Nations'.[63] 'Essentially, in the minds of Stimson and his colleagues, their prime purpose was to bring the weight of law and criminal sanctions to bear in support of the peaceful and humanitarian principles that the United Nations was to promote by consultation and collective action'.[64] Falk adds two further reasons: 'the guilty conscience of the West that not enough had been done to protect the victims of Nazi persecution before or during the war itself (for example, the regular refusal of liberal democracies to accept Jewish refugees and the failure to bomb the railroad tracks leading to Auschwitz)'.[65]

Jackson became the embodiment of the humanitarian, liberal impulse that drove the trials and illuminated his many passionate speeches. He explained the rationale for the Nuremberg trial as at once natural: '[at] length, bestiality and bad faith reached such excess that they aroused the sleeping strength of imperilled Civilisation'[66] and in the interest of sovereignty: '[t]he wrongs which we seek to condemn and punish have been so calculated, so malignant and so devastating, that civilisation cannot tolerate their being ignored, because it cannot survive their being repeated'.[67] The Charter was endorsed by many countries, which became co-signatories, meaning, in Jackson's words, that it represented 'an organised act which represents the wisdom, the sense of justice, and the will of twenty-one governments, representing an overwhelming majority of all civilised people'.[68] In his notes, Jackson added, the trials were 'demanded by the conscience of the world'.[69] As such, Jackson's speech continues, 'the real complaining party at [the IMT] bar is Civilisation'.[70]

At the same time, the specifically American elite's ultimately *economic* interest was also reflected in the opening speech:

---

63 Taylor 1992, p. 50.
64 Taylor 1992, pp. 4, 42.
65 Falk 1998–99, p. 711.
66 *IMT, Jackson Opening Address*, at 4.
67 *IMT, Jackson Opening Address*, at 3.
68 *IMT, Jackson Opening Address*, at 37.
69 Jackson 1946, p. 220.
70 *IMT, Jackson Opening Address*, at 3, 46.

> The American dream of a peace-and-plenty economy, as well as the hopes of other nations, can never be fulfilled if those nations are involved in a war every generation so vast and devastating as to crush the generation that fights and burden the generation that follows. But experience has shown that wars are no longer local. All modern wars become world wars eventually. And none of the big nations at least can stay out. If we cannot stay out of wars, our only hope is to prevent wars.[71]

We can see here an early version of the idea of the US as 'policeman of the world', and a justification for intervention in other countries' affairs for the protection and furtherance of economic interests, or the emergence of the US as an imperial force. The American *people* were addressed also, so as to come on board with the idea of this intervention in a situation which for most Americans seemed quite remote. Jackson talks of how the people of the US came to see the Nazi rulers as a 'pack of brigands', whose crimes caused a feeling of outrage, while it became more and more felt that these affected Americans at home: 'these were crimes committed against us and against the whole society of civilised nations ... I believe that those instincts of our people were right and that they should guide us as the fundamental tests of criminality'.[72] Moreover, the home public had to be persuaded that their sacrifice had been worth it: In this latter sense, the trials can be seen as a 'morality play', aimed at producing charismatic authority for the Western victor and his ideology.[73] On the other hand, the US leadership wanted to (had to) satisfy public demand for supporting the war effort, also in possible future wars. The price paid for the 'bodybags' had to be reasonable and the readiness to go to war and defend the nation had to be maintained. Moreover, trying German war criminals allowed the creation of an ideological distance between the Nazi leaders and the (also often openly anti-Semitic) Allied leaderships.[74] By painting a vivid picture of the evil of the Nazis, the Allies looked 'clean' in comparison, and in this way the trial supported the emergence of the US as global hegemonic force.

To fend off the accusation of victor's justice, finally, Jackson warned:

> We must never forget that the record on which we judge these defendants to-day is the record on which history will judge us to-morrow. To pass

71 *IMT, Jackson Opening Address*, at 3.

72 Jackson 1946, p. 220.

73 Glasbeek 2009, p. 125.

74 E.g., UK Prime Minister Eden, who refused to adopt Auschwitz survivors as refugees (*Dubois Oral History Interview*).

> these defendants a poisoned chalice is to put it to our lips as well. We must summon such detachment and intellectual integrity to our task that this trial will commend itself to posterity as fulfilling humanity's aspirations to do justice.[75]

Here, ICL is presented as applying equally to wrongdoers in an international society of formally, legally equal states. It shows the ideological force of the performance of subjecting oneself to a supranational disciplinary regime. Whether this subjection was genuine, naïve, or its presentation cynical, is assessed in this and the next chapters.[76]

In conclusion, it would seem reasonable to surmise that 'Nuremberg' came about, on the one hand, through the perseverance of lawyers, to some extent endowed with a sense of mission and ambition to be 'jurisgenerative',[77] and, like lawyers generally, being predisposed to seeking legal solutions to problems. Jackson states in 1947, '[a]s the lawyer is the most frequently chosen legislator, diplomat, executive and political leader, the intellectual discipline which we call "the law" saturates Western World statesmanship and diplomacy'. And, '[a]t the opening of this tortured and bloody century, law-trained men dominated the councils of most Western nations'.[78] On the other hand, the political leadership considered the trial-route advantageous and in line with the objective of asserting the US elite's moral leadership at this important juncture in world history. The international trial at Nuremberg would form the cornerstone of the Allies' post-World War Two policy, its main public spectacle and means of communication to home audiences and the wider world.

3 The US Occupation and Economic Reform of Germany

Behind the scenes, the plan on the US government table was for a 'pastoralised Germany' – a Germany broken up and stripped of all its economic might, that would never again be able to wage an aggressive war. This plan had been authored in 1943–44 by US Treasury Secretary Henry Morgenthau, then Roosevelt's right-hand man. The Plan connected with the ongoing programme of investigation into German industry, in particular into the US-based offices

75 *IMT, Jackson Opening Address* at 5.
76 See also Falk 1998–99, p. 706.
77 *Luban RHJ Lecture*.
78 Jackson 1949, p. 813.

and subsidiaries of German firms and the worldwide activities of some of the cartels, such as IG Farben, whose assets were frozen or expropriated.[79] Morgenthau's controversial plan was largely adopted on 25 April 1945 in the guise of Joint Chiefs of Staff Decision 1067 ('JCS 1067').[80] Some months later echoes of the plan were found in the Potsdam Agreement which was concluded at the close of the Potsdam Conference on 2 August by the USSR, the UK and the US.[81] The Potsdam Agreement established and regulated the Allied Control Council for the governance of occupied Germany, and provided for it 'to carry out programs of industrial disarmament, demilitarization, of reparations, and of approved exports and imports' as well as *complete control over all aspects of the German economy*, 'with the aim of preventing Germany from developing a war potential'.[82]

4 Nuremberg: Political Demands Translated into Law

The documentary record of negotiations spanning from 22 January 1945 to 7 October 1946 published by the US Department of State in 1949 gives some insight into the manner in which the political demands raised at the time were translated into the legal process to be followed in Nuremberg.[83] The Nuremberg Charter appended to the London Agreement, which was adopted by the four Allied powers and formally adhered to by 19 other nations,[84] provided in Article 1 for the prosecution of 'criminals whose offenses have no particular geographical location'. War criminals whose crimes could be localised would be tried in those localities once they were liberated. Allied occupation courts would be set up in their respective zones in Germany and given jurisdiction over crimes committed by Germans within the Reich.[85]

79 Including the 'oriental face of IG Farben', as described by Dubois 1952, p. 13. See also the *Kilgore Report*; and Sasuly 1952; and see Ch. 2B.

80 *JCS 1067*.

81 *Potsdam Agreement*.

82 The Control Council applied the Control Council's law by virtue of *Control Council Proclamation No. 1*.

83 Negotiation Record: Department of State Publication 3080, International Organization and Conference Series II, European and British Commonwealth 1, Released February 1949.

84 Australia, Belgium, Czechoslovakia, Denmark, Ethiopia, Greece, Haiti, Honduras, India, Luxembourg, The Netherlands, New Zealand, Norway, Panama, Paraguay, Poland, Uruguay, Venezuela, and Yugoslavia, *1945 London Agreement* and *Nuremberg Charter*.

85 Werle 2009, p. 7.

Article 6 of the Charter contained the crimes within the jurisdiction of the Tribunal: (a) crimes against peace (i.e., the crime of aggression), (b) war crimes, and (c) crimes against humanity.[86] 'Crimes against humanity' were primarily included to enable prosecution of acts committed against Germans (mainly of course German Jews) – because war crimes law does not normally cover crimes against citizens or residents within the home state. A final section of article 6 contained the crime of 'conspiracy' to commit any of the acts in the three other sections. Article 7[87] had been recommended by Mr Justice Jackson, citing the 'principle of responsible government declared some three centuries ago to King James by Lord Chief Justice Coke, who proclaimed that even a King is still "under God and the law"'.[88] Article 8 encodes the supremacy of the laws of humanity/ICL over domestic law and sovereign government orders, which was vital considering many Nazi atrocities would not have been unlawful under Reich law.[89]

4.1 *The Trial at Nuremberg*

At the next stage the defendants had to be selected, and indictments drafted. In order to produce a coherent historical narrative of the war to be communicated to the public and posterity, the trial was to focus on the grand totality (causes/origins) rather than the detail (symptoms). The IMT would also only prosecute 'Major War Criminals', leaving other suspects to be dealt with in the normal channels of military justice.[90] Chief Prosecutor Jackson stated:

> Our case against the major defendants is concerned with the Nazi master plan, not with individual barbarities and perversions which occurred independently of any central plan. The groundwork of our case must be factually authentic and constitute a well-documented history of what we are convinced was a grand, concerted pattern to incite and commit the aggressions and barbarities which have shocked the world ... Unless we write the record of this movement with clarity and precision, we cannot blame the future if in days of peace it finds incredible the accusatory generalities uttered during the war.[91]

86 See Appendix B.
87 See Appendix B.
88 *Jackson Negotiations Report*, at 64; IMT, *Jackson Opening Address* at 36.
89 See Appendix B.
90 *Taylor IC*, at 249.
91 *Jackson Negotiations Report*, Part III.

What had enabled World War Two to be started, and thus all its atrocities to be committed, had been the 'captur[e of] the form of the German state as an instrumentality for spreading their rule to other countries'.[92] The indictment was to reflect this:

> Whom will we accuse and put to their defence? We will accuse a large number of individuals and officials who were in authority in the government, in the military establishment, including the General Staff, and in the financial, industrial and economic life in Germany who by all civilised standards are provable to be common criminals.[93]

From the very start it was clear that the 'economic case' – the part of the prosecution dealing with the economic causes of, and motivations for, the war and the responsibility of economic actors and policy makers – would be key in the Nuremberg Trial.[94] From the mid-1930s the German economy had been geared up towards heavy industry, which comprised the mining of coal (Germany's main natural resource) and the manufacture of iron and steel and steel products. As a result of a deliberate policy of cartelisation implemented – through law – by the National Socialists in the 1930s,[95] these industries were in the hands of a small number of large industrial and mining combines including Krupp, Flick, Thyssen, the state-owned Reich-Werks-Hermann-Göring and the chemicals concern IG Farben. The idea behind cartel formation was for Germany to become economically self-sufficient in particular with regard to those items needed for war. Not having colonies producing rubber and oil itself, Germany's aim was to produce replacements for these resources domestically. Additionally, the occupation and colonisation of neighbouring countries was to ensure the German nation's *Lebensraum* but also the resources (including labour) that it lacked.[96]

When Justice Jackson and his staff commenced work in preparation for the trial, four indictment-drafting committees were established, each dealing with a different core aspect of the war for which charges were to be brought. Committee 1, comprised of British representatives, was to handle the aggressive war charge; Committee 2 was to deal with war crimes and crimes against humanity in the East (dealt with by the Soviets); Committee 3 with equal crimes in the

92 Ibid.

93 *Jackson Negotiations Report*, Part III.3.

94 *JCS 1067*.

95 Trainin 1945, p. 83; Neumann 1942, pp. 265–8.

96 *IMT Indictment* Count three, at (J).

West (dealt with by France), while the Americans would prepare the 'common plan and conspiracy' charge.[97] The latter charge was to cover the pre-World War Two story of Nazism, Hitler's seizure and exploitation of power, his plans and steps to occupy much of Europe, and plan to attack the United States. As the first count of the indictment, it would comprise the basic narrative of the case as a whole.[98] This committee was headed by Justice Jackson himself. As a vital part of this charge, the economic case was entrusted to the American lawyer Frank Shea.[99] Shea produced a memorandum, in which he suggested as defendants Hjalmar Schacht (former head of the Reichsbank and Minister of Economics, who had provided the financing of war production), Fritz Sauckel (primary figure in the foreign forced-labour programme), Albert Speer (architect and later Minister of Armaments and Munitions), Walter Funk (Schacht's successor)[100] as well as Alfried Krupp and six other German industrial and financial leaders. 'The guilt of the industrialists and financiers, as Shea saw it was that they had given Hitler the material means to rearm Germany, with full knowledge that Hitler planned to use these armaments to carry out a program of German aggrandizement by military conquest'.[101]

Eisenhower would later speak, in his famous farewell speech, of the military-industrial complex.[102] In the particular context of World War Two, this was called 'IG Farbenism': the inherent danger in cartel formation combined with the profit motive, or the work of the 'unholy trinity' of Nazism, militarism, economic imperialism.[103] The Soviet representative at Nuremberg, A.N. Trainin stated: 'Their political position is clear: these were the masters for whom the Fascist State machine was zealously working', adding, 'the German financial and industrial heads must also be sent for trial as criminals'.[104]

---

97 Taylor 1992, pp. 79–80.

98 Taylor 1992, p. 80.

99 Taylor 1992, pp. 90–2.

100 *Nazi Conspiracy and Aggression*, Vol. I, Ch. VIII: 'It is well known that the Nazi conspirators rearmed Germany on a vast scale. The purpose of that rearmament is revealed in the secret records of the plans and deliberations of the inner councils of the Nazis. These records show that the reorganization of the German government, the financial wizardry of Hjalmar Schacht, and the total mobilization of the German economy largely under Hjalmar Schacht, Hermann Goering, and Walter Funk, were directed at a single goal: aggressive war'.

101 Taylor 1992, p. 81.

102 Eisenhower farewell address, 17 January 1961, Press release containing the text of the address (DDE's Papers as President, Speech Series, Box 38, Final TV Talk (1)), *Eisenhower Archives*.

103 Telford Taylor in *Flick Case* (Opening Statement for the Prosecution), 32.

104 Trainin 1945, pp. 84, 85.

The 'economic case', however, gathered criticism from the start, with one critic fearing it would 'reform European economics'.[105] In the end, only the former ministers were indicted, along with Krupp, due to an apparent British-led effort to keep the list of indictees down and the trial short.[106]

The retention of Krupp, the 'main organiser of German industry', in the indictment made him the *pars pro toto* for German industry. However, there was disagreement among the different teams of lawyers working on the indictment as to whether Gustav Krupp, the man who had run the Krupp concern until 1941, or Alfried Krupp, his son, who had been in charge throughout most of the war, was the intended defendant.[107] Eventually, Gustav the elder was named on the indictment: the industrialist who had also been the president of the State Union of German Industry and high official in the Economics Ministry.[108] It soon transpired, however, that Krupp was, at 80 years of age, too ill and demented to stand trial – something the British knew, since they held Krupp Sr in detention. In September 1945 Colonel Harry Phillimore, the head of the British War Crimes Executive, wrote to the Foreign Office warning that Gustav Krupp was 'virtually dead'.[109] The US then sought to replace Gustav with his son Alfried. The prosecution of at least one Krupp family member was considered to be in the public interest, explained in the words of Justice Jackson:

> Four generations of the Krupp family have owned and operated the great armament and munitions plants which have been the chief source of Germany's war supplies. For over 130 years this family has been the focus the symbol and the beneficiary of the most sinister forces engaged in menacing the peace of Europe ... To drop Krupp von Bohlen from this case without substitution of Alfried drops the case from the entire Krupp family and defeats any effective judgment against the German armament makers ... The Krupp influence was powerful in promoting the Nazi plan to incite aggressive warfare in Europe. The Krupps were thus one of the most persistent and influential forces that made this war ... Once the war was on, Krupps, both Von Bohlen and Alfried being directly responsible therefor, led German industry in violating treaties and

105 Taylor 1992, pp. 85–7.
106 Ibid.
107 Taylor 1992, p. 92.
108 *Nazi Conspiracy and Aggression*, Vol. II, Ch. XVI, Part 13.
109 Neave 1982, p. 29.

> international law by employing enslaved laborers, impressed and imported from nearly every country occupied by Germany, and by compelling prisoners of war to make arms and munitions for use against their own countries ... Moreover, the Krupp companies profited greatly from destroying the peace of the world through support of the Nazi program ... The United States respectfully submits that no greater disservice to the future peace of the world could be done than to excuse the entire Krupp family.[110]

This request was rejected on 15 November 1945.[111] The UK had objected on the basis that it might delay the commencement of the entire trial.[112] Still, important information on what might have been the first international trial of an industrialist can be gleaned from the Indictment and the underlying prosecution file.[113]

4.2 *The Indictment*

While in Article 22 of the London Agreement a series of trials were envisaged, in fact the IMT eventually only held one large trial, indicting 24 individuals[114] and 6 groups or organisations.[115] The Indictment started with the overarching conspiracy charge, stating:

> All the defendants, with diverse other persons ... participated as leaders, organisers, instigators, or accomplices in the formulation or execution of a common plan or conspiracy to commit, or which involved the commission of, Crimes against Peace, War Crimes, and Crimes against Humanity, as defined in the Charter of this Tribunal, and in accordance with the provisions of the Charter, are individually responsible for their own acts and for all acts committed by any persons in the execution of such a plan or conspiracy.[116]

---

110 *Krupp Answer*, p. 134 ff.

111 *Krupp Order*, p. 146. See also Lippman 1995, pp. 176–9.

112 *Krupp Memorandum* 139. See also Taylor 1992, p. 92.

113 *Nazi Conspiracy and Aggression*, Vol. II, Ch. XVI, Part 13.

114 The indictees were charged individually and as members of any of the groups or organisations named in the indictment.

115 The groups and organisations were included so as to enable individuals to be held liable, if nothing more, at least for membership of these bodies. They were, the Reich Cabinet, the leadership corps of the Nazi Party, the SS, the SD, the Gestapo, the SA and the General Staff and High Command of the German Armed Forces (IMT Indictment, Appendix B).

116 *Nuremberg Trial Proceedings*, Vol. II: First day, Tuesday, 20 November 1945 Morning Session, 29–94.

This count encompassed the 'Nazi master plan'[117] including the strategic part of the 'economic case': acquiring totalitarian control of Germany and the economic planning and mobilization for aggressive war, which included using organisations of German business as instruments of economic mobilisation for war.[118]

Count two comprised crimes against the peace by planning, preparing, initiating and waging wars of aggression against 12 countries; count three comprised the violation of the laws and customs of war, which included the widespread use of slave labour, both through utilisation of camp internees and through the deportation of hundreds of thousands of Soviets, Poles, French, Belgians and Dutch civilians to work in the German industries.[119] It further included the plunder of public and private property, through, amongst other crimes, the confiscation of businesses and plants, by means of which the 'Nazi conspirators created an instrument for the personal profit and aggrandizement of themselves and their adherents'.[120] Finally, count four comprised crimes against humanity: mistreatment and persecution of Jews and other political, racial and religious groups.[121]

4.3 *The IMT Judgment*

The IMT rendered its judgment on 1 October 1946, delivering 'the world's first post mortem examination of a totalitarian regime'. Jackson added, 'That four great nations, flushed with victory and stung with injury, stay the hand of vengeance and voluntarily submit their captive enemies to the judgment of the law is one of the most significant tributes that power has ever paid to reason'.[122]

In response to the '*nullum crimen sine lege, nulla poena sine lege*' argument made by the defence against the 'crime of aggression', the IMT cited the Kellogg-Briand Pact of 1928, which renounced war as an instrument of national policy. Taking this together with the 1923 draft Treaty of Mutual Assistance (not adopted), which in Article I declared that 'aggressive war is an international crime', and an Assembly of League of Nations Declaration of 1927, which contains similar wording, the IMT accepted as evidence a rule prohibiting aggressive war. Where there is a rule containing a prohibition, the IMT argued, there must be

117 For a summary of the prosecution's case, see *Economic Aspects*.

118 See Appendix B.

119 *IMT Indictment*, Count Three Section (B) 51 (Deportation for slave labour and for other purposes of the civilian populations of and in occupied territories) and Section (H) Conscription of civilian labour.

120 *IMT Indictment*, Count Three Section (E) 55, 56.

121 *IMT Indictment*.

122 *Jackson Final Report*, p. 438.

one responsible if such is breached. It had been submitted by the defence that international law was concerned only with the actions of sovereign states, and not with individuals. However, '[c]rimes against international law are committed by men, not by abstract entities, and only by punishing individuals who commit such crimes can the provisions of international law be enforced'.[123] The tone of the judgment here suggests that IL would be ineffective without an ICL, and that, conversely, ICL saves IL from irrelevance, *completes* it.

Moreover, 'the very essence of the Charter is that individuals have international duties which transcend the national obligations of obedience imposed by the individual state. He who violates the laws of war cannot obtain immunity while acting in pursuance of the authority of the state if the state in authorizing action moves outside its competence under international law'.[124] This, one of the key principles of Nuremberg, which has persisted in ICL to date (see Chapter 4), at once responds to the liberal individualist belief in individual agency, and permits, through the absorption of blame by the individual, the system (Nazism, capitalism) to escape censure, the state and people to be rehabilitated and political-economic relations to resume post-prosecution.

4.3.1 The Judgment on the 'Economic Case'

Moreover, and despite Goering's suicide on the eve of the trial, the 'economic case' featured prominently in the Nuremberg trial, which still focused on Goering's pivotal role as 'in theory and in practice ... the economic dictator of the Reich'.[125] The judgment describes how in November 1932 a petition, signed by leading industrialists and financiers, had been presented to President Hindenburg, calling upon him to entrust the Chancellorship to Hitler.[126] Subsequently, according to evidence submitted to the Tribunal,

> On the invitation of Goering, approximately 25 of the leading industrialists of Germany, together with Schacht, attended a meeting in Berlin on 20 February 1933. This was shortly before the German election of 5 March 1933. At this meeting Hitler announced the conspirators' aim to seize totalitarian control over Germany, to destroy the parliamentary system, to crush all opposition by force, and to restore the power of the Wehrmacht. Among those present at that meeting were Gustav Krupp, head

123 *IMT Judgment*, p. 223. For a concise discussion on this 'common law' interpretation vs. civil law objections to this finding, see Burchard 2006, p. 800.

124 *IMT Judgment*, p. 223.

125 *IMT Judgment*, p. 171.

126 *IMT Judgment*, p. 177.

> of the munitions firm, Alfried Krupp, A.G.; four leading officials of the I.G. Farben Works, one of the world's largest chemical concerns; Albert Vogler, head of United Steel Works of Germany; and other leading industrialists.[127]

At this meeting Goering suggested to set up an election fund to support Hitler in the March elections (which Goering predicted would be the *last* election in Germany).[128]

Subsequent to this meeting in April 1933 Krupp submitted to Hitler – on behalf of the Reich Association of German Industry, a plan for the reorganisation of German industry. He stated the plan was 'characterized by the desire to coordinate economic measures and political necessity', and that 'the turn of political events is in line with the wishes which I myself and the board of directors have cherished for a long time'.[129] The industrialists' plan was adopted.[130] The meeting, the election fund, and the plan are mentioned again later in the 'subsequent trials'.

Funk, who had been the Minister of Economics and the president of the Reichsbank, was convicted by the IMT for crimes against the peace for his participation in the economic preparations for war.[131] However, Hjalmar Schacht, Funk's predecessor in both positions, was acquitted of the aggressive war charge as the Tribunal considered it not proven that Schacht had known of Hitler's intentions. A factor in his acquittal was that Schacht had defected before the end of the war. Additionally Speer, who had been Reich Minister for Armaments and Munitions, was acquitted on the basis that his actions were taken only after the aggressive wars had been well underway.[132]

The Soviet member of the Tribunal, Justice I. Nikitschenko, filed a dissenting opinion to the majority IMT judgment to the effect that he considered Schacht's acquittal to be in contradiction to the evidence presented to the court.[133] According to Nikitschenko, 'Schacht consciously and deliberately supported the Nazi Party and actively aided in the seizure of power in Germany by the Fascists. Even prior to his appointment as Plenipotentiary for War Economy, and immediately after the seizure of power by the Nazis, Schacht led in

127 *Economic Aspects*.
128 *Economic Aspects*.
129 *IMT Judgment*, p. 183.
130 *Economic Aspects*.
131 *IMT Judgment*, pp. 131–4.
132 *IMT Judgment*, p. 156.
133 *IMT Judgment*, pp. 342–8.

planning and developing the German armaments, Schacht provided the economic and financial basis for the creation of the Hitlerite military machine; … Schacht prepared Germany's economy for the waging of aggressive wars'.[134] However, the strong case for the recognition and condemnation of the economic instigators of the war put by the prosecution was no longer supported by the majority: an early sign of the differences to come.

5 The Turnaround: from Germany is Our Problem to Germany is Our Business

In the Spring of 1947 further signs were appearing of a changing Allied policy towards Germany, from one where Germany was to be publicly castigated and disabled (in trials and through economic policies as envisaged in the Morgenthau Plan) to one where Germany was to be rehabilitated into the world community of states and its economy rebuilt.[135] Here I focus on how the change (effectively, the start of the Cold War) is reflected in the decision-making regarding the industrialists' trials, and subsequently how its effects are reflected in the proceedings and the decisions of the tribunals. I mainly focus on US policy and sources, as the US at this point had emerged as the ideological leader of the West.

Direct economic interests initially stayed in the background in US policy towards Germany and were the subject of much internal disagreement within the US administration.[136] Morgenthau relates how already during World War Two orders were given to the military to spare German industrial plants.[137] In his memoirs, Josiah Dubois (a State Department lawyer who was to become the lead prosecutor in the *IG Farben* case) describes a *secret* State Department memorandum setting out its 'post-war program' relating to *in kind* reparations payments from Germany.[138] Such reparations could form a public justification for sparing, and where necessary, rebuilding Germany's productive capacity, as well as retaining US-German trade ties. However, the programme remained secret as at this point public and key political support was still behind the

134 *IMT Judgment*, p. 348.
135 See generally, Gimbel 1972, pp. 24–69.
136 See generally, Gimbel 1972.
137 Schild 1970, p. 64.
138 *Dubois Interview*, Oral History Interview with Josiah E. Dubois, Jr., June 29, 1973, by Richard D. McKinzie, in *Truman Library*, available at https://www.trumanlibrary.org/oralhist/duboisje.htm, p. 13.

pacific, 'pastoralised' Germany as proposed in Morgenthau's plan. Morgenthau, sensing support for his plan waning, published his book (entitled *Germany is Our Problem*) in an attempt to reinforce his stance.[139]

Incrementally over time, however, Morgenthau lost ground. Dubois tells of seeing a second secret memorandum, circulated within the US delegation at Potsdam. According to this memo, the US goal now was 'rebuilding a strong Germany as a buffer against Communism'.[140] While the *Potsdam Agreement* (and JCS 1067[141]) mirrored the Morgenthau Plan, Dubois states, 'of course, it was never followed through. The U.S. officials did do just what Morgenthau was afraid of, and in effect what the [second] State Department memorandum recommended'.[142] A strong, *indentured* economy was more attractive than a pastoralised state. Shortly after Potsdam Morgenthau was 'in effect ... fired by Truman'.[143]

The turnaround was not complete at this point, though, and elements of the plan persisted for some time. For example, the work of the Office of the Military Government of the US ('OMGUS') Decartelisation Branch – whose staff were called the 'Morgenthau Boys'[144] – continued for two years after Henry Morgenthau's departure. Many items of machinery were shipped to the United States and the other Allies by way of reparations payment. The IG Farben Control Commission, which was run by all four occupation powers, worked to split the Farben cartel into the four sections that had only come together years before: Hoechst, Agfa, Bayer and BASF.[145] The entire German economy came to be strictly controlled by the occupation authorities. Thousands of industrialists were interned, including 120 German business leaders from the banking, electrical, chemical and automobile sectors, who were interned by the British.[146] In the Eastern, Soviet occupation zone, the 'criminal concerns' were liquidated or nationalised.[147] Much has been written about the intimate relations between the US (and other, European) corporations and the German cartels.[148] In return for the (temporary) loss of these trading and scientific partnerships (and to

139 Morgenthau 1945; Schild 1970, pp. 64ff.; also Blum 1967.
140 *Dubois Oral History Interview*, p. 34.
141 Generally, *Dubois Oral History Interview*.
142 *Dubois Oral History Interview*, pp. 32, 33.
143 *Dubois Oral History Interview*, p. 25. See also, Blum 1967, pp. 451ff.
144 *Bernstein Oral History Interview* pp. 141–51, in Truman Library, available at https://www.trumanlibrary.org/oralhist/bernsten.htm; *Bernstein IG Farben Report*.
145 *Weiss Interview*.
146 Schanetzky 2003, p. 74.
147 Kahn 1952, p. 6.
148 E.g., Black 2008; Billstein 2000; Pauwels 2003.

boost government research projects), secret programmes were underway to control and harvest German scientific development. Thousands of industrial patents, even hundreds of scientists were transferred to the US as part of Operation Paperclip.[149]

The public manifestation of the turnaround eventually came on 6 September 1946, in an address entitled Restatement of Policy on Germany given in Stuttgart by US Secretary of State, James Byrnes.[150] It raised the issue of the political and economic future of Europe: 'Germany is a part of Europe and recovery in Europe, and particularly in the states adjoining Germany, will be slow indeed if Germany with her great resources of iron and coal is turned into a poorhouse'.[151] In this statement, Byrnes effectively echoed Soviet foreign minister Molotov's speech on Germany's economic future at the Paris Peace Conference in July 1946.[152] However, unlike Molotov, Byrnes omitted mention of the industrialists' role in World War Two, which by then was starting to disappear from 'Western' discourse, and would disappear all but completely after the subsequent trials.

In March 1947 Truman announced the Truman Doctrine promising economic support to those 'states resisting attempted subjugation [to communism]'.[153] Soviet representative Zhdanov responded with his 'two camps' speech in which he repeated the view that capitalist imperialism, personified in the directors of the cartels, was the true perpetrator of World War Two.[154] In July 1947, JCS1067 was replaced with Joint Chiefs of Staff Directive 1779, which codified the turn in US policy and stated: 'An orderly, prosperous Europe requires the economic contributions of a stable and productive Germany'.[155] German and generally Western European recovery took off speedily, partly through the Marshall Plan, established on 5 June 1947, which aimed to modernise Western European industry, to integrate it, and remove barriers to trade among

149 *2007 IWG Report*.

150 Restatement of Policy on Germany, Speech by James F. Byrnes, the United States Secretary of State, held in Stuttgart on 6 September 1946, US Department of State. Documents on Germany 1944–1985. Washington, DC: Department of State, [s.d.], pp. 91–9.

151 Ibid.

152 Soviet representative Viacheslav Molotov statement in Paris 10 July 1946, The Department of State, Occupation of Germany, Policy and Progress 1945–46, European Series 23, Washington, DC: US Government Printing Office, August 1947, pp. 237–41; Gimbel 1972, p. 245.

153 Merriman 2009, p. 119.

154 Wentker 2002, p. 63. Additionally, public trials focused on the Nazis' forced sterilisation and euthanasia programmes (ibid, pp. 64–5).

155 *JCS 1779*.

European countries and between Europe and the US.[156] It was also used as leverage to pressure French and Italian governments not to appoint communists to ministerial posts.[157]

On the Eastern side, the Cominform, the coordinating mechanism for all communist parties, was inaugurated in September 1947 as the successor to the Comintern, with Zhdanov installed as its chair. Soviet power in Eastern Europe was consolidating, and when Soviet troops took control of the Czech government in January 1948, and in July 1948 blocked foreign trains and truck routes into Berlin, this sent shockwaves through the US trial teams at Nuremberg. Some of the US lawyers and their families returned home,[158] and the US occupation government now put direct pressure on Taylor to wrap up the trials.[159] (West) German commentator Kröll summarises the *Umorientierung* (turnaround) as follows: 'With the re-formation of political camps during the Cold War and the open warfare in Korea, the involvement of the young Federal Republic into the Western alliance weighed heavier than crime and punishment of Nazi crimes'.[160] East German commentators accused the US of 'liquidating Potsdam'.[161]

It is against this backdrop that we must imagine the efforts of US lawyers such as Jackson, Taylor and others on their team, to persuade the US political leadership to allow further trials.

6 The Trials of the Industrialists: from Morality Play to Theatre of the Absurd

In the US military trials of the industrialists, we can see how this change and also specific historical events, such as the blockade of Berlin, left their mark. Although the other Allies' political priorities were perhaps not as explicit as the US's (partially due to the comparatively very limited publication of official documents), evidence of their political objectives can also be found reflected in the choice of defendants, and the course and outcomes of the trials in their respective occupation zones.

Not all trials discussed below are 'subsequent trials' when seen next to the main IMT trial. As early as 1944 the Allied governments had created military

156 Merriman 2009, pp. 1120–1.
157 Merriman 2009, p. 1120.
158 Dubois 1952, p.
159 Heller 2011, p. 102.
160 Kröll 1999, p. 176.
161 Kahn 1952, p. 6.

courts and commissions to deal with crimes being committed by Axis nationals.[162] The British did so under British *Royal Warrant* dated 14 June 1945.[163] The *Zyklon B Case* discussed below took place during the middle months of the IMT trial. Parallel to these military courts were the military government courts of the occupation, set up by virtue of Control Council Proclamation 1.[164] Apart from the British, the other Allied military tribunals applied the *Control Council Law No. 10 on the Punishment of Persons Guilty of War Crimes, Crimes Against Peace and Against Humanity* ('*CCL10*'),[165] which was promulgated on 20 December 1945 by the four occupying powers acting through their Zone Commanders in order to 'establish a uniform legal basis in Germany for the prosecution of war criminals and other similar offenders, other than those dealt with by the International Military Tribunal'.[166] *CCL10* is based, and according to some, an improvement, on the *Nuremberg Charter*.[167] Article II sets out the main provisions on crimes within the scope of the instrument, as well as potential defendants.[168] One of the main differences was the intended inclusion of pre-war crimes against humanity and the explicit mention of persons who have 'held high position in the financial, industrial or economic life of any such country' as potential accused.[169] *CCL10* authorised each of the four Zone Commanders to arrest suspected war criminals and to establish 'appropriate tribunals' for their trial.[170] According to Taylor, in the Soviet Zone little or nothing was done to carry *CCL10* into effect[171] although this is contradicted by the literature. The British tried Axis nationals starting from summer 1945. The major trial held by the French was that of Röchling. Of the trials carried out by the Allies and eventually also the German courts,[172] those of the US, which took place in the same Nuremberg courthouse as the IMT trial, are by far the best documented and

162 Rogers 1990, p. 787.

163 Royal Warrant, 14 June 1945, Army Order 81/45, with amendments, UNWCC Note on Zyklon B Case; Rogers 1990, pp. 788–9; *UNWCC* Vol. I, XV.

164 *Control Council Proclamation No. 1.*

165 *Control Council Law No. 10.*

166 *Control Council Law No. 10.*

167 For example, *Control Council Law No. 10* obviates the requirement for a link between crimes against humanity and war (Werle 2009, p. 783) meaning that crimes committed before the war could be included.

168 *Control Council Law No. 10* S.I. See Appendix B.

169 *Control Council Law No. 10* S.II 2. See Appendix B.

170 *Control Council Law No. 10.*

171 *Taylor IC*, p. 254.

172 As per Art. III of *Control Council Law No. 10* the French, British and Soviet commanders granted German courts jurisdiction.

most widely known. It is these trials that are cited in ICL cases to this day (see Chapter 5).[173]

6.1 *The Trials of the Industrialists at the US Military Tribunal at Nuremberg*

After the IMT judgment, the decision to proceed with 'subsequent trials' was not without hesitation on the part of the US leadership. As the IMT trial had come to a close, criticism increased.[174] Dubois and others have noted that some of the criticism can be put down to anti-Semitism within the US (and UK) governments.[175] That the US trials took place at all can be put down partly to the tenacity of the main US protagonists, Jackson, Taylor and their teams at Nuremberg.

6.1.1 Deciding Whether to Have Further Trials

Justice Jackson, in his report to the US Government on the IMT judgment, reminded the government that the US had wanted to try more industrialists besides Krupp in the IMT trial, and that his successor, Brigadier General Telford Taylor, had already 'prepared a programme of prosecutions against representatives of all the important segments of the Third Reich including a considerable number of industrialists and financiers, leading cabinet ministers, top SS and police officials, and militarists'.[176] At this point Jackson notes a lack of enthusiasm on the part of the other Allies for a second international trial. British foreign secretary Orme Sargeant feared that such a second trial would become a 'battle between capitalism and communism' and that '[t]he Russians might exploit the proceedings to discuss irrelevancies such as [the British] attitude to German rearmament'.[177] Jackson stated:

> if [the other Allies] were unwilling to take the additional time necessary to try industrialists in this case, it does not create an obligation on the United States to assume the burdens of a second international trial. The quickest and most satisfactory results will be obtained, in my opinion, from immediate commencement of our own cases according to plans which General Taylor has worked out.[178]

---

173 See Chapter 5.
174 E.g., Bloxham 2003, p. 97.
175 Dubois 1952, pp. 68–9; Bush 2009, p. 1197.
176 *Jackson Final Report*, p. 435.
177 Quoted in Bloxham 2008, p. 149.
178 *Jackson Final Report*, p. 435.

Eventually, this is what occurred.

The assumption at the time was that it would suffice for the US Military tribunals to take on the most prominent cases (British authorities handed the US administration six industrialists who had been held in the British Zone, including Alfried Krupp[179]) and that the German courts would eventually try others, on the basis of hundreds of files already prepared by the American team.[180]

The 12 trials of the US Military Tribunal at Nuremberg ('NMT'), which was established by the US Military Governor pursuant to Military Government Ordinance No. 7 of 18 October 1946,[181] each focus on a specific professional group who had together formed the elite of Nazi Germany. It includes trials of professional men – medical doctors who carried out medical experimentation in the concentration camps in the *Medical Case* and lawyers in the *Justice Case*,[182] senior SS members including camp administrators (*SS Case*) and the Police (*Einsatzgruppen Case*), industrialists and financiers (Cases 5, 6, 10 – see below), military leaders (Cases 7 and 12) and Government Ministers (2 and 11 *Ministries Case*).[183] The basis upon which the General Counsel decided whom to indict, was described thus:

> one of the first and most important responsibilities of my office was to determine, in the light of the best available information, where the deepest individual responsibility lay for the manifold crimes committed under the aegis of the Third Reich ... [I]t was necessary to scrutinise the conduct of leaders in all occupations, and to let the chips fall where they might.[184]

Bush gives a comprehensive account of the US team's deliberations on choice of defendants. At one time, the list counted 1,000 possible defendants, many of them industrialists – 'so great was the number of dirty corporations and busi-

179 Bloxham 2008, p. 152.

180 Bush 2009, p. 1228.

181 *Taylor IC*, at 363. For a discussion of the question whether the Nuremberg tribunals and Control Council Law No. 10 were international law, or as argued by the German defence and later German commentators, 'occupier's law', see, e.g., *Taylor IC*, p. 289; and Burchard 2006.

182 The movie *Judgment at Nuremberg* is based on this case.

183 *Medical Case; Justice Case; SS Case; Einsatzgruppen Case; Ministries Case.*

184 Preliminary Report to the Secretary of the Army by the Chief of Counsel for War Crimes, 12 May 1948, pp. 2–3, quoted in *Taylor IC*, p. 278.

nessmen that many, even potential "major perpetrators", just slipped through the cracks'.[185] For example, the directors of Daimler-Benz, which had used many tens of thousands of forced labourers, including women held captive as sex slaves, and Siemens, which had used slave labour from Auschwitz and Sachsenhausen, were not tried.[186]

Brigadier General Telford Taylor was appointed Chief of Counsel for War Crimes on 24 October 1946 (immediately on the resignation of Justice Jackson).[187] Josiah Dubois was the main prosecutor in the *IG Farben Case*. In his memoirs, he relates that already prior to his leaving for Germany, he was instructed by the War Department to ensure there would be no aggressive war charges against industrialists, as 'the DuPonts' (prominent US industrialists) would not like it.[188] This is an early sign of direct political pressure on the industrialists' trials.

6.1.2 Discussions of Theories of Liability

As noted, the US has published a far wider range of materials surrounding the trials than the other Allies. The documentation describing the lead-up to the industrialists' trials detail the discussion among the lawyers as to the basis ('theory' is the word used by the Americans)[189] on which the defendants were to be selected and charged. It is worth examining these at some length, as these discussions bear great resemblance to the discussions on corporate liability taking place again now (see Chapter 4C).

Among the theories for liability considered by the American team for the prosecution of industrialists was conspiracy liability as used by the IMT – a company or even a whole industry could be implicated in the conspiracy after which hundreds or thousands could be tried for membership (similar to the declaration of, e.g., the SS as an 'illegal organisation' allowing the prosecution of its members). This theory was rejected as it was specifically considered to interfere with the US policy objective of rehabilitating Germany.[190] The second theory discussed was that of trying corporations as legal entities. This was pro-

185 Bush 2009, p. 1132.
186 Bush 2009, pp. 1132–3.
187 *Taylor IC*, p. 273.
188 Dubois 1952, p. 22.
189 E.g., Dubois 1952, p. 49.
190 Bush 2009, p. 1143. At one point the US occupation authority held 74,000 persons in detention in Germany, while hundreds of thousands of German POWs were held in various other countries (Bush 2009, p. 1144).

posed by Abraham Pomerantz, a US corporate litigator who had been brought onto the team as a 'big picture strategist'.[191] He saw practical advantages to this theory including ease of proof (no need to tie individuals specifically to 'corporate' acts), and also a corporate charge could form the legal foundation for the expropriations of company property – that were already occurring. Finally, blaming the companies as such, rather than individuals, would 'disclose the industrial roots of Nazism' and 'demonstrate to the German people the real powers behind Hitler and the NSDAP'.[192] The concept of corporate liability existed in both US and UK domestic law and Pomerantz was not dissuaded by the absence of any explicit norms in international law on corporate liability or on the possible crimes that could be ascribed to corporations. However, Taylor's deputy Drexel Sprecher dismissed the suggestion, arguing that judges would be baffled by the German economy, about which they knew little, that the media would not give it the comprehensive coverage they had given individual trials and that the general public would not accept a long, 'bogged down' trial. Finally Leo Drachsler, a lawyer on the team with a background as a Hungarian refugee, fluent in German, who had previously worked on the German Cartels file for the US Government, proposed an 'institutional approach'.[193] This captured the idea that German industry had formed a 'third pillar' alongside the German military and the Nazi party, and that German big business had acted in unity.[194] This unity was evidenced in the meetings held by industrialists in the guise of industry associations, where they had reached agreement on the allotment of slave labour and other shared goals. This approach resembles the analysis by Jewish exile lawyer and political scientist Franz Neumann – who assisted the prosecution teams after publishing his book *Behemoth: The Structure and Practice of National Socialism 1933–1944*[195] – of which all members of the prosecution team were reportedly given a copy. Drachsler proposed that symbolic or representative defendants be tried.[196] Taylor 'politely rejected' this option, possibly partly as a result of the IMT judgment which had just come out – this contained Jackson's now famous phrase 'crimes are committed by men, not by abstract entities', and restricted the application of

191 Bush 2009, p. 1149.
192 Memo: A. Pomerantz, Feasibility and Propriety of Indicting I.G. Farben and Krupp as Corporate Entities, 27 August 1946, Gant Papers, Box EE (*Pomerantz Memo*); Bush 2009, p. 1150.
193 Bush 2009, pp. 1157–8.
194 Bush 2009, p. 1158.
195 Neumann 1944.
196 Bush 2009, p. 1160.

the conspiracy charge.[197] Eventually, all 'adventurous' theories were dropped and Sprecher's proposal to lay charges against a small group of individuals only, and to have no broad presentations against business and no emphasis on the planning phase of pre-1939, was selected.[198] Abraham Pomerantz quit the prosecution team and became an outspoken critic of the US handling of the trials.[199] After the first indictment, in the *Flick* case, had been drafted on the basis of individual liability, it was as if 'nothing else had ever been considered'.[200] An overall result of the chosen approach is that the prosecution of designated individuals left the 'structure' or system untouched, and as such facilitated the US objective of rebuilding the corporations as part of the economy. In this sense it resembled the prosecution of individual political leaders (at the IMT), rather than ascribing responsibility to the state as such.

Finding a middle ground between the lawyers' persistence and reluctance at the political level (an example of intra-class competition), OMGUS set a strict timetable and small budget for the 'subsequent trials'.[201] In the summer of 1947, when ten of the trials had already been completed, Telford Taylor was told that he could not proceed with the six further trials previously approved. He persuaded the Government to allow three further trials. The plan of having separate trials for Dresdner Bank and the Hermann-Goering-Werks was abandoned, but Taylor managed to agree having Dresdner Bank director Rasche and three defendants of the HGW added to the Ministries trial.[202]

6.1.3 The *Flick Case*, Case No. 5

The first of the industrialist cases, *The United States of America v. Friedrich Flick, et al.* (*Flick Case*)[203] started with the indictment of 8 February 1947 and ended on 22 December 1947. Friedrich Flick and five other officials of the Flick Concern and its subsidiary companies were accused of war crimes and crimes against humanity committed principally as officials of the Flick Concern. The charges included participation in the deportation of thousands of foreigners

197 Bush 2009, pp. 1161–2.
198 Bush 2009, p. 1157.
199 Bush 2009, pp. 1171–2, fn. 278.
200 Bush 2009, p. 1177. Bush does not present any materials showing explanations as to why the decision was made, or how the defendants were chosen.
201 Bush 2009, p. 1197.
202 Bush 2009, pp. 1217–8.
203 *Flick Case.*

including concentration camp inmates and prisoners of war to forced labour in inhuman conditions including in the Flick mines and plants; spoliation contrary to the Hague Conventions of property in occupied France and the Soviet Union; participation in the persecution (as a crime against humanity) of Jews in the pre-war years through securing Jewish industrial and mining properties in the 'Aryanisation' process; knowing participation (of Flick and Steinbrinck) in SS atrocities through membership in the 'Circle of Friends of Himmler' (a select group of industrialists and SS officers).[204] The Flick group of enterprises included coal and iron mines, steel producing and fabricating plants, and was, by around 1940, the largest steel combine, rivalled in size only by Krupp AG.[205] Flick and his colleagues were accused of having exploited more than 60,000 prisoners of war as slave labourers under atrocious conditions.

The defendants were not charged with 'conspiracy to wage a war of aggression' even though the Prosecution had found ample material evidence to support such a charge.[206] Chief Prosecutor Telford Taylor opened this first industrialist case to be tried by the Americans with a general summary of the role of industry in the Nazi war plan:

> What we are here concerned with is no mere technical form of participation in crime, or some more or less accidental financial assistance of the commission of crimes. The really significant thing, which gives the full meaning to the crimes charged, not only in this count but in all the counts of this indictment, is the fact that the defendants assisted the SS and the Nazi regime with their eyes open and their hearts attuned to the basic purposes which they were subsidizing. Their support was not merely financial. It was part of a firm partnership between these defendants and the Nazi regime that continued from before the Nazi seizure of power to the last days of the Third Reich.[207]

Flick and his colleagues argued that they had not known of the slave labour programme and the mass crimes committed by the Nazis, that their position as private, business persons shielded them from liability ('we were just doing busi-

204 *Flick Indictment*, p. 3.
205 *Flick Case* Opening Statement for Prosecution.
206 Drobisch 1999, p. 122.
207 *Flick Case*, Opening Statement for Prosecution 104.

ness'),[208] that they had acted out of 'necessity' and under orders and force and threat of the state. Flick described his ostensible agreement with Nazi ideas as a self-protective '*howling with the wolves*'.[209] They also employed the *tu quoque* argument of alleged Allied war crimes (e.g., the Allied bombing of German cities) previously heard in the IMT, and challenged the jurisdiction of the court and applicability of *CCL10*. Against the necessity argument in particular, the prosecution stated,

> The leading defendants, Flick and Steinbrinck, were not reluctant dragons. All the defendants are uncommonly able to take care of themselves, and have been phenomenally successful at accomplishing what they set out to do. To suggest that these men, whose enterprises flourished like the green bay tree under Hitler and who occupied the most powerful and privileged positions in the German industrial fabric, spent 12 years skulking about in fear and doing what they did not want to do, is ridiculous.[210]

In *Flick*, we start to see the effects of a change in US government policy. Taylor's prosecutorial statements become fiercer, while the judges adopt an excusatory tone. In its decision, the Tribunal accepted the view that the defendants (except Flick and Weiss) *had* acted under necessity, forced by the 'reign of terror' employed by the Nazi regime. According to the Tribunal, the provision in Paragraph 4(b) of Article II of Control Council Law No. 10 which states: '(b) The fact that any person acted pursuant to the order of his Government or of a superior does not free him from responsibility for a crime, but may be considered in mitigation' should not 'be employed to deprive a defendant of the defense of necessity under such circumstances as obtained in this case' (cf. *Zyklon B* below). In fact, this construction allowed the 'defense of superior orders', which was explicitly ruled out by Nuremberg Principle IV ('The fact that a person acted pursuant to order of his Government or of a superior does not relieve him from responsibility under international law, provided a moral choice was in fact possible to him'), and CCL10 II 4(b) ('The fact that any person acted pursuant to the order of his Government or of a superior does not free him from responsibility for a crime, but may be considered in mitigation'), in through the back door.

Flick and Weiss, however, were found to have *initiated* the procurement of a large number of forced labourers for two of their plants (letters by Flick and

208 *Flick Case*, p. 972.
209 *Taylor IC*, p. 304.
210 *Flick Case*, pp. 973–4.

Weiss to this effect are reproduced in the US publication) – and these 'active steps … deprive[d] the defendants Flick and Weiss of the complete defense of necessity'.[211]

Further, the tribunal declined jurisdiction over the Aryanisation activities, which the prosecution had argued amounted to persecution, as 'crimes committed before and wholly unconnected with the war' were not covered by *CCL10*, adding (obiter) that 'the compulsory taking of industrial property' did not fall in the category of acts that 'affect the life and liberty of oppressed people' so as to amount to crimes against humanity.[212]

On the count of participation in the SS crimes through membership of the Circle of Friends of Himmler, Flick and Steinbrinck (who was also an SS member), who had participated in the regular Circle meetings and contributed large sums of money to Himmler, were found guilty. However, the Tribunal considered a number of factors in mitigation, including 'fear of retribution' and the idea they may just have attended the Circle's meetings for its 'excellent dinner'.[213] This argument had not been made by the defendants themselves.

The Tribunal recounted how '[i]n 1936 [Himmler] took members of the Circle on an inspection trip to visit Dachau concentration camp which was under his charge. They were escorted through certain buildings including the kitchen where they tasted food. They saw nothing of the infamous atrocities perhaps already there begun. But Flick who was present got the impression that it was not a pleasant place'.[214] Flick was sentenced to seven years' imprisonment, Steinbrinck to five, and Weiss to two and a half, while the other three defendants were acquitted on all counts.[215] In his report, Chief Prosecutor Taylor calls the Flick judgment 'exceedingly (if not excessively) moderate and conciliatory'.[216]

The Tribunal upheld only those charges that had become incontrovertible – such as the active role in acquiring slave labour shown in letters signed by the defendants. *CCL10* was specifically drafted to include pre-war acts within the jurisdiction of the *CCL10* Tribunals as possible crimes against humanity (as mentioned above), but the Tribunal misinterpreted this. The Tribunal's applic-

211 *Flick Case* Judgment, p. 1202.
212 *Flick Case* Judgment, pp. 1213–15.
213 *Flick Case* Judgment, p. 1218.
214 Ibid.
215 *Flick Case* Judgment, p. 1223.
216 *Taylor Final Report*, p. 187.

ation of the 'necessity' defence as a stand-in for the disallowed superior orders defense was in direct contravention of *CCL10* 4(b) and Nuremberg Principle IV, which had been considered a key foundational idea of the post-World War Two accountability process. The Tribunal moreover deviated from pronouncements in previous *CCL10* cases,[217] for example on its treatment of the slave labour count when compared with the *Pohl Case's* unqualified condemnation of forced labour, regardless of the conditions:

> The freedom of man from enslavement by his fellow men is one of the fundamental concepts of civilization. Any program which violates that concept, whether prompted by a false feeling of superiority or arising from desperate economic needs, is intolerable and criminal ... [T]hese defendants today are only mildly conscious of any guilt in the kidnapping and enslavement of millions of civilians. The concept that slavery is criminal per se does not enter into their thinking ... They simply cannot realize that the most precious word in any language is 'liberty'.[218]

In that case, Pohl and three others were sentenced to death by hanging, while 11 defendants were given prison sentences ranging from ten years to life, and three were acquitted (see below).

While Flick had resented 'having been singled out to make the German industrialists look like robbers and slave-drivers',[219] the bench seems to have been persuaded by the defence's argument that the case formed an attack on German capitalism, wholesale.[220]

There was much media attention for the trials in Eastern Germany, but in the West, mainly following the change in the politico-economic environment, it began to subside.[221] This may have contributed to the tribunals' preparedness to pass light sentences despite the atrocities described by the prosecution.

---

217 The subsequent trials to some extent ran contemporaneously, which partly explains how similar facts and concepts are interpreted differently in different trials, although Dubois and others report on regular meetings between the various teams. One often-heard critique is that the judges were not trained in international law, e.g., Schwarzenberger 1946–47.

218 *Pohl Case*, p. 968.

219 Drobisch 1999, p. 131. Flick, when he had returned to head the company in his later life, gained notoriety in Germany and beyond by refusing steadfastly to contribute to a slave labour compensation fund (Drobisch 1999, p. 130; Ferencz 1979, pp. 155–70).

220 *IG Farben Case*, closing statement for defendant Weiss, at 1118.

221 Drobisch 1999, p. 131.

6.1.4 The *IG Farben Case*, Case No. 6

The United States of America v. Carl Krauch, et al. (*IG Farben Case*)[222] (indictment filed 3 May 1947, judgment 29, 30 July 1948) was the largest of the NMT proceedings, comprising 24 defendants and lasting nearly 15 months. The defendants included the members of the *Vorstand* (managing directorate) and four other important officers of what was once the biggest combine in Germany, and the biggest chemical company in Europe: the Industriegesellschaft Farben AG.[223] IG Farben had a global network of partners and subsidiaries,[224] and as the producer of both Aspirin and Nylon stockings, 'was present in every American home'.[225] The company's main industrial/military products were synthetic nitrates for the manufacture of explosives, synthetic rubber made from coal (called buna), synthetic gasoline, and various poison gases including Zyklon B. The company had come into being in 1925 through the merger of the six leading German chemicals concerns. Farben owned or part-owned 400 other German companies (including Tesch – see below) and around 500 outside of Germany, and at the peak of its activities the yearly turnover exceeded three billion Reichsmark.[226] In addition to his position within the company as Chairman of the Supervisory Board, Carl Krauch was part of Goering's staff in the office of the Four Year Plan and his principal technical and scientific advisor. The indictment was issued in August 1947 and the judgment delivered on 29 July 1948.

Before the NMT trial, Control Council Law No. 52 of 5 July 1945 placed all IG Farben companies in the American Zone under the supervision of the military representation, released the management from its functions and suspended the rights of shareholders.[227] Then through the Control Council Law No. 9 of November 1945 the Allies took control of all IG Farben property: 'In order to insure that Germany will never again threaten her neighbours or the peace of the World, and taking into consideration that I.G. Farbenindustrie knowingly and prominently engaged in building up and maintaining the German war potential'.[228] By the CC, Farben had been treated as guilty. In addition,

222 *IG Farben Case*.

223 One defendant was dropped from the case for health reasons. The combine included also IG Farben's own banks, and even a private intelligence service (Sasuly 1952).

224 *Bernstein IG Farben Report*; see, generally, Sasuly 1952.

225 Dubois 1952.

226 *IG Farben Case*, Judgment 1085.

227 *Control Council Law No. 52*.

228 *Control Council Law No. 9*.

Farben property around the world was placed under supervision, and accounts were frozen.[229] The investigation of IG Farben also led to the publication of its extensive international ties: 63 US companies had illegal agreements with IG Farben.[230]

The *Farben Case* was the only industrialist case where the defendants were actually put to proof on the charge of aggressive war (count one) (despite the War Department's warning, above). The theory of the prosecution in the case was that the acts of spoliation and slave labour 'were committed as an integral part of the planning, preparation, initiation, and waging of wars of aggression and invasions of other countries' and 'formed part of said common plan or conspiracy'.[231]

Twenty of the 24 IG Farben defendants were convicted of one or more of the following charges: war crimes and crimes against humanity through the plundering and spoliation of occupied territories, and the seizure of plants both in Austria, Czechoslovakia, Poland, Norway, France, and Russia (count two); war crimes and crimes against humanity through participation in the enslavement and deportation to slave labour on a gigantic scale of concentration camp inmates and civilians in occupied countries, and of prisoners of war, and the mistreatment, terrorisation, torture, and mass murder of enslaved persons (count three); and membership in a criminal organisation, the SS (count four).[232] The defendants were found not guilty on the charge of conspiracy (count five)[233] as the Tribunal found that – in relation to this count – they had acted merely like ordinary citizens, who, although the majority of them supported the waging of war in some way, were not the ones who planned and led a nation. They merely followed their leaders and offered no contribution greater than any other normally productive enterprise – *despite what the IMT had said in its judgment about the role of the industrialists* and despite the *CCL10*.

In *IG Farben* the tribunal emphasised the profit motive as being part of the *mens rea* (mental element) of the property crimes contained in the indictment. Farben had expropriated, confiscated and *bought* property in occupied

229 See also Chapter 2B.

230 See also, e.g., Elimination of German Resources for War, hearings before the United States Senate Committee on Military Affairs, Subcommittee on War Mobilization, Seventy-Ninth Congress, first session, IG Farben Material Submitted by the War Department, 1945 (*Kilgore Report*); see also, generally, Sasuly 1947.

231 *IG Farben Case*, Indictment at 39 and 59.

232 *IG Farben Case*, Judgment, p. 1082.

233 Ibid.

territory, which constituted spoliation and plunder contrary to the *1907 Hague Regulations*.[234]

The idea of the corporation as an instrumentality in the hands of criminal individuals was also offered in *IG Farben*: 'one may not utilise the corporate structure to achieve an immunity from criminal responsibility for illegal acts which he directs, counsels, aids, orders or abets with the knowledge of the essential elements of the crime'.[235] This precedent avoids answering the question of intent towards the criminal act in itself.

In judging the first and fifth counts of the indictment, the Tribunal relied on the IMT judgment and concluded that it had approached a finding of guilty of any defendant under the charges of participation in a common plan or conspiracy or planning and waging aggressive war with great caution. It made findings of guilt 'only where the evidence of both knowledge and active participation was conclusive'.[236] The Tribunal took a generous view on knowledge:

> While it is true that those with an insight into the evil machinations of power politics might have suspected Hitler was playing a cunning game of soothing restless Europe, the average citizen of Germany, be he professional man, farmer, or industrialist, could scarcely be charged by these events with knowledge that the rulers of the Reich were planning to plunge Germany into a war of aggression.[237]

And:

> It is argued that after the events in Austria and Czechoslovakia, men of reasonable minds must have known that Hitler intended to wage aggressive war, although they may not have known the country to be attacked or the time of initiation. This argument is not sound.[238]

Plus, most controversially, 'We reach the conclusion that common knowledge of Hitler's plans did not prevail in Germany, either with respect to a general plan to wage aggressive war, or with respect to specific plans to attack individual

234 Arts. 46, 47, 52, 53, 55 of the *1907 Hague Regulations*.
235 *IG Farben Case*, Judgment, p. 1153.
236 *IG Farben Case*, Judgment, p. 1103.
237 *IG Farben Case*, Judgment, p. 1106.
238 *IG Farben Case*, Judgment, p. 1107.

countries'.[239] Here we can see a direct contradiction of the IMT, which had detailed (amongst others) the planning and strategising meetings of Himmler's Circle of Friends, of which IG Farben defendant Buetefish had been a part (with Flick and Rasche, amongst others).[240]

The Tribunal, which at times sounds more like a defence counsel, remarked in one instance when discussing IG Farben chairman of the board Krauch, 'It may be noted that this is the only instance in which the defendant Krauch talked to Hitler'.[241] This would seem unlikely, since Krauch received an Iron Cross personally from Hitler at the start of the war, 'for his great victory on the battlefield of German industry'.[242] Even the Vermittlungsstelle Wehrmacht (War Economic Central office) of Farben, which the prosecution had considered the main clearing house between the military authorities and the three great productive divisions of IG Farben (which Goering had requested IG Farben to set up and which was headed by Krauch, who thus became an employee of Goering)[243] in 'neither its organisation nor its operation gives any hint of plans for aggressive war'.[244] In support of the claim that the Farben leaders were well aware of, and perhaps more directly involved in, planning the aggressive war for their own purposes, the prosecution had produced a letter in which Krauch argued for the take-over of neighbouring countries' industries, 'peaceably at first':

> It is essential for Germany to strengthen its own war potential as well as that of its allies to such an extent that the coalition is equal to the efforts of practically the rest of the world. This can be achieved only by new, strong, and combined efforts by all of the allies, and by expanding and improving the greater economic domain corresponding to the improved raw material basis of the coalition, peaceably at first, to the Balkans and Spain.[245]

When in 1936 Krauch joined Goering's staff on the execution of the Four Year Plan he was not authorised to make decisions relating to chemical produc-

239 *IG Farben Case*, Judgment, p. 1107.
240 Ibid.
241 *IG Farben Case*, Judgment, p. 1109.
242 Borkin 74. Cf. 'IG Farben was Hitler and Hitler was IG Farben', according to US Senator Homer T. Bone to the US Senate Committee on Military Affairs on June 4, 1943.
243 Dubois 1952, pp. 84–5.
244 *IG Farben Case*, Judgment, p. 1109.
245 *IG Farben Case*, Judgment, p. 1116.

tion, being merely retained for his 'expert advice' on 'recommending plans for expansion or erection of plants', etc.[246] While the Prosecution had argued that it must have been obvious to him as an expert that the quantities IG Farben had been asked to produce far outstripped the demands of a defensive war,[247] the Tribunal held that this knowledge could only be inferred '[i]f we were trying military men' and Krauch et al. 'were not military men at all'.[248] Whereas,

> [t]he defendants may have been, as some of them undoubtedly were, alarmed at the accelerated pace that armament was taking. Yet even Krauch, who participated in the Four Year Plan within the chemical field, *undoubtedly did not realize* that, in addition to strengthening Germany, he was participating in making the nation ready for a planned attack of an aggressive nature.[249]

Seemingly going to great lengths in its effort to 'talk right' the actions of the defendants brought up by the prosecution, the Tribunal said:

> Considering the whole report, it seems that Krauch was recommending plans for the strengthening of Germany which, to his mind, was being encircled and threatened by strong foreign powers, and that this situation might and probably would at some time result in war. But it falls far short of being evidence of his knowledge of the existence of a plan on the part of the leaders of the German Reich to start an aggressive war.[250]

Eventually the Tribunal summarised its appreciation of the further evidence submitted to it out of concern for the length of the judgment and summarily stated: 'This labor has led to the *definite* conclusion that Krauch did not knowingly participate in the planning, preparation or initiation of an aggressive war'.[251] The role of other defendants is dealt with only briefly. In regard to the 20 February 1933 meeting with Hitler and Goering (see above) after which IG Farben contributed RM 400,000 to the Nazi election fund, the Tribunal states,

246 *IG Farben Case*, Judgment, p. 1110.
247 *IG Farben Case*, Judgment, p. 1112.
248 *IG Farben Case*, Judgment, p. 1113.
249 *IG Farben Case*, Judgment, p. 1114, emphasis added.
250 *IG Farben Case*, Judgment, p. 1116.
251 *IG Farben Case*, Judgment, p. 1117, emphasis added.

'This contribution was made to a movement that had its basic origin in the unemployment and general financial chaos of a world-wide depression ... To say that this contribution indicates a sinister alliance, is to misread the facts as they then existed'.[252] Here the Tribunal neglects the sentiment expressed in Krauch's letter, cited above.[253]

On count one, waging a war of aggression, the Tribunal manages to subvert the meaning of ICL – the individualisation of responsibility in IL – as expressed by Justice Jackson at the IMT:

> The defendants now before us were neither high public officials in the civil government nor high military officers. Their participation was that of followers and not leaders. If we lower the standard of participation to include them, it is difficult to find a logical place to draw the line between the guilty and the innocent among the great mass of German people. It is, of course, unthinkable that the majority of Germans should be condemned as guilty of committing crimes against peace. This would amount to a determination of collective guilt to which the corollary of mass punishment is the logical result for which there is no precedent in international law and no justification in human relations. We cannot say that a private citizen shall be placed in the position of being compelled to determine in the heat of war whether his government is right or wrong, or, if it starts right, when it turns wrong. We would not require the citizen, at the risk of becoming a criminal under the rules of international justice, to decide that his country has become an aggressor and that he must lay aside his patriotism, the loyalty to his homeland, and the defense of his own fireside at the risk of being adjudged guilty of crimes against peace on the one hand, or of becoming a traitor to his country on the other, if he makes an erroneous decision based upon facts of which he has but vague knowledge.[254]

The Tribunal appears here to be responding to a sensitive point raised by Krauch himself during the proceedings: What if US business were to stop supporting American war efforts?[255] There was awareness on the bench that US industry was watching these trials, and that changing political circumstances

252 IG *Farben Case*, Judgment 11, p. 17.

253 As well as, amongst others, the analysis supplied in *Bernstein IG Farben Report* (*supra*).

254 IG *Farben Case*, Judgment, p. 1126.

255 IG *Farben Case*, Final statements by the Defendants, Krauch, p. 1055.

(including the start of the Cold War) may well mean the US Government would come to rely on its industrialists.[256]

With regards to the third count (participation in slave labour programme and in the holocaust) the prosecution had argued, 'Farben performed most of the research for the secret development of poison gas for war ... In 1943, Farben produced 95 percent of the poison gas in Germany'.[257] The indictment charges in Paragraph 131 that '[p]oison gases and various deadly pharmaceuticals manufactured by Farben and supplied by Farben to officials of the SS were used in experimentation upon, and the extermination of, enslaved persons in concentration camps throughout Europe. Experiments on human beings (including concentration camp inmates), without their consent, were conducted *by Farben* to determine the effects of deadly gases, vaccines, and related products'.[258] However, the Tribunal was not persuaded that the defendants *knew* the purpose of the gas supply despite the fact that a number of accused had been members of the supervisory council of Degesch, and despite the extraordinary quantities in which the gas was delivered to the extermination camps. Additionally, the Tribunal did not consider it proven, despite the 'common procedure' of the distribution of pharmaceutical preparations to medical professionals for testing, that the defendants had known of the criminal methods of the doctors, some of which had carried out their experiments at Auschwitz.

In relation to slave labour the prosecution had argued that 'the defendants, through the instrumentality of Farben and otherwise, embraced, adopted, and executed the forced labour policies of the Third Reich, thereby becoming accessories to and taking consenting part in the commission of war crimes and crimes against humanity'.[259] The Tribunal cited the IMT judgment to emphasise that at least 5,000,000 persons were deported from occupied territories to Germany. Thirteen of the IG Farben defendants were convicted on the slave labour charges with those convicted for the Auschwitz project receiving the 'heaviest of the very light sentences'.[260]

Immediately after the judgment was read, Judge Hebert made a statement to the effect that, although he concurred with the result reached by the majority

256 See also the 'liberal application of the necessity doctrine' *IG Farben Case*, p. 1175 and critique of this point in *Taylor IC*, p. 317.

257 *IG Farben Case* Indictment, p. 27.

258 *IG Farben Case* Indictment, p. 54, emphasis added.

259 *IG Farben Case*, Judgment, p. 1172.

260 *Taylor IC*, p. 319.

under counts one and five of the indictment acquitting all defendants of crimes against the peace, '[t]he judgment contains many statements with which I do not agree and in a number of respects is at variance with my reasons for reaching the result of acquittal'.[261]

Only in the Auschwitz context did the Tribunal find some evidence of Farben's proactive attitude regarding slave labour, but the area of criminal liability was still constructed very narrowly. Having considered various locations for a new synthetic rubber plant, on the recommendation of defendant Ambros, the small Polish village of Oświęcim was selected.[262] It is said that Ambros visited the construction site of the project and saw the concentration camp inmates at work. He also visited the main concentration camp at Auschwitz in the winter of 1941–42 in company with some 30 important visitors (possibly the Himmler Circle) and 'he saw no abuse of inmates and thought that the camp was well conducted'.[263]

The prosecution had shown how in 1942, at the instigation of Farben, Monowitz was built, a separate labour camp across the road from the Farben plant at Auschwitz.[264] 'Work-to-death labour' at the Farben factory is described by the Tribunal in its judgment euphemistically as '[t]hose [workers] who became unable to work or who were not amenable to discipline were sent back to the Auschwitz concentration camp or, as was more often the case, to Birkenau for extermination in the gas chambers'. Also, it is noted, '[t]he plant site was not entirely without inhumane incidents'.[265] Nevertheless, '[i]t is clear that Farben did not deliberately pursue or encourage inhumane policy with respect to the workers. In fact, some steps were taken by Farben to alleviate the situation. It *voluntarily and at its own expense* provided hot soup for the workers on the site at noon'.[266] When utilising free 'work-to-death labour', however, this appears little like generosity and even less an exculpatory factor for the Farben defendants. The fact remained, as stated by the Tribunal, that 'the labor for Auschwitz was procured through the Reich Labor Office at Farben's request. Forced labor was used for a period of approximately 3 years, from 1942 until the end of the war'.[267] Only five of the 24 defendants were found guilty under count three, and given very light sentences.[268]

261 *IG Farben Case*, Judgment, p. 1204.
262 *IG Farben Case*, Judgment, p. 1180.
263 *IG Farben Case*, Judgment, p. 1181.
264 Dubois 1952, pp. 156–7.
265 *IG Farben Case*, Judgment, p. 1184.
266 *IG Farben Case*, Judgment, p. 1185, emphasis added.
267 *IG Farben Case*, Judgment, p. 1185.
268 *IG Farben Case*, Judgment, pp. 1205–10.

Missing from the judgment is any mention of the number of worker deaths and the fact that defendant Dürrfeld actually lived at Auschwitz for three years and entertained his colleagues there, and that they socialised with Höss, the camp commander.[269] In addition, neither did the medical experiments (which had been *admitted*)[270] receive any mention in the judgment, nor the fact that IG Farben's Auschwitz plant made artificial fertiliser using ashes from the Auschwitz crematorium: 'There were times, when the production at IG Farben of fertilizers, was at a level with the production (using IG Farben chemicals) at Auschwitz of ashes'.[271]

In a manner that sought to align the German Industrialists' motivations with those present in the US in the rapidly changing global order, it was said that the Farben directors had been taken in by Hitler's fear of communism, and had acted in response to his continual warnings that Germany must be prepared to defend itself against 'danger in the East'.[272]

In his closing statement, Krauch appears to anticipate this connection, and with it, his 'amicable'[273] sentence:

> When I heard the final plea of the prosecution yesterday, I often thought of my colleagues in the United States and in England and tried to imagine what these men would think, when they heard and read these attacks hurled at us by the prosecution. For after all, they, too, are scientists and engineers; they had similar problems. They, like us, were called upon by the state to perform certain duties. That was true then, before the world war, and that is true now, as we know from information received from the United States. A citizen cannot evade the call of the state. He must submit and must obey.[274]

269 Dubois 1952, p. 212.

270 Dubois describes a scene reminiscent of the film *Schindler's List* where the camp commander lives in a large villa overlooking the camp and hosts many parties there (Dubois 1952, p. 212).

271 'Es gab Zeiten, in denen sich die Produktion der IG-Farben an künstlichen Düngemitteln mit der Produktion von Asche, gewonnen in den Vernichtungslagern bei Verwendung von Giftgasen und Brennstoffen der IG-Farben, die Waage hielten'. IG Farben 1960: Mächtiger und Gefährlicher denn je, Institut für Marxismus-Leninismus and der Technischen Hochschule für Chemie Leuna-Merseburg, 1960, p. 14. Also, Dubois 1952, p. 212.

272 DuBois 1952, p. 338.

273 Term used in Jeßberger 2009, p. 924.

274 *IG Farben Case*, Final statements by the Defendants, Krauch, p. 1055.

In particular since Farben had had close relationships with Standard Oil, this trial had been watched closely by the US home public,[275] something which Krauch had no doubt heard about, allowing him to direct his statements to his cross-Atlantic 'colleagues'. Krauch was sentenced to 6 years, Ambros to 8, and the others received sentences between 1.5 and 8 years[276] – according to Dubois, 'sentences light enough to please a chicken thief'.[277] Four were acquitted. By comparison, in the *Justices Case*, that same week, four life sentences were passed, and in the *Pohl Case* against the SS Economic and Administrative Office (who had handled the logistical and administrative side of slave labour) four death sentences were passed, and no prison sentence below 10 years with four of 20 or more.[278] The defendant Ilgner was considered innocent even of the aggressive deeds he had admitted.[279] Dubois surmises, 'no doubt they [the judges] were influenced somewhat by our foreign policy'.[280]

Decades later it emerged that Judge Hebert had drafted a dissent on the aggressive war charge in the IG Farben case, which he never submitted but which was preserved in the *Hebert Archives*. From his raw, and seemingly immediate response a similar perspective on the proceedings can be gleaned.[281] In the draft, Judge Hebert argued that all defendants should have been found guilty on count three of the indictment. He stated that 'the record shows that Farben willingly cooperated and gladly utilized each new source of manpower as it developed. Disregard of basic human rights did not deter these defendants'. And '[w]illing cooperation with the slave labor utilization of the Third Reich was a matter of corporate policy that permeated the whole Farben organization ... For this reason, criminal responsibility goes beyond the actual immediate participants at Auschwitz. It includes other Farben Vorstand plant-managers and embraces all who knowingly participated in the shaping of the corporate policy'.[282] Hebert took his time deliberating whether to submit this dissent, but instead submitted a concurring judgment six months later after the end of all *CCL10* trials. His reluctance remained: 'The issues of fact are truly so close as to cause genuine concern as to whether or not justice has

275 *Taylor Final Report*, p. 79.
276 *IG Farben Case*, Judgment, pp. 1205–10.
277 Dubois 1952, p. 339.
278 *Justices Case*; *Pohl Case*.
279 Dubois 1952, p. 355.
280 Dubois 1952, p. 357.
281 The scanned type-written document is undated. *Farben Case Hebert Dissent*.
282 Ibid.

actually been done because of the enormous and indispensable role these defendants were shown to have played in the building of the war machine which made Hitler's aggression possible'.[283] These words would seem absurd to appear in a judicial opinion, and reflect a frustrated liberal humanitarian impulse.

6.1.5 The *Krupp Case*, Case No. 10

The judgment in the last industrialist case at the NMT, *The United States v. Alfried Krupp von Bohlen und Halbach et al.* (the *Krupp Case*),[284] was delivered on 31 July 1947, the day after the sentencing in the *IG Farben Case*. As in the *IG Farben Case*, the Tribunal's task was made more difficult by the fact that a great many of the Krupp firm's files were burnt by order of Krupp officials.[285]

Alfried Krupp, the main defendant in this trial and the son of Gustav Krupp (who was still considered unfit to stand trial) had been vested with sole ownership and control of the family company by a special Reich decree (the 'Lex Krupp') of 12 November 1943. In addition to the charges levied against Alfried Krupp and eleven other Krupp officials which were comparable to the Flick charges,[286] the defendants were initially also charged with committing crimes against the peace by planning and waging aggressive wars (count one), and with conspiracy to commit such crimes against peace (count four). Those latter charges were dismissed following a defence motion[287] in a two-sentence order dated 5 April 1948 stating that the 'evidence fails to show prima facie that any of the defendants is guilty of the offense charged in count one or the offense charged in count four of the indictment'.[288] A separate opinion by Judge Anderson states that criminal liability for the planning or waging of an aggressive war must be restricted to 'leaders and policy-makers' and cannot extend to 'private citizens who participate … in the war effort'.[289]

What is remarkable in the *Krupp Case* is that the Prosecution had not argued that Krupp defendants had been part of the 'Nazi conspiracy' in the meaning of the IMT trial, but that they had been part of a '*Krupp conspiracy*' which was a manifestation of something altogether bigger:

---

283 *IG Farben Case*, Concurring Opinion by Justice Hebert, p. 1212.
284 *Krupp Case.*
285 *Krupp Case*, Judgment, p. 1331.
286 Although without SS charges nor Aryanisation-related charges.
287 *Krupp Case*, p. 356.
288 *Krupp Case*, p. 390.
289 Judge Anderson's Separate Opinion on Counts 1 and 4, at 408.

> Nazism was, after all, only the temporary political manifestation of certain ideas and attitudes which long antedated Nazism, and which will not perish nearly so easily. In this case, we are at grips with something much older than Nazism; something which fused with Nazi ideas to produce the Third Reich, but which has its own independent and pernicious vitality.[290]

What this was, was *expansionism* close to Bukharin's understanding of economic imperialism: to ensure Krupp's own continually increasing profitability, it was said to have driven the state and military to colonial expansion: what I called the imperialism at the heart of the corporation in Chapter 2.[291] Dismissing the charge, Judge Wilkins considered that Krupp's expansionism since the 1920s merely meant Krupp had acted in the firm's financial interest as behoves a businessman.[292] Taylor calls the acquittal of the aggressive war charges 'rather sketchy'.[293]

The Tribunal then considered the remaining spoliation and forced labour charges. The tribunal found, in contrast to the finding in the *IG Farben Case* (above), in terms of *knowledge* with regard to the firm's activities at Auschwitz, that the persecution of Jews by the Nazis was 'common knowledge not only in Germany but throughout the civilised World' and that the firm's officials, could not *not* have known.[294]

Apart from ignorance, the defendants had pleaded necessity, stating that production quotas were set by the Nazi government and to reach those one had to use slave labour, and had they refused to do so, they would have suffered 'dire consequences'.[295] Reviewing the Flick decision, the Tribunal held '[s]o

---

290 Judge Wilkins' Separate Opinion on Counts 1 and 4, at 412, quoting the prosecution's submission, which further argued, 'From the First World War, the Krupp firm has conspired against the peace of Europe. Like the Nazi Party, it has nurtured at all times the idea that Germany would rise to power through its military might. In 1933, it entered into an alliance with that Party for the realization of their common objectives. Its activities, both before and after this alliance, contributed materially to Germany's ability to wage its wars of aggression. As new people came into positions of control in Krupp, they continued the conspiracy which starting in 1919 lasted at least until the defeat of Germany'. Judge Wilkins' Separate Opinion on Counts 1 and 4, at 412.

291 Kröll connects this with Max Weber's 'Wilhelminismus': 'die Allianz zwischen Großindustrie und Pseudoaristokratie mit der Folge der Derationalisierung der deutschen Weltpolitik', Kröll 1999, p. 176.

292 *Krupp Case*, Judgment, p. 1412.

293 *Taylor IC*, p. 309.

294 *Krupp Case*, Judgment, p. 1434.

295 *Krupp Case*, Judgment, p. 1435.

far as we have been able to ascertain with the limited facilities at hand, the application to a factual situation such as that presented in the Nuernberg trials of industrialists is novel'.[296] Going on to consider the application of the defence in this case, the Tribunal establishes that, while the onus is on the defendants to prove they were acting under compulsion or coercion, here 'the evidence falls short in a vital particular … [T]he competent and credible evidence leaves no doubt that in committing the acts here charged as crimes, the guilty individuals were not acting under compulsion or coercion exerted by the Reich authorities within the meaning of the law of necessity'.[297] The Tribunal distinguished the *Flick* case to the extent that it had found four of the Flick defendants had not wanted to employ slave labour. The Krupp defendants' willingness to do so had been comprehensively shown: for example, in a letter from Alfried Krupp: 'As we are, under the circumstances described, very anxious to employ Russian prisoners of war in the very near future, we should be grateful if you would give us your opinion on this matter as soon as possible'. As the witness Ruemann put it, sitting round a table poring over a map while listening to the radio announcing German advances, Alfried Krupp and other industrialists had resembled 'vultures gathered around their booty'.[298]

The Tribunal thus rephrased the necessity question in the case as this proposition:

> To avoid losing my job or the control of my property, I am warranted in employing thousands of civilian deportees, prisoners of war, and concentration camp inmates; keeping them in a state of involuntary servitude; exposing them daily to death or great bodily harm, under conditions which did in fact result in the deaths of many of them; and working them in an undernourished condition in the production of armament intended for use against the people who would liberate them and indeed even against the people of their homelands.[299]

---

296 *Krupp Case*, Judgment, p. 1437.

297 *Krupp Case*, Judgment, p. 1438.

298 *Krupp Case*, Judgment, p. 1348.

299 *Krupp Case*, Judgment, pp. 1444–5; also, 'If we may assume that as a result of opposition to Reich policies, Krupp would have lost control of his plant and the officials their positions, it is difficult to conclude that the law of necessity justified a choice favorable to themselves and against the unfortunate victims who had no choice at all in the matter', id.

The Tribunal did not allow the defence, among others because it was convinced that Krupp was a close personal friend of Hitler and that all of the Krupp defendants enjoyed Hitler's protection.[300] Yet, the rephrasing of the necessity defence here contravenes Nuremberg principle IV on Superior Orders.[301] This case lends itself to comparison with *United States v. Josef Altstoetter et al* (the *Justice Case*),[302] where the Prosecution asked one of the defendants the question, 'can you imagine what effect it might have had if men of your influence had stood up against Hitler?' Moreover, it can be contrasted with examples of defendants such as Schacht, who were acquitted *because* they stood up against the Nazi regime.[303]

The comparatively heavy sentences ranged between 6 and 12 years for 10 defendants, and 3 years for one, and included the forfeiture of Alfried Krupp's real and personal property.[304] When compared with Taylor's statement, after what he called the 'Krupp snafu', that 'Alfried Krupp was a very lucky man, for, had he been named, he would almost certainly have been convicted and given a very stiff sentence by the International Military Tribunal',[305] the Krupp defendants' trial seems 'amicable' indeed.

6.1.6 The *Pohl Case*, Case No. 4

In January 1947, just before the start of *Flick*, the Military Tribunal II commenced the prosecution of Pohl and 17 other defendants in *The United States v. Oswald Pohl et al.*, with a decision being issued on 3 November 1947.[306] Oswald Pohl was the head of the SS's Main Economic and Administrative Department (Wirtschaft und Verwaltungshauptamt – WVHA), one of the 12 main departments of the SS.[307] One of the divisions of the WVHA dealt with the allocation of forced labourers to public and private employers in Germany and the occupied countries (Amtsgruppe D), and another, Amtsgruppe W, was responsible for the operation and maintenance of various industrial, manufacturing, and service enterprises throughout Germany and the occupied coun-

300 *Krupp Case*, Judgment, 1446.
301 *Nuremberg Principles.*
302 *Justice Case.*
303 See above, Section 4.3.1.
304 *Krupp Case*, Judgment, p. 1450.
305 Taylor 1992, p. 94.
306 *Pohl Case.*
307 One of the tasks that Pohl was to execute in this function was the destruction of the Warsaw Ghetto. Pohl engaged four private contracting firms, who employed forced labour. *Pohl Case*, Judgment, p. 986.

tries.[308] Another of the WVHA's activities was the management of property expropriated from Jews.[309]

A defendant of note in the *Pohl Case* is Karl Mummenthey. According to the judgment, 'In his direction and management of the German Earth and Stone Works, known as DEST, none of the defendants was more directly associated with concentration camp inmate labor than Karl Mummenthey'.[310] The DEST companies comprised 'brickworks and quarries at the Flossenbuerg, Mauthausen, Gross-Rosen, Natzweiler, Neuengamme (see below), and Stutthof concentration camps. The ceramic works of Allach and Bohemia were also subordinated to office WI under Mummenthey. The gravel works at Auschwitz and Treblinka, the granite quarry at Blizyn, the Clinker Works at Linz ... The DEST industries were strictly concentration camp enterprises'.[311] Interestingly, in his defence it had been 'Mummenthey's plan to picture himself as a private business man in no way associated with the sternness and rigor of SS discipline, and entirely detached from concentration camp routine'.[312] The picture failed to convince. 'Mummenthey was a definite integral and important figure in the whole concentration camp set-up, and, as an SS officer, wielded military power of command. If excesses occurred in the industries under his control he was in a position not only to know about them, but to do something ... The evidence in this case reveals that there was perhaps no industry which permitted such constant maltreatment of prisoners as the DEST enterprises'.[313] Viz. 'Prosecution witness Engler, testifying to conditions in the DEST plants at the Sachsenhausen-Oranienburg concentration camp, declared that ... because of the heavy work and inadequate food there was an average of from 800 to 900 deaths per month ... [T]he average life duration of a punitive company worker was four weeks'.[314]

The tone of the judges in the *Pohl Case* judgment is different from that of the other judgments. There is more *ad hominem* criticism of the defendants and less careful analysis of the applicable law. Some of the judgment adopts a cynical tone, e.g.: 'Mummenthey's assumed or criminal naivete went to the extreme of asserting that inmates were covered by accident insur-

308 *Pohl Case*, Indictment, p. 6.
309 *Pohl Case*, Judgment, p. 990.
310 *Pohl Case*, Judgment, p. 1051.
311 Ibid.
312 Ibid.
313 *Pohl Case*, Judgment, p. 1052.
314 *Pohl Case*, Judgment, p. 1052.

ance'.[315] What can be seen in this case, compared with the IMT and the earlier cases, is that there is an effort on the part of the tribunal to put business into a place subordinate to the Nazi state, even to the point that Mummenthey considers portraying himself as a businessman would make him less culpable. In the judgment, Mummenthey, as an SS officer, is considered to have had the power and authority to curb industry's excesses with regard to the prisoners. This case at the same time sends the message (to US home industry) that the responsibility for setting boundaries of propriety is with the state, not industry, hence industry can continue working on defence contracts without fear of liability.

6.1.7 Rasche in the *Ministries Case*, Case No. 11

Karl Rasche, former Chairman of Dresdner Bank, was tried in *United States v. Ernst Weizsaecker et al.* (the *Ministries Case*) as a single private banker amidst 18 former Third Reich ministers and senior civil servants, and two SS Generals.[316] In the indictment, which was served on 4 November 1947, Rasche was charged with facilitating slave labour through making loans to entities using slave labour, and economic plunder, as well as membership in the Circle of Friends of Himmler and the SS. The case took 17 months between indictment and judgment, making it the longest of the NMT cases.

The defendant Rasche directed and supervised activities of the Dresdner Bank (the 'SS Bank') and its affiliates in occupied Western areas involving economic exploitation, including particularly activities involving transfer of control of Dutch enterprises to selected German firms through the process called 'Verflechtung', which was the 'interlacing' of Dutch and German capital and economic interests with a view to creating a single market. He was convicted only on the spoliation count, as the Tribunal found Rasche had participated actively in the Reich's programme of 'Aryanisation' in The Netherlands and Czechoslovakia. In addition, he was found guilty of SS membership and sentenced to seven years.

According to the Tribunal,

> The real question is, is it a crime to make a loan, knowing or having good reason to believe that the borrower will use the funds in financing enter-

315 *Pohl Case*, Judgment, p. 1053.

316 *Ministries Case*. Other defendants on the economic side included Emil Puhl (vice president of the Reichsbank), Paul Koerner (Deputy to Goering in the Office of the Four Year Plan), Paul Pleiger (the dominant figure in the Hermann Goering Works) and Hans Kehrl (who had held a number of economic positions in the Nazi government) (*Taylor IC*, p. 331).

> prises which are employed in using labor in violation of either national or international law? Does he stand in any different position than one who sells supplies or raw materials to a builder building a house, knowing that the structure will be used for an unlawful purpose? A bank sells money or credit in the same manner as the merchandiser of any other commodity ... Our duty is to try and punish those guilty of violating international law, and we are not prepared to state that such loans constitute a violation of that law, nor has our attention been drawn to any ruling to the contrary.[317]

Rasche, in the 452-page judgment that was delivered 18 months after the indictment on 11 April 1949 'in a vastly altered international climate', received a lenient sentence, as did the other defendants in his case.[318]

Discussed sequentially, it is possible to see the changing attitude to business's role in World War Two reflected in the cases. Below the surface, a deeper US need can be discerned also: the need to reassure American industrialists, perhaps counter-intuitively *through these trials*, that production for the Korean and other, potentially *aggressive*, wars would not lead to prosecution.[319] From this perspective, the Tribunals' task was to distinguish culpable involvement with an evil regime from innocent 'business'.[320] A gradual process of exoneration takes place, which is crowned, eventually, by the clemency granted the industrialists by General John McCloy in 1951 (Section 8).

7 Industrialists in Other Zonal Trials

In Germany the other Allies also tried industrialists in their respective zones of occupation. Each of the Allies' political priorities finds its reflection in these trials too.

7.1 *Industrialists in the British Zonal Trials*

According to Bloxham, the British purposively ran a prosecutions programme disassociated from the Nuremberg programme, and from the very beginning sought to limit its scope.[321] Bush asserts that Britain's tactic was to co-opt a

317 *Ministries Case*, Judgment, p. 622.
318 *Taylor IC*, pp. 333–4.
319 Dubois 1952, p. 21.
320 Dubois 1952, p. 20.
321 Generally, Bloxham 2003.

number of industries rather than to try industrialists.[322] The British Government had been worried about the prominence of the 'economic case' at the IMT, and according to Bloxham was instrumental in preventing an 'IMT2', as (at the dawn of the Cold War) they no longer wanted to cooperate with the Soviets in what could for them be a propaganda opportunity.[323] Nevertheless, already before the end of the IMT trial, the British had tried personnel of Tesch and later also members of at least one further company, Steinöl. There is next to no secondary literature on these specific trials,[324] nor have government deliberations been published which explain why they were held.[325] The jurisdiction of the British Military Courts covered only 'war crimes', defined in Regulation 1 of the *Royal Warrant* as any violation of the laws and usages of war, and did not cover crimes against humanity or crimes against the peace.[326] This *a priori* limited the British to the prosecution of crimes against *Allied nationals only*. Handing over any 'major' war crimes suspect found in the British Occupation Zone to the Americans, the British tried mostly minor cases relating to crimes against British servicemen.[327] In the absence of published material documenting government policy on the issue, the (small) size, (short) length, (low) prominence of the trials as well as the language used in the trials would suggest that although there were some businesspersons among the accused, these trials were not intended to send a message about corporate/business involvement in the war, in the way the US trials of the industrialists' were.

7.1.1 The *Zyklon B Case*

One of the best-remembered British cases is the *Zyklon B Case*, which at the time, however, was low-profile,[328] 'a minor case that rested on the fact that British nationals were among the victims'.[329] The trial took place during the height of the IMT trial, between 1 and 8 March 1946, lasting only a week, compared to the 8–17 months of the later US cases against the industrialists. Despite being considered a minor case at the time, the trial of Bruno Tesch,

---

322 Bush 2009, p. 1134.

323 Bloxham 2003, pp. 100, 102.

324 The *Steinöl/Wittig Neuengamme Concentration Camp Case* is only mentioned in German historical reports on the Neuengamme concentration camp: see, e.g. Buggeln (2007).

325 British National Archives files on the *Steinöl/WittigNeuengamme Concentration Camp Case* and the *Zyklon B Case* do not answer these questions, nor does UNWCC 1947, but see Bloxham 2003; Ebbinghaus 1999.

326 *Royal Warrant*.

327 E.g., the famous *Stalag Luft Case* (Bloxham 2003, p. 106).

328 Bloxham 2003.

329 Bush 2009, p. 1237, but cf. *Zyklon B Case*, p. 102, 'it was not alleged that British citizens were among the victims'.

Karl Weinbacher and Joachim Drosihn at the British Military Court in Hamburg, is significant in the debate around 'corporate accountability' in that it was the first trial of industrialists accused of World War Two crimes.[330] The Tesch company was a subsidiary of IG Farben, which manufactured the Zyklon B gas sold by Tesch. While the British objective was to punish those who had killed, injured or otherwise harmed British interests/servicemen, they did not limit themselves to those directly, physically responsible for the acts. Of the defendants it was said, in the trial, that they 'at Hamburg, Germany, between 1st January, 1941, and 31st March, 1945, in violation of the laws and usages of war did supply poison gas used for the extermination of allied nationals interned in concentration camps well knowing that the said gas was to be so used'.[331]

In his summing up, the Judge Advocate General (JAG) directed the Court that for a guilty verdict they would have to be certain of three facts, 'first, that Allied nationals had been gassed by means of Zyklon B; secondly, that this gas had been supplied by Tesch and Stabenow; and thirdly, that the accused knew that the gas was to be used for the purpose of killing human beings'.[332] The JAG further stated 'when you know what kind of man Dr. Tesch was, it inevitably follows that he must have known every little thing about his business'.[333] While there was no direct evidence specifically imputing knowledge to Weinbacher, such was inferred from 'the general atmosphere and conditions of the firm'.[334] The JAG considered Drohsin to have been a subordinate employee and directed the Court that in the absence of any evidence Drohsin could have influenced matters, no knowledge as to the use of the gas could make him guilty.[335] The company officers were not shown (or required to have had) intent vis-à-vis the killings.[336]

Necessity was pleaded in mitigation of the sentences in the case. Counsel for Tesch stated that any cooperation had happened 'only under enormous pressure from the SS', and that furthermore, if he had not cooperated, the SS would surely have achieved their aims by other means.[337] Counsel for Weinbacher argued that he as a business employee might have thought that the ultimate

330 *Zyklon B Case.* Case files including appeals petitions are accessible at the UK National Archives in Kew.

331 *Zyklon B Case*, p. 93.

332 *Zyklon B Case*, p. 101.

333 Ibid.

334 See also the *Mauthausen Concentration Camp Case.* In Chapter 4C, I discuss 'corporate culture' which could be compared.

335 *Zyklon B Case*, p. 102.

336 For a discussion of the profit motive, see Ch. 5 below, and Stephens 2002.

337 *Zyklon B Case*, p. 105.

use of the gas was Tesch's responsibility as the company director and that if he had refused to supply the gas the SS would have immediately handed him over to the Gestapo.[338]

Nevertheless, after this trial of seven days, based on the JAG's directions, the Court found Tesch and Weinbacher guilty and sentenced them to death.[339] Drohsin was acquitted. Appeals were filed on behalf of Tesch and Weinbacher, but these were dismissed and the two were hanged in May 1946.[340]

7.1.2 The *Steinöl/Neuengamme Concentration Camp Case*

In January 1947, coinciding with the start of the *Pohl* case, and after the US turnaround, the British tried Professor Solms Wilhelm Wittig, the director of the Steinöl company, and two colleagues, Dr. Otto Hefter and Hans-Detlef Ohlen. They were tried together with Friedrich Ebsen, Karl Truschel, Erich Arnold Jahn, Johann Heitz, Arthur Große und Herbert Schiefelbein, six guards of the (relatively) small Neuengamme concentration camp that had been built especially to provide a workforce for the company's shale oil extraction. The camp housed mainly Spanish communists, Belgian, Dutch and French resistance fighters and Danish Jehovah's Witnesses, and seven of the defendants were convicted in relation to the unlawful deaths and maltreatment of Allied nationals. Wittig's death sentence was commuted to 20 years, by Anthony Eden, but he was released in 1955.[341] As such, being the case that ran concurrently with the NMT trials, it follows the US pattern more closely than *Tesch*.

Little can be said about the significance of the British prosecution's policy on the basis of these cases and limited discussion in the literature. However, it can be suggested that at the time, while it was a British priority to focus on crimes against British servicemen (as in the US, heavy losses among troops engaged in the liberation of Europe had to be acknowledged) and there was a willingness to draw a wide circle of complicity, a focus on industry was not apparent. According to the UNWCC commentary, 'The Military Court acted on the principle that any civilian who is an accessory to a violation of the laws and customs of war is himself also liable as a war criminal'.[342] At this point, no differentiation is made between accessories as to whether they are involved for commercial reasons or otherwise (see Chapter 4 below). The question remains

338 Ibid.

339 As is usual in such cases, there is no reasoned (written) judgment from the Court.

340 *Tesch Death Warrant.*

341 *Steinöl/Wittig Neuengamme Concentration Camp Case,* National Archives file WO 235/283. This case is not mentioned in any of the other literature mentioned in this chapter.

342 *Zyklon B Case,* p. 103.

why no further industrialists were tried by the British in their zone of occupation: for example, the Hamburg shipping firms, which employed thousands of forced labourers.[343] Ties between British and German business – which could have received the State's protection as they did in the US – undoubtedly existed, but little has been published on this topic.

7.2 *Industrialists in the French Zonal Trials*

The French were keener to prosecute industrialists, so as to strengthen their government's hand against French collaborationist industrialists,[344] because French industry had suffered considerably from 'Aryanisation', and as many more French citizens had worked as slave labourers. Successful convictions would allow for expropriations of collaborators' property and generally allow the French government to regain control over its main industries. Moreover, the specific case of Röchling was of interest to the French as Röchling's empire was built in the heavily industrialised Saar region, long the subject of German-French border disputes.

7.2.1 The Case against Hermann Roechling and Others

The *Roechling Case* is appended to Vol. XIV of the Trials of War Criminals before the Nuernberg Military Tribunals under Control Council Law No. 10.[345] The indictment is dated 25 November 1947, the judgment 30 June 1948 and the judgment on appeal 25 January 1949. The main trial, which commenced at the time of the *Pohl* judgment, thus coincided in time with the *Farben*, *Krupp* and *Ministries* cases.

Hermann Röchling and four other directors of the Röchling Enterprises were tried by the General Tribunal of the Military Government of the French Zone of Occupation in Germany at Rastatt. In what may have been the first recorded twentieth-century war crimes case against industrialists, Hermann and Robert Röchling and several associates had already been sentenced to 10 years imprisonment by a French military tribunal for wartime plunder after World War One, although the judgment was annulled for technical reasons.[346]

The post-World War Two *Röchling* judgment stands out as the only judgment after the IMT in which a defendant was found guilty of *waging* an aggressive war (distinct from planning and preparing), and the only judgment in which

343 Conversation with Joop Baars (1918–2018), whose brother Cornelis was put to labour in the Hamburg docks.

344 Bloxham 2003, p. 100.

345 *Roechling Case, Blue Series*, XIV, p. 1061.

346 Taylor 1992, p. 304, fn. 159.

an *industrialist* was found guilty on aggressive war charges.[347] In that sense, this judgment is truest to the ideas about the instigators/causes of World War Two expressed by the Allies immediately after the war.

Indeed, the Tribunal placed the *Röchling Case* in the context of the findings of the IMT on the economic aspects of war and referred to the prosecutions being prepared at the USMT in Nuremberg. The indictment stated:

> If the 'Directors of German Enterprises'[[348]] plead that they only attached themselves to Hitler in order to oppose communism or 'Social Democracy', there exists no doubt that the profound reason for their attitude can be sought in their desire, long before the coming of national socialism, to extend their undertakings beyond the frontiers of the Reich.[349]

Hermann Röchling was accused of, amongst others, urging Hitler to invade the Balkans.

According to the prosecution, Röchling further took it upon himself to take control of French industries after the invasion of France, expelling local directors and replacing them with Röchling staff. He requested to be granted ownership of enterprises in Poland, France and other occupied countries. Certain plants were removed wholesale and rebuilt in Germany, while other companies just had their capital seized.[350] Additionally, the various Röchling directors were accused of requesting, organising and employing and maltreating forced labourers from occupied countries. Urging Nazi leaders to impose compulsory labour drafting on Belgian youths between 18 and 25, Hermann Röchling said, 'If a large number of young Belgians are in our hands in loose formations, they will also serve as hostages for the good conduct of their parents'.[351] The prosecution submitted: 'This systematic exploitation of foreign workers was to produce substantial profits and royalties, mostly emanating from the sale of war material, for the shareholders and directors'.[352]

In a letter to a colleague, Hermann Röchling had written:

347 *Roechling Case*, Judgment, p. 1061.

348 Earlier on the same page, 'it is apparent that these wars of aggression and these crimes could not have been rendered possible, except with the conscious assistance of certain great German Industrialists and financiers whom we will designate under the appellation "Directors of the German Enterprises"'. (*Roechling Case*, Judgment, p. 1062).

349 *Roechling Case*, Judgment, p. 1062.

350 *Roechling Case*, Judgment, pp. 1067–8.

351 *Roechling Case*, Judgment, p. 1085.

352 *Roechling Case*, Judgment, p. 1071.

> We shall only then succeed in reaching our objective, that is, to obtain definite possession of these enterprises, if we act in the capacity of interpreters of National-Socialist principles in maintaining these in the strongest manner and in practicing them. We must also prove that we are faithful supporters of the Fuehrer's policies, that is to say, that we must follow here a policy of Germanization, as much as that is possible.[353]

Here the scenario is congruent with the IMT's 'economic case'. However, Röchling and the other defendants appealed the verdict. The Appeal judgment of 25 January 1949 took into account the decisions in *Krupp*, *Flick* and *IG Farben*, and re-examined certain fundamental considerations (relating to superior orders, necessity and other defences put forward in the original case), the preparation and waging of aggressive wars, and war crimes of an economic nature.[354] The appeal court reached the conclusion that both superior orders and necessity can only be rated as extenuating circumstances (as per *CCL10*, Art. II).[355] (In the US cases discussed in Section 7.3 I discuss different interpretations of this article.) On the defence of lack of knowledge, the tribunal stated that it is a superior's duty to know what occurs in his organisation, and if successful, such defence would lead to the situation where the executing agents would seek cover behind the superior order, while the superior would hide behind a claim of lack of knowledge.[356] Finally the tribunal considered that the excuse of a total war (the defence had cited Clausewitz's doctrines) could not be taken into consideration.

Having considered the other industrialists' judgments, the Tribunal also re-examined Speer's acquittal of the aggressive war charge, concluding that the bar had been fixed very high by the IMT and Hermann Röchling must be acquitted. On review Röchling was again found guilty of the war crimes 'as the originator of a system of spoliation of industrial, financial and commercial enterprise'.[357] Emphatically disallowing any defence of 'necessity', the appeal court found 'that Hermann Roechling, in order to execute his plan for raising the production of iron, sacrificed all human considerations and demonstrated a complete lack of respect for the rights of the civilian population in the occupied countries'.[358] Likewise Hermann and the other defendants were found

353 *Roechling Case*, Judgment, p. 1082.
354 *Roechling Case*, Judgment on Appeal, p. 1098.
355 *Roechling Case*, Judgment on Appeal, p. 1104.
356 *Roechling Case*, Judgment on Appeal, p. 1104.
357 *Roechling Case*, Judgment on Appeal, p. 1119.
358 *Roechling Case*, Judgment on Appeal, p. 1131.

guilty of maltreatment of the forced labourers. The Appeal judgment replaced the original, imposed lower sentences and upheld the property forfeiture on the Roechlings.[359] That the *Röchling* defendants' sentences were significantly reduced in 1949 shows a softening of French attitudes also.[360]

7.3 *Industrialists in the Soviet Zonal Trials*

For the Soviets and GDR leaderships, the zonal trials were about *Systemkritik* (critique of the (capitalist) system) as much as they were about nationalising German industries. As reflected in Molotov's speech (above), the Soviets held on to the idea that World War Two had been a German war of imperialism and the inevitable result of the convergence of power in the hands of fewer and fewer cartels. Bukharin's *Imperialism and World Economy*, written in 1915, and elaborated by Lenin in *Imperialism: The Highest Stage of Capitalism*, supports this analysis,[361] expressed, unsympathetically, by Bloxham as '[t]he Soviets harbored the simplistic determinist view that Hitler was an instrument of German bankers and big business'.[362] While there is no clear indication that the Soviets discounted the 'Hitler factor'[363] in this way, it is clear that the Soviet leadership at least saw a unity of purpose in the actions of the Nazi political and military leaderships and the cartels.

It is said that the Soviet Military Tribunals ('SMT') convicted over 17,000 German former members of the Gestapo, SS, SD and civilian Nazi leadership.[364] Exact numbers are difficult to gauge as most SMT trials took place in secret and were not reported.[365] Exceptions are a number of public trials which Western authors such as Wentker describe as 'political trials'. The trials relating to business must have been many, considering that the SMT over the years ordered the expropriation of business enterprises and other property under Control Council Directive No. 38 in 337 cases.[366] As stated above (Section 2), for linguistic reasons I have not been able to research official records or press reports, and there is little to no research on the Soviet trials available in German or English.[367]

---

359 *Roechling Case*, Judgment on Appeal, p. 1142.

360 Ibid.

361 Bukharin 2003; Lenin 1934.

362 Bloxham 2003, p. 100.

363 Hilger 2008, p. 180.

364 And as in August 1947, 518 persons were sentenced by German courts in the Soviet Zone applying Control Council Law No. 10 (Wentker 2002, p. 64); and see, generally, Marxen 2001, p. 159.

365 Wentker 2002, p. 64.

366 Wentker 2002, p. 69, *Control Council Directive No. 38*.

367 But see Bilkova 2014; Vormbaum 2014; Ohsterloh 2011; Van Baar and Huisman 2012; Schüle 2003; Prusin 2003.

According to Wentker, from the 1950s and the foundation of the GDR in 1955 the Nazi trials became more clearly propagandistic, aimed at showing the public how Soviet/East German authorities had uprooted fascism in Eastern Germany while in the West many key Nazi leaders once again held high positions in government. Moreover, with the restoration of liberal capitalism West Germany was considered by the East to have once again created the premises for the emergence of fascism. These warnings were wrapped into the language of the trials. In 1963 the GDR held an *in absentia* trial of the (then) West German secretary of state Hans Globke, in a direct response to Israel's Eichmann trial. Globke had been a close colleague of Eichmann and was painted by the GDR court as 'Bonn's Eichmann'.[368]

7.3.1 Topf & Söhne

One example of a case against industrialists conducted by the SMT that has received attention in the literature is that against four officials of the firm Topf & Söhne, which had delivered specially developed crematory ovens to Auschwitz and other death camps.[369] Schüle, in a company history of Topf & Söhne, emphasises the generally under-researched responsibility of business for the 'industrialisation of killing'.[370]

The firm's director, Johannes Andreas Topf, committed suicide within days of the end of the war, and his deputy, also a Topf, fled to the US occupied zone. In 1946, four further officials of the firm were detained by the Soviet Occupation Authorities, Prüfer, Braun, Schultze and Sander. Excerpts of interrogation records were published in *Der Spiegel* in 1993.[371] All admitted to their roles in designing, manufacturing and selling the ovens, and ventilation systems for gas chambers, to Auschwitz and other death camps. Sander died of a heart attack during the trial while the other three were convicted and sentenced to 25 years in a Soviet penal camp.[372] In interrogation, Schulze had said that after he and his colleague had discovered the ovens were used for the cremation of the victims of mass-murder, he continued his work. 'I and Prüfer continued, because we were bound, through our signature. We stood under obligation, with the SS, the Topf firm and the NS State'.[373]

368 Wentker 2002, pp. 72–3. In fact this 'show trial' had the effect of a change in West German attitudes to former Nazi crimes and the initiation of a number of trials.

369 Pressac 1994; Vest 2010, p. 853, fn. 7.

370 Schüle 2003, p. 215; on the industrialisation of killing see further Traverso 2003.

371 *Topf documents in Der Spiegel* 1993.

372 *Topf documents in Der Spiegel* 1993. *Der Spiegel* notes that the confessions were unlikely to have been obtained under pressure.

373 *Topf documents in Der Spiegel* 1993.

Schüle reads in this statement evidence of 'self-objectification' – the agency in the decision to place a signature on the employment and supply contracts is negated when the 'I' becomes the object of fulfilment of a duty towards customer and employer.[374] The source of such sense of duty may not necessarily be the ideological agreement with the Nazi project, but rather, a traditional mentality of blind loyalty and negation of own responsibility. Such negation is facilitated by the legal constructs and bureaucracies of the corporation: morality leaves the legal relation. This echoes the conclusion of my Chapter 2A, that the corporate 'structure of irresponsibility' 'breeds' *anomie*, or the dissociation between business(wo)men and affected individuals. At the same time, in the run of these cases, the 'necessity' defence employed in the earlier cases (protecting one's own safety) turns into Mummenthey's attempt to portray himself as a businessman, 'just doing business' once capitalism knows itself on safer ground at Nuremberg, down to 'the obligation to fulfill the contractual terms' in Topf.

An alternative explanation of the Topf defendants' involvement in the Nazis' 'industrialisation of killing' is given by criminologists van Baar and Huisman. According to them, the patent application by Sanders for a 'four storied "continuous-operation corpse incineration oven for mass use"' is 'a good example of the desire for innovation'.[375] Indeed, '"a culture of perfection" seems to form an explanation for the involvement of Topf in the *Endlösung*'.[376] If this was indeed the case, it would show the alienation that can (and, to some extent, inevitably does) take place inside the corporation *in extremis*.

8 Aftermath: the Warm Bosom of the Western Powers, the Churchill and McCloy Clemencies, McCarthyism and the Rebuilding of West Germany

In the IG *Farben case* the defendants, making their final statements to the tribunal, displayed the historical foresight that was about to render them a particularly 'amicable justice'.[377]

Krauch's former colleague Kuehne in particular stated:

> The American industry at the present time is undergoing to a much greater degree the same development that we underwent at the time

374 Schüle 2003, p. 218.
375 Van Baar and Huisman 2012, p. 1041.
376 Van Baar and Huisman 2012, p. 1042.
377 Jeßberger 2010.

> of rearmament: that is to say, demands concerning air-raid protection, mobilization plans in the event of war, counterintelligence, and much more of the same type. It is even experiencing the stockpiling of atomic bombs without any industrialists being charged on that account for participating in aggressive warfare. And you have to bear in mind, Your Honors, there is no nation on your country's borders which is a menace to you industrially or ideologically.[378]

Lawyers like Dubois and Sasuly, Judge Hebert, and to some extent also Taylor, left Germany disappointed, frustrated, and enraged. On coming home, the case they had been fighting was now taboo. The tables had turned, the capitalists emerged as victors and the prosecutors became persecuted.

Kuehne, in his final statement to the *Farben* Tribunal, cites the *New York Herald Tribune* of 4 October 1947, from a report on a speech by the secretary of defense, James Forrestal, as follows:

> Mr. Forrestal denied that there was any historical validity for the Marxist theory according to which industrialists desired war for the sake of material gains. Mr. Forrestal said that there was no group anywhere that was more in favor of peace than the industrialists.[379]

The point on which the Allies had agreed before, and at the IMT, was now a 'Marxist theory'.[380] Several of the lawyers and OMGUS staff were investigated for possible 'bolshevist' sympathies.[381] Whether these investigations (by McCarthy and his team) were intended to ensure the lawyers were subdued we will probably never know. The preface to the German edition of Sasuly's book states that this text, for political reasons, has not been available in the US for many years.[382] The legacy of this has been the 'legal amnesia' through which the industrialists' trials were forgotten until very recently.

On 21 September 1949, John McCloy replaced General Lucius Clay as High Commissioner of what was now the Federal Republic of West Germany. By September 1950, the US was at war with Korea. McCloy and Acheson strongly advocated that West Germany be rearmed.[383] According to Maguire, 'Once it

378 *IG Farben Case*, pp. 1073–4.

379 *Farben*, Final Statements of Defendants, Kuehne, p. 1073.

380 US Senator William Langer called the industrialist cases part of a communist plot: Maguire 2010, p. 169.

381 Bush 2009, p. 1240.

382 Sasuly 1952, p. 5.

383 Maguire 2010, pp. 167–9.

became official that West Germany would be rearmed, questions pertaining to the war criminals took on new significance as West German leaders from all political parties pointed to America's paradoxical role as occupying ally'.[384] German industrialists united in reconstituted trade associations again began to exert their influence, including for the release of their colleagues.[385] US and German leaderships shaped two American policies vis-à-vis the war crimes convicts: a public one to defend the validity of convictions from German attack, and a private one aimed at releasing war criminals as quickly and quietly as possible.[386] On 31 January 1951 clemency boards constituted by McCloy carried out 'extrajudicial' re-reviews of sentences handed down by the Allied occupation courts.[387] McCloy commuted 21 death sentences, reduced the sentences of 69 other individuals and released 33 other war criminals, including Alfried Krupp. The *Flick* and *Farben* defendants had already been released or had completed their sentences by this point.[388] This review greatly upset Taylor, who wrote to Eleanor Roosevelt in protest. Among the main problems Taylor found was that the clemency board based its decision on a reading of the judgments and hearing of 50 defence lawyers but not on a review of the evidence, nor did it hear anyone from the prosecution.[389] Moreover, the authority (or legality) of the reviews per se was questioned.[390] Similarly in the UK, 'immediately on his return to Downing Street [in 1951] Churchill moved to release all remaining Germans'.[391] Wittig was released in 1955.[392] The early releases are criticised as completely discrediting the original trials[393] and 'confirm[ing] the failure of

384 Maguire 2010, p. 168.

385 Schanetzky 2003, p. 80.

386 Maguire 2010, p. 162.

387 'Landsberg: A Documentary Report', *Information Bulletin*, Office of the US High Commissioner for Germany Office of Public Affairs, Public Relations Division, APO 757, US Army, February 1951, pp. 2–8, 55–67.

388 'Landsberg: A Documentary Report', p. 6. For Clay's original review and confirmation, see *Trials of War Criminals Before the Nuremberg Military Tribunals Under Control Council Law No. 10*, Vol. XV, pp. 1144–5; *Taylor Final Report*, pp. 95–7; Heller 2011, p. 332.

389 Letter to Eleanor Roosevelt dated 19 June 19 1951, Telford Taylor Papers, Arthur W. Diamond Law Library, Columbia University Law School, New York, NY, TTP-CLS: 14-4-3-53 (*Taylor Letter to Roosevelt*). Subsequently, McCarthy threatened to subpoena Taylor to appear before his committee. By December's end, however, McCarthy 'withdrew his subpoena sword'. Taylor went on to represent young Americans who refused military service in Vietnam on the basis that it was a 'war of aggression' for which they might incur individual criminal responsibility for participating (Falk 1998–99).

390 Heller 2011, pp. 356–8.

391 Bloxham 2001, p. 116.

392 UK National Archives, WO 235/283.

393 *Taylor Letter to Roosevelt*.

Nuremberg'.[394] Jeßberger writes (specifically about the IG Farben managers – but this could apply to the industrialists in general), '[the industrialists] had a soft fall, from the ranks of the Wehrmacht into the warm bosom of the Western powers'.[395]

9 Conclusion to 3A

At this point, 'Nuremberg' had turned from a morality play into theatre of the absurd. The trials served not to discover and treat real causes, but rather to express the hegemon's moral superiority, to appease home economic actors so as to further their own longer-term political-economic goals. Moreover, the trials partially failed to live up to Jackson's promise that 'justice be done', in the eyes of the home public as well as survivors, and the broader German/European publics. Ratner commented in 2009 that 'while contributing substantially to the doctrinal and procedural development of international criminal law and subjecting Nazi crime to some degree of exposure and justice, these trials, even in conjunction with their *CCL10* counterparts, were of limited value to the societies and victims involved, the ongoing debate over responsibility and reparation for Nazi atrocities is testimony to this conclusion'.[396]

So, while '[t]he masses of peoples liberated from the yoke of fascism demanded the trial of the most evil cartel leaders, in Nuremberg',[397] even those who had received sentences were soon to be freed again, and by 1952 many were already back in power at their companies.[398] The IG Farben 'parts' BASF, Bayer, and Hoechst quickly became leading companies in their sector.[399] These soon began to produce military materials again which were used by the US in the war against Korea.[400] Further, former manufacturer of German military uniforms Neckermann became a fashion mail-order giant, symbolising the rising consumer culture, while former Reich ambassador to Italy became CEO of the Coca-Cola Germany, a symbol of US–German reconciliation.[401] While Ger-

394 Maguire 2010, p. 178. 'Instead of discussing the shocking atrocities committed by many of the high-ranking convicts, American officials were forced to defend the basic legal legitimacy of the trials' ibid p. 207.

395 Jeßberger 2009, p. 802.

396 Ratner et al. 2009, p. 212.

397 Anon. 1960.

398 Along with almost all other members of 'Hitler's elite' (Frei 2003, p. 87).

399 Schanetzky 2003 p. 87.

400 Anon. 1962.

401 Schanetzky 2003 p. 88.

man industry was rebuilt, the Cold War developed, the European Coal and Steel Community, GATT and the Bretton Woods institutions took shape, further congealing capitalism, institutionalising IL. In an ironic turn, McCloy was appointed to lead the World Bank.[402] Shawcross drafted the first investment arbitration convention, which was not itself adopted, but which formed the basis for many bilateral investment treaties, and normalised the idea of private arbitration of investor-state disputes. Slave labour compensation agreements were made, Flick gained new notoriety for refusing to contribute to the compensation fund, cause lawyers litigated against banks and other companies (see Chapter 6).

From this perspective, Nuremberg had not been a failure. Rather, by producing capitalism's victor's justice it played an important part in this process of further congealing capitalism and institutionalising international law.[403]

A qualitative change came out of the contradictions thrown up by the turnaround of Nuremberg: the way in which the war was understood had altered. The 'economic case' all but disappeared from the mainstream narrative of World War Two, which today focuses almost entirely on what Frei calls the 'Hitler-factor'.[404] The 'economic case', once central to the Nuremberg prosecution, while persisting in the German Democratic Republic and Soviet literature, is now described as 'propaganda' by Western scholars.[405]

International criminal law was born out of these contradictions that existed in the aftermath of World War Two. Its potential as a powerful way of shaping narratives – highlighting some relations and 'spiriting away' others; concealing what must remain hidden – was soon realised. Through Nuremberg, international criminal law as 'commodified morality'[406] helped spirit away the material causes at the base of World War Two. At the same time, something fundamental had changed on the ground in Europe, where economic actors came to be seen as essentially peaceful, and where economic development became synonymous with peace.[407] Combined, these two moves cemented capitalism's victor's justice, functioning as a means of creating a narrative that hides the economic story of conflict, and constructs what we would now call corporate impunity.

402 Bush 2009, p. 1193.
403 Baars 2014b.
404 Generally, Frei 2010.
405 Frei 2010, front inside jacket and p. 10; Osterloh 2010, p. 37.
406 Baars 2014a.
407 See, for example, Thomas Friedman's 'Golden Arches Theory of Conflict Prevention' (Friedman 2000).

3B Japan: the Tokyo International Military Tribunal, or, How the East Was Won

1 Introduction to 3B

Once it was decided international criminal trials would be held in Germany, it seemed as if the Allies could not *not* try Japanese war crimes suspects also. While there are substantial differences, in the legal basis of the International Military Tribunal for the Far East ('IMTFE'), the content of the Charter, the composition of the bench and the shape of the indictment, the similarities with Nuremberg are perhaps more noteworthy. To some extent, 'Tokyo' was Nuremberg without frills, without Jackson's flowery language to justify it, without theatrics, and without much of an audience. Above, I have argued that the Allies (and in particular the US) at Nuremberg had as their dual aim, on the one hand, to create a lasting 'ICL', and, on the other, to immediately use this ICL to create a diversion for materially far-reaching economic reforms. Such a combination of trials and reforms I called 'capitalism's victor's justice', and its desired effect was to cement US economic hegemony as well as its charismatic authority, globally. In Japan, mostly out of view of the West, it seemed the diversion needed to be much smaller to still achieve comparably far-reaching results on the economic front.

The US had created in Japan, lasting *until today*,

> an industrial superpower under American military protection and within a stable dollar-centred global financial framework … The US need[s] Japan today … Japan's companies manufacture a range of both high value-added components and finished products on which America's technological and military supremacy totally depend. Japan's continued central role in financing the US trade and government deficits and propping up a dollar-centred international order is … the key explanation for Washington's ability to project and sustain a vast global military establishment … since the mid '70s, … it has been the Japanese elite that has acted to support the dollar, the Bretton Woods II regime and, by extension, the continuation of American hegemony.[408]

In this chapter I highlight aspects of how this effect was achieved, through the main trial, the selection (and omission) of indictees, and the occupation

408 Murphy 2009, p. 216.

policies. I also review a number of other ICL and business-related cases, which seem somehow unconnected with the future of Japan, but which play a role in how we perceive ICL and business, going forward. These trials show similarities with the secondary trials on the German side (for example, through illuminating how other states conducted trials and what the meaning of these trials was to their polities and more widely), and they also serve to 'actualise' ICL practice. These cases seem to confirm the reality of ICL and contribute to the notion that it is a mechanism that can (or will) be applied equally, if not now, then at some point soon.

1.1 *Sources*

Of the world's international war crimes trials, those at the IMTFE are probably the most under-researched. There are many reasons why these trials are largely forgotten (outside of Japan); one is the absence of a readily available version of the judgments. Unlike the Nuremberg IMT judgment, the judgments of the Tokyo IMT (the majority judgment and several separate opinions) were not published by the US government, or indeed by any of the other Allied governments participating in the Tribunal.[409] An early descriptive analysis by Solis Horwitz (who had been Assistant Prosecutor for the US at the IMTFE) was published in International Conciliation in 1950.[410] The US government deposited mimeographed copies of the entire transcript (48,288 pages of transcript and approximately 30,000 pages of exhibits) at the Department of the Army and three US universities.[411] An incomplete set is available at the British Imperial War Museum.[412] There is no statement of explanation as to the failure to publish the judgment and proceedings. ICL scholar and former practitioner Antonio Cassese simply remarks, 'There were of course political reasons for this failure to give publicity to the results of such an important trial'.[413]

---

409 Although the indictment had been published: Trial of Japanese War Criminals. Documents: 1. Opening Statement by Joseph B. Keenan, Chief of Counsel. 2. Charter of the Indictment, United States. Dept. of State, 1 v. Washington: US Govt. print. off., 1946. Apparently no explicit reason is given for this non-publication; also, I have not been able to answer the question as to why the other Allied governments did not publish.

410 Horwitz 1950, p. 477. Albertson calls this a 'rather prejudiced account of a member of the prosecution team' (Albertson 1972, p. 550).

411 Horwitz 1950, p. 576.

412 National Archives Research Guide Second World War: war crimes 1939–1945, available at: http://www.nationalarchives.gov.uk/records/research-guides/war-crimes-1939-1945.htm#16211.

413 Cassese 1994, p. 6. Cassese also mentions that Judge Pal published his dissenting opinion in Calcutta in 1953.

Not until the 1970s was the judgment published in a form accessible to the wider public, by the Dutch member of the IMTFE, Judge Röling.[414] In 1981, a 22-volume set of complete transcripts was published by Pritchard & Zaide (which is not widely available).[415] Justice Pal published his (700-page) dissenting judgment in 1953.[416] Recently a new document collection was published by Boister and Cryer, which contains the Charter, indictment and decisions.[417]

In Japan, China and the USSR various scholarly works and document collections have been published, but these did not receive a wide audience outside of their home/region, for linguistic, but also political, reasons (publications produced in the USSR or China rarely feature in 'Western' libraries).[418]

In the US, public interest in the trials was very low until the publication of a book on the Rape of Nanjing by Iris Chang.[419] Questions began to be asked: Did the US Government deliberately repress information? Did the Government grant immunity to the former Japanese Emperor Hirohito and Ishii, the notorious general in charge of Japanese Army 'Unit 731', which had been accused of practising human vivisection for bacteriological warfare research?[420] Additionally, the issue of 'comfort women' came to the fore,[421] as well as the abuse of Allied POWs by the Japanese. According to Drea, 'The rise of concern about Japanese war crimes in the 1990s reinforced the notion that most Japanese war criminals escaped punishment, either because the US government needed their cooperation against the Soviet Union during the early days of the Cold War, or to appease current Japanese economic and commercial interests'.[422]

In response to this surge in interest, the US Congress passed the Japanese Imperial Government Disclosure Act in 2000, leading to the declassification of some 100,000 pages of documents, including all of the Office of Strategic Services (a World War Two US intelligence outfit and predecessor of the CIA) files and many records of the CIA and FBI.[423] The National Archives staff produced

414 Röling 1977. It is puzzling why none of the Allies, nor indeed a publishing house, has published at least some of the documents before Röling.

415 Pritchard 1981.

416 *IMTFE Pal Dissent* 1953.

417 Boister and Cryer 2008, p. xxxiii.

418 For a bibliography that includes many Japanese texts, see Totani 2008, pp. 301–21.

419 Chang 1997.

420 Harris 2002. Harris published his original volume in 1994.

421 See Chinkin 2001, p. 335.

422 Drea et al. 2006, p. 14.

423 Under the *Nazi War Crimes Disclosure Act* (P.L. 105–246) and the *Japanese Imperial Government Disclosure Act* (P.L. 106–567), reportedly over 8.5 million pages of records related

three documents concerning declassified Japanese war crimes documents. The first is a 1,700-page archival guide, or finding aid, to Japanese World War Two war crimes records in NARA holdings, including newly released records. The second is a finding aid focused on Japanese biological warfare. The third, *Researching Japanese War Crimes: Introductory Essays*, is a book undertaken in response to concern about the alleged loss of war crimes information and the underuse of available documentation.

Very little is readily accessible about the approximately 2,200 other Allied trials held in the East after World War Two. Some of the (presumably more noteworthy?) trials are summarised by the UN War Crimes Commission.[424] Now, aside from paper archives, such documentation is becoming available online through the 'Forschungs- und Dokumentationszentrum Kriegsverbrecherprozesse' at the Philipps-Universität Marburg, the UC Berkeley War Crimes Studies Center (now the WSD Handa Center at Stanford – which no longer hosts the online archive),[425] the Hong Kong War Crimes Trials Collection,[426] the ICC Legal Tools Database,[427] and the Yale University Avalon Project.[428] In the UK, Pritchard started but abandoned a project to collect all British War Crimes Trials in the Far East.[429]

The Yamashita trial[430] is cited in contemporary texts as one of the first war crimes trials to deal extensively with the concept of command responsibility.[431] Many commentaries on the subsequent trials are based on press art-

to Japanese and Nazi War crimes have been identified among federal government records and opened to the public, including certain types of records never before released, such as CIA operational files. The declassification work is described in the *Report of the Nazi War Crimes and Japanese Imperial Government Records Interagency Working Group* (IWG), 2007. So as to facilitate and stimulate research on the topics the IWG published three research guides: Drea et al. 2006. It should be noted that many relevant documents were never classified in the first place or had already been declassified, e.g., State Department Bulletins.

424 *WCCLR* (*supra* Chapter 3A).

425 *Marburg War Crimes Project.*

426 *Hong Kong War Crimes Project.*

427 *ICC Legal Tools.*

428 *Supra.* These are works in progress, with only limited materials available as of January 2012.

429 Pritchard mentions his project of publishing the 21-volume *The British War Crimes Trials in the Far East, 1946–1948*, which is referred to as 'forthcoming, 1997' in fn. 1 of Pritchard 1996, p. 16.

430 4 United Nations War Crimes Commission, Law Reports of Trials of War Criminals 1 (1948), Trial of General Tomoyuki Yamashita (*Yamashita Case*).

431 E.g., Werle 2009, p. 500; Zahar 2008, p. 259; Van Sliedregt 2003, pp. 120–5.

icles,[432] e.g., Piccigallo's monograph *The Japanese on Trial: Allied War Crimes Operations in the Far East 1945–51*;[433] and Ramasastry's article on slave labour.[434] In 1950, the USSR published materials on the 'Chabarovsk Trial' in German and English (see below, Section 4.2.4).[435] Some trials we know of only because they are referred to in other cases (Section 4.2.3).

Like their counterparts at Nuremberg, some of the lawyers involved in the IMTFE have published memoirs and articles, as well as general texts, notably prosecutors Horwitz and Donihi, and judges Pal, Keenan, and Röling (the latter in conversation with Cassese).[436] While general ICL texts devote some attention to Tokyo,[437] outside of Japan,[438] some specialised monographs and edited volumes have been produced.[439]

The sixtieth anniversary of the trial gave rise to various reappraisals and revisits. Boister and Cryer, in their 'Reappraisal' accompanying the documents bundle, provide a retrospective.[440] The dissenting judgment of the Indian Judge Pal gave rise to a body of literature that almost rivals all that has been written on the Far East beside this.[441] Much of it celebrates Pal's 'postcolonial' stance,[442] some of it in an Orientalist manner.[443]

2 Why Tokyo?

Again, examining the history behind the trials, the context in which the tribunal was set up and organised, the official explanations given for its existence,

432 Short summaries of English-language (media) sources can be found in Welch 2001.

433 Piccigallo 1979.

434 Ramasastry 2002.

435 Prozessmaterialien in der Strafsache gegen ehemalige angehörige der Japanischen Armee wegen Vorbereitung und Anwendung der Bakterienwaffe, Verlag für Fremdsprachige Literatur, Moskau, 1950.

436 Donihi 1992–93, p. 733; Pal 1955; Keenan and Brown 1951; Röling and Cassese 1994.

437 Van Sliedregt 2003, pp. 128–30; Cryer et al. 2010, pp. 115–20; Bantekas and Nash 2007, pp. 507–8.

438 Japanese historian Yuma Totani published a monograph in English: Totani 2008; see also Futamura 2008; Hosoya, Ando, Onuma, and Minear 1986.

439 Minear 1971; Simpson 1997, p. 801; Brackman 1987.

440 Simpson 2009, pp. 608–13; Tanaka, McCormack, and Simpson 2011. Boister 2008a; Simpson 2009; Tanaka 2011.

441 Boister 2008a, p. 349; Takeshi 2011, p. 127.

442 E.g., Falk 1998–99.

443 Kopelman 1991.

as well as the unfolding of events before, during and after the trial including its 'quiet burial',[444] can tell us more about the functions and uses of ICL, in particular.

Japan's 1894 war with China had landed Japan's first colonies, and the shock of Japan's total triumph over China raised for the first time the possibility of a non-white challenge to European and US hegemony. Indeed, in his 'yellow peril' theory Emperor Wilhelm II of Germany warned of the risk of the millions of China, led by Japan, overrunning and destroying old Europe. Japan was now considered an imperial power to be reckoned with.[445] Another factor that features in the background of the Tokyo Tribunal is the racism with which Japanese immigrants had been greeted on arrival and in the US from the early twentieth century. During the 1920s (when Japan became a major competitor to the Western capitalist economies and one of the world's major powers), the US effectively placed a ban on Japanese immigration, and the racist exclusion of the 'proud' Japanese was experienced as a great insult, resulting in a long legacy of US-Japanese hostility culminating in the internment of US citizens of Japanese descent in the US during World War Two[446] – and probably also the Japanese treatment of US POWs. This history needs to be taken into account when discussing the Allies' prosecution of Japanese accused after World War Two and its aftermath.

As early as 1942 the *St James Declaration* included mention of Japanese 'acts of barbarism and violence'.[447] In the *Cairo Declaration* of 1 December 1943, which was issued at the conclusion of a meeting between Roosevelt, Churchill, and Chinese Generalissimo Chiang Kai-shek the acts were denounced as 'aggressions'.[448] In 1944, the United Nations War Crimes Commission set up the Far Eastern Sub-Committee in Chungking, specifically to collect information on Japanese crimes in East Asia.[449] The *Potsdam Declaration* (*Proclamation Defining Terms for Japanese Surrender*) of 26 July 1945 included in Paragraph (10): 'stern justice shall be meted out to all war criminals, including those who have visited cruelties upon our prisoners'.[450] A US-directed Far-Eastern Advisory Committee then (October 1945) formulated policies by which Japan was

---

444 Piccigallo 1979, p. 146.
445 Hunter 1989, p. 23.
446 Hunter 1989, pp. 27–8; also, Takemoto 2014.
447 *St James Declaration.*
448 *Cairo Declaration.*
449 Bathurst 1945, p. 570.
450 *Potsdam Declaration* (*Japanese Surrender*).

to fulfil its obligation of surrender, before this body reconstituted as the Far-Eastern Committee ('FEC') and began to concern itself also with war crimes policy.[451]

British prosecutor Comyns-Carr wrote, on behalf of the British Commonwealth prosecutors, 'the aim of this International Trial is to establish the criminality of certain acts committed by Japan'.[452] As borne out by the secondary trials in Germany and also in the 'East' (below), British priority was to deal with crimes against its servicemen/POWs. In addition, however, an Allied objective was the affirmation of Nuremberg's legal findings (in particular on individual responsibility for aggressive war[453]) – conform the 'for law' motivation described above.

Former US prosecutor Horwitz describes setting up the tribunal as a unilateral US initiative, but insists that subsequent decisions were taken jointly by the Allies and representatives of countries which had been occupied by Japan. The tribunal has rightly been accused of racism for not including Taiwanese and Korean representatives even though these countries had been victims of the war.[454] Instead, representatives of Australia, Canada, China, France, India, The Netherlands, New Zealand, the Philippine Commonwealth, the USSR and the UK only participated in the FEC.[455] Decisions taken by the commission were to be translated into Directives by the US and transmitted to the Supreme Commander for the Allied Powers ('SCAP'), US General Douglas MacArthur, who was charged with their implementation.[456] However, in reality it appears that SCAP and his team dominated not only the IMTFE, but also the organisation of post-World War Two affairs in Japan generally.[457]

451 Piccigallo 1979, p. 34. MacArthur was authorised by the Japanese Instrument of Surrender (*supra*) to 'take such steps as he deemed proper to effectuate these terms of surrender' (which was interpreted to include giving effect to the terms of the Potsdam Declaration), accorded to SCAP by a declaration of the Far Eastern Commission (FEC) founded by the foreign ministers of the United Kingdom, the United States, and the USSR, in Moscow, 27 December 1945. The FEC issued directives to the Allied Council for Japan, and the declaration establishing this council also delegated the power to General MacArthur to implement the terms of the treaty of surrender and any further directives issued by the Allies.

452 Quoted in Totani 2008, p. 66.

453 Totani 2008, p. 66.

454 Totani 2009, p. 13.

455 Horwitz 1950, p. 481.

456 Ibid.

457 E.g., generally, Finn 1992.

The main reasons given by US officials for the go-ahead of the trial were: (1) to 'impress' the Japanese;[458] (2) as a way of getting the new Japanese leadership to cooperate, to 'get down to business';[459] and (3) 'to satisfy a Japanese popular demand':

> The Japanese people at present show evidence of being in a mood for reform and change, They are now thoroughly disillusioned and there is wide and outspoken criticism of the men who misled them and brought disaster upon the country. I believe it is correct to say that the Japanese people today expect the American authorities to make more arrests and that, on the part of the great majority, they will not resent those arrests.[460]

This position is contradicted by Futamura, however, who has documented the intense resentment of the Japanese people towards the white man's, victors' trial (except insofar as they believed their leaders deserved punishment for *losing* the war).[461]

In this chapter, I argue that at least part of the reason for the trials (as in Germany) was to provide the 'public face' of the Allied administration, a morality play (or horror story) to the Japanese public, while mostly concealing to the outside world the far-reaching economic reforms implemented by the US occupation of Japan, a progamme of 'shock therapy' leading to 'Japan's stunning rise as an economic power'.[462]

3 The US Occupation and Economic Reform of Japan

The 80-month US occupation of Japan has been described as 'perhaps the single most exhaustively planned operation of massive and externally directed change in world history'.[463] Following *Potsdam*, the US published the 'US Initial Post Surrender Policy', between June and September 1945, containing a comprehensive plan for the occupation of Japan with the purpose, 'first: to prevent Japan ever again becoming a military menace, and second objective: to

458 *FRUS* 922, 7 September 1945 John McCloy Asst. Secretary of War memo to the Acting Secretary of State Acheson, and 926, discussion of the US Policy on the Apprehension and punishment of war criminals in the Far East 12 Sept, 45.

459 *FRUS* 942, 8 October 1945, Memo by Atcheson to SCAP.

460 *FRUS* 952, 6 November 1945: Atcheson 'Top Secret' memo to SCAP.

461 See, generally, Futamura 2008; see also Onuma 2002; Boister 2008b, pp. 315–22.

462 Finn 1992, p. xviii.

463 Finn 1992, p. xix, quoting Ward 1987, p. i.

bring about the eventual establishment of a peaceful and responsible government which will respect the rights of other states and which will support the objectives of the United States as reflected in the ideals and principles of the Charter of the United Nations'.[464] As in Germany, Allied occupation of Japan was to be a predominantly US affair.[465]

The policy document contained as one of its objectives: 'the eventual participation of Japan in a World economy on a reasonable basis',[466] and directives on the democratisation and the demilitarisation of Japan, economic policy, the opening up the Japanese market for foreign direct investment, and the *breaking up of the Japanese industrial and banking cartels*.[467]

In Japan during World War Two there were four main *zaibatsu* (literally plutocrats or financial clique):[468] the Mitsui, Mitsubishi, Sumitomo, and Yasuda.[469] *Zaibatsu* are horizontally structured cartels that typically include a group of subsidiary companies (usually about 10 interlinked firms that normally included a bank, an international trading firm, a real estate entity, an insurance firm, several manufacturers and a mining company)[470] arranged under a holding company, each of which was privately owned by one of Japan's well-known elite families.[471] Through generating their finance internally, *zaibatsu* were able to insulate themselves from the volatility of the pre-war Japanese capital markets.[472]

The *zaibatsu* are closely linked to the government,[473] the Royal Family[474] and the military – at the time of World War Two, for example, the Mitsubishi group was closely linked to the Imperial Japanese Navy and the *Rikken Minseito* political party, while the *Rikken Seiyukai* was considered to have been an exten-

---

464 Japanese National Diet Library, *Records of SWNCC*, Records of the Subcommittee for the Far East.

465 Ando 1991, p. 10.

466 Japanese National Diet Library, United States, *US Initial Post-Defeat Policy* Relating to Japan (SWNCC150), 11 June 1945.

467 Japanese National Diet Library, United States, *US Initial Post-Surrender Policy* for Japan (SWNCC150/4/A), 21 September 1945.

468 Ando 1991, p. 18.

469 Seita 1994, p. 143. There were also 'second-tier *zaibatsu*' such as Okura, and 'new *zaibatsu*' such as Nissan (Finn 1992, p. 57).

470 Allinson 2004, p. 24.

471 See generally, Seita and Tamura 1994, p. 129 ff.; and Vernon, R. and C. Wachenheimer 1947, 'Dissolution of Japan's Feudal Combines', *The Department of State Bulletin*, 17(419), 13 July (*Vernon and Wachenheimer DSB 1947*).

472 Allinson 2004, p. 25.

473 Seita 1994, p. 139.

474 Materialien, p. 533.

sion of the Mitsui group, which was also closely linked to the Imperial Japanese Army.[475] The *zaibatsu* are said to have had great influence over Japanese national and foreign policies.[476] By the end of the war the ten largest *zaibatsu* together controlled about 68 percent of Japan's machinery and equipment production, about 53 percent of the financial and insurance business, 50 percent of mining production, and 38 percent of chemical production.[477] This situation shows similar economic domination of key industries by a handful of enterprises (directed by a handful of individuals) to that of Germany before/during World War Two. Roth relates how the two largest combines – Mitsui and Mitsubishi – in the 1930s disagreed on the use of force for economic expansion, with Mitsubishi preferring 'economic penetration by means short of war' while eventually Fujiwara, the head of the Mitsui *zaibatsu*, 'spoke for ever wider sections of the zaibatsu' when he wrote in his *Spirit of Japanese Industry*:

> Diplomacy without force is of no value. No matter how diligent the Japanese may be, no matter how superior their technical development or industrial administration may be, there will be no hope for Japanese trade expansion if there is no adequate force to back it. Now the greatest of forces is military preparedness founded on the Army and navy. We can safely expand abroad and engage in various enterprises, if we are confident of protection. In this sense, any outlay for armament is a form of investment.[478]

Roth, writing in 1945, describes a similar scenario to that of the German industrialists' joint strategising for expansion in Europe.[479] The *zaibatsu* also greatly benefited from manufacturing military equipment.[480]

---

475 Roth 1946, pp. 61–2.

476 Finn 1992, p. 57.

477 Ibid. 'Five *zaibatsu* companies controlled the copper industry; five or six dominated other fields of mining and messages; Mitsui and Mitsubishi companies controlled half the capital in the coal-mining industry and at times built half of the ships in the merchant shipbuilding industry; and two to six *zaibatsu* companies operated factories producing seventy percent or more of all the rayon, dyestuffs, refined sugar, flour, cement and sheet glass in Japan. The significant size of the *zaibatsu* can be gauged by the number of employees in Mitsui and Mitsubishi – the two largest *zaibatsu* combines – which in 1945 was estimated to be 2.8 million and 1.0 million, respectively' (Seita 1994, p. 143).

478 Quoted in Roth 1946, p. 63.

479 During World War Two there were even attempts to imitate the German model of industrial-political relations (Cohen 2000, p. 10).

480 Allinson 2004, p. 28.

4 The International Military Tribunal for the Far East

On war criminals, the US Initial Post-Surrender Policy contained the following provision:

> 2. War criminals
> Persons charged by the Supreme Commander or the appropriate United Nations agency with being war criminals, including those charged with having visited cruelties upon United Nations prisoners or other nationals, shall be arrested, tried, and if convicted, punished. Those wanted by another of the United Nations for offenses against its nationals shall, if not wanted for trial or as witnesses or otherwise by the Supreme Commander, be turned over to the custody of such other nation.[481]

This already implies there is an attempt to minimise the scope of the trial.

On 14 August 1945, the Japanese Acceptance of Surrender was communicated by the Japanese leadership, accepting the terms of the Potsdam Declaration and as such proclaiming the unconditional surrender of Japan, placing it under authority of the SCAP.[482] On 11 September the order to arrest the major war crimes suspects was given by SCAP.[483]

On 29 October 1945, already one of the military commissions commenced a prosecution: the Yamashita trial at the Manila US Military Court.[484] The trial concluded on 7 December 1945, and Yamashita was convicted and sentenced to death for, as the commanding general of a Japanese military unit in the Philippines (which was still a US possession at the time), having failed to control his troops, who committed atrocities against American, Philippines and other nationals, that he *must have known* about.[485] The reason given for this early trial was to establish a 'precedent' or model, in the informal sense.[486]

The IMTFE was established by means of a proclamation by Douglas MacArthur, the SCAP, issued on 19 January 1946.[487] The Declaration stated that the

481 *US Initial Post-Surrender Policy.*

482 *Japanese Acceptance of Surrender.*

483 Totani 2009, p. 63.

484 *Yamashita Case.*

485 See also Van Sliedregt 2003, pp. 120–8. The decision was criticised in the literature (Piccigallo 1979, pp. 56–7), amongst others as racist; see, e.g., Prévost 1992, p. 192; Piccigallo 1979, p. 231.

486 Piccigallo 1979, p. 58; Van Sliedregt 2003, p. 124. Note that also the Soviet Union had been prosecuting cases already (Prozeßmaterialien 1950).

487 Special Proclamation by the Supreme Commander for the Allied Powers of 19 January

Tribunal was based on the Instrument of Surrender and the Potsdam Declaration, and established pursuant to 'allied authority'.[488] The Declaration received formal international sanction on 29 March 1946.[489] The Charter of the Tokyo IMT ('CIMTFE'), which was contained in the directive, was modelled on the Nuremberg Charter and closely resembled it in jurisdiction, powers and procedural provisions.[490] Article 1 establishes the Tribunal, Arts. 2–4 regulate membership, convening and voting. Article 5 delineates the Tribunal's jurisdiction over persons ('Far Eastern war criminals who as individuals or as members of organisations[491] are charged with offences which include Crimes against Peace') and offences.[492] Article 6 delineates individual responsibility.[493]

In accordance with Article 7 of the CIMTFE, the Rules of Procedure of the International Military Tribunal for the Far East were issued on 25 April 1946.[494] Article 8 provides for the appointment of one Chief of Counsel by MacArthur, this in contrast with the Nuremberg IMT where each of the four Allied Powers appointed a Chief. MacArthur appointed prosecutor Joseph Keenan as Chief Prosecutor of the International Prosecution Section, where he coordinated the work of the prosecutors appointed by the other countries.[495] Articles 9–15 deal with fair trial provisions, powers of the tribunal and conduct of trial. Article 16 provides for penalties (including the death penalty) and Article 17 finally gives the SCAP the power at any time to reduce the sentences.

A main difference of the Tokyo IMT was that all states to which Japan had capitulated were represented on the bench, along with India and the Philippines which were at the time still under UK and US colonial rule. The Tokyo

1946, superseded by General Order No. 20, 20 April 1946, available at: http://137.248.11.66/fileadmin/media/IMTFE_April_1946.pdf (*IMTFE Proclamation*).

488 Ibid. *IMTFE Proclamation*.

489 Boister 2008a, p. xxxvi.

490 Charter of the (Tokyo) International Military Tribunal for the Far East 1946, TIAS No. 1589 (*1946 IMTFE Charter*).

491 Although, like the Nuremberg Charter, the IMTFE Charter includes mention of 'as a member of a group', it was decided not to include provisions on declaring groups illegal as it was found no such groups probably existed in Japan at the relevant time (Horwitz 1950, p. 494).

492 *1946 IMTFE Charter* Art. 5. Appendix C.

493 *1946 IMTFE Charter* Art. 6. Appendix C.

494 Boister 2008a, p. 12.

495 Keenan was much criticised for his lack of legal expertise, frequent absences and alcoholism (Boister 2008a, pp. lvi–lvii).

Tribunal consisted of 11 judges, who were appointed by General MacArthur.[496] The Australian Judge Webb oversaw the bench. The Tribunal was housed in the former military academy in Tokyo, which had housed the War Ministry and Army General Headquarters during the war.[497] From a practical point of view, the trial was hampered by the Japanese destruction of official war records at the close of the war. The evidentiary standard employed by the Tribunal was relaxed ('The Tribunal shall not be bound by technical rules of evidence' – Art. 13 IMTFE).[498] The Tribunal was under pressure to deliver its judgment quickly, which was reflected in the Charter.[499] That the US generally appointed lower-level officials to functions at the tribunal could indicate US leaders considered this judicial project less important than Nuremberg.[500]

Horwitz describes US domination of the process thus: 'The first time eleven nations had agreed in a matter other than actual military operations to subordinate their sovereignty and to permit a national of one of them to have final direction and control'.[501] The much tighter US rein was to some extent a policy adopted in response to lessons learnt by Jackson and his colleagues at (and prior to) Nuremberg, who had had great trouble reaching agreement among the various representatives involved there.[502]

The indictment was lodged on 29 April 1946 charging 28 defendants with Class A (aggression), Class B (war crimes) and Class C (crimes against humanity).[503] The Indictment was a list of 55 counts related to specific occurrences (many related to maltreatment of allied POWs) with annexes setting out the general historical and political context and specifics.[504]

---

496 As per Arts 2 and 3 of the *1946 IMTFE Charter*.

497 Totani 2008, p. 8.

498 *1946 IMTFE Charter* Art. 13. Appendix C.

499 *1946 IMTFE Charter*.

500 For example, Chief Counsel Keenan was an assistant Attorney-General as opposed to Nuremberg Chief Counsel Jackson, who was a Supreme Court Justice. Horwitz comments: 'Rarely has any group of men undertaking a project of similar size and scope been less prepared for their task than were the original twenty-odd members of the legal staff of the prosecution when they began their labors on 8 December 1945 … [F]ew of them had any knowledge about Japan, the Japanese, or the principal figures involved or any real appreciation of the magnitude of the venture they were undertaking' (Horwitz 1950, p. 494).

501 Horwitz 1950, p. 487.

502 Totani 2008, p. 24.

503 The tribunal did not indict anyone who could *not* plausibly be charged with Class A crimes, possibly because at this point it was still expected that there might be further international trials.

504 Further, Section 4, 'Methods of corruption and coercion in China and other occupied territories' – includes the use of opium to 'weaken the native inhabitants' will to resist' (p. 37). Also, 'revenue from … traffic in opium and other narcotics was used to finance the preparation for and waging of the wars of aggression set forth in this Indictment and to establish

The Tribunal formally convened for the arraignment of the defendants on 3 May 1946. The first session was spent reading the indictment. The main focus again was the war of aggression and conspiracy elements. The Prosecution attempted to show that there had been a conspiracy to go to war with the UK and the US since 1928. The Prosecution's strategy was to show how Japan had been taken over by a small group of individuals, members of the political cadre, the military and industry: 'the internal and foreign policies of Japan were dominated by a criminal militaristic clique ... The mind of the Japanese people was systematically poisoned with harmful ideas of the alleged racial superiority of Japan'. The second paragraph of the indictment read: 'The economic and financial resources of Japan were to a large extent mobilised for war aims, to the detriment of the welfare of the Japanese people'. A conspiracy had been formed between the defendants, joined in by the rulers of other aggressive countries, 'the main objects of this conspiracy was to secure the domination and exploitation by the aggressive States of the rest of the world, and to this end to commit, or encourage the commission of crimes against peace, war crimes and crimes against humanity as defined in the Charter of this Tribunal'.[505]

Like in Nuremberg, the economic side of the war received much attention. The 'Appendix of Summarized Particulars showing the principal Matters and Events upon which the Prosecution will rely in support of the several Counts of the Indictment', included, e.g.:

> Section 3: Economic Aggression in China and Greater East Asia: 'During the period covered by this Indictment, Japan established a general superiority of rights in favour of her own nationals, which effectively created monopolies in commercial, industrial and financial enterprises, first in Manchuria and later in other parts of China which came under her domination, and exploited those regions not only for the enrichment of Japan and those of her nationals participating in those enterprises, but as part of a scheme to weaken the resistance of China, to exclude other Nations and nationals, and to provide funds and munitions for further aggression. This plan, as was the intention of some at least of its originators, both on its economic and military side, gradually came to embrace similar designs on the remainder of East Asia and Oceania. Later it was officially expanded into the "Greater East Asia Co-Prosperity Scheme" (a title designed to

---

and finance the puppet governments set up by the Japanese Government in the various occupied territories' (ibid).

505 *IMTFE Indictment* in Boister Documents at 17–18.

> cover up a scheme for complete Japanese domination of those areas) and Japan declared that this was the ultimate purpose of the military campaign. The same organizations as are mentioned in Section 4 hereof were used for the above purposes'.[506]

In their expansionist policy, according to the indictment, the Japanese prepared to fight both against communism ('to eradicate the Russian menace') and Western capitalism ('against Britain and America' – in particular against their interests in East Asia).[507] The Economic policy with regard to Japanese-occupied East Asia had been led by Hoshino Naoki and Kaya Okinori, two financial leaders who were charged at the IMTFE. Hoshino had held various high financial posts in Machuria/Manchuoko, while Kaya had been finance minister (twice), advisor to the finance minister (also twice), an official in the Manchurian Affairs Bureau, the Asian Development Committee and president of the North China Development Company.[508] The Japanese had used a colonial model of economic domination of China and its resources. Japanese officials took over key government posts, confiscated factories and mines, and forced all young Chinese men to work in service of the army.[509]

In the joint defence, counsel argued that Japan's economic activities had been necessary in the face of encirclement by Western powers.[510] From 1939 onwards, the US and other powers had taken measures to restrict Japanese trade (e.g., by the US terminating the Treaty of Commerce and Navigation), and the Netherlands had 'preemptively' declared war on Japan when Japan had sought to establish an economic relationship with the Dutch colony of Indonesia.[511]

The judgment was read out in full over several days from 4–12 November 1948. It contained several chapters setting down a historical narrative of the war, including its economic aspects, finding (amongst others) that Japanese

---

506 *IMTFE Indictment.*

507 Horwitz 1950, p. 510. For this purpose Japan had signed both the Anti-Comintern Pact with Germany in 1936, and the Tripartite Pact in 1940 with Germany and Italy (Horwitz 1950, pp. 513–14).

508 *IMTFE Indictment* (GPO version) at 99 (Hoshino) and 100 (Kaya).

509 Moreover, the 'narcotisation policy' generated massive income for the Japanese military (and presumably kept Chinese resistance subdued). Japan officially encouraged the production and use of drugs, Manchuoko became the centre of worldwide drug traffic and a public enterprise of the puppet governments, generating an estimated USD 300 million annually (Horwitz 1955, p. 512).

510 *IMTFE Indictment.*

511 Horwitz 1950, pp. 559–60.

economic domination over the region had been a major war objective.[512] This objective was linked to that of the Third Reich and Mussolini's Italy through the 'Tripartite Pact'.[513]

Hoshino and Kaya were convicted of conspiring to wage wars of aggression. Regarding Hoshino, the majority decision stated: 'he was able to exercise a profound influence upon the economy of Manchuoko and did exert that influence towards Japanese domination of the commercial and industrial development of that country'.[514] About Kaya it was said that 'he took part in the formulation of aggressive policies of Japan and in the financial, economic and industrial preparation of Japan for the execution of those policies'.[515] Jacobson observes that despite the fact that the tribunal held 'the guilt of the men was derived from their role as government officials rather than from any of their personal or corporate commercial activities, ... their convictions nonetheless serve as a reminder that war – and war crimes – are dependent in part upon economic support'.[516]

The majority judgment convicted and sentenced 6 defendants to death for A, B and C crimes, 1 for B and C crimes, 16 were sentenced to life imprisonment for

---

512 See, e.g., Chapter IV: The Military Domination of Japan and Preparations for War: Introductory, p. 163: 'Industrial Planning in Manchukuo after the Lukouchiao incident. Involved the creation of larger industrial units, responsive to government control'. 'Development of the war-supporting industries after the Lukouchiao incident': 'As in Manchukuo, so in Japan itself effect was given to the Army's plan for regimenting heavy industry into larger units, more susceptible of government control, The Major Industries Control Law, passed in August 1937, encouraged the formation by industrial groups of new associations or cartels, which were given wide powers of self-government'. See also, as part of Chapter V: Japanese Aggression against China: 'Japan's Economic domination and exploitation of her subject territories', (p. 179) (includes expansion of the 'yen-bloc') and 'Industrial preparations: The Synthetic oil and petroleum industry' (pp. 228–30); Chapter V, Section VII: 'Japan's Economic Domination of Manchuria and other parts of China' (*IMTFE Indictment*).

513 The Tripartite Pact between Japan, Germany, and Italy, 1940, 'The Governments of Japan, Germany, and Italy consider it the prerequisite of a lasting peace that every nation in the world shall receive the space to which it is entitled. They have, therefore, decided to stand by and cooperate with one another in their efforts in the regions of Europe and Greater East Asia respectively. In doing this it is their prime purpose to establish and maintain a new order of things, calculated to promote the mutual prosperity and welfare of the peoples concerned. It is, furthermore, the desire of the three Governments to extend cooperation to nations in other spheres of the world that are inclined to direct their efforts along lines similar to their own for the purpose of realizing their ultimate object, world peace'.

514 *IMTFE Judgment*, p. 604.

515 *IMTFE Judgment*, p. 607.

516 Jacobson 2005, pp. 196–7.

B and C crimes and 1 to 20 years, and 1 to 7. Two defendants had died of natural causes during the course of the trial and one had been declared incompetent.[517] On the same day, five judges submitted separate opinions.[518] The French judge, J. Bernard, concluded that the entire procedure had been defective and all defendants ought to be acquitted, Dutch judge Röling also criticised certain legal and procedural aspects. Judge Jaranilla of the Philippines considered the prison sentences too light, while Judge Pal of India issued a comprehensive dissent defending Japanese actions during the war as those of Asia's liberator from Western colonialism.[519]

In his dissenting opinion, Röling also discussed the claim by the defence that Japan fought in a good cause. Here Röling inquired whether the ideals, to which Japan publicly adhered in her propaganda for a New Order, were sincere. Defendants had claimed that 'Japan fought for the liberation of the peoples of Asia, and the construction of a regional economic bloc ... The New Order ... would consist ... of the liquidation of Western Imperialism, abolishment of the colonial system, and the building of a world in which all the peoples would find their proper places'.[520] Röling, however, concluded that the Greater East Asia Co-Prosperity Sphere was primarily aimed at the prosperity of the Japanese Empire.[521]

The absence of a holocaust in Asia made it harder to pathologise the defendants, and showed the conflict to be very similar to imperialist power struggles such as had taken place in the world for centuries. The Japanese defendants were racialised, however, with much of their 'cruelty' and 'deviousness' being easily ascribed to their racial identity for a Western audience.

4.1 *Missing in Action*

The Tokyo trial has been criticised (apart from on legal grounds)[522] for omitting crimes against Koreans and Taiwanese (Japanese colonial subjects at the time), for providing blanket immunity to Western powers' crimes against their own colonial subjects, and, relatedly, for ignoring the fact that 1 million Indonesians died in the war,[523] as well as ignoring the US bombing of Hiroshima and

517 Hisakazu 2011, p. 8.
518 Boister 2008a, p. lxix.
519 Boister 2008a, pp. lxxv–lxxxii.
520 *Röling Dissent*, p. 128.
521 *Röling Dissent*, p. 134.
522 For criticism on legal grounds (Judge Bernard's opinion, see generally, Boister 2008b, pp. 28–48), for violating the principle of *nullum crimen sine lege* (Piccigallo 1979, p. 25), for procedural unfairness (Boister 2008b, p. 114).
523 Boister 2008b, p. 313.

Nagasaki,[524] and the US's firebombing of 64 other Japanese cities, plus the Japanese firebombing of several Chinese cities.[525] In addition, it was criticised for not prosecuting the Japanese emperor Hirohito, and the leaders of the main business cartels. Indeed, the Soviets perceived the IMTFE as an attempt to cover up the guilt of those Japanese most responsible for the war, namely the emperor, major industrialists, capitalists and militarists.[526]

4.1.1 Hirohito

The holy emperor was exempted from trial, ostensibly for legal reasons, though perhaps rather for political, or even socio-psychological reasons.[527] According to Piccigallo, the 'strictly American decision caused perhaps more furore in Allied circles that any other relative to war crimes policy'.[528] Hirohito was said to have been a 'mere figurehead'[529] or conversely, to represent the Japanese state in the eyes of his subjects, such that trying him would be perceived as in effect an indictment of Japan itself.[530] Totani disputes Röling's assertion that Emperor Hirohito was granted immunity, but suggests the Americans kept the option of trying him open, which, however, did not happen.[531] Donihi links the decision with the feasibility of a US occupation of Japan.[532] Convinced that he had played a major role, the Soviets called Hirohito the ultimate leader of the *zaibatsu*.[533] The emperor, while exempt from prosecution, was forced by the US occupation to renounce his divine origin.[534] Otomo has argued that this was required because the US 'needed Japan to enter the emerging fraternity of States as a *secular* entity; an equal among brothers capable of recognising its others and of being sutured into the new international economic system'.[535] By

524 Hisakazu 2011, p. 18.
525 Tanaka 2011, p. 294.
526 Piccigallo 1979, p. 148: 'They are doing their utmost to whitewash and justify the aggressive policy of the Japanese imperialists. Wall Street and its agents, who direct US policy, are resurrecting militarism in Japan and converting the country into a base for the promotion of their insensate plans of world domination' (ibid).
527 Finn 1992, pp. 24–27, 71–74; Hisakazu 2011, p. 18.
528 Piccigallo 1979, p. 16.
529 Horwitz 1950, p. 497.
530 The emperor had implored MacArthur to let him assume the total burden of guilt for every political decision made and military action carried out by his people (Donihi 1992, p. 746).
531 Totani 2008, pp. 4 and, generally, 43–62.
532 Donihi 1992, p. 740.
533 Prozeßmaterialien 543.
534 Otomo 2011, p. 63.
535 Otomo 2011, p. 64.

analogy, we can say that the US needed Japan (a mostly isolated entity prior to World War Two),[536] in future, to be able to recognise it as a *formal legal* equal, for the purpose of participation in capitalist IL, and in the capitalist world system.

4.1.2 *Zaibatsu*

Although mention in the Initial Post-Surrender Policy and the Indictment gives the appearance that economic factors played an important role in Japan's war, no economic actors were indicted at the Tokyo IMT. It had been proposed to do so, however. In addition to the September/October lists drawn up by the SCAP/US State Department,[537] the Allies listed proposed indictees for the IMTFE; and, for example, the Australian completed list, presented in October 1945, contained 64 names in all including the emperor and 14 bankers and industrialists.[538] Among them were the managing director of Kawasaki Heavy Industries, and the president of the Sumitomo Bank, apparently because of their alleged profitable alliance with the militarists.[539]

Indeed, JCS 1380, which operationalised the Initial Post-Surrender Policy, the SCAP had been ordered to arrest, as rapidly as practicable, and held as suspected war criminals, 'All persons who have played an active and dominant governmental, economic, financial or other significant part in the formulation of execution of Japan's program of aggression' including, explicitly, civilians.[540] SCAP asked the US Ambassador to Japan and MacArthur's chief political advisor, George Atcheson, to advise who should be arrested and to provide evidence. Apparently largely on the basis of information from Washington, Atcheson submitted four lists in November and December.[541] By the end of 1945, 103 major

536 But see US (armed) attempts to force Japan to sign the 1852 *Treaty of Amity* (Otomo 2011, p. 64).

537 *FRUS* 940: Memo from Acting Political Advisor Atcheson to the Secretary of State dated 5 October 1945. *FRUS* 944: Response from Secretary of State *FRUS 940*, *FRUS 944*: mentioned US National War Crimes Office general list of Japanese war criminals and a special list of major war criminals of 14 September, and was agreed by State, War and Navy Departments. These lists were not disclosed to the FEC. The Chinese list of 12 major war criminals is published *FRUS 948* (dated 20 October 1945).

538 The 'No. 1 Australian List: Japanese Major War Criminals', annexed to Memorandum from Department of External Affairs, Wellington, to NZ High Commission, London, 2 February 1946, File no EA 106/3/22, Part 2, Archives New Zealand, Boister (2008b) fn118, and Sissons, D.: The Australian War Crimes Trials and Investigations, 1942–1951, *Marburg*, Pacific Theatre Document Archive.

539 Boister 2008b, p. 62.

540 *JCS 1380*.

541 Finn 1992, p. 78.

suspects had been arrested, including most of Tojo's 1941 cabinet.[542] As only the US prosecutors had arrived in Japan at this point, they took the early initiative in selecting defendants.[543]

At one point the plan was to try Class A suspects in three groups, one of them including industrialists and bankers.[544] However, it was decided only to have one single trial of 28 defendants.[545] All of the untried Class A war criminal suspects were released by General MacArthur by the end of the first and only trial in 1948.[546] According to Totani, the Japanese public believed, and continues to believe today, that the release of Class A prisoners was the result of a US change of heart with regard to the pursuit of justice at the onset of the Cold War.[547]

However, I have found no unequivocal explanation for the decision to limit Tokyo IMT cases to those with a Class A label. In reviewing the State Department Foreign Relations of the US-1945 documentation the *impression*[548] is given that the limitation to Class A Crimes was merely a practical matter, intended to

---

542 Finn 1992, p. 78.

543 Kentaro 2011, p. 57.

544 It has been implied, however, that Keenan's mention of further trials at that point may have been aimed at getting prosecution staff to agree on a small number of defendants for the first trial, rather than it being a genuine possibility (Totani 2008, p. 69).

545 Keenan recommended against further international Class A trials as they would be repetitive, lengthy and of little educational value; moreover, as soon as 'Nuremberg' was over there would be no more media interest (Totani 2008, pp. 68, 73). The IMTFE's files were handed to the US military legal team that had been carrying out trials in the Philippines, Japan and China, but, since they had been compiled with a focus on Class A crimes, they were largely useless for trying 'BC crimes' (ibid). Some of the investigations into detainees (who had, after all, now spent considerable time in Sugamo prison) continued, and a trial of eight cabinet members (the 'Pearl Harbour cabinet') was planned and organised, but did eventually not take place because the lead lawyer considered the IMTFE judgment a weak precedent for his intended case. Eventually only two 'subsequent trials' took place at Tokyo, of Tamura and Toyoda (pp. 68, 73).

546 Finn 1992, p. 79.

547 Totani 2008, p. 77. Totani suggests, however, that the decision was partly due to Keenan and MacArthur's 'inattentiveness' – as well as Washington's disinterest in Tokyo's war criminals (ibid).

548 Indeed, in the correspondence the question of 'desiderata' is raised, but not answered, and it appears that proposals were made without any specific and explicit legal, evidential or even political guidelines (although such may have existed formally or informally even if this is not evident from the correspondence) *FRUS*, 1945, Vol. VI, pp. 952–3; and *FRUS 963*: Memo by Marshall, acting Chief of Staff to the SCAP to Atcheson: 'The main difficulty is to determine just who are the war criminals in that directives to the Supreme Commander have been couched in such broad and general terms that he is unable to determine those individuals that the American Government or the Allied Governments wish to prosecute'. Note this also shows the political, rather than legal considerations that guide the choice of defendants (if only legal considerations counted the SCAP could have known himself who to arrest – as any member of a domestic police force).

speed up matters and to 'get things over with'.[549] However, even after the limitation to Class A crimes was decided, several industrialists were proposed for inclusion.[550] For example, on November 12 Atcheson sent a list of 13 names of

> major war criminal suspects, together with biographic data concerning each, which we consider sufficient evidence to support their arrest for trial under section II, Article 6(a), of the Four Power Agreement on War Crimes Trials [which relates to crimes against the peace] ... These persons are believed, with others, to have been responsible through the policies which they advocated and the influence which they exerted for the initiation and carrying on of the attacks launched by Japan on Manchuria in 1931, and on China proper in 1937, and on the United States, Great Britain and others of our Allies in 1941.

This list names Kuhara, Funanosuke, 'prominent politician, industrialist ... advocate of strong policy toward China. Involved in incident of February 26, 1936 [the "Manchuria incident"]. Ardent nationalist, closely associated with military circles and aims'.[551] The 13 names listed in the memo came from the War Crimes Office List mentioned above.[552] The second list submitted by Atcheson on 14 November includes 'Aikawa, Yoshisuke. Member, Cabinet Advisory Board, Koiso Cabinet. Brother-in-law and close associate of Fusanosuke [*sic*] Kuhara. Industrialist who worked in close cooperation, and to his great profit, with aggressive elements of Army and Government'.[553]

On 17 November 1945 Atcheson sent the secretary of state a memo enclosing the conclusion of an analysis by a Canadian called E. Norman, chief of the Research and Analysis Section of the Office of the Chief Counter Intelligence Officer of General Headquarters [of the US occupying force in Tokyo], written about the war guilt of Prince Konoye [also spelt Konoe], Fumimare, prime minister of Japan until 1941 (prior to Tojo).[554] The memo motivated the argument for Konoye's war guilt as follows:

549 *FRUS 984*: Memo from Atcheson.

550 *FRUS 960*: Communicated in the memo by Acting Chairman of the State-War-Navy Coordinating Committee to the Secretary of State with annexed Draft Message to be sent by the Joint Chiefs of Staff to the SCAP: 'Position of the US Government is that Tojo, his cabinet and other persons charged with crimes in category A in paragraph 1 of Appendix C of JCS 1512 should be tried by an international tribunal'.

551 *FRUS 963–5*: Memo from Atcheson to SCAP and Chief of Staff dated 12 November 1945.

552 Atcheson mentions this in his memo: *FRUS 962*.

553 *FRUS 968*: Subenclosure of Memo by Atcheson to SCAP and CoS.

554 Norman also authored the book, *Japan's Emergence as a Modern State* (first published by

> The most valuable service which Konoye performed on behalf of Japanese aggression was one which he alone could have accomplished – namely the fusing of all the dominant sections of the ruling oligarchy, namely the Court, Army, Zaibatsu and bureaucracy … Konoye set in motion those policies and alliances which could only lead to a collision with the Western powers. Even though he stepped aside in favour of Tojo in October 1941, be still bears a heavy responsibility both moral and legal …, since he made no move such as summoning an Imperial conference while still Premier to prevent the coming Japanese attack upon the United States and Britain.[555]

Eventually Konoye escaped trial by committing suicide, while the US had given orders to arrest Tojo and 'the entire "Pearl Harbor" Cabinet' on 11 September 1945.[556]

On 17 November, Kuhara, Funanosuke, as the only industrialist out of those mentioned here, was ordered to be arrested and held at Sugamo Prison Camp pending 'trial by an international tribunal.'[557]

However, on 27 November 1945 Atcheson advised the arrest for trial of a further two major war criminals – again with 'sufficient evidence' for an aggressive war charge, the first of which: 'Fujiwara Ginjiro: Leading Industrialist with a record of active collaboration with the military in positions of major responsibility'. The second person listed was 'Nakajima Chikuhei, Leading aircraft manufacturer (founder and president of the Nakajima Aircraft Company), war profiteer and politician'. He was described as 'closely bound up with and devoted to the developing of Japan's war machine since before the last war'. His former posts included: 'President, Seiyukai Party … Railways Minister … Member Greater East Asia Co-Prosperity Sphere Establishment Administration … Munitions Minister etc.'[558]

---

the Institute of Pacific Relations, 1940; 60th anniversary edition available from UBC Press, 2000), a fact which Atcheson mentions in each reference to Norman.

555 *FRUS* 971–2. 'Konoye was Prime Minster when Japan attacked China, entered into the Tri-Partite Alliance with Germany and Italy, invaded French Indochina … [and] laid the foundation for the command economy for total war, and abolished the old political parties' (ibid). When learning of US intent to arrest and try him as a war criminal, he committed suicide. There is considerable correspondence in *FRUS* on whether or not Konoye had been promised immunity, whether (or *as*) he was the US chosen post-war leader (Finn 1992, p. 41), and whether he had been negotiating a peace agreement with the US on the eve of the Pearl Harbor attack.

556 *FRUS* 971–2.

557 *FRUS* 972: Report by the office of the Political Advisor, dated 26 November 1945.

558 *FRUS* 977–8: Memorandum by the Acting Political Advisor in Japan (Atcheson), Tokyo, November 27 1945.

Nakajima, with his roles in industry, defence and politics embodied the idea of the *zaibatsu* elite.

It appears clearly from the US official correspondence that from the Japanese side World War Two was very much viewed as a joint effort of industrialists, military and political leaders, and that the main individuals' roles were not always clearly separated/separable. There was, in other words, a military-industrial complex. It is striking that in the correspondence published in FRUS (1945 and 1946) the selection of indictees of the IMT is only discussed in terms of whose task it is to decide, rather than on what basis a selection is made. No explanation can be found in FRUS for the omission of the industrialists. There is some discussion about the omission of the emperor; it seems likely from this that he was omitted because the Japanese public would be offended by having the still somewhat mythical figure tried as a common war criminal. Another explanation may be that he (like Konoyo) could have exposed negotiations with Western States that the Allies would wish to keep under wraps. Regarding Shigemitsu and Yamazaki it is later said that they and four others should only be arrested 'if Mr Keenan [Chief Prosecutor of the Tokyo IMT] decides to try the Tojo Cabinet en bloc, their individual records … so far fail to reveal evidence sufficient to warrant their apprehension and individual trial under the Jackson formula'.[559]

Kentaro describes how, in the IPS discussion to finalise the list of indictees, Keenan stated that, although he had wished to prosecute one of the Japanese industrialists, 'he was unable to do so because of the complex preparation that would be involved'.[560] What this preparation would have entailed is not clear.

Donihi's account of his work at the IMTFE includes this short paragraph on industrialists:

> There were no industrialists on trial, distinct from Nuremberg, where industry had used slave labour. Despite Soviet pressure, Austin Hauxhurst and I (having been assigned by Mr. Keenan to study the question) recommended against the inclusion of the industrialists (*zaibatsu*) category.[561]

Though Donihi gives no explicit reason for the exclusion, the reference to slave labour seems to suggest the Japanese industrialists did not use slave labour.

---

559 *FRUS* 986: Memo by Atcheson to the Secretary of State, dated December 19 1945.

560 Kentaro 2011, p. 61.

561 Donihi 1992–93, p. 733.

As will become clear below, Japanese industry *did* use forced labour from surrounding Asian countries as well as foreign service personnel and members of the colonial populations. According to Drea et al., 'During the war years, the Japanese government forcibly removed workers from Korea, China, and elsewhere in Asia and shipped them to Japan as unpaid labor for dangerous work in coal mines and for heavy construction. American POWs were also subjected to brutal labor details'.[562]

Horwitz described the dilemma (with echoes of the concern for US domestic industry response as per Nuremberg):

> A clear distinction must be made between the industrialist who for patriotic and economic reasons fills government orders for armaments, munitions and other implements of war to be used in connection with an aggressive war, and the industrialist, who for economic reasons, or otherwise, aids, abets, or collaborates with military and governmental leaders in the formulation and execution of a programme of aggression. No evidence was produced by the Executive Committee that any industrialist occupied the position of principal formulator of policy. Conditions in Japan made it important that the indictment of an industrialist not be undertaken unless his conviction was almost a certainty since an acquittal might well have been regarded as a blanket approval of all Japanese industry and industrialists.[563]

However, common sense would hold that convictions for war crimes (use/abuse of POWs) or crimes against humanity (forced labour) would not convey a message of blanket approval of Japanese industry and industrialists – surely not indicting/trying them would sooner convey this message.

Boister cites the *IG Farben case* as explanation for the decision not to try industrialists:

> See, for example, the IG Farben case … concerned with the prosecution of the directors of IG Farben inter alia for planning and waging an aggressive war and conspiracy to do so. The accused were acquitted following the Nuremberg IMT's lead that only political leaders with the power to control government policies could be charged with such offences. A point in the prosecution's favour was that, unlike German conglomerates, the *zaibatsu* had not used slave labour.[564]

562 Drea et al. 2006.

563 Horwitz 1950, p. 498.

564 Boister 2008b, pp. 55–6.

As shown above (Chapter 3A, Section 6.1.4), the IG Farben leaders were *not* acquitted but indeed convicted of war crimes and crimes against humanity, even if they were found *not guilty* on the aggression charge.

Röling, in the record of a long conversation with Antonio Cassesse in the 1970s, explains that the industrialists had been opposed to the war, and that it had been quite correct not to try them.[565] Cassesse conversely suggests, 'One might have thought that it was done deliberately by the Western countries, because they wanted to cooperate with the industrialists of Japan, as they would need their support in future'.[566] Finn comments on a discussion between MacArthur and Konoe, where Konoe warns the SCAP of the threat of the military-Left alliance, and warns that breaking up the *zaibatsu* will lead to communism 'immediately'.[567] In response, MacArthur is reported to have expressed his confidence in Konoe as a leader capable of safeguarding liberal/capitalist interests even in the event of a breakup of the *zaibatsu*.[568]

The USSR had asked for the indictment of three industrialists at the IMTFE.[569] The decision not to indict industrialists was not received favourably in the Soviet press.[570] The 'leaders of the giant Japanese monopolies … known as the Zaibatsu', who favoured and 'were the real instigators' of 'predatory war', had escaped trial. 'This was no accident', alleged the Communist Party daily, *Pravda*, but the results of a carefully calculated plot engineered by the *zaibatsu*'s capitalist counterparts on 'Wall Street'.[571] Another commentary suggests that Keenan did not prosecute the *zaibatsu* because of their connections with US monopolies.[572] Whatever the reason was, as in Germany, the US was later able to mobilise the industrialists so as to build a strong trading partner economy in the East.

4.2 *Other Trials of Japanese War Crimes in the Far East*

Allied governments tried more than 5,600 war crimes suspects in over 2,200 trials in 51 different venues around the Far East.[573] Australia for example held 300 B and C Class war crimes trials in a number of tribunals including in Darwin, Singapore, Hong Kong and Manus Island in the period 1949–51.[574] The

565 Röling and Cassese 1994, p. 38.
566 Röling and Cassese 1994, p. 39.
567 Finn 1992, p. 19.
568 Ibid.
569 Brackman 1987, pp. 85–6.
570 Piccigallo 1979, pp. 146–8.
571 Raginsky and Rosenblit 1948, p. 412; Markov 1946, pp. 7–10. Quoted in Piccigallo 1979, p. 147.
572 Trainin 1948, pp. 11, 12.
573 Totani 2008, p. 262.
574 Fitzpatrick 2013, p. 327; Morris 2013, p. 349.

most accessible source for information about the subsequent trials by Allies and others in the Far East is Piccigallo's monograph, with chapters on each of the Allies' war crimes trials.[575] Summaries of some of the trials are contained in the WCCLR publication.[576] Some case reviews were summarised by the Berkeley War Crimes Study Center (*supra*). Actual case reports or judgments are very difficult to find outside of (and even in) national archives.[577] Most of these trial records remain 'hidden' either literally or because, even if the records are publicly available, scholars have thus far ignored them. Narelle Morris suggests, that in the case of Australia, this was due to the deliberate creation of a 'hidden history' by the Australian government. Morris suggests that the Australian government deliberately hid the history of the approximately 300 war crimes trials it has held, by not reporting them and refusing disclosure of documents. For example, its justification of the rejection of a Japanese government request notes that the trial papers 'provide material for a trouble maker to use against the country which conducted [the trials]'.[578] Only in 1968 were 'bona fide Australian scholars' granted partial access, before full disclosure was finally made in 1975. Morris is one of the first and only to have studied the files since disclosure, and has found that, contrary to expectation, Australia prosecuted many cases relating to Asian victims.[579] A significant effort has also been made in recent years to shed light on the Hong Kong War Crimes Trials[580] through a series of symposia and edited collections organised by Zhang, Liu and Bergsmo.[581]

The case reports (or summaries/descriptions) that are easier to track down are those of cases that have become public campaigning issues (in particular where the victims included white Western citizens). For example, the case against the leaders of the Burma-Siam railroad project (the 'Bridge over the River Kwai'), where around 16,500 Allied POWs are said to have died, along with

575 Generally, Piccigallo 1979, p. 120: 306 cases tried, involving 920 accused, of whom 811 were convicted.

576 For a very brief description of the 'torrent of trials' brought by the British in various locations in South-East Asia, see Chapter 6 of Boister 2008b.

577 Pritchard echoes this sentiment (Pritchard 1996). The National Archives describe the case documents as being 'scattered among' various files (National Archives research guide, *supra*). Case compilations such as the All England Law Reports/Lexis do not include the decisions of these military commissions, not even the Oxford Reports on International Law (which does not even include the Yamashita decision).

578 Morris 2013, p. 349.

579 Morris 2013, p. 350. See for scanned documents the Marburg ICWC: https://www.uni-marburg.de/icwc/forschung/2weltkrieg/australien (last accessed 24 November 2016).

580 Linton 2013.

581 On Asian trials specifically, see Zhang and Liu 2016.

160,000 South and East Asian forced labourers.[582] Another such issue is that of the 'comfort women', thousands of women (in fact mostly girls) who were held as sex slaves for the Japanese military. Some of the brothels in which these women were held were owned and run by private contractors (see below). The victims and other activists on the 'comfort women' issue have held a citizens' tribunal,[583] and filed compensation suits.[584] The Kinkaseki mine (see below) victims have also campaigned for many years with little success.[585] In this section I highlight some examples of cases involving businesspersons.

4.2.1 Dutch Trial of Awochi at Batavia

At the Netherlands Temporary Court-Martial at Batavia (which derived its jurisdiction from Dutch law), the Japanese businessman Washio Awochi was charged with having 'in time of war and as a subject of a hostile power, namely Japan', and as 'owner of the Sakura-Club, founded for the use of Japanese civilians', committed 'war crime of enforced prostitution'.[586] He was accused of doing so 'by, in violation of the laws and customs of war, recruiting women and girls to serve the said civilians or causing them to be recruited for the purpose, and then under the direct or indirect threat of the Kempei (Japanese Military Police) should they wish to leave, forcing them to commit prostitution with the members of the said club'.[587] Among those who were forced to prostitution were girls of 12 and 14 years of age.[588] The defendant pleaded that he had operated under orders of the Japanese authorities. He was convicted and sentenced to ten years' imprisonment.[589]

This case has received praise as the only criminal prosecution in the 'comfort women' issue. However, it also illustrates the innate racism of ICL, in that the case related to Dutch victims. Of the around 200,000 women and girls (most of the victims were teenagers) who were victims of Japanese enforced

582 The Berkeley Singapore docket (part of the defunct *Berkeley War Crimes Study Center* online archive which is still accessible online) includes Burma-Siam Railway cases such as the Mizutani Case Singapore Cases: No. 235/911: https://www.ocf.berkeley.edu/~changmin/Japan/singapore/Trials/Mizutani.htm (last accessed 24 November 2016).

583 Jayasimha 2001.

584 Jayasimha 2001; Hae Bong 2005.

585 See the *Taiwan POW Camps Memorial Society*.

586 13 United Nations War Crimes Commission, Law Reports of Trials of War Criminals 122 (1949) (*Awochi Case*).

587 *Awochi Case*, p. 122.

588 *Awochi Case*, p. 123.

589 Statute Book Decree No. 46 of 1946 concerning the 'Legal Competence in respect of War Crimes', ibid.

prostitution/sexual slavery during World War Two, only around 200–300 were Dutch/European. The others were predominantly Korean, Chinese or Japanese.[590]

4.2.2 US Trials at Yokohama

Suspected Class B and C war criminals were tried in by a US military tribunal at Yokohama, Japan, between 1946 and 1948.[591] Some cases (reviews) dealt with civilian guards employed by companies who were accused and convicted of abusing POWs.[592]

This included, for example, the prosecution of Tagusari, Sukeo and Kei Kai In, civilian guards employed by the Tohoku Denki Seitetsu Company. Tagusari had worked at the plant where US and other Allied POWs from Sendai Area PW Camp No. 10 (Honshu, Japan) were forced to work. He had beaten POWs for not working hard enough, for not doing things 'the right way' or, for no reason at all. He was sentenced to 22 years confinement and hard labour, a sentence which was not reduced on review by the Judge Advocate General – Defense. Another civilian guard and interpreter, Yamauchi Kunimitsu, employed by the Mitsui Mining company (part of the Mitsui *zaibatsu*), charged with wilfully and unlawfully committing cruel, inhuman and brutal atrocities and other offences against certain POWs, was sentenced to 40 years, reduced to 33 on review. Yamauchi (who had lived in the US and attended school there) was accused of 'refusing to interpret', which had meant he had not adequately represented the complaints of American POWs, which had been his responsibility.[593] Other guards tried had been employed by Osaraizawa Mining Company, Nippon Kokan Kobushiki Kaisha and Rinko Coal Company. All were based in Japan, and all were accused of mistreatment of American and other POWs.[594]

590 See generally, Comfort Women Project: http://www.comfort-women.org/.

591 All cases in this section are taken from *Berkeley War Crimes Studies Center* (now defunct archive), Case synopses from Judge Advocate's Reviews: Yokohama Class B and C War Crimes Trials.

592 Cases reviewed by the 8th Army Judge Advocate; see http://discover.odai.yale.edu/ydc/Record/3448505. The results are housed at the *Marburg ICWC* on 5 microfilm reels titled 'Reviews of the Yokohama Class B and C war crimes Trials by the 8th Army Judge Advocate – (1946–1949)'. See for a list and summaries: https://www.uni-marburg.de/icwc/forschung/2weltkrieg/yokohama and archived online documents of the *Berkeley War Crimes Studies Center*.

593 This seems an odd case – the Reviewing Authority recommended that, as the accused had been educated in the US he 'was aware of the humanitarian ideas of Americans. The commission may have … thought it an aggravation of the offense'. Perhaps this case is one of disputed loyalty, cf. the mass internment of Japanese Americans during World War Two.

594 Archived online resources of the *Berkeley War Crimes Studies Center*.

Clearly here (as in Nuremberg) there would have been a possibility to try the directors of these companies for these crimes, including the use of slave labour especially as the cases seem to show that maltreatment was endemic. A common 'avoidance technique' in ICL (as in domestic CL) is prosecuting the lowest-ranked individuals. I discuss this further in the chapters below.

4.2.3 The British War Crimes Court in Hong Kong: the Nippon Mining Company

The British tried at least one case similar to the Yokohama cases above. In the absence of comprehensive documentation of military tribunal cases by the British, one has to rely on other means of discovering their existence. The Nippon Mining Company case we know about because it was mentioned in the Krupp case in Nuremberg:[595]

> In the trial of Mitsugu Toda and eight others, by a British Military Court in Hong Kong, 7th–28th May, 1947, the accused were charged with 'committing a war crime, in that they at Kinkaseki, Formosa, between December 1942 and May, 1945, being on the staff of the Kinkaseki Nippon Mining Coy., and as such being responsible for the safety and welfare of the British and American Prisoners of War employed in the mine under their supervisions, were, in violation of the laws and usages of war, concerned in the ill-treatment of the aforesaid Prisoners of War, contributing to the death of some of them and causing physical sufferings to the others.'[596]

The Nippon Mining Company was the owner of a hugely successful gold mine at Kinkaseki, Taiwan. 'It switched to copper production after the outbreak of the Pacific War, following the policy change of the government of Japan from promotion of gold to copper extraction. This made Kinkaseki the only mine in the colony with the ability to produce copper. The Japan [Nippon] Mining Company reportedly maintained an impressive level of productivity, making use of an array of subsidies, new infrastructure, and price control initiatives by the colonial government'.[597]

Records show that of the quarter of a million US and British POWs in Japanese detention, approximately 2,400 were brought over to Formosa/Taiwan in 1942, where they were utilised for digging, cultivating, transport, and so on,

595 Case documentation is held at the UK National Archives, file no. WO235/1028 *Mitsugu Case*. See also Totani 2013.

596 *Krupp Case*, p. 168.

597 Totani 2013, pp. 82–3.

at the Taiwan Sugar Company, the Japan Mining Company, the Taiwan Shrine compounds, and other locations within the colony: 300–400 of these came to work at the Kinkaseki mine.[598]

The main question in the trial of Toda, Mitsugu (the General Manager of the mine) and the others was whether the responsibility over the POWs was the company's or the camp commander's (or, as they were called by the victim-witnesses in the case, the 'mine hanchos' or the 'camp hanchos').[599] Each day the prisoners would leave the POW camp to work in the company mine, where they were under the supervision of company foremen. Conditions at the copper mine were admitted by all relevant parties to be dangerous, with excessive heat, deep pools, falling rocks and poor equipment. Beatings were common and admitted. The defence had argued that the POWs were not employed by the company but were being made to work at the mine by the military. The defence for Toda also argued the foremen were 'seconded' to the army and thus fell under its responsibility. Also, it was claimed that the company chose to cooperate with the Japanese Army in view of the war situation, a decision which the head office of the company in Tokyo approved. Toda testified that 'I personally did not wish to employ POWs', since the Company 'did not feel any insufficiency in obtaining the working labour' and that he was also worried about 'such enormous expenses to be defrayed for the maintenance of POW Camps' as well as the likelihood of most prisoners' lack of experience in mine extraction work.[600] Despite the fact that Toda was the general manager of the mine, he received a sentence of only one year. Two of the foremen received sentences of 10 years each.[601] This is another example devolving responsibility for international crimes in business cases to the lowest-ranked persons.

Ramasastry comments on the case that 'it can be inferred that the court held the mining company legally responsible for the deaths, injuries, and the suffering of the POWs. This is deduced from the fact that two of the defendants, Toda and Nakamura, a mining company manager and supervisor respectively, were found guilty, although they did not directly participate in the beatings or mistreatment of the prisoners'.[602] This is an illogical (incorrect) deduction often seen (e.g., Clapham[603]) in those who 'support' legal person liability – which I

598 Totani 2013, pp. 82–4.
599 National Archives file no. WO235/1028, *Mitsugu Toda et al. Case* No. 65223.
600 Totani 2013, pp. 83–4.
601 File No. WO235/1028 *Mitsugu Toda et al. Case.*
602 Ramasastry 2002, p. 115.
603 Clapham 2008, and below Ch. 4.

will discuss in Chapter 4. Ramasastry makes a lot of the fact that Toda was not directly involved in the abuse or did not know it happened, but this case concerns *command responsibility* rather than legal person liability.[604] On this distinction see Chapter 4.

Three of the former POWs who worked at the mine filed a civil compensation suit against Japan Energy Corp. in a US court in 2000, a case that was dismissed in 2007.[605] In Chapter 5, I discuss the relative merit of civil cases vs. criminal prosecutions – and the combination: civil claims attached to criminal cases, and also punitive/compensatory damages ordered in criminal cases.

4.2.4 The Soviet Trial of Unit 731

The USSR tried several Japanese war crimes suspects, among them, what may be regarded as the Japanese equivalent of the IG Farben scientists: Unit 731.[606] Like the *Topf & Söhne* trial above, this case shows the Soviet perspective on the war, on motivations for crimes, and illustrates the 'Systemkonkurrenz' [loosely: difference in ideological take on events] also seen in the West.

On 25–30 December 1949 in the city of Chabarowsk in the USSR, Yamada and 11 other former members of Unit 731 of the Japanese Imperial Army were tried for preparation and use of bacterialogical weapons. The accused, who in their final statements to the tribunal admitted the charges and expressed regret, were convicted to 3–25 years of 'improvement' through hard labour.[607] Other members of Unit 731 (including its commander, Ishii), who had surrendered to the US at the close of the war, had reportedly been granted immunity from prosecution by the US, in return for know-how.[608] Röling and others have said that these scientists were taken to the US in order for the US to benefit from their knowledge and the results of their experimentation (the US is even said to have taken one of the scientists to Korea during the war there), and also that evidence of biological warfare was deliberately withheld (and at one point quietly

604 According to Jorgensen, this is a precursor to the 'joint criminal enterprise' model used in later ICL practice (Jorgensen 2013, pp. 138 ff.) – see Chapter 5.

605 *Titherington v. Japan Energy* Corporation, filed 02/24/2000 at the Superior Court of California, County of Orange; case no. 00CC02534CO. [no further info available]; see also 'POWs fight Japan in US Court', *BBC News*, 23 February 2000.

606 On the IMT's failure to prosecute Unit 731, see Kei-Ichi 2011, pp. 177 ff.

607 Prozessmaterialien in der Strafsache gegen ehemalige angehörige der Japanischen Armee wegen Vorbereitung und Anwendung der Bakterienwaffe, Moscow, Verlag für Fremdsprachige Literatur, 1950, p. 600.

608 Röling and Cassese 1994, p. 48. See also *Vernon and Wachenheimer DSB 1947*. Vernon reports that Ishii was brought to the US along with what remained of his test result files. For a very recent accusation of US use of bacteriological warfare in its war against Korea, see Al-Jazeera 'US used "plague bomb" in Korea war', 17 March 2010.

withdrawn) from the IMTFE, despite the fact that IMTFE defendant Umuzu had been directly responsible for setting up the biological laboratory in Manchuria/Manchuoko.[609]

It would appear that one difference between the Japanese and German wars/systems was that Japan had ~~its~~ army develop, manufacture, test and ultimately apply the biological weapons, whereas Germany had used private companies for the invention, development and manufacture of poison gases.[610] The Soviet prosecutor at Chabarowsk describes how, in the pursuit of its imperialist/colonial aggressive war, Japan developed bacteriological weapons that could infect humans as well as cattle and seeds. One method of applying such bacteriological weapon was apparently the aerial bombing system 'Ishii' which was designed to drop pestilent fleas onto enemy territory.[611] This technique was apparently used by the Japanese air force a number of times in different parts of China in 1940–42.[612]

The lawyer speaking in the main accused Yamada's defence (N. Below) explains how in his view Yamada came to commit such acts. Agreeing with Locke and Rousseau that humans are innately good, he explains Marx and Engels's point of view that 'mentality, interests, will, character and moral conscience of people is a product of their historical milieu, the conditions of society and the education shaped through social relations'.[613] Yamada was born in 1881 when Japan was still very much organised through the feudal system. The four main families of Mitsui, Mitsubishi, Yasuda and Sumitomi reached their monopoly positions through an alliance with the emperor in the nineteenth century and in the 1930s decided to expand their economic empire through aggressive war. War industry (the 'bone-mill') was only additionally profitable. Precisely these 'most exploitative and rapacious of Japanese Imperialists' poisoned the people with an aggressive nationalism and chauvinism, as they knew that the war could not be fought without the broad popular masses.[614] The basis of the ideology was the holiness and infallibility of the Emperor. Below went on to explain, how the *zaibatsu*, the 'inspiration, instigators, organisers and leaders of Japanese aggression' had taken the initiative and executive role in the production of bacteriological weapons.[615] Within this

609 Röling and Cassese 1994, p. 48. See also Totani 2008, p. 3.

610 Witnesses at the Chabarovsk trial suggest that the biological warfare programme of Unit 731 fell under the direct responsibility of the emperor, which Röling considers credible Röling and Cassese 1994, p. 49; *Prozeßmaterialien* 546.

611 Indictment, *Prozeßmaterialien* 11.

612 Indictment, *Prozeßmaterialien* 23–5.

613 *Prozeßmaterialien* 533 (plea of the defence).

614 *Prozeßmaterialien* 534.

615 *Prozeßmaterialien* 539.

context Yamada had been 'one of the many instruments that carried out the nefarious crimes of the Japanese Imperialism', having had the 'misfortune' to have been born into such circumstances, a criminal and a victim at the same time.[616]

This warrants comparison with IMTFE Chief Prosecutor Keenan who was critical of Soviet motives for their call to have former emperor Hirohito tried, and denied allegations of Japanese use of bacteriological weapons.[617] Keenan asserted that as regards evidence of bacteriological warfare 'none whatever' had been introduced at the IMTFE.[618] On the other hand, the USSR is said to have used this case 'to assert its moral leadership in Asia'.[619] As in the discussion of the Soviet trial of the *Topf & Söhne* defendants (Chapter 3A, Section 8.3), the ideological character of, or motivation behind, Soviet trials is stressed. Likewise, the ideological motivations behind US/Western policy were stressed by the Soviets. Given the revelation that the US government offered General Ishii and others of Unit 731 prosecutorial immunity in return for their research findings there appears to have been as much an ideological reason behind their non-prosecution.[620]

The USSR accused the US of 'instigating a new world war, speeding revival of Japan's industrial war potential'[621] in response to the US's willingness to sign a peace treaty with Japan without the USSR. Such would lead to a Pacific military alliance with Japan as the military and economic foundation, and eventually to the US using Japan in its 'war for United States domination'.[622] Piccigallo calls the Chabarowsk trial 'part of a renewed propaganda assault against United States Policy in East Asia'.[623] In agreement with Viscount Maugham, he states, 'the USSR regards a trial as one of the organs of Government power, a weapon in the hands of the rulers of the State for safeguarding its interests'. And Lord Hankey added, 'the British and American systems treat a court as an independent agency responsible only before the law'.[624] This (positivist) portrayal of law as somehow non-political, however, also actively serves to conceal the West-

616 *Prozeßmaterialien* 540.

617 'Joseph Keenan meets the Press', American Mercury April 1950, summarised in Welch 2001, p. 88.

618 Piccigallo 1979, p. 251 fn. 56.

619 Totani 2008, p. 60.

620 Boister 2008b, p. 64.

621 Piccigallo 1979, p. 150, citing a Moscow Radio report [which is cited in the *Malay Mail*, 9 May 1949].

622 Piccigallo 1979, p. 150.

623 Piccigallo 1979, p. 154.

624 Piccigallo 1979, p. 155, quoting Maugham 1951; and L. Hankey, *Politics, Trial and Errors*, p. 9 (no further details given).

ern political goals behind the trials. One of them could plausibly have been, to divert attention from the US occupation aims in Japan, which in many ways were much more far-reaching than the 'media-genic' trials.

5 Economic Occupation Policy: *zaibatsu* Dissolution and the 'Reverse Course'

What it chose not to deal with through the courts, the US dealt with, 'with the vision and confidence of world conquerors',[625] through its economic policy as Japan's occupier. As in Germany (and more broadly in Europe through the Marshall Plan), occupation included 'anticommunism',[626] complete control over the economy, and deep reform including legal reform and even reform of the education system: 'a total restructuring of Japanese society, economy and politics was imposed within the space of only a few years'.[627] This started off with complete disarmament, making available factories and equipment for reparations,[628] and was followed by a plan for the break-up of cartels, fiscal and land reform – the Japanese version of the 'Morgenthau Plan'[629] – but soon changed direction in what became known as the 'reverse course'.

5.1 *Zaibatsu Dissolution and Other Reforms*

In 1945, US officials had reported that 'not only were the zaibatsu as responsible for Japan's militarism as the militarists themselves, but they profited immensely by it ... Unless the zaibatsu are broken up, the Japanese have little prospect of ever being able to govern themselves as free men'.[630] The conclusion of the 'Edwards Mission on economic policy' (a mission sent by the US government to advise on economic policy)[631] led to the design of a policy aimed at the formation of a broad middle class in Japan, as well as land reform, towards allowing broader private ownership of land, making these reforms similar to the policies of European colonisers (as described in Chapter 2B).[632] The Edwards Mission concluded that the existence of two classes in Japan, the rul-

625 Allinson 2004, p. 52.
626 Allinson 2004, p. 53.
627 Hunter 1989, p. 11.
628 Ando 1991, p. 14.
629 See, e.g., Japanese Post-Surrender Policy, excerpt in Appendix C.
630 Cohen 1945, p. 97; Cohen 2000, p. 426; see also Roth 1946, pp. 57–9.
631 Edwards, Corwin D., Report of the Mission on Japanese Combines, Washington, DC: Departments of State and War, 1946.
632 Finn 1992, pp. 130–2. Generally Ando 1991.

ing elite and the masses had led to Japan's aggression: 'The existence of too many peasants on too little land under the exacting tenure system imposed by feudalistic landlords was the cause of the cheap labour in Japanese industry, which in turn gave birth to a poor domestic market and militaristic expansion for overseas possessions'.[633] Effectively, in adopting this economic reform policy aimed at creating a middle class, the US government acknowledged that the Japanese aggressions had been at least in part, a war for markets, similar to European expansion starting in its feudal period. The creation of a middle class necessitated breaking up the *zaibatsu*.[634] Five *zaibatsu* were slated for dissolution by the Holding Company Liquidation Commission: Mitsui, Mitsubishi, Yasuda, Sumitomi (the big four), and Fuji Industrial.[635] The dissolution involved the surrender of vast amounts of private property.[636] The aim of the measures was to break the control the *zaibatsu* had over the economy, through liquidating the system of holding companies whose sole function it was to hold a majority share in other financial, industrial and commercial companies.[637] In December 1946, 60 additional *zaibatsu* were designated for dissolution while a further number were placed under supervision.[638] Moreover, *zaibatsu* family members' assets were frozen so as to prevent them recreating their economic power through setting up new companies.[639]

SCAP issued a directive in December 1946 ordering the removal of undesirable personnel from public office. In relation to the '*zaibatsu* problem'[640] the directive affected:

> zaibatsu personnel who at any time between July 7, 1937, and September 2, 1945, occupied a position as chairman of the board of directors, president, vice president, director, adviser, auditor, or manager of certain industrial and financial concerns or any other bank development company or institution whose foremost purpose was assisting in militaristic aggression.[641]

633 Ando 1991, p. 21.

634 FEC 230 Policy recommendation; see generally, *Vernon and Wachenheimer DSB 1947*.

635 *Vernon and Wachenheimer DSB 1947*, p. 59.

636 Generally Ando 1991, who considers aspects of the US economic policy in Japan contrary to *1907 Hague Regulations* Arts. 44 (respecting existing laws) and 55 (occupier's temporary caretaker function).

637 Ando 1991, p. 19.

638 *Vernon and Wachenheimer DSB 1947*, p. 60.

639 Ando 1991, p. 19.

640 *Vernon and Wachenheimer DSB 1947*, p. 60. According to Seita (1994) this led to the purging of 210,000 persons of all professions, including filmmakers and teachers.

641 *Vernon and Wachenheimer DSB 1947*, p. 60.

In February 1947, the first 56 members of 10 *zaibatsu* were designated for 'purging' (removal from office and exclusion from similar posts in future).[642] In total around 3,000 'leaders of private firms in finance, commerce, industry, and the media, including high-ranking managers in the largest *zaibatsu* and independent firms' were purged.[643]

To prevent the reemergence of *zaibatsu*, the US leadership proposed, and the Japanese government adopted, an 'American-style' Anti-Trust Law in April 1947.[644]

5.2 *Reverse Course*

As mentioned above in Chapter 3A, Byrnes's 1946 speech, the publication of the Truman Doctrine in March 1947 and the Marshall Plan in July 1947 marked a turning point in US policy not only in Europe but globally. In Japan, the arrival in June 1950 of John Foster Dulles marked the beginning of the end of the occupation.[645] Dulles came seeking to negotiate a treaty, needing an ally in the face of the Korean War and the rise of Mao in China.[646] The restrictions on Japanese industry, which had caused food shortages, were gradually relaxed as part of what was called the 'reverse course' effort to reindustrialise Japan as a bulwark against communism,[647] and a supplier in the Korean War.[648] Japan was to be a 'workshop of democracy in Asia'.[649] The US leadership acted partly on the advice of a group of prominent US businessmen,[650] while a Detroit banker outlined the monetary reforms that became known as

642 Ibid. Vernon adds: 'This action supplements the earlier resignation of important zaibatsu officers which took place shortly after the start of the occupation' (ibid).

643 Allinson 2004, p. 54.

644 Generally on the legality of the US economic policy in Japan, which may be considered contrary to *1907 Hague Regulations* Arts. 44 (respecting existing laws) and 55 (occupier's temporary caretaker function), see Ando 1991, Ch. 3 (The Legal Basis of the Measures in Question) and Ch. 6 (Conclusion). Ando 1991, p. 20.

645 Finn 1992, p. 241.

646 Finn 1992, p. 242.

647 Kennan 1967, p. 368. Additionally, 'as the communist movement inside Japan became active in the course of 1948, SCAP and the Japanese government resorted to [the purge] directives to remove the communist influence from the Japanese political scene. During 1949 and 1950, 61 executive committee members and editorial officers of the Japanese Communist Party, including 13 Diet members, were designated purged persons, while more than 10,000 communists or sympathizers were removed from various government posts, Several leftist organizations were ordered to liquidate and their property was seized'. (Ando 1991, p. 27).

648 Finn 1992, pp. 226, 241.

649 Allinson 2004, p. 53.

650 Ando 1991, p. 25.

the 'Dodge Line'.[651] By July 1948, 225 of the 325 companies slated for 'deconcentration measures' had been taken off the list.[652] In addition, by 1950–51 almost all of the business leaders affected by the purge law were 'depurged'.[653] A new purge targeted 20,000 alleged Communists in journalism and the labour movement.[654] In 1955 also, all those who had received prison sentences at the IMTFE were released.[655] At the same time, harassment by the US occupier of the political left in Japan continued.[656]

Some of the more far-reaching reforms the US occupation leadership had instigated, in particular land reform, fiscal reform, the opening up of the economy to foreign (US) investment, remained in place,[657] and can be said to have achieved what was set at the outset as a priority goal of the US occupation: 'the eventual participation of Japan in a World economy on a reasonable basis'.[658] The 'World economy' in this vision was the capitalist world's economy: US occupation policy had succeeded in 'integrat[ing] … Japan, economically and politically, into the Western capitalist camp and [in kickstarting] the extraordinary growth of the Japanese economy'.[659]

The 'reverse course' sentiment was not limited only to US-Japanese relations. Even though the rhetoric in news coverage of the in total 4,500 war crimes trials which resulted in convictions had insisted that all would complete their sentences, within a short time each of the governments that had carried out the trials granted all convicted war criminals some form of clemency and by 1958, all had been released.[660] According to Sandra Wilson, 'As the prosecuting governments came to believe that Japan should assume a major role in

651 Allinson 2004, p. 77.
652 Ando 1991, p. 26.
653 Seita 1994; Ando 1991, p. 27.
654 Allinson 2004, p. 54. Like in the US under the New Deal, however, past labour reforms had been aimed at organised (unionised) labour forming a countervailing power to that of large capital (Allinson 2004, p. 57).
655 Cryer 2010, p. 119.
656 Finn 1992, p. 243.
657 Ando 1991, p. 28.
658 Ibid.
659 Hunter 1989, p. 12 – who holds, however, that many factors in Japan's success pre-date the postwar reforms (p. 13), including a massive programme of change aimed at bringing Japan up to Western standards 'in the things Westerners considered important – legal system, political structure, economic legislation and a general level of "culture" and "civilization" that started in 1873 and was aimed at getting Japan to a place where it could renegotiate the unequal treaties it had signed with amongst others the US' (Hunter 1989, pp. 19–21). See also Allinson 2004, pp. 56 ff. and, generally, Ando 1991.
660 Except those whose death sentence had been carried out (Wilson 2015, pp. 746–7).

combating Communism in Asia, however, they were compelled to take more account of the views of the Japanese government and the Japanese public in order to ensure Japanese compliance with Western strategy in the Cold War'.[661] A massive Japanese lobbying campaign 'backed by powerful public figures and ... well-funded by businesses, private individuals and government', in combination with a fear on the part of the prosecuting governments to appear less than lenient to their new 'friend', contributed to the release of all, including the 'hard core' of war crimes convicts.[662]

One of the Class A war crimes suspects released from Sugamo Prison by the US occupation was Kishi Nobusuku, the former minister of industry and commerce, who became prime minister in 1957. He was responsible for the renewal of the US-Japan Security Treaty with President Eisenhower in 1960, the treaty 'which many Japanese regarded as Kishi's helping hand to entrench American military, political, and economic domination over Japan'.[663] Totani adds, 'It is perhaps not surprising that the Japanese public responded to the apparent collusion between the former Class A war crimes suspect – who had escaped prosecution by the grace of the United States – and Eisenhower *by leading one of the largest popular demonstrations ever to be seen in the history of Japan*'.[664]

6 Conclusion to Chapter 3: Capitalism's Victor's Justice

The decision to submit the authors of the war to international trials was taken in a mood of 'liberal internationalism', promoted by government lawyers, and it presented at the same time an opportunity to create both new law and a particular narrative of the war that would appease home publics and allow for the rehabilitation of Japan and German as major trading partners. While on the Western side, which was in the public limelight at least for the duration of the international trial, the 'economic case' was initially included, and industrialists were prosecuted, on the Eastern front the trial focused almost entirely on pathologising – and racialising – the Japanese military and political leadership, while the secondary trials were largely limited to cases affecting allied service personnel and ignored the Asian victims of the Japanese war machine.[665]

---

661 Wilson 2015, p. 748.

662 Wilson 2015, pp. 751–2, 760–1.

663 Totani 2008, p. 77.

664 Ibid, emphasis added.

665 Morris, however, notes that while the Tokyo Tribunal has been criticised for providing 'partial and selective justice along racial, colonial and gendered lines', there was considerable

The industrialists' trials in Europe offer a unique perspective on business in conflicts: individuals' rationalised explanations for their actions illustrate how the 'corporate anomie' generated by the corporation as a structure of irresponsibility (Chapter 2A) allows individuals to become involved in gruesome acts for profit. The very stories of the involvement of the German cartels and Japanese *zaibatsu* illustrate corporate imperialism, and the imperialism at the core of the corporate form, as argued in Chapter 2B.

In conclusion, in Japan as in Germany, the United States orchestrated/stage-managed international criminal trials so as to give the semblance of accountability of the authors of the war, while in fact ensuring that those elites considered responsible at the outset, turned from adversaries into allies. The German and Japanese industrialists and capitalists, who had been part of the national imperialist ventures, became enmeshed in the global economic system dominated by the US. Through breaking up the cartels and co-opting its leaders, the US transformed controlled, monopolised closed markets into an open Europe and Japan where US companies would find plenty of investment opportunity as well as markets for its products, access to technology and labour, stations and materiel for its military. I have argued that the trials formed the public face of a much broader post-war policy, occupation, reform, shaping the future Europe and East Asia – in ways similar to colonial times (Chapter 2B). They did so by establishing the hegemon's moral authority, which legitimised far-reaching economic intervention. The trials also served to justify involvement in Europe and Japan during and especially also *after* World War Two to the home public.

The remarkable move that happened, and that I have described here in Chapters 3A and 3B through the story of the main Tokyo and Nuremberg IMT trials, is that the *humanitarian* side of the story remains in the currently dominant liberal accounts, the story of the prosecution of criminals who threatened 'our humanity'. The ideological separation between capitalism and communism at the inception of the Cold War split 'the economic' off from the 'humanitarian' in ICL, thereby influencing not only the trials being held at the time in concretely identifiable ways, but also, and most importantly, qualitatively changing the way conflict would be understood. From now on, the role of ICL in relation to conflict would be imagined in terms of individual (or regime) pathology instead of conflict (inevitably) produced by the mode of production. The 'economic side' of World War Two only remains present in Soviet and GDR literature.[666]

---

emphasis on Asian victims of Japanese crimes in the Australian, especially the Rabaul trials (Morris 2013, pp. 348–9).

666 E.g., Institut für Marxismus-Leninismus 1960, 1962.

The economic causes of conflict were removed from ICL. Public and private, the logics of humanitarianism/peace/rights and of economy/trade (Chapter 2B) were once again discursively separated so as to create and maintain the illusion that these are unrelated issues – although we can see how economic reconstruction, development and market liberalisation remained allied to the peace (and security) narrative.[667] The UN Charter stayed clear of the structural economic causes (and effects) of the very problems it was designed to address,[668] while endorsing economic cooperation as a precondition for peace and stability. As we shall see in the following chapters, the result was a change in the way conflict came to be understood: conflict was no longer a result of imperialism, expansionism, but rather of individual and/or ethno-racial pathology.

Moreover, the prosecutions of industrialists after World War Two were largely forgotten, and only recently have 'business and conflict' been reconnected in our thinking about ICL – seemingly as a new phenomenon (Chapters 4 and 5).

The tenacity and pluck of the Nuremberg lawyers mimics the 'victory of law' over barbarism. In the clash between their liberal impulse and the capitalist logic, the liberal impulse lost out in substance if not in semblance, causing the liberal lawyers to be disciplined, and recruiting ICL to the 'capitalising mission'.

---

667 Duffield 2001, esp. pp. 22–42, 108–28.
668 Kennedy 2006, p. 162.

CHAPTER 4

Remaking ICL: Removing Businessmen and Inserting Legal Persons as Subjects

1 Introduction to Chapter 4

In the aftermath of *Nuremberg* the trials were criticised by key international lawyers on legal grounds – it was said, for example, that law had been applied retrospectively, and that by virtue of its selectivity and failure to try Allied crimes, Nuremberg had been an exercise of 'victors' justice'.[1] Refugee legal scholar Schwarzenberger, who himself had refused to become part of the prosecution team in Nuremberg[2], rather sceptically stated there was no need for an ICL, what others called ICL was simply internationalised domestic criminal law, and, citing his friend and former British IMT prosecutor Hartley Shawcross 'murder remains murder whether committed against one or a million'.[3] Schwarzenberger posited that perhaps his contemporary lawyers, enamored with ICL, were simply victims of fashion. After a 4 decade dormancy, ICL has come back into fashion. In recent years the phrases 'war crimes' and 'crimes against humanity' have become ubiquitous, in the media, on the streets, in legal practice and also in the academy.[4] There are high expectations that ICL will be deployed to remedy many ills in the world, and these have, in the first 15 years of 'mature' ICL practice, only been 'realistically tempered'.[5] ICL is popular, and seemingly critique-proof: it is a powerful pro-state ideology that has become taboo to disagree with.[6] It also accords enormous power to those tasked with

1 E.g., Kelsen 1947, p. 153; Schwarzenberger 1946–47, p. 351; Jescheck 2008, p. 408 (originally published in 1957).

2 Steinle 2004, p. 668

3 Schwarzenberger 1950, p. 266

4 E.g., Miéville 2006, pp. 296–7; Van Sliedregt 2016.

5 For example, a mood of only marginally cautious celebration pervades the ICC's 10th birthday issue of the *Journal of International Criminal Justice* – e.g., Akhavan, Schabas, Roht-Arriaza 2013. Only recently have some cracks started to appear, with the withdrawal from the ICC of Burundi, South Africa and Gambia and the withdrawal of Russia from the treaty it had not yet ratified. *The Guardian*, 27 October 2016; *The Guardian*, 16 November 2016. On the African Union's criticism of the ICC, see, e.g., Jalloh 2017.

6 Tallgren 2014, p. 75.

realising the practical side of ICL – from 'policing' the world to selecting the targets for prosecution and the creation of the narrative of a crime and its context within this process.

In the first part of this chapter, I start by asking how ICL became the accountability tool of choice more generally – not just in the realm of 'business and human rights'. In Chapter 4B, I look at *how* ICL has been developed to make it potentially applicable to business in conflict, and in Chapter 4C I raise the question of *why*, when demanding the application of ICL to business, lawyers, campaigners and others do not (or no longer) speak of individual businesspeople, but of application to the corporation *per se*.

I focus on academic[7] lawyers' role in constructing ICL's foundational narrative: the ideology that contains (constructs) its history, meaning and purpose. I also show how ICL sets the terms of the debate, forecloses any radical critique and weakens the appeal of alternative ways of addressing the problem.

It is academic lawyers' convention (or even compulsion) to take legal events set in train by political actors (such as Nuremberg and Tokyo) and make doctrinal sense of them. ICL in this mode is treated by these lawyers as a found object, or an (importantly) *unreturnable* gift left to us by a previous generation. It needs to be studied, analysed, its parts named and explained. In particular, we need to figure out how it fits into legal scholars' pre-designated categories (or whether it requires new categories) and how it fits into our broader system of law, which is an abstracted, artificial 'whole'. Academic lawyers perform a post hoc legal rationalisation of an event, attach to it a history and a logic, and send it forward into 'progressive development'. The ideological products of these lawyers' efforts are then employed by state negotiators (and the official lawmakers, e.g., Parliaments), civil society groups, business people and others (potentially members of different classes) to negotiate over and struggle for. Lawyers, as noted in Chapter 1, are thus not the 'myopic handmaidens' of this world order, but rather, as Shirley Scott has argued, 'chefs'[8] – servants to the 'system' who retain some autonomy of action – members of the (literal) 'ruling' elite, *congealing capitalism.*

The fact that ICL was taken up post-Cold War as a project for (re-)construction suggests that similar material circumstances existed in the latter half of

---

7 As, especially in ICL, there is no *clear* separation between academic and practising lawyers, it would be more accurate to say: lawyers acting in their academic capacity.

8 Scott 1998; and Alston 1997. In her article 'International Lawyers: Handmaidens, Chefs or Birth Attendants?' Scott describes chefs as 'servants who retain some autonomy of action' as opposed to Alston's 'handmaidens'.

the 1940s affecting material interests at home and abroad that required some manner of intervention (Chapter 3A, Section 3: 'Why Nuremberg?'; see also Chapter 5 below). On a more general level, the 'need' for an ICL as an element of ideology can be deduced from its significance as the missing piece of the IL project (as perceived pre-Nuremberg by, e.g., Henry Stimson). In general, as part of a broader international lawmaking effort ICL was needed to soothe the collective conscience after the barbarism of World War Two. Even though World War Two and the holocaust had by no means been 'lawless' events, law is posited as that which conquers barbarism and prevents it from re-emerging. As mentioned in Chapter 3, the making of ICL occurred in the same period as the birth of the United Nations, the creation of the first human rights treaties, the Genocide Convention, the four Geneva Conventions on conduct in war, as well as the conclusion of the first major multilateral economic instruments (the General Agreement on Tariffs and Trade) and the treaty founding the European Coal and Steel Community, the basis of what was to become the European Union, in other words, much of what makes up IL today. An additional reason for its development was that ICL was needed to operationalise the 'humanitarian' element of IL (IHRL and IHL). As such ICL serves to legitimise IL as a whole ('lending the legitimacy that comes with the enterprise of pursuing the worst criminals'[9]). 'Fashions' do not come out of nowhere, but are the expression of a dialectic between complex historical material circumstances, their past interpretations and the aspirations they evoke (or conceal) for the future. A final reason for ICL-making could be, as Schwarzenberger has suggested, that lawyers were simply following a fashion.[10] ICL is now again very much in fashion; it is the accountability tool of choice. Now I will seek to discover why.

What immediately becomes apparent when attempting to describe ICL – as a field of knowledge or ideology – is that it is not homogenous but exists in slightly different configurations in different interpreters' minds and texts. In a typology of mainstream scholarship constructing the foundational narrative (dominant or hegemonic ideology) of ICL, I distinguish four main strands: the humanitarian; the institutional; the positivist; and the pragmatist perspectives. The four strands implicitly connect with different legal traditions and cultures, consequently respond to different expectations of what 'makes' an area of law, set (slightly) different parameters, and employ different markers. Yet, I argue in this part that together these four form the mutually reinfor-

9 Mégret 2010, pp. 180–1.
10 Schwarzenberger 1950, p. 263.

cing building blocks of dominant 'ICL ideology', and I comment further on how this productive character of ICL relates to the specific function of ICL in neoliberal governance and the capitalist mode of production. I also propose an alternative, radical foundational narrative – using the commodity form theory and the notion of 'canned morality' – that I will carry forward into Chapter 6.

In Chapter 4B, I look at the 'congealing' of capitalism from deeper inside ICL, where the detailed rules are worked out ('abstracted') on the subjects, relationships and other modalities of ICL. This happens largely in the drafting of the new international tribunals' statutes, and in their case law. Academic lawyers play a role in this also, not least because academic lawyers have been doing much of the work in ICL, e.g., as judges and in other legal jobs at the tribunals, as negotiators on behalf of countries in the ICC negotiations, etc. An interesting side note here is that most ICL scholars and practitioners come from a public international law, rather than a domestic criminal law background, which somewhat explains the 'reinvention' of the basic modalities of liability in ICL. In this Part we see that in theory ICL is easily applicable to business in conflict, although this is constricted by ICL's deliberately tight boundaries, while 'expert' doctrinal debate obscures both the choices that have been made as to ICL's content (its applicability to only a narrow set of situations and actors) and its selective application in ICL practice.

Chapter 4C deals with ICL's internal contradiction when it comes to ICL's focus on the individual, and the putative *corporate* liability of businesses. ICL post-World War Two complemented the enlightened liberal *Individualisierung* (individualisation/atomisation, below Section 2.3) of society, law, and responsibility.[11] Human rights became synonymous with ICL prosecution: behind every human rights violation, which produces one or more individual 'victims', there must be a (pathologised) individual responsible. In the past decade, however, the *Individualisierung* that ICL forces has come to be challenged by scholars proposing various perspectives on 'system crime'. Among these new critiques, discussed in Chapter 4C, is the discussion of (actual or potential) corporate liability in ICL, which is taking place subsequent to the reification of the corporation in IL described in Chapter 2B. The putative corporate ICL springs from the contradiction of corporate international personality in ILIP on the one hand, and the development of a regime of responsibility in IL to be applied to an area in which business involvement is increasingly visible on the other.

11 Pashukanis 1978, p. 178.

In the final section of 4C, I analyse the narratives feeding these developments and relate them also to domestic 'corporate crime' scholarship.

In my conclusion I comment further on how this productive character of ICL relates to the specific function of ICL in neoliberal governance and the capitalist mode of production. I also raise the possibility of a radical critique dissolving dominant ICL ideology.

4A The (Re-)Making of ICL: Lawyers Congealing Capitalism[12]

1 Introduction to 4A: Constructing ICL's Foundational Ideology

Academic lawyers' post hoc provision of a foundational narrative (ideology) of ICL, providing it with a history, a sense of 'where it came from' can be contrasted with the way history has been written out of the mainstream company law texts. In Chapter 2A I argued that this is because company law is considered mature and settled in its identity as opposed to ICL, which to some extent is still fluid and subject to appropriation for different purposes. Yet while ICL is acknowledged to be 'new',[13] there is also a felt need to historicise it, for it to gain venerability.[14] Although lawyers' construction of ICL ideology serves partly to *congeal* ICL's fluidity, it has resulted in different views on the related questions of the meaning of 'international criminal law', what constitutes an 'international crime', and subsequently what ICL's purpose is (Sections 2.1–2.4). A further, more recent debate is over who are the actual or potential subjects (or objects) of ICL – who is a potential 'international criminal': does this include the individual company director or officer or business person, the company as a collective, or, the company *per se* as a legal person?

This chapter proceeds as follows: I first describe the construction of ICL's ideology, or *the making of ICL*, which occurred after the World War Two trials at Nuremberg. The parameters and markers delimiting ICL now range from the cosmopolitan 'justice' approach of Cassese, to the strict doctrinal (positivist) approach adopted by Werle and others, and the very narrow approach

12 An earlier version of Chapter 4A has been published as Baars 2014.

13 Boas 2010, p. 501. Boas notes: 'It must be recalled that international criminal law, at least in its modern manifestation is merely 15 years in existence' (2010, p. 501, fn. 1).

14 On this term, see Marks 2003, pp. 19–20.

(one could call this an institutional approach) adopted by Cryer et al. These first three approaches I discuss here are variants of what Kreß in the *Max Planck Encyclopaedia of International Law* calls ICL '*stricto sensu*';[15] a fourth is the 'omnibus' approach espoused by policy-oriented authors.[16] In the penultimate section of this chapter, I show how each of these four approaches contributes to the overall making of ICL – by forming ICL's 'ideological backbone'. The descriptive exercise – making us see that which is so close to us that we normally do not see it[17] – of the production of ICL ideology evinces the 'productive character' of ICL. Each of the four approaches I identify produces, within scholarship and what we could call the 'policy-world', its own critique. Each such 'pre-fab' critique serves to resolve the 'problematic' suggested by the approach itself. This insight reveals that *current ICL critique*, such as it is, is produced by, and remains within the parameters of, hegemonic ICL ideology. Moreover, as I will show, critiques that reach beyond are foreclosed.

In the final section, I offer a more detailed example of one such foreclosed, or radical, critique, namely that of what I call 'canned morality'.

1.1 *Against All Atrocities: a Distinction Based on Morality*

The ICL narrative with by far the strongest appeal, including outside of legal academia, is the 'humanitarian' school of thought on ICL, of which the late Antonio Cassese was a major proponent.[18] With clear echoes of Jackson's Nuremberg orations, Cassese – the Italian professor of Public International Law who became the first president of the ICTY and the STL – described, in one of the first textbooks of ICL, the *telos* of international criminal law (in line with the ICC Statute Preamble) as 'protecting society against the *most harmful transgressions* of legal standards of behaviour perpetrated by *individuals*'.[19] In this perspective, international crimes are something qualitatively different from 'ordinary' crimes, and should have their own, exclusive, 'area' of law. Calling ICL a *new* branch of international law, Cassese explicitly excluded piracy, as, in his view, the concept has not only become obsolete, but it 'does not meet the requirements of *international crimes proper*'.[20] Piracy was not pun-

15 Kreß 2009.
16 Cryer 2005, p. 1; Ratner 2009, p. 12.
17 Orford 2013, p. 618.
18 Besides Cassese, followers of this approach include, e.g., Ferencz. See, e.g., Ferencz 1979.
19 Cassese 2008, p. 20, emphasis added.
20 Cassese 2008, p. 12.

ished for the purpose of protecting a *community value*, and not thought so *abhorrent* as to amount to an international crime. Cassese further stated: 'the notion of international crimes does not include illicit traffic in narcotic drugs and psychotropic substances, the unlawful arms trade, smuggling of nuclear and other potentially deadly materials, or money laundering, slave trade or traffic in women'.[21] This is because these are normally perpetrated by private individuals or criminal organisations, 'states usually fight against them, often by joint action ... [A]s a rule these offences are committed against states'.[22] Apartheid is also excluded since, according to Cassese, the prohibition has not yet reached the status of a customary international law norm.[23] Cassese restricts ICL to offences occurring predominantly in the 'public sphere', and perpetrated mostly by public actors for political motives.[24] He includes as international crimes war crimes, crimes against humanity, genocide, torture, aggression and terrorism, which shows that even among the authors who limit their understanding of ICL to 'core crimes', crimes *stricto sensu* (see below, Section 3.3) or 'international crimes proper', there is disagreement over what those crimes may be.[25] In the 'humanitarian' ideology, ICL expresses, and to some extent constitutes, the values of the international community.[26]

1.2 *Optimists and Sceptics: a Distinction Based on Enforcement Mechanisms*

The next most prominent perspective is one that builds on historical ICL enforcement attempts. It anchors ICL's foundational narrative in international legal institutional development. Cryer et al. in *An Introduction to International Criminal Law* (the 'first authoritative'[27] and now 'market-leading'[28] textbook on the subject) define ICL as the law of the crimes over which international courts

---

21 Cassese 2008, p. 13.

22 Ibid.

23 Ibid.

24 Cassese 2003, p. 1. Cassese in his second, 2008 edition, omits the first chapter of the 2003 edition, which was entitled 'The Reaction of the International Community to Atrocities' and appraised non-judicial responses to atrocities, such as UN Security Council sanctions, countermeasures, revenge (in the biblical sense) and *forgetting*. Examples of what Cassese meant by atrocities were the violence and bloodshed caused by the growing disparity between rich and poor, increasing poverty and hopelessness, nationalism religious fundamentalism, etc.

25 Cassese 2008, p. 3.

26 Kyriakakis 2017.

27 O'Keefe 2009, p. 485.

28 Cryer 2010 (second edition, back cover).

and tribunals have been granted jurisdiction in general international law.[29] This covers what are also called 'core crimes', namely genocide, war crimes, crimes against humanity and the crime of aggression. Those that delineate ICL in relation to international enforcement mechanisms (but also other *stricto sensu* proponents) normally commence any discussion of substantive ICL with a narrative of historical progress which traces ICL's origin to the legendary trial of Peter von Hagenbach in 1474[30] or the Allies' attempts at prosecuting the German Kaiser Wilhelm II, and end at the present-day ICC.[31] In effect, the narrative suggested by the lawyers at Nuremberg as a putative justification for the IMT trial – which emphasised that IL would only *make sense* with a working enforcement mechanism – is here taken and naturalised. This narrative would list certain key moments in the development of the ICL enforcement regime, starting just before *Versailles*. Following World War One, seemingly unwilling to allow the Kaiser's self-imposed exile in The Netherlands to secure his immunity from prosecution for the heinous acts committed by Germany, the victorious Allies created a commission to look into the question of responsibility of the 'authors of the war'. The Commission reported to the 1919 Preliminary Peace Conference that the Central Powers (the losing side in World War One) had committed numerous acts in violation of established laws and customs of war and the elementary laws of humanity.[32] This led to the inclusion in the 1919 *Treaty of Versailles* of three clauses in which the states party ordered the prosecution of the Kaiser and almost 900 others[33] by an international tribunal.[34] The Versailles Treaty marks the first time the concept of

---

29 Cryer 2007, p. 2; Cryer 2010, p. 4.

30 Cryer 2007, p. 91. According to Scharf and Schabas, 'After it was discovered that his troops had raped and killed innocent civilians and pillaged their property during the occupation of Breisach, Germany, Hagenbach was tried before a tribunal of twenty-eight judges from the allied states of the Holy Roman Empire, which at that time included Austria, Bohemia, Luxembourg, Milan, the Netherlands, and Switzerland. Hagenbach was found guilty of murder, rape, and other crimes against the "laws of God and man", stripped of his knighthood, and sentenced to death' (2002, p. 39).

31 See, e.g., Cassese 2008, pp. 30–1; Werle 2007, pp. 1–30; Cryer 2005, pp. 9–72 (Cryer starts in antiquity); Bassiouni and Schabas, include von Hagenbach's 1474 trial (Bassiouni 1974, p. 414; Schabas 2007, p. 1). Ratner gives a 'History of individual accountability' (2009, pp. 3–9); Guilfoyle lists 10 incidences and trials as 'possible precursors to the Nuremberg IMT' (2016, pp. 59–60).

32 *1919 WWI Commission Report*. The Report names 32 charges, including 'systematic terrorism' and the 'abduction of women and girls for the purpose of enforced prostitution', adding that the list is not exhaustive (pp. 114–15).

33 Werle 2007, p. 8.

34 *1919 Versailles Treaty*, excerpt in Appendix D; Schabas 2007, p. 2.

individual criminal responsibility was explicitly mentioned in an international treaty.[35] Thus, in this narrative, the ICL notions of war crimes and an emerging concept of crimes against the laws of humanity had been introduced at this point.[36] Histories of this kind then narrate the very tentative 1920 proposals for an ICC,[37] and following this the concrete proposal (which was supported by only 13 member states)[38] by the League of Nations following the assassination of King Alexander of Yugoslavia in 1934.[39] Eventually, the determination of the World War Two Allies led to the conclusion in 1945 of the 'London Agreement', with annexed to it the Nuremberg Charter, and the establishment of the two international military tribunals at Nuremberg and Tokyo.[40] While the Allied post-World War Two trials are thus construed as laying the foundation for contemporary *global* ICL, its further development was taken over by the UN system. The United Nations General Assembly tasked its International Law Commission in 1947 to draft a 'Code of Offenses Against the Peace and Security of Mankind' based on the IMT Charter principles and judgment.[41] After formulating the *Nuremberg Principles* in 1950[42] and presenting the draft code in 1954,[43] the ILC suspended its work until it neared the end of the Cold War impasse in 1983.[44]

Such histories invariably describe the development of international criminal law gaining momentum after the end of the Cold War with the establishment of the International Criminal Tribunal for the former Yugoslavia (ICTY) and the International Criminal Tribunal for Rwanda (ICTR). These momentous events were followed by the completion in 1996 of a new *Draft Code*, which then

35 Werle 2007, p. 13.

36 No individuals were in fact prosecuted under these provisions, although some were tried by domestic German tribunals in the 'Leipzig Trials': Schabas 2007, p. 4; Werle 2007, p. 8; Ratner 2009, p. 6.

37 Phillimore 1922–23; *1927 Draft Statute for an ICC*.

38 Werle 2009, p. 18.

39 ICC Convention 1937; Cryer 2007, p. 92.

40 On the latter, see esp. Boister and Cryer 2008.

41 General Assembly Resolution 177 (II) Formulation of the Principles recognized in the Charter of the Nurnberg Tribunal and in the Judgment of the Tribunal, 21 November 1947, UN Doc. A/RES/177(II). See *Nuremberg Principles Commentary*. See also Ratner 2009, p. 8.

42 *Nuremberg Principles*.

43 *Draft Code 1954*.

44 Ratner 2009, p. 8. It has been suggested that the 'undermining' turnaround and the reverse course in (mostly the US's political interest in) Asia and Europe resulting in the early release of those convicted post-World War Two, led to prosecutions of war crimes suspects not to be attempted again on such scale (Wilson 2015, p. 761).

formed a basis for the negotiations over the International Criminal Court (ICC) Statute. Thus, the history of ICL *culminates* in the establishment of the ICC.[45] In this narrative, the ICC Statute forms the embodiment of a *maturing* system of ICL.[46] It is therefore perhaps more accurate to describe this narrative as one of the enforcement (possibilities) of ICL on the international level, rather than one of ICL in general. Strikingly, all cast their histories back *before* Nuremberg, not accepting that as its moment of origin (as Werle does, by calling the London Charter the 'birth certificate of ICL'[47]), but rather considering Nuremberg as just one step in a logical sequence. This has the effect of rendering the flaws many saw in Nuremberg (retrospectivity; selectivity) as specific to Nuremberg rather than *innate* to ICL.

1.3 *German Positivists: a Distinction Based on Doctrine*

The third narrative is *internal to law*, the 'legal scientist's perspective' – the lawyer whose task it is to explain law and 'legal happenings' resulting from legal processes, as part of, and in terms of, a coherent, autonomous system of law. This perspective is dominant in German-speaking legal academia,[48] where *Völkerstrafrecht* ('criminal law of nations' – equivalent terms exist in Portuguese, Spanish, French and Italian but not in English – Kreß diplomatically suggests 'international criminal law *stricto sensu*')[49] is defined as 'all norms of PIL, that directly create, exclude, or in another way regulate criminal liability'.[50] In their narrative, *Völkerstrafrecht* must be distinguished from *Internationales Strafrecht* ('international criminal law').[51] In the French literature the same distinction is made between *droit international pénal*, on the one hand, and *droit pénal international*, on the other.[52] Thus, the international crimes within this definition are what authors writing in English may call 'core crimes' (war crimes, crimes against humanity, genocide and aggression).[53] The subtle dif-

45 See Schabas 2007, pp. 1–21; De Than and Shorts 2003, pp. 271–341; Schwarzenberger 1950, p. 263; Ambos 2002 (uses the term 'gipfelt' which translates as 'culminates').
46 Werle 2007, p. v. See also Sliedregt 2003, p. 3; Werle 2009, pp. 4, 18; Ambos 2002 (in the title of his book).
47 Werle 2007, p. 14.
48 Werle 2007, fn. 153.
49 See also Kreß 2009; Vitzthum 2010, p. 19.
50 Werle 2007, p. 34, fn. 153; see also Werle 2014, p. 31.
51 Werle 2007, p. 35.
52 The distinction on the same basis also exists in the Portuguese, Italian and Spanish legal tradition (Cassese 2003, p. 15). See also Hollán 2000; Schwarzenberger 1950.
53 Cryer 2010, p. 4; Werle 2014, p. 32.

ference in terms of the content of the enforcement narrative above is that this includes CIL crimes that do not fall under the jurisdiction of the ICC or the international tribunals, such as certain specific crimes in internal armed conflicts,[54] and single occurrences of war crimes and crimes against humanity and the CIL norms on crimes in civil war (some of) which are included in the jurisdiction of the ICTR and ICTY. The core crimes covered in *Völkerstrafrecht* are *as a category* included in the ICC jurisdiction and defined there; however, *Völkerstrafrecht* generally includes custom and other sources, where these crimes are also regulated.[55] Implicitly, Art. 22(3) of the ICC Statute itself evidences that there exist other IL crimes than those listed in the Statute. The bigger difference is the motivation for the distinction, in that the 'German' approach includes as *Völkerrechtsverbrechen* (international law crimes) all those crimes the substantive content of which is found in IL, regardless of where (or even whether) these crimes may be prosecuted. It is thus a distinction that finds its source in doctrine *per se*. The substantive content of the *Völkerrechtsverbrechen* should be found *directly* in IL itself. Whether a domestic constitution does or does not permit the direct application of the international norm containing the crime in domestic law does not affect the validity of the norm in IL.[56] Crimes such as torture (in the sense of the 1984 Convention Against Torture)[57] or certain crimes against air traffic are thus not ICL *stricto sensu*, but 'international criminal law in the meaning of internationally prescribed/authorized municipal criminal law'.[58]

In the German understanding, when *Völkerrechtsverbrechen* occur in the context of a systematic or massive attack or use of force, for which a collective, normally a state, is responsible, the collective deed is the sum of all individual deeds.[59] *Völkerstrafrecht* thus forms part of a gapless system of IL, and borders the law on state responsibility. *Völkerstrafrecht* forms part of *Internationales Strafrecht* (lit. international criminal law), which includes all areas of criminal law that have international aspects.[60] This encompasses supranational criminal law (criminal law made by supranational organisations, which thus far

54 Werle 2007, p. 942.
55 E.g., Ferdinandusse 2006, p. 11.
56 Werle 2007, p. 111.
57 For the view these and other crimes attracting universal jurisdiction should be counted as 'Völkerrechtsverbrechen', see also Dahm 2002, p. 999.
58 Schwarzenberger 1950, p. 266; and Werle 2007, p. 111.
59 Werle 2007, p. 40.
60 Werle 2007, p. 52.

does not exist), the law on the international cooperation in matters of criminal law (which includes, e.g., extradition treaties), and national choice of law and jurisdiction norms.[61]

A key aspect for the German approach is the *Individualisierung* of responsibility provided by ICL. Werle, moving outside of the *internal* perspective, explains, with a reference to Jackson's famous IMT opening speech, how (*that*) this view of ICL correctly and appropriately mirrors our material experience:

> The individual allocation shows that international crimes are committed not by abstract entities such as states, but always require the cooperation of individuals. This individualization is important for the victims and their families because they have a right to the whole truth. The individualization of the perpetrators provides an opportunity to process their personal stake in the system crimes. Finally, it is important for society, because it rejects a theory of collective guilt.[62]

This approach aligns with the deliberate absence in German domestic law of corporate (legal person) criminal liability. Since the *stricto sensu* approach excludes most corporate activities in peacetime (and thus liability of individual corporate officers in ICL), this approach seems most amenable to 'corporate impunity'.

1.4 *No Distinction: the Catch-All 'Omnibus' Approach*

Alternative narratives of ICL compared to the ones discussed above *do* start their account of its origins with the international norms applicable to piracy.[63] According to these, since the time of the Phoenicians piracy has been condemned as a crime against the law of nations.[64] In this view, the activities of pirates, committing acts on the open seas that under most national jurisdictions would amount to crimes, led to the development and application of international rules.[65] These histories also include early regulation of the slave trade, the opium trade, and other phenomena, *in addition to* the events and

61 In Werle's view, the source of the universal jurisdiction principle for Völkerrechtsverbrechen is domestic law (Werle 2007, p. 54).

62 Werle 2007, p. 43.

63 Bantekas 2007, p. 1.

64 Ferencz 1995, p. 1123.

65 E.g., *ATS* in the US, see further below Ch. 6. See also, e.g., *In re Piracy Jure Gentium* [*1934*] *A.C. 586*.

developments described above.[66] In this narrative, slave trade and piracy were both crimes in CIL.[67] The norm prohibiting piracy did not have a specific international enforcement mechanism attached to it,[68] but 'every state may seize a pirate ship … and arrest the persons and seize the property on board' (*In re Piracy*) according to treaty law of the capturing state, and according to CIL, applying universal jurisdiction, *any* State may prosecute the pirate.[69] The prohibitions, violations of which amount to crimes in this approach constitute *erga omnes* obligations, meaning that every state in the world has an interest in their observance. As the enforcement of the norms on piracy occurred only in national courts, *stricto sensu* authors argue that the CIL rule on piracy is merely jurisdictional.[70] Counter to this stands the 'omnibus' view that the crime of piracy is defined in IL (both the content of the crime and the fact that it is a crime), regardless of where that norm may be enforceable. Crimes like piracy are thus considered 'international crimes' in this perspective irrespective of enforcement, or even whether they are explicitly designated as 'crimes' or indeed 'international crimes' in international law.[71] Whether the ICL norm can be directly applied in a domestic court or needs the intermediation of a piece of domestic legislation does not detract from the 'international' nature of the crime.[72] This approach is the most *catholic*,[73] pragmatic, problem-solving-oriented approach.

As opposed to the German positivist approach, which is to explain doctrinal inconsistencies or lacunae as deliberate exceptions or distinctions, the policy approach deals with a 'messy' reality by overriding inconsistencies in the name of a desired policy outcome. Such inconsistencies and lacunae exist, for example, where IL instruments do not clearly specify whether a crime in question is an '*international* crime',[74] or whether a crime is subject to international jurisdiction, to universal jurisdiction in national[75] or international fora, or whether the treaty only obligates or authorises states to criminalise a cer-

66 Ferencz 1995, p. 1126; Cryer 2005, p. 57; Schabas 2007, p. 10.

67 According to Ferencz (1995, p. 1123), since the time of the Phoenicians and the Vikings, piracy has been condemned as a crime against the law of nations. Art. 15 *1958 High Seas Convention*; Art. 101 *UNCLOS 1982*.

68 *In re Piracy*.

69 For a discussion of contemporary forms of piracy, see Guilfoyle 2008.

70 Cassese 2008, p. 28.

71 Bantekas and Nash 2007, p. 6.

72 Ibid.

73 Ratner 2008, p. 12.

74 E.g., Art. 1 *1948 Genocide Convention*.

75 E.g., Art. 105 *1982 UNCLOS*.

tain event in domestic law[76] and/or to prosecute or extradite a suspect.[77] In the omnibus approach, this situation is dealt with on a case-by-case basis, with authors coming to occasionally different conclusions.[78] Generally the crimes that Werle would designate as 'international crimes' are included.

This is the broadest approach, including the largest number of crimes. It is also potentially the most receptive to 'business crimes'. For example, under the 'German' approach above, slavery as such (without the required contextual elements and 'gravity' requirement, see Chapter 4B) is not seen as a crime under international law, while this approach would include the many slavery-related practices – such as enslavement, slave trading, forced labour and human trafficking – which are seen by the others as 'transnational crimes'.[79] It is worth giving some further examples, in particular as they relate to legal persons. Certain international instruments, such as the OECD Convention on Combating Bribery of Foreign Public Officials in International Business Transactions[80] and the United Nations Convention against Transnational Organized Crime[81] require states to criminalise the behaviour of legal persons if this is congruent with national legal principles. Likewise, the 2000 Optional Protocol to the Convention on the Rights of the Child on the Sale of Children, Child Prostitution and Child Pornography requires states to establish criminal or civil liability of legal persons in line with a state's legal principles – and this makes it the only international human rights instrument with such a clause.[82] Another category exemplified by conventions such as the Basel Convention on the Control of Transboundary Movements of Hazardous Waste seems to encompass the criminalisation of behaviour in international law, while leaving it to states to choose the *object* (individual human and/or legal person) of domestic law criminalisation.[83]

---

76 E.g., Arts. 5, 6, 8 *2000 Transnational Organized Crime Convention*. See also Rodriguez-Lopez 2017.

77 E.g., Art. 4 Convention Against Torture.

78 Cf. lists of crimes considered ICL crimes in Van den Wijngaert 1996 and Steiner 2007, p. 1136.

79 Jeßberger 2016, p. 331.

80 *1997 Bribery Convention*, excerpt in Appendix D.

81 *2000 Transnational Organized Crime Convention*, excerpt in Appendix D.

82 Art. 3, para. 4, then reads: 'Subject to the provisions of its national law, each State Party shall take measures, where appropriate, to establish the liability of legal persons for offences established in paragraph 1 of the present article. Subject to the legal principles of the State Party, such liability of legal persons may be criminal, civil or administrative'. As of August 2016, 173 States are party to the Optional Protocol and another nine States have signed but not yet ratified it.

83 *Basel Convention*, excerpt in Appendix D.

The tiff amongst legal scholars of various plumes over the inclusion or exclusion of certain crimes within the remit of international criminal law may seem of only semantic importance; however, even semantic (ideological) differentiation harnesses distributive power (material effects). In the next section I further explore the ideological processes within and around ICL.

2 ICL Ideology, Pre-fab Critiques and Foreclosed Critiques

Soederberg, in a Gramscian vein, has noted that neoliberal hegemony is not static and must continually renegotiate and re-establish itself 'through complex social struggles and contradictions that emerge within, are shaped by, and shape, the structures and processes of capital accumulation'.[84] For ICL, this renegotiation becomes apparent in the description of the production of 'pre-fab critiques' and 'foreclosed critiques' by ICL's dominant ideology.

2.1 *ICL Ideology*

Each of the four narratives described above contributes one of the vital elements of current accepted ICL ideology. What we see is that the apparent disparities between the approaches, in fact serve to support a more or less coherent dominant ideology. Each of the approaches links with the others; they complement each other. This linkage becomes apparent when authors acknowledge the validity of others' narratives implicitly and occasionally explicitly.

First, Cassese's approach provides ICL with the key element of the ideological justification, almost the emotional *need*, for intervention in 'foreign' jurisdiction 'for the protection of higher values'.[85] This at once *universalises* ICL, purports to serve us, further our community interest and represent us, and our collectively held values.[86] It does not seem to matter that Cassese does not further explain what those values are and how we may discover them. Instead, in an attempt to defend and legitimate his position, he uncomfortably moves into positivist territory, stating: 'The values at issue are not propounded by scholars or thought up by starry-eyed philosophers. Rather, they are laid down in a string of international instruments, which, however, do not necessarily spell them out in so many words'.[87]

84 Soederberg 2010, pp. 16–17.
85 Cassese 2008, p. 11, emphasis in original.
86 See also Mégret 2010, p. 210.
87 Cassese 2008, p. 11.

Likewise moving outside of their comfort-zone, positivists would recognise that broad aspirational statements of 'values' are regularly found in preambles to treaties. Triffterer, for example, notes that those declarations found in the Preamble to the ICC Statute 'echo, in the arena of international affairs, the loftiest aspirations of an ever advancing society'.[88] The 'humanitarian' here shines through for positivists as both an explanatory (this is why we have ICL) as well as a legitimating factor.

Aside from such departures, the 'German' variant seems to approach law from a purely analytical, scientific perspective. It thus appears to be technical, value neutral. The differences and distinctions found by adherents to this school of thought may appear of limited value other than from the intellectual pursuit of studying law as a system. For example, Kreß's remark that the ICC Statute contains crimes that are not in fact 'international crimes'[89] is likely to find resonance with only the smallest circle of specialists and would not likely concern even the ICC itself – something Kreß must realise. Yet, precisely such debates serve to give ICL *doctrinal credibility*.

Proponents of the 'omnibus approach', presumably like the ICC itself, display a more 'relaxed' approach to such questions, preferring to be more practice-oriented. Bantekas and Nash, for example, conceptualise ICL as a 'fusion of IL and domestic criminal law' and include in their textbook on ICL discussion of the efforts of IOs and NGOs on issues such as human trafficking.[90] Grant and Barker's *Deskbook of International Criminal Law* (a documents bundle, aimed at the ICL practitioner) contains conventions ranging from the 1926 Slavery Convention to the European Convention on Cybercrime.[91] Dugard and van den Wijngaert see ICL as a means for states to help each other in the application of their respective domestic criminal laws, necessitated by the internationalisation of crime – and thus come closest to interpreting ICL in the practical sense permitted in Schwarzenberger's critique.[92] Ramasastry, possibly at the pragmatic extreme of this group of scholars, expresses no view on the doctrinal nature of ICL, but asks only 'what it can do for us'.[93]

Within the narrative focused on the enforcement mechanisms and possibilities of ICL, two strands can be detected: those that consider the court half full[94]

88 Triffterer 2008, p. 6.
89 Kreß 2009.
90 Bantekas and Nash 2007, p. 1.
91 Grant and Barker 2006.
92 Dugard and van den Wijngaert 1996, p. 1.
93 Ramasastry 2002.
94 E.g., Roht-Arriaza 2013.

and those that consider it half empty.[95] Both provide us with a history of how ICL was built up brick by brick, how this logical development *culminated* in an overarching ICC. What binds the two together, then, is that the ultimate desire, objective, and mark of success is a *full* court, working to capacity,[96] something they share first and foremost with the pragmatists. The assumption that ICL is a good thing, and should be improved, implemented, and promoted, is not called into question by anyone within the four approaches.

Viewing these approaches as key ingredients of today's ICL, we can see that ICL is a mixture (in varying quantities) of emotions, rationality, pragmatics and 'legal soundness' – altogether, an irresistible combination to lawyers, policy makers and the general public. The pragmatic element gives it flexibility, for example to develop new rules/policies in the 'war on terror' context, the positivist foundational narrative gives it 'academic kudos', while the enforcement focus supports efforts to strengthen institutions. Moreover, as ICL symbolises 'justice' in IL,[97] it has become something to believe in: it 'carries a religious exercise of hope that is stronger than the desire to face everyday life'.[98] Its crimes have become reasons (or rather, justifications) to invade other countries. *This* is why ICL is in fashion. It is something to propose as a remedy to a perceived problem (such as 'business in conflict'),[99] and something to rally around, to continually work to improve. Most of all, ICL communicates to us, reassuringly, its *exceptionality* (e.g., Cassese's effort to exclude certain 'less grave' crimes), while also confirming to us that *these select international crimes are the ills of international society*. All other problems pale in comparison or even disappear altogether. One can see that in the seemingly insignificant debate over the inclusion or exclusion of certain 'economic crimes' in ICL discussed above. Whether, for example, forced labour is considered an international crime or a transnational crime may have no *direct* bearing on whether the relevant offences are committed or in which venue they may be prosecuted, but the doctrinal (legal scholarly) acceptance of the classification of these acts does belie an implicit normalisation if not acceptance of the exclusion of, for example, most 'economic' acts having social and environmental repercussions from the purview of the ICC, the institution that is arguably the most powerful, if not in enforcement capacity then certainly in ideological terms. ICL has been very deliberately constructed to encompass only a certain type of activity, in a par-

95 E.g., Schabas 2013.

96 For Roht-Arriaza, this is a full domestic court enforcing ICL rather than a full ICC (ibid).

97 Mégret 2010, pp. 210, 220, 224; see also Tallgren 2002a, p. 580.

98 Tallgren 2002a, p. 593.

99 E.g., Stewart 2013.

ticular type of context. By no means do all international human rights law violations – no matter how severe – amount to crimes under ICL.[100] Just as 'accountability' is a legal construct, so is 'impunity'. Moreover, once 'impunity' is 'discovered', or is used to label 'inaction' with regard to certain harm that triggers media and legal attention, it automatically generates the call for 'punity' or prosecution. The marked absence of ICL then *creates the desire for ICL*.

At the same time, the introduction of the concept of corporate criminal liability in 'transnational crime' treaty law (despite the limited ratifications these instruments normally attract, or their regional nature) when there is no consensus yet on corporate crime in domestic jurisdictions, also normalises, and perhaps stimulates the development of a concept of corporate crime in international law.[101]

The seeming contradictions between the four approaches described above do not pull apart, but rather serve to strengthen the cohesion of the dominant ideology. They do so by implicitly accepting the main parameters of the ideology, being silent as to the ontology of the ideology itself *and also* by keeping much of the critical debate within the parameters of the ideology itself.

2.2 *Pre-fab Critiques and Foreclosed and Subjugated Critiques*

This makes ICL seemingly 'critique-proof'. This is not to say that there is no ICL critique – on the contrary, each of the four narratives outlined above generates its own specific set of critiques[102] and a lively academic debate around them.[103] It would be more precise to say that critique *is rarely radical*.[104] Radical critique is foreclosed by the stated purpose of ICL as the manifestation of the moral conscience of mankind. ICL ideology is so overwhelming (akin to the

100 This is explained in more detail in Chapter 4B.

101 Ratner 2009, p. 17; mixed academic-practitioner workshops can play an important role in this process, see e.g. the *'Transnational Business and International Criminal Law'*, symposium held at Humboldt University (Berlin 15–16 May 2011), proceedings in *Journal of International Criminal Justice*, 9(1). The majority of these instruments require national authorities to legislate so as to give effect to the terms of the treaty – it leaves it to states to decide whether to legislate for the possible imposition of 'corporate crime' sanctions or administrative sanctions or measures on corporations, or indeed criminal sanctions on individual company officials (the principle of 'functional equivalence'): Bantekas and Nash 2007, pp. 47–9.

102 In Marx's and Horkheimer's terms, these ought rightly to be called 'criticisms' rather than critiques (Marx 1972; Horkheimer 1972).

103 E.g., Van Sliedregt 2013.

104 Not even when part of feminist critique of TWAIL – Tallgren 2014, p. 75. The CAICL collection edited by Christine Schwöbel contains some of the few more radical critiques of ICL.

'oceanic feeling' generated by human rights and justice) that it has made criminal accountability the sacred cow of international politics. To offer a radical critique, to be 'against' ICL, would be equivalent to 'advocating letting those guilty of genocide walk free'.[105] In this section I briefly outline the types of pre-fab critiques produced by each approach, and I offer some pointers as to what a radical, transformative critique might look like.

The most commonly aired critique today is of ICL's selectivity when it comes to situations and defendants.[106] This critique – and more generally questions regarding effectiveness and how to improve the workings of ICL institutions – is produced by the enforcement approach. Other critiques address the inadequate representation or protection by one or another group in the judicial process (witnesses, victims, women; the focus on some crimes but not on others[107] – e.g., failure to address sexual crimes). In respect of the latter two points, rather than arguing for an improved regime of inclusion, a more intricate, transcendental or *radical* critique could be made, e.g., regarding the way women are constructed as victims (and thus denied agency and responsibility in conflict) in trials relating to sexual offences.[108]

The implication of the pre-fab enforcement critiques is that all ICL's problems will be resolved when we have strong, professional international institutions that apply the rules equally to all. The latter is also a concern for the German positivists. Both, however, assume that it is a structural possibility for this to become reality: these approaches therefore enable a 'progressive' debate and practical activity on improving and expanding ICL's institutions. Curiously, at the same time, it also allows for the argument *not* to expand ICL enforcement: we must not grow too fast. Crawford has suggested that the current limitation of the ICC's jurisdiction is quite simply motivated by the risk of the court being 'swamped' otherwise.[109]

Both enforcement and pragmatic approaches favour the question of 'how can we ...?' over 'why are we not ...?'. This becomes clear when examining Crawford's argument more closely. The 'size' of the court merely depends on the funding that governments make available. An analogous argument on the domestic level is almost inconceivable. This is despite the fact that more generally, restrictions impeding ICL's effectiveness are often considered to be financial. For example, in his monograph, Cryer lays the cause of selectivity at

105 Tallgren 2014, p. 76.
106 E.g., Cryer 2005, esp. Ch. 5; Heller 2010; Jalloh 2009; Eberechi 2009; Dugard 2013.
107 E.g., Charlesworth 1999.
108 E.g., Engle 2005.
109 Crawford 2002, p. 122.

the dependence of courts on states' contributions – although he expects this situation to change with time. Finance appears as an external 'fact of life' to ICL. Any more fundamental critique, such as that which asks why governments are generally outwardly very supportive of ICL, but leave the courts to struggle with very limited funds, would be unconstructive, and almost *unsportsmanlike*. Already, Cryer states, 'the [ICC] represents a quantum leap beyond what went before'.[110] Radical critiques could start from the bureaucratic and political decision-making processes behind the budgeting of the ICL institutions or even the drafting of budgetary provisions pre-adoption. It is interesting for a start – something rarely mentioned in the literature – that the ICC and the other tribunals are expected to, and in fact do, actively seek private, including corporate, funding for their activities.[111] A study of, for example, the independent auditor's recommendations as to the reinforcement and clarification of the roles of the Prosecutors and the Registrar of the ICC could reveal budgetary constraints on the prosecutor's independence.[112]

Rather than expressing disappointment with the achievements of the ICC 10 years since it opened its doors, most authors of the JICJ special anniversary issue urge readers to display pragmatic realism, e.g., 'the hangover after the euphoria [of 1992] should be used to correct the sky-high expectations'.[113] Yet, our faith in ICL is sustained (at most, pending another 'Pinochet moment')[114] by the fantasy that one day, the likes of G.W. Bush and Tony Blair, or their equivalents in a different time, *will* face justice.

What Cryer and others overlook is the fact that the impunity gap, which exists as a result of selectivity, is itself also created through ICL. As suggested above, the makers of ICL create its inclusions as well as its exclusions. For example, the fact that the ICC – as the general, universal ICL institution – was created (through its statute) with a highly specific and narrow mandate (more about this in Chapter 4B) constitutes either innocence or 'impunity' (depending on our position) for those that fall outside its remit. By analogy to Marks's 'planned misery' in relation to poverty, we could term this 'planned whitewash' or 'planned impunity'.[115] The recognition of the planned nature of such innocence/impunity is also a recognition that selectivity cannot simply be 'correc-

110 Cryer 2005, p. 231.

111 1998 ICC Statute; Del Ponte 2005; Project on International Courts and Tribunals *'The Financing of the International Criminal Court: A Discussion Paper'*, n.d., available at: http://www.pict-pcti.org/publications/ICC_paprs/FinancingICC.pdf.

112 *ICC Financial Statement* 2012, pp. 9–10.

113 Roht-Arriaza 2013, p. 537.

114 Schabas 2013.

115 Marks 2011.

ted'. Why, by whom and how such impunity is planned and what mechanisms are in place to cause us to believe it can be overcome are the questions I am seeking to respond to here.

Similarly, the almost anti-intellectualist pragmatist perspective forecloses fundamental theoretical/political questions in favour of constructive critiques aimed at achieving maximum *effectiveness* in the face of immediate, urgent and 'real' problems ('while babies are dying'). For example, Stewart offers an – in his view – urgent, pragmatic, corrective to theories of corporate liability that are 'not sensitive to the complexities of reality'.[116] What this 'spirits away' though is the fact that those theories are themselves reflective, and reconstitutive of that very same reality that produces the corporate exploitation Stewart wishes to eradicate. Such eradication requires *instead* a radical critique of the corporation itself.

A second often-heard critique relates to doctrinal issues. The positivist approach invites debate over whether this rule or that concept is properly interpreted, or within the purview of ICL. Much of the debate surrounds the proper interpretation by the three main international tribunals of their constituent instruments. For example, debates abound about the ICC Prosecutor's actions in relation to former Sudanese president Omar Al-Bashir.[117] Here, problems are often seen to be due to the inexperience of the courts' officials and critiques can also be *ad hominem*. Others surround the progressive development in the courts of ICL doctrine where such matters are not covered by the instruments – and where problems are thus thrown up by ICL being a 'new' and as yet not fully developed discipline. One example here is the debate over the correctness or otherwise of the joint criminal enterprise (JCE) doctrine.[118] Lost in doctrinal detail, these metanarratives produced by the doctrinal approach guarantee that bigger questions on the meaning and purpose of ICL will not be asked. Most important, it sets the 'legal scientist' – who rightly only concerns herself with questions of legal doctrine – apart from the *politician* and thus denies (obscures) lawyers' role in, amongst others, congealing capitalism.

What ICL allows for, and what cannot be 'done' in any way that fits law's configuration as it stands, is to intervene in other states to criminalise through supranational law acts that are not criminal in the relevant domestic law (or not prosecuted domestically), and to allow for their prosecution externally (or post-regime). In other words, by 'lifting' certain behaviour, events and individuals into international law, ICL creates the option of *centralising* the admin-

116 Stewart 2012, p. 38.
117 E.g., Luban 2013.
118 E.g., JICJ Symposium 2006 and see further Chapter 4B.

istration and management of this regime according to the interests (or lack of interest) of the global ruling class directly. What it also allows is the protection of the GCC – indeed, just like the law on international investment arbitration ICL functions to keep Western/Northern parties out of host-state courts. When stripped of the practical justifications, what remains is the violence of ICL, made possible by its ideology – namely the way that ICL designates certain behaviour as '*international crimes which form an attack on the fundamental values of the international community*'.[119] This ideological element has very real practical uses: one is (through ICL prosecutions) to create specific explanations of conflicts that exempt/exonerate the economic/capitalism, as seen in Chapter 3, often in the process of what Klein has called the post-intervention 'human rights clean-up operation'.[120] Another is to form the diversion or Trojan Horse for the intervention in states that goes much further than ICL,[121] for the purpose of 'regime change', 'civilisation', or, indeed, 'capitalisation'. Both we have seen in Nuremberg and Tokyo, and also in the contemporary context in e.g., the former Yugoslavia.[122] ICL thus forms an important function in legitimating other parts of, and actions under, international law.

This function appears to be beyond enquiry. Cassese's refusal to engage in the question of where ICL's universal values come from – insisting instead they must thus be self-evident to us, forecloses, most importantly, the *why* question – and with that, any ontological critique of ICL ideology. As noted, Schwarzenberger's reservations regarding the need for an ICL still stand today. Yet, the question is no longer posed.[123] ICL continues to be constructed, and 'believed in',[124] on various grounds.[125]

Ultimately the designation 'more harmful' used by Cassese appears to be Cassese's own, to reflect his moral indignation. Yet, aside from the harm caused, a transcendental critique might note that Cassese also seems to imply that the emotive reaction to his 'international crimes proper' ('so abhorrent as to offend the international community as a whole')[126] is universally felt and

---

119 1998 ICC Statute.

120 Klein 2007, p. 126.

121 The *1948 Genocide Convention* appears 'based on the assumption of virtuous governments and criminal individuals, a reversion of the truth in proportion to the degree of totalitarianism and nationalism practised in any country' (Schwarzenberger 1950, p. 292).

122 Baars 2013; Baars 2012.

123 Cryer 2005, p. 2.

124 Tallgren 2002a, p. 593. On IL, generally, as secular religion, Koskenniemi 2007.

125 Tallgren 2002a, p. 593; also generally, Koskenniemi 2007; JICJ 2013.

126 As per *1998 ICC Statute* Preamble.

absent (or less) in the case of other crimes, or, for example, in the face of mass starvation, tens of thousands of children dying preventable deaths each day.[127]

Schmitt famously quoted Proudhon, 'Whoever invokes humanity wants to cheat'.[128] The humanitarian narrative was reconstructed, re-invented, re-emphasised after Nuremberg (and Tokyo). Importantly, it allows assertion of the moral high ground, a positioning of us (good) vs. them (bad). Ferdinandusse recognises such normative claims in ICL 'as techniques in a hegemonic struggle for greater control between different actors in international law'.[129] As a starter for a transcendental critique, therefore, ICL can be said to play an instrumental role in the distribution of power among global actors.

A critique of the 'humanitarian' narrative of ICL may be made analogously to Marks's critique of the concept of 'Humanitarian Intervention'.[130] Presenting ICL as a necessity for the benefit of humanity, against atrocities, works as a rhetorical move, the function of which is to justify *inaction* of the political field vis-à-vis certain situations of suffering, and to ignore the root causes.[131] This critique can be made in both a constructive way ('if only global political focus was less selectively pointed towards hot conflict/away from structural problems')[132] and a transgressive way, as demonstrated by Franzki and Olarte, through interrogating why the global leadership's accusatory finger is pointed in that direction and not another.[133]

The essential contradiction between the factual and normative in Miller's constructive, 'if only' critique is also visible in a slightly different way in Ambos: 'the worldwide impunity for grave human rights violations leads to a factual accountability gap, the closure, or at least the narrowing, of which ICL has made as its highest priority task'. The author adds in a footnote: 'It concerns a *factual*, not a *normative* accountability gap, because the impunity can be traced back not to a lack of norms on international crimes, but on a lack of States' political will to prosecute'.[134] Why, one might ask (Ambos does not), would state leaders create a body of norms to do something that they do not in fact *want* to do? It only makes sense, if (a) that body of law is not, in fact, designed to do this

127 Beckett 2012; http://www.unicefusa.org/.
128 Schmitt 1996, p. 54.
129 Ferdinandusse 2006, p. 158.
130 Marks 2006.
131 Marks 2006, p. 344; Marks 2011.
132 Miller 2008.
133 E.g., Franzki and Olarte 2013.
134 Ambos 2000, p. 39.

thing, or (b) it is so designed, but only in relation to specific others, or exceptional, acceptable situations, or, (c) if it is done in response to a felt need (or public call) to be 'doing something' and the creation of these norms alone, with the promise of enforcement, satisfies this need – perhaps we can call regulation in this sense 'law-washing'. ICL gives us faith that 'something is being done'. In a realist/transcendental critique, Akhavan posits,

> In contrast to the prevention of ongoing atrocities through military intervention or peacekeeping, and substantial postconflict economic assistance and social rehabilitation, resort to international tribunals incurs a rather modest financial and political cost. However, the attractive spectacle of courtroom drama, which pits darkness against the forces of light and reduces the world to a manageable narrative, could lead international criminal justice to become an exercise in moral self-affirmation and a substitute for genuine commitment and resolve.[135]

Mégret calls it a 'palliative to sovereign failure'.[136] We might also call it a cloak for the systemic root causes of 'crimes', which may be endemic to the current mode of production.

A popular demand for justice for certain occurrences in certain places is thus produced based on criminal law's visceral appeal,[137] and deployed, with Cassese's emotive discourse providing the legitimising element. Critique following an historical materialist methodology should serve to elucidate exactly how ICL 'works' in this regard. It is towards what and whom is 'excluded' from ICL that we should look. Indeed, ICL allows those that fall outside of the narrow scope of ICL (covering only certain crimes, committed in certain contexts by certain persons), to remain 'innocent'. As Tallgren suggests,

> Perhaps [ICL's] task is to naturalize, to exclude from the political battle, certain phenomena which are in fact the preconditions for the maintenance of the existing governance; by the North, by wealthy states, by wealthy individuals, by strong states, by strong individuals, by men, especially white men, and so forth.[138]

135 Akhavan 2001, p. 30.
136 Mégret 2003, p. 334.
137 Tallgren 2002a, p. 591.
138 Tallgren 2002a, p. 595.

In Chapters 4B and 4C I discuss the debates around the inclusion/exclusion of individual businesspeople and corporations in light of this. First, I explore further what narratives and critiques the pre-fab critiques may have foreclosed, subjugated or spirited away.

3 An Alternative Foundational Narrative for ICL

Schwarzenberger's 1950 critique of a putative ICL as mere 'fashion' and moreover practically unnecessary, metaphorically pulls the rug from under the preceding justifications of ICL. If ICL, new ICL norms and institutions are not in fact needed to try 'murderers' and 'torturers', then why do we call for them? What is ICL and what is it for?

3.1 *Canned Morality: a Commodity Form Theory of ICL*

We cannot *directly* attach to ICL the explanation for domestic criminal law commonly proposed by Marxist theorists, namely that it serves to maintain its class rule and suppress the lower classes – as 'organised class terror'.[139] ICL crimes are mostly 'leadership crimes', and those tried in ICL courts have been mostly members of elites. Yet, according to Pashukanis, 'Every historically given system of penal policy bears the imprint of the class interests of that class which instigated it'.[140] Perhaps indeed ICL trials can be reduced to intra-class competition, and *Systemkonkurrenz*. 'Society as a whole', in whose name ICL is created, does not exist. What then are the GCC's interests in ICL? In Chapter 2 I showed how a 'public' domain was shaped, a separate sphere in which new, humanitarian, areas of law (such as the laws of war, human rights and also ICL) could develop, to apply only in a limited 'public' sphere. This humanitarian side serves to legitimise the IL enterprise as a whole. Currently, however, the contradiction in the artificial public/private divide described in Chapter 2B is making it (more) permeable, hence the consideration now also of the corporate person in ICL (Chapter 4C). Pashukanis analysed the particular element that makes [I]CL so attractive, and seem so necessary, and as something we cannot do without. Applying the commodity form theory to criminal law on the domestic level, he notes 'this [criminal] procedure contains particular features which are not fully dealt with by clear and simple considerations of social purpose, but represent an irrational, mystified, absurd element. We wish … to demonstrate

139 Tallgren 2002a, p. 575; Pashukanis 1978, p. 173.

140 Pashukanis 1978, p. 174.

that it is precisely this which is the specifically legal element'.[141] The practical social purpose he refers to is the compensation of victims (which is often absent in CL in any case), the protection of society (which could be achieved better in other ways) or the treatment and rehabilitation of the offender (which is likewise not normally a priority).[142] The value in CL, according to Pashukanis, lies in its 'morality' – which is present both in its demonstrative function and in the 'compulsory atonement' it demands of the convicted criminal.[143] Criminal law functions as the 'remoralisation' of society post-cash nexus (Chapter 2A, and analogous to the 'humanitarian makeover' of IL in Chapter 2B, Section 5). Once law has replaced human relationships with legal relationships, law is – or lawmakers are – there to inform us what is right. 'Law creates right by creating crime'.[144] This commodified morality[145] tells us when to feel revulsion, or when to forgive, who to grieve; it is the 'canned morality' served up in the 'bourgeois theatre'[146] of international criminal trials. It can be fostered, deployed at opportune moments, and instrumentalised – and develop on its own according to the logic of the market.[147]

Canned morality thus produces 'accountability' in the Weberian sense – meaning that by means of 'calculable law' costs, benefits and risks of political actions can be calculated, managed, and even optimised.[148] In other words, commodified morality can be deployed to control and optimise public sentiment in this or that situation (viz. the prosecution of Milošević, or, more recently the domestic US prosecution of Viktor Bout once he had lost his utility).[149] As the independence of the ICC prosecutor and thus the supposed unpredictability of the court's activity is a major factor in ICL's legitimacy, in particular a study of the financial and other constraints on the prosecutor could reveal the actual power relations behind the scenes of ICL. Akhavan has noted that ICL produces spectator's justice.[150] The 'bourgeois theatre' public become passive consumers of spectacle (cf. 'opium for the masses') and simultaneously

141 Pashukanis 1978, p. 177.
142 Pashukanis 1978, pp. 176–8.
143 Pashukanis 1978, pp. 185, 187.
144 Pashukanis 1978, p. 167.
145 Or what Shamir calls 'market-embedded morality', Shamir 2008; see also Baars 2011.
146 Orzeck 2012.
147 In Ch. 6, I elaborate on this latter aspect further in § 4.4 on the 'market for responsibility'.
148 Weber 1982, p. 277.
149 See, finally, *Viktor Bout, aka Victor Anatoliyevich Bout, aka Viktor Bulakin, aka Viktor Butt, aka Vadim Markovich Aminov, aka Viktor Budd, aka Viktor But, Petitioner v. United States, Supreme Court of the United States*, No. 16–1024, petition for certiorari denied 3 April 2017.
150 Akhavan 2013, p. 530.

producers and reproducers of canned morality – and reproducers of ICL, when baying for ICL blood. Despite, and at the same time because of, ICL's individualising function, it unites us (significantly, in this pluralist time) *with* the state/elite against the accused, and *away* from structural questions. *This* is what ICL is for.

4 Conclusion to 4A

I have tried to show in this chapter how lawyers and legal scholars have played an important role in the construction of the ideology known as ICL. They have created an almost critique-proof system through its four building blocks, of which the most important is the humanitarian. The 'epidermic' humanitarian aspect contains the values that 'ennoble ICL'[151] and cause an overwhelming 'oceanic feeling'[152] that we cannot possibly resist, or politely refuse. I have argued that each of the four approaches within ICL ideology creates its own 'constructive critique' which serves to strengthen ICL and perpetuate both ICL's and implicitly, as part of IL, capitalism's *status quo*. In certain instances also, the ready-made constructive critique silences other critiques.[153] While this descriptive process in itself should create its own ideology, I have also pointed to various different ways in which our critique can transcend problem-solving and create radical critique, and how we can start to think about what ICL really is, and what it is really for.

I pick this up again in Chapter 5. First, I must finish my analysis of the 'direction of development', which may, or may not, be heading towards the inclusion of the company as a legal person in ICL rules, if probably not in ICL practice.

4B '*No Soul to Damn and No Body to Kick*'? Attribution, Perpetration and *Mens Rea* in Business

1 Introduction to 4B

At Nuremberg and Tokyo, and in the other trials after World War Two, the Allied lawyers and politicians worked out who they conceived of as 'subjects' of ICL (to whom they wanted ICL to apply) and what relation between person

151 Tallgren 2014, p. 212.
152 Schabas 2013, p. 549.
153 Tallgren 2014.

and act, result and/or victim(s) needed to exist (both in the factual *actus reus* and the *mens rea* or 'fault' sense) before such a person could be considered guilty. After the reanimation of ICL post-Cold War these modalities were to some extent worked out afresh, *ostensibly* because both were criticised on legal grounds.[154] The lawyers of the ICTY and ICTR (and those who had negotiated their statutes) developed the more intricate modalities of this 'New ICL', performing the abstraction of real (or imagined) persons and relationships into legal categories and modes of responsibility, allowing the calculation of the transactional value of each mode of responsibility, and determining in which new geopolitical contexts ICL was to be applied: the further congealing of ICL.

As argued in the previous part, lawyers' role is also to move the debate from substantive questions of justice (the 'what', 'why' and 'in whose interest' questions), to the technical meta-questions of the 'how' of a particular preferred solution that is circumscribed by legal rules. These meta-questions serve to obscure the process of how, at whose behest, and as a result of which power differentials, that solution came to be 'preferred' – by some, and eventually, by most. Moreover, this congealing serves to further *rationalise* criminal justice policy: both in the sense of determining and legitimising of the transactional value (or reducing the cost) of each mode of responsibility,[155] and to make it seem 'as if there are good reasons why things [here: ICL, narrowly interpreted and applied] are as they are'.[156] Moreover, and 'invisibly', by determining the categories, modes, and contexts in which ICL was to be applied, the ICL-makers also effected the exclusions of, and future demands from, ICL.

As I argued in the previous chapter, academic lawyers played an important role, both indirectly by providing ICL, post hoc, with its foundational narrative (Chapter 4A) and generating this meta-narrative, as scholars, 'experts', but also directly because of the overlap between practising and academic lawyers in ICL. In this part, I take a closer look at the process of, what Kennedy has called, experts' 'ruling by argument and assertion',[157] in order to discover how the existence of ICL has given rise to the call for corporate ICL accountability as it manifests today.

The most remarkable change in ICL post-Cold War is in relation to business involvement in conflict and other scenarios that could give rise to accus-

154 Chapter 4A, §1.
155 Pashukanis 1978, p. 179.
156 Marks 2000, p. 19.
157 Kennedy 2016, p. 135.

ations of human rights violations or international crimes (what I have roughly gathered under the popular term 'business and human rights' in this book). It seems that the experience of applying ICL to several businessmen post-World War Two has been erased from collective scholarly memory. The cause of this will have been the rehabilitation of the businessmen in the 'turnaround' and the start of the Cold War as discussed in Chapter 3A, helped by the fact that ICL lay fallow[158] for almost four decades until the end of the Cold War and capitalism moving to its late, neoliberal stage.

So despite the post-World War Two trials of several dozen businessmen, many of the scholars writing in on ICL today claim that ICL is *not clear* on whether or not it *could be* applied to business in conflict.[159] Some argue that business involvement is somehow *different* from the involvement of other participants (including other private actors) in a conflict,[160] and as a consequence many in the debate consider that there is a need for *new rules* on the topic, for example in the form of a '*Wirtschaftsvölkerstrafrecht*'.[161]

I show in Sections 1.2–1.5 that current ('New') ICL has several doctrines similar to those used at Nuremberg that could (if desired) very well be applied to businesspersons as individuals and indeed even to the corporation as a legal person. I discuss these doctrines in some detail in this section. The post-World War Two trials, plus the existence of these doctrines raises the question of how legal ideology has worked to dissociate business from ICL. I suggest that the reification of the corporation (emptying it of people), and the perception of the *sui generis* nature of business actors fostered in IL in general, plus the separation of 'economic' and 'political' spheres (Chapter 2B) are responsible for this 'indecisiveness' and eventually the privileged treatment of business 'humans' over others, as well as the eventual legitimising inclusion of the corporate legal person in ICL.

Also, despite the discussions both at Nuremberg and later on during the negotiation of the ICC Statute on the inclusion of legal persons, ICL tribunals' constituent instruments only explicitly grant them jurisdiction over natural

158 Phrase used by Drumbl 2011, p. 23.

159 See, e.g., Vest 2010; Cryer 2007, p. 453; Cryer 2010, p. 587. In the latter the *2008 JICJ Symposium* is referenced in the footnote, evidencing the perspective that it is the study performed by academic lawyers that creates legal rules.

160 Note that the legal distinction between 'armed groups' and 'corporations' is another technique that allows the differential treatment of persons carrying out particular activities in some form of cooperation depending on the context, purpose, class membership or relation to capital etc. See, generally, Clapham 2006.

161 Jeßberger coins this term, literally meaning 'ICL of the economy' (Jeßberger 2009).

persons, and they have indeed only ever tried individual natural persons.[162] In the following chapter (4C) I explore how it is precisely this jarring contradiction that gives rise to the *discovery* (by lawyers committed to justice over law) of 'corporate impunity' and thus the 'pre-fab' call for the prosecution of corporations in ICL, and particularly now the call for the ICC's jurisdiction to be extended to cover corporations. Once businessmen have been removed from the narrative of ICL, there is space for the corporate legal person to be introduced into it, and even for the individual to 'temporarily' stand in for the corporation while we wait for legal person liability to (finally!) be ratified. It is my argument that the logic of capitalism produces this narrative (and that, counterintuitively, this direction of development will thus not carry emancipatory potential).

In the next sections I focus mainly on the law of the ICC, ICTY, ICTR and the STL, as 'representative' ICL venues while acknowledging that there are of course others.

2 'No Soul to Damn and No Body to Kick'?[163] Attribution, Perpetration and Mens Rea in Business

In the ICTY and ICTR jurisprudence, and lately also in the ICC, ICL is applied to individuals who form part of state or military structures, which have role-delineations, functional hierarchies and power relations. The ICL tribunals and the ICC have jurisdiction only over the international crimes in the narrow sense, and those crimes normally require a 'contextual element' of war or large-scale human rights abuse. This means that individual acts of, say, killing or torture can only be prosecuted if they occurred in a context of large-scale violence or war. This has, of course, been a choice, and therefore excludes relatively isolated, single or smaller-scale occurrences of such crimes in peacetime and 'business as usual'. It also means that the international crimes over which the tribunals have jurisdiction are not normally committed by one person in isolation, but by a number of persons together over a stretch of time, and place. ICL has developed doctrines, both at Nuremberg and Tokyo, and as part of the 'New ICL', 'modes of responsibility' to allocate and apportion blame to individu-

162 E.g., *1993 ICTY Statute* Art. 6; *1998 ICC Statute* Art. 25(3). On the debate on the inclusion of legal persons in the negotiation of the Rome Statue – see Ch. 4C.

163 Coffee 1980–81, quoting Edward Thurlow 1731–1805.

als playing a variety of lesser and greater roles, both physically and in terms of design in the events or processes in question. Different levels of fault are ascribed to, for example, those giving the orders, those designing the policies, and those carrying them out, and those that helped along the way. In many ways the relationships within state apparatuses and armies are comparable to those in companies,[164] as recognised also in the post-World War Two trials of industrialists. In terms of the material facts of crimes (what in law is called the '*actus reus*' or guilty act), in military and civil administrations, like in companies, those may be outwardly innocuous or involve mainly desk activity, words alone or no activity (omissions), or may involve acts by a single individual within the organisational structure or by several individuals that together result in a crime. Analogous to the way domestic criminal law has doctrines which allow for the prosecution of members of criminal gangs, and wide and amorphous organisations such as the mafia, transnational crime networks, or individuals in instances of 'mob violence', ICL's modes of responsibility, such as direct or indirect perpetration, command responsibility and joint criminal enterprise (JCE, see below), enable its application to members of state/military and non-state groups (such as armed opposition groups) alike. For example at Nuremberg, the concept of 'conspiracy' was used to reflect the idea of a group of persons acting collectively, and the notion of an 'illegal organisation' allowed persecution of individuals for membership of such a body. While in 4C I show that the possibility of explicitly including legal person liability in the ICC's jurisdiction was discussed, but dismissed, here I show that, just as there wasn't post-World War Two, in the 'New ICL' there is nothing in principle that precludes its application to business actors in many situations.

In this section I seek to imagine the modes of responsibility developed in ICL as mapped onto relations between individual businesspersons and those affected by their activities (or indeed their inaction or failure to act). If corporate *legal person* liability is accepted in ICL, corporations as legal persons could likewise be considered, e.g., as principal perpetrators, or part of a JCE, conceivably, together with military or government officials and/or with individuals 'inside' the corporation. The mental element of the crime, the *mens rea* ('guilty mind') of a corporation could be conceived (or avoided) analogously to domestic law (Chapter 4C) through doctrines such as strict liability, vicarious liability, attribution through a 'directing mind' (an example of the identifica-

164 See, generally, Farrell 2010.

tion doctrine) or through aggregation, the concept of 'corporate culture' and other doctrines developed in domestic law on corporate crime.[165]

Although Art. 6 of the ICTR Statute, Art. 7 of the ICTY Statute, Art. 6 of the SCSL Statute (which correspond in all material respects: see Appendix D, and which set out the conditions for individual responsibility applied by the tribunals) do not distinguish hierarchies of perpetration, in their decisions these tribunals have differentiated between perpetration as principal (commission as perpetrator, joint criminal enterprise) and accessory liability (planning, ordering, instigating, aiding and abetting a crime).[166] Legal scholar and practitioner Norman Farrell (who is currently the SCSL's prosecutor) has argued that co-perpetration/joint criminal enterprise and complicity/aiding and abetting are the two modes of liability most likely to be applicable to both individual businesspersons and legal persons.[167] Perpetration as a principal, however, is generally considered to form the gravest mode of criminal liability in ICL doctrine.[168] The ICC recognises at least three modes of perpetration: direct individual perpetration; co-perpetration; and perpetration by means. This hierarchical differentiation carries some ideological weight and mystificatory potential (Chapter 4C). Here I discuss these modes together with command responsibility (see further below, Section 1.4) and the putative doctrine of 'perpetration through an organisation' (see Section 1.5).

3 Direct (Individual) Perpetration

The ideologically most culpable mode is that of the perpetrator who 'with his own hands' carries out all material facts of the crime, and thus the one normally near or at the bottom of the (military or indeed corporate) hierarchical structure. This type of perpetration is reserved for the soldier (or other) who himself rapes, tortures, or kills in war or other widespread conflict, or who violates fundamental human rights in some other way as part of a campaign of systemic abuse.

165 Simester 2010, pp. 274–9; French 2009, pp. 636–9.
166 Werle 2009, p. 168.
167 Farrell 2010, p. 873.
168 Werle 2009, p. 170.

4 Co-perpetration and Joint Criminal Enterprise

The second mode exists for individuals who 'jointly with another perpetrate a crime'.[169] Emulating the Nuremberg conspiracy idea, the ICTY and the SCSL have developed the concept of 'joint criminal enterprise' ('JCE') to include both direct and indirect co-perpetration.[170] The difference between joint criminal enterprise and mere participation lies in the *mens rea* – joint perpetration / JCE requires a 'common plan, design or purpose' which must be aimed at committing one or more crimes against international law,[171] while other forms of joint perpetration may come in three categories ranging from the same *mens rea* as JCE, down to intention to participate in a group with the aim of committing *an* offence.[172] Importantly for the business context (where crimes may result from what are seen as 'neutral acts'[173] or 'business as usual'), an accused's contribution to the JCE need not be criminal in itself.[174] The JCE construct can be applied to situations where business leaders (managers, decision makers) work together to perpetrate crimes through organised structures of power. The hypothetical example Farrell gives is that of a corporation and a governmental authority cooperating in order to forcibly remove local people from an area where oil may be extracted.[175] The provision of means by the company (e.g., trucks or weapons) may then constitute the 'significant contribution' required for the JCE. Further elements required (for war crimes or crimes against humanity) would depend on the context in which the alleged offences took place (see further below).

The ICC Statute's Art. 25(3)(d) covers a 'group of persons with a common purpose', which broadly corresponds to the JCE construct – while in the early decisions the ICC has placed emphasis on control as mentioned above.[176] In particular, joint perpetration involves the responsibility of all for the acts of others in the group acting according to a common plan (*Lubanga*).[177] A slightly

169 E.g., *1998 ICC Statute* Art. 25(3)(a).

170 *Krasjisnik Appeals Judgment*; *Sesay Appeals Judgment*; Werle 2009, pp. 171–8; Cryer 2010, pp. 363–74; Boas 2010, pp. 510–19.

171 *Tadić 1999 Appeal* 188.

172 *Tadić 1999 Appeal* 204, 228, see also Van der Wilt 2009, pp. 158–9; Werle 2009, pp. 174–5; Van Sliedregt 2003, pp. 94–110.

173 See, e.g., Farrell 2010, p. 878.

174 *Krasjisnik Appeals Judgment* 218.

175 Farrell 2010, p. 879.

176 See also Manacorda 2011.

177 *Lubanga Charges Decision* 513; Lubanga Decision on Art. 74, paras. 1018, 1351, 1358.

different form was employed in *Al-Bashir*,[178] namely co-perpetration which relies on joint control, meaning that each member of the group could frustrate the commission of the crime by withdrawing.[179] Katanga was convicted in 2014 for being part of a rebel organisation with which they attacked a village with the intention of wiping out its population and the Hema ethnic group under Art. 25(3)(d)(ii)[180] – which does not contain a requirement that the contribution be made with the intent to commit the crime, or for the purpose of assisting the crime, only intention towards the contribution, and knowledge of the crime is required. This would work to capture a corporate actor at some distance removed from events.[181] *In casu*, while Katanga had initially been charged using a mode which required 'control of the crime', the ICC Trial Chamber found it sufficient for conviction that Katanga had had a role in establishing a coalition with regional authorities and in devising a military strategy, impressed on those authorities the importance of fighting against the Hema group, had a role in facilitating good communications between the various parties, and had a role in the distribution of weapons.[182] By analogy, it is conceivable that this role could be played by a businessperson involved for ulterior (commercial) reasons with an authority or militia who will clear land or eradicate local resistance to corporate activity. Also, the co-perpetrators may initially plan to achieve a non-criminal goal altogether, while being aware of the risk that implementing the plan will result in the commission of an offence – 'in the ordinary course of events'.[183] This may cover the situation where a private company is involved in immigration detention.[184]

JCE is criticised, for example, by Van der Wilt who argues that the doctrine, as (over)used by the tribunals, enables the lax application of criminal law standards on individual involvement in order to 'catch' a maximum number of members of the group.[185] This critique approximates a 'collective punishment' critique (see further below, Chapter 4C).

178 *Al-Bashir Arrest Warrant*; and see, generally, on this point Jeßberger 2008, p. 853.
179 *Lubanga Charges Decision* 342; Cryer 2009, pp. 364–5.
180 *Katanga Judgment* para. 1620.
181 Farrell 2010, p. 881.
182 *Katanga Judgment* para. 1671; Guilfoyle 2016, p. 354.
183 *Lubanga Appeals Judgment*, para. 450.
184 *Global Legal Action Network ICC Complaint* re. Nauru, p. 98.
185 E.g., Van der Wilt 2009, p. 181. See also Zahar 2008, pp. 224–34.

5 'Complicity', Aiding and Abetting

A key phrase in the business and human rights discourse is 'corporate complicity'[186] (see below 4C). The popularity of the phrase 'corporate complicity' over notions of corporations/corporate individuals as direct perpetrators evokes the idea that corporations (businesspersons) may, perhaps *inadvertently*, get tangled up in others' HR or IHL violations, but are never the initiators or main perpetrators.[187] As a mode of liability to capture individual businesspeople and potentially legal persons, the main advantage of the complicity / aiding and abetting mode is that there is, in ICTY, ICTR and SCSL law, no need for the aider and abetter to share the intent of the principal perpetrator.[188] As such, it covers the situation where the businessperson's intent is *only* commercial (e.g., selling weapons that are then used in a genocide), as opposed to *ultimately* commercial in the forced displacement example above.

The standard developed by the ICTY and ICTR for accomplice liability has come to be seen as part of general international law.[189] It has been defined by the ICTY as 'providing practical assistance that has a substantial effect on the perpetration of the crime, with knowledge that these acts would substantially assist the commission of the offence'.[190] The complicit corporate actor need not share the intent of the principal offender – the aider and abettor merely needs to know, or be aware, that her act assists in the commission of the crime.[191] A person need not have consciously decided to act for the purpose of the assistance of a crime.[192] As to causation, in *Kayishema* (ICTR), it was held that 'substantial' contribution suffices.[193] Further, the ICTY has included intangible assistance, for example, moral support and encouragement. Relying on a survey of CIL on aiding and abetting, the ICTY also found that actual physical presence at the scene of the crime was not required. Authority and presence can constitute a form of assistance, particularly when a person with the authority to stop an act from occurring (e.g., by ordering subordinates to desist) fails to do so.[194]

186 E.g., Schabas 2001; Jacobson 2005; Clapham 2001; Tófalo 2006; *ICJurists Complicity Report* Vol. 2 (2008).

187 Clapham 2002.

188 Farrell 2010, p. 882.

189 This is accepted, for example, by the US courts in *ATS* litigations, and by the Dutch courts, in the recent case *Van Anraat* 2005.

190 *Furundzija Judgment*.

191 *Krnojelac Judgment*.

192 *Mrksić Appeals Judgment* 159.

193 *Kayishema Judgment* 199.

194 *Furundzija Judgment* 249; on moral support, see 232.

Article 25(c) of the ICC Statute also includes accomplice liability for those who 'otherwise assist in its commission, ... including providing the means for its commission'.[195] In contrast to the ICTY and ICTR statutes and their interpretation in case law, the ICC Statute contains no requirement for the accomplice to make a direct or substantial contribution to the commission of crime.[196] In *Lubanga*, it was held that the accused must have made an 'essential contribution',[197] and in *Ngudjolo Chui* the ICC judges understood 'essential contribution' to mean that the Defendant's acts had 'an immediate impact on the way in which the material elements of the crime were realised'.[198] On the other hand, the *mens rea* requirement includes 'the purpose of facilitating the commission of such a crime', which appears to be more specific than the rule of CIL employed by the tribunals. Farrell illustrates – (by using the US *Talisman* Alien Tort Statute (ATS) case [see below Chapter 6] which adopts the ICC *mens rea* standard, the Dutch *Van Anraat* case [id.] which adopts a Dutch law standard equivalent to the CIL/ICTY standard, and the ICTY *Blagojević and Jokić* decision) that the ICC regime, if it were to congeal into CIL, would be less useful for capturing corporate actors.[199] It remains to be seen how the ICC develops this in its own jurisprudence, and how member-state domestic systems deal with this when complying with the requirement to bring their domestic laws in line with the ICC Statute.[200] The fact that international courts do look to domestic law as an informal persuasive authority[201] and that the US is the place where IL is considered most regularly, especially in ATS cases, it may well be that the ICC/ATS view will persist. This, despite the fact that the *Talisman* court's finding that the ICC standard is the standard in general IL, rather than the ICTY standard which is part of CIL, is erroneous.[202]

---

195 *1998 ICC Statute*.

196 Schabas suggests the absence of the word 'substantially' in the *1998 ICC Statute* may imply that the Diplomatic Conference meant to reject the higher threshold of the recent case law of The Hague (Schabas 2001, p. 448).

197 *Lubanga Decision on Art. 74*, para. 1018 (Mar. 14, 2012).

198 *Prosecutor v. Ngudjolo Chui*, Case No. ICC-01/04-02/12 paras. 44–6 (Dec. 18, 2012).

199 Farrell 2010, pp. 883–5. But see, *Global Legal Action Network ICC complaint*, pp. 98–9.

200 This may of course depend to some extent on the doctrines of accomplice liability already in use in these respective systems.

201 For example, the ICJ in the *Arrest Warrant Case*.

202 Farrell 2010, p. 887. In addition, the *Talisman* court erroneously sought to rely on the USMT *Ministries case* (*supra*) while in this case the knowledge standard was explicitly cited. In addition, this was in line with other USMT cases such as the *Einstatzgruppen Case*, *Flick*, *IG Farben*, and the British trial of *Tesch* (Farrell 2010, pp. 888–9 and Ch. 3 above). The question was once again in front of the US Supreme Court, in *Jesner v. Arab Bank*.

As to the CIL standard, the contribution of an aider and abettor need not be 'direct' but must be 'substantial', with the former being an evidentiary issue depending on the *mens rea*.[203] A substantial contribution may include moral support or be an accumulation of acts of support.[204] For example, this could include the company director's acquiescence in military oppression of union leaders for the benefit of the company.

6 Command and Other Superior Responsibility

The term 'superior responsibility' has come to replace the older 'command responsibility', in a development that sees the broader recognition of non-military leaders' responsibility for crimes committed by their subordinates. Yet, the *mens rea* element (in the ICC Statute variant)[205] is more 'lenient' with regard to civilian leaders, who do not have the same level of 'should have known' regarding their subordinates' activities as military commanders. The doctrinal classification of the construct of 'command' or 'superior' responsibility is in dispute.[206] Some argue that it is a specific crime where superiors fail to comply with their own obligations in IL (the duty to look after/control subordinates), yet others argue a superior is effectively responsible for the crime of a subordinate which they fail to prevent or punish/report (both see superior responsibility as a crime of omission, effectively).[207] The latter interpretation gives rise to a 'collective responsibility' critique (Chapter 4C, Section 1). The Tokyo Tribunal took a very broad view of command responsibility (see above, Chapter 3, Section 4). Article 28(b) ICC Statute, which deals with hierarchical relationships outside the military sphere, may be applied to business.[208] Subparagraph (b)(ii) states that the subordinates' crimes must concern activities within the superior's *effective* responsibility and control, which is interpreted to mean the superior may not be responsible for acts falling outside of the scope of her duties.[209] This may give rise to a debate along the line of that regarding functional immunity in IL – can the commission of crimes ever be considered to be part of someone's role or job description? In ICC law superi-

203 Farrell 2010, p. 891.
204 *Blagojević and Jokić* TC *Decision*.
205 1998 ICC Statute Art. 28(a) cf. 28 (b); Werle 2014, p. 226 ff.
206 Werle 2014, p. 222; Cryer 2010, p. 397.
207 Werle 2014, pp. 222–3. See also, generally, the JICJ Symposium on command responsibility in JICJ 5 2007, p. 599–682.
208 E.g., Vest 2010, p. 869.
209 1998 ICC Statute; *Mucić* TC *Decision* 593.

ors may be liable if they 'knew or consciously disregarded information which clearly indicated, that the subordinates were committing or about to commit such crimes' – this high standard clearly omits the information the superior *should have known* about considering the scope of their role and responsibility within the organisation. According to Art. 28 ICC Statute, civilian superiors may be liable if they subsequently 'failed to take all necessary and reasonable measures within [their] power to prevent or repress the acts in question' or to report them to appropriate authorities.[210] Hypothetically, for example, where superiors know that their employees are intimidating or even killing local union activists and has the power to stop them, they could be liable if they fail to do so, or also, if they take only perfunctory measures, for instance, if they tell their employees to be respectful but do nothing when they continue their activities. The moment when a superior's 'should have known' turns into 'actively looking away' is hard to pinpoint in practice. A doctrine of superior responsibility could only be effective in reducing crime if it encouraged, rather than discouraged, superiors from playing an active role in the supervision of subordinates, and if it were possible to avoid the situation where employees commit offences outside of their 'official' job description while superiors actively 'look away'. While turning a blind eye to known or suspected crimes may be caught by the provision, arms-length management (often involving significant geographical distance) delegating jobs with a wide mandate while keeping information streams strictly 'need to know' would not be. Of course, the accusation that states hire private contractors specifically to 'privatise responsibility' (an element of 'plausible deniability') is commonly made.[211]

7 Perpetration through an Organisation?

Article 25(3)(a) of the ICC Statute includes the notion of perpetration 'through another person'. This could be the perpetration by a 'perpetrator behind the perpetrator' who pulls the strings, or perpetration though a non-culpable person (someone who cannot be prosecuted) such as a minor. In *Prosecutor v. Katanga and Chui*, the ICC Pre-Trial Chamber used this concept where crimes were said to be committed through the control of a hierarchical organisation.[212] Explicitly referring to the German concept of *Organisationsherrschaft*

210 *1998 ICC Statute* Arts. 28(a)(i) and (b)(i).

211 E.g., Whyte 2006, Scahill 2007, Klein 2007, *GLAN ICC Complaint* p. 99.

212 *Katanga Charges Decision*; Werle 2014, pp. 178–80; Cryer 2010, p. 366.

(translated by the court as perpetration through an 'organised and hierarchical apparatus of power'), the ICC Trial Chamber defined the necessary elements of an 'organisation', which

> must be based on hierarchical relations between superiors and subordinates. The organisation must also be composed of sufficient subordinates to guarantee that superiors' orders will be carried out, if not by one subordinate, then by another. These criteria ensure that orders given by the recognised leadership will generally be complied with by their subordinates.[213]

The perpetrators behind the scene, or removed from the physical site of the crime 'decide whether or how the offence will be committed'[214] and 'the leader's control over the apparatus allows him to utilise his subordinates as a mere gear in a giant machine'.[215] Citing *Eichmann*, the Pre-Trial Chamber confirms that 'the degree of responsibility increases as we draw further away from the man who uses the fatal instrument'.[216] In *Eichmann in Jerusalem: A Report on the Banality of Evil*, Hannah Arendt describes the now-proverbial 'desk murderer' – the man who claimed he bore no responsibility with regard to the crimes of the holocaust, because he was 'just doing his job', a 'small cog in a big machine' and 'never himself laid a finger on anyone'.[217] From the descriptions of the factual situations in corporations as related in Chapters 3 and 4 (and 5), it is clear how this analysis may approximate corporate actuality.

Weigend, however, has queried

> whether this doctrine is helpful in analysing the cases of indirect perpetration in the context of systemic crime; it might be preferable to ask what it takes to control the will of another person to such an extent as to 'make him' commit a crime. The existence of an organization controlled by the perpetrator may be no more than one factor relevant for answering that question.[218]

213 *Katanga Charges Decision* 512. This construct was also used in the trial of Fujimori in Peru, and the junta in Argentina, Werle 2014, pp. 207–13.

214 *Katanga Charges Decision* 485.

215 *Katanga Charges Decision* 515.

216 *Katanga Charges Decision* 503, citing Adolf Eichmann 1961, p. 197.

217 Arendt 1963. The term 'desk murderer' is first used by Arendt not in *Eichmann* but in the foreword to Bernd Naumann's report on the Frankfurt Auschwitz trials (Naumann 1966), see also *Neue Zürcher Zeitung* 2017.

218 Weigend 2011, p. 91.

Arguing that the constructs of 'instigation' and 'ordering' already can be employed to cover the kinds of situations in *Katanga and Chui*, Weigend suggests that the design of the concept of 'perpetration through an organisation' satisfies 'our sense of judicial aesthetics' rather than a doctrinal need.[219] The important question to ask, however, is whether 'perpetration through an organisation' lets 'organisation'/company in through the back door – considering the ICC membership have not utilised the opportunity of the review conference to include legal person liability.[220] Weigend notes, however, that domestically in Germany (where this construct was used to prosecute GDR border guards)[221] the proposal to employ this doctrine in the business context 'has been widely criticized by legal scholars, mainly because a business enterprise lacks all the main characteristics (tight hierarchical structure, general lawlessness, fungibility of members) that might justify the imposition of liability as a perpetrator to the leaders of a military or political organization'.[222] Such an attempt to curb the use of a doctrine to particular types of organisation seems clearly ideological. Very controversially, the ICC Trial Chamber itself rewrote the charges against Katanga, and convicted him under Art. 25(3)(d) as discussed above – a mode that neither the prosecution nor the defence had addressed at trial.[223]

8 Contextual Elements and Gravity

Two further ICL requirements that potentially limit the effectiveness of ICL (or more specifically, the ICC) in the business and human rights context warrant discussion. First, the ICC Statute limits the jurisdiction of the court to those situations of sufficient gravity (Arts 17(1)(d) and 53(1)(c)). The Prosecutor must assess a potential case's gravity as against any other cases that may arise from the same situation, and she must limit herself to those who bear the greatest responsibility for the crimes alleged, and avoid 'peripheral' and 'insignificant' crimes.[224] The criteria for gravity concern the 'scale, nature, manner of

---

219 Weigend 2011, p. 102. Weigend holds: 'There is certainly nothing to even remotely suggest that the concept of "perpetration through an organisation" is a form of criminal liability recognized as customary international law' (Weigend 2011, p. 106).

220 See generally, https://asp.icc-cpi.int/en menus/asp/reviewconference/Pages/review%20conference.aspx.

221 Weigend 2011, p. 98.

222 Weigend 2011, p. 99.

223 Guilfoyle 2016, p. 353.

224 Pre-trial Chamber II, Case No. ICC-01/09, Decision Pursuant to Art. 15 of the *Rome Statute*

commission and impact of the crimes'.[225] The gravity requirement is aimed at 'maximiz[ing] the Court's deterrent effect'.[226] However, the requirements are vague and subjective (similar to the distinctions made by Cassese at al regarding which crimes 'deserve' to be ICL crimes – see Chapter 4A), allowing the exclusion of those who are merely 'complicit' or those whose crimes are less bloody but have effects that may spread more slowly, less visibly, though far more widely (e.g., the less immediately apparent effects of corporate capitalism on the environment, health, quality of life).

Secondly, where corporate involvement in human rights violations occurs outside of interstate war (which is covered by war crimes law), then they could be classified as crimes against humanity. Crimes against humanity (such as killing, torture, persecution), however, must occur 'as part of a widespread or systematic attack directed against any civilian population, with knowledge of the attack' in order to be prosecutable. Under Art. 7(2)(a) ICC Statute, moreover, an 'attack directed against any civilian population' is defined as 'a course of conduct involving the multiple commission of acts referred to in paragraph 1 against any civilian population, pursuant to or in furtherance of a State or organizational policy to commit such attack'.[227] Such an attack may be non-violent, even legislative[228] – or an 'accumulation of bureaucratic and administrative procedures'.[229] The question whether the policy element requires if not a state, a state-like organisation, is currently being debated. The majority view at the ICC is that the term 'organisation' merely presumes the existence of a group of persons lasting for a certain period of time and possessing established structures – while the crucial element is the organisation's potential, in terms of both personnel and physical capacity, to commit a widespread or systematic attack on a civilian population.[230] According to Jeßberger, in the corporate context, such an organisation could include the corporation itself, a corporate board, or even a part of a corporate board.[231] It could also include a subsidiary, a division or department, or a team.

---

on the Authorization of an Investigation into the Situation in the Republic of Kenya, para. 58; 56 (Mar. 31, 2010).

225 International Criminal Court Office of the Prosecutor, Policy paper on case selection and prioritisation para. 32 (Sept. 15, 2016).

226 *Prosecutor v. Dyilo*, Case No. ICC-01-04-01/06, Decision on the confirmation of the charges, para. 48 (Jan. 29, 2007). For a discussion of this requirement, see Heller 2010.

227 Art. 7 *1998 ICC Statute*; *Elements of Crimes (2002 and 2010)*.

228 E.g., *Prosecutor v. Jean-Paul Akayesu* TC, Case No. ICTR-96-4-T, Judgment, 2 September 1998, para. 581.

229 *GLAN ICC Complaint*, p. 60.

230 Jeßberger 2016, pp. 334–5.

231 Jeßberger 2016, p. 335.

Even though it is possible usually to argue that corporate abuse could be covered by ICL/ICC law, it is clear that the limitations that have been imposed serve to create obstacles to prosecution of corporate cases. These obstacles appear practically justified, but also again serve to disqualify corporate abuse as 'grave' or potentially 'widespread or systematic' – basically more than merely incidental or accidental – rather than an inevitable effect of the structures of corporate capitalism.

9 Conclusion to 4B: so Many Men, so Many Modes

One can see that it can at times become difficult to distinguish between the various modes of responsibility. The point to take away from this is that it would seem that *in principle* ICL modes are flexible enough (and ICL practice clearly flexible enough) to cover every conceivable scenario of 'business in conflict' – including that of business actors perpetrating or otherwise being involved in international crimes, just as they had been in World War Two. In Chapter 5, I will show that despite this development, and despite the World War Two business trials, *in practice* there has been virtually no 'mapping' of these modes onto the relations within the corporation and between the businessperson and 'victims' or persons affected by their acts or omissions in recent years. In this sense, the corporation remains a 'structure of irresponsibility' as proposed in Chapter 2A. The fact, that ICL is (almost wholly) not applied to business, supports the findings in the previous chapters of ICL being a legal technology not for 'justice', but indeed for the funnelling of affect into a specific place / onto a specific body, for the creation of a specific narrative about conflict (excluding economic actors/factors), perhaps also for the production of 'spectacle' that focuses on individual 'enemy' state or military leaders but distracts us from particular other happenings and structural dynamics in the world, while ensuring legal risk-free 'business as usual'.

The fact that business – even in conflict – is not normally discussed in terms of, or, is effectively shielded from, ICL's modes of responsibility (except by, e.g., Farrell, Jeßberger, and Stewart, mentioned above) points toward two main findings. Firstly, it highlights lawyers' role in the congealing of capitalism, and the effectiveness of legal and corporate ideology. The 2016 JICJ special issue on slavery contained two articles arguing that ICL could be applied to corporations / individual corporate officers in international and domestic tribunals, that concluded that the problem is that it just isn't.[232] The debate has not moved on

232 Jeßberger 2016; and Amol and Shay 2016.

in recent years from an analysis of the various legal rules that could be applied, without speculation as to precisely why they are currently not, as if 'not' is simply an oversight due to limited understanding of the law, rather than a deliberate exclusion or shielding – which exists in the choice of crimes, but also in the 'contextual elements' and especially the controversial 'gravity' requirements of ICL prosecution as set by the Rome Statute negotiators.[233]

This is how the remedial 'ICL 101' – or the depoliticised doctrinal 'metadebate' with clear echoes of the foundational disputes in 4A – plays out in Jeßberger:

> The norms of transnational criminal law do not establish criminal responsibility directly under international (treaty) law, but establish legal duties for state parties to provide for criminal responsibility for the respective transnational crime under their domestic law. This doctrinal distinction becomes relevant when we consider slavery: many slavery-related practices, including enslavement, slave trading, forced labour and human trafficking are transnational crimes. At the same time, slavery as such is not a crime under international law. Some of the pertinent practices, however, including enslavement, sexual slavery and forced labour, may qualify as crimes under international law if (and only if) additional requirements (armed conflict; attack against the civilian population, etc.) are present.[234]

This analysis ignores the fact that all distinctions exist as a result of *choices* made by lawmakers at various points of time in the history of ICL. Jeßberger's own unusual stance as an ICL scholar in holding onto the 'German' position against legal person liability and who focuses on individuals, claiming that 'the tools [for effective business and human rights prosecution] are there' – belies the fact that the in- or exclusion of legal person liability in ICL is also a choice, driven by the structures of corporate capitalism, allowing zero-risk corporate involvement in conflict, at least from a legal perspective.

ICL has become a field where 'expert' doctrinal debate obscures the very specific political goals of ICL, and spirits away the relationships of oppression it does not want us to focus on or append responsibility to. Secondly, it aligns with the creation – in international investment protection law, for example – of a *sui generis* position for individuals engaged in business, for ideological reasons. In ICL this separation creates a space between business persons (good)

233 Jeßberger 2016, p. 334ff.

234 Jeßberger 2016, pp. 330–1 (footnotes omitted).

and, say, members of armed groups and other (private) non-state actors potentially involved in conflict (bad) in a way set up by the Nuremberg Industrialists, even though in legal doctrine / positive law they are of the same kind. So does the attempt to argue that business involvement is somehow inexplicably, *but obviously* qualitatively different from the involvement of other participants in a conflict situation, and thus requires its own, yet to be developed, area of law (*Wirtschaftsvölkerstrafrecht*).[235] Here we clearly see the analogy with the deliberate separation into public and private spheres, and the fragmentation of legal regulation in the context of FDI discussed in Chapter 2B. These rhetorical moves go in the same direction: making it more difficult for us to imagine individual businesspersons in the framework of general ICL, leading at best to a resigned 'it just isn't'. However, this contradiction, as one might have expected, becomes the logical premise of a new pre-fab dissent. 'Impunity' is found, the desire for 'punity' is created, resulting in the fact that the development of such a *Wirtschaftsvölkerstrafrecht* is indeed now well underway – more about this in Chapter 6. First, I find who is to be the object of this 'punity' and examine the attempts to get legal persons included/excluded within ICL's enforcement remit.

4C Re-making ICL: Who Wants to Be an International Criminal? Casting Business in Contemporary ICL

1 Introduction to 4C

In the preceding two chapters, I have outlined how ICL became the accountability tool of choice (4A), and I have looked at the 'congealing' deeper inside ICL by examining how the 'New ICL' reworked the abstraction of relations of responsibility of Post-World War Two ICL to allow the calculation of the transactional value of each mode of responsibility in the new geopolitical landscape (4B). In the current chapter, I examine a striking phenomenon, namely that, compared to the discourse of the Nuremberg Industrialists' trials, the current legal literature on business in conflict centres almost exclusively on the putative liability of the corporate legal person.

One fact is rarely, if at all, mentioned in ICL histories. This is that in the early 1950s, the ILC (see Chapter 4A, Section 2.2) and the Committee on International Criminal Jurisdiction considered including corporate liability in the draft statute. In the discussion of Art. 25 (Jurisdiction as to Persons) of the revised draft

235 Generally Jeßberger 2009; Pearce 1990, p. 424.

statute, '[t]he member from Australia ... argued that the criminal responsibility of corporations was not excluded [from IL] either by doctrine or by jurisprudence, and that the mere fact that the responsibility of corporations under existing international criminal law was not entirely clear should not mean that all possibility of conferring Jurisdiction over them should be denied'.[236] However, the Committee on International Criminal Jurisdiction decided: 'In view of the experience at the Nürnberg and Tokyo trials, it was undesirable to include so novel a principle as corporate criminal responsibility in the draft statute'.[237] The Committee rejected the Australian proposal by 11 votes to one, with four abstentions. One factor motivating the Australian call for corporate liability may be the Australian POWs lost to Japanese mining companies in World War Two. While it is not clear what precisely is meant by 'in view of the experience at the Nürnberg and Tokyo trials', one possibility is that it refers to the punishment of military suppliers who at this point in the 1950s were once again urgently required to supply the global arms race. Australian manufacturers would not have played a major role here, but Australia did seek to recruit and retain soldiers to fight in Korea.[238] The abandonment of the ICL project soon after rendered both concerns moot.

In this part I examine how, post-1989, as part of the 'New ICL', the proposed corporate ICL has come out of the developments described in 4A and 4B. Here we see ICL ideology at work: abstracting relationships, creating divisions, naturalising 'difference' and spiriting away that which is not included – generating planned impunity on the one hand, and the opportunity for canned morality on the other.

While ICL has been about the *Individualisierung* of IL,[239] and while the requisite modes of responsibility still exist (as shown in 4B) – the current response to the much more acute awareness of the role of business actors in human rights abuse, conflict and environmental destruction has not been, and is overwhelmingly *not* to call for the prosecution of individual business leaders.

Instead, the combination of the erasure of the Nuremberg Industrialists' trials from legal memory, and corporate ideology inducing ILIP's reification of the corporation (Chapter 2B, Section 3), now posits *it* as a putative 'individual' subject of ICL.[240] As a result of both factors, 'corporate impunity' comes to demand

---

236 Report of the Committee on International Criminal Jurisdiction, UN Doc. A/2136 (1952).

237 Report of the Committee on International Criminal Jurisdiction, UN Doc. A/2645 (1953).

238 McLean 2001, p. 298.

239 Cf. Stahn and Van den Herik who speak of the 'de-individualisation' of ICL (Stahn 2010, p. 315).

240 Interestingly, the ILC committee preparing the draft statute for a permanent criminal

corporate 'punity' and, although 'corporate liability' in ICL is considered by most only *lex ferenda* (what the law should be – in the future), some argue it already exists, or, should for pragmatic reasons, be presumed to exist.[241] The proposals for corporate ICL spring from the contradiction between corporate ILP in the 'private' side of IL, increasingly visible harm caused by business and the development of a regime dealing with responsibility. The (non-)existence of corporate liability in ICL thus becomes the pre-fab constructive critique that shapes the direction of development for ICL, where 'while we wait', exceptionally, the individual businessperson can 'stand in' for legal person liability.

Here I examine in some depth the ideology of 'CICL' and its constituent elements. Broadly three types of argument are made by those who consider corporate liability in ICL *lex ferenda*. The first is not an argument strictly speaking, although it is often phrased as such, but rather a description or explanation in the style of a progress narrative, reflected for example when describing the number of states that have 'already accepted', 'recognised', or 'acknowledged' corporate liability. Here, we can see the 'trend' ('progress'/'fashion') of ICL at work.[242] For example, the International Commission of Jurists, in its first major contribution to the debate, the three-volume 'Corporate Complicity' report, notes that 'significant opposition to the imposition of criminal sanctions on companies as legal entities remains';[243] however, this opposition is 'broadly conceptual' and based on a memory of 'national criminal laws developed many centuries ago'.[244] Also, 'the fact that increasing numbers of jurisdictions are applying criminal law to companies is evidence that these difficulties can be overcome'.[245] In fact, in its 2016 report, the International Commission of Jurists sees this prediction confirmed: the Convention on the Rights of the Child Optional Protocol containing a legal person liability provision [mentioned in 4A above] has 173 States party – and another nine States have signed but not yet ratified it, allowing the International Commission of Jurists to claim that the principle '*societas delinquere non potest* (society cannot commit a crime) is in retreat in all regions of the world'.[246]

court did in fact discuss, but dismissed, jurisdiction over legal persons, specifically corporations.

241 In the latter category, e.g., Clapham 2000; Ramasastry 2002; Chiomenti 2006.

242 E.g., *FAFO* (*Ramasastry*) 2006; *FAFO* (*Ramasastry*) 2004; Ramasastry 2002.

243 ICJurists Complicity Report Vol. II, 59.

244 Ibid.

245 The Panel gives as its only two reasons why CICL might be a good thing, the possibility of financial redress for victims, and the chance that 'corporate culture' might improve after the imposition of a criminal sanction on a company (*ICJurists Complicity Report* Vol. II, 59).

246 In its 2016 report, the ICJ still notes 'unclear modalities' and 'insufficient state practice'.

The second type of argument for corporate liability is based on a pragmatic or rational need to close a doctrinal gap, or 'accountability gap': 'the lack of a norm of corporate liability in ICL leaves business involvement in crimes unaddressed'.[247] The narrative holds that, since the multinational corporation exists, we must create law to deal with it: 'just as the concept of corporate criminal responsibility emerged as a reaction to the industrialization process in the common law jurisdictions over a century ago, so should the concept now be lifted to the international level in order to address the demands and realities of the relentless globalization process'.[248] Again, the direction of development is 'clear' here, and logical.

Both these arguments are grounded in the almost complete reification of the corporation, 'spiriting away' the individuals that operate it.[249]

A third argument for the existence or creation of a norm allowing a finding of corporate liability in ICL that is being made by some scholars, forms part of a broader debate on 'system criminality' (see also Chapter 3A). Nollkaemper, in the introduction to his edited volume on the subject, explains system criminality as 'the phenomenon that international crimes – notably crimes against humanity, genocide and war crimes – are often caused by collective entities in which the individual authors of these acts are embedded'.[250] The most recent iteration of this debate revolves around the notion of 'shared responsibility': the idea that corporations and states together bear responsibility for human rights fulfilment.[251]

Recent legal developments bear out, and seemingly concretise, this latter notion, as I will show and discuss in Section 4 below.

'Recommendations for the content of a treaty on business and human rights', ICJ Submission to the OEIWG, October 2016, available at: https://www.icj.org/the-icj-releases-its-proposals-for-the-content-of-a-treaty-on-business-and-human-rights/ (*ICJ Proposals for Elements 2016*).

247 Van den Herik 2010, p. 362.

248 Van den Herik 2010, p. 358.

249 I would like to note upfront that my assessment of current developments does not indeed lead me to argue for a return to a focus on the human individual businessperson for ICL prosecution.

250 Nollkaemper 2009, p. 1. Nollkaemper has since gone on to publish on the concept of shared responsibility between states and non-state actors as well as the process of 'diffusion' of responsibility between different actors, e.g., Nollkaemper 2015, pp. 49–67.

251 Karavias 2015.

2 The 'New ICL' and Re-opening the Debate on Collective Liability

Now that the 'new ICL' has had two decades to develop, scholars and practitioners alike are starting to reflect on and criticise it in the ways discussed in Chapter 4A – and to map out (im)possible, probable and desired directions for future development. On the one hand, ICL has been about the *Individualisierung* of responsibility, the neat delineation of each human individual's agency in a complex situation;[252] on the other, it deals mostly with 'collective' acts (in a broader situation of conflict where many persons are involved) that some critics say cannot be ascribed to individuals singly.[253] Questions are also asked, for example, as to whether individuals behave differently as part of a 'pack' or within a particular system, and if so, whether this should affect the level of responsibility they can be ascribed, or even to whom responsibility can be ascribed.[254] Some authors (not necessarily structural Marxists) argue that some actions are in fact not those of individuals but of the structure within which they operate: the corporation, or the government, or 'the system' (Section 4).[255] ICL is being criticised precisely for leaving 'system criminality' unaddressed.[256] The solution offered by most authors is corporate liability in ICL.

Many of the arguments both for and against corporate criminal liability echo those made in the last century regarding the question of state criminality.[257] The concept of state crime was discussed at length in the context of the development of the rules on state responsibility.[258] The International Law Commission removed Art. 19[259] on state criminal liability from the Draft Articles on State Responsibility in 1998[260] (reportedly because of the clause's

252 Werle 2007, p. 48.

253 E.g., Nollkaemper 2009, p. 2.

254 Ceretti 2009, pp. 5–15. Ceretti in particular discusses the group dynamics of collective violence from a sociological perspective and emphasises the importance of denial of individual moral culpability by perpetrators and denial of what happened to them by those affected (2009, pp. 5, 13).

255 See, e.g., generally, Arendt 1994, and to a lesser extent Nollkaemper 2009, p. 1; Herik 2010, pp. 364–5: 'social scientists … view corporations increasingly as more than the aggregation of a number of individuals … In these situations, … the "guilt" does not lie principally with easily identifiable specific individuals but rather with the corporation as such'.

256 Nollkaemper 2009, p. 1. See also Drumbl 2011.

257 E.g., Weiler 1989; Pellet 1999.

258 See, e.g., Brownlie 2008, p. 433 ff. Crawford's view on this issue of state criminality was that it was unnecessary and divisive and had the potential of destroying the project as a whole (Crawford 1999, p. 442). For a contemporary reappraisal, see Doucet 2010.

259 Art. 19.2 *ILC Draft Articles 1970*.

260 *ILC 1998 Report* 319–31.

problematic wording and some states' vehement opposition to the concept of state crime),[261] and the Articles adopted by the General Assembly in 2001 did not contain the concept.[262] Nonetheless, the idea of state crime persists, implicitly if not explicitly, in the popular political discourse of 'rogue states', and in the practice of state sanctions. In academic scholarship it persists in the discourse of state-corporate crime (a relatively new research area, network and journal),[263] and most recently in the new 'shared responsibility' project – on the latter, see further below.[264] The debate on 'collective responsibility' is being reopened.

The common objection to state crime (or other forms of 'collective' criminality) is that enforcement of the concept would result in collective punishment.[265]

Interestingly, current *individualised* ICL practice of the ICTY, ICTR is *also* being criticised for leading to collective punishment[266] when punishing senior leaders for the crimes (physically) committed by (usually junior) personnel 'on the ground'. This critique is made in relation to the use of the concept of command or superior responsibility (Chapter 4B, Section 1.4).[267]

Both of these critiques hinge on how we see a crime, and foreground the physical, violent, 'bloody' end of crime over the 'invisible' 'intellectual' crime of the individual who designed the policy, gave the order, authorised the operation, or who has the overall command over those on the ground. This person is the minister, the senior civil servant, the proverbial desk-killer, white-collar criminal or 'Schreibtischtäter' as Arendt has it, or, general in a grey suit, in Dubois's words.[268]

This downward shift presupposes the freedom to choose not to comply with an order (the freedom to walk away), a question that was discussed at length also at Nuremberg (see above Chapter 3A). The 'freedom' presupposed here, as

261 *ILC 1998 Report* 241–59.

262 *UN General Assembly Resolution 589*; *ILC State Responsibility Articles*; see also *Serbia Genocide Convention Case*.

263 International State Crime Initiative, http://www.statecrime.org/.

264 Also the ICJ held that a state could be found liable for genocide: *Bosnia v. Serbia*, para. 180. 'The Court accordingly concludes that state responsibility can arise under the Convention for genocide or complicity, without an individual being convicted of the crime or an associated one' (para. 182).

265 E.g., Van Sliedregt 2003, pp. 343–4.

266 Van den Herik 2010, p. 362.

267 Werle 2009, p. 188. See also, generally, Meloni 2007; Meloni 2010; Guilfoyle 2016.

268 Dubois 1952 (title of the book).

it is the freedom of the one at the bottom of the hierarchy, is analogous (or identical) to the 'freedom' (unfreedom) of labour in the Marxist sense.[269]

A related critique is made in relation to the doctrine of joint criminal enterprise (4B, Section 1.2). Boas calls the ICTY's practice in regard to the latter 'an increasingly obsessive preoccupation with the apportionment of responsibility to political leaders for *committing* crimes from which they are physically and structurally very far removed'.[270] Boas posits that JCE is (over)used to attach the special stigma of being a committer, rather than an instigator or aider or abettor.[271] Again, this critique hinges on individuals' perceived and actual role in a larger structure. If a special stigma is indeed attached to being a *committer* as Boas suggests, then a complicity conviction of a leader would signal a lower level of culpability, perhaps that of someone only marginally involved in an action directed by others, perhaps even 'from below'. What this allows is the portrayal of a conflict as resulting from 'leaders failing to control the masses', rather than leaders actively perpetrating acts of conflict and ordering/forcing 'the masses' to participate and carry out the dirty work. In Chapter 5, I will query whether the conflicts in Rwanda and the former Yugoslavia can be (and were) characterised as such.

Again, as a solution to both these concerns around collective responsibility (as well as the supposed difficulty of allocating responsibility fairly), corporate criminal liability is offered.

3 'De-individualising ICL': towards Legal Person Liability?

It is not clear which way IL will develop with regard to legal person criminal liability. After a flurry of events, scholarly publications and UN and NGO reports between around 1996 and 2012,[272] the issue seems to have gone relatively quiet, apart from the work of ICAR, Business and Human Rights Resource Centre, the UNHRC OEIWG on binding treaty, and the Global Movement for a Binding Treaty mentioned in Chapter 1 – see also Chapter 6.[273] Yet, as evidenced in

269 Gray 2006, p. 875.

270 Boas 2010, p. 502, emphasis in original.

271 On the significance of this stigma, see also Guilfoyle 2011.

272 For an overview of government and NGO engagement on the issue starting at a turning point in 1996, see Human Rights Watch Corporations and Human Rights, at: https://www.hrw.org/legacy/about/initiatives/corp.html.

273 Specific fora for discussion of business in ICL in the past years have been the *JICJ (2008) Workshop*, the *Humboldt Symposia*, and the *ICJurists Complicity Report*.

recent literature, the trend is still to argue for, or to *find*, legal person liability.[274] It is this putative legal person liability that I focus on in the remainder of this section. I start with the debate between the negotiators at the drafting stage of the ICC Statute because, as I argued in 4A, the ICC tends to be seen as the 'culmination' of ICL and as such as an authoritative gauge of ICL development as a whole.[275]

3.1 *The ICC Negotiations on Legal Persons*

The Preparatory Commission's draft, which formed the basis for the ICC Statute negotiations included in Art. 23:

> 5. The Court shall also have jurisdiction over legal persons, with the exception of States, when the crimes were committed on behalf of such legal persons or by their agencies or representatives
> 6. The criminal responsibility of legal persons shall not exclude the criminal responsibility of natural persons who are perpetrators or accomplices in the same crimes.[276]

In the negotiations the French delegation proposed and argued strongly in favour of the inclusion of legal persons in the ICC's jurisdiction.[277] The article they initially proposed on 16 June 1998 was a mirror image of Art. 10 of the IMT Charter (on criminal organisations – see Chapter 3A). It envisaged the declaration by the ICC of an organisation/company as a 'criminal organisation' under certain circumstances.[278] It went one step further than the IMT Charter by allowing the imposition of fines on the criminal organisation. France considered this important in terms of restitution and compensation orders for victims (effectively displaying the same priority it had during the *Röchling* trial, Chapter 3A, Section 8.2).[279] The 19 June 1998 proposal put forward was significantly different. It proposed giving the ICC jurisdiction to try legal persons in

274 E.g., Clapham 2006, p. 31; and generally, Van den Herik 2010, pp. 350–68; Voiculescu 2007, pp. 418–30; generally, Chiomenti 2006; Stoitchkova 2010; for an exploratory perspective, see Burchard 2010.

275 Others have discussed it in terms of the application of ICL on the domestic level: Kyriakakis 2010; Wanless 2009.

276 *ICC PrepCom Report 1998*.

277 Ambos 2008, p. 746.

278 *French Corporate Crime Proposal*: Art. 23: Appendix E.

279 Ambos 2008, p. 746. It may be a funding point – the French government may have considered it preferable for victims to be compensated from the funds of perpetrators rather than the court (members) itself.

the same way it would try natural persons. It was limited to cover only companies (and thus *not* the myriad of other groups/persons that could potentially be included such as political parties, organised armed groups, etc.), linking their criminal responsibility to that of leading members of those corporations who were in positions of control and who committed the crime 'acting on behalf of and with explicit consent of the corporation and in the course of its activities'.[280] France emphasised that '[t]here was nothing in the proposal to permit the concealment of individual responsibility behind that of an organisation'.[281] Eventually this proposal, too, was rejected. The delegates of the Scandinavian countries stated that the inclusion of legal persons would detract from the purpose of the ICC, which was the prosecution of individuals.[282] The representative for Syria noted that the inclusion of corporate legal persons would beg the question of why States, though legal persons, could not be prosecuted.[283] The Greek representative said categorically that there is no criminal responsibility which cannot be traced back to individuals.[284] The representative of China emphasised that the 'criminal organisation' provisions in the Nuremberg Charter had not been intended as a means of prosecuting legal persons as such. He added that the political context existing at the time of the Nuremberg trials was very different from the sensitive political context pertaining today. Also, he reminded the meeting that the Nuremberg trials had been conducted by victorious over defeated countries.[285]

In preparing this draft, France had been closely collaborating with the Solomon Islands – which were being represented by Andrew Clapham, one of the main academic proponents of corporate liability in ICL.[286] Eventually, France withdrew the proposal, apparently due to time constraints.[287] The Statute that was adopted on 17 July 1998 limits the Court's jurisdiction to natural persons.[288] The ICC's Art. 25(1) reads: 'The Court shall have jurisdiction over

280 The term 'juridical person' was defined as 'a corporation whose complete, real or dominant objective is seeking private profit or benefit, and not a State of other public body in the exercise of state authority, a public international body or an organisation registered, and acting under the national law of a State ad a non-profit organization'. *WGGP Working Paper on Art. 23*, pp. 1–2.

281 Ibid, see also *Committee of the Whole Record*, pp. 32, 33.

282 *Committee of the Whole Record*, pp. 43, 55.

283 *Committee of the Whole Record*, p. 56.

284 *Committee of the Whole Record*, p. 57.

285 *Committee of the Whole Record*, p. 36.

286 Clapham 2000, fn. 1.

287 Clapham 2006, p. 31.

288 *1998 ICC Statute (supra)*.

natural persons pursuant to this Statute'.[289] The extension of the ICC Statute to cover legal persons was not proposed at the 2010 ICC Statute Review Conference, which focused mainly on the definition of the crime of aggression.[290]

So just as the ILC put aside the issue of state crime at a time when no consensus could be reached, the ICC membership put corporate (and armed group *qua* group) liability aside, potentially to be picked up again in the future. In the meantime, consensus is emerging, evidenced by statements such as 'The striking phenomenon is that many other international instruments have been adopted which, unlike the Rome Statute, introduce, at the international level, the concept of corporate criminal liability'.[291] While this statement relies on a misreading of the international instruments (see Chapter 4A, Section 2.4), this argument is increasingly made, contributing to the naturalisation of the idea of corporate ICL, which is the first step to its adoption in law.

3.2 *Legal Person Liability for Business in ICL: The 'Progress View'*

Much of the corporate liability debate in the NGO literature employs the concept of 'corporate complicity' – which is part of the 'legalising CSR' push (see further Chapter 6), and posits that while (or so long as) corporations cannot be liable *per se*, they can still be 'complicit' in violations committed by or on behalf of a state.[292] Human Rights Watch ('HRW') Director Kenneth Roth has commented on the way that the concept of complicity – deliberately used in a non-legal sense in HRW reporting in the 1980s – was developed into a criminal law concept.[293] The non-legal concept of 'complicity' was picked up and given legal content by the International Commission of Jurists, UN Special Representative on Business and Human Rights John Ruggie (see above and Chapter 6) and legal scholars.[294] The road to legalisation is one of 'narrativisation' and 'naturalisation':[295] a discursive process in which NGOs, legal scholars and UN offi-

289 The ICTY and ICTR also confine jurisdiction to natural persons: Art. 6 *1993 ICTY Statute*; Art. 5 *1994 ICTR Statute*.

290 See, generally, https://asp.icc-cpi.int/en menus/asp/reviewconference/Pages/review%20conference.aspx.

291 Swart 2008, p. 947. Another such misreading is Seck 2011, who argues (incorrectly) that Ruggie found ICL corporate liability to exist. In the same volume, Drumbl gives the opposite reading: 'corporate entities [are] relevant actors who currently fall outside the reach of international criminal law'.

292 *ICJurists Complicity Report*.

293 Roth 2008, p. 960 – see also below, Ch. 6. Kenneth Roth has been Executive Director of Human Rights Watch since 1993.

294 E.g., Clapham 2008; Stoitchikova 2010; Černič 2010.

295 Marks 2000, p. 19.

cials played the main roles – and where the same individuals often switch between roles within this process. Andrew Clapham, for example, an influential scholar who has published widely on corporations and human rights and international criminal law, besides representing the Solomon Islands in the ICC negotiations (above) also served as the Special Adviser on Corporate Responsibility to High Commissioner for Human Rights Mary Robinson.[296] He has said, about corporate liability in ICL, 'it will happen if we say it enough times' – in other words, if the idea is *naturalised*.[297] Even if formal adoption of the concept for example through extension of the ICC's jurisdiction is not achieved, the desired effect (see Chapter 6) may be reached even if it is not in fact enforced internationally but there is '*expert opinio iuris*' – and/or a common understanding among the 'thought leaders' such as Ruggie and Clapham that it exists. Similarly, Surya Deva and David Bilchitz, prominent scholars in business and human rights, are deeply embedded in the current negotiations on a binding treaty on business and human rights.[298]

Above (Section 1.1) I quoted Larissa van den Herik's view that corporate liability 'should' be adopted, just as it was adopted on the domestic level, in response to the 'relentless globalization process'. I also mentioned texts that cite those that have not *yet* adopted corporate criminal liability as *traditional*.[299] The US tort litigation where corporations are accused of international crimes (see Chapter 6) also plays a part in the normalisation of the idea of corporate criminal liability.[300] Other arguments in the 'progress' vein seem to be limited to simply stating corporate liability should be adopted because corporations are here, exist, or because corporations hold great power, or because not doing so would leave 'corporate crime' unaddressed.[301] These are all arguments that make sense on the superficial level, that 'ring true' and therefore have traction, and the effect of their repetition may well be that

296 *Clapham website.*

297 Conversation with Clapham at *Humboldt Symposium.*

298 See, e.g., Deva and Bilchitz (eds) 2017.

299 See, e.g., Stessens 1994, p. 493: 'Though some jurisdictions (e.g., the United States) have taken this step earlier, other criminal law systems in Europe apparently still have not been able to ...'; Cockayne 2008, p. 955.

300 Generally, *Harvard Law Review*, which asks the question of corporate liability in IL from the point of view of *ATS* cases, which it says, '[t]he international community should view ... as a call to collective action' (Anon. 2001, p. 2049).

301 Van den Herik 2010, p. 362. *That* it exists is also sometimes argued on the basis that it *should* exist, e.g., Chiomenti 2006, p. 295: 'In conclusion, the concept of criminal responsibility for corporations is now generally accepted at the level of both national and international law'.

these ideas are internalised, and that the norms come to exist by some sort of ideological socialisation process rather than through their formal adoption.

Many who argue for corporate criminal liability do not explain why such liability would be a good thing – this appears as a given: indeed, to deny this would mean to deny 'this idea that corporations should be prohibited from assisting governments in violating international law'[302] and to leave corporations 'largely immune from liability'.[303] The question of responsibility here presupposes the subjectivity in IL of the corporation. Moreover, corporate liability in ICL is thus presented as *the* solution, while no evidence is produced how, or *that* it would 'work', for example by showing that corporate crime regimes on the domestic level have reduced corporate offending, and most importantly, no indication of how corporate crime enforcement would actually be executed on the international level. There is no elaboration of how the mental element of a crime (or indeed the *actus reus*) would be established in the case of multinational corporate groups, or which doctrines of attribution or identification (common to domestic systems) would be proposed or suitable. Finally, and most significantly, no explanation is given of how such a norm would even come to be formally adopted at all, considering 'the ... realities of the relentless globalization process'[304] (the nature of which remains unexplained). The desirability of corporate ICL is supposed to be self-evident to the point where criminal law must be fundamentally changed in order to enable corporate liability: e.g., 'It is thus necessary to reconceptualize the parameters of guilt and blame in order to develop a criminal law theory that is tailored to corporations'.[305]

Other arguments for corporate liability appear practical: for example, 'when there is not one individual that can be blamed given the collective decision-making, because the individual who originally took decision [*sic*] already left, or as a result of unclear corporate structures'.[306] The modes of liability developed by the tribunals (see 4B) are assumed to be inadequate, even if they have at times been applied to individuals as part of 'unclear structures'.[307] Here,

302 Clapham 2008, p. 899.

303 This argument is made in the *Harvard Law Review* (Anon. 2001, p. 2026): 'Corporations thus remain immune to liability, and victims remain without redress'; Steinhardt 2005, p. 177; Cockayne 2008, p. 955. For a discussion of the dangers of critique, see Tallgren 2014.

304 Van den Herik 2010, p. 358.

305 Van den Herik 2010, p. 364.

306 Van den Herik 2010, p. 368.

307 Viz. the cases employing a 'joint criminal enterprise' construct, e.g., *Krajisnik Appeals Judgment*.

the evidentiary difficulty inherent in pinning criminal blame on one (or, possibly more than one) legal person within the group structure of multinationals (the parent company, which may be a holding company, a local subsidiary close to the physical site of the crime, or the whole group) is not examined. ICL is, of course, formally equipped to deal with a person who has 'already left' the company or indeed the country. A further situation in which corporate liability is argued to be appropriate is 'where collective decision-making in the company makes it hard to see who exactly should be liable'.[308] Again, these arguments may sound rational and attractive, but as discussed above, the ICL tribunals have tackled exactly these questions in the context of military, state and other group structures, and on the domestic level such questions are addressed when dealing with organised crime, mob violence, etc. It becomes difficult to assess why these scholars would make ('perform') such arguments about corporate criminal liability – perhaps one partial explanation, as Schwarzenberger has suggested (above Chapter 4A, Section 1), is that these lawyers are simply susceptible to fashions in the realm of political ideology – and argue within a certain liberal capitalist 'mood of the time'.[309] The absence of discussion on attribution doctrines suggests these authors implicitly consider liability of the corporation per se the desired option, as per Pomerantz (Chapter 3A, Section 6.1.2), who saw the practical advantage of not having to tie specific individuals to 'corporate acts'. As the trend ('fashion') may be corporate reification in other areas of IL (e.g., in ILIP, Chapter 2B – and arguably in international human rights law),[310] this may be catching on in ICL too. The notion of legal scholars arguing within a (structural/ideological) trend shows the limits of their agency (see Chapter 1, Section 4) and provides clues as to the creation of the 'unbreakable circle' referred to in Chapter 1.

3.3 *Legal Person Liability: the Systems View*

In the UK and other domestic legal systems that include the concept of corporate liability, it is possible to distinguish between 'artificial' corporate liability (i.e., liability based on the actions and/or intent of one or more individuals within the company using attribution or identification doctrines)[311] and what

308 *ICJurists Report*, p. 56.

309 Schwarzenberger 1950, p. 263.

310 E.g., Muchlinski 2007.

311 On the basis of the vicarious liability of the company for the acts of its agents, on the basis of the 'identification doctrine' where the state of mind of a 'directing mind' (a senior manager/director who is in actual control) and the acts of what Denning called the hands

the English criminal law standard text Simester et al. call '*corporate* corporate guilt'.[312] In domestic jurisdictions, there appears to be a trend towards the adoption of the latter construct. For example, in the UK the *Corporate Manslaughter and Corporate Homicide Act 2007* expresses the grounds of corporate liability in organisational terms,[313] while in Australia *corporate* corporate liability is independent of the liability of individuals through the idea of 'corporate culture'.[314] Authors (explicitly, as opposed to impliedly – above) arguing from an analogous perspective in ICL regard a company (or in Nollkaemper et al.'s term: a system) as something qualitatively different from the sum of the individuals 'inside' it. *Corporate* corporate liability, according to Van den Herik, serves where 'indicting one individual may not capture what really happened, may not provide an appropriate narrative, may not address the crime properly, and may not place the responsibility where it belongs'.[315] What *really* happened, according to this view, is that a 'corporate culture' has 'induce[d] employees to act in a certain way that they would not do outside the corporation'[316] (taking the notion of corporate *anomie* one step further) and what is therefore really responsible is the corporation *itself*. In many ways this line of thought echoes that of the turn of the last century (see Chapter 2A), that of Frankenstein, Inc.,[317] the idea that corporations, like robots, would become intelligent and outgrow their makers ('it's not me, it's the corporation').[318] The interesting twist or contradiction, though, is that current scholars now take this reified model, the 'structure of irresponsibility', to be part of the solution, rather than the source of the problem.

The 'corporate culture' construct responds to the argument that corporations cannot have criminal intent as such[319] by assuming intent from the

(workers) is attributed to the corporation, or on the basis of aggregation – where the acts and intentions of a number of individuals within the corporation are aggregated so as to constitute 'the company's crime' even if such acts were not criminal on their own – see generally, Simester 2010, pp. 279–80. See also Lederman 2001.

312 Simester 2010, pp. 281–3.

313 Appendix E.

314 Where 'corporate culture means an attitude, policy, rule, course of conduct or practice existing within the body corporate generally or in the part of the body corporate in which the relevant activities takes place', The Criminal Code Act 1995, Art. 12.3(6) (Australia). See also, generally, Wells 2001.

315 Van den Herik 2010, p. 365.

316 Van den Herik 2010, p. 364.

317 Wormser 1931.

318 Steinbeck 1939, p. 38 (Ch. 2A, § 6).

319 Other arguments may include, for example, that holding corporations to account in (international) criminal law would not actually reduce the incidence of 'corporate crime' in

culture prevailing amongst (and presumably created/generated by) company employees and directors.[320] Criminal intent can, on the other hand, be seen as only an extension of the abstraction in other areas of law: while a corporation is frequently assumed to have 'intent to create legally binding obligations' in contract law, why could it not have 'intent to permanently deprive' in criminal law, or even 'intent to destroy all or part of a group' in ICL? It would seem easier to imagine 'intent' in 'purely economic' transactions, while seemingly non-economic, seemingly irrational behaviour (which may and indeed *must* also be rational – Chapter 2A) requires more imagination, and perhaps more convoluted 'theories' to be applied. However, CSR and corporate crime in domestic law is making such much easier. Indeed, such is acceptance of the abstraction of law, that '[t]he social constructedness of these concepts [intentionality and agency] make them amenable to credible reformulations that are suitable for a new paradigm of corporate agency and responsibility'.[321] I discuss this further in Chapter 6. For now, it is worth pausing with (a rare critic) Jeßberger at the question, 'do we really want to punish the establishment of a "culture" encouraging or tolerating illegal behaviour like slavery?'[322]

Aside from its use in the formulation of ideas around corporate liability, 'system criminality' *could* be a useful term when employed to identify, analyse and criticise exactly those *structural* factors causing 'deviant' behaviour, as per the 'Systemkritik' offered in the Chabarovsk trial. The inherently 'psychopath' corporation (as Bakan described it – Chapter 2A), conducive to immoral behaviour (the 'amoral calculator'), the 'structure of irresponsibility', creates a distance between the employee/manager and affected party – not to mention even the physical distance between bosses at desks in London or New York vs. workers on hunger wages carrying out orders in a 'host state' (Marx's term *alienation* could be used by analogy), and in fact *mandate* amoral behaviour solely focused on surplus value extraction. Thus far, such analyses have been mostly left to criminologists who have not yet started work on ICL.[323]

The concept of 'system criminality' obscures real power relations within a corporate structure, where some individuals have more agency to decide

general, or that such an 'artificial' idea as corporate criminal liability negatively affects the 'special nature' of criminal law.

320 Schwarzenberger 1952, p. 263.

321 Voiculescu 2007.

322 Jeßberger 2016, p. 339.

323 See further Ch. 6, and the work of Tombs, Pearce, Gray and others cited there. But see Van Baar and Huisman 2012 as a rare contemporary application of domestic criminology to an ICL case.

courses of action (within the frame of the corporate profit mandate), while others (subordinates/workers) do not have the freedom to refuse orders. The contradiction between individual/collective (structure/agency) does not (even logically, as I will argue below) mean that corporate liability is the answer.

3.4 *'Shared Responsibility'*

The latest iteration in international law theory of large-scale, multi-actor crime is that of 'shared responsibility' – again proposed by one of Andre Nollkaemper's large EU-funded research projects at the University of Amsterdam.[324] It responds, and to some extent concretises, the idea of system crime by seeking to discover how responsibility (in ICL but also in non-criminal international law) can be allocated to different parties involved in, and somehow considered to bear partial/joint responsibility for, a situation.[325] In 1996, *The Economist* editorialised, that when governments fail to uphold international human rights, the moral burden of responsibility shifts to corporate management.[326] The theory of shared responsibility seeks to *legalise* that responsibility (connecting it to the move to legalise CSR – Chapter 6). Ostensibly motivated by the same pragmatic stand HRW displayed in 1996, and called for by authors such as Stewart,[327] the 'shared responsibility' approach lifts corporate (and other non-state actors such as armed groups) into responsibility-carrying subject status in international law. The consequent flip side of placing expectation on corporations operating in 'failed' or weak states pragmatically is that it allocates responsibility in both senses of the word – liability for failure as well as legitimate authority to govern and fulfil/provide. The latter is the main effect in terms of corporate legitimacy translating into corporate power. Moreover, the 'shared responsibility' project envisages responsibility shared not only in the context of weak states, but generally. It furthermore reopens the question of state crime, alongside that of corporate crime.[328] In international law, some argue that state crime never went away, or indeed is now again an 'emerging norm',[329] which, if

---

324 Generally, see the 'Shares' project at the University of Amsterdam: http://www.sharesproject.nl/about/project/project-description/.

325 On MNEs specifically, see Karavias 2015.

326 Anon. *The Economist* 1996, pp. 15–16, as cited by Human Rights Watch, https://www.hrw.org/legacy/about/initiatives/corp.html.

327 Stewart 2012.

328 State responsibility (non-criminal) for Genocide was discussed, and found, in the Bosnian genocide case at the International Court of Justice: *Application of the Convention on the Prevention and Punishment of the Crime of Genocide (Bosnia and Herzegovina v. Serbia and Montenegro)*, Judgment, ICJ Reports 2007, 43, at 116, para. 173.

329 E.g., Jørgensen 2003; Bonafè 2009.

taken together with the criminological movement on 'state crime',[330] comes to appear realistic. Although, given that the dividing line between 'state' and 'corporation' seems harder to draw than ever, it is difficult to imagine concretely how 'shared responsibility' would work, the concept does reflect the coincidence of interests (and thus responsibility) between members of the global capitalist class engaged in either, or often both, state and corporation. Altogether, these theoretical developments through scholarly projects support the emergence or existence of a norm of corporate ICL.

4 From Theory to Practice: Recent Developments

In his 'Mapping' Report of 2007, Special Representative on Business and Human Rights John Ruggie stated,

> corporate responsibility is being shaped through the interplay of two developments: one is the expansion and refinement of individual responsibility by the international ad hoc criminal tribunals and the ICC Statute; the other is the extension of responsibility for international crimes to corporations under domestic law. The complex interaction between the two is creating an expanding web of potential corporate liability for international crimes – imposed through national courts ... In this fluid setting, simple laws of probability alone suggest that corporations will be subject to increased liability for international crimes in the future.[331]

In this chapter, I have discussed the 'refinement of individual responsibility' by the international tribunals, and I will continue on this theme in Chapter 5. Domestic corporate crime was discussed in Chapter 2A and will return in Chapter 6. Ruggie here 'forgets' the role of scholars and scholarship in the development of IL. The negotiators of the Rome statute were not able to agree on the inclusion of corporate liability – reportedly because of the lack of a broad support for the concept induced by scholarship and public discourse more widely. The fact that this situation is now changing – as reflected in current developments in IL practice – is partly through the increasing scholarly support for CICL discussed above. In other words, legal development is driven by a practice-theory dialectic, which of course on closer inspection looks more

330 E.g., the International State-Crime Initiative, see http://www.statecrime.org/.

331 *Ruggie* (2007) *'Mapping' Report*, para. 27.

like a 'panlectic' operating in a more complex environment. I discuss below how the development of corporate ICL is (1) driven by the IL scholars embedded within the internal bureaucracies of international law, here, specifically the UN's International Law Commission, and (2) how this is induced by the demand for 'punity' created by the obvious involvement of business actors in violations, and finally (3) how this is driven by specific individual lawyers driving the development of law and making use of a tipping point moment.

4.1 *ILC Crimes against Humanity*

The UN International Law Commission, mentioned above in 4A and in the introduction to this Chapter 4C, was established by the General Assembly in 1947 to 'initiate studies and make recommendations for the purpose of ... encouraging the progressive development of international law and its codification'.[332] From the early post-Nuremberg and Tokyo period, it has been deeply engaged in the development of ICL (see Chapter 4A), while also drafting the definitive rules on, most notably, state responsibility (mentioned above – the deleted Art. 19 on state crime) and producing a draft statute for a permanent international criminal tribunal (Introduction, above). From 2014 the ILC has been working on crimes against humanity (CaH). The ILC recognised that of the three main areas of ICL, genocide (criminalised in the 1948 Genocide Convention), war crimes (defined by the 1949 Geneva Conventions and Protocol I) and crimes against humanity, only the latter has not been addressed through a global treaty that requires states to prevent and punish such conduct and to cooperate with other states toward those ends.[333] As such, a 'global convention on crimes against humanity appears to be a key missing piece in the current framework of international humanitarian law, international criminal law, and international human rights law'.[334] Thus, in the years following the ILC has commissioned reports by a special rapporteur (IL scholar Sean D. Murphy), sought views from member states, and instructed a drafting committee to prepare articles for a new convention. According to its report, '[t]he Commission decided to include a provision on liability of legal persons for crimes against humanity, given the potential involvement of legal persons in acts committed as part of a widespread or systematic attack directed against a civilian popu-

332 21 November 1947, the General Assembly adopted resolution 174 (II) on the Establishment of the International Law Commission.

333 ILC 2013 recommendation of the Working-Group on the long-term programme of work (see syllabus: A/68/10, annex B) (*ILC 2013 Recommendation*).

334 Ibid. para. 3.

lation'.[335] Discussions have followed on the desirability of corporate liability for CaH amongst member states,[336] and the ILC Drafting Committee has provisionally adopted on first reading a number of articles including Art. 5(7):

> Subject to the provisions of its national law, each State shall take measures, where appropriate, to establish the liability of legal persons for the offences referred to in this draft article. Subject to the legal principles of the State, such liability of legal persons may be criminal, civil or administrative.[337]

This provision draws inspiration from the provisions found in environmental, terror financing and anti-corruption treaties mentioned above (4A, Section 2.3), and specifically, it is modelled on the 2000 Optional Protocol to the Convention on the Rights of the Child on the Sale of Children, Child Prostitution and Child Pornography (see 4A),[338] the instrument supported by the vast majority of states.[339]

Several states expressed satisfaction with the proposed CaH convention provision, while others seemed somewhat hesitant to take this next big step in the context of CaH instead of child rights.[340] One limiting factor currently is that

335 Report of the International Law Commission on the Work of its Sixty-Eighth Session UN Doc. A/71/10, 2016, para. 42.

336 Id. paras. 36–46 (commentary on draft Art. 5(7)) Crimes against humanity: Text of draft articles 5, 6, 7, 8, 9 and 10 provisionally adopted by the Drafting Committee on 25, 26, 30 and 31 May and 1 and 2 June 2016, and of draft article 5, paragraph (f), provisionally adopted on 7 July 2016, A/CN.4/L.873, 3 June 2016; Third Report on Crimes against Humanity by the Special Rapporteur by Sean Murphy UN Doc. A/CN.4/704 (*3rd report of Sean Murphy*).

337 Sixty-Ninth Session: Crimes against humanity: Texts and titles of the draft preamble, the draft articles and the draft annex provisionally adopted by the Drafting Committee on first reading, UN Doc. A/CN.4/L.892.

338 Statement of the Chairman of the Drafting Committee, Mr. Pavel Šturma, 21 July 2016 on presenting the report on liability of LP: 'the formulation of the proposed paragraph 7 was based on that contained in article 3, paragraph 4, of the Optional Protocol to the Convention on the Rights of the Child on the Sale of Children, Child Prostitution and Child Pornography, adopted in 2000, and which had been widely accepted by States. Currently, 173 States are parties to the Optional Protocol. The paragraph also reflected the core aspects of the corresponding article in the Convention against Corruption, and would be supplemented by an explanation in the commentary that the liability identified in the paragraph was without prejudice to the criminal liability of natural persons provided for elsewhere in the draft article'.

339 Report of the International Law Commission on the work of its sixty-eighth session A/71/10 Chapter VII Crimes against humanity, para. 43.

340 E.g., '107. Slovenia welcomed the progressive approach taken by the Commission in includ-

the accompanying extradition procedures in the document are drafted to apply to natural persons only.[341] This signals that the presence of the norm per se is considered more important (or more readily available) than its enforcement. Enforcement is not discussed either in the ILC's Drafting Committee, or by the Special Rapporteur, or by the states whose comments are included in the ILC's reports.[342] Enforcement is, however, specifically desired by the drafters of the Malabo Protocol.

4.2 *Malabo Protocol*

On 27 June 2014, the African Union (AU) adopted the Protocol on Amendments to the Protocol on the Statute of the African Court of Justice and Human Rights (Malabo Protocol),[343] which extends the jurisdiction of the (not yet established) African Court of Justice and Human Rights to crimes under international law and transnational crimes. In response to the selectivity or anti-African bias of the ICC (see 4A), the Malabo Protocol seeks to create the African Union's own international criminal chamber as part of the larger African Court.[344] The Malabo Protocol, explicitly in recognition of the suffering experienced by African Union subjects at the hands of corporate actors,[345] moreover provides that 'the Court shall have jurisdiction over legal persons, with the exception of States' (Art. 46C).[346]

---

ing liability of legal persons for the commission of crimes against humanity in article 5, paragraph 7. As rightly noted by the Special Rapporteur, the criminal liability of legal persons had become a feature of several national jurisdictions. Legal persons could have significant involvement in the suffering of victims of crimes against humanity. While recognizing the need to address that aspect, his delegation supported the inclusion of paragraph 7, which was progressive in nature but allowed States considerable flexibility in its implementation. That paragraph could constitute a notable novelty and an important contribution to the ongoing work'. Report of the International Law Commission on the work of its sixty-eighth session (A/71/10).

341 *ILC Third report on crimes against humanity* by the Special Rapporteur Sean Murphy, para. 34. A/CN.4/704, 23 January 2017.

342 Treaties with legal person criminalisation provisions often contain a provision aimed at excluding states from criminal liability.

343 Protocol on Amendments to the Protocol on the Statute of the African Court of Justice and Human Rights Assembly/AU/Dec.529(XXIII) (2014) (*Malabo Protocol*).

344 *AfricLaw* 2016, 28 October, 'South Africa's Intention to Withdraw from the Rome Statute of the International Criminal Court: Time to Seriously Consider an African Alternative?'.

345 Sirleaf 2017, p. 77.

346 Article 46C.
Corporate Criminal Liability
1. For the purpose of this Statute, the Court shall have jurisdiction over legal persons, with the exception of States.

Thus far (June 2017) the Malabo protocol has been signed by nine out of 54 AU member states, and ratified by none.[347] However, a recent call by the AU for African states to withdraw from the ICC,[348] as well as some states' responses to this call,[349] may increase this number.

As well as the selectivity point combined with the 'devastating impact of corporate malfeasance in Africa',[350] the judicial treatment of corporate abuse by the African Committee on Human and Peoples' Rights will have motivated the development. Notably, in *Social and Economic Rights Action Centre v. Nigeria* of 2001,[351] Nigeria was held to have violated a number of articles of the African Charter,

> 1. The communication alleges that the military government of Nigeria has been directly involved in oil production through the State oil company, the Nigerian National Petroleum Company (NNPC), the majority shareholder in a consortium with Shell Petroleum Development Corporation (SPDC), and that these operations have caused environmental degradation and health problems resulting from the contamination of the environment among the Ogoni People.
> 2. The communication alleges that the oil consortium has exploited oil reserves in Ogoniland with no regard for the health or environment of the local communities, disposing toxic wastes into the environment and local waterways in violation of applicable international environmental standards. The consortium also neglected and/or

---

2. Corporate intention to commit an offence may be established by proof that it was the policy of the corporation to do the act which constituted the offence.
3. A policy may be attributed to a corporation where it provides the most reasonable explanation of the conduct of that corporation.
4. Corporate knowledge of the commission of an offence may be established by proof that the actual or constructive knowledge of the relevant information was possessed within the corporation.
5. Knowledge may be possessed within a corporation even though the relevant information is divided between corporate personnel.
6. The criminal responsibility of legal persons shall not exclude the criminal responsibility of natural persons who are perpetrators or accomplices in the same crimes.

347 *Malabo Protocol.*

348 AU Assembly/AU/Dec 590 (XXVI) 30–31 January 2016 (*African Union ICC Decision*); see also Eberechi 2009.

349 *Mail & Guardian* 2017, 8 March, 'South Africa Revokes ICC Withdrawal'.

350 Sirleaf 2017, p. 77. For an argument that corporate abuse, especially in the Niger Delta, warrants the ICC's extension to corporations, see Ezeudu 2011, p. 11.

351 155/96 Social and Economic Rights Action Center (SERAC) and Center for Economic and Social Rights (CESR) / Nigeria.

failed to maintain its facilities causing numerous avoidable spills in the proximity of villages. The resulting contamination of water, soil and air has had serious short and long-term health impacts, including skin infections, gastrointestinal and respiratory ailments, and increased risk of cancers, and neurological and reproductive problems.

3. The communication alleges that the Nigerian Government has condoned and facilitated these violations by placing the legal and military powers of the state at the disposal of the oil companies. The communication contains a memo from the Rivers State Internal Security Task Force, calling for 'ruthless military operations'.

The AHRC's decision, however, is non-binding, and it remains to be seen whether its urging Nigeria (which did not participate in the proceedings) to prosecute past offences, compensate appropriately and respect human and environmental rights, partly through controlling its state oil company and the Shell venture's activities, has any effect. The Commission decided it was not competent to give its views about the conduct of the private companies, directly. A more recent civil case against Shell for its alleged complicity in the killing of Ken Saro Wiwa and other activists in the Dutch (home state) courts would suggest past wrongs have not been repaired.[352] The Malabo Protocol seeks to compensate for the AHRC's lack of competence over corporations as well as Western host states' 'laissez-faire' when it comes to their MNCs' activities extraterritorially.[353]

4.3 *STL Contempt Cases*

Special Tribunal for Lebanon Prosecutor Norman Farrell is a well-known scholar and proponent of corporate ICL. Even though criminal jurisdiction over legal persons is not expressly provided for in the statute of the Special Tribunal for Lebanon (a tribunal 'of international character set up by the UN Security Council to prosecute those responsible for the assassination of Lebanon's former Prime Minister Rafiq Hariri'), the prosecutor commenced cases against

352 'Nigeriaanse Weduwen klagen Shell aan wegens executies', De Volkskrant 29 June 2017, http://www.volkskrant.nl/4503351.

353 But see European Coalition for Corporate Justice, 'France adopts corporate duty of vigilance law: a first historic step towards better human rights and environmental protection', 21 February 2017, available at: http://corporatejustice.org/news/393-france-adopts-corporate-duty-of-vigilance-law-a-first-historic-step-towards-better-human-rights-and-environmental-protection.

two companies at the Tribunal. Farrell was replaced in his role in these cases by an independent (amicus curiae) prosecutor. The cases concerned the release by two media companies (and two individual journalists) of information about two tribunal STL trial witnesses, which the prosecutor considered amounted to 'contempt of court' and 'obstruction of justice' and which potentially endangered the witnesses and the ongoing judicial process.[354] The Defence in the first case against Al Jadeed and New TV challenged the Tribunal's jurisdiction over legal persons on the basis that this is not provided for by the tribunal's statute. In July 2014, the Contempt Judge found that the Tribunal lacked jurisdiction over legal persons mainly because the term 'person' in ICL has hitherto always been understood to mean natural persons.[355] An Appeals Panel overturned this decision by a two-to-one majority on 2 October 2014, holding that the 'ancillary jurisdiction' of the court (i.e., the jurisdiction to hear cases necessary to ensure the proper running of the tribunal and fair trial of the defendants) could extend to legal persons, meaning that the case against Al Jadeed could proceed.[356] It was held that 'the existence of criminal responsibility for legal persons best enables the Tribunal to achieve its goals to administer justice in a fair and efficient manner by ensuring that no one is beyond the reach of the law' and (after a thorough review of corporate criminal liability in domestic jurisdictions) that the Contempt Judge had given 'insufficient weight to the relevance of state practice on the criminalization of the conduct of legal persons in the interpretation of the word "person"'.[357] Moreover, having reviewed ICL starting with Nuremberg cases, it found 'corporate criminal liability is on the verge of attaining, at the very least, the status of a general principle of law applicable under international law'.[358] Here we see the scholarly lines of argumentation discussed above echoed in a court setting.

The Tribunal ultimately found that Al Jadeed was not guilty because it was not shown that the journalist in question acted on authority of the company.[359]

---

354 The charges were brought under Rule 60 *bis* (A) of the Rules of Procedure and Evidence (STL-BD-2009-01-Rev.9), which states that the Tribunal may hold in contempt persons who knowingly and wilfully interfere with its administration of justice.

355 *New TV S.A.L. Karma Mohamed Tashin Al Khayat*, Case No. STL-14-05/PT/CJ, Decision on motion challenging jurisdiction and on request for leave to amend order in lieu of an indictment, 24 July 2014.

356 *New TV S.A.L. Karma Mohamed Tashin Al Khayat*, Case No. STL-14-05/PT/AP/AR126.1, Appeals Panel, Decision of 2 October 2014 on interlocutory appeal concerning personal jurisdiction in contempt proceedings, at para. 58 ('the practice concerning criminal liability of corporations and the penalties associated therewith varies in national systems').

357 Ibid, at para. 60.

358 Ibid, at para. 67.

359 See *Al Jadeed S.A.L./New T.V.S.A.L. Karma Mohamed Tahsin Al Khayat*, Case No. STL-14-

In the 2016 Appeal judgment the court once again thoroughly examined corporate liability, (para 174ff.) mentioning the work of the Human Rights Council International Open Ended Working Group and the Malabo Protocol's Art. 46(c). It confirmed corporate liability and found Lebanese law the appropriate source for a model of attribution in *casu*.[360]

In the second case, Akhbar Beirut S.A.L. was on 16 July 2016 found guilty of knowingly and wilfully interfering with the administration of justice and fined €6,000.[361] In this judgment, the tribunal judge noted the absence of a mode of attribution specific to corporate *corporate* liability in ICL, and again applied the Lebanese legal standard.[362] Both cases show that when needed, courts can and *will* find a solution in law to close any gaps left by ICL rules. Most significantly, the *New TV* Appeals Panel echoed precisely the scholarly arguments at the center of this book: 'many corporations today wield far more power, influence and reach than any one person' and '[e]xcluding them from the reach of the Tribunal and in essence shielding them from prosecution for contempt, therefore, makes little sense'.[363]

4.4 *The Practice-Theory Dialectic*

The ILC performs a standard-setting role in IL and from its inclusion of corporate liability in the draft Convention on Crimes against Humanity we can see that CICL is starting to make headway in IL. In the Malabo Protocol's adoption of a specific CICL provision, we can see how this is spurred on by the demand for and denial of 'corporate punity' in the face of decades-long abuses by corporate actors in a Third World setting. Finally at this tipping point, the CICL legal scholar Norman Farrell was, in a pragmatic move, able to set in motion the first-ever prosecution of corporations in an 'international' tribunal, leading

05/T/CJ, Contempt Judge, Public redacted version of judgment on 18 September 2015, Special Tribunal for Lebanon, para. 55; *Al Jadeed S.A.L./New T.V.S.A.L. Karma Mohamed Tahsin Al Khayat*, Case No. STL-14-05/A/AP, Appeals Panel, Decision of 8 March 2016. One of the three judges dissented on the company's acquittal, holding that the acts of the director could be attributed to the corporation: *Al Jadeed S.A.L./New T.V.S.A.L. Karma Mohamed Tahsin Al Khayat*, Case No. STL-14-05/A/AP Public redacted version of judgment on Appeal 8 March 2016 Nosworthy Dissent para. 26.

360 *Al Jadeed S.A.L./New T.V.S.A.L. Karma Mohamed Tahsin Al Khayat*, Case No. STL-14-05/A/AP, Public redacted version of judgment on Appeal 8 March 2016 paras. 174–96.

361 *Akhbar Beirut S.A.L. & Mr Al Amin*, Case No. STL-14-06/T/CJ Public redacted version of judgment, 16 July 2016.

362 Ibid, paras. 44–5.

363 *New TV S.A.L. Karma Mohamed Tashin Al Khayat*, Case No. STL-14-05/PT/AP/AR126.1, Appeals Panel, Decision of 2 October 2014 on interlocutory appeal concerning personal jurisdiction in contempt proceedings, at paras 82, 84.

ions hailed to be 'of great significance' for business and human rights development, and of 'utmost symbolic importance'.[364]

5 Conclusion to 4C

We can see now that in spite of the distaste (partly motivated by the fear of collective punishment) for the idea of corporate liability in the style of Nuremberg (declaring an organisation criminal so as to enable prosecution of its 'members'), and in the absence of rational justifications for it, CICL seems to be on the verge of being widely accepted. Moreover, attribution models of corporate crime (holding a corporation liable for the acts of one of its members, usually a 'controlling officer') are not finding traction in the literature, but '*corporate* corporate liability' or corporate crime emptied of or detached from individuals (as the corporation itself, Chapter 2A), is now gaining popularity.

In his most managerial mode, Ruggie suggests,

> Some operating environments, such as conflict-affected areas, may increase the risks of enterprises being complicit in gross human rights abuses committed by other actors (security forces, for example). Business enterprises should treat this risk as a legal compliance issue, given the expanding web of potential corporate legal liability arising from extraterritorial civil claims, and from the incorporation of the provisions of the Rome Statute of the International Criminal Court in jurisdictions that provide for corporate criminal responsibility.[365]

So, while 'corporate complicity' is in business terms nothing more than 'risk management' issue (giving rise to a whole new compliance and certification industry, liability insurance and derivatives market), I will argue in Chapter 6 that *corporate* corporate liability has the effect (if enforced and even if not enforced) of legitimising the corporation and corporate capitalism, and of 'collectively punishing' both workers and the rest of society and the environment.

---

364 Bernaz 2015, pp. 313 and 321.

365 *Ruggie (2011) Report*, pp. 25–6.

6 Conclusion to 4A, 4B and 4C: Who Let the *Dogmatisierung* out?

It is said that 'in the latter period of ICL's lifespan [one] can ... speak of (some extent of) doctrinalisation of ICL'.[366] The relevance of analysing the 'competing narratives' (on 'what is ICL' and 'what is it for', 'how is ICL liability allocated/distributed' and 'who is a subject of ICL') is that 'norm production is also, transnationally, increasingly the result of professional networks of experts who control certain fields'.[367] The system produces scholars like Cassese, Clapham, Nollkaemper and Farrell, and their work in turn affects the direction of development of ICL.

Although some authors speak of ICL as a 'maturing' system, which is undergoing doctrinalisation or *Dogmatisierung*, from the first part of this chapter this may appear as mere wishful thinking. There is no consensus on the nature, sources, content and subjects of ICL. 'There is no international legislative policy'[368] on international criminal law, and '[n]one of the proponents so far has developed a doctrinal framework, nor a methodology, that combines the approaches of international law, comparative criminal law and procedure, and international human rights law'.[369] I have argued that what is driving ICL development is not policy, but structure, the form of law and the logic of capitalism. Within this structure, the development of ICL has many different instigators (and those wishing to be), with different interests: practitioners on the defence, prosecution or judicial sides, NGO activists and careerists, market-orientated non-government organisations or MaNGOs,[370] legal and other scholars, public servants, elected leaders of powerful and less powerful states, etc.[371] *A propos* Ferdinandusse, the various claims regarding the content of law serve 'as techniques in a hegemonic struggle for greater control between different actors in international law'.[372] Those victorious in this struggle (at any given point, on any given issue) can employ ICL ideology: ICL's 'canned morality' (and appeals to and channelling of affect to the ICL PO Box) to support their interests. The competition between these actors takes place within the structural constraints of the form of law and the logic of capitalism. In Chapters 5 and 6 below I assess

---

366 See, generally, Bassiouni 2003; Van Sliedregt 2003, Ch. 1.

367 Dezalay and Garth 1996 (no pagination), cited by Mégret 2010, para. 33.

368 Bassiouni 1987, p. xxxiii.

369 Bassiouni 1987, p. xxxiv.

370 Shamir 2004, pp. 680–1.

371 And those playing more than one of these roles, e.g., Cassese: the passage in Cassese's textbook about a dissenting opinion at the ICTY by Judge Cassese, which the textbook author declares is obviously the correct view (Cassese 2008, p. 23).

372 Ferdinandusse 2006, p. 158.

this dynamic further, and examine how ICL shapes our responses to certain instances of suffering differently from others, and who wins and who loses as a result of this.

Notwithstanding the 'constructive' efforts of scholars in the first four approaches outlined above, Schwarzenberger's scepticism has taken us to the 'dark side' of ICL.[373] Moreover, Pashukanis's analysis of criminal law generally suggests, in Clapham and Marks's words, that 'international criminal processes are more a matter of asserting authority and monopolising virtue than of curbing violence and reducing security [*sic*]'.[374] I would add to this, shielding corporate actors from relationships of responsibility and/or rendering risk accountable alongside profit. The 'ICL industry' producing 'canned morality' would almost implicitly divert our attention from the structural causes of conflict – even if they are hiding in plain sight, right in front of us.

Clapham and Marks query, 'Can individual responsibility be pursued in ways that do not impede efforts to understand and *address* the political, economic, social, and indeed legal, conditions within which international crime becomes possible?'[375] To this question I turn next.

373 Cf. Kennedy 2005.

374 Clapham and Marks 2005, p. 234.

375 Clapham and Marks 2005, pp. 234–5, emphasis added.

CHAPTER 5

Contemporary *Schreibtischtäter*: Drinking from the Poisoned Chalice?

1 Introduction

In the preceding chapter, I discussed the construction of a humanitarian 'foundational narrative' for ICL and showed that ICL has developed a reasonably intricate scheme that would seem to be capable of application to business actors – including even the 'desk murderers' or Schreibtischtäter carrying out the seemingly innocuous tasks that lead or contribute to 'physical' crimes at some distance removed from the office. It might seem logical, after the various wars and other serious conflicts in the past decades, that, as in Nuremberg, the international community would seek to prosecute those military, civilian, business and professional elites thought to have been responsible for the outbreak of the conflicts and any violations committed in it. This would seem appropriate (that is, fitting within the discourse and *raison d'être* given to ICL), especially considering the vast rise of reports detailing business involvement in conflict in the past two decades (mostly by Western, multinational corporations). It would also honour Justice Jackson's promise to 'drink from the poisoned chalice' – or face ICL scrutiny – when the cup was offered back to the victorious powers of World War Two. An informal survey reveals that since the 1940s no individual businessperson has been tried for international crimes in an international forum, with minor exceptions, some of which are discussed below.[1] Domestic courts likewise have not often applied ICL to businesspeople. In fact, commentators treated the trial of Dutch chemicals broker Frans Van Anraat in the Netherlands in 2004 as a novelty. Here I analyse and discuss these exceptional cases, paying particular attention to the modes of responsibility employed in the case, the discussion of *mens rea*, the identity of the initiator of the case and the political context of the crime as well as the prosecution. I include also a section on 'host state cases', a particularly interesting category

1 Those I have been able to check: I rely on various networks, mailing lists and personal contacts here, including with the Center for Constitutional Rights in New York, the American Civil Liberties Union, Sherpa, Business and Human Rights Resource Centre, European Coalition for Corporate Justice, CorpWatch, CorporateWatch, The European Centre for Constitutional and Human Rights, Reprieve, Redress, the Universal Jurisdiction Yahoo group, and others.

that, considering the importance attached to the 'principle of complementarity' – that is, the idea that the international criminal tribunals should be a last resort only used when a relevant state is unable or unwilling to prosecute suspects itself – in ICL,[2] should be, but clearly is not, the main category here.

I argue here, that, as was the case in Nuremberg and Tokyo, the international criminal trials, held at the ICTR, ICTY, SCSL and other venues, exclude economic causes from the explanations of the conflicts. In fact, these trials serve to cover up the economic causes. We also see ICL being used to 'open up' the legal market, to carry through wholesale political and legal reforms largely for the benefit of capital. In conclusion it can again be said, as Telford Taylor suggested, that 'humanitarian' laws are at base really commercial laws, despite appearances.

I conclude that the non-application of ICL to businesses and businesspersons has given rise to NGOs and so-called 'cause lawyers' stepping in and, in a variety of ways, seeking to change this situation by 'strategic lawyering' (see further Chapter 6). I discuss a number of cases against business actors – but since these are exceptional I also devote some attention to situations that have not been the subject of court action.

As noted above (Chapter 4A, Section 1) after the Cold War, the time was finally considered right for a 'New ICL' to be institutionalised on the supranational level. In 1993 the International Tribunal for the Former Yugoslavia was founded, on an ad hoc basis; the Rwanda Tribunal followed soon after; and the negotiations for the final piece of the IL puzzle, a permanent international criminal court, began. The ICTY was created at a moment when the UN Security Council was stepping up its peace enforcement activities, implementing a new 'internationalism' with a strong liberal foundation, or varnish, depending on one's point of view.[3] However, although the Security Council forms a broader coalition than the post-World War Two Allies, it is a more selective, elitist group of leaderships than what would become the membership of the ICC. Moreover, both the ICTY and ICTR were set up to intervene in *internal* armed conflicts, which supports the argument that global institutionalised ICL forms part of an effort to shift power to a global governance regime, and is aimed to allow for intervention in less powerful states/against individuals less favourable to prevailing power structures, further breaking down (or keeping porous) sovereignty and penetration of GCC interest/hegemony or eventually, allowing for intra-class competition (as per Chapters 2B and 4A).

2 Reflected in, e.g., Art. 1 of the *1998 ICC Statute*.

3 Koskenniemi 2002.

2 The Balkans and the ICTY

It is perhaps fitting that the first concerted international application of ICL post-Cold War would come in the context of a conflict borne out of an economy in systemic transition. According to Woodward, the cause of the Balkans War was the process of transformation from a communist state to a market economy by means of a shock therapy stabilisation.[4] A critical element was a programme designed to resolve the sovereign debt crisis.[5] Yugoslavia was struggling to repay its IMF loans, and ten years of 'austerity measures' (combined with a loss of the health and education benefits of communism) fuelled resentment against the Serbian and other local elites who were seen to be benefitting from the market liberalisation. The reforms demanded by creditors demanded political suicide: to reduce the state's ability to govern internally.[6] At the same time, Europe/the West saw the opportunity to embrace the new territories 'coming in from the cold', territories they saw as forming part of, in Zbigniew Brzezinski's words, the so-called '"Eurasian Balkans" – the vast, unstable, but energy-rich region extending from South-eastern Europe and the Horn of Africa, through the Middle East, into Central Asia, Afghanistan and Pakistan'.[7] Where in Nuremberg and Tokyo ICL had been used to ward off communism, here it was being used to 'welcome back' nations coming out of communism, into the (Western) European fold.[8]

The UN Security Council (UNSC) adopted the resolution founding the Tribunal under Chapter VII of the UN Charter, which governs the UNSC's power to take measures aimed at restoring international peace and security. The hope was expressed in the resolution's preamble that prosecution of the crimes committed in the former Yugoslavia would restore international peace and security.[9] The establishment of the tribunal – an unprecedented move by the UNSC – followed the failure to reach agreement on military intervention. Aside from this stated objective, what could have been the reasons behind the ICTY? Was this the opportunity that the international leadership had been waiting for, to revive ICL? It was also the opportunity to create a particular narrative of the

---

4 Woodward 1995, esp. Ch. 5 and p. 114ff.

5 Woodward 1995, p. 15.

6 Woodward 1995, p. 114. See also Woodward 2002.

7 Callinicos 2009, p. 217, citing Brzezinski 1998.

8 Cooperation with the ICTY was and is seen as a precondition for the former Yugoslav republics to join the European Union; see, e.g., Del Ponte 2005; Serbian leaders recently relinquished Ratko Mladic in an effort to smooth EU-entry; see, e.g., *The Guardian*, 26 May 2011.

9 *UNSC Res. establishing the International Criminal Tribunal for the former Yugoslavia*. For a discussion of the legality of this basis, see Zahar and Sluiter 2008, pp. 6–9 who conclude it was probably lawful.

conflict,[10] to distract from, and to *justify*, the controversial 'illegal but legitimate' nature of the NATO intervention[11] (as with Tokyo/Hiroshima and Nuremberg/Allied bombing of German cities), and to divert arguments as to the West's early inaction and later arguably ineffective or counterproductive intervention in the conflict[12] – as an 'insurance policy' for being found complicit by 'posterity'.[13] There had been much media coverage of the atrocities committed, and public demand for action was great.[14] Also, it was a way of ensuring 'regime change' in an area where the leadership was still very popular despite the allegations (and later convictions) of atrocities.[15] In this sense the West's campaign had been successful: when Serbia proved unwilling to implement the economic reform demands imposed by the West, NATO could rely on public support for a bombing campaign supposedly to 'save' Kosovar Albanians, which would force Milošević's (and Yeltsin's) hand – as was later testified by Strobe Talbott, US Deputy Secretary of State at the time.[16] The ICTY's cases, however, would only confirm this, the 'ethnic strife' version of the story.

The ICTY case files and decisions do not give the impression that business played a major role in the Balkan conflict. However, there is mention of an important role for arms and drugs, and even organ traffickers, the illicit business ventures finding a profit opportunity in the war.[17] Woodward mentions deliberate intervention by Western bankers which served to escalate the pace of political disintegration in Yugoslavia[18] and describes how the German government persuaded the EU to recognise Croatia's independence (in 1992) to serve German economic interests and substantial investments in the area.[19] With a focus on the local, and the illicit, the role in the story of the macro-level and the 'normal' is excluded from the historical record created by the ICTY.[20] It suited both internal and external interests to portray the conflict as caused by ethnic nationalism rather than by socio-economic circumstances. According

10 Carla del Ponte specifically mentioned this objective in her speech (Del Ponte 2005).

11 See *The Kosovo Report*, pp. 185–98, which labeled the Kosovo intervention as illegal, but legitimate.

12 Woodward 1995, p. 374.

13 Megret 2002, p. 1273.

14 Zahar and Sluiter 2008, p. 6, fn. 13.

15 Del Ponte 2005.

16 Talbott 2005, p. xxiii.

17 Del Ponte 2005.

18 Woodward 1995, p. 145.

19 Woodward 1995, pp. 185–6.

20 On the (tenuous) distinction between illicit and 'normal' business, see Chiomenti 2006, p. 288.

to Woodward: 'contrary to those who argue that these wars represent a clash of civilizations – between civilized and barbarian, Western and Balkan, Roman Catholic and Eastern Orthodox, Christian and Muslim – the real clash is social and economic. Territorial war for new states does not put an end to the political, economic, and social conflicts raised by the policies of global integration but that lost out to the nationalist juggernaut; they are simply played out under the guise of ethnic conflict'.[21] Creating such a narrative secures the systemic causes from attack, and moreover helps to create the impression (aimed at the external audience) that the economic system will not lead to conflict in *our* communities, which do not share the same peculiar ethnic divisions and history.[22]

In relation to business, the ICTY may have served another goal. Carla del Ponte, the ICTY's Chief Prosecutor at the time gave a speech at Goldman Sachs in London in 2005 (as part of a fundraising tour), in which she explained the purpose of the tribunal, and international criminal justice more broadly, in different terms.[23] She told the audience,

> It is dangerous for companies to invest in a State where there is no stability, where the risk of war is high, and where the rule of law doesn't exist. This is where the long term profit of the UN's work resides. We are trying to help create stable conditions so that safe investments can take place. In short, our business is to help you make good business.[24]

ICL can thus be seen as a way to insert (a particular type of) law into a system that may have been developed or run on a different basis. ICL as law reform would fit into the national law reforms already ongoing as part of the IMF intervention – which may have been threatened by a break-up of the state – and fits into the broader legal (and economic) reform programmes carried out by the international intervention in the various former Yugoslav republics.[25] Ultimately these EU and UN administrations would also have had the purpose to restore such law and order as would be conducive to 'good business', presumably with the ultimate aim of the new states joining the EU.

Towards the end of her speech in London, Carla del Ponte said, 'International justice is cheap. The yearly cost of the Tribunal is less than one day of US milit-

21 Woodward 1995, p. 271.
22 This point is also made by Kamola 2008, p. 54.
23 Del Ponte 2005.
24 Ibid.
25 Generally, Tzouvala 2016, especially Ch. 5.

ary presence in Iraq ... Our annual budget is well under 10 % of Goldman Sachs' profit during the last quarter. See, I can offer you high dividends for a low investment'.[26]

The ICTY receives part of its funding from non-state voluntary donors.[27] In the ICTY such donations are not regulated by the Tribunal's Statute.[28] The ICC, however, is explicitly entitled to receive donations from amongst others, corporations, according to Art. 116 of its Statute. Although such donations would have to conform to the UN Policy on Voluntary Donations,[29] corporate funding of ICL institutions is not likely to be conducive to corporate accountability in the sense that is mainly used now, although it will aid *accountability* in the Weberian sense (Chapter 2A) – the ability of corporate actors to calculate costs and benefits and therefore optimise their exposure to human rights-relevant situations.

3 International Criminal Tribunal for Rwanda

A year after the ICTY was founded, the ICTR was created on the same basis. The ICTR did in fact indict and prosecute a small number of businesspersons. I first examine these, before placing them in context in Section 2.2.6 below.

3.1 *Kabuga and Rutaganda*

Félicien Kabuga was first indicted by the ICTR in August 1997.[30] As of today Kabuga remains listed as 'accused at large' by the ICTR.[31] In the 2004 indictment Kabuga is 'at all times referred to in this indictment: (a) a wealthy and influential businessman'.[32] The indictment states that under President Habyar-

26 Del Ponte 2005.

27 See the ICTY website, section 'Support and Donations', http://www.icty.org/en/content/support-and-donations. In the ICTY such donations are not regulated by the tribunal's Statute. The ICC, however, is explicitly entitled to receive donations from, amongst others, corporations, see Art. 116 1998 ICC Statute. See also *PICT Financing Report*.

28 It would be interesting to see if Goldman Sachs did indeed donate; it is not mentioned in the ICTY's annual reports of 2005 or 2006; the financial reports are not linked on the ICTY website. ICTY officials have thus far (25 November 2018) not responded to my correspondence on this matter (dated 29 June 2011).

29 Although this policy is mentioned on the ICTY website, I was unable to locate the document itself and have written (in 2011) to the UN information desk requesting it – no response received as of 29 August 2017.

30 *Kabuga Indictment*.

31 Accused at large, ICTR website, http://www.unictr.org/Cases/tabid/77/default.aspx?id=12&mnid=12.

32 In addition, he is described as (b) President of the Comité Provisoire of the Fonds de

imana's rule, political and financial power in Rwanda was consolidated within a tight circle (known as the Akazu).[33] Kabuga was a prominent member. As such, he 'wielded great power and influence', having de facto control and authority over (among others) the Interahamwe,[34] while he also had control of the employees of the business enterprises that he headed, such as Kabuga ETS.[35]

Kabuga is accused in the indictment of (count 1) conspiracy to commit genocide, (count 2) genocide, or alternatively, (count 3) complicity in genocide, (count 4) direct and public incitement to commit genocide, and (count 5) extermination as a crime against humanity.[36] It describes how, allegedly, Kabuga, with other powerful and influential figures (including Nahimane and Barayagwiza, about whom below), agreed on a plan to destroy in whole or in part the Tutsi ethnic group, and to this end 'to plan, fund, launch and operate a radio station (RTLM) in a manner to further ethnic hatred between the Hutu and the Tutsi'.[37] As president of the radio station, Kabuga had *de jure* control of the programming, operations and finances of the station, and by virtue of his chairmanship of the management committee, also *de facto* control. The radio station, during the genocide, functioned as a major source of information to the population of Rwanda, broadcasting information identifying the location of Tutsi and urging members of the Rwandan population to find and kill all Tutsi.[38]

In addition, Kabuga is said to have chaired a number of meetings where the *Fonds de Défense Nationale* ('FDN') was established, a fund to provide financial and logistical support and arms to the Interahamwe. The indictment states: 'At least one of these meetings was attended by a large number of businessmen from Gisenyi and other major trading centres'.[39] The support received from FDN is said to have facilitated the Interahamwe in attacking, killing and injuring thousands of civilian Tutsis.[40] Specifically, logistical support in the form of vehicles said to have been provided by Kabuga were used to transport arms

Défense Nationale, or the National Defence Fund (the 'FDN'); and (c) President of the Comité d'Initiative of Radio Television Libre des Milles Collines SA ('RTLM'), *Kabuga Indictment* 1.

33 Literally, 'little house', a term used for the inner circle of the President (Glossary, *Nahimana TC Judgment* 5).

34 Literally, 'those who kill together', the Hutu militia (Glossary, *Nahimana TC Judgment* 5).

35 *Kabuga Indictment*, p. 2.

36 Ibid.

37 *Kabuga Indictment*, p. 6.

38 *Kabuga Indictment*, p. 9.

39 *Kabuga Indictment*, p. 14.

40 *Kabuga Indictment*, p. 15.

and Interahamwe militia to massacre and killing sites, and transport Tutsis to a site where they were killed. Kabuga is also said to have ordered the employees of his company ETS to import machetes, and to have ordered members of the Interahamwe to distribute these among their group. The Interahamwe is then said to have used machetes during the period between 7 April and 17 July 1994 to exterminate the ethnic Tutsi population.[41]

Not much more can be said about Kabuga, other than that his indictment shows (alleges) a situation in Rwanda similar to those of Nazi Germany and Japan, with a small group of political, military and business leaders directing the conflict. According to a Kenyan newspaper, senior US official Mr Stephen Rapp, the ambassador-at-large for War Crimes, claims Kabuga is presently in Kenya,[42] despite a USD five million bounty on his head.[43] In 2003 the UNSC called on all states and Rwanda, Kenya and neighbouring states in particular, to intensify cooperation with the ICTR, and specifically to help bring Kabuga and all other at large indictees to the ICTR.[44] Nevertheless, Kabuga is said to be able to travel freely, including trips to Sweden and Norway in 2008.[45]

Rutaganda, who was also a prominent businessman from an elite family, had joined the MRND party, as he thought it would best protect his economic interests.[46] He became the second vice president of the Interahamwe on the national level. He was convicted of genocide for ordering massacres in Kigali and elsewhere, and two counts of crimes against humanity (murder and extermination) for (among others) also directly participating in the massacres.[47] In his case, the Prosecutor had submitted: 'He endorsed the genocidal plan of the interim government. At the same time, he seized the occasion for his personal gain'.[48]

3.2 *Government 1*

Due to his failure to appear before the court, Kabuga's case was separated from that of the other accused in what was to become known as the trial of

41 *Kabuga Indictment*, p. 29.

42 *Nation*, February 10, 2010; see also *ICG Rwanda Report*, pp. 15–16.

43 Rewards for Justice Website, U.S. Department of State's Counter-Terrorism Rewards Program, available at: https://rewardsforjustice.net/english/.

44 *UNSCRes. 1503*.

45 African Press International, 8 May 2008.

46 *Rutaganda TC Decision*, pp. 24–30.

47 *Rutaganda TC Decision*, p. 472. Rutaganda was portrayed in the movie *Hotel Rwanda*.

48 *Rutaganda TC Decision*, p. 460 (iii).

'Karemera et al.',[49] which reached its final judgment on 21 December 2011 with Ngirumpatse and Karemera being given life sentences.[50]

In this trial, Karemera (a lawyer by training and a minister in the Interim Government of 8 April 1994), Ngirumpatse (also a lawyer, president of the MRND political party, former diplomat and general manager of an insurance company), and Nzirorera (a former MRND parliamentarian and Minister for Industry) were accused of (amongst other charges) conspiracy to commit genocide, direct and public incitement to genocide, genocide or alternatively complicity in genocide.[51] In order to commit the crimes alleged, they are said to have formed a 'joint criminal enterprise' together with groups of named political leaders and prominent businessmen. The businessmen named include Barayagwiza, Kabuga, Musema and Bagaragaza (*among others*) – the indictment details some of the meetings that are said to have taken place between the accused and these businessmen, including one meeting organised by Kabuga with the aim of setting up a fund 'to support the interim Government in combating the enemy and its accomplices'.[52] Ngirumpatse is also accused of having participated in the creation and financing of RTLM, which counts toward his incitement charge.

3.3 *Nahimana/Radio Cases*

The other case of relevance here is that against Ferdinand Nahimana (a Professor of History and Dean of the Faculty of Letters of the Rwanda National University), Jean-Bosco Barayagwiza (a lawyer) and Hassan Ngeze (journalist and editor with the Kangura newspaper),[53] co-founders and board members of RTLM. This case is known as the 'media case', as it deals with the power of those in control of the media to 'create and destroy fundamental human values'.[54] These accused had been part of the Akuza and co-founders, promoters and contributors to RTLM.[55]

The Appeals Chamber upheld the Trial Chamber's findings that RTLM's broadcasts after 6 April 1994 contributed significantly to the commission of

---

49 *Karemera Kabuga Severance Decision.* Kabuga was also included in a second indictment: *Bizimana Indictment Decision.*

50 *Karemera TC Decision.*

51 *Karemera Indictment*, p. 1.

52 *Kabuga Indictment*, p. 50.

53 *Nahimana TC Decision; Nahminana Appeals Judgment.*

54 *Nahminana Appeals Judgment*, p. 3.

55 Other businessmen involved in RTLM were shareholder Georges Rutagando (above) and Joseph Serugendo, also a board member of RTLM and a radio engineer; see *Serugendo Decision.*

acts of genocide.[56] The significance of this is that if Kabuga is brought to trial this will be an important point in his disfavour. While the Appeal Chamber dismissed the genocide charges against Nahimana, it confirmed his 'command responsibility', in that he had been a superior of RTLM staff who had the material ability to prevent or punish the broadcast of criminal utterances by such staff, and that there was no doubt that he knew or had reasons to know that his subordinates at RTLM were about to, or had already, broadcast utterances inciting the killing of Tutsi, and that he had not taken necessary and reasonable steps to prevent or punish incitement by RTLM staff. Thus Nahimana's conviction on the count of direct and public incitement to commit genocide pursuant to Art. 6(3) of the ICTR Statute was upheld, as was the finding of guilt for persecution as a crime against humanity.[57] Zahar has criticised this judgment amounting to 'judicial activism', arguing the radio broadcasts did not amount to incitement nor did Nahimana and Barayagwiza have 'command responsibility' over the radio station.[58]

3.4 *Musema*

Another example of the application in the business context is the ICTR prosecution of *Musema*.[59] The *Musema* case concerned the director of one of the largest state-owned tea factories who had been present at the site of mass killings of Tutsi, and on several occasions had actually participated alongside his employees. His employees on some of these occasions wore the company uniform and drove the company cars. The Trial Chamber found that also for those acts where he had not himself participated, 'Musema incurs individual criminal responsibility, on the basis of Article 6(1) of the [ICTR] Statute, for having ordered, and, by his presence and participation, aided and abetted in the murder of members of the Tutsi group'. The Chamber established that Musema had *de jure* and *de facto* control over his employees and was personally present at the attack sites. From this the court inferred that 'he knew, or at least ought to have known, that his subordinates were about to commit [the acts in question] ... Musema, nevertheless, failed to take the necessary and reasonable measures to prevent the commission of said acts by his subordinates, but rather abetted

56 *Nahimana Appeals Judgment.*

57 The hate speeches and speeches calling for violence against Tutsi that were broadcast on RTLM themselves were considered acts of persecution (pp. 310–13). Should Kabuga ever face trial, he, having been the president in overall charge – his role as such is mentioned in the discussion (p. 796) – may be convicted on the same basis.

58 Zahar and Sluiter 2008, p. 195, fn. 205.

59 *Musema TC Decision; Musema Appeals Decision.*

in their commission, by his presence'.[60] For these events, and also for the occasions where he had participated[61] Musema was found guilty of genocide and extermination as a crime against humanity[62] and sentenced to life imprisonment.[63]

3.5 *Bagaragaza*

Bagaragaza was the Director General of OCIR/Thé, the government office that controlled the tea industry in Rwanda.[64] In this capacity, he controlled 11 tea factories, which employed approximately 55,000 persons. He was also the vice president of Banque Continentale Africaine au Rwanda ('BACAR') and a member of the comité préfectoral of the MRND political party in Gisenyi préfecture.[65] He was also a member of the Akazu.[66]

Bagaragaza pleaded guilty and the ICTR accordingly found him guilty of complicity pursuant to Art. 6(1) of the Statute for complicity in genocide pursuant to Art. 2(3)(e) of the ICTR Statute.[67] The tribunal found Bagaragaza had substantially contributed to the killings of more than 1,000 Tutsis who sought refuge at Kesho Hill and at Nyundo Cathedral. His contribution consisted in allowing the Interahamwe to use company vehicles and fuel, allowing the company employees to participate [the indictment had accused him of having *ordered* those over whom he had authority and/or *instigated* those over whom he did not][68] in the attacks, being heavily armed, having concealed arms in company factories since 1993. He also paid a significant sum of money to the militia leader after having been told money was needed to buy alcohol as an incentive for the Interahamwe to carry out its attacks. Bagaragaza *knew* about the attacks and the Interahamwe's genocidal intent through several meetings with the group's leaders. He did not himself share the genocidal special intent.[69]

60 *Musema TC Decision*, p. 905.

61 In the indictment around 15 very similar events all with slightly different details, sometimes he is said to have joined, sometimes just watched, sometimes he ordered persons to carry out certain acts, e.g., 4.6–4.10.

62 *Musema TC Decision*, p. 7.

63 *Musema TC Decision*, p. 8.

64 *Bagaragaza TC Decision*, p. 18.

65 Ibid.

66 *Bagaragaza TC Decision*, p. 19.

67 *Bagaragaza TC Decision*, p. 27.

68 *Bagaragaza TC Decision*, p. 16.

69 *Bagaragaza TC Decision*, pp. 24, 25.

3.6 *Discussion*

These cases paint the picture of the Akazu as the small group of political and military leaders plus businessmen and members of various professions centred around President Habyarimana, similar to the leadership exercised by the 'Himmler Circle of Friends' in Nazi Germany and the *zaibatsu* families with the court of the emperor in Japan. While showing this element, the 'economic case' as it was told at Nuremberg is not made here. The indictments and decisions do not go into *why* Musema and the others did what they did. Of course, in criminal law generally *motive* is only of evidentiary interest as opposed to *mens rea*, which is an essential element of a crime. Yet even the motivation behind, e.g., the 'intent to destroy, in whole or in part' is not discussed in these cases. The ICTR indictments give a limited historical context to the occurrences of 1994. The judgments give only a brief account, a summing up of events. The bigger question of why the powerful majority Hutus seem to have wanted to exterminate a minority is not answered in the court documents or in the (legal) scholarly writing on the ICTY cases.[70]

Economist Michel Chossudovsky has asserted that 'the civil war was preceded by the flare-up of a deep-seated economic crisis. It was the restructuring of the agricultural system which precipitated the population into abject poverty and destitution'.[71] His assessment of the cause of the genocide can be summarised as follows. Rwanda had inherited a colonial export economy based on coffee (constituting 80 percent of its foreign exchange earnings) and a colonial rentier administration based on local chiefs who each controlled local plantation labour forces. The Germans and later the Belgians used a system of 'divide and rule' between the ethnic groups, placing one in control of the other (a tactic that has prevailed during the various Western interventions undertaken since). Communal lands were transformed into individual plots for cash crop production. When the International Coffee Agreement collapsed, coffee prices plummeted, and famines erupted throughout the Rwandan countryside. The state fell into disarray, and austerity measures imposed by the IMF made the health and education systems collapse. At the high point of the economic crisis and the moment fighting started, multilateral 'balance of payment aid' came in but was likely at least partly diverted to arms acquisition, which was aided by a French bilateral military aid package.[72]

---

70 Chossudovsky 1996, pp. 938–41. See also Ansoms 2005; Reyntjens 2006; Reyntjens 2004; Ansoms 2009; Reyntjens 2011; Marysse 2007.

71 Chossudovsky 1996, p. 938.

72 Chossudovsky 1996, p. 938. A very similar account is given by Kamola 2008.

Jeffremovas describes a situation similar to that of the ICTY above: 'The media have emphasized the role of ethnicity and ethnic politics in [the Rwandan genocide] and imbued them with an air of inevitability as one more example of "tribal violence" in Africa. [In fact,] economic recession, economic restructuring, population growth, patterns of elite access to power, regional politics, civil war, "democratization", the politics of other countries of the Great Lakes Region, and international policies al; played a role in the move to the genocide'.[73] She also shows how the violence was not strictly Hutu/Tutsi but instead the elite, which in places consisted both of Hutus and Tutsis, against the people. Keane and Jeffremovas both argue the killings were systematic and planned well in advance, with Keane adding that '[t]he theology of hate espoused by the extremists was remarkably similar to that of the Nazis in their campaign against the Jews prior to the outbreak of the Second World War'[74] and 'Hutu extremism was essentially a useful tool by which the corrupt elite that ran the country could hold on to power'.[75]

Peter Uvin has described how the *Bazungu* (lit. 'white folk') had played out the Hutus, Tutsis and Twa against each other from the nineteenth century onward, creating local elites through allying one or the other group to their own economic and political leadership.[76] After decolonisation, those *Bazungu* that remained in Rwanda controlled the large financial resources coming in through the development aid system, fostering a system of clientalism. Uvin also argued that the international aid system contributed to a climate of structural violence: inequality, exclusion, prejudice and hatred, which fed the frustration and enmity that led to the killings.[77]

In this context we can reassess the case against Musema. An economic study into the 1994 genocide carried out at Leuven specifically mentions Musema:

> The tea-plantations and tea-factory in Gisovu Commune were the only object of interest for the Habyarimana regime [in this region]. The plantation and the factory were managed by Ocir-thé and directed by Alfred Musema, member of the Akazu. Since Rwanda only had six tea-plantations, the Gisovu plantation was of considerable importance for export earnings. With the decline in the price of coffee at the end of the eighties, an increase in tea production and tea export became an import-

73 Jefremovas 2002. For similar arguments, see also the book by BBC reporter Fergal Keane: Keane 1995, p. 21.

74 Keane 1995, p. 10.

75 Keane 1995, p. 25. This view is also expressed by Uvin 1998, p. 54.

76 Uvin 1998, esp. pp. 13–39, and see also Kamola 2008, pp. 63–7.

77 Uvin 1998, p. 103ff. On the role of international aid, see also Van der Walle 2001.

> ant objective for the Habyarimana government. The local peasant population was very hostile to the establishment of the tea-plantation since their land was expropriated. The peasant families had to move to other, less fertile land or even migrate.[78]

Uvin, moreover, concludes that only the Akazu members really benefited from the tea production, and that the tea industry was a good example of rent-seeking by the Akazu members, most of the tea producing facilities having been financed by donor agencies.[79] This scenario is reminiscent of the clearances described in Chapter 2A and also the colonial land reform in Chapters 2B and 3B.

The fact that genocide is often discussed in terms of irrational, emotional racist ideologies may lead to the subconscious exclusion of business actors from the scope of possible perpetrators because business actors are thought to make decisions on rational grounds. However, looking at Musema above, plus the particular economic context of the region, it is conceivable that Musema wanted to exterminate (part of) the Tutsi in order to clear land for the tea plantation, for example. Uvin has suggested that 'it is ... possible that some participated in the genocide in the hope to appropriate other people's land'.[80] With Musema's deeper motivation remaining unexplored, this open question is answered by our expectations and the common emotive discourse of ICL rather than by a number of possible alternatives.[81]

It is not my aim here (nor in this book in general) to give definitive explanations for historical events or the motivations of actors, but rather to comment on the interaction between law and material reality. While ICL purports to allocate responsibility to some causes, the responsibility of many others (persons, factors, processes) is concealed. In particular, the narrative generated by the ICTR cases discussed here, while to some limited extent including local economic disparity, excludes the wider role of the market, and in particular, the international economic angle in the form of colonial processes, post-colonial processes, and possibly neo-colonial processes of the World Bank, the IMF and

78 Verwimp 2001.

79 Ibid, citing Uvin 1998; see also Longman 2001, p. 169.

80 Uvin 1998, p. 55.

81 The *Musema* decision is criticised elsewhere as having '*nothing* to do with business activities at all' (Wilt 2010, p. 871). Vest states, 'it seems absolutely clear that the production of tea as such does not constitute any risk of perpetrating or contributing to war crimes, crimes against humanity and genocide at all', which stands in contrast with his recital of the example of business leaders' involvement in forced displacement earlier in the article (2010, p. 868) but is perhaps emblematic of the attitude that 'neutral' acts are unlikely to amount to crimes (generally, 2010, pp. 863–4).

the donor community in general.[82] The role of particular Western corporations is, even in the critical literature, difficult to find.[83]

A better source on more detailed information of third state and company involvement is NGO reports. The international human rights NGO Human Rights Watch ('HRW') in its January 1994 report, 'Arming Rwanda', describes six foreign governments supplying arms to Rwanda before, during and after the Rwandan war with Uganda. Corporate involvement, among others, was alleged by means of credit guarantees by the French bank Credit Lyonnais.[84] HRW suggests another hidden responsibility in its 1995 report 'Rwanda/Zaire: Re-arming with Impunity: International Support for the Perpetrators of the Rwandan Genocide' written by Kathi Lynn Austin (see below).[85] HRW's report and further reports led to an UNSC Resolution on the basis of which a Commission of Inquiry was set up to investigate arms supplies. The Commission published its Interim Report, S/1996/67, in which it describes approaching governments of Bulgaria, China, France, Seychelles, South Africa and Zaire, each of which was accused of having exported arms to Rwanda.[86] So while the ICTR includes Rwandese businesspersons on its case list, it also excludes, and thereby potentially conceals the involvement of Western banks and arms companies.

4 Special Court for Sierra Leone

Moving to the West of Africa, the indictment of former Liberian president Charles Taylor by the Special Court for Sierra Leone ('SCSL') (which was established pursuant to a bilateral agreement between the UN and Sierra Leone)[87] is of interest here because of its potential impact as a persuasive precedent for prosecuting arms dealers and others who aid and abet perpetrators through financing or engaging in trade with a violating party. Charles Taylor was indicted while still a sitting president for (amongst other offenses) having aided and

82 Also, post-genocide Rwanda went through a programme of drastic privatisation. Gisuvo Tea Company was bought by an Indian-owned British company, McLeod-Russell, the largest tea producer in the world: *All Africa*, 14 February 2011, while the bulk of coffee production was bought up by US giants Costco and Starbucks: *Development Afrique*, 10 November 2009.

83 Slapper and Tombs have suggested that academics may self-censor research on corporate crime (especially on specific companies) for fear of loss of research funding or libel suits by corporations, which may be winnable but are expensive to defend (Slapper and Tombs 1999, pp. 231–2).

84 *HRW Arming Rwanda Report*.

85 *HRW Rearming Rwanda Report*.

86 *UNSC Commission of Inquiry on Great Lakes Arms Flow*.

87 *SCSL Agreement*.

abetted abuses perpetrated by the Sierra Leoneans.[88] While Charles Taylor is generally seen as a political leader and not a businessman as such, he is said to have supplied arms to the Revolutionary United Front ('RUF') in Liberia in exchange for 'diamonds and other riches'.[89] In the 2003 indictment this is phrased as follows:

> 20. To obtain access to the mineral wealth of the Republic of Sierra Leone, in particular the diamond wealth of Sierra Leone, and to destabilize the State, the ACCUSED provided financial support, military training, personnel, arms, ammunition and other support and encouragement to the RUF, led by FODAY SAYBANA SANKOH, in preparation for RUF armed action in the Republic of Sierra Leone, and during the subsequent armed conflict in Sierra Leone.[90]

Writing in 2004, HRW heralds the Taylor indictment, saying it will set a precedent to prosecute other arms dealers around the world for complicity in international crimes.[91] In the same publication, HRW noted that 'the SCSL is also currently investigating other arms suppliers'.[92] Considering Charles Taylor's well-publicised international relations, amongst others with supermodel Naomi Campbell and the Russian arms dealer Viktor Bout, the SCSL had the opportunity to prosecute a significant number of businesspersons on the conflict diamond and arms circuits.

On 17 March 2006, an Amended Indictment was filed in the Taylor case in which the paragraph above no longer appears,[93] nor does it appear in the Second Amended Indictment of 2007, which is rather brief, and vague about the exact way in which Taylor may have aided and abetted the crimes committed by the RUF and others:

> By his acts or omissions in relation to the below described events, the ACCUSED, pursuant to Article 6.1. and, or alternatively, Article 6.3. of the Statute, is individually criminally responsible for the crimes alleged below.[94]

88 *Taylor 2007 Indictment.*

89 *HRW Weapons Report* 2. See also *BBC News*, 20 May 2010, 'Noami Campbell may be subpoenaed to appear as a witness at Taylor trial for receiving blood diamonds'.

90 *Taylor 2003 Indictment.*

91 *HRW Weapons Report.*

92 *HRW Weapons Report.*

93 *Taylor 2006 Indictment.*

94 Ibid. The crimes below include, 'crimes against humanity, violations of Article 3 Com-

Once again, it seemed the case would focus on ethnic differences rather than economic resources that could potentially involve many Western individuals and companies. Nevertheless, Charles Taylor was convicted in April 2012 in a 2,539-page judgment – with his crimes including aiding and abetting, as well as planning (through arming, training and financing), war crimes and crimes against humanity, including summary executions and numerous massacres, widespread and systematic rape, mutilation and torture, and large-scale forced conscription and use of child combatants, committed by the Revolutionary United Front (RUF) and the Armed Forces Revolutionary Council (AFRC), which were Sierra Leonean rebel groups.[95] His dealings with international arms dealers Viktor (here: Victor) Bout, Sanjivan Ruprah, Leonard Minin and the Oriental Timber company (Kouwenhoven's company – see below) are mentioned,[96] as are companies harmed by Taylor's and the RUF's activities, such as the international mining company Sierra Rutile,[97] and a passing mention of private military company Executive Outcomes being asked for help in running Freetown (and later to protect diamond interests in Kono)[98] occurs on the same page.[99] The judgment found a mixture of political and profit motivations behind the various crimes,[100] and was widely and positively received, especially by the human rights community; it was criticised only for omitting the crimes within Liberia.[101] The judgment relies on the reports of the panel of experts established by Security Council Resolution 1306,[102] for some of its data on arms and diamond trading and more international company names appear in the sections describing this report – e.g., a Ukrainian company and one based in

mon to the Geneva Conventions and of Additional Protocol II and other serious violations of International Humanitarian Law, in violation of Articles 2, 3 and 4 of the [SCSL] Statute'.

95 *Taylor Trial Judgment*, pp. 2476–7.

96 *Taylor Trial Judgment*, pp. 1656, 1766.

97 Now, a subsidiary of Australian mining company Iluka Resources: http://www.sierra-rutile.com/media/merger-with-iluka-resources.

98 *Taylor Trial Judgment*, p. 838.

99 *Taylor Trial Judgment*, p. 20, see also p. 856.

100 *Taylor Trial Judgment*, e.g., p. 846 (attack on Kono because it was a diamondiferous area).

101 E.g. Human Rights Watch: 'Fugitives take notice: Justice can be done', May 15, 2012 https://www.hrw.org/news/2012/05/15/africa-fugitives-take-note-justice-can-be-done. Crimes within Liberia did not fall under the jurisdiction of the Special Court for Sierra Leone.

102 See Resolution 1306 (2000) Adopted by the Security Council at its 4168th meeting, on 5 July 2000, UN Doc. S/RES/1306 (UN S Res. establishing the panel of experts on Sierra Leone); Report of the Panel of Experts appointed pursuant to Security Council Resolution 1306 paragraph 19, relating to Sierra Leone, dated 20 December 2000, UN Doc. S/2000/1195.

Gibraltar.[103] Undoubtedly a vast number of other local and international corporations will have been involved in the trading, transport and financing of these crimes, but only Charles Taylor is accused here. While Charles Taylor can conveniently be described as an opportunist warlord and playboy, the 'business as usual' supply chains stay out of reach of ICL. The omission of other local and international corporate actors was not accidental: according to an anonymous lawyer at the SCSL: 'the court knows who the people supplying arms/buying diamonds are (outside of CT) but they aren't in any way pursuing them'.[104] Similar then to the ICTR, the SCSL paints a picture of conflict that conceals Western involvement and profit.

5 The ICC

Although the ICC does not have jurisdiction over legal persons, it could prosecute individual businesspersons (see Chapter 4B). The first Chief Prosecutor of the ICC, Louis Moreno Ocampo, has often expressed his wish to prosecute business actors, but neither Ocampo nor his successor Fatou Bensouda has thus far indicted any.[105]

5.1 *The Democratic Republic of Congo*

Sometimes business involvement in conflict comes up in other venues. For example, the International Court of Justice in *DRC v. Uganda* cited evidence that Ugandan military commanders had planned to exploit the DRC resources for business purposes; that Ugandan military aircraft had been used by businessmen to transport resources out of the DRC; and in conclusion that the Ugandan government was liable for acts of the military.[106] The ICJ is not in a position to tackle this issue, but the ICC could. An ICC statement of 2003 has

103 *Taylor Trial Judgment*, p. 1765.

104 Email to the author, 10 June 2010. In 2011 a US court convicted Viktor Bout of conspiracy to kill US citizens and officials, deliver anti-aircraft missiles and provide aid to a terrorist organisation (FARC), United States Department of Justice Press Release, 'International Arms Dealer Viktor Bout Convicted in New York of Terrorism Crimes: Bout Convicted on All Four Counts, Including Conspiring to Kill Americans and Conspiring to Provide Material Support to Terrorists'. Wednesday, November 2, 2011, available at: https://www.justice.gov/opa/pr/international-arms-dealer-viktor-bout-convicted-new-york-terrorism-crimes.

105 E.g., at *BLIHR* 2005.

106 *Armed Activities* 2005; Okowa 2007.

signalled the Prosecutor's interest in investigation of corporate involvement in international crimes in the DRC:

> the prosecutor will work together with national investigators and prosecutors in order to determine the contribution, if any, that these businesses are making to the commission of crimes in the DRC ... The Prosecutor of the ICC hopes that the prosecution of these cases [of alleged business practices fuelling atrocities] will contribute to the ongoing peace process [in the DRC] and ultimately yield stability for the DRC, fostering not just political stability but also *healthy markets*.[107]

However, the DRC list does not contain business actors as of June 2017.[108] According to one former ICC employee, this was, and still is, definitely an issue for many Congolese – in fact, one of the reasons that many Congolese have lost faith in the ICC precisely is that the ICC is only pursuing relatively low-level suspects (Lubanga, Katanga and Chui), not the big leaders nor the corporations.[109]

Ifeonu Eberechi has similarly argued that the ICC's failure to inquire into and effectively deal with the role of international actors and Western powers in promoting and exacerbating the various conflicts in Africa the ICC has in its docket, functions as a disincentive for African Union cooperation with the court.[110] In Chapter 4C, I discussed how this has led to the planning of an African Court of Human Rights, potentially with jurisdiction over corporations.

5.2 *Kenya*

In May of 2010 it was announced that the ICC would prosecute six 'political and business leaders' who are thought to have been responsible for the election violence in Kenya that claimed 1,200 lives in 2007/8.[111] The Prosecutor has whittled down an initial 20 potential defendants presented in March 2010,[112] to

---

107 *ICC Ituri PR*, emphasis added; see also *ICC Ituri Communications PR*.

108 See the ICC website, Situations, The Democratic Republic of Congo, available at https://www.icc-cpi.int/drc.

109 D. De Vos, 'Complementarity's Gender Justice Prospects and Limitations – Examining normative interactions between the Rome Statute and national accountability processes for sexual violence crimes in Colombia and the Democratic Republic of Congo', Ph.D. Thesis, European University Institute, submitted 2017; see also the ICC's 'Situation in the Democratic Republic of the Congo' page, available at: https://www.icc-cpi.int/drc.

110 Eberechi 2009.

111 *France 24*, 12 May 2010.

112 'The Office has presented a preliminary list of 20 political and business leaders to the

six. The Kenyan file raised the interest of the Pre-Trial Chamber for utilising the concept of 'state or organisational policy' in the latter, rather than the former meaning. In response to a request for clarification, the Office of the Prosecutor explained that 'state or organisational policy' can apply to non-state actors (here, political parties).[113] Making it clear that a political party can, in the Prosecutor's view, amount to an organisation for the purposes of the ICC Statute, the Prosecutor may be paving the way (indirectly) for corporate liability in ICL (see Chapters 4 and 6).[114] However, in this particular case no precedent was set, as in 2014 the case against Uhuru Kenyatta was vacated, while the charges against William Ruto, Kenya's deputy president, and former broadcaster, Joshua arap Sang, were dropped for lack of evidence in 2016, and the three other cases also failed, while three suspects remain at large.[115] Kenya is being accused of violating its obligation to cooperate with the ICC on all cases, and the Kenyan government is accused by Human Rights Watch of having 'set out to undermine the ICC while it turned its back on its responsibilities to provide justice and to stop threats against witnesses and human rights defenders'.[116]

6 Alternative Ways of Dealing with Business in Conflict

There are limited international interventions in business involvement in conflict by other means, mostly diplomatic.

6.1 *The UNSC Embargoes, Sanctions and Fact-Finding Missions*

When the UNSC decides that the use of force or the creation of a tribunal is not the appropriate option, Chapter VI of the UN Charter provides for other options of dealing with past, present or potential future international crimes. It seems that the preferred method for dealing with arms trade (when the need is felt

---

Judges, belonging to or associated with both parties, the PNU and ODM. As you know, this list was just indicative. It is not binding'. *Ocampo Kenya Statement* 2010.

113 *Prosecutor Organisation Indicators*, Appendix F.

114 On 31 March, Kenya filed a request to the Pre-Trial Chamber to declare the case inadmissible, on the basis that Kenya is investigating the issue itself: *Kenya Art. 19 Application*.

115 ICC Republic of Kenya page, available at: https://www.icc-cpi.int/kenya.

116 *Human Rights Watch, ICC*: Kenya Deputy President's Case Ends Witness Interference Undermined Trial, 5 April 2016, available at: https://www.hrw.org/news/2016/04/05/icc-kenya-deputy-presidents-case-ends. In the meantime, Kenyan claimants have filed a case against Unilever Plc in the UK courts, claiming that the UK-Dutch company failed to protect them – workers on a Unilever tea plantation – during the election violence: *AAA & Ors v Unilever* [2017]. On this type of litigation, see below Ch. 6.

to 'do something') is UNSC arms embargoes. Violations of such embargoes do not necessarily attract the same publicity as court cases do, and can be resolved diplomatically (or ignored).

In 2000, the President of the Security Council asked the UN Secretary General to appoint a panel of experts to examine the illegal exploitation of natural resources in the Democratic Republic of the Congo and the connection between such exploitation and the conflicts in the area.[117] This move was the first time at this level that conflict and private economic activity in the natural resources sector was the subject of investigation. The Panel's mandate was extended four times, ending with a *final* Final Report in October 2003. In its previous, 2002 Final Report, the Panel described having found three 'elite networks' of politicians, military and business leaders that each controlled the natural resources in three separate areas controlled by the governments of the DRC, Uganda and Rwanda.[118] It also found a direct link between the exploitation of natural resources and the ongoing conflict in the region and abuses that included the use of child forced labour.[119] In this report, it also made the 'unparalleled' move of naming 29 companies and 54 individuals, whose association with the elite groups was well documented.[120] The Panel recommended the imposition of financial restrictions and travel bans. It further listed 85 companies (among which many UK, Belgian and other Western firms) that it found to be in breach of the OECD Guidelines for Multinational Enterprises.[121]

117 *UNSC Congo Panel Request*, Appendix F.

118 *UN SC Congo 2003 Report*, pp. 25–64. 'The networks consist of a small core of political and military elites and business persons and, in the case of the occupied areas, selected rebel leaders and administrators. Some members of the elite networks occupy key positions in their respective Governments or rebel groups ... The elite networks ensure the viability of their economic activity through control over the military and other security forces ... The networks monopolize production, commerce and fiscal functions ... The elite networks form business companies or joint ventures that are fronts through which members of networks carry on their respective commercial activities' (p. 21).

119 *UN SC Congo 2002 Report*, pp. 149–54.

120 *UN SC Congo 2002 Report*, Annex I and Annex II.

121 *UN SC Congo 2003 Report*, Annex III. The OECD Guidelines for Multinational Enterprises are 'recommendations addressed by governments to multinational enterprises operating in or from adhering countries. They provide non-binding principles and standards for responsible business conduct in a global context consistent with applicable laws and internationally recognised standards. The Guidelines are the only multilaterally agreed and comprehensive code of responsible business conduct that governments have committed to promoting' (Guidelines for Multinational Enterprises, Annex to the Declaration of 11 June 1976 by Governments of OECD Countries on Investment and Multinational Enterprises, last updated in 2011, available at: http://mneguidelines.oecd.org/guidelines/) (*OECD Guidelines*).

However, in its 2003 Final report, the Panel removed a number of these companies and indicated others as 'resolved', which commentators have taken to show that

> the panel did not manage to counter political pressure by business lobbies and governments generated by its unprecedented step of naming specific TNCs [transnational corporations]. This is reflected in the Panel's 2003 Final Report, which raises many questions with respect to the Panel's ultimate categorization of companies and its listing of cases as resolved without including further information.[122]

In addition to the Panel's findings, the Security Council imposed an arms and 'related material' embargo on the Kivu and Ituri districts of the DRC[123] and established a panel of experts (sanctions committee) to monitor compliance with the embargo.[124] One of the tasks of the group was:

> (b) To examine, and to take appropriate action on, information concerning alleged violations of the measures imposed by paragraph 20 of resolution 1493 and information on alleged arms flows highlighted in the reports of the Panel of Experts on the Illegal Exploitation of Natural Resources and Other Forms of Wealth in the Democratic Republic of the Congo, identifying where possible individual and legal entities reported to be engaged in such violations, as well as aircraft or other vehicles used.

Kathi Lynn Austin, one of the Experts appointed to the panel, at an international conference in The Hague stated that the Security Council informally instructed the panel to disregard information related to non-African companies and individuals violating the embargo or otherwise contributing to the arms flow into the relevant localities.[125] Nevertheless, the panel gathered this information, and Austin is now hoping to bring Western corporate involvement in the Congo conflict to light by taking this information to US and possibly other domestic courts (see below, Chapter 6).[126]

---

122 Papaioannou 2006, p. 283.

123 *UN S Res.1493 – Congo Arms Embargo.*

124 *UN S Res. 1533 – On the establishment of a committee to examine the implementation of the measures imposed by resolution 1493* (2003).

125 Austin 2010.

126 Ibid. See also, https://www.conflictawareness.org.

The absence of business representatives from the ICC's DRC trial list, the UN Security Council's decision to opt for an embargo instead of setting up a tribunal or urging the ICC to prosecute, and the Security Council's apparent wish to protect Western corporate interests, as alleged by Kathi Lynn Austin, would seem to underline the unlikeliness of Western corporate actors becoming the subject of an ICL prosecution. What is remarkable, at the same time, is the fact that Austin, having described the abuse of power in the political institution of the UN, continues to have faith in law itself, and to believe that domestic legal institutions will recognise the truth of her story and deliver 'justice'. It is on this 'faith' by cause lawyers and others in the (domestic) legal system that the system continues to thrive. I focus on this briefly in the next section and again in Chapter 6.

7 ICL on the Domestic Level

If reading ICL literally, taking ICL's word seriously, then according to the 'principle of complementarity', the enforcement of ICL should occur primarily on the domestic level.[127] Pursuant to the *Geneva Conventions* of 1949 (and other conventions such as the ICC Statute, for member states) states have obligations to enact national laws criminalising certain specific activities, and in respect of a number of these, they have the obligation to seek out and prosecute or extradite individuals suspected of these crimes.[128] According to the principle of universal jurisdiction (which exists in CIL as well as in treaties), certain crimes that violate obligations of a *ius cogens* nature (e.g., torture, genocide, apartheid) can potentially be tried by any state, regardless of the nationality of the perpetrator or the place where the crime is said to have occurred.[129] All in all, it would seem, that according to the discourse ICL can (*should*) be used on the domestic level with the ability to make serious inroads into combating the prevalence of international crimes. Depending on national laws of the jurisdiction, cases can either be brought by prosecutorial authorities at their own instigation (which is rare for various reasons, not least cost), by private parties if such is possible in a domestic legal system (e.g., in France) or as a result of a complaint lodged on behalf of victims (by NGOs, victims' groups or private (cause) lawyers). Immigration authorities play a role in the detection and detention

---

127 See generally, Ferdinandusse 2008, pp. 482–520; Ferdinandusse 2009.

128 See further Arts. 1 and 146 of the *Fourth Geneva Convention, 1949*.

129 On the principle of universal jurisdiction, see, e.g., Cryer et al. 2010, pp. 50–63; Zahar and Sluiter 2008, pp. 496–503.

(or expulsion) of war crimes suspects.[130] In particular, Rwandan refugees have been under scrutiny in their host states – leading to deportations and/or prosecutions in Germany, Belgium and elsewhere.[131] From the examples below of ICL on the domestic level, we can see that ICL contains within it the empirical impossibility of its promised 'accountability', amounting to 'planned impunity'.

7.1 *Van Anraat and Kouwenhoven, the Exception and the Rule*

Media attention and public interest in a case can persuade prosecution authorities to proceed with a case. Sometimes, such as in the case of Frans Van Anraat, a suspect appearing in the media boasting about his pursuits renders it politically difficult for the public prosecutor to decline prosecution.[132] That, combined with the Dutch treaty-monist system (meaning that international conventional law prevails over domestic law in case of conflict), made The Netherlands a relatively receptive venue for a first case against a Western businessman for crimes against IL.[133]

Above I noted that the Van Anraat case forms the exception that confirms the rule of 'impunity' for business actors. The Kouwenhoven case, on the other hand, (thus far) conforms to the more regular pattern of impunity for business involvement in conflict.[134]

7.2 *Van Anraat*

The Van Anraat case bears resemblance to the *Zyklon B Case* discussed in Chapter 3 (both in content and in law), in that it provides another example

130 See, e.g., Ratner et al. 2009, pp. 281–5.

131 Ibid. This includes the case in Belgium of Rwandan businessmen Etienne Nzabonimana and Samuel Ndashykirwa ('The Two Brothers' case), concerning crimes committed during the 1994 genocide. Prosecutors said the two businessmen provided weapons, vehicles and beer for militias in Rwanda's south-eastern Kibungo region during the April 1994 killings. The brothers were sentenced to 12 and 10 years in June 2005: *BBC News*, 29 June 2005, 'Rwandans sentenced for genocide'.

132 Van Anraat appeared on national Dutch television boasting about his relationship with Saddam Hussein. The Dutch secret service had paid Van Anraat and accommodated him in a safe house in return for intelligence on Iraq but the public revelation made it difficult to ignore him: see, among others, Karskens 2006.

133 *Dutch Constitution*, Ch. 5(2), Arts. 90 ff., e.g., 'Article 94 Statutory regulations in force within the Kingdom shall not be applicable if such application is in conflict with provisions of treaties that are binding on all persons or of resolutions by international institutions'. An obstacle in non-monist/dualist systems occurs when the international law obligations are not brought into domestic law (a domestic statute is usually needed for this), which leaves the international norms non-actionable on the domestic level by domestic actors.

134 On the *Van Anraat* and *Kouwenhoven* cases generally, see Huisman 2010; Van Sliedregt 2007; Van der Wilt 2006; Van der Wilt 2008.

of inferred knowledge vis-à-vis an act of assistance. Van Anraat was a chemicals broker. The significance of Van Anraat being a broker rather than supplier is that the products never entered the European Union's jurisdiction, and that Van Anraat himself did not personally hold or handle them.[135] He was tried for having brokered the supply of chemicals to former Iraqi president Saddam Hussein. The chemicals were then used to manufacture mustard gas with which the Kurdish populations of northern Iraq and Iran were attacked (the Anfal Campaign). Van Anraat claimed in his defence that he believed the chemicals were for use in the garment industry. However, the court found, that although the type of chemical sold were commonly used in the garment industry, the quantities requested by the Iraqi President *must have* given Van Anraat cause to think his customer may have had another purpose for them.[136] Additionally, as Van Anraat was an experienced chemicals dealer, he *must have known* the chemicals could be used as a component in the manufacture of poison gas, and finally, as a regular newspaper reader and someone who had spent considerable time in Iraq, Van Anraat *must have known* that, considering that Iraq was at war with its neighbour and in conflict with the Kurds in Northern Iraq, *in the ordinary course of things*, the mustard gas, once manufactured, *would be used*, and eventually was used, to gas the Kurds.[137] Importantly, Van Anraat delivered another shipment of the chemicals after the Halabja attack in 1988 which had been widely covered in the news. On this basis Van Anraat was considered to have aided and abetted Saddam Houssein in his war crimes: he was not required to have had *intent* towards crimes carried out by Saddam. In other words, Van Anraat was not required to have *wanted* the Kurds to be gassed, it was sufficient that he *knew* (*must have known*) the chemicals would be used to this end and he supplied them nonetheless.[138] Van Anraat was sentenced to 17 years' imprisonment.[139]

7.3 *Kouwenhoven*

Also in The Netherlands, businessman Guus Kouwenhoven is being prosecuted on the accusation of having delivered arms to Liberia and of being involved in war crimes committed by Liberian troops and/or militias during the reign of Charles Taylor. Kouwenhoven was convicted of the weapons supply charges but

135 *Mark Thomas Documentary*.

136 *Van Anraat Appeal Decision*, 12.1.1.

137 *Van Anraat Appeal Decision*, 11.17.

138 See also Van der Wilt 2008.

139 On 1 July 2009, the Dutch Supreme Court upheld the judgment, but shortened Van Anraat's sentence by six months due to the length of the trial. The Supreme Court also ordered the lower court to reconsider the compensation claims made by Kurdish victims, *Van Anraat Supreme Court Decision*.

acquitted of the war crimes charges by a lower court in 2006,[140] then released in 2007[141] and fully acquitted by the Court of Appeal in 2008,[142] but on 20 April 2010 the Dutch Supreme Court ordered a retrial, finding that the Court of Appeal had neglected to hear important witnesses in the case.[143] In April 2017, the retrial was completed, and the Court of Appeal sentenced Kouwenhoven to 19 years imprisonment for complicity in war crimes, committed multiple times, and for supplying arms and ammunition to (the regime of) Charles Taylor in violation of arms embargoes.[144] The court noted:

> Until today, the defendant has denied the facts and has not provided any clarity about his motives for his criminal activities. In conclusion, it must be assumed that the defendant did not act out of political or ideological motives, but acted in fear of losing his investments in Liberia and losing his income from the logging companies. Thus, his actions were committed for financial gain and apparently with the acceptance of the serious consequences.[145]

What this means (cf. Chapter 4B, Section 1.4) is that, like in the case of Van Anraat, the court did not require the defendant to share the principal perpetrator's intent; he need only have intentionally assisted (e.g., through supplying the means, weapons, ammunitions, training, etc) while knowing of the cruel nature of the war, and knowingly accepting the risk of what Charles Taylor and his men (unnamed co-perpetrators) would do with the means (indiscriminately firing at unarmed civilians, beheading people, forcing people into houses and setting them on fire, throwing live babies into wells, etc. etc.) and what that would result in (death and rape etc.).

Kouwenhoven had stated (in his defence), amongst others, 'that a war in African countries is fought differently than in Europe and that human life has less value'.[146]

Kouwenhoven had been put on a UN travel ban list in 2000 because of his alleged arms and diamond dealings for Charles Taylor and the RUF.[147] The

140 *Kouwenhoven 2006 Judgment.*

141 *Kouwenhoven Interim Judgment.*

142 *Kouwenhoven Acquittal.*

143 *Kouwenhoven Supreme Court Judgment 2010.*

144 *Kouwenhoven Retrial Judgment 2017.*

145 *Kouwenhoven Retrial Judgment 2017*, English translation available at: https://uitspraken.rechtspraak.nl/inziendocument?id=ECLI:NL:GHSHE:2017:2650.

146 *Kouwenhoven Retrial Judgment 2017*, English translation.

147 *UNSC Liberia Asset Freeze List*; *UN Liberia 2007 Report; Bankrolling Brutality.*

Global Witness report 'The Usual Suspects' claims that OTC, the company managed by Kouwenhoven, ran a militia of 2,500 armed fighters.[148] Kouwenhoven is also mentioned by name in the UN Panel of Experts Reports on Liberia,[149] but only as the 'manager of Oriental Timber Company' in the Charles Taylor decision.[150] The company Kouwenhoven ran was registered in Liberia and part of a Chinese-owned group, which may explain why Kouwenhoven was indicted as an individual in The Netherlands, and the company was not.[151]

The fact that Frans Van Anraat was prosecuted is partly the result of an investigation carried out by a journalist, Arnold Karskens, and partly the result of 'prosecuterial activism'. Although The Netherlands had one of the first 'war crimes units' as part of the office of the public prosecutor,[152] international cases such as those against Van Anraat and Kouwenhoven are expensive to investigate and run – plus, there normally is little public pressure to spend 'taxpayers' money' on cases relating to victims in remote countries. As a result of this, the outside help of journalists such as Karskens, or NGOs such as Global Witness, can be a *sine qua non*. However, according to the prosecutors, the case of Kouwenhoven fell apart when NGO-produced evidence was rejected by the court,[153] witnesses were shown to have been bought, and so on.[154] Viewing the situation from a different angle, when such prosecutions depend to such a large extent on external assistance, it also shows us something about the government's/public prosecutor's budgeting priorities.

The two Dutch prosecutions are essentially 'progressive' cases. However, Van Anraat and Kouwenhoven both acted as loners, even outlaws. Van Anraat incriminated himself when by boasting on TV about his dealings with Saddam Hussein. Kouwenhoven's company OTC was not prosecuted *per se*. The US company that manufactured the TCG that Van Anraat brokered was fined USD 200,000 for sanctions-busting.[155]

---

148 *Global Witness Liberia Report*, p. 13.

149 E.g., *UN Liberia 2007 Report*.

150 *Taylor Trial Judgment*, p. 1658.

151 In a magazine interview in 2007, Kouwenhoven's lawyer claims that Global Witness's report is tainted by the fact that the organisation received funding from OSI-West Africa, where at the relevant time Ellen Johnson-Sirleaf was the Chair of the Board. She has served as the President of Liberia since 2006 and, according to Kouwenhoven's lawyer, had an interest in eliminating her rival Taylor's main source of finance, the timber trade (of which the OTC was the main producer). He also accuses Global Witness of pressing for a timber embargo from the UNSC on the same grounds: Vrij Nederland, 31 March 2007, p. 77.

152 Office of the Public Prosecutor: http://www.om.nl/onderwerpen/international-crimes-0/.

153 Conversation with members of the War Crimes Unit, 29 October 2010.

154 *Karskens blog*.

155 Karskens 2006, p. 169.

It is perhaps the model case for what we (a putative 'ideal' college of liberal lawyers, as well as an 'ideal' general public) imagine ICL could be (or, what ICL promises to be): a greedy villain, an evil dictator, a firm but fair judge, a long jail sentence and a reassured public. Van Anraat and Kouwenhoven are both mediagenic 'James Bond baddies' with a certain charm. This turns prosecuting them into a popular spectacle. The Van Anraat case is being turned into a film.[156] At the same time, it creates an artificial distinction between these two bad guys, and 'legitimate', normal, clean corporate business. Van Anraat, and Kouwenhoven are thus the 'fall guys' for the 'backlash' (Chapter 6).

8 Host State Cases

It is rare to hear of corporate actors (especially Western/Northern actors) being prosecuted in 'host states' – the states where these individuals and companies do business, and where violations of the kind discussed here generally occur. Part of the reason for this is that these cases are not widely reported in the Western media. However, some examples deserve mention. When such prosecutions do occur, reports of obstacles and buying off of judges/authorities also appear (e.g., Trafigura in Côte d'Ivoire[157]). Additionally, in cases such as the prosecution of Warren Anderson, CEO of Union Carbide/Dow, which has been ongoing since 1987, it would be difficult to get the suspect to appear in court or even be extradited.[158] The 2010 Bhopal Court decision lists Anderson as an 'absconder'.[159] A claim for USD 489 million worth of damages that a Nicaraguan court awarded plaintiffs (who had suffered injury from pesticides) against Shell Chemicals, Dow Chemicals, Standard Fruit was declared unenforceable by a California court in 2003.[160] A documentary on Al-Jazeera mentioned a local Colombian lawsuit against Chiquita, which is accused of killing local trade union leaders, workers and social activists. I have not found further details on this local case, but the ATS case in the US is well documented.[161] On 4 January 2012, a court in Ecuador ordered Chevron to pay USD 18 billion for dumping oil-drilling waste in unlined pits, polluting the forest and causing

156 *Het Parool*, 1 July 2010.
157 *De Volkskrant*, 24 August 2009.
158 *BBC News*, 7 June 2010.
159 *Bhopal Indian Criminal Case*.
160 Joseph 2004, p. 150 (case not reported).
161 *Chiquita* documentary.

illness and deaths among indigenous people.[162] Chevron's staff immediately denounced the decision: 'the decision is another glaring example of the politicisation and corruption of Ecuador's judiciary that has plagued this fraudulent case from the start'.[163] This has led (amongst other matters) to Chevron taking Ecuador to arbitration under the US-Ecuador Bilateral Investment Treaty, and to Ecuador losing – with the arbitrator ordering all states where Ecuador is currently trying to enforce the award, to desist from doing so.[164] This shows that private arbitration trumps domestic public courts, and that, especially where law does generate a seemingly emancipatory outcome, the system will correct itself. Chevron brought a second arbitration suit which led to Ecuador having to pay out USD 112 million, while the award was confirmed (that is, the writ of *certiorari* was denied) in June 2016 by the US Supreme Court,[165] perhaps showing what happens when a small, poor country takes on a global corporate giant.

In the Democratic Republic of Congo, on 14 December 2006, three former employees of the Australian mining company Anvil Mining (together with nine Congolese soldiers) went on trial on charges of complicity in war crimes over a 2004 massacre in the DRC. Pierre Mercier, the Canadian who was the general manager of Anvil Mining Ltd.'s Congolese subsidiary, as well as two South Africans stood accused of having 'knowingly facilitated' war crimes committed by Congolese troops when the military suppressed an uprising near Anvil's Dikulushi mine in the Katanga Province, allegedly killing at least 70 civilians.[166] The trial ended six months later in the acquital of all accused.[167]

On 17 July 2007, RAID and Global Witness together with two Congolese NGOs published a report, 'The Kilwa Trial: A Denial of Justice', which presents a detailed chronology of events from October 2004 to June 2007. The report argues that the proceedings were 'plagued with obstructions and political interference'[168] and documents 'serious flaws and irregularities' in the trial of the

162 *The Independent*, 5 January 2012.

163 Ibid.

164 *Chevron Corporation and Texaco Petroleum Corporation v. The Republic of Ecuador*, UNCITRAL, PCA Case No. 2009–23.

165 *Republic of Ecuador v. Chevron Corp*. 2016 BL 179029, U.S., No. 15–1088, *cert. denied* 6/6/16.

166 See Australian Broadcasting Corporation list of articles on the subject, available at: http://www.abc.net.au/4corners/content/2005/s1408730.htm. See also *ABC Kilwa Documentary*.

167 *Anvil Mining Press Release* 28 June 2007.

168 E.g., Global Witness, RAID Press Release, 7 April, 2008 *'Human Rights Defenders Prevented from Meeting Victims of the Kilwa Massacre'*.

three Anvil employees.[169] RAID together with the Congo-based Action Against Impunity and Human Rights (ACIDH) and the Institute for Human Rights and Development in Africa (IHRDA) from Gambia subsequently took their complaint (on behalf of 8 victims) to the African Commission on Human and Peoples' Rights, which in August 2017 found the government of the Democratic Republic of Congo responsible for the 2004 massacre of over 70 persons in Kilwa, and granted compensation of USD 2.5 million to the victims and their families. The Commission also 'publicly rebuked [Australian mining company Anvil Mining] for its role in the violations, which included providing logistical support to soldiers who indiscriminately shelled civilians, summarily executed at least 28 people and disappeared many others after a small group of lightly armed rebels tried to take control of the town'.[170] The fact that the Commission did not mention the three Anvil employees individually as responsible, and can only 'rebuke' a global multinational and urge the DRC to 'take all due measures to prosecute and punish agents of the state and Anvil Mining Company staff' contributes to the desire for a Malabo Protocol (Chapter 4). Quite aside from it being extremely unlikely that the claimants, NGOs and the Commission – or a future African human rights court – could meaningfully restrain a global multinational the size of Anvil, prosecute its officers and make it pay out the compensation, it is my argument in this book that law is not designed to produce this effect, and in fact incapable of doing so except where ultimately favourable to the structures of corporate capitalism.

In Chapter 1, I commented on the notion of 'corporate power' and quoted statistics such as 'the combined sales of four of the largest corporations in the world exceed the gross domestic product of Africa'.[171] Likewise, over 90 percent of Nigeria's foreign exchange earnings are said to come from Shell,[172] which would make local litigation, let alone prosecution, very difficult. Moreover, Shell is said to have someone on their payroll in every government department in Nigeria.[173] Also, in Chapter 2B I mentioned how 'stabilisation clauses' and other provisions in BITs leave host states very little room to adopt or strengthen human rights and other 'restrictive' legislation, as well as lawsuits as seen in the

169 Global Witness, RAID Press Release, 7 April, 2008.

170 RAID, *'African Commission: Landmark $2.5 Million Award to DR Congo Massacre Victims'*, 4 August 2017.

171 Ch. 1, § 1.1.

172 Usman 2011, p. 294.

173 *The Guardian*, 8 December 2010.

case of Ecuador. While Third World elites enjoy the benefits of Western (and East Asian) MNCs, the global working classes are virtually[174] powerless in the face of exploitation and abuse.[175]

9 Conclusion

There are many other examples of recent conflicts where we may have expected international criminal trials to have been brought against the businesspersons or companies.

One such example (I mention others in Chapter 6) is South Africa, where the South African Truth and Reconciliation Commission held three days of 'Business Sector hearings'.[176] In a submission, the Center for Conflict Resolution (University of Cape Town) asserted,

> Sections within the business community, through their extensive involvement in domestic arms production, and as an active participant in Total Strategy,[177] provided the material means for the maintenance and defence of apartheid, both domestically and in the context of South Africa's destabilisation campaign of the Southern African region. As such, elements within the business community are guilty of directly and indirectly perpetuating the political conflict and associated human rights abuses which characterised South Africa between March 1960 and May 1994.[178]

---

174 See Chapter 6 below.

175 This includes African Human Rights NGOs, e.g., Africa Legal Aid (AFLA), who published *The Cairo-Arusha Principles*: 'The Principles provide that universal jurisdiction applies to gross human rights offences committed "even in peacetime." The Principles also provide that universal jurisdiction should not be limited only to natural persons, but that it should extend to legal entities as well. The Principles suggest that crimes such as acts of plunder and gross misappropriation of public resources, trafficking in human beings and serious environmental crimes, which have "major adverse economic, social or cultural consequences," should be added to the list of crimes subject to universal jurisdiction'.

176 *TRC Business Sector Hearings* Excerpt in Appendix F.

177 The strategy developed by the South African government over the years aimed at repelling the 'communist onslaught' it expected, and which included recruitment of the private sector, and 'depended on the active participation of private sector business'. *CCRSA TRC Submission.*

178 *CCRSA TRC Submission.*

It further asserted the emergence of a 'military-industrial complex' functioning 'on the basis of a structural pairing between business and military that inevitably develops into mutual interests'.[179]

The Truth and Reconciliation Commission's Final Report weighed up two dominant points of view that had been represented at the hearings:

> One view, which sees apartheid as part of a system of racial-capitalism, held that apartheid was beneficial for (white) business because it was an integral part of a system premised on the exploitation of black workers and the destruction of black entrepreneurial activity. According to this argument, business as a whole benefited from the system, although some sections of the business community (most notably Afrikaner capital, the mining houses and the armaments industry) benefited more than others did. This position is most clearly articulated in submissions by the African National Congress (ANC), the South African Communist Party (SACP), the Congress of South African Trade Unions (COSATU), Professor Sampie Terreblanche of the University of Stellenbosch and the Black Management Forum (BMF) ... The other position, argued mainly by business, claims that apartheid raised the costs of doing business, eroded South Africa's skill base and undermined longterm productivity and growth. In this view, the impact of apartheid was to harm the economy.[180]

The TRC's finding on business was, first and foremost: 'Business was central to the economy that sustained the South African state during the apartheid years. Certain businesses, especially the mining industry, were involved in helping to design and implement apartheid policies. Other businesses benefited from co-operating with the security structures of the former state. Most businesses benefited from operating in a racially structured context'.[181] No prosecutions ensued, with 'truth and reconciliation' being the chosen strategy for transition. That this was not satisfactory to many victims of apartheid can be concluded from the class actions in the US brought in their name against a number of corporations (Chapter 6).

Another example is the situation in Iraq. One could have imagined prosecutions, by analogy to the prosecution of Tesch in the *Zyklon B Case*, of the *other* manufacturers and suppliers of the gas that Saddam Hussein used to kill the Kurds of Halabja and across the border in Iran. Likewise, we could imagine

---

179 *CCRSA TRC Submission*, citing Smith 1983, p. 74.
180 *TRC Final Report*, Volume 4, C.2, p. 18ff., deal with the business sector hearings.
181 *TRC Final Report*, p. 48. See further, Appendix F.

prosecutions for complicity in war crimes committed in post-2003 Iraq by probably every major arms supplier who supplied the US military, the banks that provided the finance, the companies that supplied the manpower in the form of mercenaries or private military contractors.[182] I have argued that Van Anraat's prosecution is the exception that confirms the rule: it appears that ICL is *not designed* to do this, that this is not what ICL is for. As I have argued in the previous chapter, and illustrated in the present chapter, ICL's purpose is partly for pro-capital intervention, partly ideological: to create a particular narrative of conflict which excludes economic causes.

While in Iraq, one trial was organised for Saddam Hussein and seven of his colleagues (a trial that has received much criticism in itself),[183] the US occupation put through a programme of economic and legal reform in Iraq that was in many ways similar to that in Japan, in Yugoslavia, and generally the reforms that accompany World Bank and IMF finance. In Iraq, US-appointed Paul Bremer passed orders allowing 100 percent foreign ownership of Iraqi companies, leaving the oil industry in the hands of a professional management team independent from political control and headed by a former Shell CEO, major tax reforms, the creation of a US-Iraq free trade area, etc.[184] Saddam's trial formed only a thin veil over those reforms. But while many (lawyers and others) focus on the legality or illegality of the war, legal issues surrounding detention in Guantanamo and elsewhere, and torture[185] (one could call this 'law's CNN effect'), very little if any research focuses on the dispossession of the resources in Iraq. Our faith in ICL is important to the capitalist IL, partly because it keeps activists' and leftist legal academics' focus on prosecuting suspected war criminals. Tallgren suggests: 'Focusing on the idea of international criminal justice helps us to forget that an overwhelming majority of the crucial problems of the societies concerned are not adequately addressed by criminal law'.[186] (Nor, indeed and most importantly, that many of them are enabled by, and actualised *through* law.)

ICL thus forms an integral part of the structure of rules congealing the economically exploitative relationships between the GCC and the GWC.

182 See, generally, Klein 2007, pp. 323–82; Scahill 2007.

183 See, e.g., Alvarez 2004; Shany 2004; Zolo 2004.

184 See Gathii 2010, pp. 71–93; Klein 2007, p. 323ff.; Coalition Provisional Authority website: http://www.iraqcoalition.org/ [now defunct].

185 Viz., e.g., the case brought in Germany against Donald Rumsfeld, the case in Spain against John Yoo et al., attempted arrests of George W. Bush in Switzerland and Canada, etc. – the work of cause lawyers (see Ch. 6 below).

186 Tallgren 2002a, p. 593.

Koskenniemi and Ratner both contend that the ICTY and ICTR were created for political ends. Ratner asserts: 'the [UN Security] Council created [the ICTY and ICTR] as substitutes for robust international action to prevent or stop the atrocities in these two regions'.[187] The visual performance of the trials at those tribunals masks the failure to prevent the tragedies in the first place. The Nuremberg, Tokyo and associated courts have overwhelmingly received the same criticism. Brownlie has stated that 'political considerations, power and patronage will continue to determine who is tried for international crimes and who not'.[188] Rather than presenting ICL as a triumph of law enforcement (and the recognition of individual criminal responsibility) over politics that should be improved by eliminating 'selectivity',[189] we should speak of the instrumentalisation of individual responsibility for political ends. These ends would include not only the accountability of, say, Serbian leaders or African warlords, but also (for example) the *impunity* of Western (business and political) leaders and, e.g., NATO commanders.[190] Here we see in practice how impunity, too, is a *legal* construct.[191]

Moreover, Akhavan has suggested that the purpose of ICL is utilitarian in the sense that accountability may contribute to post-conflict peace building and the long-term prevention of mass violence.[192] In the East-Timorese example, he suggests why this is important: 'Accountability for atrocities and corruption ... is the key to obtaining the international investment and aid Indonesia desperately needs'.[193] Similarly, former Chief Prosecutor Carla del Ponte said in a speech that the function of the ICTY was 'to bring law where there is none, so that we can invest'.[194] This suggests that when peace and justice are good for business, we use it to hide this effect, but when ICL is bad for business, ICL remains our vital dream, forever deferred. In the next chapter, I elaborate specifically on the value for corporate capitalism of the ideological power of (corporate) ICL.

---

187 Ratner et al. 2009, p. 9. See also Koskenniemi 2002.
188 Brownlie 2008, p. 604. See also Mégret 2003.
189 This is the conclusion of Cryer 2005.
190 *ICTY NATO Bombing Report*. See also Benvenuti 2001.
191 Cf. Susan Marks, who asserts 'empire is a *legal* construct' (Marks 2006, p. 347).
192 Akhavan 2001, p. 30.
193 Akhavan 2001, p. 29.
194 Del Ponte 2005.

CHAPTER 6

Corporate Imperialism 3.0: from the Dutch East India Company to the American South Asia Company

1 Introduction: Corporate Imperialism 3.0: the American South Asia Company*

In Chapter 1, I recounted the story of Erik Prince, who went on Fox News in order to sell to US President Trump the idea that it was time to reintroduce the East India Company model, in the shape of a American South Asian Company, with a viceroy at its helm,[1] which would both administer Afghanistan (in the way that General MacArthur had administered Japan, changing economic and property laws) and ship the trillions of dollars worth of oil, gas and minerals there back to the US. Prince here played to Trump's own expressed wish to 'bomb the shit out of ISIS' and to ship Iraqi oil back to the US with the help of Exxon Mobil.

What we see in this story is late capitalism coming full circle and reverting back to the private, corporate-run armies of the early colonial era, pillaging as well as administrating and spreading its law and ideology to far-flung but resource-rich places.

The connection with corporate ICL is *this* – *CICL* which has lent (will lend) the corporation its legitimacy in taking up this 'public', governance function. Corporate rule is here, perhaps counter-intuitively, because corporations have posited themselves (or rather, corporate CEOs have posited their legal vehicles) as 'good corporate citizens' capable of the same errors as humans, and account-

* An earlier version of Chapter 6 has been published as '"It's Not Me, It's the Corporation": The Value of Corporate Accountability in the Global Political Economy', *London Review of International Law*, 4(1) (2016): 127–63; and as 'Capital, Corporate Citizenship and Legitimacy: The Ideological Force of "Corporate Crime" in International Law', in Baars, G. and A. Spicer (eds) 2017, *The Corporation: A Critical, Multidisciplinary Handbook*, Cambridge: Cambridge University Press.

1 See also, 'Erik Prince offers Private Military force in Afghanistan', *Financial Times*, 7 August 2017; Josh Rogan, 'Inside Erik Prince's secret proposal to outsource the war in Afghanistan', *Washington Post*, 9 August 2017; Erik Prince, 'The MacArthur Model for Afghanistan; Consolidate authority into one person: an American viceroy who'd lead all coalition efforts', *Wall Street Journal*, 31 May 2017.

.e same laws as individual people. Law still constructs the seemingly world of Corporate Imperialism 3.0.

ɔther part of it is that corporations do in fact rule our lives now to an ˌecedented degree. Our health, our sleep,[2] our death,[3] and even our political activism are now managed, or governed, by corporations.[4] Corporations are participating in 'governance' directly, by providing policing, healthcare, education, benefits assessments, and many other formerly public services. These also include national security, including the above-mentioned military services but also intelligence, detention, borders. Even the most sensitive and most vulnerable parts of the state, like the UK's nuclear arsenal, are now in private hands.[5] Such direct provision of services formerly seen as public leads to the population starting to expect certain governance functions from corporations. For example, the giant 'global town square' Facebook has come to be expected to govern its vast public domain, and to police it: 'Facebook could have prevented Lee Rigby murder'.[6] Facebook marks us safe at times of terrorist incidents (those deadly events it deems worthy of listing)[7] and reports us when we call for riots,[8] or show particular types of nipples.[9] It also leads to people supporting the idea that corporations now have rights, the right to freedom of speech, the right to a religion, etc.[10] We have come to truly see rights provision and protection as a *shared responsibility* between state and corporation. Besides being involved in every manner of 'public' service provision today, corporations are also participating in governance (familiarising us with their public role) through, for example, sponsoring major public events,[11] handing out free ice-cream in electoral registration campaigns in

2 A. Spicer, 'The road to hell is paved with corporate wellness', *New Scientist*, 7 December 2016.

3 *The Guardian*, 'NHS cancer care could switch to private contracts in £700m plans' 2 July 2014.

4 'Revealed: Rio Tinto's plan to use drones to monitor workers' private lives', *The Guardian*, 8 December 2016.

5 'Command and control contract for Britain's armed nuclear police outsourced to Capita', *The Independent*, 18 May 2015.

6 'Facebook could have prevented Lee Rigby Murder', *The Telegraph*, 26 November 2014.

7 Aaron Balick, 'Why I won't be marking myself as "safe" on Facebook today', *The Independent*, 4 June 2017.

8 'Facebook riot calls earn men four-year jail terms amid sentencing outcry', *The Guardian*, 16 August 2011.

9 'Facebook still has a nipple problem', 12 October 2016, *The Verge*.

10 Brown 2015.

11 Such as Pride, which in many places has attracted criticism and resistance because of its corporate sponsorship, see, e.g., Michael Edison Hayden, 'LGBTQ pride marches marked by protests across US', *ABC News*, 25 June 2017; and more generally, 'Pride in London: Why

Britain's most deprived areas,[12] and, most recently, by seeking to 'brand' a variety of social issues and movements – e.g., the Pepsi Black Lives Matter ad,[13] 'that' Heineken ad,[14] H&M's 'transgender' ad,[15] the Danish 'all that we share' ad.[16]

Corporations have become so 'natural' and so inevitable that we can hardly imagine a world without them. The unprecedented privatisation has erased the distinction between public and private (the public has collapsed into the private). Moreover, procurement of 'public' services from private providers, increased privatisation of formerly public benefits such as pensions, student loans as well as public bail-outs, threatens to dissolve the distinction between 'taxpayer' and 'shareholder'. To paraphrase Marx, 'social capital makes the enterprise appear as social enterprise'.[17] We (at least many of us) have started to see corporations as part of the solution, rather than as part of the problem. Some even believe that corporations have an equal, legitimate and deserved, seat at the governance table. The potential for change lies in the contradiction between our acceptance of the corporation in this role and our increasing awareness that it cannot be sustained.

In this final chapter, I round out my counter-narrative to the popular mainstream literature on the call for the use of international criminal law to restrain business in conflict, in order to make a much broader argument about the 'actual' relationship between law and capital, and what we could call its motor, the corporation.

---

businesses are backing Pride', *BBC News*, 8 July 2017; The Business of Gay Pride, *Financial Times*, 11 August 2016.

12 *TimeOut*, 'Ben & Jerry's are giving away FREE ice cream to encourage Londoners to vote', 31 March 2016.

13 Daniel Victor, 'Pepsi Pulls Ad Accused of Trivializing Black Lives Matter', *New York Times*, 5 April 2017.

14 The DiDi Delgado, 'The Heineken Ad Is Worse Than The Pepsi Ad, You're Just Too Stupid To Know It', *Medium*, 28 April 2017.

15 'One Million Moms attack "transgender" H&M model … but she's not actually trans', *PinkNews*, 5 October 2016.

16 'This Danish TV Ad Is What The World Needs To Remember Now More Than Ever', *Huffington Post*, 30 January 2017.

17 Marx 1981, p. 567.

2 The Story so far …

The broader relationship lies in the ways in which the corporation, as the motor (engine, progeny even) of capitalism, has managed despite (in dialectical relationship with) ongoing challenge and resistance, to create, maintain and recover its legitimacy, its reputation, through corporate ideology.

For as long as 'the corporation' has existed, it has had to fight for its reputation.[18] Variously called a 'worm[s] in the entrails of men', a Frankensteinian monster or a psychopath, the suspicion has long persisted that there is something fishy about this odd, ungraspable, 'artificial entity' called 'the corporation'. Although wounds to reputations often attach only to specific corporations and are healed through a locally applied remedy, or by corporate atonement, sometimes the challenge extends beyond the individual corporation to the concept of the corporation *per se* and to *all* corporations or to 'corporate capitalism' as a whole. The 1720 scandal of the South Sea Bubble discussed in Chapter 2A, for example, was linked to the very concept of the corporation, which was called into question as a result, but managed to survive nonetheless. At other moments, particular corporations have become a symbolic target for a political movement because of their perceived power or privilege. This was the case with the British East India Company – which received preferential tax treatment by the British over rival American companies – leading to the Boston Tea Party and kicking off the American Revolution. So-called 'misuse' of the corporate form has shown the public what a powerful and malevolent tool the corporation can be. In the nineteenth century, the abuses by the International Congo Society, owned by King Leopold and responsible for the deaths of millions, led to the growth of the abolitionist movement in Europe, which deflected criticism of the corporation per se.[19] Instances of corporations employed as instruments of foreign policy, in the 'banana wars'[20] and in the Pinochet takeover of Chile, have only recently been written into history.[21] More complex entanglements of corporations in political-economic historical events such as the 1920s crisis,[22] the involvement of *zaibatsu* and the German cartels in Japanese and Nazi imperialism, as we saw in Chapter 3, at the time led to a temporary clampdown on vanquished industrial power. In fact, some

18 See, e.g., Yamamoto 2017; Taylor 2006.
19 Renton, Seddon, and Zeilig 2006.
20 Litvin 2004.
21 Klein 2007.
22 Polanyi 2002.

company directors and officers were prosecuted. Before long, however, a swift (if messy) restoration unfolded, once the political landscape had changed.

Despite – or, I suggest, because of – these periodic backlashes, the structure of the corporation has not only survived but continues to thrive. The German businessmen prosecuted at Nuremberg, as I showed in Chapter 3A, got off with 'sentences light enough to please a chicken thief' before several of them resumed their prior positions. In fact, the individual people who owned and/or ran corporations have remained largely immune – as shown for instance in Chapter 5. The interests (and indeed often the identity and class membership) of capitalist and governmental elites – though at times at odds or in competition with each other – in fact largely coincide and it is this dynamic that has driven the legal-economic development of the corporation. The Anglo-Saxon model of the corporation with its key characteristics of separate legal personality, limited liability, indefinite lifespan, and profit mandate, has been adopted (or imposed) around the world. Over its three-century history, the corporation has become the key apparatus that facilitates the surplus value-extracting function of global capitalism. This has been due to the parallel development of the 'corporate form' (Chapter 2A) and a specific 'corporate ideology' – an ideology which is in constant flux and constantly under (re)construction in a dialectical relationship with the material effects (harms) of corporate capitalism. This final chapter focuses on the development and 'value' of this corporate ideology as it props up the corporate form, and seeks to find the cracks in these seemingly unbreakable bonds, in which the 'seed of the new' may germinate.

The latest series of backlashes against multinational corporations appears stronger than before. However, the debates of the ten years between 2007 and 2017 no longer attack the corporate form as such, but only corporate 'behaviour'. The corporate form itself is no longer questioned. The current debates centre, at one end of the spectrum, on 'corporate wrongdoing' or the 'excesses of capitalism' that proper regulation can minimise and, at the other end, on the fundamental contradictions between corporate capitalism, and the global ecosystem and world peace. At the same time, in the cracks of the system, the ultra-left's anti-corporate sentiment, which has built up within and alongside the anti-globalisation movement, is slowly starting to filter through to a broader public.[23] Bigger questions are being asked – by a so far small but vocal number of activist-critics – about the desirability and ultimate sustainability of corpor-

23 See, e.g., the work of CorporateWatch in the UK, see: https://corporatewatch.org and 'Fuck Off Google' in Berlin, see: https://fuckoffgoogle.de/.

ate capitalism *per se*. The 2016 US elections marked a crossroads where half of the US electorate voted in a corporate CEO, while another sizeable sector sided with Bernie Sanders, a candidate with a strong suspicion of corporate capitalism. In the UK, socialist Labour leader Jeremy Corbyn managed to mobilise and activate a massive, previously despondent contingent of the electorate, some of whom were undoubtedly spurred into action by a shock result following the 2016 British referendum result to leave the EU ('Brexit'). Is corporate ideology still as strong now as Erik Prince hopes?

Even respectable 'centrist' activists in the US have challenged corporate campaign funding, as well as the right of corporations to refuse employees (elements of) medical insurance on religious grounds.[24] In Europe, when Volkswagen (a 'trustworthy' company) was said to have been cheating environmentally conscious consumers, this troubled a significant section of the increasingly not-so-comfortable middle class.[25] The increasing distrust of large corporations has led to the growth of 'buy local' and 'small, independent', fair trade and organic 'locally grown' movements, some of which are reformative while others have more revolutionary agendas.[26] At the same time, it has also triggered forceful 'legitimacy recovery' efforts on the part of corporate capitalism.

In this book I have taken these legitimacy backlashes seriously. My specific focus in this final chapter is the evolution of the debate on 'corporate accountability' (CA) in the past ten years (2007–17). Today the call to 'hold corporations to account' as an answer to the latest corporate backlash is heard far and wide.[27] Apart from corporate criminal liability, the main focus of this book, CA is generally understood to mean the efforts to force corporations to account for (explain, justify, excuse, compensate, make good) the negative effects of corporate activity on its 'victims' and the public at large. The methods employed for this include both 'self-accounting', through or with the help of various NGOs, lawyers, media, activists, states and international bodies,

---

24 *Citizens United v. Federal Election Commission*, Supreme Court No. 08-205, 21 January 2010; *Burwell v. Hobby Lobby Stores, Inc.* 573 U.S. (2014).

25 *BBC News* 2015, 10 December.

26 See, e.g., projects like OrganicLea in London, see: http://www.organiclea.org.uk/; The Landworkers' Alliance, see: https://landworkersalliance.org.uk/; UK Food Sovereignty Network, see: http://foodsovereigntynow.org.uk; the People's Grocery now Community Foods Market in Oakland, California, see: http://communityfoodsmarket.com/learn-more/; and studies such as 'People Powered Money: Designing, developing and delivering community currencies', *New Economics Foundation*, 18 May 2015. On the reform vs. revolution dilemma, see Baars 2013.

27 E.g., the work on accountability of the Business and Human Rights Resource Centre, at: http://business-humanrights.org/en/corporate-legal-accountability.

corporate-produced corporate social responsibility (CSR) programmes, drawing up voluntary guidelines, standards, creating schemes for compliance, monitoring or (self-)certification, working with PR and the media on corporate image, etc. It also includes the work of states and courts in legally regulating, permitting self-regulation, prosecuting or threatening to prosecute, subjecting to licensing and other bureaucratic procedures, and a variety of actors in advocating and lobbying for or participating in negotiations around CA instruments and policies. CA in this sense is thought of as a vital method of restraining corporate activity, limiting wrongdoing and reducing negative effects of corporate profit-making activities.

I proposed in Chapter 2A that corporate accountability also has a second, closely related but more (or increasingly less) hidden meaning based on Weber's *literal* understanding of 'accountability' – the ability to account the cost/benefit effects of certain events and processes. In Chapter 4C, we saw that Ruggie considers corporate criminal liability as a 'risk management issue'. The exact value of CA work in the ordinary sense can be calculated (think: money spent on CSR/BHR consultants, CSR projects and gestures, fees for certification, advertising and PR, lobbying, legal fees defending CA cases or indeed spying on and suing anti-corporate activists,[28] etc. and the effects on company share prices, brand value, and goodwill as a result).[29] My key argument in this book has been that rather than thinking of CA as restraining corporate value-extracting activity, we should think of it as *facilitating* corporate profit making and corporate capitalism as a whole. Corporate reputational risk becomes calculable through the ability to account – to predict, know, and thus manage, manipulate, exchange or 'bank on', future events, relations, dynamics, through 'investment' in CA efforts, which adds value in itself. Secondly and most significantly, CA work, in shaping how we think of, feel about, deal with, and what we expect from, the corporation (again, canned morality), has a legitimising effect – the value of which to the corporation and corporate capitalism more generally is not directly calculable. It is 'priceless' – because of the power it accords corporations within global governance.

In the first chapters of this book I described how the corporation was created as a legal structure to function as the surplus-value-extracting motor of capitalism. I commented on its main elements and the main moments in its creation, the notion of corporate legal personality, limited liability, the profit

28 J. Scahill, 'Blackwater's Black Ops', *The Nation*, 15 September 2010.

29 Indeed, 'A 2013 study of 1000 brands found that 28% of brand value relates to corporate social responsibility', G. LeBaron and J. Lister, 'Ethical Audits and the Supply Chains of Global Corporations', SPERI Global Political Economy Brief No. 1 (2016) 6.

the corporation was created as an 'amoral calculator' and 'exter- ıchine', its growing power and what we now call 'negative extern- e corporation's ability to shift responsibility – cost – for the harm it ıto others) are inevitably challenged, and the question arises, 'why do we up with it all'?[30] The answer lies in the creation of corporate ideology legitimising both the internal structure and workings of the corporation as well as general public acceptance of corporations as essentially normal or indeed a good thing. In this chapter I discuss corporate ideology production predominantly through CA in the form of corporate self-portrayal as a good and 'socially responsible' and 'law-abiding' citizen.

In Section 3 below I first discuss CSR's material and intellectual provenance and its development into a movement for the promotion of non-binding rules on corporate behaviour. The subsequent development is that of CA cause lawyering and the multiple attempts by NGOs and cause lawyers to 'hold corporations to account' in Western domestic courts.[31] Such cause lawyering forms a civil society response to the CSR movement, which in turn has ramped up its game to alleviate the 'bad corporation' accusations of the cause lawyers.[32] This dynamic then produces the call for the *legalisation* of CSR, which seeks to form a compromise between the first two responses and has advocates in the corporate, NGO/practice world as well as in academia.[33] One particular demand often expressed within the 'legalised CSR' ambit is the inclusion of corporate criminal liability in international law or, the formation of a specific field of 'corporate international criminal law', as highlighted in Chapter 1.

Building on my argument that corporate accountability should be seen as (value-producing) accountability in the literal, Weberian sense, in the penultimate section I underscore the *distributive effects* of the CA tools created within these three strategies. Most important, the contribution CA makes to the reification/anthropomorphisation of the corporation changes ('spirits away')[34] the relationship of responsibility for harm from individual to affected communities or society at large, to one of individual victims with 'the corporation'. The practical effect of this is that individuals affected by the particular excesses of capitalism (normally in the Global South) are constituted as victims who, in

30 I take this evocative phrase from Allott 2002, p. 400.

31 See, e.g., *Amnesty Dignity Report*: Amnesty International: Demand Dignity: Close the accountability gap: Corporations, human rights and poverty (2009); Global Witness and Sherpa, Report: Bankrolling Brutality – Why European timber company DLH should be held to account for profiting from Liberian conflict timber (2009).

32 Shamir 2004, p. 635.

33 E.g., the various contributions in McBarnet et al. (eds) 2007.

34 Arthur, 'Editor's Introduction', in Pashukanis 1978, p. 31.

a legal relationship as formal equals (a relationship that hides the inequalities of power between the parties) with the corporation, can seek to negotiate the 'price' of the harm done to them, under the commodified responsibility relationship, where 'planned impunity' thus furthers contemporary corporate imperialism.[35] 'Calculable' value is created in the specific internal mechanism of CA, namely that of channelling difficult-to-predict risk to business (the potential repercussions of suffering produced by capitalism) into calculable avenues of exchange between the corporation and individual victims. Finally, and importantly, the broader effect of the availability of accountability mechanisms (whether used or not) is that of absorbing a large chunk of critique of capitalism and grassroots anticapitalist resistance into a struggle where capitalism's violence is reduced to 'corporate wrongdoing' and where, once accountability mechanisms exist, the backlash is reversed and the corporation and thus capitalism are 'fixed'.[36] CSR, corporate cause lawyering, and advocacy towards a 'corporate international criminal law (CICL)' – together 'corporate accountability' – form the main part of what Klein has called 'the 50 year campaign for total corporate liberation'.[37] In particular, as I discuss in the final section, (putative) corporate ICL serves to complete the corporation as a political citizen and legitimate participant in global governance. The greatest value of CA is that it (albeit always only temporarily) legitimises and therefore perpetuates and even strengthens the current system of surplus value extraction, enabling, or continuing to enable, imperialist accumulation and exploitation of the working class both at home and abroad.[38]

CA thus serves as an illustration of the *commodity form theory of law*'s central claim regarding law's emancipatory potential. CA shows how capitalist law generates seemingly emancipatory discourses and practices that, on closer inspection, turn out to follow the logic of capitalism itself. In my final section I also briefly consider alternatives, which must entail a move beyond law.

35 An example is Shell's activities in the Ogoni Valley, Nigeria: Shell has already agreed a number of compensation deals with those affected, yet continues its activities with the same claimed effect on local communities. See the discussion on Shell in Chapter 5, and also for another example, Leigh Day, 'Shell agrees £55 m compensation deal for Niger Delta community', 7 January 2015; and Leigh Day, '40,000 Nigerians take Shell to the UK High Court following oil spills', 21 November 2016.

36 Aside from imperialist wars, etc., but perhaps an argument can be made that these are placed outside of capitalism in the public imaginary.

37 Klein 2007, p. 19. In *The Shock Doctrine*, Klein describes this process as represented in the economic reforms including privatisations and corporate involvement in, among other places, occupied Iraq and post-Katrina New Orleans.

38 Cf. Suárez-Krabbe, in Dhawan 2014, pp. 211–26.

…reation of the Corporate Soul: Corporate Citizenship and …porate Social Responsibility as the 'Last Maginot Line of …pitalism'

Th… orate form, the company as an 'amoral calculator',[39] induces its individual operatives to make 'economically rational', arms' length, amoral decisions – a form of capitalist *anomie*.[40] The fact that – as noted in 2A – the corporation's history is now rarely discussed, its characteristics rarely questioned, that it is mostly seen as given, precisely maintains this anomie. The modern corporation as 'the end of history' in economic organisation[41] continues to produce knowledge, policy and legal decisions and instruments, that self-perpetuate capitalism and reproduce current socio-economic hierarchies. This ideological achievement is the key source of corporate power. Maintaining this power in the face of intermittent attack, did, however, mean that the corporation, as the reification of capital, 'Monsieur le Capital', the corporate 'psychopath',[42] would require some humanisation,[43] or the creation of a corporate *soul*.

Glasbeek has called CSR the 'last *Maginot* line of capitalism', which it has 'dug' in the face of the latest remaining resistance to its main bearer, the corporation.[44] The first resistance to the corporation was overcome through reification (creation of the corporation as a separate legal person, emptied of its members) and mass public buy-in to corporate capitalism, and in the twentieth century, corporate ideology continued to develop as part of capitalist ideology more generally. The humanisation of 'Monsieur le Capital', corporate citizenship, the CSR industry and corporate legal accountability are corporate ideology tools created in response to backlashes against the legitimacy of the corporate form and profit-making activities. In Europe and the US, the growing power of large monopoly corporations and cartels caused public concern in the first two decades of the twentieth century while the depression of the 1930s caused another backlash, this time against the system of free enterprise itself. Nineteenth-century reification then had to be followed by the creation

39 Sutherland 1983, pp. 236–8, arguing the corporation comes closer to 'economic man' than any person or organisation.

40 Passas 1990, p. 157, excerpted in Whyte 2008, pp. 153, 155.

41 Ireland 2002, p. 120.

42 Bakan 2005, p. 134.

43 *Coca-Cola* (n.d.), 'Is it true that Santa traditionally wears red because of Coca-Cola?'. See also Marchand 2001.

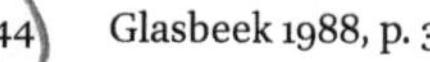

44 Glasbeek 1988, p. 363.

of the corporate soul, to portray the corporation as a 'good citizen' – 'institution in the service of mankind' rather than 'amoral calculator'.[45] In 1908, the US telecommunications giant AT&T was one of the first to launch an advertising campaign aimed at getting the public to 'love and hold affection for' the corporation. US historian Roland Marchand has evocatively described how corporate ideology was re-constructed when the major US corporations used advertising and later in-house public relations officers, and even iconic architecture, to portray themselves as benevolent and socially responsible.[46] Moreover, in the 1930s, crisis corporations started to address the public as voters rather than 'just' buyers, positioning themselves alongside the state as benevolent providers of public goods in what was the 'best strategy ... to restore people's faith in corporations and reverse their growing fascination with big government'.[47] A parallel development to the creation of the corporate soul is the pinpointing of a 'body to kick' and emerging ideas around corporate crime in the first half of the twentieth century.[48] The 'obvious' involvement of the major German corporations in World War Two had led to the prosecution of individual German businessmen but not the corporations per se, as shown in Chapter 3. Any more fundamental critique of corporate capitalism was staved off then through the Allied governments' realisation of their dependence on the major manufacturers for future war efforts. Instead, the major US corporations were given key roles in rebuilding war-ravaged Europe, allowing them to demonstrate public service and 'good neighbourliness'.[49] Complaints from this point onwards were no longer fundamental challenges to the corporation but rather focused on the 'corporate excesses' and 'abuses' of 'bad apples'. Wormser's demand that the Frankensteinian corporate monster be made to respect its maker[50] seemed to have been satisfied, at least ostensibly.

In legal scholarship the debate centred on the corporation's objective, with CSR and 'corporate citizenship' advocates arguing that the corporation's mandate is (or should be) wider than simple maximisation of shareholder return: that it should act for the benefit of other 'stakeholders' (workers, local communities, etc.), though doing so may also be, and indeed normally is, profitable. Although the profit/shareholder return objective had, in English law, just been introduced in 1844 as the only *lawful* objective for the corporation, in the 1883

45 Marchand 2001; Shamir 2008, p. 1.
46 Marchand 1998, p. 203 ff.
47 Bakan 2005, p. 19.
48 Coffee 1981, p. 386.
49 Marchand 1998, p. 361.
50 Wormser 1931, p. 21.

case of *Hutton v. West Cork Railway Co* the court held that a company board could make a decision that at first sight went against shareholders' interests. This would be lawful when the decision indirectly makes business sense: 'The law does not say that there are to be no cakes and ale, but there are to be no cakes and ale except such as are required for the benefit of the company'.[51] While CSR entails a calculation as to its value for the company, the ideological move this allows is to highlight the 'generous' provision of 'cakes and ales': for example, to workers or the local community, while the corporate benefit of such provision – for example pacifying workers and thereby reducing risk of industrial action or other loss of productivity – remains hidden. As Marchand surmises, corporations create their soul, making us believe they are serving humanity, while in fact they serve capital[52] – a move that law permits and masks.

In this light, the 1930s *Harvard Law Review* debate between Adolf Berle and E. Merrick Dodd on the proper purpose of the corporation[53] comes to appear moot, or indeed purely ideological – rephrased according to the prevailing political climate. In the economically more secure US of the 1950s, the economist Milton Friedman in 1952 again floated the idea that any managerial concern with interests outside of shareholder interests *reduces* social wealth due to increased agency cost.[54] Friedman reraised the 'just business' model dismissed in the 1920s, asking whether it should not rather be up to the state to set the rules on, e.g., wages, the environment, other 'stakeholder' issues, and that businessmen could not presume to know, and that it is not their task to decide, what is best for society in general.[55] The debate in the US and UK rests for now on the 'enlightened shareholder model', which allows attention to stakeholders to be seen as a generous gesture or progressive move.[56] In particular, the currently popular notion of 'shared value' communicates the possibility of a win-win resolution for society and corporate capitalism, even if it is acknowledged to be important that the discussion continue so as to offer a space for concerns over corporate activity to be aired, and discontent to be absorbed.[57] This is an important achievement of/for the 'CSR industry' which can be ascribed to the dialectical development between popular concerns over corporate activity and

51 *Hutton v. West Cork Railway Co* (1883) 23 *Ch D* 654, 673.
52 Marchand 1998, pp. 1–5.
53 Berle 1931, p. 1049; Dodd 1932, p. 1145; Berle 1932, p. 1365. See also Sommer 1991, p. 33.
54 Glasbeek 1988, p. 384.
55 Friedman and Friedman 1962, pp. 133–4, n. 26.
56 In the sense that (English) corporate boards are only legally obliged to *consider* the interests of stakeholders: s. 172 Companies Act 2006.
57 Bakan 2015, pp. 279, 292. See further Fleming and Jones 2013.

the realisation that this presents a lucrative business opportunity as well as a vital value-creating legitimising process (regardless of whether one lives up to it).[58] The responsibility for this can even be shifted to 'consumers': 'Whether we like it or not, this [the emergence of the corporation] is what has happened ... The dangers are obvious. But history cannot usually be reversed. Until engineers and economic forces give us a way by which anyone can manufacture an automobile in his back yard we will continue to have organizations the size of General Motors or Ford – as long as people want Chevrolets or Fords'.[59]

The more confrontational quest for 'corporate accountability' as part of the structured process of corporate ideology picked up in the economically abundant (in the West, at least) and politically activist 1960s, when companies came under more exacting public scrutiny.[60] Ralph Nader in 1965 published *Unsafe At Any Speed: The Designed-In Dangers of the American Automobile* in which he criticised the American automobile industry, which had found it economically rational to produce unsafe cars and pay out compensation to accident victims after lawsuits. This caused a scandal – and revealed a key tendency of corporate anomie.[61] In addition, the anti-Vietnam war movement of the 1960s rallied against companies such as General Motors, General Dynamics and Chrysler, which were seen to be making large profits from the war, and against Dow Chemical, which produced both the napalm and Agent Orange used in Vietnam and almost two decades later the devastating chemical spill at Bhopal.[62] During the 1970s crisis and decolonisation, the *global* class struggle intensified, and resulted in (amongst other things) the assertiveness in the face of increasing global corporate power of the G77 countries that resulted in the various New International Economic Order Resolutions.[63] These growing accountability efforts gave impetus – in what has been called the 'private regulation revolution'[64] – to the development of the first series of soft law CSR instruments: the 1976 Organisation for Economic Cooperation and Development Guidelines for Multinational Enterprises, the 2000 United Nations Global Compact, and the 2003 Norms on the Responsibilities of Transnational Corporations and Other Business Enterprises with Regard to Human

58 Marchand 1998, p. 363.

59 Berle 1957, p. 15. CSR is most popular among producers of consumer goods, for obvious reasons.

60 Broad 2002, p. 6; Bakan 2005, p. 60; Lang 2011, p. 61ff.

61 See, generally, Nader 1965.

62 Glasbeek 1988, p. 363. Dow also produced Agent Orange, which would later become the subject of the *Agent Orange* ATS suit, and was responsible for the Bhopal disaster.

63 *UN General Assembly NIEO Resolution.*

64 Shamir 2010, p. 531.

Rights,[65] as well as a whole raft of corporate and NGO-produced documents. These instruments, while doing little to curb harmful corporate activity, especially in the Global South, were ideologically highly significant, as they fed into the development of a new expanded notion of *global* 'corporate citizenship' and of the legitimate role of corporations as partakers in neoliberal global governance and *providers* of socio-economic and civil rights[66] – as, for example, builders of schools and hospitals in the Global South.

The triumphant 'Gordon Gecko' capitalism of the 1980s and 1990s – neoliberalism's 'golden age' – tripped up on the corporate scandals of Enron (2001) and WorldCom (2002).[67] What is interesting is that these scandals led to a highly visible application of individual criminal liability.[68] Perhaps this – as well as the rise of the anti-globalisation movement starting in the late 1980s – was the last push the CSR movement needed to start moving towards professionalisation, formalisation and eventually legalisation beyond the judicial endorsement of 'cakes and ale' spending. The result is that corporations maintain or increase their capacity to extract surplus value. The sizeable part of, or arguably all of, CSR which concerns business impact on the enjoyment of human rights,[69] was institutionalised through the work of UN Special Representative on Business and Human Rights John Ruggie,[70] contributing to CSR's development into a lucrative industry in its own right, with a willing market of 'fair trade' importers and 'socially responsible investors', meeting 'ethical consumers' with a multitude of non-binding standards and guidelines, private and (semi-)public labelling and certification schemes and associated monitoring agencies.[71] For producers of consumer products a visible CSR strategy is now an essential badge of corporate legitimacy.

3.1 *Legalising CSR*

The 1980s and 1990s saw a 'private regulation revolution'[72] signalling the growing legitimacy of a governance function for corporations through the acceptance of their self-regulation by governments and (much of) civil society alike. Currently, however, some business representatives are joining 'progressive'

65 *OECD Guidelines*; *UN Global Compact*; *UN Norms*.
66 Fleming 2013, p. 34.
67 Karstedt and Farrall 2006, pp. 1011, 1013.
68 Glasbeek 2010, pp. 248–9.
69 Views differ over whether the scope of 'business and human rights' is broader or narrower than that of CSR. López 2013, pp. 58, 59.
70 See, e.g., *Ruggie (2011) Report*; Baars 2011, pp. 415, 425–7.
71 For a critique, see Ferrando 2017.
72 Bakan 2015.

domestic and international NGOs in responding to a more sceptical section of the public's concern that CSR may amount only to window-dressing by calling for a 'legalised' CSR consisting of binding rules and enforcement mechanisms. There was widespread disappointment among business and human rights professionals when the United Nations Special Representative's final report did not propose a treaty clearly setting out corporations' legal responsibilities.[73] This has led to a 'Global Movement for a Binding Treaty' joined by 402 organisations and 745 individuals[74] and, in July 2014, the adoption of a resolution (adopted on a vote of 20 against 14 with 13 abstentions[75]) signalling the start of negotiations on a binding CSR Treaty at the United Nations Human Rights Council. The 'Open-Ended Intergovernmental Working Group on transnational corporations and other business enterprises with respect to human rights', which was mandated 'to elaborate an international legally binding instrument',[76] published the draft report of its first session in July 2015.[77] The first two sessions of the OEIGWG were 'dedicated to conducting constructive deliberations on the content, scope, nature and form of the future international instrument'.[78] Building on the first session, the second session in October 2016 continued the discussion so as to enable the OEIGWG Chairperson-Rapporteur to 'prepare elements for the draft legally binding instrument for substantive negotiations at the commencement of the third session' (see the report of the second session).[79]

---

73 Lopez 2013, p. 58.

74 Global Movement for a Binding Treaty, available at: http://www.treatymovement.com/statement.

75 Adopted by a recorded vote of 20 to 14, with 13 abstentions. The voting was as follows:
In favour:
Algeria, Benin, Burkina Faso, China, Congo, Côte d'Ivoire, Cuba, Ethiopia, India, Indonesia, Kazakhstan, Kenya, Morocco, Namibia, Pakistan, Philippines, Russian Federation, South Africa, Venezuela (Bolivarian Republic of), Viet Nam
Against:
Austria, Czech Republic, Estonia, France, Germany, Ireland, Italy, Japan, Montenegro, Republic of Korea, Romania, the former Yugoslav Republic of Macedonia, United Kingdom of Great Britain and Northern Ireland, United States of America
Abstaining:
Argentina, Botswana, Brazil, Chile, Costa Rica, Gabon, Kuwait, Maldives, Mexico, Peru, Saudi Arabia, Sierra Leone, United Arab Emirates.

76 *UN HRC OEIGWG Resolution.*

77 *UN HRC OEIGWG 2016 Report.*

78 *UN HRC OEIGWG 2017 Report.*

79 Ibid.

An international law CSR Treaty could include the obligation on states to ensure civil and criminal accountability in domestic law (mostly home-state law / legal systems as host state legal systems are often considered to be lacking), as well as specific legislation providing for liability for civil wrongs or crimes, including international crimes, committed extraterritorially. After the academic and activist calls (Chapter 1) for a legalised CSR also to include extending ICL to corporations,[80] the OEIWG is indeed considering this very matter. The OEIWG's Second Report on its second session, published on 4 January 2017, briefly notes the discussion:

> 85. Regarding criminal liability, a binding instrument *could correct a historical failure* by making legal persons liable, as was expected for article 25 of the Rome Statute, and by attributing criminal responsibility to corporations ...
>
> 87. One delegation mentioned the 2016 report of the International Law Commission, which included a section in which the Commission's Special Rapporteur on crimes against humanity outlined arguments to support the international criminal liability of legal entities.[81]

The latter point I discussed in Chapter 4C, and we can see here how the influence of the ILC (again) plays out in practice. We can see here a repeat of the narrative that sees 'closing the accountability gap' – that gap which must have been missed though mere oversight/error, as the (long overdue) imperative solution now on the domestic and international level. While in UN jargon this situation – a 'company, between one government that can't levy a punishment and another that won't, gets away with actions it could never carry out at home'[82] – is termed 'the governance gap', I suggest here that it is this very gap, as well as the closure of this gap with CICL, that constitutes corporate (governance) or Monsieur Le Capital's power.

In most jurisdictions, including the UK, the laws necessary for corporate legal accountability for human rights abuses already exist. Britain was at the forefront of adopting Ruggie's three pillars and the first to publish a national action plan in 2013, with an update published in May 2016.[83] We can see the role of

80 See, e.g., McBarnet 2007, p. 9; Stoitchkova 2010; Bernaz 2016.

81 *UN HRC OEIGWG 2017 Report*, emphasis added.

82 Mike Baab 'I Live My Life One Professional Conference At A Time', 21 February 2017.

83 See also the updated Plan, published in 2016 and heavily criticised by various NGOs and IOs; and for a critique, see: CORE Coalition n.d., 12 May 2016.

NGO lawyers and activists in this through, for example, the work of the British NGO Traidcraft. This campaigning organisation in a 2015 report 'Above the Law' noted that the remaining problem is that the political will to enforce these norms is lacking. The solution Traidcraft offers is a new legal framework – and at first glance this seems illogical considering the political will required to pass (and indeed enforce) such new laws. Traidcraft's report also notes that directors of 69 percent of UK companies agree that companies should be accountable for harms caused abroad.[84] Viewed in light of the dia/panlectical development of corporate ideology as described in this section, however, this makes sense. Following Bakan, who has argued that corporations participate in CSR processes in order to shape the narrative and ensure that any resulting private regulation regimes are optimally calibrated to business interests,[85] we could argue that the engagement in advocating and negotiating *legal* changes is likewise an effort to 'control the field' and possibly even *erode* existing legal standards or change liability models or enforcement policies with similar effect.[86]

Shamir has argued that a corporate conscience, or 'soul', had to be constructed – the corporation had to be 'remoralised', in order for self-regulation to be viewed as a legitimate mechanism.[87] Likewise, by extension, it is corporate right (corporate good citizenship), which creates corporate wrong/crime and, dialectically, vice versa: corporate accountability creates the 'good corporation'.[88] Corporate accountability thus equals 'commodified (and canned) morality' or 'moral' behaviour with a clear economic benefit. The value of this dynamic is the legitimation of the corporation as the main surplus-value extracting mechanism – but also, as a 'good corporate citizen', as an actor in global governance with an as yet undefined mandate – as an enthusiastic participant in all important global fora, from Davos to Paris for COP21. In the next section, I set out how CA cause lawyering inadvertently contributes to this.

3.2 *CA Cause Lawyering*

In recent years the focus of those raising concerns about corporations has shifted largely to the Global South – possibly because a 'kinder capitalism'

84 Traidcraft, 27 November 2015.
85 Bakan 2015, p. 295.
86 Which, in fact, it does. See below and Traidcraft 2015, pp. 10–12.
87 Shamir 2010, p. 536.
88 See also Baars 2011, p. 415; Shamir 2008, p. 1.

at home has limited, or concealed from scrutiny, 'corporate excess' in the metropole to all but the most eagle-eyed,[89] and because Western corporations have a global reach not seen since the British East India Company.[90] CA cause lawyers have mostly worked on these, rather than Western companies' domestic activities also because of the internationalisation of NGO activities (and funding), and the seemingly useful legal tools in international law. Accountability solutions have mainly been sought in international human rights and criminal law applied domestically in home states (for extraterritorial activities) rather than domestic (host state) law per se. Particularly, the availability of ICL norms and the growth of the international human rights industry with a new focus on private actors, producing hard-hitting reports about business involvement in 'foreign'/international conflict, extraordinarily exploitative labour conditions and environmental destruction, and in general the increasing litigiousness of human rights / social justice practice has led 'cause lawyers' to attempt to hold corporations (and occasionally individuals) to account for violations in home state courts.[91] In a parallel, and dialectically connected, development, broader publics have been mobilised, and have responded to, the emotive discourse around 'corporate impunity'. The CA lawsuits appear to form the counterpoint to CSR, being aimed at 'bad corporations', making cause lawyers the designated (and thus far *only*) putative 'enforcers' of (legalised/'weaponised') CSR and corporate ICL. This puts them in a position of potentially, counter-intuitively, creating value for the corporation and corporate capitalism.

Cause lawyers and legal/human rights NGOs have found various ways of bringing claims in national courts ultimately based on violations of international human rights law and ICL.[92] Best known of these are the compensation suits brought against corporations (normally as legal persons, sometimes in conjunction with key corporate officers) under the Alien Tort Statute (ATS) and other provisions of US law, which have been numerous and highly publi-

89 Scrutiny of, and resistance against, domestic corporate activity does continue in the work of organisations such as Corporate Watch, Reclaim the Power, and Plane Stupid: https://corporatewatch.org/; https://reclaimthepower.org.uk/; http://www.planestupid.com/.

90 Also, some Chinese, Indian and Gulf corporations have a global reach – but CA focuses largely on Western corporations.

91 Sarat and Scheingold are credited with coining the term 'cause lawyers', which they define as 'lawyers who commit themselves and their legal skills to a vision of the good society'. Sarat and Scheingold 1998, p. 3.

92 See, e.g., Business and Human Rights Legal Accountability Portal, available at: http://business-humanrights.org/en/corporate-legal-accountability.

cised.[93] A small number of similar cases have been brought in Canada[94] and in Europe.[95] Where civil compensation claims for ICL violations are not possible, cause lawyers have found other strategic litigation methods around corporate involvement in conflict.[96] Public interest lawyers in France have taken some more imaginative public law and contract law cases that are ultimately based on the allegation of an international crime.[97]

The US has seen exponentially more CA cases than anywhere else in the world. A rush of cases started when Peter Weiss, chairman of the Center for Constitutional Rights (CCR), unearthed the long-forgotten ATS in the 1970s while searching for a legal means to hold to account those responsible for the My Lai massacre. He drew on his experience as one of the Morgenthau Boys investigating the German industrialists preceding their prosecution at Nuremberg when applying the instrument to litigation against corporations allegedly involved in international crimes.[98] In 1996 CCR filed cases under the ATS against *Unocal*, accusing the US oil company[99] of using slave labour in its plants in Burma, in collusion with the Burmese dictatorship.[100] Similar cases at the time were brought against the major Western oil and mining companies[101] and against financiers of, and suppliers to, oppressive regimes such as the South

93 This US instrument allows aliens (and Americans) to bring civil suits in US courts against parties who have, or are accused of having, committed a violation of international law. Alien Tort Statute, 28 U.S.C. 1350.

94 *Bil'in (Village Council) v. Green Park and Green Mount*, QCCS 2011 2 May 2011. See Yap 2010, p. 631.

95 In the UK, human rights abuse-related tort cases have been brought against, amongst others, Cape Plc. *Adams v. Cape Industries plc* [1990] BCLC 479 520. Evidence of a growing interest in such cases is the recent number of conferences and workshops on the issue, such as an effort by the European Centre for Constitutional and Human Rights, available at: http://www.ecchr.eu/en/events/archive-2013.html.

96 *In re Agent Orange Product Liability Litigation* 323 F. Supp. 2d 7 (EDNY 2005) (No. 04–400), a product liability case.

97 L'Association France Palestine Solidarité (AFPS) v. ALSTOM and VEOLIA TRANSPORT, Tribunal de Grande Instance de NANTERRE, March 2007. See AFPS 19 March 2007. Global Witness, 'Complaint accuses international timber company DLH of trading illegal timber and funding Liberian war', Press Release, 12 March 2014.

98 'Gespräch mit Peter Weiss', in *ECCHR TNU Konferenz Bericht* (ECCHR, 2008) 22, 26; Baars 2013, pp. 163–92.

99 This section in particular draws on Baars 2006, p. 97.

100 *Doe v. Unocal Corp.*, 963 F. Supp. 880 (C.D. Cal.1997); *Roe v. Unocal Corp.*, 70 F. Supp. 2d 1073 (C.D. Cal. 1999).

101 See, e.g., *The Presbyterian Church of Sudan, et al. v. Talisman Energy Inc., et al.*, USDC SDNY 2005, US Dist. 30 August 2005.

African apartheid government.[102] A major series of cases that are subject to a complex settlement mechanism is the *Holocaust Litigation* – including against Ford – for the use of forced labour.[103] Cases were also filed in relation to corporate atrocities during colonialism,[104] and against suppliers of the means to commit atrocities in war zones such as Vietnam and Palestine.[105]

US Courts have found that corporations could be held directly responsible for slave trade, genocide, war crimes, and other so-called 'offences of universal concern'.[106] They have also accepted the principle of corporate liability for *complicity* in state acts of torture and summary execution, crimes against humanity, cruel, inhuman or degrading treatment, torture, violation of the right to life, liberty and security of the person, prolonged arbitrary detention, and peaceful assembly.[107]

Yet none of the ATS corporate cases – nor indeed most of the cases brought elsewhere[108] – have resulted in a court win for the claimants. The claims relate to atrocities that have usually affected large numbers of people. Many of these cases have taken several years, and amicus briefs have been filed by other NGOs, churches, victim support groups, trade associations, legal scholars and governments. Courts have generally dismissed these cases on technical grounds, without consideration of the merits. In certain cases, in order to avoid, or settle, a mass of lawsuits against particular companies, states have set up mechanisms to channel compensation payments to individuals who have suffered losses as a result of companies' actions or inactions. Some of these settlements have been challenged (unsuccessfully) as infringements of *individual* rights to redress.[109]

---

102 Barclays and Citigroup, amongst others, in the *Apartheid Litigation Cases*: *In re South African Apartheid Litigation: Ntsebeza et al. v. Daimler et al. and Khulumani et al. v. Barclays et al.*, 02 MDL 1499 (SAS) – 03 Civ. 4524 (SAS), 8 April 2009.

103 See, e.g., *In re. Assicurazioni Generali SpA. Holocaust Insurance Litigation*, MDL 1374, M21–89 (MBM) Opinion and Order, 25 September 2002.

104 *The Herero People's Reparations Corporation and the Herero v. Deutsche Bank AG et al.* (First Amended Complaint, 18 September 2001).

105 *In re Agent Orange Product Liability Litigation* 323 F. Supp. 2d 7 (EDNY 2005) (No. 04–400); *Corrie et al v Caterpillar Inc.*, No. 05–36210 (9th Cir. 2007); Baars 2006.

106 In the sense that motions to strike out these cases brought by the defendant, for example, on the basis that (the specifically claimed provisions of) ICL did not apply to corporations (and thus that the plaintiff failed to state a claim, or the court lacked jurisdiction), were dismissed.

107 Baars 2006, p. 121.

108 Among the exceptions is *Lubbe et al v. Cape* [2000] UKHL 41.

109 See, e.g., *In re Holocaust Victim Assets Lit.*, 302 F. Supp. 2d 89 (EDNY 2004).

In other cases, such as in the *Wiwa v. Royal Dutch Petroleum* case, a settlement was reached directly by the (representatives of the) company and (representatives of) victims where thousands of victims are to receive nominal sums for the injury to their bodies, families, communities and environments, in return for abandoning the right to file future claims.[110]

The 2013 US Supreme Court decision in *Kiobel* (on a claim brought on behalf of Ogoni Valley claimants against Royal Dutch Shell) changed the future of corporate ATS litigation.[111] The Court of Appeal for the Second Circuit held that the ATS does not confer jurisdiction on the federal courts to hear claims filed under the ATS against corporations.[112] Originally this point was to be the question in front of the Supreme Court for certiorari, however, the Court *proprio motu* changed this to the more general question of 'whether and under what circumstances courts may recognize a cause of action under the ATS' thus allowing for a potentially far-reaching reformulation of ATS law while remaining vague on corporate liability. The Supreme Court unanimously dismissed the claim because of the 'presumption against extraterritorial application of US jurisdictional statutes'.[113] Subsequently, *Cardona v. Chiquita* confirmed that no US corporation shall be held liable for conduct that took place outside the US.[114] Yet, parts of the *Cardona* case continue in a federal district court in Florida.[115] Cause lawyers, though 'baffled' by this latest string of cases, continue to litigate.[116] We can see the dialectic at work here between legitimacy challenge and legitimacy reproduction, as these cases generated a significant amount of discovery and media coverage of corporate 'crimes' and 'human rights abuses' – which in turn have spurred on corporate CSR development and the current call for legalised CSR/corporate ICL. In 2017 the original *Kiobel* question of corporate liability in IL has once again made its way to the US Supreme Court in *Jesner et al. v. Arab Bank* – asking, 'Whether the Alien Tort Statute, 28 USC §1350, categorically forecloses corporate liability'.[117] This time,

110 *Centre for Constitutional Rights Wiwa docket.*

111 *Kiobel v. Royal Dutch Petroleum Co.*, No. 10–1491 2010 U.S. App. LEXIS 19382 (2d Cir. 2010) (*Kiobel v. Shell* (2010)). The *Kiobel case* had been consolidated with the *Wiwa* case, but Kiobel et al. refused to settle. See CCR Wiwa docket.

112 *Kiobel v. Shell* (2010) 48; *Kiobel v. Royal Dutch Petroleum Co.*, 133 S. Ct. 1659 (2013).

113 *Kiobel v. Royal Dutch Petroleum Co.*, 133 S. Ct. 1659 (2013). For a detailed discussion, see Ferrando 2015, pp. 183–235.

114 *Cardona, et al. v. Chiquita Brands International, et al.*, No. 12–14898 (11th Cir. 2014).

115 Earth Rights International, 20 April 2015.

116 Ferrando 2015.

117 *Joseph Jesner et al. v. Arab Bank PLC*, On Petition for a Writ of Certiorari to the United States Court of Appeals for the Second Circuit, No. 16–499, granted April 3 2017.

it appears in a case which commentators feel is much more likely to lead to a confirmative finding, considering the accused is the Arab Bank, in a case concerning alleged 'terrorist funding'. The claimants are relatives of Israeli victims and survivors of suicide attacks carried out by Palestinians over the past decades since the first *intifada*.[118] Unsurprisingly, far fewer amicus briefs were filed in support of the Arab Bank's argument.[119] The various parts of the US state (State Department against the Treasury and Justice Department) have in the earlier stages of this case already claimed contradicting stakes in this case, perhaps reminding us of the intra-governmental disagreements around the appropriate treatment of the German industrialists discussed in Chapter 3.[120]

3.3 *Legalising CSR and Cause Lawyering*

We can see how legalised CSR and cause lawyering feed off and stimulate one another. Collaboration between civil society and international legal institutions/officials has favoured CICL increasingly since in 2003 the then ICC Prosecutor Luis Moreno-Ocampo suggested that he was minded – with the help of aid organisations on the ground – to pursue corporate actors complicit in the DRC genocide[121] – seemingly undeterred by the ICC's lack of jurisdiction. No actual prosecutions ensued, but the issue of corporate wrongdoing has continued to be brought to the attention of the ICC. The DRC, in the context of its self-referral, has brought to the ICC's attention the alleged complicity of (Western) MNCs in the genocide (see Chapter 5, Section 2.1). Over ten years – and no corporate prosecutions later – in Autumn 2016 the current ICC Prosecutor, Fatou Bensouda, in her new case-selection policy also expressed willingness to receive complaints about corporate actors – mentioning in particular the issue of land grabs.[122] A new form of weaponised CSR cause lawyering is starting to emerge, and involves filing complaints at the ICC against corporate

---

118 *Jesner v. Arab Bank* S. Ct. No. 16–499 (2017).

119 See http://www.scotusblog.com/case-files/cases/jesner-v-arab-bank-plc/.

120 'The quandary facing the administration stems from the unusual trade-offs between issues that are rarely linked, including diplomatic efforts to achieve Middle East peace, the rights of American victims of terrorism, and an American campaign to tear down Swiss banking secrecy laws that have long aided tax evasion'. *New York Times*, 1 April 2014.

121 *Ocampo 2003 Report to States Parties*; *Ocampo Complicity Speech 2005*.

122 Office of the Prosecutor, Policy on Case Selection and Prioritization, 15 September 2016.

actors. In 2014, for example, Cambodian victims of land grabs amounting to crimes against humanity by sugar company officers filed their complaint,[123] which was followed by a submission targeting Chevron for the destruction in the Lago Agrio region of Ecuador, also claimed (but denied) to amount to crimes against humanity.[124] More recently, submissions have been made relating to Chiquita's alleged complicity in the murder, forced displacement, enforced disappearance, sexual violence, torture, and persecution of civilians carried out by a paramilitary group,[125] and corporate participation in the off-shore detention of refugees by Australia.[126] In the meantime other semi, quasi and metajudicial bodies with international gravitas have urged the accountability of corporations: for example, the statements by the Liberia Truth and Reconciliation Commission urging the further investigation of 19 multinational corporations allegedly involved in the Liberian civil war.[127] This general movement has been supported by civil society initiatives such as the International Corporate Accountability Roundtable's Corporate Accountability Principles.[128]

Combined with the findings reported in Chapter 4C (Malabo Protocol, ILC Crimes against Humanity draft convention, STL contempt cases) we can see that there is a movement toward the adoption of CICL in scholarship as well as practice, in a variety of environments.

4 Legalised CSR, CA Cause Lawyering and Corporate ICL Problematised

Just as it was argued in the 1940s that international human rights law would only 'make sense' if there were a way to hold individuals to account for violations, which became ICL, so (global) corporate citizenship now only 'makes sense' when it is linked to the possibility of holding corporations to account in ICL. Subjection to corporate ICL validates the moralisation of Monsieur Le Capital, and completes the process of CSR. Here I comment on the value, as part of corporate ideology, of CSR and corporate ICL, as generated through the

123 *FIDH* 7 October 2014; see also Ferrando 2017.

124 *Chevron Texaco ICC Complaint*; see also above Ch. 5.

125 *FIDH* May 2017.

126 *Global Legal Action Network* 2017.

127 *Liberia Truth and Reconciliation* 2006. See also: International Centre for Transitional Justice 2010.

128 *ICAR*, Independent Commission of Experts, The Corporate Crimes Principles: Advancing Investigations and Prosecutions in Human Rights Cases, October 2016.

work of cause lawyers as well as the proponents of legalised CSR. Although the CA efforts discussed here have many positive effects, not least the vastly increased public knowledge of corporate activities globally, I argue here that the strategies are *part of the problem* along four axes. I first look at compliance and class, then enforcement and imperialism. I then comment on cause lawyering as the reproduction of white privilege, before discussing the idea of a 'market for responsibility' – which is where corporate ICL, CSR and cause lawyering potentially meet. I conclude on corporate power, legitimacy and the logic of law.

4.1 *Corporate Crime, Compliance and Class*

A preliminary critique of the development of a 'corporate ICL' or *Wirtschaftsvölkerstrafrecht*[129] is that it excludes business actors from a general legal regime on the basis that they are *sui generis* and should thus have their own set of rules and enforcement policies. Additionally, the mere existence of a corporate crime rule inevitably removes the focus from individual businesspeople and thus contributes to the reification of the corporation 'emptied of individuals' – further facilitating the relative risk-free extraction of surplus value by the protected owners of the means of production.

The main lesson from English law is that 'corporate crime', despite having been 'on the books' for decades, has not been used to prosecute corporations except in a small number of cases.[130] On the domestic level, under neoliberal regimes, rather than enforcement/punishment models, compliance models of corporate regulation are predominant.[131] This is a function of corporate economic power and common class interest among business and legal/political elites. For this reason, there is likely only to be a semantic/ideological difference between existing voluntary and any new *legally binding* norms, as the latter are unlikely to be enforced with much rigour. Nevertheless, the mere existence of binding CSR/corporate ICL combined with a 'compliance culture' has the power to deflate the complaint of 'corporate impunity'. Building and invoking a compliance culture has two main effects described (in the domestic context) by Hawkins, Snider, Slapper and Pearce and Tombs in the 'punishment model versus compliance school debate' of the early 1990s.[132] The first

129 Literally, 'economic international criminal law' (Jeßberger 2009, p. 924).

130 Whyte 2008, p. 103. One such exceptional case is *R v. P&O Ferries (Dover) Ltd.* [1991] 93 Cr App Rep 72.

131 Gray 2006, pp. 875, 887.

132 On the punishment versus compliance models debate in criminal law generally, see the debate in the *British Journal of Criminology* between Pearce and Tombs (for punishment)

is that a corporation can shield itself from criminal liability by adopting programmes that provide technical compliance while not actually reducing the incidence of crime, and the so-called 'due diligence defence' could be invoked (by arguing managers had followed protocol) to ward off the risk of a finding of non-compliance. The second is the class-effect.

The *Afrimex* case exemplifies how CSR (specifically, the adoption of a CSR policy or document) can function to insulate against a finding of violation of the *OECD Guidelines*.[133] From this it is not difficult to imagine how CA court litigation may be decided in a similar way: companies show readiness to cooperate by emphasising their CSR policies, promise to adopt such policies, etc. This would prove pivotal as grounds for dismissing the claim. The UN Special Representative on Business and Human Rights has defined the 'responsibility to respect' human rights as 'in essence mean[ing,] to act with due diligence to avoid infringing on the rights of others'.[134] Legalised CSR, which would likely be based on the Guiding Principles[135] and would have the same effect as domestic corporate crime law. Due diligence works through the delegation of responsibility: each lower-level employee has her specific task list and has received training on compliance and has to sign off on compliance on tasks. This constitutes a 'compliance system' put in place by a senior manager (who has thus acted with due diligence) such that all aberrant results are the result of worker deviance.[136] This means that, even with corporate ICL, the most likely target of enforcement action (if any) is an individual low-ranking worker. As such, corporate responsibility/liability immunises the corporation itself, and the directors and managers, by shifting the blame to the workers. Compliance, especially certified compliance, obviates corporate 'command responsibility'.[137] For instance, a corporation could institute a programme in which low-level managers were instructed not to overwork their subordinates. The corporation then sets quotas that the managers cannot meet unless they overwork their subordinates. In this way, the low-level managers take all the blame if discovered. At the same time, it is very hard to investigate such claims because only someone who thoroughly understands a business could tell whether quotas

and Hawkins (for the compliance model): Pearce and Tombs 1990, p. 423; Hawkins 1990, p. 444; Hawkins 1991, p. 427; Gray 2006.

133 Final Statement by the UK National Contact Point for the OECD Guidelines for Multinational Enterprises: Afrimex (UK).

134 *Ruggie* (2009) *Report*, 2.

135 *Ruggie* (2011) *Report*.

136 Gray 2006, pp. 875, 885.

137 Certification and labelling schemes have a similar risk spreading/displacing rationale, see, e.g., LeBaron and Lister 2016.

were unrealistic.[138] Here we see how capital works to protect itself (preserve value) seemingly in the face of mechanisms formulated to restrain it – amounting to 'planned impunity' for the corporate 'structure of irresponsibility'. Thus it is no longer hard to see why British businesses would support the change to a due diligence, or 'failure to prevent' liability model.[139]

Should legalised CSR or corporate ICL be enforced (beyond worker discipline) in an exceptional case (and no 'deferred prosecution agreement' be made), a financial penalty, or indeed any penalty that in a practical sense translates into a financial penalty (e.g., revoking the licence of a 'blood diamond' trader) will likely be accounted for by raising prices of products or services; cutting workers' numbers, pay or conditions; or cutting expenditure on, say, measures to decrease the corporation's negative effects on the environment.[140] As such punishment of the corporation is 'socialised' like any other risk, and may lead to the (collective) punishment of workers or external parties. Nader described in the 1970s how corporations can opt to pay a fine rather than employ technology to conform to safety or environmental regulation, if the latter is more costly.[141] The key barrier to 'effectiveness' of sanctions in the sense normally used in criminal law is that a sanction would not change the rational basis for corporate decision-making, nor the individuals who made the relevant decisions, but the burden of compliance would affect the global working class.[142] Corporate accountability here maintains and reproduces, with renewed legitimacy, the value-extracting rationale of the corporation and corporate capitalism.

4.2 *Enforcement and Imperialism*

Forcese has described CSR as only being necessary because Third World countries, with 'underdeveloped legal systems', are simply not able to write and enforce their own rules for corporate behaviour.[143] Such countries in his view, moreover, may have 'oppressive leaders' making it even more necessary for developed-country multinationals to seek (voluntarily) to set standards of good behaviour. Forcese suggests that CSR could be 'administered' by the interna-

138 For further such examples, see Gray 2006.

139 *Traidcraft* 2015, pp. 11–12: 'Companies and directors would be able to call upon an adequate procedures defence to show that systems were in place to prevent harms'.

140 Simester 2010, p. 283. Keep in mind the negative effects of fines on employees, creditors, and shareholders not implicated in wrongdoing. Other options, such as corporate probation or equity fines, are fraught with practical and theoretical difficulties.

141 Nader 1965.

142 Gray 2006, p. 875.

143 Forcese 2009, p. 723.

tional investment dispute resolution mechanisms, and/or by means of 'smart sanctions'.[144] Such language clearly echoes that of international law's racist 'civilising mission', the export of 'Western' law through IFIs (Chapter 2B), and ICL as a tool for intervention.

It is well known that the shift of most manufacturing and extraction industries to the Global South suits business due to lower costs (as a result of factors such as low wages and less stringent regulation or enforcement), and where the 'crimes' are not normally visible to us, and the victims are not known to Western publics.[145] With increased CA and public scrutiny, however, the risk of brand-name damage as a result of a 'scandal' is real. It is exactly that brand value that enables a story to be spun that the scandal is the fault of a, at most, 'badly chosen' subcontractor rather than a result of supply chain power distribution and price squeeze.

If we combine this with Forcese's point (or *attitude*) above, we can see how corporate crime, warded off by the adoption of CSR compliance programmes, may create a distinction between 'civilised' Western-based multinational corporations on the one hand, and 'backward' host state companies on the other. Legalised CSR creates the possibility of selective enforcement against 'uncivilised' corporations, to 'level the playing field',[146] or eliminate that which 'by its unpopularity poisons the pond in which we all must all fish'.[147]

An example of potentially 'imperialist ICL' is the OSI pillage litigation project, which has as its aim to intervene in the (mainly) African context of conflict resources. It could become the paragon of pro-business use of ICL, if it activates the proposals aimed at regulating the natural resource market in the conflict zones of Africa so as to enable prosecution of 'rogue' traders and miners connected to armed groups, thus enabling international corporations to mine and trade without the (costly) 'blood diamond' label.[148] In sum, legalised CSR and Corporate ICL appear to be deployed particularly in order to facilitate continued value extraction particularly by metropolitan corporations, and thus the continued exploitation of mostly Third World workers.

144 Forcese 2009, p. 283.

145 In any case, acts committed by non-customer-facing industries, e.g., shipping, are much less susceptible to such public exposure.

146 Traidcraft specifically refers to 'cowboys' who 'act … as if they are above the law' and '[i]n doing so … also damage the reputation of responsible British companies', echoing David Cameron's 2013 speech to the World Economic Forum. Traidcraft 2015, p. 3.

147 Cryer 2005, pp. 191 ff.; Marchand 1998, p. 203.

148 Stewart 2010.

4.3 *Cause Lawyering as the Domestication of Class Struggle and Reproduction of White Privilege*

If we look at the matter from the point of view of those engaged in legal practice, we can see that in recent decades the promise of ICL has turned civil rights and criminal defence lawyers into lawyers seeking criminal prosecution. The romantic ideal of the civil rights movement, of 'little people and landmark decisions',[149] of 'speaking law to power', has – in the context of ICL – turned lawyers to voicing traditionally statist carceral claims for order and control through criminal law. Viewed through a Marxist theoretical lens, such cause lawyering might be seen as a form of resistance or class struggle, as a tactical 'principled opportunism'[150] that may be successful when it coincides with 'judicial activism'.[151] Although these attempts do amount to resistance, they are not emancipatory, and their (unintended) effect is rather, on the one hand, to domesticate class struggle, and, on the other, to actualise, legitimate, and strengthen the existing structures of power and, thus value extraction.[152]

CA cause lawyering, based on extraterritorial claims and CSR legalised by means of a treaty, 'lifts' corporate behaviour out of local host state jurisdictions and potential local control (the locality of the harm and thus the affected persons) into a de facto Western capitalist realm of international normativity. In particular, compensation claims and settlements create an exchange relationship where the 'victim' sells her right and the corporate offender calculates risk.[153] We thus have a situation of 'calculable law' where value is created for the corporation and corporate capitalism through predictability of risk, as well as, and more so, through the ideological effect of the existence and operation of an accountability mechanism (even if partial or selective).

The active agent in actualising the legal relationship between the individual 'victim' and the corporation are the cause lawyers themselves. While human rights claims are 'claims for admittance to law',[154] the role of lawyers persuading people to bring cases in (Western) foreign courts is in some way the equivalent of 'spreading capitalist law' (as part of the civilising or *capitalising* mission) as

149 *Ha'aretz*, 28 November 2008. The byline of the article reads, 'Sometimes all it takes to right a wrong is for one person to stand up and make his or her voice heard'.

150 See, generally, Knox 2009, p. 413.

151 See, generally, Marks 2007, p. 199.

152 This is the conclusion of Ziv and Shamir 2001, p. 287; Sfard 2009, p. 37; Barzilai, 'The Ambivalent Language of Lawyers in Israel: Liberal Politics, Economic Liberalism, Silence, and Dissent', in Halliday, Karpik and Feeley 2007, p. 247.

153 However, these cases do have limited value for promoting mobilisation and demystification: Baars 2012.

154 Douzinas 2010, p. 95.

done by the corporate colonisers in the nineteenth century.[155] claim to be valid and recognised, the human being must becom ject, she must articulate her needs, grievances and desires in lega and in a Western courtroom, through the mouth of (usually) a w She must 'join the system' in the same way that 'decolonised' peoples had to join the Western state system and European international law. As a Western lawyer I may think I am the enabler, the empowering medium in this equation, but in fact I am the opposite, as I produce (constitute) the 'victim'[157] and demand her surrender to my expertise, and I become a rights-entrepreneur.[158] I, the white lawyer, claim to speak for the oppressed, for justice, but I speak for capitalism, as its enforcer.[159] Thus, inadvertently, such cause lawyers come to create value for the corporation/corporate capitalism – extracted from those on whom the suffering has been inflicted as well as (often) the natural environment, and barely 'compensated', if at all.

A harrowing account of one former NGO worker's experience of the UN's Annual Forum on Business and Human Rights describes the change from a forum where real constructive debate was held between activists, policy makers and corporate leaders, to a 'trade show'.[160] Capitalism's ability to adapt when challenged leads it to commodify or consume genuine resistance efforts, where the players desperate for funding are morphed into MaNGOs, grass roots becomes Astroturf. Where lawyers settle and activist take jobs in corporate CSR departments.

4.4 *Settlements and Selling Rights: a Market for Responsibility*

Through the lens of the *commodity form theory of law*, compensation claims and settlements create an exchange relationship where the 'victim' sells her right and the corporate offender calculates the risk (price). The corporate decision maker gets to calculate the benefit of the violation (e.g., conflict diamonds are likely to be cheaper than 'clean' diamonds), the chance that those affected will speak out or find (or be found by) a human rights organisation (or UN appointed expert), the chance that they will commence litigation, the

155 Baars 2015.

156 Cf. Neocosmos 2006, pp. 356, 357.

157 Madlingozi 2010, p. 208.

158 Davis uses this term for cause lawyers (Davis 2008, p. 44).

159 A more cynical scenario is that of some cause lawyers 'creating' victims, instrumentalising them for their own political or personal career goals.

160 Michael Hobbes, 'Saving the World, One Meaningless Buzzword at a Time: How corporations, activists, and politicians turned the language of human rights into meaningless babble', *Foreign Policy*, 21 February 2017.

chance a court will keep the case going for a few years while the human rights NGO publicises the issue, the expected drop in sales and or share price, lawyers' fees, in the process of determining whether, finally, to come to a settlement. The decision whether to cause the harm has a *calculable* price tag. For the 'victim', the need, desire to be free of injury, becomes a 'right' which can be worth investing in through, for example, lawyers' fees, time away from regular productive labour, in return for a calculable chance of success. What is my price, for what sum will I relinquish all further claims? Victim and violator negotiate as *formal legal equals*.

The question arises of why businesses or the individuals behind them would settle such cases at all if the record shows that the likelihood of the petitioners winning in court is next to nil.[161] To analogise Sfard, who asks a similar question in the context of anti-occupation cause-lawyering in the Israeli courts, such settlements are beneficial to the company both *directly* as it allows them to look generous and recover from bad press, as well as to get claimants to sign statements relinquishing future claims, and *indirectly* as it 'supplies the oxygen' of the system of capitalism itself, helping to render it sustainable and legitimate.[162]

The essence of my critique here is that ATS and similar cases (including, potentially, legalised CSR and corporate liability in ICL with mainly financial penalties or penalties that can ultimately be converted into a mere financial penalty)[163] turn the 'international crime' from a problem of international society into a problem between the individual victim (or group) and a powerful 'fictional' economic entity in a powerful state – a quantifiable problem if it is 'settled' or receives a financial penalty.[164] However, criminal fines could partially be allocated to victims, meaning that a successful criminal conviction, should such occur, would 'yield' the same result as a successful civil complaint. For example, in December 2011, Trafigura was convicted in a Dutch court of hav-

---

161 I adapt this point from Sfard 2009, p. 44: 'Why are the authorities ready to compromise "in the shadow of the court" when reality shows that the Court rarely, if ever, decides in favour of the Palestinian petitioners?'.

162 Sfard 2009, p. 45 by analogy. On this notion see Barzilai 2007, p. 270: 'Defying silence through litigation has also further legitimated the state, its main narratives, and state courts as markers of state and society relations'.

163 E.g., licensing penalties or 'corporate death penalty', which can be overcome through alternative licenses and the formation of new companies, at a cost.

164 For the current 'enforcers' such as CCR and other private cause lawyers, it is not financially feasible to file criminal cases (aside from whether criminal cases can be brought/initiated by private parties) because they normally also rely on settlement deals for their own funding.

ing concealed the dangerous nature of the waste aboard the *Probo Koala* ship. The company's fine was decreased by the court to €1m because the company had set up a compensation fund for victims.[165] This 'solution' serves to take the 'victim' out of the picture as an agent and merely positions her as a recipient of goodwill gestures from the corporation.[166] Subsequent cases, filed in The Netherlands, France and the UK, seeking compensation for the harm to thousands of Ivory Coast citizens affected by toxic waste dumped from Trafigura's ship, resulted in dismissals and out-of-court settlements.[167] Corporate accountability commodifies the 'right' of the individual to be protected from crime (to remain free from harm); the individual is *forced* to sell by means of a material and (thus) power differential. I say 'forced', because the situation is comparable to 'free' labour and may be necessary for survival just as a Third World worker cannot walk out on a situation where her rights are being abused. As such, the rights/crimes paradigm is liberalism's essence: in global governance, it is each individual's own responsibility to 'valorise' or to claim (negotiate, exchange) her right: claim your prize! Responsibility for violating a right (causing harm) exists only insofar as (and to the value of) the right (which is) claimed: *accountability* is achieved.

By participating in the efforts to legalise CSR and to create the possibility for corporate ICL, corporations are not just turning a bad situation into a profitable one, but at the same time, they are again owning the process, 'controlling the field'. It is noteworthy that the breakdown of participants at the 4th UN Annual Forum on Business and Human Rights is as follows: 32% NGOs, 22% business (including executives from Shell, Unilever and Newmont Mining), 12% government, 15% academics.[168] The result is the creation of corporate ideology of 'canned morality' – the dispensing of commodified moral disapproval in order to conceal the transactions that lie below the surface of corporate accountability. The most important transaction is paying off the victims that have been created and placed into a relation of exchange, which results in a return to a balanced account, and to innocence. This transaction also conceals the structure, the broader effects on society and the natural environment, beyond that individual victim. This means that 'canned morality' is deployed

165 Trafigura, LJN: BU9237, Gerechtshof Amsterdam, 23 December 2011, Case No. 23-003334-10.

166 Shamir 2010, pp. 531–53.

167 'Trafigura lawsuits (re Côte d'Ivoire)', Business and Human Rights Resource Centre; 'Ivory Coast Toxic Waste Victims Still Await Payments', VOANEWS, 12 November 2015.

168 The remainder is made up of members of national human rights institutes and unions. Business and Human Rights Resource Centre Weekly Update, 18 November 2015.

to achieve precisely the opposite of what it is said to achieve: namely, liability is socialised, shifted to wider society and the natural environment. This move legitimises the corporation, all corporations, and corporate capitalism itself. This is allowed to occur, because, as Berle has suggested, accountability (canned morality applied to corporations) in the 'mainstream' sense responds to a demand, and on a deeper level, to expectations of democracy. Generally, the link between accountability and legitimacy is as old as the separation of powers, the rule of law, and democracy itself. Yet, 'canned morality' is as far away from democracy as we can get.

4.5 *Corporate Power, Legitimacy and Law*

On the domestic level, Glasbeek has argued, corporate criminal responsibility was a 'major response developed by law-makers trying to put their fingers in the dyke holding back the flood of illegitimacy threatening to drown the corporate form'.[169] I noted above that corporate power has material and ideological elements. Corporate ICL, legalised CSR, actualised through claims by cause lawyers, *constitutes* and *completes* the corporation as a person. It also facilitates the spread of capitalist law, maintains global class differences, puts a price tag on rights, and absorbs emancipatory energy. Corporate liability constitutes the corporation not as an amoral calculator (pathological 'monster'), but as a *political citizen who occasionally errs*.[170] Criminal law is a regime of exception, where corporate transgressions would be constituted as exceptional rather than the normal, inevitable and a *necessary* consequence of the prevailing mode of production.

In a move that may have surprised some, the US Government on 21 December 2011 filed an *amicus curiae* brief in support of the claimants in *Kiobel*, arguing that it is for the federal courts exercising their 'residual' common law powers to determine whether and when corporate liability is appropriate. Taking into account the arguments raised in this chapter, it is clear to see why the US government would wish to keep the corporate liability for international law violations option open. The US Government itself phrases its interest in the case thus: 'The United States has an interest in the proper application of the ATS because such actions can have implications for the Nation's foreign and commercial relations and for the enforcement of international law'.[171]

---

169 Glasbeek 2004, p. 17.

170 Pearce and Tombs 1990, p. 423.

171 *Kiobel v. Royal Dutch Petroleum Co.*, Brief for the United States as Amicus Curiae Supporting Petitioners, p. 1.

Having corporate criminal liability 'on the books' can be highly valuable for use against scapegoats or bad apples. Such liability is conceived as states' residual sovereign right to control its own corporations (or to punish those of others). On the majority CA-engaged civil society point, Daniel Augenstein argues that CA must be seen instead as the obligation on home states to provide Third World victims with a right of redress.[172] However, this vision still depends on global power elites to grant *and fulfil* that right – which will only rarely be in their interest.[173] Further, it depends on a vision of law as an unqualified good, operating autonomously from power/capital according to a logic of (social) justice, which, I hope to have shown, it does not.

Finally, the UK government was the first in the world to publish its 'Action Plan' in fulfilment of its obligations to implement the UN Guiding Principles on Business and Human Rights, the purpose of which it summarises as follows:

- Helping to protect and enhance a company's reputation and brand value;
- Protecting and increasing the customer base, as consumers increasingly seek out companies with higher ethical standards;
- Helping companies attract and retain good staff, contributing to lower rates of staff turnover and higher productivity, and increasing employee motivation;
- Reducing risks to operational continuity resulting from conflict inside the company itself (strikes and other labour disputes), or with the local community or other parties (social licence to operate);
- Reducing the risk of litigation for human rights abuses;
- Appealing to institutional investors, including pension funds, who are increasingly taking ethical, including human rights, factors into account in their investment decisions;
- Helping companies to become a partner/investor of choice for other businesses or governments that are concerned to avoid human rights risks.[174]

This summary is remarkable for at least three reasons. First, it seems wholly and brashly premised on the 'business case', addressing business as its main audience, signifying the primacy of capital. Second, 'victims' or those affected by abuses of British corporations abroad[175] are entirely absent. And third, taken as a whole, this statement signifies the effectivity or 'confidence' of corporate

172 Augenstein 2014, p. 41.

173 See also Business and Human Rights Resource Centre, Corporate Legal Accountability Annual Briefing: 'Corporate Impunity is common and remedy for victims is rare', April 2017.

174 *UK BHR Action Plan.*

175 See, e.g., Core Coalition, 'The Bottom Line: UK Corporate Abuse Abroad', October 2015.

capitalism in its legitimacy, such that only a modicum of 'canned morality' is required for acceptance. Assigning responsibility here does not therefore create a tighter connection between acts and consequences, or strengthen accountability (in its common understanding); instead it is an ideological achievement, namely the development of intuitive comfort with the current logic of empathy redistribution.[176] Corporate legitimacy has become calculably 'cheap' – or rather – *cheaply produced* with a large profit margin.

4.6 *The Dark Side of 'Corporate Accountability'*

Although CA efforts may occasionally serve to restrain business involvement in conflict or improve the situation of persons affected by such involvement, added together they are only cosmetic changes on the surface of ongoing corporate-led human and environmental exploitation.[177] They are *significant* cosmetic changes in that they, in fact, sustain our illusion of the possibility, forever deferred, of systemic change through law. They are, as Peter Fleming has put it, contextualised truth-telling functions as a tactic of mystification.[178] Human rights law, ICL, and so on, thus serve as a 'ruse to perpetuate class rule'.[179] To be precise, global class rule. Human rights risk management is perhaps the new term for CA, according to Ruggie. In a letter to the heads of the Global Commission on Business and Sustainable Development, he speaks of 'a tremendous opportunity' for businesses 'to find new customers, investors, partners and employees'.[180] Here I have focused on CA. But we have other ways of reducing the room for legal manoeuvre in the states hosting our FDI and providing the workers that sew our garments and extract the resources we 'dispossess' from them.[181] The effect of these efforts is, on the one hand, to domesticate

---

176 Cf. Konings 2015, p. 111.

177 Sfard 2009, p. 39.

178 Fleming 2017.

179 Glasbeek 2010, p. 250: 'it is important for law to mask that it exists for capitalism'.

180 Ruggie is writing in his capacity as chair of Shift, a project with the aim of advising business on GP implementation, available at: https://www.shiftproject.org/resources/viewpoints/sustainable-development-goals-guiding-principles/; see also the resignation letter of the former chair of the UN Working Group of Human Rights and Transnational Corporations and Other Businesses, Puvan Selvanathan, complaining that UN 'fossils' do not understand what motivates corporations, and that 'there is a strong symbiosis between states, business and civil society for global governance, economics and politics. More things are better because more of us from different sectors work together' in line with the 'shared responsibility' approach. Letter dated 15 May 2015, available at: https://business-humanrights.org/sites/default/files/documents/Letter%20to%20the%20President%20HRC.pdf.

181 I use the word 'dispossess' to refer to Harvey's 'accumulation by dispossession' (Harvey 2003, p. 137).

class struggle, and on the other, to actualise, legitimate and thu the existing structures of power.[182] All that is challenged and all without sanction is implicitly declared innocent. All that is *not* ch 'rights-entrepreneurs' *never even happened*.[183]

At the same time, an active human rights/cause lawyering scene willing to engage corporations in court creates the impression (illusion) that the system is democratic, that there is access to 'justice' and a remedy, that capitalism is rule-governed, with the broader implication being a 'sociological and psychological process of transference of moral responsibility from the individual ... to the justice system'.[184] As such, cause lawyering is a profoundly liberal 'in-power' activity.[185]

ICL can be seen as the 'completion piece' of international law, which served, along with other elements of 'humanitarian' international law, to legitimise the international law enterprise. By analogy, it can be said that CSR, corporate litigation, and also 'corporate ICL' – together 'corporate accountability' – complete the reification of the corporation that began in the eighteenth century. As such, 'corporate accountability' forms the main part of what Klein has called 'the 50 year campaign for total corporate liberation'.[186] By constituting the corporation as a responsible citizen, who 'like everyone else' risks criminal penalty for doing wrong, the global capitalist class has completed the corporation's reification, thus allowing the corporation to exercise legitimate authority within 'global governance'. For example, in an almost implausible tour de force, in September 2015 the *Financial Times* reported that Shell, BHP and GE will advise governments on climate change.[187] The re-moralisation of the corporation described in this chapter at first sight appears to be the reverse of the project achieved by 'calculable law'. However, the corporation is infused with 'canned morality', not a commodity form ethic. Corporate accountability is still, 'corporate accountability'. 'Marketised morality',[188] the 'responsibilised' corporation, has, moreover, dissolved the epistemological distinction between society and the market (more or less, the public and the private, or the economic and the political). In pluralist global governance conceptions, corporations, states

182 Barzilai 2007, p. 270.

183 Pashukanis 1978, p. 167: 'the normal as such is not prescribed at first; it simply does not exist'.

184 Sfard 2009, p. 45.

185 Barzilai 2007.

186 Klein 2007, p. 19.

187 See, e.g., Clark, 'Shell, BHP and GE to advise governments on climate change', *Financial Times*, 24 September 2015.

188 Shamir 2008, p. 9; Shamir 2010, p. 531; Baars 2011, pp. 427–30.

and individuals can now interact as formal legal equals. 'Corporate rule', or the multiplication of global capitalist class rule through corporations, is here, and legitimate. Thus, corporate capitalism can continue its unending search for surplus value, now even through an 'American South Asia Company'. At the same time, the contradiction inherent in this situation, the cracks in the bond, is that such legally constructed 'irresponsibility' (planned impunity) contributes to the anarchy of capitalism, which will inevitably lead to its collapse.[189] This, together with the global 99 percent's growing consciousness – the active factor in the coming revolution – is the '*seed of the new*'.

5 Consciousness-Building and the Seed of the New

Kenneth Roth, director of Human Rights Watch, relates the origin of 'corporate ICL' as something that developed through systemic forces rather than through his or his civil society colleagues' agency – or perhaps even despite them:

> Out of the blue, we came up with the concept of complicity. It is very interesting watching it evolve into a criminal concept, because that was not what we had in mind at all ... The way we enforce rights is, in a sense, by appealing to peoples' [*sic*] moral sense of what is right and wrong and building up that popular sentiment as a source of pressure on the actor concerned, whether it is a government or a rebel force or, in this case, a corporation.[190]

It would seem that the move Roth describes needs to be reversed, and Roth's initial intention recovered. The global capitalist class rule, to a significant degree, through and with the corporate form, which 'hides the essential brutality and indifference to the plight of others that characterises [corporate] profit-making activities'.[191] Their 'corporate rule', is, as we have seen, not only material, but also ideological[192] – the corporation rules with a 'combination of force and guile'.[193] The two depend on, and mutually reinforce, one another. We need to 'undo' corporate ideology so as both to de-normalise the idea of the corporation and ultimately the corporate structure itself. Recently, in particular in the

189 Luxemburg, 'Reform or Revolution, and Mass Strike', in Scott 2008, p. 45.
190 Roth 2008, p. 960.
191 Glasbeek 2010, p. 249.
192 Pearce and Tombs 1990, p. 428.
193 Ollman 2003, p. 11.

context of the Occupy Wall Street movement, activism directed against corporate personhood has come to the fore.[194] However, the point is not (just) to get rid of corporate personhood or to realise or remember that there are human individuals behind the corporate shield, wielding corporate power, making the decisions that lead to harm, and pocketing corporate profits. The point is *not* then to seek to prosecute those individuals – there are many arguments aside from the argument in this book against carceral solutions to societal problems.[195] The point is to realise that the property-owning classes (the global capitalist class) are employing the law in this way, to enable exploitation, 'shift' or sell risk, to protect themselves as individuals, and to create the ideology that means we put up with it all. As the foundational norm of law is the legal ownership of private property, however, law *cannot but* function in this way: the form of law is not simply an empty vessel into which we can pour any (progressive or even socialist) content.[196] Our resistance must turn against the concept of private property, against capitalism and *against law*: away from *legal* emancipation and toward *human* emancipation.[197] Our imagination and our organising must turn towards the creation of alternative forms of relating, producing, and distributing.[198]

If the corporation is indeed the motor of capitalism, corporate 'excesses' (deaths in factory collapses and fires, widespread environmental, health and livelihood destruction as a result of oil and mining) are the directly visible manifestations of capitalism's 'dark side' – or, conversely, the corporation is singled out as the author of capitalism's 'excesses'. The corporation, as capitalism's visible persona, 'capital personified' or Monsieur Le Capital, becomes the *pars pro toto* taking the hit for the team, for capitalism as a whole. There is value not only to the corporation itself, but to the system of capitalism more broadly, in creating, repairing and maintaining the corporation's legitimacy, its standing, as the 'face' of capitalism. I have examined the labour that goes into maintaining that value, and translating human and environmental damage into quantifiable, and exchangeable risk. While the corporation takes the hit for capitalism, the converse is that once the corporation is 'fixed', and rendered

194 Shut Down the Corporations, available at: http://www.shutdownthecorporations.org; 'Target Ain't People' flashmob, video available at: https://www.youtube.com/watch?v=9FhMMmqzbD8.

195 E.g., Davis 2003.

196 Pashukanis 1978, p. 160; Arthur 1978, p. 29.

197 Marx, 'On the Jewish Question', excerpted in McLellan 2000, pp. 46, 64.

198 Parker, Cheney, Fournier, and Land, in Baars and Spicer (eds) 2017. See also, e.g., the work of the members of the Calafou Post-capitalist Eco-industrial Colony, available at: https://calafou.org/en.

accountable, this immunises (temporarily) the broader structures of capitalism from critique. When the problems in the world are framed as 'criminal', 'policing' and prosecution come to be seen as the solution. When our critique of capitalism and our activism focuses on creating avenues for or instances of corporate accountability, we inadvertently strengthen, rather than restrain, capitalism. Our labour then creates value for capitalism.

Let us instead work towards the world we *actually* want to live in.

Appendix A

CERD

Charter of Economic Rights and Duties of States, GA Res 3281 (1974) UN Doc A/RES/29/3281.

The Charter includes, e.g.:

2. Each State has the right:
   (a) To regulate and exercise authority over foreign investment within its national jurisdiction in accordance with its laws and regulations and in conformity with its national objectives and priorities ...;
   (b) To regulate and supervise the activities of transnational corporations within its national jurisdiction and take measures to ensure that such activities comply with its laws, rules and regulations and conform with its economic and social policies. Transnational corporations shall not intervene in the internal affairs of a host State ...;
   (c) To nationalize, expropriate or transfer ownership of foreign property, in which case appropriate compensation should be paid by the State adopting such measures, taking into account its relevant laws and regulations and all circumstances that the State considers pertinent. In any case where the question of compensation gives rise to a controversy, it shall be settled under the domestic law of the nationalizing State ...

Appendix B

Potsdam Agreement

Potsdam Agreement of 2 August 1945, between the USSR, the USA and the UK.

B. ECONOMIC PRINCIPLES.

11. In order to eliminate Germany's war potential, the production of arms, ammunition and implements of war as well as all types of aircraft and sea-going ships shall be prohibited and prevented. Production of metals, chemicals, machinery and other items that are directly necessary to a war economy shall be rigidly controlled and restricted to Germany's approved post-war peacetime needs to meet the objectives stated in Paragraph 15. Productive capacity not needed for permitted production shall be removed in accordance with the reparations plan recommended by the Allied Commission on Reparations and approved by the Governments concerned or if not removed shall be destroyed.
12. At the earliest practicable date, the German economy shall be decentralized for the purpose of eliminating the present excessive concentration of economic power as exemplified in particular by cartels, syndicates, trusts and other monopolistic arrangements.
13. In organizing the German Economy, primary emphasis shall be given to the development of agriculture and peaceful domestic industries.
14. During the period of occupation Germany shall be treated as a single economic unit. To this end common policies shall be established in regard to:
    (a) mining and industrial production and its allocation;
    (b) agriculture, forestry and fishing;
    (c) wages, prices and rationing;
    (d) import and export programs for Germany as a whole;
    (e) currency and banking, central taxation and customs;
    (f) reparation and removal of industrial war potential;
    (g) transportation and communications.

    In applying these policies account shall be taken, where appropriate, of varying local conditions.
15. Allied controls shall be imposed upon the German economy but only to the extent necessary:
    (a) to carry out programs of industrial disarmament, demilitarization, of reparations, and of approved exports and imports.
    (b) to assure the production and maintenance of goods and services required to meet the needs of the occupying forces and displaced persons in Ger-

many and essential to maintain in Germany average living standards not exceeding the average of the standards of living of European countries. (European countries means all European countries excluding the United Kingdom and the USSR).

(c) to ensure in the manner determined by the Control Council the equitable distribution of essential commodities between the several zones so as to produce a balanced economy throughout Germany and reduce the need for imports.

(d) to control German industry and all economic and financial international transactions including exports and imports, with the aim of preventing Germany from developing a war potential and of achieving the other objectives named herein.

(e) to control all German public or private scientific bodies research and experimental institutions, laboratories, *et cetera* connected with economic activities.

16. In the imposition and maintenance of economic controls established by the Control Council, German administrative machinery shall be created and the German authorities shall be required to the fullest extent practicable to proclaim and assume administration of such controls. Thus it should be brought home to the German people that the responsibility for the administration of such controls and any break-down in these controls will rest with themselves. Any German controls which may run counter to the objectives of occupation will be prohibited.

17. Measures shall be promptly taken:

(a) to effect essential repair of transport;

(b) to enlarge coal production;

(c) to maximize agricultural output; and

(d) to erect emergency repair of housing and essential utilities.

18. Appropriate steps shall be taken by the Control Council to exercise control and the power of disposition over German-owned external assets not already under the control of United Nations which have taken part in the war against Germany.

19. Payment of Reparations should leave enough resources to enable the German people to subsist without external assistance. In working out the economic balance of Germany the necessary means must be provided to pay for imports approved by the Control Council in Germany. The proceeds of exports from current production and stocks shall be available in the first place for payment for such imports.

The above clause will not apply to the equipment and products referred to in paragraphs 4 (a) and 4 (b) of the Reparations Agreement.

III. REPARATIONS FROM GERMANY.

1. Reparation claims of the USSR shall be met by removals from the zone of Germany occupied by the USSR, and from appropriate German external assets.
2. The USSR undertakes to settle the reparation claims of Poland from its own share of reparations.
3. The reparation claims of the United States, the United Kingdom and other countries entitled to reparations shall be met from the Western Zones and from appropriate German external assets.
4. In addition to the reparations to be taken by the USSR from its own zone of occupation, the USSR shall receive additionally from the Western Zones:
   (a) 15 per cent of such usable and complete industrial capital equipment, in the first place from the metallurgical, chemical and machine manufacturing industries as is unnecessary for the German peace economy and should be removed from the Western Zones of Germany, in exchange for an equivalent value of food, coal, potash, zinc, timber, clay products, petroleum products, and such other commodities as may be agreed upon.
   (b) 10 per cent of such industrial capital equipment as is unnecessary for the German peace economy and should be removed from the Western Zones, to be transferred to the Soviet Government on reparations account without payment or exchange of any kind in return.

   Removals of equipment as provided in (a) and (b) above shall be made simultaneously.
5. The amount of equipment to be removed from the Western Zones on account of reparations must be determined within six months from now at the latest.
6. Removals of industrial capital equipment shall begin as soon as possible and shall be completed within two years from the determination specified in paragraph 5. The delivery of products covered by 4 (a) above shall begin as soon as possible and shall be made by the USSR in agreed installments within five years of the date hereof. The determination of the amount and character of the industrial capital equipment unnecessary for the German peace economy and therefore available for reparation shall be made by the Control Council under policies fixed by the Allied Commission on Reparations, with the participation of France, subject to the final approval of the Zone Commander in the Zone from which the equipment is to be removed.

IMT Charter

London Agreement Establishing the Nuremberg Tribunal, 82 UNTS 279 (no. 251).

Article 5.
In case of need and depending on the number of the matters to be tried, other Tribunals may be set up; and the establishment, functions, and procedure of each Tribunal shall be identical, and shall be governed by this Charter.

Article 6.
The Tribunal established by the Agreement referred to in Article 1 hereof for the trial and punishment of the major war criminals of the European Axis countries shall have the power to try and punish persons who, acting in the interests of the European Axis countries, whether as individuals or as members of organizations, committed any of the following crimes.

The following acts, or any of them, are crimes coming within the jurisdiction of the Tribunal for which there shall be individual responsibility:

(a) CRIMES AGAINST PEACE: namely, planning, preparation, initiation or waging of a war of aggression, or a war in violation of international treaties, agreements or assurances, or participation in a common plan or conspiracy for the accomplishment of any of the foregoing;

(b) WAR CRIMES: namely, violations of the laws or customs of war. Such violations shall include, but not be limited to, murder, ill-treatment or deportation to slave labor or for any other purpose of civilian population of or in occupied territory, murder or ill-treatment of prisoners of war or persons on the seas, killing of hostages, plunder of public or private property, wanton destruction of cities, towns or villages, or devastation not justified by military necessity;

(c) CRIMES AGAINST HUMANITY: namely, murder, extermination, enslavement, deportation, and other inhumane acts committed against any civilian population, before or during the war; or persecutions on political, racial or religious grounds in execution of or in connection with any crime within the jurisdiction of the Tribunal, whether or not in violation of the domestic law of the country where perpetrated.

Leaders, organizers, instigators and accomplices participating in the formulation or execution of a common plan or conspiracy to commit any of the foregoing crimes are responsible for all acts performed by any persons in execution of such plan.

Article 7.
The official position of defendants, whether as Heads of State or responsible officials in Government Departments, shall not be considered as freeing them from responsibility or mitigating punishment.

Article 8.

The fact that the Defendant acted pursuant to order of his Government or of a superior shall not free him from responsibility, but may be considered in mitigation of punishment if the Tribunal determines that justice so requires.

CCL10

Control Council Law No. 10, 20 December 1945, in Enactments and Approved Papers of the Control Council and Coordinating Committee, Applied Control Authority, Germany, 1945, Vol. 1, p. 306.

1. Each of the following acts is recognized as a crime:

(a) Crimes against Peace. Initiation of invasions of other countries and wars of aggression in violation of international laws and treaties, including but not limited to planning, preparation, initiation or waging a war of aggression, or a war of violation of international treaties, agreements or assurances, or participation in a common plan or conspiracy for the accomplishment of any of the foregoing.

(b) War Crimes. Atrocities or offenses against persons or property constituting violations of the laws or customs of war, including but not limited to, murder, ill treatment or deportation to slave labour or for any other purpose, of civilian population from occupied territory, murder or ill treatment of prisoners of war or persons on the seas, killing of hostages, plunder of public or private property, wanton destruction of cities, towns or villages, or devastation not justified by military necessity.

(a) Crimes against Humanity. Atrocities and offenses, including but not limited to murder, extermination, enslavement, deportation, imprisonment, torture, rape, or other inhumane acts committed against any civilian population, or persecutions on political, racial or religious grounds whether or not in violation of the domestic laws of the country where perpetrated.

(d) Membership in categories of a criminal group or organization declared criminal by the International Military Tribunal.

CCL 10 II 2. Any person without regard to nationality or the capacity in which he acted, is deemed to have committed a crime as defined in paragraph 1 of this Article, if he was (a) a principal or (b) was an accessory to the commission of any such crime or ordered or abetted the same or (c) took a consenting part therein or (d) was connected with plans or enterprises involving its commission or (e) was a member of any organization or group connected with the commission of any such crime or (f) with reference to paragraph 1 (a) if he held a high political, civil or military (including General Staff) position in Germany or in one of its Allies, co-belligerents or satellites or *held high position in the financial, industrial or economic life of any such country.*

3. Any persons found guilty of any of the crimes above mentioned may upon conviction be punished as shall be determined by the tribunal to be just …

4. (a) The official position of any person, whether as Head of State or as a responsible official in a Government Department, does not free him from responsibility for a crime or entitle him to mitigation of punishment.

(b) *The fact that any person acted pursuant to the order of his Government or of a superior does not free him from responsibility for a crime, but may be considered in mitigation.*

5. …[1]

IMT Indictment

Indictment of the International Military Tribunal: The United States of America, The French Republic, The United Kingdom of Great Britain and Northern Ireland, and the Union Of Soviet Socialist Republics against Hermann Wilhelm Goering, in 1 Trial of the Major War Criminals before the International Military Tribunal 27 1947.

Indictment Count I section (E) at p. 35.

Having gained political power the conspirators organized Germany's economy to give effect to their political aims.

1. In order to eliminate the possibility of resistance in the economic sphere, they deprived labor of its rights of free industrial and political association as particularized in paragraph (D) 3 (c) (1) herein.
2. They used organizations of German business as instruments of economic mobilization for war.
3. They directed Germany's economy towards preparation and equipment of the military machine. To this end they directed finance, capital investment, and foreign trade.
4. The Nazi conspirators, and in particular the industrialists among them, embarked upon a huge re-armament program and set out to produce and develop huge quantities of materials of war and to create a powerful military potential.

1 Emphasis added.

5. With the object of carrying through the preparation for war the Nazi conspirators set up a series of administrative agencies and authorities. For example, in 1936 they established for this purpose the office of the Four Year Plan with the Defendant GORING.

Indictment Individual responsibility, Krupp von Bohlen von Halbach

KRUPP:

The Defendant KRUPP was between 1932 and 1945: Head of Friedrich KRUPP A.G., a member of the General Economic Council, President of the Reich Union of German Industry, and head of the Group for Mining and Production of Iron and Metals under the Reich Ministry of Economics. The Defendant KRUPP used the foregoing positions, his personal influence, and his connection with the Fuehrer in such a manner that: He promoted the accession to power of the Nazi conspirators and the consolidation of their control over Germany set forth in Count One of the Indictment; he promoted the preparation for war set forth in Count One of the Indictment; he participated in the military and economic planning and preparation of the Nazi conspirators for Wars of Aggression and Wars in Violation of International Treaties, Agreements, and Assurances set forth in Count One and Count Two of the Indictment; and he authorized, directed, and participated in the War Crimes set forth in Count Three of the Indictment and the Crimes against Humanity set forth in Count Four of the Indictment, including more particularly the exploitation and abuse of human beings for labor in the conduct of aggressive wars.

Appendix C

Charter of the (Tokyo) International Military Tribunal for the Far East 1946, TIAS No. 1589

ARTICLE 5. Jurisdiction Over Persons and Offenses. The Tribunal shall have the power to try and punish Far Eastern war criminals who as individuals or as members of organization are charged with offenses which include Crimes against Peace. The following acts, or any of them, are crimes coming within the jurisdiction of the Tribunal for which there shall be individual responsibility:

Crimes against Peace: Namely, the planning, preparation, initiation or waging of a declared or undeclared war of aggression, or a war in violation of international law, treaties, agreements or assurances, or participation in a common plan or conspiracy for the accomplishment of any of the foregoing;

Conventional War Crimes: Namely, violations of the laws or customs of war;

Crimes against Humanity: Namely, murder, extermination, enslavement, deportation, and other inhumane acts committed before or during the war, or persecutions on political or racial grounds in execution of or in connection with any crime within the jurisdiction of the Tribunal, whether or not in violation of the domestic law of the country where perpetrated. Leaders, organizers, instigators and accomplices participating in the formulation or execution of a common plan or conspiracy to commit any of the foregoing crimes are responsible for all acts performed by any person in execution of such plan.

ARTICLE 6. Responsibility of Accused. Neither the official position, at any time, of an accused, nor the fact that an accused acted pursuant to order of his government or of a superior shall, of itself, be sufficient to free such accused from responsibility for any crime with which he is charged, but such circumstances may be considered in mitigation of punishment if the Tribunal determines that justice so requires.

ARTICLE 13. The Tribunal shall not be bound by technical rules of evidence. It shall adopt and apply to the greatest possible extent expeditious and non-technical procedure, and shall admit any evidence which it deems to have probative value.

Japanese National Diet Library US Initial Post-Surrender Policy for Japan (SWNCC 150/4/A), 21 September 1945

(Part I (1)), 'The occupation forces will be under the command of a Supreme Commander designated by the United States. Although every effort will be made, by consultation and by constitution of appropriate advisory bodies, to establish policies for the conduct of the occupation and the control of Japan which will satisfy the principal

Allied powers, in the event of any differences of opinion among then, the policies of the United States will govern', war criminals, Part II(2), Democratisation: 'The Japanese people shall be afforded opportunity and encourage to become familiar with the history, institutions, culture, and the accomplishments of the United States and the other democracies', the economy (Part IV) which includes the break up of cartels (para 2 (a)), a '*prohibition on the retention in or selection of individuals for places of importance in the economic field of individuals who do not direct future Japanese economic efforts solely towards peaceful ends*', reparations payments (para 4, 'Reparations for Japanese aggression shall be made ... (b) Through the transfer of such goods or existing capital equipment and facilities as are not necessary for a peaceful Japanese economy or the supplying of the occupying forces') and opening the market for FDI (para 8 'Equality of Opportunity for Foreign Enterprise within Japan').[1]

1 Emphasis added.

Appendix D

Versailles Treaty
Treaty of Peace, June 28, 1919, 225 Consol. T.S. 188, 285–286.

Article 227
The **Allied and Associated Powers** publicly arraign **William II of Hohenzollern**, formerly **German Emperor**, for a supreme offence against international morality and the sanctity of treaties.

A special tribunal will be constituted to try the accused, thereby assuring him the guarantees essential to the right of defence. It will be composed of five judges, one appointed by each of the following Powers: namely, the **United States of America**, **Great Britain**, **France**, **Italy** and **Japan**.

In its decision the tribunal will be guided by the highest motives of international policy, with a view to vindicating the solemn obligations of international undertakings and the validity of international morality. It will be its duty to fix the punishment which it considers should be imposed.

The Allied and Associated Powers will address a request to the Government of the **Netherlands** for the surrender to them of the ex-Emperor in order that he may be put on trial.

Article 228
The German Government recognises the right of the Allied and Associated Powers to bring before military tribunals persons accused of having committed acts in violation of the laws and customs of war. Such persons shall, if found guilty, be sentenced to punishments laid down by law. This provision will apply notwithstanding any proceedings or prosecution before a tribunal in Germany or in the territory of her allies.

The German Government shall hand over to the Allied and Associated Powers, or to such one of them as shall so request, all persons accused of having committed an act in violation of the laws and customs of war, who are specified either by name or by the rank, office or employment which they held under the German authorities.

Article 229
Persons guilty of criminal acts against the nationals of one of the Allied and Associated Powers will be brought before the military tribunals of that Power. Persons guilty of criminal acts against the nationals of more than one of the Allied and Associated Powers will be brought before military tribunals composed of members of the military tribunals of the Powers concerned. In every case the accused will be entitled to name his own counsel.

Article 230

The German Government undertakes to furnish all documents and information of every kind, the production of which may be considered necessary to ensure the full knowledge of the incriminating acts, the discovery of offenders and the just appreciation of responsibility.

1997 Convention on Combating Bribery of Foreign Public Officials inInternational Business Transactions

Article 2 – Responsibility of Legal Persons

Each Party shall take such measures as may be necessary, in accordance with its *legal principles*, to establish *the liability of legal persons* for the bribery of a foreign public official.

Article 3 – Sanctions

1. The bribery of a foreign public official shall be punishable by effective, proportionate and dissuasive criminal penalties …
2. In the event that, under the legal system of a Party, criminal responsibility is not applicable to legal persons, that Party shall ensure that legal persons shall be subject to effective, proportionate and dissuasive non-criminal sanctions, including monetary sanctions, for bribery of foreign public officials.

2000 Transnational Organized Crime Convention

Article 10 – Liability of legal persons

1. Each State Party shall adopt such measures as may be necessary, consistent with its legal principles, to establish the liability of legal persons for participation in serious crimes involving an **organized** criminal group and for the offences established in accordance with articles 5, 6, 8 and 23 of this **Convention.**
2. Subject to the legal principles of the State Party, the liability of legal persons may be criminal, civil or administrative.

1989 Basel Convention on the Control of Transboundary Movements of Hazardous Waste

14. 'Person' means any natural or legal person.

Appendix E

ICTY Statute Article 7 Individual criminal responsibility

Statute of the International Criminal Tribunal for the Former Yugoslavia 1993 UN Doc. S/RES/827 (1993).

1. A person who planned, instigated, ordered, committed or otherwise aided and abetted in the planning, preparation or execution of a crime referred to in articles 2 to 5 of the present Statute, shall be individually responsible for the crime.
2. The official position of any accused person, whether as Head of State or Government or as a responsible Government official, shall not relieve such person of criminal responsibility nor mitigate punishment.
3. The fact that any of the acts referred to in articles 2 to 5 of the present Statute was committed by a subordinate does not relieve his superior of criminal responsibility if he knew or had reason to know that the subordinate was about to commit such acts or had done so and the superior failed to take the necessary and reasonable measures to prevent such acts or to punish the perpetrators thereof.
4. The fact that an accused person acted pursuant to an order of a Government or of a superior shall not relieve him of criminal responsibility, but may be considered in mitigation of punishment if the International Tribunal determines that justice so requires.

ICTR Statute Article 6 Individual Criminal Responsibility

Statute of the International Criminal Tribunal for Rwanda 1994 UN Doc S/Res/955 (1994).

1. A person who planned, instigated, ordered, committed or otherwise aided and abetted in the planning, preparation or execution of a crime referred to in articles 2 to 4 of the present Statute, shall be individually responsible for the crime.
2. The official position of any accused person, whether as Head of State or Government or as a responsible Government official, shall not relieve such person of criminal responsibility nor mitigate punishment.
3. The fact that any of the acts referred to in articles 2 to 4 of the present Statute was committed by a subordinate does not relieve his or her superior of criminal responsibility if he or she knew or had reason to know that the subordinate was about to commit such acts or had done so and the superior failed to take the necessary and reasonable measures to prevent such acts or to punish the perpetrators thereof.
4. The fact that an accused person acted pursuant to an order of a Government or of a superior shall not relieve him or her of criminal responsibility, but may be

considered in mitigation of punishment if the International Tribunal for Rwanda determines that justice so requires.

SCSL *Agreement* Article 6 Individual criminal responsibility

Agreement between the United Nations and the Government of Sierra Leone on the Establishment of a Special Court for Sierra Leone, 2178 UNTS 138.

1. A person who planned, instigated, ordered, committed or otherwise aided and abetted in the planning, preparation or execution of a crime referred to in articles 2 to 4 of the present Statute shall be individually responsible for the crime.
2. The official position of any accused persons, whether as Head of State or Government or as a responsible government official, shall not relieve such person of criminal responsibility nor mitigate punishment.
3. The fact that any of the acts referred to in articles 2 to 4 of the present Statute was committed by a subordinate does not relieve his or her superior of criminal responsibility if he or she knew or had reason to know that the subordinate was about to commit such acts or had done so and the superior had failed to take the necessary and reasonable measures to prevent such acts or to punish the perpetrators thereof.
4. The fact that an accused person acted pursuant to an order of a Government or of a superior shall not relieve him or her of criminal responsibility, but may be considered in mitigation of punishment if the Special Court determines that justice so requires.
5. Individual criminal responsibility for the crimes referred to in article 5 shall be determined in accordance with the respective laws of Sierra Leone.

ICC *Statute* Article 25 Individual criminal responsibility

International Criminal Court Statute 1998, 2187 UNTS 91.

1. The Court shall have jurisdiction over natural persons pursuant to this Statute.
2. A person who commits a crime within the jurisdiction of the Court shall be individually responsible and liable for punishment in accordance with this Statute.
3. In accordance with this Statute, a person shall be criminally responsible and liable for punishment for a crime within the jurisdiction of the Court if that person:
   (a) Commits such a crime, whether as an individual, jointly with another or through another person, regardless of whether that other person is criminally responsible;
   (b) Orders, solicits or induces the commission of such a crime which in fact occurs or is attempted;

(c) For the purpose of facilitating the commission of such a crime, aids, abets or otherwise assists in its commission or its attempted commission, including providing the means for its commission;

(d) In any other way contributes to the commission or attempted commission of such a crime by a group of persons acting with a common purpose. Such contribution shall be intentional and shall either:

(i) Be made with the aim of furthering the criminal activity or criminal purpose of the group, where such activity or purpose involves the commission of a crime within the jurisdiction of the Court; or

(ii) Be made in the knowledge of the intention of the group to commit the crime;

(e) In respect of the crime of genocide, directly and publicly incites others to commit genocide;

(f) Attempts to commit such a crime by taking action that commences its execution by means of a substantial step, but the crime does not occur because of circumstances independent of the person's intentions. However, a person who abandons the effort to commit the crime or otherwise prevents the completion of the crime shall not be liable for punishment under this Statute for the attempt to commit that crime if that person completely and voluntarily gave up the criminal purpose.

4. No provision in this Statute relating to individual criminal responsibility shall affect the responsibility of States under international law.

French Corporate Crime Proposal

United Nations Diplomatic Conference of Plenipotentiaries on the Establishment of an International Criminal Court, UN Doc A/CONF.183/C.1/L.3, 16 June 1998, PROPOSAL SUBMITTED BY FRANCE

Article 23 Individual criminal responsibility
Legal persons
Paragraphs 5 and 6 (criminal organizations)

[5. When the crime was committed by a natural person on behalf or with the assent of a group or organization of every kind, the Court may declare that this group or organization is a criminal organization.

6. In the cases where a group or organization is declared criminal by the Court, this group or organization shall incur the penalties referred to in article 76, and the relevant provision of articles 73 and 79 are applicable.

In any such case, the criminal nature of the group or organization is considered proved and shall not be questioned, and the competent national authorities of any State party shall take the necessary measures to ensure that the judgment of the Court shall have binding force and to implement it.]

[Article 76
Penalties applicable to criminal organizations
A criminal organization shall incur one or more of the following penalties.
(i) Fines;
(ii) deleted
(iii) deleted
(iv) deleted
(v) Forfeiture of [instrumentalities of crime and] proceeds, property and assets obtained by criminal conduct;] [and]
[(vi) Appropriate forms of reparation].]

Corporate Manslaughter Act and Corporate Homicide Act 2007
Corporate Manslaughter and Corporate Homicide Act 2007 c.19
1 The offence
(1) An organisation to which this section applies is guilty of an offence if the way in which its activities are managed or organised –
  (a) causes a person's death, and
  (b) amounts to a gross breach of a relevant duty of care owed by the organisation to the deceased.
(2) The organisations to which this section applies are –
  (a) a corporation;

...

(3) An organisation is guilty of an offence under this section only if the way in which its activities are managed or organised by its senior management is a substantial element in the breach referred to in subsection (1).
(4) For the purposes of this Act –
  (a) 'relevant duty of care' has the meaning given by section 2, read with sections 3 to 7;
  (b) a breach of a duty of care by an organisation is a 'gross' breach if the conduct alleged to amount to a breach of that duty falls far below what can reasonably be expected of the organisation in the circumstances;
  (c) 'senior management', in relation to an organisation, means the persons who play significant roles in –
    (i) the making of decisions about how the whole or a substantial part of its activities are to be managed or organised, or
    (ii) the actual managing or organising of the whole or a substantial part of those activities.

...

(6) An organisation that is guilty of corporate manslaughter or corporate homicide is liable on conviction on indictment to a fine.

...

Appendix F

Prosecutor Organisation Indicators

The Prosecutor laid out 'relevant indicators to determine the existence of an organization' as follows:

- Existence of pre-determined objectives, whether formally or informally adopted by the members of the organization.
- Existence of a common identity, whether political, ethnic, religious, etc.
- Activities carried out by the group, including meetings, financial transfers, fund raising, logistical arrangements, etc.
- Public discourse, including communications, writings, broadcast, etc.
- Ability to pursue their objectives through certain agreed methods and active involvement such as directing or instigating the crime.
- Sufficient resources (material and personnel) to pursue their objectives.

UNSCP Congo Panel Request

The Security Council requests the Secretary-General to establish this panel, for a period of six months, with the following mandate:

- To follow up on reports and collect information on all activities of illegal exploitation of natural resources and other forms of wealth of the Democratic Republic of the Congo, including in violation of the sovereignty of that country;
- To research and analyse the links between the exploitation of the natural resources and other forms of wealth in the Democratic Republic of the Congo and the continuation of the conflict;
- To revert to the Council with recommendations.

TRC Business Sector Hearings

The Commission further found that: '162 Businesses were reluctant to speak about their involvement in the former homelands. A submission by Mr Sol Kerzner and Sun International would have facilitated the work of the Commission.

163 The Land Bank and the Development Bank of South Africa, in particular, were directly involved in sustaining the existence of former homelands.

164 The denial of trade union rights to black workers constituted a violation of human rights. Actions taken against trade unions by the state, at times with the cooperation of certain businesses, frequently led to gross human rights violations.

165 The mining industry not only benefited from migratory labour and the payment of low wages to black employees; it also failed to give sufficient attention to the health and safety concerns of its employees.

166 Business failed in the hearings to take responsibility for its involvement in state security initiatives specifically designed to sustain apartheid rule. This included

involvement in the National Security Management System. Several businesses, in turn, benefited directly from their involvement in the complex web that constituted the military industry.

167 The white agricultural industry benefited from its privileged access to land. In most instances, it failed to provide adequate facilities and services for employees and their dependants'.

References

Books, Book Chapters, Journal Articles, Other

Abass, A. 2013, 'Prosecuting International Crimes in Africa: Rationale, Prospects and Challenges', *European Journal of International Law*, 24(3): 933–46.

Akhavan, P. 2001, 'Beyond Impunity: Can International Criminal Justice Prevent Future Atrocities', *American Journal of International Law*, 95(7): 7–31.

Akhavan, P. 2013, 'The Rise, and Fall, and Rise, of International Criminal Justice', *Journal of International Criminal Justice*, 11 (3): 527–36.

Albertson, T. 1972, 'Review of R. Minear, *Victor's Justice: The Tokyo War Crimes Trial*, Princeton University Press', *Harvard International Law Journal*, 13: 550–4.

Allott, P. 2001, *Eunomia: New Order for a New World*, Oxford: Oxford University Press.

Allott, P. 2002a, 'The Emerging International Aristocracy', *NYU Journal of International Law and Politics*, 35(2): 309–38.

Allott, P. 2002b, *The Health of Nations: Society and Law beyond the State*, Cambridge: Cambridge University Press.

Alston, P. 1997, 'The Myopia of the Handmaidens: International Lawyers and Globalization', *European Journal of International Law*, 8(3): 435–48.

Alston, P. 2005, *Non-State Actors and Human Rights*, Oxford: Oxford University Press.

Alston, P. 2006, 'The "Not-a-cat" Syndrome: Can the International Human Rights Regime Accommodate Non-State Actors?', in Alston 2005.

Alvarez, J.E. 2001, 'Are Corporations "Subjects" of International Law?' *Santa Clara Journal of International Law*, 9(1): 1–36.

Alvarez, J.E. 2004, 'Trying Hussein: Between Hubris and Hegemony', *Journal of International Criminal Justice*, 2(2): 319–29.

Ambos, K. 2000, 'Individual Criminal Responsibility in International Criminal Law: A Jurisprudential Analysis – From Nuremberg to The Hague', in *Substantive and Procedural Aspects of International Criminal Law*, Vol. 1, edited by G. McDonald and O. Swaak, The Hague: Kluwer Law International.

Ambos, K. 2004, *Der Allgemeine Teil des Völkerstrafrechts: Ansätze einer Dogmatisierung*, Berlin: Duncker u. Humblot GmbH.

Ambos, K. 2008, 'Article 25: "Individual Criminal Responsibility"', in *Commentary on the Rome Statute of the International Criminal Court: Observers' Notes*, edited by W. Triffterer, Munich: Nomos Verlagsgesellschaft.

Amerson, J.M. 2012. '"The End of the Beginning?": A Comprehensive Look at the UN's Business and Human Rights Agenda from a Bystander Perspective', *Fordham Journal of Corporate and Financial Law*, 17(4): 871–941.

Anderson, K. 1994, 'Nuremberg Sensibility: Telford Taylor's Memoir of the Nuremberg Trials', *Harvard Human Rights Journal*, 7(1): 41–53.

Anderson, K. 2009, 'The Rise of International Criminal Law: Intended and Unintended Consequences', *European Journal of International Law*, 20(2): 331–58.

Ando, N. 1991, *Surrender, Occupation and Private Property in International Law: An Evaluation of US Practice in Japan*, Oxford: Clarendon.

Anghie, A. 2007, *Imperialism, Sovereignty and the Making of International Law*, Cambridge: Cambridge University Press.

Anghie, A. and B.S. Chimni 2003, 'Third World Approaches to International Law and Individual Responsibility in Internal Armed Conflicts', *Chinese Journal of International Law*, 2(1): 77–103.

Anievas, A. 2008, 'Theories of a Global State: A Critique, Review Article', *Historical Materialism*, 16: 167–236.

Anon. 1945, 'Current Notes', *American Journal of International Law*, 39(3): 565–70.

Anon. 2001, 'Developments – International Criminal Law, v. Corporate Liability for Violations of International Human Rights Law', *Harvard Law Review*, 114: 2025–48.

Ansoms, A. 2005, 'Resurrection after Civil War and Genocide: Growth, Poverty and Inequality in Post-Conflict Rwanda', *European Journal of Development Research*, 17(3): 495–508.

Ansoms, A. 2009, 'Re-Engineering Rural Society: The Visions and Ambitions of the Rwandan Elite', *African Affairs*, 108(431): 289–309.

Aoki, M. 2010, *Corporations in Evolving Diversity: Cognition, Governance and Institutions*, Oxford: Oxford University Press.

Archer, J. 1973, *The Plot to Seize the White House: The Shocking True Story of the Conspiracy to Overthrow FDR*, New York: Hawthorn Books.

Arendt, H. 1994 [1963], *Eichmann in Jerusalem: A Report on the Banality of Evil*, London: Penguin.

Armour, J., H. Hansmann and R. Kraakman 2009, 'What Is Corporate Law?', in *The Anatomy of Corporate Law: A Comparative and Functional Approach*, edited by R. Kraakman, J. Armour, P. Davies, L. Enriques, H. Hansmann, G. Hertig, H. Kanda, and E. Rock, Oxford: Oxford University Press.

Armour, J. and M. Whincop 2007, 'The Proprietary Foundations of Corporate Law', *Oxford Journal of Legal Studies*, 27: 429–65.

Arthur, C. 1978, 'Editor's Introduction', in *Law & Marxism: A General Theory*, by E. Pashukanis, London: Ink Links.

Ashworth, J. 1987, 'The Relationship between Capitalism and Humanitarianism', *American Historical Review*, 92(4): 813–28.

d'Aspremont, J., A. Nollkaemper, I. Plakokefalos, and C. Ryngaert 2015, 'Sharing Responsibility between Non-State Actors and States in International Law: Introduction', *Netherlands International Law Review*, 62(1): 49–67.

Augenstein, D. 2014, 'The Crisis of International Human Rights Law in the Global Market Economy', *Netherlands Yearbook of International Law*, 44: 41–64.

Avi-Yonah, R. 2011, '*Citizens United* and the Corporate Form', *Accounting, Economics and Law: A Convivium*, 1(3), available at: https://www.degruyter.com/view/j/ael.2011.1.issue-3/2152-2820.1048/2152-2820.1048.xml.

Baars, G. 2007, 'Corrie et al. v. Caterpillar: Litigating Corporate Complicity in Israeli Violations of International Law in the US Courts', *Yearbook of Islamic and Middle Eastern Law, 2005–2006*, 21: 97–134.

Baars, G. 2011, 'Reform or Revolution: Marxian vs. Polanyian Approaches to the Regulation of "the Economic"', *Northern Ireland Legal Quarterly*, 17(4): 415–31.

Baars, G. 2012, 'Law(yers) Congealing Capitalism: On the (Im)possibility of Restraining Business in Conflict through International Criminal Law', Ph.D. thesis, University College London.

Baars, G. 2013, 'Capitalism's Victor's Justice? The Hidden Story of the Prosecution of Industrialists Post-WWII', in *Untold Stories: Hidden Histories of War Crimes Trials*, edited by G. Simpson and K. Heller, Oxford: Oxford University Press.

Baars, G. 2014a, 'Making ICL History: On the Need to Move beyond Prefab Critiques', in *Critical Approaches to International Criminal Law: An Introduction*, edited by C. Schwöbel, New York: Routledge.

Baars, G. 2014b, 'Remarks on Andrew Lang's World Trade Law After Neo-Liberalism', *Social and Legal Studies*, 23(3): 433–6.

Baars, G. 2015, 'From the Dutch East India Company to the Corporate Bill of Rights: Corporations and International Law', in *Political Economy and Law: A Handbook of Contemporary Practice, Research and Theory*, edited by U. Mattei and J. Haskell, Cheltenham: Edward Elgar.

Baars, G. 2016, '"It's Not Me, It's the Corporation": The Value of Corporate Accountability in the Global Political Economy', *London Review of International Law*, 4(1): 127–63.

Baars, G. 2017, 'Capital, Corporate Citizenship and Legitimacy: The Ideological Force of "Corporate Crime" in International Law', in Baars and Spicer (eds) Baars, G. and A. Spicer (eds), *The Corporation: A Critical, Multidisciplinary Handbook*, Cambridge: Cambridge University Press.

Baars, G. and A. Spicer (eds) 2017, *The Corporation: A Critical, Multidisciplinary Handbook*, Cambridge: Cambridge University Press.

Baars, G. et al. (The IGLP Law and Global Production Working Group) 2016, 'The Role of Law in Global Value Chains: A Research Manifesto', *London Review of International Law*, 4(1): 57–79.

Bakan, J. 2005, *The Corporation: The Pathological Pursuit of Profit and Power*, London: Constable & Robinson Publishing.

Bakan, J. 2015, 'The Invisible Hand of Law: Private Regulation and the Rule of Law', *Cornell International Law Journal*, 48(2): 279–300.

Baker, J.H. 1979, 'The Law Merchant and the Common Law Before 1700', *Cambridge Law Journal*, 38(2): 295–322.

Baker, J.H. 2002, *An Introduction to English Legal History*, 4th edn, Oxford: Oxford University Press.

Baker, J.H. 2003, *The Oxford History of the Laws of England*, Volume 5: 1483–1558, Oxford: Oxford University Press.

Bantekas, I. and S. Nash 2007, *International Criminal Law*, London: Routledge-Cavendish.

Barkan, J. 2013, *Corporate Sovereignty: Law and Government under Capitalism*, Minneapolis, MN: University of Minnesota Press.

Barker, C. and J. Grant 2005, *Deskbook of International Criminal Law*, London: Routledge-Cavendish.

Barnet, R. and R. Muller 1974, *Global Reach: The Power of Multinational Corporations*, New York: Simon & Schuster.

Barreto Jose-Maria 2013, *Human Rights from a Third World Perspective: Critique, History and International Law*, Newcastle upon Tyne: Cambridge Scholars Publishing.

Barzilai, G. 2007, 'The Ambivalent Language of Lawyers in Israel: Liberal Politics, Economic Liberalism, Silence, and Dissent', in *Liberalism and Lawyers*, edited by M. Feeley, T. Halliday, and L. Karpik, Oxford: Hart Publications.

Bassiouni, M. 1987, *A Draft International Criminal Code and Draft Statute for an International Criminal Tribunal*, The Hague: Kluwer Law International.

Bastid, S., R. David, and F. Luchaire 1960, *La personnalité morale et ses limites: études de droit comparé et de droit international public*, Paris: Travaux et recherches de l'institut de droit comparé de l'Université de Paris.

Bathurst, M. 1945, 'The United Nations War Crimes Commission', *American Journal of International Law*, 39: 565–70.

Beckett, J. 2012, 'Critical Legal Thought in Public International Law', in *New Critical Legal Thinking: Law and the Political*, edited by C. Douzinas, M. Stone, and I. Wall, London: Taylor & Francis Group.

Beirne, P. 1977, 'Introduction to "Juridical Socialism"', *Politics & Society*, 7(2): 199–201.

Benvenisti, E. and G. Downs 2007, 'The Empire's New Clothes: Political Economy and the Fragmentation of International Law', *Stanford Law Review*, 60(2):595–631.

Benvenuti, P. 2001, 'The ICTY Prosecutor and the Review of the NATO Bombing Campaign Against the Federal Republic of Yugoslavia', *European Journal of International Law*, 12(3): 503–28.

Bergsmo, M. and O. Triffterer 2008, 'Preamble', in *Commentary on the Rome Statute of the International Criminal Court*, 2nd edn, edited by O. Triffterer, Munich: Nomos Verlagsgesellschaft.

Berle, A.A. 1931, 'Corporate Powers as Powers in Trust', *Harvard Law Review*, 44: 1049–74.

Berle, A.A. 1932, 'For Whom Corporate Managers Are Trustees: A Note', *Harvard Law Review*, 45: 1365–72.

Berle, A.A. 1947, 'The Theory of Enterprise Entity', *Columbia Law Review*, 47: 343–58.

Berle, A.A. 1957, *Economic Power and the Free Society: A Preliminary Discussion of the Corporation*, The Fund for the Republic.

Berle, A.A. and G.C. Means 1991, *The Modern Corporation and Private Property*, New Brunswick, NJ: Transaction Publishers.

Berman, N. 1993, '"But the Alternative is Despair": European Nationalism and the Modernist Renewal of International Law', *Harvard Law Review*, 106(8): 1792–1903.

Berman, N. 1998–99, 'In the Wake of Empire', *American University International Law Review*, 14: 1521–000.

Bernaz, N. 2015, 'Corporate Criminal Liability under International Law: The New TV S.A.L. and Akhbar Beirut S.A.L. Cases at the Special Tribunal for Lebanon', *Journal of International Criminal Justice*, 13: 313–30.

Bernaz, N. 2016, *Business and Human Rights: History, Law and Policy – Bridging the Accountability Gap*, New York: Routledge.

Bernstein, E. 2010, 'Militarized Humanitarianism Meets Carceral Feminism: The Politics of Sex, Rights, and Freedom in Contemporary Antitrafficking Campaigns', *Signs*, 36(1): 45–72.

Bilkova, V. 2014, 'Post-Second World War Trials in Central and Eastern Europe', in *Historical Origins of International Criminal Law*, Volume 2, edited by M. Bergsmo, W. Ling Cheah, and P. Yi, Brussels: Torkel Opsahl.

Billstein, L. 2004, *Working for the Enemy: Ford, General Motors, and Forced Labor in Germany During the Second World War*, Oxford: Berghahn Books.

Bilsky, L. and N.R. Davidson 2012, 'A Process-Oriented Approach to Corporate Liability for Human Rights Violations', *Transnational Legal Theory*, 4(1): 1–43.

Bilsky, L., R. Citron, and N.R. Davidson 2014, 'From Kiobel back to Structural Reform: The Hidden Legacy of Holocaust Restitution Litigation', *Stanford Journal of Complex Litigation*, 2: 139–84.

Bishop, R., J. Crawford, and W. Reisman 2005, *Foreign Investment Disputes: Cases, Materials and Comments*, The Hague: Kluwer Law International.

Bittle, S. 2015, 'Beyond Corporate Fundamentalism: A Marxian Class Analysis of Corporate Crime Law Reform,' *Critical Sociology*, 41(1)1: 133–151.

Bittle, S. and L. Snider 2015, 'Law, Regulation, and Safety Crime: Exploring the Boundaries of Criminalizing Powerful Corporate Actors', *Canadian Journal of Law and Society / Revue Canadienne Droit et Société*, 30: 445–464.

Black, E. 2008, *IBM and the Holocaust: The Strategic Alliance Between Nazi Germany and America's Most Powerful Corporation*, Dialog Press.

Blackford, M. 2008, *The Rise of Modern Business: Great Britain, The United States, Germany, Japan & China*, Chapel Hill, NC: University of North Carolina Press.

Blair, M. 1995, *Ownership and Control: The American Corporation in the Twenty-First Century*, Washington, DC: Brookings Institution.

Blair, M. 2003, 'Locking in Capital: What Corporate Law Achieved for Business Organizers in the Nineteenth Century', *UCLA Law Review*, 51: 387–455.

Blair, M. and Stout, L. 1999, 'A Team Production Theory of Corporate Law', *Virginia Law Review*, 85: 247–328.

Blank, Y. 2006, 'Localism in the New Global Legal Order', *Harvard International Law Journal*, 47: 263–81.

Bloxham, D. 2003, 'British War Crimes Trial Policy in Germany, 1945–1957: Implementation and Collapse', *Journal of British Studies*, 42(1): 91–118.

Bloxham, D. 2006, 'Pragmatismus als Programm: Die Ahndung deutscher Kriegsverbrechen durch Großbritannien', in *Transnationale Vergangenheitspolitik: Der Umgang mit deutschen Kriegsverbrechern in Europa nach dem Zweiten Weltkrieg*, edited by N. Frei, Göttingen: Wallstein Verlag.

Bloxham, D. 2009, *The Final Solution: A Genocide*, Oxford: Oxford University Press.

Blum, J. (ed.) 1967, *From the Morgenthau Diaries*, Years of War: 1941–45, Boston, MA: Houghton Mifflin.

Blumberg, P.I. 1993, *The Multinational Challenge to Corporate Law: The Search for a New Corporate Personality*, Oxford: Oxford University Press.

Boas, G. 2010, 'The Difficulty with Individual Criminal Responsibility in International Criminal Law', in *Future Perspectives on International Criminal Justice*, edited by C. Stahn and L.J. van den Herik, The Hague: TMC Asser Press.

Böckli, P. 2004, *Schweizer Aktienrecht*, Zurich: Schulthess.

Boister, N. and R. Cryer 2008a, *Documents on the Tokyo International Military Tribunal: Charter, Indictment, and Judgments*, Oxford: Oxford University Press.

Boister, N. and R. Cryer 2008b, *The Tokyo International Military Tribunal: A Reappraisal*, Oxford: Oxford University Press.

Bonafè, B.I. 2009, *The Relationship Between State and Individual Responsibility for International Crimes*, Leiden: Brill.

Borchard, E. 1925, 'The Mavrommatis Concessions Cases', *American Journal of International Law*, 19: 728–38.

Borkin, J. 1978, *The Crime and Punishment of I.G. Farben*, New York: Free Press.

Boyle, A.J. and J. Birds 2014, *Boyle and Bird's Company Law*, 9th edn, Bristol: Jordan Publishers.

Brackman, A. 1987, *The Other Nuremberg: The Untold Story of the Tokyo War Crimes Trials*, New York: William Morrow & Co.

Brandon, P. 2010, 'Military Investment and the Rise of Capitalism: The Case of the Dutch Republic', unpublished draft paper.

Brandon, P. 2011, 'Marxism and the "Dutch Miracle": The Dutch Republic and the Transition-Debate', *Historical Materialism*, 19(3): 106–46.

Brandon, P. 2017, 'Between Company and State: The Dutch East and West India Companies as Brokers between War and Profit', in Baars and Spicer (eds) 2017, *The Cor-*

poration: A Critical, Multidisciplinary Handbook, Cambridge: Cambridge University Press.

Bratton, W. 1989, 'The New Economic Theory of the Firm: Critical Perspectives from History', *Stanford Law Review*, 41: 1471–527.

Braudel, F. 1983, *The Wheels of Commerce: Civilization and Capitalism, 15th–18th Century*, Volume 2, New York: HarperCollins.

Broad, R. (ed.) 2002, *Global Backlash: Citizen Initiatives for a Just World Economy*, Lanham, MD: Rowman & Littlefield Publishers, Inc.

Brook, T. 2001, 'The Tokyo Judgment and the Rape of Nanking', *Journal of Asian Studies*, 60(3): 673–700.

Brown Weiss, E. 2002, 'Invoking State Responsibility in the Twenty-First Century', *American Journal of International Law*, 96(4): 798–816.

Brownlie, I. 2008, *Principles of Public International Law*, Oxford: Oxford University Press.

Brzezinski, Z. 1998, *The Grand Chessboard: American Primacy and Its Geostrategic Imperatives*, New York: Basic Books.

Buggeln, M. 2007, 'Schandelah', in: W. Benz, B. Distel (Eds.): *Der Ort des Terrors. Geschichte der nationalsozialistischen Konzentrationslager, Vol. 5: Hinzert, Auschwitz, Neuengamme*. München: C.H. Beck.

Bukharin, N. 2003, *Imperialism and World Economy*, London: Bookmarks.

Burchard, C. 2006, 'The Nuremberg Trial and Its Impact on Germany', *Journal of International Criminal Justice*, 4(4): 800–29.

Burchard, C. 2010a, 'The International Legal Process: Towards a Realistic Model of International Criminal Law', in *Future Perspectives on International Criminal Justice*, edited by C. Stahn and L.J. van den Herik, The Hague: TMC Asser Press.

Burchard, C. 2010b, 'Ancillary and Neutral Business Contributions to "Corporate-Political Core Crime": Initial Enquiries Concerning the Rome Statute', *Journal of International Criminal Justice*, 8(3): 919–46.

Burroughs, P. (ed.) 1998, *Managing the Business of Empire: Essays in Honour of David Fieldhouse*, London: Cass.

Buscher, F.M. 1989, *The US War Crimes Trial Program in Germany, 1946–1955*, New York: Greenwood Press.

Bush, J.A. 2009, 'The Prehistory of Corporations and Conspiracy in International Criminal Law: What Nuremberg Really Said', *Columbia Law Review*, 109: 1094–1257.

Busscher, F. 2006, 'Bestrafen und Erziehen: "Nuremberg" und das Kriegverbrecherprogramm der USA', in *Transnationale Vergangenheitspolitik: Der Umgang mit deutschen Kriegsverbrechern in Europa nach dem Zweiten Weltkrieg*, edited by N. Frei, Göttingen: Wallstein Verlag.

Byers, M. (ed.) 2001, *The Role of Law in International Politics: Essays in International Relations and International Law*, Oxford: Oxford University Press.

Byers, M. and G. Nolte 2003, *US Hegemony and the Foundations of International Law*, Cambridge: Cambridge University Press.

Cain, M. and A. Hunt (eds) 1979, *Marx and Engels on Law*, London: Academic Press.

Callinicos, A. 2004, *Making History: Agency, Structure, and Change in Social Theory*, Leiden: Brill.

Callinicos, A. 2009, *Imperialism and Global Political Economy*, Cambridge: Polity Press.

Calvocoressi, P. 1947, *Nuremberg: The Facts, The Law and The Consequences*, London: Chatto & Windus.

Cameron, P. 2011, *International Energy Investment Law*, Oxford: Oxford University Press.

Canfield, G. 1914, 'Corporate Responsibility for Crime', *Columbia Law Review*, 14(6): 469–81.

Carty, A. 2007, *Philosophy of International Law*, Edinburgh: Edinburgh University Press.

Carty, T. 2008, 'Marxism and International Law: Perspectives for the American (Twenty-First) Century?', in *International Law on the Left*, edited by S. Marks, Cambridge: Cambridge University Press.

Cassese, A. 2008, *International Criminal Law*, Oxford: Oxford University Press.

Cassese, A. et al. (eds) 2009, *The Oxford Companion to International Criminal Justice*, Oxford: Oxford University Press.

Cattan, H. 1967, *The Evolution of Oil Concessions in the Middle East and North Africa*, New York: Oceana Publications.

Caudwell, C. 1905, *Studies in a Dying Culture*, London: John Lane.

Ceretti, A. 2009, 'Collective Violence and International Crimes', in *The Oxford Companion to International Criminal Justice*, edited by A. Cassese, Oxford: Oxford University Press.

Černič, J. 2010, *Human Rights Law and Business: Corporate Responsibility for Fundamental Human Rights*, Groningen: Europa Law Publishing.

Černič, J.L. and T. Van Ho (eds) 2015, *Human Rights and Business: Direct Corporate Accountability for Human Rights*, Nijmegen: Wolf Legal Publishers.

Chambliss, W.J. and R. Seidman 1982, *Law, Order and Power*, 2nd edn, Reading, MA: Addison-Wesley Publishing Company.

Chambliss, W.J. et al. 2010, *State Crime: Current Perspectives*, New Brunswick, NJ: Rutgers University Press.

Chandler, D.G. 2001, 'The Road to Military Humanitarianism: How the Human Rights NGOs Shaped a New Humanitarian Agenda', *Human Rights Quarterly*, 23(3): 678–700.

Chang, I. 1997, *The Rape of Nanking: The Forgotten Holocaust of World War II*, New York: Basic Books.

Cheffins, B. 2010, 'The Stewardship Code's Achilles Heel', *Modern Law Review*, 73(6): 1004–25.

Chimni, B.S. 2010, 'Prolegomena to a Class Approach to International Law', *European Journal of International Law*, 21(1): 57–82.

Chinkin, C. 2001, 'Women's International Tribunal on Japanese Military Slavery', *American Journal of International Law*, 95(2): 335–41.

Chiomenti, C. 2006, 'Corporations and the ICC', in *Transnational Corporations and Human Rights*, edited by O. De Schutter, Oxford: Hart.

Chossudovsky, M. 1996, 'Economic Genocide in Rwanda', *Economic and Political Weekly*, 31(15): 938–41.

Chua, A. 2000, 'The Paradox of Free Market Democracy: Rethinking Development Policy', *Harvard International Law Journal*, 41(2): 287–379.

Clapham, A. 2000, 'The Question of Jurisdiction under International Criminal Law over Legal Persons: Lessons from the Rome Conference on an International Criminal Court', in *Liability of Multinational Corporations under International Law*, edited by M. Kamminga and S. Zia-Zarifi, The Hague: Kluwer Law International.

Clapham, A. 2002, 'On Complicity', in *Le droit penal à l'epreuve de l'internationalisation*, edited by M. Henzelin and R. Roth, Paris: LGDJ.

Clapham, A. 2006, *Human Rights Obligations of Non-State Actors*, Oxford: Oxford University Press.

Clapham, A. 2008, 'Extending International Criminal Law Beyond the Individual to Corporations and Armed Opposition Groups', *Journal of International Criminal Justice*, 6(5): 899–926.

Clapham, A. 2011, 'Corporations and Criminal Complicity', in *Human Rights, Corporate Complicity and Disinvestment*, edited by G. Nystuen, A. Follesdal, and O. Mestad, Cambridge: Cambridge University Press.

Clapham, A. and S. Jerbi 2001, 'Categories of Corporate Complicity in Human Rights Abuses', *Hastings International & Comparative Law Review*, 24: 339–49.

Clark, R.C. 1986, *Corporate Law*, Boston, MA: Little, Brown.

Clarkson, C. 1996, 'Kicking Corporate Bodies and Damning Their Souls', *Modern Law Review*, 59(4): 557–72.

Cockayne, J. 2008, 'Discussion', *Journal of International Criminal Justice*, 5: 955–000.

Coffee, J. 1981, 'No Soul to Damn: No Body to Kick: An Unscandalized Inquiry into the Problem of Corporate Punishment', *Michigan Law Review*, 79(3): 386–459.

Cohen, F. 1935, 'Transcendental Nonsense and the Functional Approach', *Columbia Law Review*, 35: 809–49.

Cohen, G.A. 2000, *Karl Marx's Theory of History: A Defence*, Oxford: Oxford University Press.

Cohen, I. 1982, 'Introduction', in *General Economic History*, by M. Weber, New Brunswick, NJ: Transaction Books.

Cohen, J. 2000 [1949], *Japan's Economy in War and Reconstruction*, Minneapolis, MN: University of Minnesota Press. Republished in Janet Hunter, *Japanese Economic History 1930–1960*, Volume 2, New York: Routledge.

Coliver, S., J. Green, and P. Hoffman 2005, 'Holding Human Rights Violaters Accountable by Using International Law in US Courts: Advocacy Efforts and Complementary Strategies', *Emory International Law Review*, 19(1): 169–226.

Collier, P. and A. Hoeffler 2004, 'Greed and Grievance in Civil War', *Oxford Economic Papers*, 56(4): 563–95.

Collins, H. 1982. *Marxism and Law*, Oxford: Clarendon.

Cook, W.W. 1891, *The Corporation Problem: The Public Phases of Corporations, Their Uses, Abuses, Benefits, Dangers, Wealth, and Power, with a Discussion of the Social Industrial, Economic, and Political Questions to Which They Have Given Rise*, New York: G.P. Putnam's sons.

Cooke, C. 1950, *Corporation Trust and Company: An Essay in Legal History*, Manchester: Manchester University Press.

Cornish, W. et al. 2010, *The Oxford History of the Laws of England, Volume 12: 1820–1914 Private Law – Joint Stock Companies*, Oxford: Oxford University Press.

Cozian, M., A. Viandier, and F. Deboissy 2005, *Droit des sociétés*, Paris: Litec.

Craven, M. 2009, *The Decolonization of International Law: State Succession and the Law of Treaties*, Oxford: Oxford University Press.

Craven, M. 2010, 'Statehood, Self-Determination, and Recognition', in *International Law*, edited by M. Evans, Oxford: Oxford University Press.

Craven, M. 2012 'Colonialism and Domination', in *The Oxford Handbook of the History of International Law*, edited by B. Fassbender and A. Peters, Oxford: Oxford University Press.

Craven, M. 2016, 'Theorizing the Turn to History in International Law', in *The Oxford Handbook of the Theory of International Law*, edited by A. Orford and F. Hoffmann, Oxford: Oxford University Press.

Crawford, J. 1999, 'Revising the Draft Articles on State Responsibility', *European Journal of International Law*, 10(2): 442–60.

Crawford, J. 2002, *The International Law Commission's Articles on State Responsibility: Introduction, Text and Commentaries*, Oxford: Oxford University Press.

Crawford, J. 2010, 'The System of International Responsibility', in *The Law of International Responsibility*, edited by J. Crawford, A. Pellet, and S. Olleson, Oxford: Oxford University Press.

Crouch, C. 2011, *The Strange Non-Death of Neoliberalism*, Cambridge: Polity.

Cryer, R. 2005, *Prosecuting International Crimes: Selectivity and the International Criminal Law Regime*, Cambridge: Cambridge University Press.

Cryer, R., H. Friman, D. Robinson and E. Wilmshurst 2007, *An Introduction to International Criminal Law and Procedure*, Cambridge: Cambridge University Press.

Cryer, R., H. Friman, D. Robinson and E. Wilmshurst 2010, *An Introduction to International Criminal Law and Procedure*, Cambridge: Cambridge University Press.

Cutler, A. 2008, 'Toward a Radical Political Economy Critique of Transnational Economic Law', in *International Law on the Left*, edited by S. Marks, Cambridge: Cambridge University Press.

Cutler, A.C. 2001, 'Artifice, Ideology and Paradox: The Public/Private Distinction in International Law', *Review of International Political Economy*, 4(2): 261–85.

Cutler, A.C. 2003, *Private Power and Global Authority: Transnational Merchant Law in the Global Political Economy*, Cambridge: Cambridge University Press.

Cutler, A.C. 2005, 'Gramsci, Law, and the Culture of Global Capitalism', *Critical Review of International Social and Political Philosophy*, 8(4): 527–42.

Dahm, G. et al. 2002, *Völkerrecht*, Band 1/3, Berlin: De Gruyter Verlag.

Dallas, L. 1988, 'Two Models of Corporate Governance: Beyond Berle and Means', *University of Michigan Journal of Law Reform*, 22(1): 19–116.

Damaska, M. 2008, 'What is the Point of International Criminal Justice?', *Chicago-Kent Law Review*, 83: 329–65.

Danielsen, D. 2005, 'How Corporations Govern: Taking Corporate Power Seriously in Transnational Regulation and Governance', *Harvard International Law Journal*, 46(2): 411–425.

Danielsen, D. 2006, 'Corporate Power and Global Order', in, *International Law and its Others*, edited by Anne Orford, Cambridge: Cambridge University Press.

Danielsen, D. 2011, 'Economic Approaches to Global Regulation: Expanding the International Law and Economics Paradigm', *Journal of International Business & Law*, 10(1) 23–90.

Danielsen, D. 2015, 'Beyond Corporate Governance: Why a New Approach to the Study of Corporate Law is Needed to Address Global Inequality and Economic Development', in Research Handbook on Political Economy and Law, edited by U. Mattei and J. Haskell, Cheltenham: Edward Elgar.

Danielsen, D. 2015, 'Corporate Power and Instrumental States: Toward a Critical Reassessment of the Role of Firms, States, and Regulation in Global Governance', in *International Law and its Discontents: Confronting Crises*, edited by Barbara Stark, Cambridge: Cambridge University Press.

Darcy, S. 2017, '"The Elephant in the Room": Corporate Tax Avoidance and Business and Human Rights', *Business and Human Rights Journal*, 2: 1–30.

Davies, P. 1997, *Gower and Davies Principles of Modern Company Law*, 6th edn, Oxford: Oxford University Press.

Davies, P. 2003, *Gower and Davies: The Principles of Modern Company Law*, London: Sweet & Maxwell.

Davies, P. 2012, *Gower and Davies: Principles of Modern Company Law*, 9th edn, Oxford: Oxford University Press.

Davies, P. and S. Worthington 2016, *Gower's Principles of Modern Company Law*, 10th edn, London: Sweet & Maxwell.

Davis, A. 2003, *Are Prisons Obsolete?*, New York: Seven Stories Press.

Davis, J. 2008, *Justice Across Borders: The Struggle for Human Rights in US Courts*, Cambridge: Cambridge University Press.

Dawson, W.H. 1973, *Bismarck and State Socialism: An Exposition of the Social and Economic Legislation of Germany since 1870*, New York: Howard Fertig.

De Nevers, R. 2009, 'Private Security Companies and the Laws of War', *Security Dialogue*, 40(2): 169–90.

De Schutter, O. (ed.) 2006, *Transnational Corporations and Human Rights*, Oxford: Hart.

De Vitoria, F. 1964a [1532], *De Indis et De Ivre Belli Relectiones*, Section 3, translated by Ernest Nys, New York: Oceana Publications.

De Vitoria, F. 1964b [1557], *Relectiones Theologicae, Volume 12: De Indes et de Iure Belli*, Part 2 – *On the Indians Lately Discovered*, New York: Oceana Publications, available at: http://en.wikisource.org/wiki/De_Indis_De_Jure_Belli.

De Vos, D. 2017, 'Complementarity's Gender Justice Prospects and Limitations – Examining normative interactions between the Rome Statute and national accountability processes for sexual violence crimes in Colombia and the Democratic Republic of Congo', Ph.D. Thesis, European University Institute.

De Vroey, M. 1975, 'The Corporation and The Labor Process: The Separation of Ownership and Control in Large Corporations', *Review of Radical Political Economy*, 7(2): 1–10.

Deakin, S. 2012, 'The Corporation as Commons: Rethinking Property Rights, Governance and Sustainability in the Business Enterprise', *Queen's Law Journal*, 37(2): 339–81.

Deakin, S. 2017, 'The Corporation in Legal Studies', in Baars and Spicer (eds) 2017.

Deakin, S. and A. Supiot (eds) 2009, *Capacitas: Contract Law and the Institutional Preconditions of a Market Economy*, Oxford: Hart.

Defoe, D. 1721, 'A vindication of the Honour & Justice of Parliament against a most scandalous libel Entitled, "The Speech of John A---, Esq. (London)"', 15.

Defoe, D. 1722[?], 'A brief Debate upon the Dissolving the late Parliament', probably published March 1722.

Deitelhoff, N. and K.D. Wolf 2013, 'Business and Human Rights: How Corporate Norm Violators Become Norm Entrepreneurs', in *The Persistent Power of Human Rights: From Commitment to Compliance*, edited by T. Risse, S.F. Ropp, and K. Sikkink, Cambridge: Cambridge University Press.

Deva, S. and D. Bilchitz (eds) 2013, *Human Rights Obligations of Business: Beyond the Corporate Responsibility to Respect?* Cambridge: Cambridge University Press.

Deva, S. and D. Bilchitz (eds) 2017, *Building a Treaty on Business and Human Rights: Context and Contours*, Cambridge: Cambridge University Press.

Dewey, J. 1925, *Experience and Nature*, Chicago: Open Court.

Dewey, J. 1926, 'The Historic Background of Corporate Legal Personality', *Yale Law Journal*, 35(6): 655–73.

Dezalay, Y. and B. Garth 1996, *Dealing in Virtue: International Commercial Arbitration and the Construction of a Transnational Legal Order*, Chicago: University of Chicago Press.

Di Sabato, F. 1995, *Manuale della Società*, 5th edn, Torino: Utet.

Dignam, A. 2011, *Hicks & Goo's Cases and Materials on Company Law*, Oxford: Oxford University Press.

Dignam, A. and J. Lowry 2009, *Company Law*, Oxford: Oxford University Press.

Dignam, A. and J. Lowry 2010, *Company Law: Core Text*, Oxford: Oxford University Press.

Dine, J. and A. Fagan 2006, *Human Rights and Capitalism: A Multidisciplinary Perspective on Globalization*, Cheltenham: Edward Elgar.

Dodd, E. 1932, 'For Whom Are Corporate Managers Trustees?', *Harvard Law Review*, 45: 1145–63.

Donihi, R. 1992–93, 'War Crimes', *St. John's Law Review*, 66: 733–71.

Doucet, S. 2010, 'The Inter-American Court of Human Rights and Aggravated State Responsibility: Operationalizing the Concept of State Crime', in *Future Perspectives on International Criminal Justice*, edited by C. Stahn and L.J. van den Herik, The Hague: TMC Asser Press.

Douzinas, C. 2010, 'Adikia: On Communism and Rights', in *The Idea of Communism*, edited by S. Žižek and C. Douzinas, London: Verso.

Drago, L. and E. Nettles 1928, 'The Drago Doctrine in International Law and Politics', *Hispanic American History Review*, 8: 204–23.

Drescher, S. and P. Finkelman 2012, 'Slavery', in *The Oxford Handbook of the History of International Law*, edited by B. Fassbender and A. Peters, Oxford: Oxford University Press.

Drobisch, K. 1999, 'Fall 5: Der Prozeß gegen Industrielle (gegen Friedrich Flick und andere)', in *Der Nationalsozialismus vor Gericht: Die alliierten Prozesse gegen Kriegsverbrechen und Soldaten 1943–1952*, edited by G. Ueberschär and R. Blasius, Berlin: Fischer Taschenbuch Verlag.

Drumbl, M.A. 2011, 'Collective Responsibility and Post-Conflict Justice', in *Accountability for Collective Wrongdoing*, edited by T. Isaacs and V. Richard, Cambridge: Cambridge University Press.

Dubois, A.B. 1938, *The English Business Company After the Bubble Act 1720–1800*, New York: Commonwealth Fund.

DuBois, J.E. 1952, *The Devil's Chemists: 24 Conspirators of the International Farben Cartel Who Manufacture Wars*, Boston: Beacon Press.

Duffield, M. 2001, *Global Governance and the New Wars: The Merging of Development and Security*, New York: Zed Books.

Dugard, J. 2013, 'Palestine and the International Criminal Court: Institutional Failure or Bias?', *Journal of International Criminal Justice*, 11(3): 563–70.

Dugard, J. and C. Van Den Wyngaert 1996, *International Criminal Law and Procedure*, Aldershot: Dartmouth Publishing Co. Ltd.

Dunoff, J. and J. Trachtman (eds) 2009, *Ruling the World?*, Cambridge: Cambridge University Press.

Easterbrook, F. and D. Fischel 1991, *The Economic Structure of Corporate Law*, Cambridge, MA: Harvard University Press.

Ebbinghaus, A. 1999, 'Der Prozeß gegen Tesch & Stabenow. Von der Schädlingsbekämpfung zum Holocaust', *Zeitschrift für Sozialgeschichte des 19. und 20. Jahrhunderts*, 13: 16–71.

Eberechi, I. 2009, 'Armed Conflicts in Africa and Western Complicity: A Disincentive for African Union's Cooperation with the ICC', *African Journal of Legal Studies*, 3: 53–76.

Edgerton, H. 1927, 'Corporate Criminal Responsibility', *Yale Law Journal*, 36: 827–44.

Edwards, A. 2006, 'The "Feminizing" of Torture under International Human Rights Law', *Leiden Journal of International Law*, 19(2): 349–91.

Eizenstat, S. 2003, *Imperfect Justice: Looted Assets, Slave Labor, and the Unfinished Business of World War II*, New York: Public Affairs.

Engels, F. 1894, 'Letter to Borgius, London 25 January 1894', available at: http://www.marxists.org/archive/marx/works/1894/letters/94_01_25.htm.

Engels, F. 1950 [1886], *Ludwig Feuerbach and the End of Classical German Philosophy*, Moscow: Foreign Language Publishing House.

Engels, F. and K. Kautsky 1977, 'Juridical Socialism', *Politics & Society*, 7(2): 203–20.

Engle, K. 2005, 'Feminism and Its (Dis)Contents: Criminalizing Wartime Rape in Bosnia and Herzegovina', *American Journal of International Law*, 99(4): 778–816.

Evans, M. 2014, *International Law*, 4th edn, Oxford: Oxford University Press.

Ezeudu, M. 2011, 'Revisiting Corporate Violations of Human Rights in Nigeria's Niger Delta Region: Canvassing the Potential Role of the International Criminal Court', *African Human Rights Law Journal*, 11(1): 23–56.

Falk, R. 1998–99, 'Telford Taylor and the Legacy of Nuremberg', *Columbia Journal of Transnational Law*, 37(3): 693–723.

Fanon, F. 1963, *The Wretched of the Earth*, New York: Grove Press Inc.

Farrar, J. 2008, *Corporate Governance: Theories, Principles and Practice*, Oxford: Oxford University Press.

Farrar, J. and B. Hannigan (eds) 1998, *Farrar's Company Law*, 4th edn, London: Butterworth.

Farrell, N. 2010, 'Attributing Criminal Liability to Corporate Actors: Some Lessons from the International Tribunals', *Journal of International Criminal Justice*, 8(3): 873–94.

Fassbender, B. and A. Peters 2012, *The Oxford Handbook of the History of International Law*, Oxford: Oxford University Press.

Ferdinandusse, W.N. 2006, *Direct Application of International Criminal Law in National Courts*, The Hague: Asser Press.

Ferdinandusse, W.N. 2009, 'The Prosecution of Grave Breaches in National Courts', *Journal of International Criminal Justice*, 7(4): 703–21.

Ferencz, B. 1979, *Less Than Slaves: Jewish Forced Labor and the Quest for Compensation*, Cambridge, MA: Harvard University Press.

Ferencz, B. 1995, 'International Criminal Court', in *Encyclopedia of Public International Law*, Volume 2, edited by R. Bernhardt, Burlington: Elsevier.

Ferencz, B. 1999, 'A Prosecutor's Personal Account: Nuremberg to Rome', *Journal of International Affairs*, 52(2): 455–69.

Ferrando, T. 2017a, 'Certification Schemes and Labelling as Corporate Governance: The Value of Silence', in Baars and Spicer (eds).

Ferrando, T. 2017b, 'Land Rights at the Time of Global Production: Leveraging Multi-Spatiality and "Legal Chokeholds"', *Business and Human Rights Journal*, 2(2): 275–95.

Ferro, M. 1997, *Colonization: A Global History*, New York: Routledge.

Finn, R.B. 1992, *Winners in Peace: MacArthur, Yoshida and Postwar Japan*, Stanford: University of California Press.

Fisse, B. and J. Braithwaite 1993, *Corporations, Crime and Accountability*, Cambridge: Cambridge University Press.

Fitzpatrick, G. 2013, 'War Crimes Trials, "Victor's Justice" and Australian Military Justice in the Aftermath of the Second World War', in *Untold Stories: Hidden Histories of War Crimes Trials*, edited by G. Simpson and K. Heller, Oxford: Oxford University Press.

Fleming, P. 2017 'Bad Parresia: CSR and Corporate Mystification Today', in Baars and Spicer (eds).

Fleming P. and M.T. Jones 2013, *The End of Corporate Social Responsibility: Crisis and Critique*, London: Sage.

Fleming, P. and A. Spicer 2007, *Contesting the Corporation: Power, Resistance and Struggle in Organizations*, Cambridge: Cambridge University Press.

Forbath, P. 1977, *The River Congo: The Discovery, Exploration and Exploitation of the World's Most Dramatic Rivers*, New York: Harper & Row.

Forcese, C. 2009, 'Regulating Multinational Corporations and International Trade Law', in *The Oxford Handbook of International Trade Law*, edited by D. Bethlehem et al., Oxford: Oxford University Press.

Ford, H. 2010, *The International Jew*, Mansfield Centre, CT: Martino Publishing.

Fox, D.R. 1993, 'Where's the Proof That Law is a Good Thing?', *Law and Human Behavior*, 17(2): 257–8.

Franzki, H. and M.C. Olarte 2013, 'Understanding the Political Economy of Transitional Justice: A Critical Theory Perspective', in *Transitional Justice Theories*, edited by S. Buckley-Zistel et al., New York: Routledge.

Franzki, H. and M.C. Olarte 2016, 'Criminal Trials, Economic Dimensions of State

Crime, and the Politics of Time in International Criminal Law: A German-Argentine Constellation', Ph.D. thesis, Birkbeck College, University of London.

Fraser, N. 2009, *Scales of Justice: Reimagining Political Space in a Globalized World*, Cambridge: Cambridge University Press.

Frei, N. (ed.) 2003, *Hitlers Eliten nach 1945*, Munich: Deutscher Taschenbuch Verlag.

Frei, N. (ed.) 2006, *Transnationale Vergangenheitspolitik: Der Umgang mit deutschen Kriegsverbrechen in Europa nach dem Zweiten Weltkrieg*, Göttingen: Wallstein Verlag.

Frei, N. and T. Schanetzky 2010, *Unternehmen im Nationalsozialismus: Zur Historisierung einer Froschungskonjunktur*, Göttingen: Wallstein Verlag.

French, D., S. Mayson, and C. Ryan 2009, *Mayson, French and Ryan on Company Law*, Oxford: Oxford University Press.

Friedman, M. and R.D. Friedman 1962, *Capitalism and Freedom*, Chicago: University of Chicago Press.

Friedmann, W. et al. (eds) 1953, *Transnational Law in a Changing Society: Essays in Honor of Philip C. Jessup*, New York: Columbia University Press.

Fruin, R. 1925 [1868], *Een Onuitgegeven Werk van Hugo de Groot*, Bibliotheca Visseriana.

Fuchs, D. 2013, 'Theorizing the Power of Global Companies', in *The Handbook of Global Companies*, edited by John Mikler, Chichester: John Wiley & Sons, Ltd.

Fukuyama, F. 1992, *The End of History and the Last Man*, New York: Free Press.

Futamura, M. 2008, *War Crimes Tribunals and Transitional Justice: The Tokyo Trial and the Nuremberg Legacy*, New York: Routledge.

Gathii, J.T. 2010, *War, Commerce, and International Law*, Oxford: Oxford University Press.

Geldart, W.M. 1911, 'Legal Personality', *Law Quarterly Review*, 27: 90–108.

Getzler, J. and M. McNair 2006, 'The Firm as an Entity before the Companies Acts', University of Oxford Faculty of Law Legal Studies Research Paper Series Working Paper 47.

Gewald, J.-B. 2009, 'Rumours of Mau Mau in Northern Rhodesia, 1950–1960', *Afrika Focus* 22(1): 37–56.

Gierke, O. 1900, *Political Theories of the Middle Age*, translated by F. Maitland, Cambridge: Cambridge University Press.

Gierke, O. 1903, *Das Deutsche Genossenschaftsrecht*, Berlin: Weidmannche Buchhandlung.

Gierke, O. 1958, *Political Theories of the Middle Age*, Boston: Beacon Press.

Gimbel, J. 1972, 'On the Implementation of the Potsdam Agreement: An Essay on US Postwar German Policy', *Political Science Quarterly*, 87(2): 242–269.

Gindis, D. 2009, 'From Fictions and Aggregates to Real Entities in the Theory of the Firm', *Journal of Institutional Economy*, 5(1): 25–46.

Gindis, D. 2015, 'Legal Personhood and the Firm: Avoiding Anthropomorphism and Equivocation', *Journal of Institutional Economy*, 12(3): 499–513.

Girvin, S. 2010, *Charlesworth's Company Law*, 18th edn, London: Sweet & Maxwell.

Glasbeek, H. 1987–88, 'The Corporate Social Responsibility Movement: The Latest in Maginot Lines to Save Capitalism', *Dalhousie Law Journal*, 11: 363–402.

Glasbeek, H. 2002, *Wealth by Stealth: Corporate Crime, Corporate Law, and the Perversion of Democracy*, Toronto: Between the Lines.

Glasbeek, H. 2004, 'Crime, Health and Safety and Corporations: Meanings of the Failed Crimes (Workplace Deaths and Serious Injuries) Bill', University of Melbourne Centre for Employment and Labour Relations Law, Working Paper No. 29, available at: http://celrl.law.unimelb.edu.au/assets/wp29.pdf.

Glasbeek, H. 2010, 'The Corporation as Legally Constructed Site of Irresponsibility', in *The International Handbook of White-Collar and Corporate Crime*, edited by H. Pontell and G. Geis, Berlin: Springer.

Glaser, Stefan 2008, 'The Charter of the Nuremberg Tribunal and New Principles', in *Perspectives on the Nuremberg Trials*, edited by G. Mettraux, Oxford: Oxford University Press.

Gower, L. 1952, 'A South Sea Heresy?', *Law Quarterly Review*, 68(4): 214–25.

Gower, L.C.B. 2003, *Gower and Davies: The Principles of Modern Company Law*, 7th edn, London: Sweet & Maxwell.

Grant, J. and C. Barker 2006, *International Criminal Law Deskbook*, London: Cavendish.

Gray, G. 2006, 'The Regulation of Corporate Violations: Punishment, Compliance and the Blurring of Responsibility', *British Journal of Criminology*, 46(5): 875–92.

Grear, A. 2007, 'Challenging Corporate "Humanity": Legal Disembodiment, Embodiment and Human Rights', *Human Rights Law Review*, 7(3): 511–43.

Greiff, P. De (ed.) 2006, *The Handbook of Reparations*, Oxford: Oxford University Press.

Grewe, W.G. 1984, *Epochen der Volkerrechtsgeschichte*, 1st edn, Munich: Nomos Verlagsgesellschaft.

Grotius, H. 1925 [1604–08], 'De Jure Praedae', in *Een Onuitgegeven Werk van Hugo de Groot*, edited by R. Fruin, Bibliotheca Visseriana.

Grotius, H. 2004 [1605], *Mare Liberum* [The Free Sea], edited by D. Armitage, Indianapolis: Liberty Fund, available at: http://oll.libertyfund.org/index.php?option=com_staticxt&staticfile=show.php%3Ftitle=859&layout=html.

Grotius, H. 2005 [1625], *The Rights of War and Peace*, edited by R. Tuck, Indianapolis: Liberty Fund.

Guilfoyle, D. 2008, 'Piracy off Somalia: UN Security Council Resolution 1816 and IMO Regional Counter-Piracy Efforts', *International and Comparative Law Quarterly*, 57(3): 690–9.

Guilfoyle, D. 2011, 'Responsibility for Collective Atrocities: Fair Labelling and Approaches to Commission in International Criminal Law', *Current Legal Problems*, 64(1): 255–86.

Guilfoyle, D. 2016, *International Criminal Law*, Oxford: Oxford University Press.

Gunningham, N., R.A. Kagan, and D. Thornton 2004, 'Social License and Environmental Protection: Why Businesses Go beyond Compliance', *Law and Social Inquiry*, 29(2): 307–41.

Hadden, T. 1977, *Company Law and Capitalism*, 2nd edn, London: Weidenfeld & Nicolson.

Hae Bong, S. 2005, 'Compensation for Victims of Wartime Atrocities: Recent Developments in Japan's Case Law', *Journal of International Criminal Justice*, 3(1): 186–206.

Hajjar, L. 1997, 'Cause Lawyering in Transnational Perspective: National Conflict and Human Rights in Israel/Palestine', *Law and Society Review*, 31: 473–504.

Hale, C., K. Hayward, A. Wahidin, and E. Wincup 2009, *Criminology*, Oxford: Oxford University Press.

Hannigan, B. 2009, *Company Law*, Oxford: Oxford University Press.

Hannigan, B. 2016, *Company Law*, 4th edn, Oxford: Oxford University Press.

Hansmann, H. 1996, *The Ownership of Enterprise*, Cambridge, MA: Belknap Press.

Hansmann, H. 2006, 'How Close is the End of History?', *Journal of Corporation Law*, 31(3): 745–51.

Hansmann, H. and R. Kraakman 2000a, 'Organisational Law as Asset Partitioning', *European Economic Review*, 44: 807–17.

Hansmann, H. and R. Kraakman 2000b, 'The Essential Role of Organizational Law', *Yale Law Journal*, 110: 387–440.

Hansmann, H. and R. Kraakman 2001, 'The End of History for Corporate Law', *Georgetown Law Journal*, 89: 439–68.

Hansmann, H., R. Kraakman, and R. Squire 2006, 'Law and the Rise of the Firm', *Harvard Law Review*, 119: 1333–403.

Harris, D. 2010, *Cases and Materials on International Law*, London: Sweet & Maxwell.

Harris, R. 1994, 'The Bubble Act: Its Passage and Its Effects on Business Organization', *Journal of Economic History*, 54(3): 610–27.

Harris, R. 1997, 'Political Economy, Interest Groups, Legal Institutions and the Repeal of the Bubble Act in 1825', *Economic History Review*, 50(4): 675–96.

Harris, R. 2000, *Industrializing English Law: Entrepreneurship and Business Organization, 1720–1844*, Cambridge: Cambridge University Press.

Harris, R. 2006, 'The Transplantation of a Legal Discourse: Corporate Personality Theories from German Codification to British Political Pluralism and American Big Business', *Washington and Lee Law Review*, 63(4): 1421–78.

Harris, S. 2002, *Factories of Death: Japanese Biological Warfare 1932–45 and the American Cover-Up*, New York: Routledge.

Hart, H.L.A. 1983, 'Essay 1: Definition and Theory in Jurisprudence', in *Essays in Jurisprudence and Philosophy*, Oxford: Clarendon Press.

Harvey, D. 2003, *The New Imperialism*, Oxford: Oxford University Press.

Harvey, D. 2010, *The Enigma of Capital: And the Crises of Capitalism*, London: Profile Books.

Hawkins, K. 1990, 'Compliance Strategy, Prosecution Policy and Aunt Sally: A Comment on Pearce and Tombs', *British Journal of Criminology*, 30(4): 444–66.

Hawkins, K. 1991, 'Enforcing Regulation: More of the Same from Pearce and Tombs', *British Journal of Criminology*, 31(4): 427–30.

Hayes, P. 2000, *Industry and Ideology: IG Farben in the Nazi Era*, Cambridge: Cambridge University Press.

Hazeltine, D. et al. (eds) 1936, *Maitland: Selected Essays*, Cambridge: Cambridge University Press.

Head, M. 2007, *Evgeny Pashukanis: A Critical Reappraisal*, London: Routledge-Cavendish.

Heller, K.J. 2010, 'Situational Gravity under the Rome Statute', in *Future Perspectives on International Criminal Justice*, edited by C. Stahn and L.J. van den Herik, The Hague: TMC Asser Press.

Heller, K.J. 2011, *The Nuremberg Military Tribunals and the Origins of International Criminal Law*, Oxford: Oxford University Press.

Henn, H. and J. Alexander 1983, *Laws of Corporations and other Business Enterprises*, St. Paul, MN: West Publishing Co.

Hertz, N. 2001, *The Silent Takeover: Global Capitalism and the Death of Democracy*, London: Arrow.

Hicks, A. and S. Goo 2008, *Cases and Materials on Company Law*, 6th edn, Oxford: Oxford University Press.

Higgins, R. 1995, *Problems and Process: International Law and How We Use It*, Oxford: Clarendon Press.

Higgins, R. 1999, 'Natural Resources in the Case Law of the International Court', in *International Law and Sustainable Development: Past Achievements and Future Challenges*, edited by A. Boyle and D. Freestone, Oxford: Oxford University Press.

Hilger, A. 2006, '"Die Gerechtigkeit nehme ihren Lauf"? Die Bestrafung deutscher Kriegs- und Gewaltverbrecher in der Sowjetunion und der SBZ/DDR', in *Transnationale Vergangenheitspolitik: Der Umgang mit deutschen Kriegsverbrechern in Europa nach dem Zweiten Weltkrieg*, edited by N. Frei, Göttingen: Wallstein Verlag.

Hirsch, F. 2008, 'The Soviets at Nuremberg: International Law, Propaganda and the Making of the Postwar Order', *American Historical Review*, 113: 701–30.

Hisakazu, F. 2011, 'Humanity's Justice v. Victor's Justice', in *Beyond Victor's Justice? The Tokyo War Crimes Trial Revisited*, edited by Y. Tanaka, T. McCormack, and G. Simpson, Leiden: Martinus Nijhoff.

Hobbes, T. 1651, *Leviathan*, available at: http://oregonstate.edu/instruct/phl302/texts/hobbes/leviathan-contents.html.

Hochschild, A. 2006, *King Leopold's Ghost: A Story of Greed, Terror and Heroism in Colonial Africa*, London: Pan.

Hoffmann, F. 2016, 'International Legalism and International Politics', in *The Oxford Handbook of the Theory of International Law*, edited by A. Orford and F. Hoffmann, Oxford: Oxford University Press.

Hohfeld, W. 1913–14, 'Some Fundamental Legal Conceptions as Applied in Judicial Reasoning', *Yale Law Journal*, 23(1): 16.

Hohfeld, W. 1923, 'Some Fundamental Conceptions as Applied in Judicial Reasoning', in *Fundamental Legal Conceptions as Applied in Judicial Reasoning and Other Legal Essays by W.N. Hohfeld*, edited by W. Cook, New Haven: Yale University Press.

Holdsworth, W. 1925, *History of English Law*, 8 Volumes, London: Methuen & Co. Ltd.

Hollán, M. 2000, 'Globalisation and Conceptualisation in the Sphere of International Criminal Law', *Acta Juridica Hungarica*, 41(3–4): 225–46.

Hopkins, A.G. 1980, 'Property Rights and Empire Building: Britain's Annexation of Lagos, 1861', *Journal of Economic History*, 40(4): 777–98.

Horkheimer, M. 1972, 'Traditional and Critical Theory', in *Critical Theory: Selected Essays*, New York: Continuum.

Horwitz, S. 1950, 'Tokyo Trial', *International Conciliation: Carnegie Endowment for International Peace*, 465: 477–98.

Horwitz, Y. 2013, 'The Prisoner of War Camps Trials', in *Hong Kong War Crimes Trials*, edited by S. Linton, Oxford: Oxford University Press.

Hosoya, C., N. Ando, Y. Onuma, and R. Minear (eds) 1986, *The Tokyo War Crimes Trial: An International Symposium*, Tokyo: Kodansha.

Huisman, W. and E. van Sliedregt 2010, 'Rogue Traders: International Crimes and Corporate Complicity in the Netherlands', *Journal of International Criminal Justice*, 8(3): 803–28.

Hunt, C. 1936, *The Development of the Business Corporation in England, 1800–1867*, Cambridge, MA: Harvard University Press.

Hunter, J. 1989, *The Emergence of Modern Japan: An Introductory History since 1853*, London: Longman.

Hurst, J.W. 1970, *The Legitimacy of the Business Corporation in the US 1780–1970*, Charlottesville: University of Virginia Press.

Igwe, C.S. 2008, 'The ICC's Favourite Customer: Africa and International Criminal Law', *Comparative and International Law Journal of South Africa*, 41(2): 294–323.

Institut für Marxismus-Leninismus 1960, *IG Farben: Mächtiger und Gefährlicher denn je*, Berlin: Institut für Marxismus-Leninismus and der Technischen Hochschule für Chemie Leuna-Merseburg.

Institut für Marxismus-Leninismus 1962, *IG Farben: Macht und Verbrechen: Ein auf exaktem Material beruhender Beitrag zur nationalen Frage in Deutschland un dem Weg zu ihrer Lösung*, Berlin: Institut für Marxismus-Leninismus and der Technischen Hochschule für Chemie Leuna-Merseburg.

Ireland, P. 1999, 'Company Law and the Myth of Shareholder Ownership', *Modern Law Review*, 62(1): 32–57.

Ireland, P. 2002, 'History, Critical Legal Studies and the Mysterious Disappearance of Capitalism', *Modern Law Review*, 65(1): 120–40.

Ireland, P. 2009, 'Limited Liability, Rights of Control and the Problem of Corporate Irresponsibility', *Cambridge Journal of Economics*, 34(5): 837–56.

Ireland, P. 2017, 'Finance and the Origins of Modern Company Law', in Baars and Spicer (eds) 2017.

Ireland, P., I. Grigg-Spall, and D. Kelly 1987, 'The Conceptual Foundations of Modern Company Law', *Journal of Law and Society*, 14(1): 149–65.

Ittersum, M. 2006, *Hugo Grotius, Natural Rights Theories and the Rise of Dutch Power in the East Indies 1595–1615*, Leiden: Brill.

Jackson, R. 1946, 'The Significance of the Nuremberg Trials to the Armed Forces: Previously Unpublished Personal Observations by the Chief Counsel for the United States', *Military Affairs*, 10(4): 2–15.

Jackson, R. 1949, 'Nuremberg in Retrospect, Legal Answer to International Lawlessness', *American Bar Association Journal*, 35(10): 813–87.

Jacobson, K.R. 2005, 'Doing Business with the Devil: The Challenges of Prosecuting Corporate Officials whose Business Transactions Facilitate War Crimes and Crimes Against Humanity', *Air Force Law Review*, 56: 167–231.

Jalloh, C.C. 2009, 'Regionalizing International Criminal Law?', *International Criminal Law Review*, 9(3): 445–99.

Jalloh, C.C. 2015, 'The Law and Politics of the Charles Taylor Case', *Denver Journal of International Law and Policy*, 43(3): 229–76.

Jalloh, C.C. 2017, 'The African Union, the Security Council, and the International Criminal Court', in *The International Criminal Court and Africa*, by C.C. Jalloh and I. Bantekas, Oxford: Oxford University Press.

Jannaca-Small, K. 2010, *Arbitration Under International Investment Agreements: A Guide to the Key Issues*, Oxford: Oxford University Press.

Jayasimha, S. 2001, 'Victor's Justice, Crime of Silence and the Burden of Listening: Judgment of the Tokyo Tribunal 1948, Women's International War Crimes Tribunal 2000 and Beyond', *Law, Social Justice and Global Development Journal*, (1), available at: https://warwick.ac.uk/fac/soc/law/elj/lgd/2001_1/jayasimha/.

Jefremovas, V. 2002, *Brickyards to Graveyards: From Production to Genocide in Rwanda*, Albany: State University of New York Press.

Jensen, M. 2005, 'Value Maximisation, Stakeholder Theory, and the Corporate Objective Function', *Journal of Applied Corporate Finance*, 14(3): 8–21.

Jensen, M. and W. Meckling 1976, 'Theory of the Firm: Managerial Behavior, Agency Costs and Capital Structure', *Journal of Financial Economics*, 3: 305–60.

Jescheck, H.-H. 1995, 'International Crimes', in *Encyclopedia of Public International Law*, Volume 2, edited by R. Bernhardt, Burlington: Elsevier.

Jescheck, H.-H. 2008, 'The Development of International Criminal Law after Nuremberg', in *Perspectives on the Nuremberg Trials*, edited by G. Mettraux, Oxford: Oxford University Press.

Jeßberger, F. 2009, 'Die I.G. Farben vor Gericht: Von den Ursprüngen eines "Wirtschaftsvölkerstrafrechts"', *Juristenzeitung*, 64(19): 924–32.

Jeßberger, F. 2010, 'On the Origins of Individual Criminal Responsibility under International Law for Business Activity: IG Farben on Trial', *Journal of International Criminal Justice*, 8(3): 783–802.

Jeßberger, F. 2016, 'Corporate Involvement in Slavery and Criminal Responsibility under International Law', *Journal of International Criminal Justice*, 14(2): 327–41.

Jeßberger, F. and J. Geneuss 2008, 'On the Application of a Theory of Indirect Perpetration in Al Bashir: German Doctrine at The Hague?', *Journal of International Criminal Justice*, 6(5): 853–69.

Jessop, B. 1990, *State Theory: Putting Capitalists in Their Place*, Cambridge: Polity Press.

Jessop, B. 1997, 'Capitalism and Its Future: Remarks on Regulation, Government and Governance', *Review of International Political Economy*, 4(3): 561–81.

Jessup, P.C. 1956, *Transnational Law*, New Haven: Yale University Press.

Johns, F. 1995, 'The Invisibility of the Transnational Corporation: An Analysis of International Law and Legal Theory', *Melbourne University Law Review*, 19(4): 893–923.

Johns, F. 2007, 'Book Review: A. Orford, (ed.), *International Law and Its Others*, Cambridge: Cambridge University Press, 2006', *Melbourne Journal of International Law*, 8(2): 516–35.

Johns, F. (ed.) 2010, *International Legal Personality*, Farnham: Ashgate.

Johns, F. 2016, 'Theorizing the Corporation in International Law', in *The Oxford Handbook of the Theory of International Law*, edited by A. Orford and F. Hoffmann, Oxford: Oxford University Press.

Johns, F., R. Joyce, and S. Pahuja 2010, *Events: The Force of International Law*, London: Routledge-Cavendish.

Jones, C. and A. Spicer 2009, *Unmasking the Entrepreneur*, Cheltenham: Edward Elgar.

Jørgensen, N.H.B. 2003, *The Responsibility of States for International Crimes*, Oxford: Oxford University Press.

Jørgensen, N.H.B. 2013, 'On Being "Concerned" in a Crime: Embryonic Joint Criminal Enterprise?', in *Hong Kong War Crimes Trials*, edited by S. Linton, Oxford: Oxford University Press.

Joseph, S. 2004, *Corporations and Transnational Human Rights Litigation*, Oxford: Hart Publishing.

Kahn, S. 1952, 'Preface', in *IG Farben*, edited by R. Sasuly, Berlin: Verlag Volk und Welt GMBH.

Kalls, S. and C. Nowotny et al. 2008, *Österreichisches Gesellschaftsrecht*, Vienna: Manzsche Verlags- und Universitätsbuchhandlung.

Kamminga, M.T. 2000, *Liability of Multinational Corporations Under International Law*, Leiden: Brill.

Kamola, I. 2008, 'Coffee and Genocide: A Political Economy of Violence in Rwanda', *Transition*, 99: 54–72.

Karavias, M. 2015, 'Shared Responsibility and Multinational Enterprises', *Netherlands International Law Review*, 62(1): 91–117.

Karskens, A. 2006, *Geen cent spijt: De jacht op oorlogsmisdadiger Frans van Anraat*, Amsterdam: Meulenhoff.

Karstedt, S. and S. Farrall 2006, 'The Moral Economy of Everyday Crime: Markets, Consumers and Citizens', *British Journal of Criminology*, 46(6): 1011–36.

Keane, F. 1995, *Seasons of Blood: A Rwandan Journey*, New York: Viking.

Keay, A. 2008, 'Ascertaining the Corporate Objective: An Entity Maximisation and Sustainability Model', *Modern Law Review*, 71(5): 663–98.

Keay, A. 2010, 'Getting to Grips with the Shareholder Value Theory in Corporate Law', *Common Law World Review*, 39(4): 358–78.

Keenan, J. and B. Brown 1951, *Crimes Against International Law*, Washington, DC: Public Affairs.

Keene, E. 2002, *Beyond the Anarchical Society: Grotius, Colonialism and Order in World Politics*, Cambridge: Cambridge University Press.

Kei-Ichi, T. 2011, 'Reasons for the Failure to Prosecute Unit 731 and Its Significance', in *Beyond Victor's Justice? The Tokyo War Crimes Trial Revisited*, edited by Y. Tanaka, T. McCormack, and G. Simpson, Leiden: Martinus Nijhoff.

Kelsen, H. 1947, 'Will the Judgment in the Nuremberg Trial Constitute a Precedent in International Law?', *International Law Quarterly*, 1(2): 153–71.

Kelsen, H. 2008, *Reine Rechtslehre: Einleitung in die Rechtswissenschaftliche Problematik*, Tubingen: Mohr Siebeck.

Kennan, G.F. 1967, *Memoirs, 1925–1950*, New York: Little Brown and Company.

Kennan, G.F. 1983, *Memoirs 1925–50*, New York: Pantheon.

Kennedy, D. 1987, *International Legal Structures*, Munich: Nomos.

Kennedy, D. 1997, 'International Law and the Nineteenth Century: History of an Illusion', *Quinnipiac Law Review*, 17: 99–138.

Kennedy, D. 1999, 'The Disciplines of International Law and Policy', *Leiden Journal of International Law*, 12(1): 9–133.

Kennedy, D. 2005, *The Dark Sides of Virtue: Reassessing International Humanitarianism*, Princeton: Princeton University Press.

Kennedy, D. 2006, *Of War and Law*, Princeton: Princeton University Press.

Kennedy, D. 2006–07, 'One, Two, Three, Many Legal Orders: Legal Pluralism and the Cosmopolitan Dream', *New York Review of Law and Social Change*, 31: 641–59.

Kennedy, D. 2013, 'Law and the Political Economy of the World', *Leiden Journal of International Law*, 26: 7–48.

Kennedy, D. 2016, *A World of Struggle: How Power, Law, and Expertise Shape Global Political Economy*, Princeton: Princeton University Press.

Kennedy, D.L.M. and J.D. Southwick 2008, *The Political Economy of International Trade Law: Essays in Honor of R.E. Hudec*, Cambridge: Cambridge University Press.

Kennedy, Duncan 1983, *Legal Education and the Reproduction of Hierarchy: A Polemic Against the System*, self-published.

Kennedy, Duncan 1998, *A Critique of Adjudication*, Cambridge, MA: Harvard University Press.

Kentaro, A. 2011, 'Selecting Defendants at the Tokyo Trial', in *Beyond Victor's Justice? The Tokyo War Crimes Trial Revisited*, edited by Y. Tanaka, T. McCormack, and G. Simpson, Leiden: Martinus Nijhoff.

Kingsbury, B. 2001, 'Reconciling Five Competing Conceptual Structures of Indigenous Peoples' Claims in International and Comparative Law', *NYU Journal of International Law and Politics*, 34: 189–250.

Kingsbury, B. and B. Straumann 2010, 'State of Nature versus Commercial Sociability as the Basis of International Law: Reflections on the Roman Foundations and Current Interpretations of the International Political and Legal Thought of Grotius, Hobbes, and Pufendorf', in *The Philosophy of International Law*, edited by S. Besson and J. Tasioulas, Oxford: Oxford University Press.

Kinley, D. and D. Augenstein 2013, 'When Human Rights "Responsibilities" become "Duties": The Extra-Territorial Obligations of States that bind Corporations', in *Human Rights Obligations of Business: Beyond the Corporate Responsibility to Respect?*, edited by S. Deva and D. Bilchitz, Cambridge: Cambridge University Press.

Kinley, D., J. Nolan, and N. Zerial, 2007, '"The Norms Are Dead! Long Live the Norms!": The Politics behind the UN Human Rights Norms for Corporations', in *The New Corporate Accountability: Corporate Social Responsibility and the Law*, edited by D. McBarnet, A. Voiculescu, and T. Campbell, New York: Cambridge University Press.

Klabbers, J. 2003, *An Introduction to International Institutional Law*, Cambridge: Cambridge University Press.

Klausner, M. 2006, 'The Contractarian Theory of Corporate Law: A Generation Later', *Journal of Corporation Law*, 31(3): 779–98.

Klein, N. 2001, *No Logo: No Space, No Choice, No Jobs*, London: Flamingo.

Klein, N. 2007, *The Shock Doctrine: The Rise of Disaster Capitalism*, London: Allen Lane.

Knox, R. 2009, 'Marxism, International Law, and Political Strategy', *Leiden Journal of International Law*, 22(3): 413–36.

Knox, R. 2010, 'Review of *The Degradation of the International Legal Order? The Rehabilitation of Law and the Possibility of Politics*, by Bill Bowring, Routledge-Cavendish, 2008', *Historical Materialism*, 18(1): 193–207.

Knox, R. 2012, 'Strategy and Tactics', *Finnish Yearbook of International Law*, 21: 193–229.

Knox, R. 2016a, 'Valuing Race? Stretched Marxism and the Logic of Imperialism', *London Review of International Law*, 4: 81–126.

Knox, R. 2016b, 'Marxist Approaches to International Law', in *The Oxford Handbook of the Theory of International Law*, edited by A. Orford and F. Hoffmann, Oxford: Oxford University Press.

Konings, M. 2015, *The Emotional Logic of Capitalism: What Progressives Have Missed*, Stanford: Stanford University Press.

Konoplyanik, A. 2004, 'Energy Security and the Development of International Energy Markets', in *Energy Security: Managing Risk in a Dynamic Legal and Regulatory Environment*, edited by B. Barton, Oxford: Oxford University Press.

Kopelman, E. 1991, 'Ideology and International Law: The Dissent of the Indian Justice at the Tokyo War Crimes Trial', NYU *Journal of International Law and Politics*, 23(2): 373–444.

Korhonen, O. 1996, 'New International Law: Silence, Defence or Deliverance', *European Journal of International Law*, 7(1): 1–28.

Korten, D. 2001, *When Corporations Rule the World*, West Hartford: Kumarian Press.

Koskenniemi, M. 1995, 'Police in the Temple, Order, Justice and the UN: A Dialectical View', *European Journal of International Law*, 6(1): 325–48.

Koskenniemi, M. 2002a, 'Between Impunity and Show Trials', *Max Planck Yearbook of United Nations Law*, 6: 1–35.

Koskenniemi, M. 2002b, 'The Lady Doth Protest Too Much: Kosovo and the Turn to Ethics in International Law', *Modern Law Review*, 62(2): 159–75.

Koskenniemi, M. 2002c, *The Gentle Civilizer of Nations: The Rise and Fall of International Law 1870–1960*, Cambridge: Cambridge University Press.

Koskenniemi, M. 2002d, '*The Epochs of International Law*, by Grewe Wilhelm, translated and revised by Michael Byers [Berlin: De Gruyter, 2001]', *International and Comparative Law Quarterly*, 51(3): 746–51.

Koskenniemi, M. 2004a, 'What Should International Lawyers Learn from Karl Marx?', *Leiden Journal of International Law*, 17(2): 229–46.

Koskenniemi, M. 2004b, 'Why History of International Law Today?', *Rechtsgeschichte*, 4: 61–6.

Koskenniemi, M. 2006 [1989], *From Apology to Utopia: The Structure of International Legal Argument*, Cambridge: Cambridge University Press.

Koskenniemi, M. 2007a, 'International Legal Theory and Doctrine', in *Max Planck Encyclopedia of Public International Law*, edited by R. Wolfrum, online edition, available at: http://opil.ouplaw.com/abstract/10.1093/law:epil/9780199231690/law-9780199231690-e1618?prd=EPIL.

Koskenniemi, M. 2007b, 'The Fate of Public International Law: Between Technique and Politics', *Modern Law Review*, 70(1): 1–30.

Koskenniemi, M. 2010, 'What is International Law for?', in *International Law*, edited by M. Evans, Oxford: Oxford University Press.

Koskenniemi, M. 2016a, 'Expanding Histories of International Law', *American Journal of Legal History*, 56: 104–12.

Koskenniemi, M. 2016b, 'Colonial Laws: Sources, Strategies and Lessons?', *Journal of the History of International Law*, 18: 248–77.

Kraakman, R. et al. (eds) 2009, *The Anatomy of Corporate Law: A Comparative and Functional Approach*, Oxford: Oxford University Press.

Krasner, S. 1999, *Sovereignty: Organized Hypocrisy*, Princeton: Princeton University Press.

Kreß, C. (n.d.), 'International Criminal Law', in *Max Planck Encyclopedia of Public International Law*, edited by R. Wolfrum, online edition, available at: http://opil.ouplaw.com/abstract/10.1093/law:epil/9780199231690/law-9780199231690-e1423?prd=EPIL.

Krisch, N. 2009, 'The Case for Pluralism in Postnational Law', LSE Legal Studies Working Paper 12.

Krisch, N. 2010, *Beyond Constitutionalism: The Pluralist Structure of Postnational Law*, Oxford: Oxford University Press.

Kropotkin, P. 1886, 'Law And Authority: An Anarchist Essay', London: International Publishing Co.

Kröll, F. 1999, 'Fall 10: Der Krupp-Prozess', in *Der Nationalsozialismus vor Gericht: Die alliierten Prozesse gegen Kriegsverbrechen und Soldaten 1943–1952*, edited by G. and R. Blasius, Berlin: Fischer Taschenbuch Verlag.

Kuran, T. 2005, 'The Absence of the Corporation in Islamic Law: Origins and Persistence', *American Journal of Comparative Law*, 53(4): 785–834.

Kyaogly, T. 2010, *Legal Imperialism: Sovereignty and Extraterritoriality in Japan, the Ottoman Empire, and China*, Cambridge: Cambridge University Press.

Kyd, S.A. 1795, *Treatise on the Law of Corporations*, London: J. Butterworth.

Kyriakakis, J. 2010, 'Prosecuting Corporations for International Crimes: The Role for Domestic Criminal Law', in *International Criminal Law and Philosophy*, edited by L. May and Z. Hoskins, Cambridge: Cambridge University Press.

Kyriakakis, J. 2017a, 'Corporations before International Criminal Courts: Implications for the International Criminal Justice Project', *Leiden Journal of International Law*, 30(1): 221–40.

Kyriakakis, J. 2017b, 'Article 46C: Corporate Criminal Liability at the African Criminal Court (September 1, 2016)', in *African Court of Justice and Human and People's Rights in Context*, edited by C. Jalloh, K. Clarke, and V. Nmehielle, available at: https://ssrn.com/abstract=2970864.

Lahey, K. and S. Salter 1985, 'Corporate Law in Legal Theory and Legal Scholarship: From Classicism to Feminism', *Osgoode Hall Law Journal*, 23: 543–72.

Lang, A. 2011, *World Trade Law After Neoliberalism: Reimagining the Global Economic Order*, Oxford: Oxford University Press.

Laski, H. 1916, 'The Personality of Associations', *Harvard Law Review*, 29: 404–26.

Lauterpacht, H. 1968, *International Law and Human Rights*, London: Stevens and Sons.

Lawson, T. 2014, 'The Nature of the Firm and the Peculiarities of the Corporation', *Cambridge Journal of Economics*, 39: 1–32.

Leal-Arcas, R. 2010, *International Trade and Investment Law: Multilateral, Regional and Bilateral Governance*, Cheltenham: Edward Elgar.

LeBaron G. and J. Lister 2016, 'Ethical Audits and the Supply Chains of Global Corporations', *SPERI Global Political Economy Brief No. 1*, 6, available at: http://speri.dept.shef.ac.uk/wp-content/uploads/2016/01/Global-Brief-1-Ethical-Audits-and-the-Supply-Chains-of-Global-Corporations.pdf.

Lederman, E. 2001, 'Models for Imposing Corporate Criminal Liability: From Adaptation and Imitation towards Aggregation and the Search for Self-Identity', *Buffalo Criminal Law Review*, 4(1): 642–708.

Lenin, V.I. 1943, *State and Revolution*, New York: International Publishers.

Lenin, V.I. 1963, *Imperialism, the Highest State of Capitalism*, in *Lenin's Selected Works*, Volume 1, Moscow: Progress Publishers.

Lesaffer, R. 2002, 'The Grotian Tradition Revisited: Change and Continuity in the History of International Law', *British Yearbook of International Law*, 73(1): 103–39.

Linton, S. (ed.) 2013, *Hong Kong War Crimes Trials*, Oxford: Oxford University Press.

Lippman, M. 1995, 'War Crimes Trials of German Industrialists: The Other Schindlers', *Temple International and Comparative Law Journal*, 9(2): 173–267.

Litvin, D. 2004, *Empires of Profit: Commerce, Conquest and Corporate Responsibility*, Mason: Thomson.

Liu, D. and Zhang, B. (eds) 2016, *Historical War Crimes Trials in Asia*, Brussels: Torkel Opsahl Academic E-Publisher.

Longman, P. 2001, 'Review of P. Uvin, Aiding Violence: Development Enterprise in Rwanda, Kumarian Press, 1998', *Human Rights Review*, 2(3): 169–72.

López, C. 'The "Ruggie Process": From Legal Obligations to Corporate Social Responsibility?', in *Human Rights Obligations of Business: Beyond the Corporate Responsibility to Respect?*, edited by S. Deva and D. Bilchitz, Cambridge: Cambridge University Press.

Lowe, V. 2010, 'Injuries to Corporations', in *The Law of International Responsibility*, edited by J. Crawford, A. Pellet, and S. Olleson, Oxford: Oxford University Press.

Lowenfeld, A.F. 2008, *International Economic Law*, Oxford: Oxford University Press.

Lowry, J. and A. Reisberg 2012, *Pettet's Company Law: Company and Capital Markets Law*, New York: Longman.

Luban, D. 2008, 'The Legacies of Nuremberg', in *Perspectives on the Nuremberg Trials*, edited by G. Mettraux, Oxford: Oxford University Press.

Luban, D. 2011, 'Hannah Arendt as a Theorist of International Criminal Law', *Georgetown Public Law and Legal Theory Research Paper 11*, 30.

Luban, D. 2013, 'After the Honeymoon: Reflections on the Current State of International Criminal Justice', *Journal of International Criminal Justice*, 11(3): 505–15.

Luxemburg, R. 2008, 'Reform or Revolution, and Mass Strike', in *The Essential Rosa Luxemburg: Reform or Revolution and the Mass Strike*, edited by H. Scott, Chicago: Haymarket Books.

Machen, A. 1911, 'Corporate Personality', *Harvard Law Review*, 24(4): 253–67.

MacKay, C. 2001 [1841], *Extraordinary Popular Delusions, and the Madness of Crowds*, Amherst, NY: Prometheus.

Macklem, P. 2005, 'Corporate Accountability under International Law: The Misguided Quest for Universal Jurisdiction', *International Law Forum*, 7(4): 281–9.

Madlingozi, T. 2010, 'On Transitional Justice Entrepreneurs and the Production of Victims', *Journal of Human Rights Practice*, 2(2): 208–28.

Maguire, P. 2010, *Law and War: International Law and American History*, New York: Columbia University Press.

Maine, F. 1861, *Ancient Law, Its Connection With the Early History of Society, and Its Relation to Modern Ideas*, available at: http://en.wikisource.org/wiki/Ancient_Law.

Maitland, F.W. 1898, *Township and Borough, Being the Ford Lectures, Delivered in the University of Oxford in the October Term of 1897*, Cambridge: Cambridge University Press.

Maitland, F.W. 1900, 'Introduction', in Gierke, O. 1900, *Political Theories of the Middle Age*, translated by F. Maitland, Cambridge: Cambridge University Press.

Maitland, F.W. 1905, 'Moral Personality and Legal Personality', *Journal of the Society of Comparative Legislation*, 6: 192–200.

Maitland, F.W. 1936, 'Moral Personality and Legal Personality', in *Maitland: Selected Essays*, edited by H.D. Hazeltine et al., Cambridge: Cambridge University Press.

Mamolea, A. 2011, 'The Future of Corporate Aiding and Abetting Liability Under the Alien Tort Statute: A Roadmap', *Santa Clara Law Review*, 51(1): 153–216.

Manacorda, S. and C. Meloni 2011, 'Indirect Perpetration versus Joint Criminal Enterprise: Concurring Approaches in the Practice of International Criminal Law?', *Journal of International Criminal Justice*, 9(1): 159–78.

Marchand, R. 2001, *Creating the Corporate Soul: The Rise of Public Relations and Corporate Imagery in American Big Business*, Berkeley: University of California Press.

Marks, S. 1997, 'The End of History: Reflections on Some International Legal Theses', *European Journal of International Law*, 8(3): 449–77.

Marks, S. 2001, 'Big Brother is Bleeping Us: With the Message that Ideology Doesn't Matter', *European Journal of International Law*, 12(1): 109–23.

Marks, S. 2002, 'Reflections on a Teach-in Walk-out', *Canadian Journal of Law and Jurisprudence*, 15(2): 175–89.

Marks, S. 2003, *The Riddle of All Constitutions: International Law, Democracy, and the Critique of Ideology*, Oxford: Oxford University Press.

Marks, S. 2006, 'State-Centrism, International Law, and the Anxieties of Influence', *Leiden Journal of International Law*, 19(2): 339–47.

Marks, S. 2007, 'International Judicial Activism and the Commodity-Form Theory of International Law', *European Journal of International Law*, 18(1): 199–211.

Marks, S. 2008, *International Law on the Left: Re-examining Marxist Legacies*, Cambridge: Cambridge University Press.

Marks, S. 2009, 'False Contingency', *Current Legal Problems*, 62(1): 1–21.

Marks, S. 2011a, 'Human Rights and Root Causes', *Modern Law Review*, 74(1): 57–78.

Marks, S. 2011b, 'What has Become of the Emerging Right to Democratic Governance?', *European Journal of International Law*, 22(2): 507–24.

Marks, S. and A. Clapham 2005, *International Human Rights Lexicon*, Oxford: Oxford University Press.

Marks, S. and M. Craven et al. 2013, 'The London Review of International Law begins, Editorial', *London Review of International Law*, 1–5 June.

Martinez, J.S. 2008, 'Antislavery Courts and the Dawn of International Human Rights Law', *Yale Law Journal*, 117(4): 550–641.

Marx, K. 1853, 'Capital Punishment. – Mr. Cobden's Pamphlet. – Regulations of the Bank of England', 28 January; *New York Daily Tribune*, 17–18 February, available at: http://www.marxists.org/archive/marx/works/1853/02/18.htm.

Marx, K. 1976, *Capital: Critique of Political Economy*, Volume 1, London: Penguin.

Marx, K. 1979, *Capital: Critique of Political Economy*, Volume 2, London: Penguin.

Marx, K. 1982, *Capital: Critique of Political Economy*, Volume 3, London: Penguin.

Marx, K. 2000a, *Critique of the Gotha Programme*, excerpted in *Karl Marx, Selected Writings*, edited by D. McLellan, Oxford: Oxford University Press.

Marx, K. 2000b, *Grundrisse*, excerpted in *Karl Marx, Selected Writings*, edited by D. McLellan, Oxford: Oxford University Press.

Marx, K. 2000c, *On the Jewish Question*, excerpted in *Karl Marx, Selected Writings*, edited by D. McLellan, Oxford: Oxford University Press.

Marx, K. 2000d, *Preface to a Critique of Political Economy*, in *Karl Marx, Selected Writings*, edited by D. McLellan, Oxford: Oxford University Press.

Marx, K. 2000e, *The German Ideology*, excerpted in *Karl Marx, Selected Writings*, edited by D. McLellan, Oxford: Oxford University Press.

Marx, K. 2000f, *Theses on Feuerbach*, excerpted in *Karl Marx, Selected Writings*, edited by D. McLellan, Oxford: Oxford University Press.

Marx, K. and F. Engels, 1969, *Manifesto of the Communist Party*, in *Marx/Engels Selected Works*, Vol. One, Progress Publishers, Moscow.

Marx, K. and F. Engels, 1979, *The German Ideology: The Ruling Class and the Ruling Ideas*, excerpted in *Marx and Engels on Law*, edited by M. Cain and A. Hunt, London: Academic Press.

Marxen, K. 2001, 'Die Bestrafung von NS-Unrecht in Ostdeutschland', in *Der Umgang mit Kriegs- und Besatzungsunrecht in Japan und Deutschland*, edited by K. Marxen, K. Miyazawa, G. Werle, Berlin: Berlin Verlag.

Marxen, K., K. Miyazawa, and G. Werle (eds) 2001, *Der Umgang mit Kriegs- und Besatzungsunrecht in Japan und Deutschland*, Berlin: Berliner Wissenschafts-Verlag.

Marysse, S., A. Ansoms, and D. Cassimon 2007, 'The Aid "Darlings" and "Orphans" of the Great Lakes Region in Africa', *European Journal of Development Research*, 19(3): 433–58.

May, L. and Z. Hoskins (eds) 2010, *International Criminal Law and Philosophy*, Cambridge: Cambridge University Press.

Mayer, M.S. 1955, *They Thought They Were Free: The Germans, 1933–45*, Chicago: University of Chicago Press.

Mayson, S., D. French, and C. Ryan 2015–16, *Company Law*, 32nd edn, Oxford: Oxford University Press.

Mazlish, B. and E.R. Morss 2005, 'A Global Elite?', in *Leviathans: Multinational Corporations and the New Global History*, edited by A.D. Chandler and B. Mazlish, Cambridge: Cambridge University Press.

McBarnet, D. 2007, 'Corporate Social Responsibility beyond Law, through Law, for law: The New Corporate Accountability', in McBarnet, Aurora, and Campbell 2007.

McBarnet, D., A. Voiculescu, and T. Campbell (eds) 2007, *The New Corporate Accountability: Corporate Social Responsibility and the Law*, Cambridge: Cambridge University Press.

McCorquodale, R. 2010, 'The Individual and the International Legal System', in *International Law*, edited by M. Evans, Oxford: Oxford University Press.

McCorquodale, R. and P. Simons 2007, 'Responsibility beyond Borders: State Responsibility for Extraterritorial Violations by Corporations of International Human Rights Law', *Modern Law Review*, 70: 598–625.

McLean, D. 2001, 'Australia in the Cold War: A Historiographical Review', *International History Review*, 23(2): 299–321.

McLean, J. 2004, 'The Transnational Corporation in History: Lessons for Today?', *Indiana Law Journal*, 79(2): 363–77.

McLean, J. 2013, 'Ideologies in Law Time: The Oxford History of the Laws of England', *Law and Social Inquiry*, 38(3): 746–64.

McNally, D. 2011, *Monsters of the Market: Zombies, Vampires and Global Capitalism*, Chicago: Haymarket Books.

McQueen, R. 2009, *A Social History of Company Law: Great Britain and the Australian Colonies 1854–1920*, Farnham: Ashgate.

Mégret, F. n.d., 'Globalization and International Law', *Max Planck Encyclopedia of Public International Law*, online edition.

Mégret, F. 2002, 'The Politics of International Criminal Justice', *European Journal of International Law*, 13(5): 1261–84.

Mégret, F. 2003, 'Justice in Times of Violence', *European Journal of International Law*, 14: 327–45.

Mégret, F. 2010, 'In Search of the "Vertical": An Exploration of What Makes International Criminal Tribunals Different (and Why)', in *Future Perspectives on International Criminal Justice*, edited by C. Stahn and L.J. van den Herik, The Hague: TMC Asser Press.

Mégret, F. 2016, 'The Anxieties of International Criminal Justice', *Leiden Journal of International Law*, 29(1): 197–221.

Mehra, A. and K. Shay 2016, 'Corporate Responsibility and Accountability for Modern Forms of Slavery', *Journal of International Criminal Justice*, 14 (2): 453–68.

Meier-Hayoz, A. and P. Forstmoser 2007, *Schweizerisches Gesellschaftsrecht*, Bern: Stämpfli Verlag AG.

Meloni, C. 2007, 'Command Responsibility: Mode of Liability for the Crimes of Subordinates or Separate Offence of the Superior?', *Journal of International Criminal Justice*, 5(3): 619–37.

Meloni, C. 2010, *Command Responsibility in International Criminal Law*, The Hague: TMC Asser.

Meron, T. 2000, 'The Humanization of Humanitarian Law', *American Journal of International Law*, 94(2): 239–78.

Meron, T. 2006, *The Humanization of International Law*, The Hague: Academy of International Law.

Merriman, J. 2010, *A History of Modern Europe: From the Renaissance to the Present*, New York: W.W. Norton & Company.

Mettraux, G. (ed.) 2008, *Perspectives on the Nuremberg Trials*, Oxford: Oxford University Press.

Miéville, C. 2004, 'The Commodity-Form Theory of International Law: An Introduction', *Leiden Journal of International Law*, 17: 271–302.

Miéville, C. 2006, *Between Equal Rights: A Marxist Theory of International Law*, London: Pluto Press.

Miéville, C. 2007, 'Multilateralism as Terror: International Law, Haiti and Imperialism', *Finnish Yearbook of International Law*, 19(1): 63–91.

Miéville, C. et al. 2008, 'Roundtable: "War, Force & Revolution"', ASIL Proceedings.

Miles, K. 2013, *The Origins of International Investment Law: Empire, Environment and the Safeguarding of Capital*, Cambridge: Cambridge University Press.

Miliband, R. 1969, *The State in Capitalist Society*, London: Littlehampton Book Services Ltd.

Miller, Z. 2008, 'Effects of Invisibility: In Search of the "Economic" in Transitional Justice', *International Journal of Transitional Justice*, 2(3): 266–91.

Millon, D. 1993, 'New Directions in Corporate Law: Communitarians, Contractarians, and the Crisis in Corporate Law', *Washington and Lee Law Review*, 50(4): 1373–1723.

Minear, R. 1971, *Victor's Justice: The Tokyo War Crimes Trial*, Princeton: Princeton University Press.

Moisel, C. (ed.) 2006, *Transnationale Vergangenheitspolitik: Der Umgang mit deutschen Kriegsverbrechern in Europa nach dem Zweiten Weltkrieg*, Göttingen: Wallstein Verlag.

Molotov, V. 1946, *Speeches of V.M. Molotov, Minister for Foreign Affairs of the USSR and Head of the Soviet Delegation at the Conference*, London: Soviet News.

Moran, T.H. 1977, *Multinational Corporations and the Politics of Dependence: Copper in Chile*, Princeton: Princeton University Press.

Morgenthau, H. 1945, *Germany is Our Problem*, New York: Harper & Brothers.

Morris, N. 2013, 'Justice for "Asian" Victims: The Australian War Crimes Trials of the Japanese, 1945–51', in *Untold Stories: Hidden Histories of War Crimes Trials*, edited by G. Simpson and K. Heller, Oxford: Oxford University Press.

Morse, G. et al. 2005, *Charlesworth's Company Law*, 17th edn, London: Sweet & Maxwell.

Morse, G. et al. 2010, *Charlesworth's Company Law*, 18th edn, London: Sweet & Maxwell.

Moses, M. 2012, *The Principles and Practice of International Commercial Arbitration*, Cambridge: Cambridge University Press.

Muchlinski, P. n.d., 'Corporations in International Law', in *Max Planck Encyclopedia of Public International Law*, online edition.

Muchlinski, P. 1987, 'The Bhopal Case: Controlling the Ultrahazardous Industrial Activities Undertaken by Foreign Investors', *Modern Law Review*, 50(5): 545–87.

Muchlinski, P. 2007a, *Multinational Enterprises and the Law*, 2nd edn, Oxford: Oxford University Press.

Muchlinski, P. 2007b, 'Corporate Social Responsibility and International Law: The Case of Human Rights and Multinational Enterprises', in D. McBarnet et al. (eds), *The New Corporate Accountability: Corporate Social Responsibility and the Law*, Cambridge: Cambridge University Press.

Muchlinski, P. 2008, 'Corporate Social Responsibility', in P. Muchlinski et al. (eds), *The Oxford Handbook of International Investment Law*, Oxford: Oxford University Press.

Muchlinski, P. 2011, 'The Changing Face of Transnational Business Governance: Private Corporate Law Liability and Accountability of Transnational Groups in a Post Financial Crisis World', *Indiana Journal of Global Legal Studies*, 18(2): 665–705.

Murphy, T. 2006, 'East Asia's Dollars', *New Left Review*, 2(40): 39–66.

Mwangi, W., L. Rieth, and H.P. Schmitz 2013, 'Encouraging Greater Compliance: Local Networks and the United Nations Global Compact', in *The Persistent Power of Human Rights: From Commitment to Compliance*, edited by T. Risse, S.F. Ropp, and K. Sikkink, Cambridge: Cambridge University Press.

Mwaura, K. 2012, 'Internalization of Costs to Corporate Groups: Part-Whole Relationships, Human Rights Norms and the Futility of the Corporate Veil', *Journal of International Business and Law*, 11: 85–110.

Nader, R. 1965, *Unsafe at any Speed: The Designed-In Dangers of the American Automobile*, New York: Grossman Publishers.

Naumann, B. 1966, *Auschwitz: A Report on the Proceedings Against Robert Karl Ludwig Mulka and Others Before the Court at Frankfurt*, London: Pall Mall Press.

Neave, A. 1982, *Nuremberg*, London: Hodder & Stoughton Ltd.

Neff, S. 1990, *Friends but No Allies: Economic Liberalism and the Law of Nations*, New York: Columbia University Press.

Neff, S. 2010, 'A Short History of International Law', in *International Law*, edited by M. Evans, Oxford: Oxford University Press.

Nekam, A. 1938, *The Personality Conception of the Legal Entity*, Cambridge, MA: Harvard University Press.

Neocleous, M. 2003, 'Staging Power: Marx, Hobbes and the Personification of Capital', *Law and Critique*, 14: 147–65.

Neocosmos, M. 2006, 'Can a Human Rights Culture Enable Emancipation? Clearing Some Theoretical Ground for the Renewal of a Critical Sociology', *South African Review of Sociology*, 37(2): 356–79.

Neumann, F.B. 1942, *Behemoth: The Structure and Practice of National Socialism*, New York: Harper & Row.

Nielsen, C. 2008, 'From Nuremberg to The Hague: The Civilizing Mission of International Criminal Law', *Auckland University Law Review*, 14: 81–114.

Nijman, J.E. 2004, *The Concept of International Legal Personality: An Inquiry into the History and Theory of International Law*, The Hague: Asser Press.

Nollkaemper, A. 2009, 'Introduction', in *System Criminality in International Law*, edited by A. Nollkaemper and H. Van der Wilt, Cambridge: Cambridge University Press.

Nollkaemper, A. 2015, 'The Problem of Many Hands in International Law', Amsterdam Law School Research Paper No. 2015-35, Amsterdam Center for International Law No. 2015-15.

Nollkaemper, A. and H. Van der Wilt (eds) 2009, *System Criminality in International Law*, Cambridge: Cambridge University Press.

Novak, M. 2003, *Daniel Defoe: Master of Fictions, His life and Ideas*, Oxford: Oxford University Press.

Nowrot, K. 2004, *Global Governance and International Law*, Halle: Institute of Economic Law.

Nussbaum, A.A. 1954, *Concise History of the Law of Nations*, New York: Macmillan.

O'Keefe, R. 2009, 'Review of R. Cryer, et al. (eds.), International Criminal Law (2007)', *International and Comparative Law Quarterly*, 58(2): 485–6.

O'Kelly, C. and S. Wheeler 2012, 'Internalities and the Foundations of Corporate Governance', *Social and Legal Studies*, 21(4): 469–89.

Okowa, P. 2007, 'Congo's War: The Legal Dimension of a Protracted Conflict', *British Yearbook of International Law*, 77: 203–55.

Okowa, P. 2010, 'Admissibility and the Law on International Responsibility', in *International Law*, edited by M. Evans, Oxford: Oxford University Press.

Ollman, B. 2003, *Dance of the Dialectic: Steps in Marx's Method*, Urbana: University of Illinois Press.

Onuma, Y. 2002, 'Japanese War Guilt and Postwar Responsibilities in Japan', *Berkeley Journal of International Law*, 20(3): 600–20.

Oppenheim, L. 1973, *International Law: A Treatise by L. Oppenheim*, edited by H. Lauterpacht, Volume 1, New York: David McKay Co.

Orford, A. 1999, 'Muscular Humanitarianism: Reading the Narratives of the New Interventionism', *European Journal of International Law*, 10: 679–711.

Orford, A. 2001, 'Globalisation and the Right to Development', in *Peoples' Rights*, edited by P. Alston, Oxford: Oxford University Press.

Orford, A. 2006, 'A Journal of the Voyage from Apology to Utopia', *German Law Journal*, 7(12): 993–1010.

Orford, A. 2009, *International Law and its Others*, Cambridge: Cambridge University Press.

Orford, A. 2012, 'In Praise of Description', *Leiden Journal of International Law*, 25: 609–25.

Osterloh, J. 2010, 'Die Monopole und ihre Herren: Marxistische Interpretationen', in *Unternehmen im Nationalsozialismus: Zur historisierung einer Forschungskonjunktur*, edited by N. Frei and Tim Schanetzky, Göttingen: Wallstein Verlag.

Otomo, Y. 2011, 'The Decision not to Prosecute the Emperor', in *Beyond Victor's Justice? The Tokyo War Crimes Trial Revisited*, edited by Y. Tanaka, T. McCormack, and G. Simpson, Leiden: Martinus Nijhoff.

Pahuja, S. 2011, *Decolonising International Law: Development, Economic Growth and the Politics of Universality*, Cambridge: Cambridge University Press.

Pal, R. 1955, *Crimes in International Relations*, Calcutta: University of Calcutta.

Parfitt, R. 2016, 'Theorizing Recognition and International Personality', in *The Oxford Handbook of the Theory of International Law*, edited by A. Orford and F. Hoffmann, Oxford: Oxford University Press.

Parisi, F. and G. Dari-Mattiacci 2004, 'The Rise and Fall of Communal Liability in Ancient Law', *International Review of Law and Economics*, 24(4): 489–505.

Pashukanis, E. 1925–27, 'International Law', in C. Miéville 2006, *Between Equal Rights: A Marxist Theory of International Law*, London: Pluto Press.

Pashukanis, E. 1978, *Law and Marxism: A General Theory*, London: Ink Links.

Passas, N. 1990, 'Anomie and Corporate Crime', *Contemporary Crises*, 14(2): 157–78, excerpted in D. Whyte (ed.) 2009, *Crimes of the Powerful: A Reader*, New York: McGraw Hill.

Paulus, A. 2001, 'International Law After Postmodernism: Towards Renewal or Decline of International Law?', *Leiden Journal of International Law*, 14(4): 727–55.

Pauwels, J. 2003, 'Profits "Über Alles!" American Corporations and Hitler', *Labour/Le travail*, 51: 223–49.

Pearce, F. and L. Snider (eds) 1995, *Corporate Crime: Contemporary Debates*, Toronto: University of Toronto Press.

Pearce, F. and S. Tombs 1990, 'Ideology, Hegemony and Empiricism: Compliance Theories and Regulation', *British Journal of Criminology*, 30(4): 423–443.

Pearce, F. and S. Tombs 1997, 'Hazards, Law and Class: Contextualizing the Regulation of Corporate Crime', *Social and Legal Studies*, 6(1): 79–108.

Pearce, F. and S. Tombs 1998, 'Foucault, Governmentality, Marxism', *Social and Legal Studies*, 7(4): 567–75.

Pellet, A. 1999, 'Can a State Commit a Crime? Definitely, Yes!', *European Journal of International Law*, 10(2): 425–434.

Pellet, A. 2010, 'The Definition of Responsibility in International Law', in *The Law of International Responsibility*, edited by J. Crawford, A. Pellet, and S. Olleson, Oxford: Oxford University Press.

Pennington, R.R. 2001, *Pennington's Company Law*, London: Butterworth.

Peters, A. 2016, 'Fragmentation and Constitutionalization', in *The Oxford Handbook of the Theory of International Law*, edited by A. Orford and F. Hoffmann, Oxford: Oxford University Press.

Phillimore, L. 1922–23, 'An International Criminal Court and the Resolutions of the Committee of Jurists', *British Yearbook of International Law*, 3: 79–86.

Piccigallo, D. 1979, *Japanese on Trial: Allied War Crimes Operations in the East, 1945–51*, Austin: University of Texas Press.

Pies, I. 2010, 'Sustainability in the Petroleum Industry: Theory and Practice of Voluntary Self-Commitments', (1 February), *University of Wittenberg Business Ethics Study No. 2010-1*, available at: http://ssrn.com/abstract=1595943.

Plomp, C. 2014, 'Aiding and Abetting: The Responsibility of Business Leaders under the Rome Statute of the International Criminal Court', *Utrecht Journal of International and European Law*, 30(79): 4–29.

Polanyi, K. 2002, *The Great Transformation: The Political and Economic Origins of Our Time*, Boston: Beacon Press.

Pollock, F. and F.W. Maitland 1911, *The History of English Law Before the Time of Edward I*, Cambridge: Cambridge University Press.

Posner, E. 2009, *The Perils of Global Legalism*, Chicago: University of Chicago Press.

Poulantzas, N. 1978, *State, Power, Socialism*, London: Verso.

Pressac, J.-C. 1994, *Die Krematorien von Auschwitz: Die Technik des Massenmordes*, Munich: Piper Verlag.

Prévost, A. 1992, 'Race and War Crimes: The 1945 War Crimes Trial of General Tomoyuki Yamashita', *Human Rights Quarterly*, 14(3): 303–38.

Pritchard, R.J. 1996, 'The Gift of Clemency Following British War Crimes Trials in the Far East, 1946–1948', *Criminal Law Forum*, 7: 15–50.

Prusin, A.V. 2003, '"Fascist Criminals to the Gallows!": The Holocaust and Soviet War Crimes Trials, December 1945–February 1946', *Holocaust and Genocide Studies*, 17(1): 1–30.

Prusin, A.V. 2010, 'Poland's Nuremberg: The Seven Court Cases of the Supreme National Tribunal, 1946–1948', *Holocaust and Genocide Studies*, 24(1): 1–25.

Punch, M. 2009, 'Why Corporations Kill and Get Away with It: The Failure of Law to Cope with Crime in Organisations', in *System Criminality in International Law*, edited by A. Nollkaemper and H. Van der Wilt, Cambridge: Cambridge University Press.

Pynchon, T. 2007, *Gravity's Rainbow*, new edn, New York: Vintage.

Qureshi, A. and A. Ziegler 2011, *International Economic Law*, London: Sweet & Maxwell.

Radin, M. 1932, 'The Endless Problem of Corporate Personality', *Columbia Law Review*, 32: 643–667.

Raiser, T. and R. Veil 2006, *Recht der Kapitalgesellschaft*, Munich: Verlag Franz Vahlen.

Rajagopal, B. 2003, *International Law from Below: Development, Social Movements and Third World Resistance*, Cambridge: Cambridge University Press.

Ramasastry, A. 2002, 'Corporate Complicity: From Nuremberg to Rangoon – An Examination of Forced Labour Cases and Their Impact on the Liability of Multinational Corporations', *Berkeley Journal of International Law*, 20: 91–159.

Rasulov, A. 2008, 'Bringing Class Back into International Law', 6 September, available at: http://ssrn.com/abstract=1675447.

Rasulov, A. 2010, 'The Nameless Rapture of the Struggle: Towards a Marxist Class-Theoretic Approach to International Law', *Finnish Yearbook of International Law*, 19: 259.

Ratner, S. et al. 2009, *Accountability for Human Rights Atrocities in International Law: Beyond the Nuremberg Legacy*, 3rd edn, Oxford: Oxford University Press.

Reinisch, A. 2006, 'The Changing International Legal Framework for Dealing with Non-State Actors', in *Non-State Actors and Human Rights*, edited by P. Alston, Oxford: Oxford University Press.

Renton, D., D. Seddon, and L. Zeilig 2006, *The Congo: Plunder and Resistance*, London: Zed Books.

Reyntjens, F. 2004, 'Rwanda, Ten Years On: From Genocide to Dictatorship', *African Affairs*, 10(411): 177–210.

Reyntjens, F. 2006, 'Post-1994 Politics in Rwanda: Problematising Liberation and Democratisation', *Third World Quarterly*, 27(6): 1103–1117.

Reyntjens, F. 2011, 'Constructing the Truth, Dealing with Dissent, Domesticating the World: Governance in Post-Genocide Rwanda', *African Affairs*, 110(438): 1–34.

Robé, J.-P. 2011, 'The Legal Structure of the Firm', *Accounting, Economics and Law*, 1, available at: http://globalization-jp-robe.over-blog.com/article-the-legal-structure-of-the-firm-66397678.html.

Robins, N. 2012, *The Corporation That Changed the World*, London: Pluto Press.

Robinson, D. 2008, 'The Identity Crisis of International Criminal Law', *Leiden Journal of International Law*, 21(4): 925–63.

Rodley, N. 2014, 'International Human Rights Law', in *International Law*, 4th edn, by M. Evans, Oxford: Oxford University Press.

Rodriguez-Lopez, C.S. 2017, 'Criminal Liability of Legal Persons for Human Trafficking Offences in International and European Law', *Journal of Trafficking and Human Exploitation*, 1: 95–114.

Rogers, A.P.V. 1990, 'War Crimes Trials under the Royal Warrant: British Practice, 1945–1949', *International and Comparative Law Quarterly*, 39(4): 780–800.

Roht-Arriaza, N. 2013, 'Just a "Bubble"? Perspectives on the Enforcement of International Criminal Law by National Courts', *Journal of International Criminal Justice*, 11(3): 537–43.

Röling, B. and C. Rüter (eds) 1977, *The Tokyo Judgment: The International Military Tribunal for the Far East*, Amsterdam: Amsterdam University Press.

Röling, B. and A. Cassese (ed.) 1994, *The Tokyo Trial and Beyond*, Cambridge: Polity Press.

Root, E. 1910, 'The Basis of Protection to Citizens Residing Abroad', *American Journal of International Law*, 4(3): 517–28.

Rosenblum, D. and V. Magnier 2014, 'Quotas and the Transatlantic Divergence of Corporate Governance', *Northwestern Journal of International Law and Business*, 34(2): 249–98.

Roth, A. 1946, *A Dilemma in Japan*, London: Victor Gollancz Ltd.

Roth, G. and C. Wittich (eds) 1978, *Max Weber, Economy and Society: An Outline of Interpretive Sociology*, Volume 2, Berkeley: University of California Press.

Roth, K. 2008, 'Discussion', *Journal of International Criminal Justice*, 6(5): 947–79.

Sampson, A. 1973, *The Sovereign State: Secret History of ITT*, London: Hodder & Staughton.

Santos, B. and C.A. Rodríguez-Garavito (eds) 2005, *Law and Globalization from Below: Towards a Cosmopolitan Legality*, Cambridge: Cambridge University Press.

Sarat, A. and S. Feingold (eds) 2001, *Cause Lawyering and the State in a Global Era*, Oxford: Oxford University Press.

Sarat, A. and S. Feingold (eds) 2006, *Cause Lawyers and Social Movements*, Stanford: Stanford University Press.

Sasuly, R. 1947, *IG Farben*, New York: Boni & Gea.

Sasuly, R. 1952, *IG Farben*, Berlin: Verlag Volk und Welt GMBH.

Scahill, J. 2007, *Blackwater: The Rise of the World's Most Powerful Mercenary Army*, London: Serpent's Tail.

Schabas, W. 2001, 'Enforcing International Humanitarian Law: Catching the Accomplices', *International Committee of the Red Cross Review*, 83(842): 439–59.

Schabas, W. 2007, *An Introduction to the International Criminal Court*, Cambridge: Cambridge University Press.

Schabas, W. 2013, 'The Banality of International Justice', *Journal of International Criminal Justice*, 11(3): 545–51.

Schacherreiter, J. 2009, 'Un Mundo Donde Quepan Muchos Mundos: A Postcolonial Legal Perspective Inspired by the Zapatistas', *Global Jurist*, 9(2): 1–40.

Schacht, H. 1956, *Confessions of 'The Old Wizard': The Autobiography of Hjalmar Horace Greeley Schacht*, Boston: Houghton Mifflin.

Schachter, O. 1977, 'The Invisible College of International Lawyers', *Northwestern University Law Review*, 72: 217–26.

Schanetzky, T. 2003, 'Unternehmer: Profiteure des Unrechts', in *Hitlers Eliten nach 1945*, edited by N. Frei, Munich: Deutscher Taschenbuch Verlag.

Schermers, H. and N. Blokker 2003, *International Institutional Law: Unity within Diversity*, Leiden: Martinus Nijhoff.

Schild, H. (ed.) 1970, *Das Morgenthau Tagebuch: Dokumente des Anti-Germanismus*, Leoni: Druffel Verlag.

Schlag, P. 1991, 'The Problem of the Subject', *Texas Law Review*, 69: 1627–743.

Schmitt, C. 2007, *The Concept of the Political*, expanded edn, Chicago: University of Chicago Press.

Schrijver, N. 2008, *Sovereignty Over Natural Resources: Balancing Rights and Duties*, Cambridge: Cambridge University Press.

Schüle, A. 2003, 'Technik ohne Moral, Geschäft ohne Verantwortung: Topf & Söhne – die Ofenbauer von Auschwitz', in *Im Labyrinth der Schuld. Jahrbuch 2003 zur Geschichte und Wirkung des Holocaust*, edited by I. Wojak and S. Meinl, Frankfurt am Main: Campus Verlag.

Schwarzenberger, G. 1947, 'The Judgment of Nuremberg', *Tulsa Law Review*, 21: 351.

Schwarzenberger, G. 1950, 'The Problem of an International Criminal Law', *Current Legal Problems*, 3: 263–96.

Schwarzenberger, G. 1955, 'The Standard of Civilization in International Law', *Current Legal Problems*, 8(1): 212–34.

Schwarzenberger, G. 1970, *Economic World Order? A Basic Problem of International Economic Law*, Manchester: Manchester University Press.

Scott, S. 1994, 'International Law as Ideology: Theorizing the Relationship between International Law and International Politics', *European Journal of International Law*, 5(3): 313–25.

Scott, S. 1998, 'International Lawyers: Handmaidens, Chefs, or Birth Attendants? A Response to Philip Alston', *European Journal of International Law*, 9(4): 750–6.

Sealy, L.S. and S. Worthngton 2013, *Sealy's Cases and Materials in Company Law*, 10th edn, Oxford: Oxford University Press.

Seck, S. 2011, 'Collective Wrongdoing and Transnational Corporate Conduct', in *Accountability for Collective Wrongdoing*, edited by T. Isaacs and R. Wachenheimer, New York: Cambridge University Press.

Seita, A. and J. Tamura 1994, 'The Historical Background of Japan's Antimonopoly Law', *University of Illinois Law Review*, 1: 115–85.

Sfard, M. 2009, 'The Price of Internal Legal Opposition of Human Rights Abuses', *Journal of International Criminal Justice*, 1(1): 37–50.

Shamir, R. 2004, 'Between Self-Regulation and the Alien Tort Claims Act: On the Contested Concept of Corporate Social Responsibility', *Law and Society Review*, 38(4): 635–64.

Shamir, R. 2005, 'Corporate Social Responsibility: A Case of Hegemony and Counter-Hegemony', in *Law and Globalization from Below: Towards a Cosmopolitan Legality*, edited by Boaventura de Sousa Santos and César A. Rodríguez-Garavito, Cambridge: Cambridge University Press.

Shamir, R. 2008a, 'The Age of Responsibilization: On Market-Embedded Morality', *Economy and Society*, 37(1): 1–19.

Shamir, R. 2008b, 'Corporate Social Responsibility: Towards a New Market-Embedded Morality?', *Theoretical Inquiries in Law*, 9(2): 371–94.

Shamir, R. 2010, 'Capitalism, Governance and Authority: The Case of Corporate Social Responsibility', *Annual Review of Law and Social Sciences*, 6(1): 531–53.

Shamir, R. and N. Ziv 2001, 'State-Oriented and Community-Oriented Lawyering for a Cause: A Tale of Two Strategies', in *Cause Lawyering and the State in the Global Era*, edited by A. Sarat and S. Scheingold, Oxford: Oxford University Press.

Shany, 'Does One Size Fit All? Reading the Jurisdictional Provisions of the New Iraqi Special Tribunal Statute in the Light of the Statutes of International Criminal Tribunals', *Journal of International Criminal Justice*, 2(2): 338–46.

Sharlett, R. and P. Beirne 1980, *E. Pashukanis: Selected Writings on Marxism and Law*, London: Academic Press Inc.

Shelley, M. 2003, *Frankenstein: Or, the Modern Prometheus*, London: Longman.

Shelton, D. 2003, *Commitment and Compliance: The Role of Non-binding Norms in the International Legal System*, new edn, Oxford: Oxford University Press.

Shepperd, S. (ed.) 2003, *The Selected Writings of Sir Edward Coke*, Volume 1, Indianapolis: Liberty Fund.

Silbey, S. 1997, '1996 Presidential Address: Let Them Eat Cake: Globalization, Postmodern Colonialism and the Possibilities of Justice', *Law and Society Review*, 31(2): 207–35.

Simester, A. et al. 2010, *Simester and Sullivan's Criminal Law: Theory and Doctrine*, 4th edn, Oxford: Hart Publishing.

Simmonds, K. 1961, 'The Interhandel Case', *International and Comparative Law Quarterly*, 10(3): 495–547.

Simpson, G. 1997, 'Didactic and Dissident Histories in War Crimes Trials', *Albany Law Review*, 60: 801–39.

Simpson, G. 2004, *Great Powers and Outlaw States: Unequal Sovereigns in the International Legal Order*, Cambridge: Cambridge University Press.

Simpson, G. 2009, 'Revisiting the Tokyo War Crimes Trial', *Pacific Historical Review*, 78: 608–13.

Simpson, G.J. 2007, *Law, War and Crime: War Crimes Trials and the Reinvention of International Law*, Cambridge: Polity Press.

Singer, P.W. 2003, 'War, Profits, and the Vacuum of Law: Privatized Military Firms and International Law', *Columbia Journal of Transnational Law*, 42: 521–50.

Sirleaf, M. 2017, 'The African Justice Cascade and the Malabo Protocol', *International Journal of Transitional Justice*, 11(1): 71–91.

Skinner, G. 2008, 'Nuremberg's Legacy Continues: The Nuremberg Trials' Influence on Human Rights Litigation in US Courts Under the Alien Tort Statute', *Albany Law Review*, 71: 321–67.

Sklair, L. 1997, 'Social Movements for Global Capitalism: The Transnational Capitalist Class in Action', *Review of International Political Economy*, 4(3): 514–38.

Skouteris, T. 2009, *The Notion of Progress in International Law Discourse*, The Hague: TMC Asser Press.

Slapper, G. and S. Tombs 1999, *Corporate Crime*, London: Longman.

Slaughter, A.-M. 2005, *A New World Order*, Princeton: Princeton University Press.

Sloterdijk, P. 1987, *Critique of Cynical Reason*, translated by M. Eldred, Minneapolis: University of Minnesota.

Smith, A. 1994 [1776], *An Inquiry into the Nature and Causes of the Wealth of Nations*, New York: Modern Library.

Snider, L. 1993, *Bad Business: Corporate Crime in Canada*, Scarborough: Nelson.

Snider, L. 2000, The Sociology of Corporate Crime: An Obituary: (Or: Whose Knowledge Claims have Legs?). *Theoretical Criminology*, 4(2), 169–206.

Soederberg, S. 2010, *Corporate Power and Ownership in Contemporary Capitalism: The Politics of Resistance and Domination*, London: Routledge/RIPE Series in Global Political Economy.

Somers, J. 2001, *De VOC als Volkenrechtelijk Actor*, Rotterdam: Gouda Quint.

Sommer, A. 1991, 'Whom Should the Corporation Serve? The Berle-Dodd Debate Revisited Sixty Years Later', *Delaware Journal of Corporate Law*, 16(1): 33–56.

Sornarajah, M. 2010, *The International Law on Foreign Investment*, Cambridge: Cambridge University Press.

Stahn, C. and L. van den Herik 2010, *Future Perspectives on International Criminal Justice*, The Hague: Asser Press.

Stanley, C. 1988, 'Corporate Personality and Capitalist Relations: A Critical Analysis of the Artifice of Company Law', *Cambrian Law Review*, 19: 97–109.

Stapelbroek, K. 2012, 'Trade, Chartered Companies, and Mercantile Associations', in *The Oxford Handbook of the History of International Law*, edited by B. Fassbender and A. Peters, Oxford: Oxford University Press.

Steiner, J. and P. Alston 2007, *International Human Rights in Context*, Oxford: Oxford University Press.

Steinhardt, R. 2006, 'Corporate Responsibility and the International Law of Human Rights: The New Lex Mercatoria', in *Non-State Actors and Human Rights*, edited by P. Alston, Oxford: Oxford University Press.

Steinle, S. 2004, 'Georg Schwarzenberger (1908–1991)', in *Jurists Uprooted: German-Speaking Emigré Lawyers in Twentieth Century Britain*, edited by J. Beatson and R. Zimmermann, Oxford: University Press.

Stephens, B. 2005, 'The Amorality of Profit: Transnational Corporations and Human Rights', *Berkeley Journal of International Law*, 20(1): 45–90.

Stephens, B. and M. Ratner 1996, *International Human Rights Litigation in US Courts*, Ardsley, NY: Transnational Publishers Inc.

Stephens, B., M. Ratner, and J. Chomsky 2008, *International Human Rights Litigation in US Courts*, 2nd edn, Leiden: Brill.

Stephenson, C. 1933, *Borough and Town: A Study of Urban Origins in England*, The Cambridge, MA: Medieval Academy of America.

Stern, P.J. 2011, *The Company-State: Corporate Sovereignty and the Early Modern Foundations of the British Empire in India*, Oxford: Oxford University Press.

Stessens, G. 1994, 'Corporate Criminal Liability: A Comparative Perspective', *International and Comparative Law Quarterly*, 43(3): 493–520.

Stewart, J. 2010, 'Corporate War Crimes: Prosecuting Pillage of Natural Resources', Open Society Foundations, New York, October, available at: http://ssrn.com/abstract=1875053.

Stewart, J. 2013, 'A Pragmatic Critique of Corporate Criminal Theory: Lessons from the Extremity', *New Criminal Law Review*, 16(2): 261–99.

Stewart, J. 2014, 'The Turn to Corporate Criminal Liability for International Crimes: Transcending the Alien Tort Statute (February 19, 2014)', *NYU Journal of International Law and Politics*, 47(1): 121–206.

Stimson, H. 1946–47, 'The Nuremberg Trial: Landmark in Law', *Foreign Affairs*, 25: 179.

Stoitchkova, D. 2010, *Towards Corporate Liability in International Criminal Law*, Oxford: Intersentia.

Stokes, M. 1986, 'Company Law and Legal Theory', in *Legal Theory and the Common Law*, edited by W. Twining, Malden, MA: Blackwell.

Stone, C. 1972, 'Should Trees Have Standing? Toward Legal Rights for Natural Objects', *Southern California Law Review*, 45: 450–501.

Stuchka, P. 1988, 'State and Law in the Period of Socialist Construction', excerpted in *Selected Writings on Soviet Law and Marxism*, edited by R. Sharlet, P. Maggs, and P. Byrne, London: M.E. Sharpe.

Suárez-Krabbe, J., 2014, 'The Other Side of the Story: Human rights, race and gender from a historical transatlantic perspective', in *Decolonizing Enlightenment: Transnational Justice, Human Rights and Democracy in a Postcolonial World* edited by N. Dhawan, Leverkusen: Barbara Budrich Publishers.

Subedi, S.P. 2008, *International Investment Law: Reconciling Policy and Principle*, Oxford: Hart Publishing.

Sutherland, E. 1983, *White Collar Crime: The Uncut Version*, New Haven: Yale University Press.

Swart, B. 2008, 'Discussion: International Trends towards Establishing Some Form of Punishment for Corporations', *Journal of International Criminal Justice*, 6(5): 947–79.

Takemoto, T. 2014, 'Looking for Jiro Onuma: A Queer Meditation on the Incarceration of Japanese Americans during World War II', *GLQ: A Journal of Lesbian and Gay Studies*, 20(3): 241–75.

Takeshi, N. 2011, 'Justice Pal (India)', in *Beyond Victor's Justice? The Tokyo War Crimes Trial Revisited*, edited by Y. Tanaka, T. McCormack, and G. Simpson, Leiden: Martinus Nijhoff.

Talbot, L. 2013, 'Why Shareholders Shouldn't Vote: A Marxist-Progressive Critique of Shareholder Empowerment', *Modern Law Review*, 76(5): 791–816.

Talbot, L. 2014, *Great Debates in Company Law*, Basingstoke: Palgrave.

Talbot, L. 2015, *Critical Company Law*, 2nd edn, New York: Routledge.

Talbott, S. 2005, 'Foreword', in *Collision Course: Nato, Russia and Kosovo*, by J. Norris, New York: Praeger.

Tallgren, I. 2002a, 'The Sensibility and Sense of International Criminal Law', *European Journal of International Law*, 13(3): 561–95.

Tallgren, I. 2002b, 'La Grande Illusion', *Canadian Journal of Law and Jurisprudence*, 15(2): 297–316.

Tallgren, I. 2014, 'Who are "We" in International Criminal Law? On Critics and Membership', in *Critical Approaches to International Criminal Law*, edited by C. Schwöbel, New York: Routledge.

Tanaka, Y., T. McCormack, and G. Simpson (eds) 2011, *Beyond Victors' Justice? The Tokyo War Crimes Trial Revisited*, Leiden: Martinus Nijhoff.

Taylor, J. 2006, *Creating Capitalism: Joint-Stock Enterprise in British Politics and Culture, 1800–1870*, London: Boydell & Brewer.

Taylor, T. 1953, 'The Krupp Trial – Fact v. Fiction', *Columbia Law Review*, 53(2): 197–210.

Taylor, T. 1992, *The Anatomy of the Nuremberg Trials*, New York: Bloomsbury.

Teitel, R. 2002, 'Humanity's Law: Rule of Law for the New Global Politics', *Cornell International Law Journal*, 35: 355–87.

Teschke, B. 2009, *The Myth of 1648: Class, Geopolitics, and the Making of Modern International Relations*, London: Verso.

Teubner, G. 1988, 'Enterprise Corporatism: New Industrial Policy and the Essence of the Legal Person', *American Journal of Comparative Law*, 36: 130–55.

Than, C. de and E. Shorts 2003, *International Criminal Law and Human Rights*, London: Sweet & Maxwell.

Thomas, M. 2007, *As Used on the Famous Nelson Mandela: Underground Adventures in the Arms and Torture Trade*, London: Ebury Press.

Thompson, E.P. 1963, *The Making of the English Working Class*, London: Penguin.

Thompson, E.P. 1973, *Writing by Candlelight*, London: Merlin Press.

Tigar, M. and T. Emerson 2005, *Law and the Rise of Capitalism*, Delhi: Aakar Books.

Tófalo, I. 2006, 'Overt and Hidden Accomplices: Transnational Corporations' Range of Complicity for Human Rights Violations', in *Transnational Corporations and Human Rights*, edited by O. de Schutter, Oxford: Hart.

Tombs, S. and D. Whyte 2003, 'Unmasking the Crimes of the Powerful', *Critical Criminology*, 11(3): 217–36.

Toporowski, J. 2010, 'Corporate Limited Liability and the Financial Liabilities of Firms', *Cambridge Journal of Economics*, 34(5): 885–93.

Totani, Y. 2008, *Tokyo War Crimes Trial: The Pursuit of Justice in the Wake of World War II*, Cambridge, MA: Harvard University Press.

Trainin, A.N. 1945, *Hitlerite Responsibility Under Criminal Law*, edited by A.Y. Vishinski, London: Hutchinson & Co. Ltd.

Traverso, E. 2003, *The Origins of Nazi Violence*, New York: New Press.

Tugendhat, C. 1971, *The Multinationals*, London: Eyre & Spottiswoode.

Tzouvala, K. 2016, 'Letters of Blood and Fire: A Socio-Economic History of International Law', Ph.D. thesis, Durham University.

Udovitch, A.L. 1970, *Partnership and Profit in Medieval Islam*, Princeton: Princeton University Press.

Ueberschär, G. and R. Blasius (eds) 1999, *Der Nationalsozialismus vor Gericht: Die alliierten Prozesse gegen Kriegsverbrechen und Soldaten 1943–1952*, Berlin: Fischer Taschenbuch Verlag.

Umfahrer, M. 2008, *Die Gesellschaft mit beschränkter Haftung*, 6th edn, Vienna: Manz Verlag.

Unger, R.M. 2015, *Critical Legal Studies Movement*, London: Verso.

Usman, S. 2011, 'The Opacity and Conduit of Corruption in the Nigeria Oil Sector: Beyond the Rhetoric of the Anti-Corruption Crusade', *Journal of Sustainable Development in Africa*, 13(2): 294.

Uvin, P. 1996, 'Tragedy in Rwanda: The Political Ecology of Conflict', *Environment*, 38(3): 7–29.

Uvin, P. 1998, *Aiding Violence: Development Enterprise in Rwanda*, West Hartford, CT: Kumarian Press.

Vagts, D. 1970, 'The Multinational Enterprise: A New Challenge for Transnational Law', *Harvard Law Review*, 83: 738–92.

Van Baar, A. and W. Huisman 2012, 'The Ovenbuilders of the Holocaust', *British Journal of Criminology*, 52: 1033–50.

Van den Herik, L. 2010, 'Corporations as Future Subjects of the International Criminal

Court: An Exploration of the Counterarguments and Consequences', in *Future Perspectives on International Criminal Justice*, edited by C. Stahn and L.J. van den Herik, The Hague: TMC Asser Press.

Van den Wijngaert, C. and J. Dugard (eds) 1996, *International Criminal Law and Procedure*, Farnham: Ashgate.

Van der Walle, N. 2001, *African Economies and the Politics of Permanent Crisis, 1979–1999*, Cambridge: Cambridge University Press.

Van der Wilt, H. 2006, 'Genocide, Complicity in Genocide and International v. Domestic Jurisdiction: Reflections on the Van Anraat Case', *Journal of International Criminal Justice*, 4: 239–57.

Van der Wilt, H. 2008, 'Genocide v. War Crimes in the Van Anraat Appeal', *Journal of International Criminal Justice*, 6(3): 557–67.

Van der Wilt, H. 2009, 'Joint Criminal Enterprise and Functional Perpetration', in *System Criminality in International Law*, edited by A. Nollkaemper and H. van der Wilt, Cambridge: Cambridge University Press.

Van Schilfgaarde, P. 2006, *Van de BV en de NV*, Deventer: Kluwer.

Van Sliedregt, E. 2003, *The Criminal Responsibility of Individuals for Violations of International Humanitarian Law*, The Hague: TMC Asser Press.

Van Sliedregt, E. 2007, 'International Crimes before Dutch Courts: Recent Developments', *Leiden Journal of International Law*, 20(4): 895–908.

Van Sliedregt, E. 2016, 'International Criminal Law: Over-studied and Underachieving?', *Leiden Journal of International Law*, 29(1): 1–12.

Veitch, S. 2007, *Law and Irresponsibility: On the Legitimation of Human Suffering*, London: Routledge-Cavendish.

Vermeer-Künzli, A. 2013, 'Diallo: Between Diplomatic Protection and Human Rights', *Journal of International Dispute Settlement*, 4(3): 487–500.

Vernon, R. 1971, *Sovereignty at Bay: The Multinational Spread of US Enterprise*, New York: Basic Books.

Verwimp, P. 2001, 'A Quantitative Analysis of Genocide in Kibuye Prefecture, Rwanda', Catholic University of Leuven Center for Economic Studies Discussions Paper Series 10, available at: http://www.econ.kuleuven.be/ces/discussionpapers/default.htm.

Verzijl, J. 1968, *International Law in Historical Perspective*, Leiden: Sijthof.

Vest, H. 2010, 'Business Leaders and the Modes of Individual Criminal Responsibility under International Law', *Journal of International Criminal Justice*, 8(3): 851–72.

Vitali, S., J.B. Glattfelder, and S. Battiston 2011, 'The Network of Global Corporate Control', *Public Library of Science*, 6(10).

Vitzthum, W. 2010, 'Begriff, Geschichte und Rechtsquellen des Völkerrechts', in *Völkerrecht*, edited by W. Vitzthum, Gruyter Recht.

Vitzthum, W. 2010, 'Begriff, Geschichte und Rechtsquellen des Völkerrechts', in W. Vitzthum (ed.), *Völkerrecht*, Berlin: De Gruyter.

Voiculescu, A. 2007, 'Changing Paradigms of Corporate Criminal Responsibility: Lessons for Corporate Social Responsibility', in *The New Corporate Accountability: Corporate Social Responsibility and the Law*, edited by D. McBarnet et al., Cambridge: Cambridge University Press.

Voiculescu, A. 2009, 'Human Rights and the New Corporate Accountability: Learning from Recent Developments in Corporate Criminal Liability', *Journal of Business Ethics* (Supp. 2), 87: 419–32.

Von Knieriem, A. 1953, *Nürnberg: Rechtliche und Menschliche Probleme*, Stuttgart: Ernst Klett Verlag.

Von Savigny, F. 1840, *System des heutigen römischen Recht*, Volume 2, available at: http://www.deutschestextarchiv.de/book/show/savigny_system02_1840.

Vormbaum, M. 2014, 'An "Indispensable Component of the Elimination of Fascism": War Crimes Trials and International Criminal Law in the German Democratic Republic', in *Historical Origins of International Criminal Law*, Volume 2, edited by M. Bergsmo, W.L. Cheah, and P. Yi, Florence: Torkel Opsahl Academic ePublisher.

Wanless, W.C. 2009, 'Corporate Liability for International Crimes under Canada's Crimes Against Humanity and War Crimes Act', *Journal of International Criminal Justice*, 7(1): 201–21.

Ward, R.E. and S. Yoshikazu (eds) 1987, *Democratizing Japan: The Allied Occupation*, Honolulu: University of Hawaii Press.

Webb, L.C. 1958, *Legal Personality and Political Pluralism*, Melbourne: Melbourne University Press.

Weber, M. 1978, *Economy and Society: An Outline of Interpretive Sociology*, Berkeley: University of California Press.

Weber, M. 1982, *General Economic History*, New Brunswick, NJ: Transaction Books.

Weber, M. 2003 [1889], *The History of Commercial Partnerships in the Middle Ages*, translated by Lutz Kaelber, Lanham, MD: Rowman & Littlefield.

Weigend, T. 2008a, 'Discussion', *Journal of International Criminal Justice*, 6(5): 958.

Weigend, T. 2008b, 'Societas delinquere non potest? A German Perspective', *Journal of International Criminal Justice*, 6(5): 927–45.

Weigend, T. 2011, 'Perpetration through an Organization: The Unexpected Career of a German Legal Concept', *Journal of International Criminal Justice*, 9(1): 91–111.

Weil, P. 1983, 'Towards Relative Normativity in International Law', *American Journal of International Law*, 77(3): 413–42.

Weiler, J. et al. (eds) 1989, *International Crimes of State: Critical Analysis of the ILC's Draft Article 19 on State Responsibility*, Berlin: De Gruyter.

Welch, J. 2001, *The Tokyo Trial: A Bibliographic Guide to English-Language Sources*, Westport, CT: Greenwood Press.

Wells, C. 2001, *Corporations and Criminal Liability*, Oxford: Oxford University Press.

Wentker, H. 2002, 'Die juristische Aufarbeitung von NS-Verbrechen in der Sowjetischen Besatzungszone und in der DDR', *Kritische Justiz*, 35(1): 60–78.

Werle, G. 2007, *Völkerstrafrecht*, Tübingen: Mohr Siebeck.

Werle, G. 2009, *Principles of International Criminal Law*, The Hague: Asser Press.

Werle, G. and F. Jeßberger 2014, *Principles of International Criminal Law*, 3rd edn, Oxford: Oxford University Press.

Wheeler, S. 2002a, 'An Ethical Frame for Corporate Behaviour', in *Essays in International Corporate Law*, Volume 11, edited by F. Macmillan, Oxford: Hart Publishing.

Wheeler, S. 2002b, *Corporations and the Third Way*, Oxford: Hart Publishing.

Wheeler, S. 2016, 'Independence and Diversity in Board Composition', in *The Routledge Handbook of Corporate Law*, edited by R. Tomasic, New York: Routledge.

White, N.D. and S. MacLeod 2008, 'EU Operations and Private Military Contractors: Issues of Corporate and Institutional Responsibility', *European Journal of International Law*, 19(5): 965–88.

Whyte, D. 2006, 'The Crimes of Neo-Liberal Rule in Occupied Iraq', *British Journal of Criminology*, 47(2): 177–95.

Whyte, D. (ed.) 2008, *Crimes of the Powerful: A Reader*, Milton Keynes: Open University Press.

Wilhelm, J. 2009, *Kapitalgesellschaftsrecht*, Berlin: De Gruyter.

Williams, E. 1966 [1944], *Capitalism and Slavery*, New York: Capricorn Books.

Williams, G. 2002, '"No Participation Without Implication": Understanding the Wrongs We Do Together', *Res Publica*, 8(2): 201–10.

Williston, S. 1888a, 'History of the Law of Business Corporations before 1800. I'. *Harvard Law Review*, 2(3): 105–24.

Williston, S. 1888b, 'History of the Law of Business Corporations before 1800. II', *Harvard Law Review*, 2(4): 149–66.

Wilson, E. 2008, *Savage Republic: De Indis of Hugo Grotius, Republicanism and Dutch Hegemony within the Early Modern World System (c. 1600–1619)*, Leiden: Martinus Nijhoff.

Wilson, S. 2015, 'The Sentence is Only Half the Story: From Stern Justice to Clemency for Japanese War Criminals, 1945–1958', *Journal of International Criminal Justice*, 13(4): 745–61.

Wishart, D. 2010, 'A Reconfiguration of Company and/or Corporate Law Theory', *Journal of Corporate Law Studies*, 10(1): 151–78.

Wolfrum, R. 2005, 'State Responsibility for Private Actors: An Old Problem of Renewed Relevance', in *International Responsibility Today: Essays in Memory of Oscar Schachter*, edited by M. Ragazzi, Leiden: Brill.

Wood, E.M. 2002, *The Origin of Capitalism: A Longer View*, London: Verso.

Woods, N. 2006, 'Center for Global Development Brief', available at: http://www.globaleconomicgovernance.org/wp-content/uploads/CGDEV%20BRIEF%20Woods.pdf.

Woodward, S. 1995, *Balkan Tragedy: Chaos and Dissolution after the Cold War*, Washington, DC: The Brookings Institution.

Woodward, S. 2002, 'The Political Economy of Ethno-Nationalism in Yugoslavia', in *Fighting Identities: Race, Religion and Ethno-Nationalism*, edited by L. Panitch and C. Leys, London: Merlin Press.

Wormser, M. 1931, *Frankenstein Incorporated*, New York: McGraw-Hill.

Yamamoto, K. 2011, 'Piety, Profit and Public Service in the Financial Revolution', *English Historical Review*, 126: 806–34.

Yamamoto, K. 2017, 'Early Modern Business Projects and a Forgotten History of Corporate Social Responsibility', in Baars and Spicer (eds) 2017.

Yap, J. 2010, 'Corporate Civil Liability for War Crimes in Canadian Courts: Lessons from Bil'in (Village Council) v. Green Park International Ltd.', *Journal of International Criminal Justice*, 8(2): 631–48.

Zahar, A. and G. Sluiter 2008, *International Criminal Law: A Critical Introduction*, Oxford: Oxford University Press.

Zahraa, M. 1995, 'Legal Personality in Islamic Law', *Arab Law Quarterly*, 10(3): 193–206.

Zanotti, L. 2011, *Governing Disorder UN Peace Operations, International Security, and Democratization in the Post-Cold War Era*, University Park, PA: Penn State University Press.

Zeck, W.A. 1947, 'Nuremberg: Proceedings Subsequent to Goering et al.', *North Carolina Law Review*, 26: 350–89.

Zegveld, L. 2002, *Accountability of Armed Opposition Groups in International Law*, Cambridge: Cambridge University Press.

Zerk, J. 2006, *Multinationals and Corporate Social Responsibility*, Cambridge: Cambridge University Press.

Ziv, N. and R. Shamir 2001, 'State-Oriented and Community-Oriented Lawyering for a Cause: A Tale of Two Strategies', in *Cause Lawyering and the State in the Global Era*, edited by A. Sarat and S. Scheingold, Oxford: Oxford University Press.

Zolo, D. 2004, 'The Iraqi Special Tribunal: Back to the Nuremberg Paradigm?', *Journal of International Criminal Justice*, 2(2): 313–18.

Treaties, International Reports and Declarations, Cases, Proceedings, and Hybrid Cases

Treaties

1648 Treaty between Spain and the United Netherlands, concluded at Münster, 30 January, in *European Treaties Bearing on the History of the United States and Its Dependencies until 1648*, edited by F. Davenport, Carnegy Institute, 2004 (*1648 Peace of Münster*).

1885 General Act of the Berlin Conference, 26 February, C 4361 1885 (General Act), in E. Hertslet, *The Map of Africa by Treaty*, vol. 2, 3rd ed. (HMSO, 1909) 128, 468 (*1885 Berlin General Act*).

1907 Convention (IV) Respecting the Laws and Customs of War on Land and its annex: Regulations concerning the Laws and Customs of War on Land, UKTS (1910) 9 (*1907 Hague Regulations*).

1907 Convention Respecting the Limitation of the Employment of Force for the Recovery of Contract Debts, October 18, 36 Stat. 2241, UNTS 537 (*1907 Hague Convention on Debt Recovery*).

1919 Treaty of Peace, Versailles, June 28, 1919, 225 Consol. T.S. 188, 285–286. Excerpt in Appendix A (*1919 Versailles Treaty*).

1920 Statute of the Permanent Court of International Justice, LNTS, vol. 6, 380–413.

1937 Convention for the Creation of an International Criminal Court, League of Nations Official Journal Special Supplement 156, 1938.

1945 Potsdam Agreement of 2 August 1945, between the USSR, the USA and the UK, available at: http://avalon.law.yale.edu/20th_century/decade17.asp. Excerpt in Appendix A.

1945 Agreement for the prosecution and punishment of the major war criminals of the European Axis, London Agreement of 8 August Establishing the Nuremberg Tribunal, 82 UNTS 279 (no. 251) (*London Agreement*) with its Annex, the Charter of the International Military Tribunal (*Nuremberg Charter*).

1945 Charter of the United Nations, 1 UNTS xvi (*1945 UN Charter*).

1946 Charter of the International Military Tribunal for the Far East, TIAS No. 1589 (*1946 IMTFE Charter*).

1948 Convention for the Prevention and Punishment of the Crime of Genocide, 78 UNTS 277 (*1948 Genocide Convention*).

1949 Convention I for the Amelioration of the Conditions of the Wounded and Sick in Armed Forces in The Field; II for the Amelioration of the Condition of the Wounded, Sick and Shipwrecked Members of Armed Forces at Sea; III relative to the Treatment of Prisoners of War; IV relative to the Protection of Civilian Persons in Time of War, 75 UNTS 3 (Nos. 970–973) (*1949 Geneva Conventions*).

1958 Geneva Convention on the High Seas, 450 UNTS 82 (*1958 High Seas Convention*).

1965 Washington Convention on the Settlement of Investment Disputes between States and Nationals of Other States, 575 UNTS 532 (*1965 ICSID Convention*).

1966 International Covenant on Economic, Social and Cultural Rights, 993 UNTS 3 (No. 14531) (*1966 ICESCR*).

1969 Vienna Convention on the Law of Treaties, 1155 UNTS, 331 (*1969 Vienna Convention on the Law of Treaties*).

1977 Protocols Additional to the Geneva Conventions of 1949, 1125 UNTS 3 (No. 17512).

1982 United National Convention on the Law of the Sea, 1833 UNTS 3 (*1982 UNCLOS*).

1984 Convention Against Torture and Other Cruel, Inhuman and Degrading Treatment and Punishment, 1465 UNTS 85 (*1984 Torture Convention*).

1989 Basel Convention on the Control of Transboundary Movements of Hazardous Waste, adopted on 22 March, 1673 UNTS 57. Excerpt in Appendix D.

1993 Statute of the International Criminal Tribunal for the Former Yugoslavia UN Doc. S/RES/827 (*1993 ICTY Statute*).

1994 Statute of the International Criminal Tribunal for Rwanda UN Doc. S/Res/955 (1994) (*1993 ICTR Statute*).

1997 Convention on Combating Bribery of Foreign Public Officials inInternational Business Transactions, Organisation of Economic Cooperation and Development, 17 December, 37 ILM 1 (1998). Excerpt in Appendix D.

1998 International Criminal Court Statute, 2187 UNTS 91 (*1998 ICC Statute*)

2000 Convention Against Transnational Organized Crime, 2225 UNTS 209. Excerpt in Appendix D.

2002 Agreement between the United Nations and the Government of Sierra Leone on the Establishment of a Special Court for Sierra Leone, 2178 UNTS 138.

2000 Optional Protocol to the Convention on the Rights of the Child on the Sale of Children, Child Prostitution and Child Pornography of 25 May 2000, A/RES/54/263.

World War II and Aftermath Declarations/Instruments/Cases/Other Documents

Allied Declarations

Joint Declaration on Punishment for War Crimes made on 13 January 1942 (at St James) in London, by the Government of Belgium, the Government of Czechoslovakia, the Free French National Committee, the Government of Greece, the Government of Luxembourg, the Government of the Netherlands, the Government of Norway, the government of Poland and the Government of Yugoslavia, reprinted in Current Notes, AJIL 39(3) 1945, at 565–79 (*1942 St James Declaration*).

Declaration on German Atrocities in Occupied Europe, 1 November 1943, reprinted in 1 T.W.C., at viii (*1943 Declaration on Atrocities*). The Cairo Declaration on future military operations against Japan, jointly released by the United States, the Republic of China and Great Britain on December 1, 1943, National Diet Library, available at http://www.ndl.go.jp/constitution/e/shiryo/01/002 46/002 46tx.html (*1943 Cairo Declaration*). Proclamation Defining Terms for Japanese Surrender, issued by the United States, the Republic of China and Great Britain, at Potsdam on July 26, 1945, National Diet Library, available at http://www.ndl.go.jp/constitution/e/etc/c06.html (*1945 Potsdam Proclamation on Japanese Surrender*).

Collections

Trial of the Major War Criminals before the International Military Tribunal, Nuremberg, 14 November 1945–1 October 1946, a 42-volume series of books containing the official record of the proceedings of the International Military Tribunal at Nuremberg, published by the IMT, Nuremberg, 1947, known as the Blue Series, available at https://www.loc.gov/rr/frd/Military_Law/NT_major-war-criminals.html (*Blue Series*).

Trials of War Criminals Before the Nuremberg Military Tribunals Under Control Council Law No. 10, October 1946–April 1949, Washington: United States Government Printing Office, n.d., available at https://www.loc.gov/rr/frd/Military_Law/NTs_war-criminals.html (*Green Series*).

'Nazi Conspiracy and Aggression', an 8-volume, 12-book series, with the subtitle 'Collection of Documentary Evidence and Guide Materials Prepared by the American and British Prosecuting Staffs for Presentation before the International Military Tribunal at Nurnberg, Germany', known as the Red Series, United States Government Printing Office, 1946, available at https://www.loc.gov/rr/frd/Military_Law/NT_Nazi-conspiracy.html (*Red Series*).

Law Reports of Trials of War Criminals, Selected and prepared by the United Nations War Crimes Commission, London: His Majesty's Stationery Office, 1947–1949, available at https://www.loc.gov/rr/frd/Military_Law/law-reports-trials-war-criminals.html (*WCCLR*).

Pritchard, J. and S.M. Zaide (eds) 1981, *The Tokyo War Crimes Trial: The Complete Transcripts of the Proceedings of the International Military Tribunal for the Far East*, Vols. 1–22, New York: Garland.

Online Archives and Archive Guides

Berkeley War Crimes Studies Center, Pacific Theatre Document Archive, available at: http://socrates.berkeley.edu/~warcrime/documents/Sissons%20Final%20War%20Crimes%20Text%2018-3-06.pdf.

Berkeley War Crimes Studies Center, Singapore docket, available at: http://socrates.berkeley.edu/~warcrime/Japan/singapore/Trials/Case_details.htm.

Berkeley War Crimes Studies Center, 'Reviews of the Yokohama Class B and C war crimes Trials by the 8th Army Judge Advocate (1946–1949)'. See for a list and summaries: http://socrates.berkeley.edu/~warcrime/Japan/Yokohama/Reviews/PT-yokohama-index.htm.

Comfort Women Project, available at: http://www.comfort-women.org/.

Forschungs- und Dokumentationszentrum Kriegsverbrecherprozesse an der Philipps-Universität Marburg, available at: http://www.uni-marburg.de/icwc/dokumente.

Hong Kong War Crimes Project, available at: http://hkwctc.lib.hku.hk/exhibits/show/hkwctc/home.

Hong Kong War Crimes Trials Collection, 'Snapshots of Cases', available at: http://hkwctc.lib.hku.hk/exhibits/show/hkwctc/documents/listing.

National Archives Research Guide, *Second World War: War Crimes 1939–1945*, available at: http://www.nationalarchives.gov.uk/records/research-guides/war-crimes-1939-1945.htm#16211.

Nazi Crimes on Trial Project, 'Die deutschen Strafverfahren wegen NS-Tötungsverbrechen', available at: http://www.junsv.nl.

Swiss Banks Holocaust Settlement, available at: http://www.swissbankclaims.com/.

Taiwan POW Camps Memorial Society, available at: http://www.powtaiwan.org.

Personal Online Archives and Libraries

Ben Ferencz Library: http://www.benferencz.org/ (*Ferencz Library*).

Hebert Nuremberg Collection, Louisiana State University Paul M. Hebert Law Center: https://digitalcommons.law.lsu.edu/nuremberg/ (*Hebert Nuremberg Collection*).

Robert H. Jackson Centre Archive: http://www.roberthjackson.org/ and http://www.youtube.com/profile?user=RobertHJacksonCenter#g/u. (*Jackson Archive*).

Columbia University Libraries, Arthur W. Diamond Law Library, Telford Taylor Archive: http://www.columbia.edu/cu/lweb/archival/collections/ldpd_10199444/ (*Taylor Archive*).

Letter to Eleanor Roosevelt dated 19 June 19 1951, *Telford Taylor Archive*, TTP-CLS: 14-4-3-53 (*Taylor Letter to Roosevelt*).

Harry S. Truman Presidential Library & Museum Online Documents: https://www.trumanlibrary.org/online-collections.htm (*Truman Library*).

Oral History Interview with Josiah E. Dubois, Jr., Camden, N.J., 29 June 1973, by Richard D. McKinzie, in *Truman Library*, available at https://www.trumanlibrary.org/oralhist/duboisje.htm (*Dubois Oral History Interview*).

Oral History Interview with Bernard Bernstein, New York, 23 July 1975, in *Truman Library* available at https://www.trumanlibrary.org/oralhist/bernsten.htm (*Bernstein Oral History Interview*).

International Military Tribunal at Nuremberg

Indictment of the International Military Tribunal: The United States of America, The French Republic, The United Kingdom of Great Britain and Northern Ireland, and the Union of Soviet Socialist Republics against Hermann Wilhelm Goering, in I Trial of the Major War Criminals before the International Military Tribunal 27 1947; Appendix B (*IMT Indictment*).

Jackson, R. IMT Opening Address, I International Military Tribunal, The Trial of German Major War Criminals by the International Military Tribunal Sitting at Nuremberg Germany (Commencing 20 November, 1945) 3 1946 (*IMT, Jackson Opening Address*).

International Military Tribunal, Judgment of 1 October 1946, in I The Trial of German Major War Criminals by the International Military Tribunal Sitting at Nuremberg Germany (Commencing 20 November 1945) 22 (22 August 1946–1 October 1946) (*IMT Judgment*).

Motion on Behalf of Defendant Gustav Krupp von Bohlen for Postponement of the Trial as to Him, dated 4 November 1945, in I Trial of the Major War Criminals Before the International Military Tribunal 124 (*Krupp IMT Motion*).

Memorandum of the British Prosecution on the motion, in I Trial of the Major War Criminals Before the International Military Tribunal 139 (*Krupp IMT Memorandum*).

Answer of the United States Prosecution to the Motion on Behalf of Defendant Gustav Krupp Von Bohlen, dated 12 November 1945, in I Trial of the Major War Criminals Before the International Military Tribunal 134–5 (*Krupp IMT Answer*).

Order of the Tribunal Rejecting the Motion to amend the Indictment, dated 15 November 1945, in I Trial of the Major War Criminals Before the International Military Tribunal 146 (*Krupp IMT Order*).

Economic Aspects of the Conspiracy, Chapter VIII, I 'Nazi Conspiracy and Aggression', 349 (*Economic Aspects*).

International Military Tribunal for the Far East (Tokyo)

Trial of Japanese War Criminals. Documents: 1. Opening Statement by Joseph B. Keenan, Chief of Counsel. 2. Charter of the International Military Tribunal for the Far East. 3. Indictment, United States. Dept. of State, 1 vol. Washington, DC: US Govt. print off, 1946 (*IMTFE Indictment*).

International Military Tribunal for the Far East, Judgment of 12 November 1948 20 1 The Tokyo War Crimes Trial 1. *Pal Dissent* (1953): in N. Boister and R. Cryer 2008a, *Documents on the Tokyo International Military Tribunal: Charter, Indictment, and Judgments*, Oxford: Oxford University Press (*IMTFE Judgment*).

Dissenting Opinion of the Member from India on Judgment, in: B. Röling and C. Rüter (eds) 1977, *The Tokyo Judgment: The International Military Tribunal for the Far East*, Amsterdam: Amsterdam University Press (*IMTFE Röling Dissent*).

US Military Court Cases and Proceedings[1]

Case No. 1 United States v. Karl Brandt et al. (*Medical Case*), U.S. Military Tribunal Nuremberg, judgment of 19 August 1947, in *Trials of War Criminals before the Nuremberg Military Tribunals under Control Council Law No. 10*, Vol. II, pp. 171 et seq.

Case No. 3 United States v. Josef Altstoetter et al. (*Justice Case*), U.S. Military Tribunal Nuremberg, judgment of 3 December 1947, in *Trials of War Criminals before the Nuremberg Military Tribunals under Control Council Law No. 10*, Vol. III, pp. 945 et seq.

Case No. 4 United States v. Oswald Pohl et al. (*Pohl Case*), U.S. Military Tribunal Nuremberg, judgment of 3 November 1948, in *Trials of War Criminals before the Nuremberg Military Tribunals under Control Council Law No. 10*, Vol. V, pp. 958 et seq.

Case No. 5 United States v. Friedrich Flick et al. (*Flick Case*), U.S. Military Tribunal Nuremberg, judgment of 22 December 1947, in *Trials of War Criminals before the Nuremberg Military Tribunals under Control Council Law No. 10*, Vol. VI, pp. 1187 et seq.

Case No. 6 United States v. Carl Krauch et al. (*Farben Case*), U.S. Military Tribunal Nuremberg, judgment of 30 July 1948, in *Trials of War Criminals before the Nuremberg Military Tribunals under Control Council Law No. 10*, Vol. VIII, pp. 1081 et seq.

Draft of Judge Hebert's dissent on the aggressive war charge in IG Farben, available at: https://digitalcommons.law.lsu.edu/nuremberg_docs/46/ (*Farben Case Hebert dissent*).

Case No. 7 United States v. List (*Hostage Case*), U.S. Military Tribunal Nuremberg, judgment of 19 February 1948 in *Trials of War Criminals before the Nuremberg Military Tribunals under Control Council Law No. 10*, Vol. XI, pp. 1230 et seq.

Case No. 9 United States v. Otto Ohlendorf et al. (*Einsatzgruppen Case*), U.S. Military Tribunal Nuremberg, judgment of 8 April 1948, in *Trials of War Criminals before the Nuremberg Military Tribunals under Control Council Law No. 10*, Vol. IV, pp. 411 et seq.

Case No. 10 United States v. Alfried Krupp et al. (*Krupp Case*), U.S. Military Tribunal Nuremberg, judgment of 31 July 1948, in *Trials of War Criminals before the Nuremberg Military Tribunals under Control Council Law No. 10*, Vol. IX, pp. 1230 et seq.

Case No. 11 United States v. Ernst Weizsaecker et al. (*Ministries or Wilhelmstrasse Case*), U.S. Military Tribunal Nuremberg, judgment of 11 April 1949, in *Trials of War Criminals before the Nuremberg Military Tribunals under Control Council Law No. 10*, Vol. XIV, pp. 308 et seq.

Trial of General Tomoyuki Yamashita, 4 United Nations War Crimes Commission, Law Reports of Trials of War Criminals 1 (1948) (*Yamashita Case*).

1 I have followed here the case citation commonly used in the literature, and the short form in parenthesis (e.g. *Medical Case*) is used in the footnotes.

Mauthausen Concentration Camp Case: Trial of Martin Gottfried Weiss and Thirty-Nine Others, Case No. 60, The Dachau Concentration Camp Trial, General Military Government Court of the United States Zone, Dachau, Germany, 15 November–13 December, 1945 Law Reports of Trials of War Criminals, The United Nations War Crimes Commission, Volume XI, London, HMSO, 1949.

British Military Courts

Death Warrant Bruno Tesch, 16 May 1946, National Archives, File Nos. WO311/423 (*Tesch Death Warrant*).

Trial of Mitsugu Toda and 8 others, Case No. 65223; National Archives file no. WO235/1028 (*Trial of Mitsugu Toda*).

In re Tesch & Others (Zyklon B Case) (British Mil. Ct. 1946), in 1 *UN War Crimes Comm'n, Law Reports of Trials of War Criminals* 93 (1947); National Archives WO208/2169; 309/625; WO309/625; WO3091602; WO309/1603; WO235/83; WO235/641 (*Zyklon B Case*).

Trial of Solm Wilhelm Wittig et al., 1947, National Archives file no. WO 235/283; FO1060/509 (unsorted documents) (*Steinöl/Neuengamme Concentration Camp Case*).

Soviet Military Courts

Prozeßmaterialien in der Strafsache gegen ehemalige angehörige der Japanischen Armee wegen Vorbereitung und Anwendung der Bakterienwaffe, Verlag für Fremdsprachige Literatur Moskau 1950 (Materials in the case of former servicemen of the Japanese Army charged with manufacturing and employing bacteriological weapons), Moscow: Foreign Languages Publishing House, 1950 (*Prozeßmaterialien*).

'Protokolle des Todes, Verhörprotokolle der Auschwitz-Ingenieure Prüfer, Sander und Schultze', *Der Spiegel*, 1993, 47(40): 151–62, available at: http://www.spiegel.de/spiegel/print/d-13679718.html and http://www.spiegel.de/spiegel/print/d-13679727.html (*Töpf Documents in Der Spiegel*).

Dutch Military Courts

Trial of Washio Awochi, Case No. 76, 13 United Nations War Crimes Commission, *Law Reports of Trials of War Criminals* 122 (1949) (*Awochi Case*).

French Military Court

The Government Commissioner of the General Tribunal of the Military Government of the French Zone of Occupation in Germany v. Hermann Roechling, Ernst Roechling, Hans Lothar von Gemming Jacksonen-Hornberg, Albert Maier, Wilhelm Rodenhauser, Directors of the Roechling Enterprises (*'Roechling Case'*), Indictment dated 25 November 1947; Judgment dated 30 June 1948; Judgment on appeal dated 25 January 1949 (German National Archive at Koblenz).

Documents of the Allied Occupation of Germany

Control Council Proclamation No. 1, Berlin, 30 August 1945, in *Enactments and Approved Papers of the Control Council and Coordinating Committee, Applied Control Authority, Germany, 1945*, Vol. 1, p. 44 (*Control Council Proclamation No. 1*).

Control Council Law No. 9, 30 November, 1945, Military Government, Germany (Territory under Allied occupation, 1945–1955: US Zone). Providing for the seizure of property owned by I.G. Farbenindustrie and the control thereof, published in, Military Governor / *Property control in the US-occupied area of Germany, 1945–1949. Special report, July 1949* ([1949]), p. 87 (*Control Council Law No. 9*).

Control Council Law No. 10, 20 December 1945, in *Enactments and Approved Papers of the Control Council and Coordinating Committee, Applied Control Authority, Germany, 1945*, Vol. 1, p. 306 (*Control Council Law No. 10*).

Control Council Law No. 52, amended 3 April 1945, Military Government, Germany, supreme commander's area of control, law No. 52 (blocking and control of property), published in: Germany (territory Allied occupation, 1945–1955: US Zone). Office of Military Government. Civil Administration Division. / *Denazification, cumulative review. Report, 1 April 1947–30 April 1948.* no. 34 (1948), pp. 46–8 (*Control Council Law No. 52*).

Control Council Directive No. 38, 12 October 1945, in Enactments and Approved Papers of the Control Council and Coordinating Committee, Applied Control Authority, Germany, 1945, Vol. V, p. 12 (*Control Council Directive No. 38*).

Directive to Commander-in-Chief of United States Forces of Occupation Regarding the Military Government of Germany; April 1945, US Archives, available at: http://www.archives.gov/research/holocaust/finding-aid/military/rg-260.html#OMGUS (*JCS 1067*).

Directive to the Commander-in-Chief of United States Forces of Occupation Regarding the Military Government of Germany (J.C.S. 1779) Germany 1947–1949, pages 33–41, Department of State Bulletin, July 27, 1947, pages 186–193 (*JCS 1779*).

Documents of the US Occupation of Japan

FRUS: *United States Department of State/Foreign Relations of the United States* diplomatic papers, 1945. The British Commonwealth, the Far East, Volume VI (1945), available at: http://digicoll.library.wisc.edu/cgi-bin/FRUS/FRUS-idx?id=FRUS.FRUS1945v06.

FRUS 922: John McCloy, Asst. Secretary of War, memo to the Acting Secretary of State Acheson, 7 September 1945.

FRUS 926: Discussion of the US Policy on the Apprehension and punishment of war criminals in the Far East, 12 September 1945.

FRUS 942: Memo by Atcheson to SCAP 8 October 1945.

FRUS 940: Memo from Acting Political Advisor Atcheson to the Secretary of State, 5 October 1945.

FRUS 944: Response from Secretary of State mentioned US National War Crimes Office general list of Japanese war criminals and a special list of major war criminals, 14 September 1945.

FRUS 948: The Chinese list of 12 major war criminals, 20 October 1945.

FRUS 952: Atcheson 'Top Secret' memo to SCAP, 6 November 1945.

FRUS 952-3: Memorandum by Atcheson to SCAP, 6 November 1945.

FRUS 960: Memorandum by Acting Chairman of the State-War-Navy Coordinating Committee to the Secretary of State with annexed Draft Message to be sent by the Joint Chiefs of Staff to the SCAP.

FRUS 963: Memo by Marshall, acting Chief of Staff to the SCAP to Atcheson, 12 November 1945.

FRUS 963-5: Memo from Atcheson to SCAP and Chief of Staff, 12 November 1945.

FRUS 968: Subenclosure of Memo by Atcheson to SCAP and CoS.

FRUS 971-2: Memo of the Political Advisor in Japan Atcheson to the Secretary of State, 17 November 1945.

FRUS 972: Report by the Office of the Political Advisor, dated 26 November 1945.

FRUS 977-8, Memorandum by the Acting Political Advisor in Japan (Atcheson), Tokyo, 27 November 1945.

FRUS 986: Memo by Atcheson to the Secretary of State, dated 19 December 1945.

IMTFE Proclamation: Special Proclamation by the Supreme Commander for the Allied Powers of 19 January 1946, superseded by General Order No. 20, 20 April 1946, available at: http://137.248.11.66/fileadmin/media/IMTFE_April_1946.pdf.

US Initial Post-Defeat Policy: United States Initial Post-Defeat Policy Relating to Japan (SWNCC150), 11 June 1945.

US Initial Post-Surrender Policy: US Initial Post-Surrender Policy for Japan (SWNCC150/4/A), 21 September 1945.

Joint Chiefs of Staff Directive 1380/15, Basic Initial Post Surrender Directive to Supreme Commander for the Allied Powers for the Occupation and Control of Japan, 2 November 1945.

Further International Reports/Documents/Resolutions

African Commission on Human and Peoples' Rights

Communication 155/96 Social and Economic Rights Action Center (SERAC) and Center for Economic and Social Rights (CESR) / Nigeria, 27 October 2001.

African Union

Protocol on Amendments to the Protocol on the Statute of the African Court of Justice and Human Rights Assembly/AU/Dec.529(XXIII) (2014) (*Malabo Protocol*).

Decision on the International Criminal Court Doc. EX.CL/952(XXVIII), Assembly/AU/Dec 590 (XXVI) 30–31 January 2016.

United Nations

International Law Commission

Principles of International Law Recognized in the Charter of the Nuremberg Tribunal and in the Judgment of the Tribunal 1950, UN Doc. A/CN.4/SER.A/1950/Add.1 (*Nuremberg Principles*).

Report of the International Law Commission on its Second Session, 5 June to 29 July 1950, Official Records of the General Assembly, Fifth session, Supplement No. 12 (A/1316), UN Doc. A/CN.4/34, Commentary, p. 374 (*ILC Nuremberg Principles Commentary*).

Draft Articles on the Responsibility of States for internationally wrongful acts, Yearbook of the International Law Commission, 1970, Vol. II, UN Doc. A/CN.4/233 (*ILC Draft Articles 1970*).

First Report on State Responsibility, by Mr. James Crawford, Special Rapporteur, 24 April 1998, UN Doc. A/CN.4/490 (*ILC 1998 Report*).

Responsibility of States for internationally wrongful acts, UN Doc. A/RES/56/83 2001 (*ILC State Responsibility Articles*).

Report of the study group on the fragmentation of international law, finalised by Martti Koskenniemi, UN Doc. A/CN.4/L.682 13 April 2006 (*ILC Fragmentation Report (2006)*).

Draft Articles on the Responsibility of International Organizations, Yearbook of the International Law Commission, 2011, Vol. II, Part Two, UN Doc. A/66/10 (*ILC Draft Articles on IOs*).

Recommendation of the Working-Group on the long-term programme of work, UN Doc. A/68/10, annex B (*ILC 2013 Recommendation*).

Report of the International Law Commission on the Work of its Sixty-Eighth Session UN Doc. A/71/10, 2016; Crimes against humanity: Text of draft articles 5, 6, 7, 8, 9 and 10 provisionally adopted by the Drafting Committee on 25, 26, 30 and 31 May and 1 and 2 June 2016, and of draft article 5, paragraph (f), provisionally adopted on 7 July 2016, A/CN.4/L873, 3 June 2016.

Report of the International Law Commission on the Work of its Sixty-Ninth Session: Crimes against humanity: Texts and titles of the draft preamble, the draft articles and the draft annex provisionally adopted by the Drafting Committee on first reading, UN Doc. A/CN.4/L.892.

Third Report on Crimes against Humanity by the Special Rapporteur Sean Murphy, A/CN.4/704, 23 January 2017.

United Nations Environment Programme

Solanas, M. 'Revisiting Privatization, Foreign Investment, Arbitration and Water', United Nations Publication (UNEP/CEPAL) 2007 (*CEPAL FDI: Arbitration and Water Report*).

United Nations General Assembly

General Assembly Resolution 177 (II) Formulation of the Principles recognized in the Charter of the Nurnberg Tribunal and in the Judgment of the Tribunal, 21 November 1947, UN Doc. A/RES/177(II).

General Assembly Resolution 1803 (XVII) Permanent Sovereignty over Natural Resources, 14 December 1962, UN Doc. A/RES/1803 (*UN General Assembly PSNR Resolution*).

General Assembly Resolution 2158 (XXI) Permanent Sovereignty over Natural Resources, 25 November 1966, UN Doc. A/RES/2158.

General Assembly Resolution 3171 (XXVIII) Permanent Sovereignty over Natural Resources, 17 December 1973, UN Doc. A/RES/3171.

General Assembly Resolution 3201 (S-VI). Declaration on the Establishment of a New International Economic Order, UN Doc. A/RES/S-6/3201, 1 May 1974. (*UN General Assembly NIEO Resolution*).

General Assembly Resolution 3281 Charter of Economic Rights and Duties of States, (1974) UN Doc A/RES/29/3281 (*UN General Assembly CERD*)

General Assembly Resolution Adopted by the General Assembly 28 January 2002 [on the report of the Sixth Committee (A/56/589 and Corr.1) Responsibility of States for Internationally Wrongful Acts] (*UN General Assembly Resolution 589*).

General Assembly *CERD* Voting Record, available at: http://unbisnet.un.org:8080/ipac20/ipac.jsp?session=1307019CJ2I95.47059&profile=voting&uri=link=3100028~!202794~!3100029~!3100070&aspect=alpha&menu=search&ri=3&source=~!horizon&term=A%2FRES%2F3281%28XXIX%29&index=Z791AZ

UN Global Compact

The Ten Principles (n.d.), available at https://www.unglobalcompact.org.

Human Rights Commission; Human Rights Council

Norms on the Responsibilities of Transnational Corporations and Other Business Enterprises with Regard to Human Rights, UN Doc. E/CN.4/Sub.2/2003/12/Rev.2, 13 August 2003 (*UN Norms*).

Report of the Working Group on an Optional Protocol to the International Covenant on Economic, Social and Cultural Rights on Its Fifth Session, 18 June 2008 (UN Doc. A/HRC/RES/8/7) (*UN Legalising CSR Report*).

Resolution: Elaboration of an international legally binding instrument on transnational corporations and other business enterprises with respect to human rights, UN Doc. A/HRC/RES/26/9, 14 July 2014 (*UN HRC OEIGWG Resolution*).

Report of the First session of the open-ended intergovernmental working group on transnational corporations and other business enterprises with respect to human rights, UN Doc. A/HRC/31/50 (*UN HRC OEIGWG 2016 Report*).

Report of the Second session of the open-ended intergovernmental working group on transnational corporations and other business enterprises with respect to human rights, UN Doc. A/HRC/34/47, 4 January 2017 (*UN HRC OEIGWG 2017 Report*).

Special Representative of the Secretary-General on Human Rights and Transnational Corporations and Other Business Enterprises

Commission on Human Rights Resolution 2005/69, 20 April 2005, UN Doc. E/CN4/RES/2005/69 (*Ruggie Appointment Resolution*).

'Mapping International Standards of Responsibility and Accountability for Corporate Acts', Report of the Special Representative of the Secretary-General on the Issue of Human Rights and Transnational Corporations and Other Business Enterprises, John Ruggie, 19 February 2007, UN Doc. A/HRC/4/35, (*Ruggie (2007) Mapping Report*).

'Protect, Respect and Remedy: A Framework for Business and Human Rights', Report of the Special Representative of the Secretary-General on the Issue of Human Rights and Transnational Corporations and Other Business Enterprises, John Ruggie, 7 April 2008, 8th Session, UN Doc. A/HRC/8/5 (*Ruggie (2008) Report*).

'Towards operationalizing the "protect, respect and remedy" framework', Report of the Special Representative of the Secretary-General on the Issue of Human Rights and Transnational Corporations and Other Business Enterprises, John Ruggie, 22 April 2009, UN Doc. A/HRC/11/13 (*Ruggie (2009) Report*).

'Further Steps Toward the Operationalizing of the 'Protect, Respect and Remedy' Framework', Report of the Special Representative of the Secretary-General on the Issue of Human Rights and Transnational Corporations and Other Business Enterprises, John Ruggie, United Nations Human Rights Council, 9 April 2010, UN Doc. A/HRC/14/27 (*Ruggie (2010) Report*).

'Guiding Principles on Business and Human Rights: Implementing the United Nations "Protect, Respect and Remedy" Framework', Report of the Special Representative of the Secretary-General on the Issue of Human Rights and Transnational Corporations and Other Business Enterprises, John Ruggie, 21 March 2011, UN Doc. A/HRC/17/31 (*Ruggie (2011) Report*).

'Business and human rights in conflict-affected regions: challenges and options towards State responses' Report of the Special Representative of the Secretary-General on the Issue of Human Rights and Transnational Corporations and Other Business Enterprises, John Ruggie, 27 May 2011, UN Doc. A/HRC/17/32.

Security Council

Resolution 827 of 25 May 1993, UN Doc. S/Res/827 (1993) (*UN SC Res. 827 establishing the International Criminal Tribunal for the former Yugoslavia*).

Letter dated 96/01/26 from the Secretary-General addressed to the President of the

Security Council, UN Doc. S/1996/67, containing the Interim report of the International Commission of Inquiry to investigate reports of the sale or supply of arms to former Rwandan Government forces in violation of the Security Council arms embargo and allegations that those forces are receiving training to destabilize Rwanda (*UNSC Commission of Inquiry into Great Lakes Arms Flow Interim Report*).

Statement of the President of the Security Council, dated 2 June 2000, UN Doc. S/PRST/2000/20, (*UNSCP Congo Panel Request*), see Appendix F.

Resolution 1306 (2000) Adopted by the Security Council at its 4168th meeting, on 5 July 2000 UN Doc. S/RES/1306 (*UN SC Res. establishing the panel of experts on Sierra Leone*).

Report of the Panel of Experts appointed pursuant to Security Council Resolution 1306 paragraph 19, relating to Sierra Leone, dated 20 December 2000, UN Doc. S/2000/1195.

Final Report of the Panel of Experts on the Illegal Exploitation of Natural Resources and Other Forms of Wealth of the Democratic Republic of the Congo, 16 October 2002, UN Doc. S/2002/1146 (*UN SC Congo 2002 Report*).

Final Report of the Panel of Experts on the Illegal Exploitation of Natural Resources and Other Forms of Wealth of the Democratic Republic of the Congo, 23 October 2003, UN Doc. S/2003/1027 (*UN SC Congo 2003 Report*).

Resolution 1493 of 2003, UN Doc S/Res/1493 (2003) (*UN SC Res.1493 – Congo Arms Embargo*)

Resolution 1503 of 2003, UN Doc S/Res/1503 (2003) (*UN SC Res. 1503 – Implementation of ICTY and ICTR completion strategies*).

Resolution 1533 of 2004, UN Doc S/Res/1533 (2004). (*UN SC Res. 1533 – On the establishment of a committee to examine the implementation of the measures imposed by resolution 1493 (2003)*)

List of Individuals and Entities Subject to the Measures Contained in Paragraph 1 of Security Council Resolution 1532 (2004) Concerning Liberia (*UNSC Liberia Assets Freeze List*), available at: http://www.un.org/sc/committees/1521/aflist.shtml.

Report of the Panel of Experts on Liberia submitted pursuant to Paragraph 5 (e) of Security Council resolution 1792 (2007) concerning Liberia, 12 June 2008, UNDoc. S/2008/371 (*UN SC Liberia 2007 Report*).

Organisation for Economic Cooperation and Development (OECD)

Guidelines for Multinational Enterprises, Annex to the Declaration of 11 June 1976 by Governments of OECD Countries on Investment and Multinational Enterprises, last updated in 2011, http://mneguidelines.oecd.org/guidelines/ (*OECD Guidelines*).

Final Statement by the UK National Contact Point for the OECD Guidelines for Multinational Enterprises: Afrimex (UK) Ltd, 28 August 2008, available at: http://www.oecd.org/daf/inv/mne/ncpstatements.htm.

Other International Courts, Hybrid Tribunals, Arbitral Awards, Cases, Documents and Proceedings

Permanent Court of International Justice

Mavrommatis Palestine Concessions Case (Jurisdiction), Greece v. UK (1924), PCIJ Reports, Series A, No. 2, 12 (*Mavrommatis (1924)*).

Mavrommatis Jerusalem Concessions Case (Jurisdiction), Greece v. UK (1925), PCIJ Reports, Series A, No. 5, 6 (*Mavrommatis (1925)*).

Case concerning the Factory at Chorzów, 1927 PCIJ (ser. A), No. 9 (jurisdiction); 1928 PCIJ (ser. A) No. 17 (merits) (*Factory at Chorzów*).

International Court of Justice

Reparations for Injuries suffered in the Service of the United Nations, Advisory Opinion, ICJ Rep. 1949, 174 (*Reparations for Injuries*).

Interhandel Case (Switzerland v. United States), Preliminary Objections, ICJ Rep. 1959, 6 (*Interhandel*).

Anglo-Iranian Oil Case (United Kingdom v. Iran), Judgment, ICJ Rep. 1952, 93 (*Anglo-Iranian Oil Case*).

Certain Expenses of the United Nations, Judgment, ICJ Rep. 1962, 151 (*Certain Expenses Case*).

Barcelona Traction Light & Power Co. Case (Belgium v. Spain), Judgment, ICJ Rep. 1970, 3. (*Barcelona Traction*).

Arrest Warrant of 11 April 2000 (Democratic Republic of the Congo v. Belgium), Judgment, ICJ Rep. 2002, 3 (*Arrest Warrant Case*).

Armed Activities on the Territory of the Congo (Democratic Republic of Congo v. Rwanda), Judgment, ICJ Rep. 2005, 168 (*Armed Activities*).

Application of the Convention on the Prevention and Punishment of the Crime of Genocide (Bosnia and Herzegovina v. Serbia and Montenegro), Judgment, ICJ Rep. 2007, 43 (*Bosnia Genocide Convention Case*).

Application of the Convention on the Prevention and Punishment of the Crime of Genocide (Croatia v. Serbia), Preliminary Objections, Judgment, ICJ Rep. 2008, 412 (*Serbia Genocide Convention Case*).

Ahmadou Sadio Diallo (Republic of Guinea v. Democratic Republic of the Congo), Judgment, ICJ Rep. 2010, 582 (*Ahmadou Sadio Diallo Case*).

International Arbitration

Instruments

Iran-US Claims Tribunal Rules of Procedure, available at: http://www.iusct.org/tribunal-rules.pdf (*Iran-US Tribunal Rules*).

Awards

Opinion and Award of the United States and Paraguay Commission, August 28, 1860, New York Times, https://www.nytimes.com/1860/08/28/archives/opinion-and-award-of-the-united-states-and-paraguay-commission.html.

Cayuga Indians: Cayuga Indians Case (Great Britain v. United States), 1926, 6 RIAA 173.

Island of Palmas Case: Island of Palmas (Netherlands v. United States), 1928, 2 RIAA 829.

Abu Dhabi Award: In The Matter of an Arbitration Between Petroleum Development (Trucial Coast) Ltd. and the Sheikh of Abu Dhabi, ICLQ (1952), 247.

Texaco Award: Texaco Overseas Petroleum Co and California Asiatic Oil Co v. Libyan Arab Republic (1977), 53 ILR 389.

Aminol Award: Government of the State of Kuwait v. American Independent Oil Co., 21 ILM (1982) 976.

ARAMCO Award: Saudi Arabia v. Arabian American Oil Company, 27 ILR 156–68.

LIAMCO Award: Libyan American Oil Co. (LIAMCO) v. Libya, Award on Jurisdiction, Merits and Damages, 20 ILM (1981) 1.

Metalclad Award: Metalclad Corp v. Mexico, Award, ICSID Case No. ARB(AF)/97/1, IIC 161 (2000).

Methanex Award: Methanex v. United States, Final Award, IIC 167 (2005).

Chevron v Ecuador Award: Chevron Corporation and Texaco Petroleum Corporation v. The Republic of Ecuador (2009), UNCITRAL, PCA Case No. 2009-23.

Bernhard von Pezold and Others v. Republic of Zimbabwe, ICSID Case No. ARB/10/15 (2015).

International Criminal Tribunal for the Former Yugoslavia Documents and Cases

Final Report to the Prosecutor by the Committee Established to Review the NATO Bombing Campaign Against the Federal Republic of Yugoslavia (2000), available at: http://www.icty.org/x/file/About/OTP/otp_report_nato_bombing_en.pdf (*ICTY NATO Bombing Report*).

Prosecutor v. Mucić et al. (IT-96-21), Trial Chamber Judgment of 16 November 1998 (*Mucić TC Decision*).

Prosecutor v. Furundzija (IT-95-17/1-T), Trial Chamber 10 December 1998 (*Furundzija TC Decision*).

Prosecutor v. Tadić (IT-94-1), Appeals Chamber Judgment of 15 July 1999 (*Tadić 1999 Appeals Decision*).

Prosecutor v. Krnojelac (IT-97-25-T), Trial Chamber 15 March 2002 (*Krnojelac TC Decision*).

Prosecutor v. Blagojević and Jokić (IT-02-60), Trial Chamber Judgment 1 September 2004 (*Blagojević and Jokić TC Decision*).

Prosecutor v. Krajisnik (IT-00-39), Appeals Chamber 19 March 2009 (*Krasjisnik Appeals Decision*).

Prosecutor v. Mrksić et al. (IT-95-13/1-A), Appeals Chamber 5 May 2009 (*Mrksić Appeals Decision*).

International Criminal Tribunal for Rwanda Cases

The Prosecutor v. Félicien Kabuga (ICTR-97-22-I), Indictment 30 October 1997 (*Kabuga Indictment*).

The Prosecutor v. Augustin Bizimana, Édouard Karemera, Callixte Nzabonimana, André Rwamakuba, Mathieu Ngirumpatse, Joseph Nzirorera, Félicien Kabuga, Juvénal Kajelijeli (ICTR-98-44-I), Confirmation and Non Disclosure of the Indictment, 29 August 1998 (*Bizimana Indictment Decision*).

The Prosecutor v. Jean-Paul Akayesu TC, Case No. ICTR-96-4-T, Judgment, 2 September 1998.

The Prosecutor v. Kayishema and Ruzindana (ICTR-95-1), Trial Chamber, May 21, 1999 (*Kayishema TC Decision*).

The Prosecutor v. Georges Rutaganda (ICTR-96-3-T), Trial Chamber decision 6 December 1999 (*Rutaganda TC Decision*).

The Prosecutor v. Alfred Musema (ICTR-96-13-T), Trial Chamber Judgment, 27 January 2000 (*Musema TC Decision*).

The Prosecutor v. Alfred Musema (ICTR-96-13-A), Appeals Chamber Decision of 16 November 2001 (*Musema Appeals Decision*).

The Prosecutor v. Félicien Kabuga (ICTR-98-44B-I), 1 October 2004 (*Kabuga TC Decision*).

The Prosecutor v. Édouard Karemera et al. (ICTR-98-44-I), Decision on the Prosecutor's Motion for Severance of Félicien Kabuga's Trial and for Leave to Amend the Accused's Indictment (TC), 1 September 2003 (*Karemera Kabuga Severance Decision*).

The Prosecutor v. Ferdinand Nahimana, Jean-Bosco Barayagwiza and Hassan Ngeze (ICTR-99-52-T), Trial Chamber decision 3 December 2003 (*Nahimana TC Judgment*).

The Prosecutor v. Serugendo (ICTR-2005-84-I), Judgment 12 June 2006 (*Serugendo Decision*).

The Prosecutor v. Ferdinand Nahimana, Jean-Bosco Barayagwiza and Hassan Ngeze (ICTR-99-52-A), Appeals judgment of 28 November 2007 (*Nahimana Appeals Judgment*).

The Prosecutor v. Édouard Karemera, Mathieu Ngirumpatse, Joseph Nzidorera (ICTR-97-24), amended Indictment dated 25 August 2005 (*Karemera Indictment*).

The Prosecutor v. Michel Bagaragaza (ICTR0-05-86-S), Trial Chamber Judgment 17 November 2009 (*Bagaragaza TC Decision*).

The Prosecutor v. Édouard Karemera et al. (ICTR-98-44-I), Trial Chamber, 2 February 2012 (*Karemera TC Decision*).

International Criminal Court Documents (Includes Documents Preceding the ICC's Establishment)

Violation of the laws and customs of war: reports of majority and dissenting reports of American and Japanese members of the Commission of Responsibilities, Conference of Paris, 1919, by the Commission on the Responsibility of the Authors of the War and on Enforcement of Penalties, Oxford: Clarendon Press (*1919 WWI Commission Report*).

Draft Statute for an International Criminal Court, International Law Association, Report of the 34th Conference, 1927 (*Draft Statute for an ICC 1927*).

Convention for the Creation of an International Criminal Court, (1938) League of Nations Official Journal Special Supplement 156, 1937 (*Convention for an ICC 1937*).

Report of the Committee on International Criminal Jurisdiction, UN Doc. A/2136 (1952).

Report of the Committee on International Criminal Jurisdiction, UN Doc. A/2645 (1953).

Draft Code of Offences Against the Peace and Security of Mankind 1954, UN Doc. A/2693 (1954) (*Draft Code 1954*).

Draft Code of Offences Against the Peace and Security of Mankind 1996, UN Doc. A/48/10 (1996) (*Draft Code 1996*)

United Nations Diplomatic Conference of Plenipotentiaries on the Establishment of an International Criminal Court, Rome, Italy 15 June–17 July 1998, 1st meeting of the Committee of the Whole, UN Doc. A/CONF.183/C.1/SR.1 (*Committee of the Whole Record*).

United Nations Diplomatic Conference of Plenipotentiaries on the Establishment of an International Criminal Court, UN Doc. A/CONF.183/C.1/L.3, 16 June 1998, Proposal submitted by France: Article 23: Excerpt in Appendix D (*French Corporate Crime Proposal*).

United Nations Diplomatic Conference of Plenipotentiaries on the Establishment of an International Criminal Court, Report of the Working Group on General Principles of Criminal Law, UN Doc A/CONF.183/C.1/WGGP/L.5/Rev.2 (*WGGP Working Paper on Art. 23*).

The Elements of Crimes, Official Records of the Assembly of States Parties to the Rome Statute of the International Criminal Court, First session, New York, 3–10 September 2002 (United Nations publication, Sales No. E.03.V.2 and corrigendum).

ICC Press Release: Communications received by the Office of the Prosecutor of the ICC, ICC-OTP-20030716-27 of 16 July 2003 (*ICC Ituri Communications PR*).

Report of the Prosecutor of the International Criminal Court to Second Assembly of States Parties to the Rome Statute, 8 September 2003 (*Ocampo 2003 report to States Parties*).

ICC Press Release: The Prosecutor on the cooperation with Congo and other States regarding the situation in Ituri, DRC, Office of the Prosecutor, ICC-OTP20030926-37 of 26 September 2003 (*ICC Ituri PR*).

International Criminal Law and Business, speech by ICC Prosecutor Luis Moreno Ocampo, The 2005 Business & Human Rights London Seminar: Exploring Responsibility and Complicity, 8 December 2005, available at: https://www.business-humanrights.org/en/pdf-the-2005-business-human-rights-seminar-report-exploring-responsibility-and-complicity (*Ocampo Complicity Speech 2005*).

The Elements of Crimes (adopted at the 2010 Review Conference), Official Records of the Review Conference of the Rome Statute of the International Criminal Court, Kampala, 31 May–11 June 2010 (International Criminal Court publication, RC/11).

Prosecutor Moreno-Ocampo's Statement, OTP Press Conference on Kenya, 1 April 2010 (*Ocampo Kenya Statement*).

Financial statements for the period 1 January to 31 December 2012, ICC-ASP/12/12 (*ICC Financial Statement 2012*).

International Criminal Court Office of the Prosecutor, Policy paper on case selection and prioritisation (15 September 2016).

International Criminal Court Cases

Prosecutor v. Katanga and Ngudjolo Chui (ICC 01/04-01/07), Pre-Trial Chamber I, Decision on Confirmation of Charges, 30 September 2008 (*Katanga Charges Decision*).

Prosecutor v. Al Bashir, Decision on the Prosecution's Application for a Warrant of Arrest, Unreported 4 March 2009 (*Al-Bashir Arrest Warrant*).

Prosector v. Katanga, ICC Trial Chamber, 17 March 2014 (*Katanga Judgment*).

Prosecutor v. Lubanga (ICC 01/04-01/06), Pre-Trial Chamber I, Decision on Confirmation of Charges, 29 January 2007 (*Lubanga Charges Decision*).

Prosecutor v. Dyilo, Case No. ICC-01-04-01/06, Decision on the confirmation of the charges (29 January 2007).

Prosecutor v William Samoei Ruto and Joshua Arap Sang, Pre-trial Chamber II, Case No. ICC-01/09, Decision Pursuant to Art. 15 of the *Rome Statute* on the Authorization of an Investigation into the Situation in the Republic of Kenya (31 March 2010) (*Kenya Investigation Decision*).

Prosecutor v. William Samoei Ruto, Henry Kiprono Kosgey, Joshua Arap Sang and Prosecutor v. Francis Kirimi Muthaura, Uhuru Muigai Kenyatta And Mohammed Hussein Ali Prosecution's Response to Decision Requesting Clarification and Additional Information, ICC-01/09-16 03-03-2010 5/19 CB PT, 3 March 2010, Excerpt Appendix F (*Ruto Prosecutor Organisation Indicators*).

Prosecutor v. William Samoei Ruto, Henry Kiprono Kosgey, Joshua Arap Sang and Prosecutor v. Francis Kirimi Muthaura, Uhuru Muigai Kenyatta And Mohammed Hussein Ali Application by Kenya, ICC-01/09-01/11-19 31-03-2011 1/30 CB PT (*Kenya Art. 19 Application*).

Prosecutor v. Lubanga (ICC-01/04-01/06-2842) Trial Chamber I, Decision on Art. 74 of the Statute, 4 April 2012 (*Lubanga Decision on Art. 74*).

Special Court for Sierra Leone

Prosecutor v. Charles Ghankay Taylor, also known as Charles Ghankay MacArthur Dapkpana Taylor, Case No. SCSL-03-01-I dated 3 March 2003 (*Taylor 2003 Indictment*).

Prosecutor v. Charles Ghankay Taylor, also known as Dakpannah Charles Ghankay Taylor, also known as Dakpannah Charles Ghankay MacArthur Taylor, Case No. SCSL-03-01-I, Amended indictment dated 17 March 2006 (*Taylor 2006 Indictment*).

Prosecutor v. Charles Taylor, Case No. SCSL-03-01-PT, Prosecution's second amended indictment, dated 29 May 2007 (*Taylor 2007 Indictment*).

Prosecutor v. Sesay, Kallon, Gbao (SCSL-04-15-A), Appeals Chamber Judgment 26 October 2009 (*Sesay Appeals Decision*).

Prosecutor v. Charles Taylor, Case No. SCSL-03-01-T-1283, 26 April 2012 (*Taylor Trial Judgment*).

Special Tribunal for Lebanon

New TV S.A.L. Karma Mohamed Tashin Al Khayat, Case No. STL-14-05/PT/AP/AR126.1, Appeals Panel, Decision of 2 October 2014 on interlocutory appeal concerning personal jurisdiction in contempt proceedings.

Al Jadeed S.A.L./New T.V.S.A.L. Karma Mohamed Tahsin Al Khayat, Case No. STL-14-05/A/AP, Public redacted version of judgment on Appeal 8 March 2016.

Al Jadeed S.A.L./New T.V.S.A.L. Karma Mohamed Tahsin Al Khayat, Case No. STL-14-05/A/AP Public redacted version of judgment on Appeal 8 March 2016, Nosworthy Dissent.

Akhbar Beirut S.A.L. & Mr Al Amin, Case No. STL-14-06/T/CJ Public redacted version of judgment, 16 July 2016.

National Laws, Cases, Documents

United States of America

US Statutes

Alien Tort Statute (28 U.S.C. 1350) (*ATCA/ATS*).

Japanese Imperial Government Disclosure Act (P.L. 106–567).

Nazi War Crimes Disclosure Act (P.L. 105–246).

Transparency in Supply Chains Act (California) (S.B. 657, 2010).

US Cases

People v. Corporation of Albany, XII Wendell 539 (1834).

State v. Morris Essex RR, 23 Zabrinski's NJR 360 (1852).

New York Central & Hudson River Railroad Company v. United States, 212 US 481 (1909).

Beanal v. Freeport-McMoran, Inc., 969 F. Supp. 362, 373, 382–84 (E.D. LA. 1997).

Doe v. Unocal: Doe v. Unocal Corp., 963 F. Supp. 880 (C.D. Cal. 1997).

Roe v. Unocal Corp., 70 F. Supp. 2d 1073 (C.D. Cal 1999).

Titherington v. Japan Energy Corporation, filed 02/24/2000, the Superior Court of California, County of Orange; case no. 00CC02534.

Wiwa v. Royal Dutch Petroleum Co., F.3d, (2d Cir. 2000) (*Wiwa*).

Bowoto, et al. v. Chevron, et al., Case No. C99-2506 (N.D. Cal. 2000).

The Herero People's Reparations Corporation and the Herero v. Deutsche Bank AG et al. (First Amended Complaint, 18 September 2001), available at: http://www.business-humanrights.org/en/german-cos-lawsuit-by-hereros.

In re. Assicurazioni Generali SpA. Holocaust Insurance Litigation, MDL 1374, M21–89 (MBM), Opinion and Order, 25 September 2002.

In re Holocaust Victim Assets Lit., 302 F. Supp. 2d 89 (E.D. N.Y. 2004).

In re Agent Orange Product Liability Litigation 323 F. Supp. 2d 7 (E.D. N.Y. 2005) (No. 04-400).

John Roe I et al. v. Bridgestone Corporation et al. (Complaint), 7 November 2005, available at: http://www.iradvocates.org/bfcase.html (*2005 Firestone Complaint*).

The Presbyterian Church of Sudan, et al. v. Talisman Energy Inc. et al., USDC SDNY 2005 US Dist. 30 August 2005.

Corrie et al. v. Caterpillar Inc., No. 05-36210 (9th Cir. 2007).

In re South African Apartheid Litigation: Ntsebeza et al. v. Daimler et al.; and Khulumani et al. v. Barclays et al, 02 MDL 1499 (SAS) – 03 Civ. 4524 (SAS), 8 Apr 2009 (*Apartheid Litigation Cases*).

Citizens United v. Federal Election Commission, Supreme Court, No. 08-205, 21 January 2010.

Viktor Bout, aka Victor Anatoliyevich Bout, aka Viktor Bulakin, aka Viktor Butt, aka Vadim Markovich Aminov, aka Viktor Budd, aka Viktor But, Petitioner v. United States, Southern District of New York in November 2010.

Kiobel v. Royal Dutch Petroleum Co., No. 10-1491 2010 U.S. App. LEXIS 19382 (2d Cir. 2010) (*Kiobel v. Shell* (*2010*))

Kiobel v. Royal Dutch Petroleum Co., 133 Supreme Court, No. 1659 (2013).

Kiobel v. Royal Dutch Petroleum Co., Brief for the United States as Amicus Curiae Supporting Petitioners, available at: http://www.americanbar.org/content/dam/aba/publications/supreme_court_preview/briefs/10-1491_petitioner_amcu_unitedstates.authcheckdam.pdf.

Cardona, et al. v. Chiquita Brands International, et al., No. 12-14898 (11th Cir. 2014).
Burwell v. Hobby Lobby Stores, Inc., 573 US __ (2014).
Republic of Ecuador v. Chevron Corp., 2016 BL 179029, U.S., No. 15-1088, *cert. denied*, 6 June 2016.
Joseph Jesner et al. v. Arab Bank PLC, On Petition for a Writ of Certiorari to the United States Court of Appeals for the Second Circuit, No. 16-499, *granted* 3 April 2017.
Viktor Bout, aka Victor Anatoliyevich Bout, aka Viktor Bulakin, aka Viktor Butt, aka Vadim Markovich Aminov, aka Viktor Budd, aka Viktor But, Petitioner v. United States, Supreme Court, No. 16-1024, *cert. denied*, 3 April 2017.

US Government Documents

Special Committee on Un-American Activities, Investigation of Nazi Propaganda Activities and Investigation of Certain Other Propaganda Activities, 73rd Congress, 1934.
IG Farben: US Congress, Senate, Committee on Military Affairs, Cartel Practices and National Security, Hearings Before a Subcommittee of the Committee on Military Affairs, 78th Cong., 2nd Sess., 1944 (*Bernstein IG Farben Report*).
Elimination of German Resources for War: Hearing on S. Res. 107 and S. Res. 146 Before a Subcomm. of the Senate Comm. on Military Affairs, 79th Cong. 941–42 (1945) (*Kilgore Report*).
Restatement of Policy on Germany, Speech by James F. Byrnes, the United States Secretary of State, held in Stuttgart on 6 September 1946, US Department of State. Documents on Germany 1944–1985. Washington, DC: Department of State, [s.d.], pp. 91–9.
Report to the President by Mr Justice Jackson, United States Representative to the International Conference on Military Trials, June 6, 1945, published as Section VIII (p. 42) of the record of negotiations at the London Conference of June 26 to August 8, 1945, in Department of State Publication 3080, International Organization and Conference Series II, U.S. Government Printing Office, Released February 1949 (*Jackson Negotiations Report*).
Memo: A. Pomerantz, Feasibility and Propriety of Indicting I.G. Farben and Krupp as Corporate Entities, 27 August 1946, Gant Papers, Box EE (*Pomerantz Memo*).
Report to the President by Mr Justice Jackson, October 7, 1946, published as document LXIII of *Jackson Negotiations Report*, available at: http://www.loc.gov/rr/frd/Military_Law/pdf/jackson-rpt-military-trials.pdf (*Jackson Final Report*).
Edwards, Corwin D., Report of the Mission on Japanese Combines, Washington, DC: Departments of State and War, 1946.
Vernon, R. and C. Wachenheimer 1947, 'Dissolution of Japan's Feudal Combines', *The Department of State Bulletin*, 17(419), 13 July (*Vernon and Wachenheimer DSB 1947*).
Final Report to the Secretary of the Army on the Nuernberg War Crimes Trials under Control Council Law No. 10, Telford Taylor, et al., (1949) (*Taylor Final Report*).

Appendix B to *Taylor Final Report*: Nuremberg Trials: War Crimes and International Law, 27 International Conciliation 1 April 1949, No. 450 (*Taylor IC*).

Negotiation Record: Department of State Publication 3080, International Organization and Conference Series II, European and British Commonwealth 1, Released February 1949.

Eisenhower farewell address, 17 January 1961, Press release containing the text of the address (DDE's Papers as President, Speech Series, Box 38, Final TV Talk (1)), Eisenhower Archives online documents, available at: http://www.eisenhower.archives.gov/research/online_documents/farewell_address.html.

Drea, E. et al. 2006, *Researching Japanese War Crimes: Introductory Essays*, Washington, DC: GPO, 14.

Nazi War Crimes and Japanese Imperial Government Records Interagency Working Group, Final Report to the United States Congress, Published April 2007, Report available at: http://www.archives.gov/press/press-releases/2007/nr07-143.html (*2007 IWG Report*).

United States Department of Justice Press Release, 'International Arms Dealer Viktor Bout Convicted in New York of Terrorism Crimes: Bout Convicted on All Four Counts, Including Conspiring to Kill Americans and Conspiring to Provide Material Support to Terrorists', Wednesday, 2 November 2011, available at: https://www.justice.gov/opa/pr/international-arms-dealer-viktor-bout-convicted-new-york-terrorism-crimes.

Rewards for Justice Website, U.S. Department of State's Counter-Terrorism Rewards Program, available at: https://rewardsforjustice.net/english/.

Union of Socialist Soviet Republics

Soviet Government Documents

Soviet representative Viacheslav Molotov statement in Paris 10 July 1946. Published in English in, The Department of State, Occupation of Germany, Policy and Progress 1945–46, European Series 23, Washington, DC: US Government Printing Office, August 1947, pp. 237–41.

United Kingdom

English/British Statutes

Statute of Westminster I: 1275, 3 Edw. ch. 15.

The Royal Exchange and London Assurance Corporation Act 1719, 6 Geo.1 c.18 (Bubble Act)

The Regulating Act for India 1773, 13 Geo. 3 c. 63 (*Regulating Act*).

Joint Stock Companies Act 1844, 7 & 8 Vict, c.110.

Limited Liability Act 1855, 18 & 19 Vict. c.47.

Companies Act 1856, 19 & 20 Vict. c.47.

Companies Act 1862, 25 & 26 Vict. c.89.
Limited Liability Partnerships Act 2000, c.12.
Companies Act 2006 c.46.
Corporate Manslaughter and Corporate Homicide Act 2007 c.19 (Excerpt in Appendix F).

British Cases

Case of Sutton's Hospital [1612] 77 Eng Rep 960, 973.
Case of the Right Honorable John Aislabie, Esq. ([London]: Printed for J. Roberts, near the Oxford-Arms in Warwick-Lane [1721]).
Birmingham and Gloucester Rly Co [1842] *3 QB 223.*
Edwards v. Midland Railway Company (1880) 6 QBD 281.
Hallett v. Dowdall [1852] Exchequer Chambers 18 QB2.
Hutton v. West Cork Railway Co (1883) 23 Ch D 654.
Salomon v. A. Salomon and Co. Ltd [1897] AC 22.
Mousell Bros Ltd v. London and North-Western Rly Co [1917] 2 KB 836.
In re Southern Rhodesia [1919] AC 211.
In re Piracy Jure Gentium [1934] AC 586.
Rex v. ICR Haulage [1944] 1 KB 551.
DPP v. Kent and Sussex Contractors [1944] 1 KB 146.
HL Bolton (Engineering) Co Ltd v. T.J. Graham & Sons Ltd [1957] 1 QB 159.
Parke v. Daily News Ltd. [1962] (Ch. D. 1962) Ch. 927.
Adams v. Cape Industries plc [1990] BCLC 479 520.
R v. P&O Ferries (Dover) Ltd [1991] 93 Cr App Rep 72.
Lubbe et al. v. Cape [2000] UKHL 41.
AAA & Ors v Unilever Plc & Anor [2017] EWHC 371.

British Government Documents

Royal Warrant, 14 June 1945, Army Order 81/45, with amendments, UNWCC Note on *Zyklon B Case.*
Company Law Review Steering Group (2000) 'Modern Company Law for a Competitive Economy: Developing the Framework' (URN 00/656), London: Department for Trade and Industry.
UK Foreign & Commonwealth Office 2013, 'Good Business: Implementing the UN Guiding Principles on Business & Human Rights', 4 September, available at: https://www.gov.uk/government/uploads/system/uploads/attachment_data/file/236901/BHR_Action_Plan_-_final_online_version_1_.pdf (*UK BHR Action Plan*).
Haldane, A. (Chief Economist, Bank of England), 'Who Owns a Company?', speech given at the University of Edinburgh Corporate Finance Conference on Friday 22 May 2015, available at: http://www.bankofengland.co.uk/speech/2015/who-owns-a-company.

Australia

Australian Statutes

The Criminal Code Act 1995, Act No. 12 of 1995.

India

Indian Cases

Bhopal Indian Criminal Case: State of Madhya Pradesh through CBI v. Warren Anderson et al., Judgment, Court of Chief Judicial Magistrate Bhopal, Cr. Case No. 8460 / 1996, Date of Institution 01.12.1987, Judgment of 7 June 2010, available at http://www.countercurrents.org/UCIL.pdf.

The Netherlands

Dutch Statutes

Dutch Constitution: Grondwet voor het Koninkrijk der Nederlanden van 24 augustus 1815, available at: https://wetten.overheid.nl/BWBR0001840/2008-07-15.

Dutch Documents

Office of the Public Prosecutor International Crimes prosecution information, available at: https://www.om.nl/onderwerpen/international-crimes-0/.

Dutch Cases

Van Anraat 2005 Decision: Van Anraat, Rechtbank 's-Gravenhage, Judgment of 23 December 2005, Case No. 09/751003-04.

Kouwenhoven 2006 Judgment: Judgment in the case against Guus K., District Court of The Hague, 7 June 2006, Case No. 09/750001-05.

Kouwenhoven Interim Judgment: Interim Judgment in the Kouwenhoven case, 19 March 2007, District Court of the Hague, Case No. 09-750001-05.

Van Anraat Appeal Decision: *Van Anraat*, Court of Appeal The Hague, 9 May 2007, Case No. 2200050906-2.

Kouwenhoven Acquittal: Judgment in the case against Guus K., District Court of the Hague, 10 March 2008, Case No. 220043306.

Van Anraat Supreme Court Decision: Van Anraat, Dutch Supreme Court, 30 June 2009, Case No. 07/10742.

Kouwenhoven Supreme Court Judgment: Kouwenhoven, LJN: BK8132, Hoge Raad, Supreme Court Judgment 20 April 2010, Case no. 08/01322.

Trafigura Appeal Court Decision: Trafigura, LJN: BU9237, Gerechtshof Amsterdam, 23 December 2011, Case No. 23-003334-10.

Kouwenhoven Retrial Judgment 2017: Case K. Court of Appeal 's-Hertogenbosch, 21 April 2017, Case No. 20-001906-10 ECLI:NL:GHSHE:2017:1760.

France

French Cases

L'Association France Palestine Solidarité (AFPS) *v. Alstom and Veolia Transport*, Tribunal de Grande Instance de Nanterre, March 2007, available at: http://www.france-palestine.org/article5863.html?var_recherche=veolia. (*AFPS v. Alstom*).

L'association Sherpa et al. contre la société DLH France et al., Plainte, Tribunal de Grande Instance de Nantes, 2009; Press release available at: http://www.asso-sherpa.org/nos-programmes/gdh/campagne-rec/dlh (*DLH Complaint*).

Israel

Israeli Cases

The Attorney General v. Adolf Eichmann, Jerusalem District Court, Criminal Case 40/61, Judgment, 36 ILR 5–14, 18–276, 12 December 1961.

Canada

Canadian Cases

Bil'in (Village Council) v. Green Park and Green Mount, QCCS 2011, 2 May 2011.

South Africa

South African Documents

Truth and Reconciliation Commission Business Sector Hearings: Volume 4, 18ff., available at: http://www.justice.gov.za/trc/special/index.htm#bh (*TRC Business Sector Hearings*).

Truth and Reconciliation Commission Final Report (1998), available at: http://www.justice.gov.za/trc/report/index.htm (*TRC Final Report*).

Liberia

Liberian Documents

Liberia Truth and Reconciliation Commission, '19 companies identified for further investigation': https://web.archive.org/web/20170415020206/http://trcofliberia.org/press_releases/41.

Japan

Japanese Documents

Japanese National Diet Library, Records of SWNCC, Records of the Subcommittee for the Far East (*Records of SWNCC*).

Japanese Acceptance of Surrender, ICC Legal Tools Database, available at: http://www.legal-tools.org/en/go-to-database/record//ltdetails/21729/535bf15abcd9b52b37548ed31f891e46993424c75225e7206f5f5c48d09dbc68/ (*Japanese Acceptance of Surrender*).

News Media and NGO Reports, Films, Lectures and Miscellaneous

News Media

AfricLaw 2016, 28 October, 'South Africa's Intention to Withdraw from the Rome Statute of the International Criminal Court: Time to Seriously Consider an African Alternative?', available at: https://africlaw.com/2016/10/28/south-africas-intention-to-withdraw-from-the-rome-statute-of-the-international-criminal-court-time-to-seriously-consider-an-african-alternative/#more-1238

African Press International 2008, 8 May, 'Kabuga arrived in Norway on the 23rd of March this year after crossing the Swedish/Norway border in Svinesund by car', available at: https://africanpress.wordpress.com/2008/05/08/kabuga-arrived-in-norway-on-the-23rd-of-march-this-year-after-crossing-the-swedishnorway-border-in-svinesund-by-car/?iframe=true&theme_preview=true/amp/.

Al-Jazeera 2010, 17 March, 'US used "plague bomb" in Korea war', available at: http://english.aljazeera.net/news/asia-pacific/2010/03/2010317341226367o.html.

All Africa 2011, 14 February, 'Rwanda Approves Takeover of Gisovu', available at: http://allafrica.com/stories/201102140796.html.

Australian Broadcasting Corporation 2005, list of articles on the subject, available at: http://www.abc.net.au/4corners/content/2005/s1408730.htm.

BBC 2015, 10 December, 'Volkswagen: The Scandal Explained', available at: http://www.bbc.co.uk/news/business-34324772.

BBC *News* 2000, 23 February, 'POWs Fight Japan in US Court', available at: http://news.bbc.co.uk/2/hi/uk_news/652633.stm.

BBC *News* 2005, 29 June, 'Rwandans Sentenced for Genocide', available at: http://news.bbc.co.uk/2/hi/africa/4635637.stm.

BBC *News* 2010, 20 May, 'Naomi Campbell May be Subpoenaed to Appear as a Witness at Taylor Trial for Receiving Blood Diamonds', available at: http://news.bbc.co.uk/1/hi/world/europe/10133754.stm.

BBC *News* 2010, 7 June, 'Bhopal Gas Leak Convictions Not Enough, Say Campaigners', available at: http://www.bbc.co.uk/news/10260109.

BBC *News* 2011, 21 December, 'Rwanda Genocide: Ngirumpatse and Karemera Given Life', available at: http://www.bbc.co.uk/news/world-africa-16287169.

BBC *News* 2017, 8 July, 'Pride in London: Why businesses are backing Pride', available at https://www.bbc.co.uk/news/uk-40517036.

Daily Nation 2010, 10 February, 'Kabuga in Kenya, claims US envoy', available at: http://www.nation.co.ke/News/-/1056/859834/-/vq2lsl/-/index.html.

Development Afrique 2009, 10 November, 'Rwanda replaces genocide with economic ambition', available at: http://developmentafrique.com/?tag=starbucks (last accessed 2015).

Financial Times 2015, 24 September, 'Shell, BHP and GE to Advise Governments on Climate Change', available at: http://www.ft.com/cms/s/0/ebd4ae20-62bd-11e5-a28b-50226830d644.html#axzz3mfaCBZv8.

Financial Times 2016, 11 August, The Business of Gay Pride, https://www.ft.com/content/228207c6-5f46-11e6-ae3f-77baadeb1c93.

Foreign Policy 2017, 21 February, 'Saving the World, One Meaningless Buzzword at a Time: How Corporations, Activists, and Politicians Turned the Language of Human Rights into Meaningless Babble', available at: http://foreignpolicy.com/2017/02/21/saving-the-world-one-meaningless-buzzword-at-a-time-human-rights.

Fox News 2017, 17 May, *Tucker Carlson Tonight*, 'Blackwater Founder: Ironically 'The Left Loved The USSR' 30 Years Ago', available at: http://insider.foxnews.com/2017/05/17/blackwater-erik-prince-democrats-loved-russia-during-cold-war.

France 24 2010, 12 May, 'ICC to Prosecute six Kenyans over Poll Chaos', available at: http://www.france24.com/en/20100512-six-kenyans-prosecuted-over-poll-chaos-international-criminal-court-mwai-kibaki-moreno-ocampo.

The Guardian 2010, 8 December, 'WikiLeaks Cables: Shell's Grip on Nigerian State Revealed', available at: http://www.guardian.co.uk/business/2010/dec/08/wikileaks-cables-shell-nigeria-spying.

The Guardian 2011, 26 May, 'Ratko Mladic Arrested: What it Means for Serbia's EU Membership', available at: https://www.theguardian.com/world/2011/may/26/ratko-mladic-serbia-eu-membership.

The Guardian 2011, 16 August, 'Facebook Riot Calls Earn Men Four-Year Jail Terms amid Sentencing Outcry', available at: https://www.theguardian.com/uk/2011/aug/16/facebook-riot-calls-men-jailed.

The Guardian 2014, 2 July, 'NHS cancer care could switch to private contracts in £700m plans', available at: https://www.theguardian.com/uk-news/2014/jul/02/cancer-care-nhs-outsourcing-ccgs-unison-virgin.

The Guardian 2016, 27 October, 'African Revolt Threatens ICC's Legitimacy', available at: https://www.theguardian.com/law/2016/oct/27/african-revolt-international-criminal-court-gambia.

The Guardian 2016, 16 November, 'Russian Withdraws Signature from International Criminal Court Statute', available at: https://www.theguardian.com/world/2016/nov/16/russia-withdraws-signature-from-international-criminal-court-statute.

The Guardian 2016, 8 December, 'Revealed: Rio Tinto's Plan to Use Drones to Monitor Workers' Private Lives', available at: https://www.theguardian.com/world/2016/dec/08/revealedrio-tinto-surveillance-station-plans-to-use-drones-to-monitors-staffs-private-lives.

Ha'aretz 2008, 28 November, 'Of Little People and Landmark Decisions', available at: http://www.acri.org.il/en/2008/12/17/of-little-people-and-landmark-decisions/.

Huffington Post 2017, 30 January, 'This Danish TV Ad is What the World Needs to Remember Now More Than Ever', available at: https://www.huffingtonpost.ca/2017/01/30/danish-tv-ad-all-that-we-share_n_14504328.html.

Intercepted podcast 2017, 31 May, 'There's Something about Jared', available at: https://theintercept.com/2017/05/31/intercepted-podcast-theres-something-about-jared/.

The Independent 2015, 18 May, 'Command and Control Contract for Britain's Armed Nuclear Police Outsourced to Capita', available at: http://www.independent.co.uk/news/uk/politics/command-and-control-contract-for-britains-armed-nuclear-police-outsourced-to-capita-10258611.html.

The Independent 2017, 4 June, 'Why I Won't be Marking Myself as "Safe" on Facebook Today', available at: http://www.independent.co.uk/voices/facebook-safety-check-london-bridge-terror-attack-a7772211.html.

Jurist 2011, 13 April, 'Spanish Court Turns Torture Investigation over to US', available at: http://jurist.org/paperchase/2011/04/spain-court-turns-over-guantanamo-torture-investigation-to-US.php.

Mail & Guardian 2017, 8 March, 'South Africa Revokes ICC Withdrawal', available at: https://mg.co.za/article/2017-03-08-south-africa-revokes-icc-withdrawal.

Medium, The DiDi Delgado 2017, 28 April, 'The Heineken Ad is Worse Than the Pepsi Ad, You're Just Too Stupid to Know It', available at: https://medium.com/@thedididelgado/the-heineken-ad-is-worse-than-the-pepsi-ad-youre-just-too-stupid-to-know-it-5580e7c40cb1.

The Nation 1951, 24 February, 'The Nazis Go Free: Justice and Mercy or Misguided Expediency?', 172(8).

The Nation 2009, 4 August, 'Blackwater Founder Implicated in Murder', available at: http://www.thenation.com/article/blackwater-founder-implicated-murder.

The Nation 2010, 15 September, 'Blackwater's Black Ops', available at: http://www.thenation.com/article/blackwaters-black-ops/.

Neue Zürcher Zeitung 2017, 17 January, 'Die Täter hinter den Tätern', available at: https://www.nzz.ch/feuilleton/schreibtischtaeter-die-taeter-hinter-den-taetern-ld.140108.

New Scientist 2016, 7 December, 'The Road to Hell is Paved with Corporate Wellness', available at: https://www.newscientist.com/article/mg23231031-700-the-road-to-hell-is-paved-with-corporate-wellness/.

New York Times 2014, 1 April, 'Terror Suit Against Jordanian Bank Tests US Diplomacy and Secrecy Laws', available at: https://www.nytimes.com/2014/04/02/us/terror-suit-against-jordanian-bank-tests-us-diplomacy-and-secrecy-laws.html?_r=0.

New York Times 2016, 29 December, Norimitsu Onishi, 'Germany Grapples with Its African Genocide', New York Times, available at: https://www.nytimes.com/2016/12/29/world/africa/germany-genocide-namibia-holocaust.html?ref=world&_r=0

New York Times 2017, 5 April, 'Pepsi Pulls Ad Accused of Trivializing Black Lives Matter', available at: https://www.nytimes.com/2017/04/05/business/kendall-jenner-pepsi-ad.html.

Open Democracy 2009, 25 February, 'Lawfare in Gaza: Legislative Attack', available at: http://www.opendemocracy.net/article/legislative-attack.

Het Parool 2010, 1 July, 'Boek Karskens over van Anraat verfilmd', available at: http://www.parool.nl/parool/nl/21/FILM/article/detail/303275/2010/07/01/Boek-Karskens-over-Van-Anraat-verfilmd.dhtml.

PinkNews 2016, 5 October, 'One Million Moms Attack "Transgender" H&M Model ... But She's Not Actually Trans', available at: http://www.pinknews.co.uk/2016/10/05/one-million-moms-attack-transgender-hm-model-but-shes-just-a-butch-woman/.

Salon 2017, 3 June, 'Erik Prince's Dark Plan for Afghanistan: Military Occupation for Profit, Not Security', available at: http://www.salon.com/2017/06/03/erik-princes-dark-plan-for-afghanistan-military-occupation-for-profit-not-security/.

Der Spiegel 1993, 4 October, 'Protokolle des Todes, Verhörprotokolle der Auschwitz-Ingenieure Prüfer, Sander und Schultze', available at: http://www.spiegel.de/spiegel/print/d-13679718.html and http://www.spiegel.de/spiegel/print/d-13679727.html.

The Telegraph 2013, 29 April, 'Bangladesh building collapse death toll approaches 1,300', available at https://www.telegraph.co.uk/news/worldnews/asia/bangladesh/10026421/Bangladesh-building-collapse-death-toll-approaches-1300.html.

The Telegraph 2017, 6 September, 'Facebook "Could Have Prevented Lee Rigby Murder"', available at: http://www.telegraph.co.uk/news/uknews/terrorism-in-the-uk/11253518/Facebook-could-have-prevented-Lee-Rigby-murder.html.

Time 1947, 28 July, 'Conferences: Pas de Pagaille', available at: http://www.time.com/time/magazine/article/0,9171,887417,00.html.

Time 2013, 15 February, 'Viewpoint: Why was the Biggest Protest in World History Ignored?', available at: http://world.time.com/2013/02/15/viewpoint-why-was-the-biggest-protest-in-world-history-ignored/.

VOANEWS 2015, 12 November, 'Ivory Coast Toxic Waste Victims Still Await Payments', available at: http://www.voanews.com/content/ivory-coast-toxic-waste-victims-still-await-payments/3056111.html.

Time Out 2016, 31 March, 'Ben & Jerry's are Giving Away FREE Ice Cream to Encourage Londoners to Vote', available at: http://www.timeout.com/london/blog/ben-jerrys-are-giving-away-free-ice-cream-to-encourage-londoners-to-vote-033116?cid=GB_LON~NL~1400851511~~Title~.

The Verge 2016, 12 October, 'Facebook Still has a Nipple Problem', available at: https://www.theverge.com/2016/10/12/13241486/facebook-censorship-breast-cancer-nipple-mammogram.

Volkskrant 2009, 24 August, 'Trafigura moet rapport geheimhouden', available at: http://www.volkskrant.nl/nieuws-achtergrond/trafigura-om-moet-rapport-geheimhouden~bd139716/.

Volkskrant 2017, 29 June, 'Nigeriaanse Weduwen klagen Shell aan wegens executies', available at: http://www.volkskrant.nl/4503351.

Vrij Nederland 2007, 31 March, 'Dit is an absolute nachtmerrie', 77.

Washington Post 1951, 1 February, 'US Saves 21 Convicted Nazi War Criminals from Gallows, Confirms 7 Death Sentences',

NGO *Reports, Press Releases and Other Documents*

Africa Legal Aid (AFLA)

- The Cairo-Arusha Principles on Universal Jurisdiction in Respect of Gross Human Rights Offences: An African Perspective, 18–20 October 2002, available at https://www.africalegalaid.com/download/policy_document/Policy_Document.pdf

Amnesty International

- 'Demand Dignity: Close the Accountability Gap: Corporations, Human Rights and Poverty', 2009, available at: http://www.amnesty.org/en/library/info/ACT35/006/2009/en.

Association France Palestine Solidarite

- 'Communiqué sur l'action de l'AFPS concernant le tramway en Palestine', 19 March 2007, available at http://www.france-palestine.org/Communique-sur-l-action-de-l-AFPS.

Business Leaders' Human Rights Forum

- BLIHR 2005, 8–9 December, Business Leaders' Initiative on Human Rights Seminar, London.

Business & Human Rights Resource Centre

- Business & Human Rights Legal Accountability Portal: https://www.business-humanrights.org/en/corporate-legal-accountability
- n.d., 'Trafigura Lawsuits (Re Côte d' Ivoire)', available at: http://business-humanrights.org/en/trafigura-lawsuits-re-côte-d'ivoire.
- *Weekly Update* 2015, 18 November, available at: http://us3.campaign-archive1.com/?u=bdd1a6a40fffad39c8719632f&id=0b6eb798e4&e=b59c4119fa
- Corporate Legal Accountability Annual Briefing: 'Corporate Impunity is common and remedy for victims is rare', April 2017, available at: https://business-humanrights.org/en/corporate-legal-accountability-annual-briefing.

Center for Constitutional Rights-New York

- CCR Wiwa docket n.d., Centre for Constitutional Rights Wiwa docket, available at: http://ccrjustice.org/ourcases/current-cases/wiwa-v.-royal-dutch-petroleum,

Chevron Toxico

- Chevron Texaco ICC Complaint, available at: http://chevrontoxico.com/assets/docs/2014-icc-complaint.pdf.

Centre for Conflict Resolution

- Submission to the Truth and Reconciliation Commission: Business Sector Hearing, Laurie Nathan, Peter Batchelor and Guy Lamb, Centre for Conflict Resolution, University of Cape Town, South Africa, October 1997, available at: http://ccrweb.ccr.uct.ac.za/archive/staff_papers/guy_trc.html.

Core Coalition
- 'The Bottom Line: UK Corporate Abuse Abroad', October 2015, available at: http://corporate-responsibility.org/wp-content/uploads/2015/10/The-Bottom-Line-report_final-digital-version.pdf.
- 'UK Publishes Updated Business and Human Rights Action Plan', 12 May 2016, available at https://corporate-responsibility.org/uk-publishes-updated-business-and-human-rights-action-plan/.

Earth Rights International
- 'Supreme Court Allows US Corporation to Finance Terrorism Without Accountability', Press Release, 20 April 2015, available at: http://www.earthrights.org/media/supreme-court-allows-us-corporation-finance-terrorism-without-accountability.

European Centre for Constitutional and Human Rights
- 'Gespräch mit Peter Weiss' (Weiss interview), conducted by Kamil Majchrzak, 12 October, Berlin, published in European Centre for Constitutional and Human Rights 2008, Conference on Transnational Enterprises and Human Rights, Berlin, October, Report, 22–32, available at: https://www.scribd.com/document/82979434/ECCHR-TNC-Conference-Report

European Coalition for Corporate Justice
- 'France adopts corporate duty of vigilance law: a first historic step towards better human rights and environmental protection', 21 February 2017, available at: http://corporatejustice.org/news/393-france-adopts-corporate-duty-of-vigilance-law-a-first-historic-step-towards-better-human-rights-and-environmental-protection.

Fafo
- 'Business and International Crimes: Assessing the Liability of Business Entities for Grave Violations of International Law', by A. Ramasastry for Fafo & International Peace Academy 2004, available at: http://www.ipacademy.org/media/pdf/publications/businessand_intcrime.pdf.
- 'Commerce, Crime and Conflict: Legal Remedies for Private Sector Liability for Grave Breaches of International Law', by A. Ramasastry and R. Thompson for FAFO Institute of Applied International Studies 2006, available at: http://www.fafo.no/pub/rapp/536/536.pdf.

FIDH *(International Federation for Human Rights)*
- 'The contribution of Chiquita corporate officials to crimes against humanity in Colombia Article 15 Communication to the International Criminal Court', May 2017, available at: https://www.fidh.org/IMG/pdf/rapport_chiquita.pdf.
- Cambodia: ICC preliminary examination requested into crimes stemming from mass land grabbing, 7 October 2014, available at https://www.fidh.org/en/region/asia/cambodia/16176-cambodia-icc-preliminary-examination-requested-into-crimes-stemming-from

Global Justice Now
- 'What is Food Sovereignty?' available at https://www.globaljustice.org.uk/what-food-sovereignty.

Global Legal Action Network
- Communiqué to the Office of the Prosecutor of the International Criminal Court Under Article 15 of the Rome Statute, on The Situation in Nauru and Manus Island: Liability for crimes against humanity in the detention of refugees and asylum seekers, by Global Legal Action Network 2017, available at: http://www.glanlaw.org/single-post/2017/02/13/Communication-made-to-International-Criminal-Court-requesting-investigation-of-Australia-and-corporate-contractors.

Global Movement for a Binding Treaty
- Statement (n.d.), available at http://www.treatymovement.com/statement

Global Witness
- 'The Usual Suspects: Liberia's Weapons and Mercenaries in Côte d'Ivoire and Sierra Leone, Why It's Still Possible, How It Works and How to Break the Trend', Global Witness Report, 31 March 2003, available at https://reliefweb.int/report/liberia/usual-suspects-liberias-weapons-and-mercenaries-c%C3%B4te-divoire-and-sierra-leone
- 'Complaint Accuses International Timber Company DLH of Trading Illegal Timber and Funding Liberian War', Press Release, 12 March, 2014 available at: https://www.globalwitness.org/archive/complaint-accuses-international-timber-company-dlh-trading-illegal-timber-and-funding-0/.

Global Witness, RAID, ACIDH, and ASADHO
- Global Witness, RAID Press Release, 7 April, 2008 'Human Rights Defenders Prevented from Meeting Victims of the Kilwa Massacre', available at: https://www.globalwitness.org/en/archive/human-rights-defenders-prevented-meeting-victims-kilwa-massacre/

Global Witness and Sherpa
- Global Witness and Sherpa Report, 'Bankrolling Brutality: Why European Timber Company DLH Should Be Held to Account for Profiting from Liberian Conflict Timber', 2009, available at: http://www.globalwitness.org/library/bankrolling-brutality-why-european-timber-company-dlh-should-be-held-account-profiting.

Human Rights Watch
- 'Arming Rwanda: The Arms Trade and Human Rights Abuses in the Rwandan War', Vol. 6 Issue 1, January 1994, available at https://www.hrw.org/sites/default/files/reports/RWANDA941.PDF (*HRW Arming Rwanda Report*).
- 'Rearming with Impunity: International Support for the Perpetrators of the Rwandan Genocide', 1995, available at https://www.hrw.org/report/1995/05/01/rearming-impunity/international-support-perpetrators-rwandan-genocide (*HRW Rearming Rwanda Report*)

– 'Weapons and War Crimes: The Complicity of Arms Suppliers', Misol, L.: Human Rights Watch World Report 2004, available at: http://hrw.org/wr2k4/13.htm.
– 'Courting History: The Landmark International Criminal Court's First Years', 2008, available at https://www.hrw.org/report/2008/07/11/courting-history/landmark-international-criminal-courts-first-years.
– 'Fugitives take notice: Justice can be done', May 15, 2012 https://www.hrw.org/news/2012/05/15/africa-fugitives-take-note-justice-can-be-done.
– 'Kenya Deputy President's Case Ends Witness Interference Undermined Trial', 5 April 2016, available at: https://www.hrw.org/news/2016/04/05/icc-kenya-deputy-presidents-case-ends (*Human Rights Watch, ICC*).

International Crisis Group
– 'International Criminal Tribunal for Rwanda: Delayed Justice', ICG Africa Report No. 30, 7 June 2001.

International Commission of Jurists
– 'Criminal Law and International Crimes', International Commission of Jurists (ICJ) Expert Legal Panel on Corporate Complicity in International Crimes, Corporate Complicity & Legal Accountability, Vol. 2, 2008 (*ICJurists Complicity Report 2008*).
– 'Proposals for Elements of a Legally Binding Instrument on Transnational Corporations and Other Business Enterprises', ICJ Submission to the OEIWG, October 2016, available at: https://www.icj.org/wp-content/uploads/2016/10/Universal-OEWG-session-2-ICJ-submission-Advocacy-Analysis-brief-2016-ENG.pdf (*ICJ Proposals for Elements 2016*).

New Economics Foundation
– 'People Powered Money: Designing, developing and delivering community currencies' 2015, 18 May, available at: https://neweconomics.org/2015/05/people-powered-money/.

Oxfam
– Oxfam International Briefing, 'Land and Power: The Growing Scandal Surrounding the New Wave of Investments in Land', September 2011, available at: http://corporate-responsibility.org/about-core/history/.

Project on International Courts and Tribunals
– 'The Financing of the International Criminal Court: A Discussion Paper', n.d., available at: http://www.pict-pcti.org/publications/ICC_paprs/FinancingICC.pdf

Rights and Accountability in Development
– 'African Commission: Landmark $2.5 Million Award to DR Congo Massacre Victims', 4 August 2017, available at: http://www.raid-uk.org/blog/african-commission-landmark-2-5-million-award-dr-congo-massacre-victims.

Stop Corporate Impunity
– 'The International Peoples Treaty on the Control of Transnational Corporations',

2014, available at: http://www.stopcorporateimpunity.org/wp-content/uploads/2016/11/PeoplesTreaty-EN-mar2015-1.pdf.

Traidcraft

– 'Above the Law: Time to hold irresponsible companies to account', 27 November 2015, available at: http://www.traidcraft.co.uk/media.ashx/above-the-law-nov-15-final.pdf.

Transnational Institute

– 'The State of Power, 2016: Democracy, Sovereignty and Resistance', available at: https://www.tni.org/files/publication-downloads/state-of-power-2016.pdf.

War on Want

– 'What is TTIP?', n.d. http://www.waronwant.org/what-ttip

Lectures, Symposia

Del Ponte, C. 2005, 'The Dividends of International Criminal Justice', Goldman Sachs, London, 6 October, available at: http://www.icty.org/x/file/Press/PR_attachments/cdp-goldmansachs-050610-e.htm.

Luban, D. 2007, 'The Poisoned Chalice: Humanity at Nuremberg and Now', at Stanford University, 31 March, available at: iTunes U, under 'Luban (2007) Lecture'.

Harvey, D. 2010, Berkeley, 22 October, http://davidharvey.org/.

Austin, K. 2010, 'Corporate Involvement in Resource Wars', Presentation at the Conference on Corporate War Crimes: Prosecuting Pillage of Natural Resources, 29–30 October, The Hague, available at: http://www.pillageconference.org/speakers/.

'Transnational Business and International Criminal Law', symposium held at Humboldt University (Berlin 15–16 May 2010), proceedings published in *Journal of International Criminal Justice*, 9(1) 2011 (*Humboldt Symposium*).

Orzeck, R. 2012, 'International Criminal Trials as Bourgeois Theater', paper presented at the Workshop New Marxist Writing in International Law, 3 November, City, University of London.

Brown, W. 2015, 'When Firms Become Persons and Persons Become Firms: Neoliberal Jurisprudence in Burwell v. Hobby Lobby Stores', LSE Public Law Lecture, London School of Economics, 1 July.

Films; Documentaries

Judgment at Nuremberg, see: http://www.imdb.com/title/tt0055031/.

Nuremberg: Its Lessons for Today, see: http://www.nurembergfilm.org/.

Rat der Götter, see: http://www.imdb.com/title/tt0042877/.

Schindler's List, see: http://www.imdb.com/title/tt0108052/.

Al Jazeera International, 2009, 'People & Power' documentary: 'Chiquita: Between Life and Law', in *Corporations on Trial*, a special series, available at: http://english

.aljazeera.net/programmes/peopleandpower/2009/05/200951912718478492.html (*Chiquita Documentary 2009*).

Mark Thomas, 2006, 'Mark Thomas' After School Arms Club', Channel 4 'Dispatches', available at: http://www.markthomasinfo.com/section_writing/default.asp?id=5.

ABC, Four Corners (Kilwa documentary), 2005 transcript available at: http://www.abc.net.au/4corners/content/2005/s1386467.htm.

Miscellaneous

Woodland Trust (n.d.), Aislabie walk leaflet, available at: http://www.woodlandtrust.org.uk/mediafile/100048013/aislabie-walk-leaflet.pdf.

Coca-Cola (n.d.), 'Is it true that Santa traditionally wears red because of Coca-Cola?', available at: https://www.coca-colaanswers.co.uk/en/qtile.html/rumours/is-it-true-that-santa-traditionally-wear-red-because-of-coca-coal/.

London Stock Exchange, Our History (n.d.), http://www.londonstockexchange.com/about-the-exchange/company-overview/our-history/our-history.htm [website no longer available].

South Sea Company Harvard Business School Project: http://www.library.hbs.edu/hc/ssb/index.html

The Internationale, original text by Pottier, E. (n.d. 1890–1900), Chants Révolutionnaires. Paris, Comité Pottier, translated for Marxists.org by Mitchell Abodor, available at http://www.marxists.org/history/ussr/sounds/lyrics/international.htm (*The Internationale*).

'The suppression of the Herero uprising' Speech by Federal Minister Heidemarie Wieczorek-Zeul at the commemorations of the 100th anniversary of the suppression of the Herero uprising, Embassy of the Federal Republic of Germany Windhoek, 14 August 2004, available at: http://www.windhuk.diplo.de/Vertretung/windhuk/en/03/Commemorative__Years__2004__2005/Seite__Speech__2004-08-14__BMZ.html.

Anvil Kilwa PR 2007, 28 June, Anvil Mining Press Release, available at: http://www.anvilmining.com/files/NewsReleasereMilitaryCourtAnnouncement.pdf [link no longer available; for more on this topic, see: https://www.ejatlas.org/conflict/kilwa-mine].

The White House, Office of the Press Secretary, The President's Remarks in a Speech at Cairo University, 4 June 2009, available at https://obamawhitehouse.archives.gov/the-press-office/remarks-president-cairo-university-6-04-09.

'Target Ain't People' flashmob, The Other 98%, 15 August 2010, footage available at: https://other98.com/target-aint-people/

Explainer Museum of London Docklands, 21 September 2010.

Karskens, A., 'De zaak Kouwenhoven herbegint en afgesloten', 2017, 8 December, available at: https://thekarskenstimes.com/weblog/item/661-de-zaak-kouwenhoven-herbegint (*Karskens blog*).

Portland General Assembly 2012, 1 January, National Call to Action to Shut Down the Corporations, available at: http://https://snuproject.wordpress.com/2012/02/07/f29-shut-down-the-corporations-national-call-to-action-made-by-the-portland-general-assembly/.

Trump Campaign Speech, *'Donald Trump on ISIS, 'I'm gonna bomb the SHIT out of 'em!''*, 16 November, 2015, available at: https://www.youtube.com/watch?v=OES7kbWZ70Y.

Andrew Clapham, Graduate Institute, Geneva, http://graduateinstitute.ch/home/study/academicdepartments/international-law/people/resources/prof-clapham.html (*Clapham Website*).

Mike Baab 'I Live My Life One Professional Conference At A Time', 21 February 2017, available at https://rottenindenmark.wordpress.com/2017/02/21/i-live-my-life-one-professional-conference-at-a-time/ (*Rotten in Denmark blog*).

Mutual Aid Disaster Relief, see: https://mutualaiddisasterrelief.org/.

It's Going Down Podcast, see: https://itsgoingdown.org/category/podcast/.

Index